LEARNING MATHEMATICS

in Elementary and Middle Schools

W. George Cathcart
University of Alberta

Yvonne M. Pothier
Mount Saint Vincent University

James H. Vance
University of Victoria

Nadine S. Bezuk
San Diego State University

Merrill
an imprint of Prentice Hall
Upper Saddle River, New Jersey   Columbus, Ohio

This edition is dedicated to my husband, Steve, and my son, Peter,
whose encouragement and support made this work possible.

—N.S.B.

Library of Congress Cataloging-in-Publication Data

Learning mathematics in elementary and middle schools / W. George
  Cathcart . . . [et al.].
      p.   cm.
    Includes bibliographical references and index.
    ISBN 0–13–011681–5
    1. Mathematics—Study and teaching (Elementary)   2. Mathematics—
  –Study and teaching (Middle school)   I. Cathcart, W. George.
  QA135.5.L398   2000
  372.7—dc21   99–33271
                                                          CIP

Editor: Bradley J. Potthoff
Developmental Editor: Linda Ashe Montgomery
Production Editor: JoEllen Gohr
Text Designer and Production Coordination: Elm Street Publishing Services, Inc.
Design Coordinator: Diane C. Lorenzo
Cover Designer: Curt Besser
Cover Art: Stephan Schildbach
Production Manager: Pamela D. Bennett
Director of Marketing: Kevin Flanagan
Marketing Manager: Meghan Shepherd
Marketing Coordinator: Krista Groshong

This book was set in Times Roman by The Clarinda Company and was printed and bound by Courier/Kendallville, Inc.
The cover was printed by Phoenix Color Corp.

©2000 by Prentice-Hall, Inc.
Pearson Education
Upper Saddle River, New Jersey 07458

The Standards Links boxes are from *Curriculum and Evaluation Standards for Teaching Mathematics* (1989), *Professional
Standards for Teaching Mathematics* (1991), and *Assessment Standards for School Mathematics* (1995), National Council of
Teachers of Mathematics, Reston, VA. Used with permission.

Printed in the United States of America

10 9 8 7 6 5 4 3 2 1

ISBN: 0-13-011681-5

Prentice-Hall International (UK) Limited, *London*
Prentice-Hall of Australia Pty. Limited, *Sydney*
Prentice-Hall Canada, Inc., *Toronto*
Prentice-Hall Hispanoamericana, S. A., *Mexico*
Prentice-Hall of India Private Limited, *New Delhi*
Prentice-Hall of Japan, Inc., *Tokyo*
Prentice-Hall (Singapore) Pte. Ltd., *Singapore*
Editora Prentice-Hall do Brasil, Ltda., *Rio de Janeiro*

This book is about *children* learning mathematics. It is also about *teachers* learning to create an environment that encourages and supports children to help them build understandings, make connections, reason, and solve problems in mathematics.

About the Audience

This book is for preservice and inservice elementary and middle school mathematics teachers. Preservice teachers will develop an understanding of the content of school mathematics programs and formulate a teaching methodology for the meaningful learning of mathematics. Inservice teachers who wish to explore current thinking about mathematics teaching and learning will find the book a valuable source of theoretical and practical ideas for involving students in meaningful problem-solving tasks and for having students reflect, talk, and write about mathematics.

Teachers will be challenged to reflect on their personal views of mathematics, on how children learn mathematics, and on classroom environments that help children understand mathematics. The more readers become actively involved with the activities, problems, and Video Links in this book, the greater both the quantity and quality of that reflection will be, and ultimately, the greater their learning will be.

About the Approach to Mathematics Learning

The vision of mathematics learning presented in this text places the student at its center. Supporting this vision are the following beliefs:

- Students construct for themselves the mathematics they come to know. Therefore, the approach to mathematics learning is an *active* one in which students engage in problem-solving activities that are discovery-oriented or open-ended. Chapter 3 in this text describes the importance of teaching problem solving to children and discusses the problem-solving process and problem-solving strategies. Subsequent chapters reinforce the critical role that problem solving plays in teaching children to reason and to make mathematical connections.
- Communication is an important part of the mathematics learning process. Readers will find questions embedded in activities in the text. These questions encourage students to reflect on the math they are doing in order to clarify their own ideas. Also, they invite students to share their mathematical understanding of

a concept with classmates. In addition, there are frequent requests in the text for students to record their work or findings using drawings, diagrams, descriptions, or symbols.

- An active, student-centered approach requires the use of manipulative materials and technology. Each chapter identifies appropriate manipulative materials and technology for the concepts presented and includes numerous activities that incorporate their use.
- The teacher's role is to provide children with opportunities to explore mathematics using manipulative materials and technology, and to help children observe and describe patterns and make generalizations about the mathematics topics and relationships they examine. To support teacher development, chapter topics link classroom practice and the NCTM Standards connecting real-world problems, concrete models, language, symbols, and hands-on activities.

We believe the ideas presented in this text reflect the vision of learning and teaching mathematics encouraged by the *Curriculum and Evaluation Standards for School Mathematics,* the *Professional Standards for Teaching Mathematics,* and the *Assessment Standards for School Mathematics,* all published by the National Council of Teachers of Mathematics in 1989, 1991, and 1995, respectively. These documents promote teaching mathematics from a problem-solving perspective and making communication, reasoning, and connections the primary foci of mathematics learning. These recommendations, highlighted throughout the text in the *Standards Link* feature, help readers connect the recommendations of the Standards to the topics in each chapter.

About the Text Features

There are several unique features in this book aimed at helping readers learn how to teach children mathematics. Readers are encouraged to use all of these features to maximize their own learning.

- **Key Concepts** at the beginning of each chapter list the most important topics included in the chapter and serve as an advance organizer to the reader.
- **Focus Questions** at the beginning of each chapter address the chapter's key concepts to help focus the readers' attention on pertinent topics.
- **Standards Links,** throughout each chapter, connect the content of each chapter with the NCTM *Curriculum and Evaluation Standards,* the *Professional Standards for Teaching Mathematics,* and the *Assessment Standards.* The *Standards Link* feature helps the

reader understand the importance and relevance of chapter content.

- **Video Links** connect topics presented in the textbook to videos of outstanding teachers teaching the same topics to children in classrooms. Each *Video Link* concludes with questions designed to strengthen the reader's understanding of the topic and to emphasize its link to practice.

- **Activities,** prolific throughout each chapter, provide practical applications related to chapter topics. These activities may be done in university classes and with small groups of children.

- **For Your Journal,** at the end of each chapter, is a means for readers to strengthen and reflect on their understanding of chapter topics by responding in math journals to concept-related questions. Later, the journal can serve as a convenient teaching resource. Instructors may choose to require students to respond to one or more questions as part of a course assignment.

- **For Your Portfolio,** at the end of each chapter, describes activities or assignments that readers may complete to help them connect the chapter's key concepts to classroom practice. Instructors may choose to include one or more of these items as course assignments.

- **Resources for Teachers,** at the end of each chapter, is a listing of exemplary children's books or professional resources for teachers related to the chapter topic.

- **Links to the Internet,** also located at the end of each chapter, lead readers to helpful Web destinations where they can find valuable resources to assist their development of teaching strategies.

- **Blackline Masters,** collected at the end of the text, are formatted so they may be photocopied and used as manipulatives in K–8 classrooms. In studying this text, it is helpful for a reader to employ these blackline masters to enhance his or her own understanding of the mathematical concepts.

About Text Supplements

A *Companion Website* is available for professors and students who adopt this text. It can be accessed via the Internet at *http://www.prenhall.com/cathcart*. Please review page v in this text for specific information about Website features.

An *Instructor's Manual* has been produced for course instructors and includes chapter objectives, strategies for developing major concepts presented in each chapter, transparency masters, and additional projects and discussion questions. The *Instructor's Manual* is free to adopters.

In addition, five videos, free to adopting professors, accompany this text. These videos are part of the *Annenberg/CPB Math and Science Collection* and are the ones referred to in the Video Links. They are:

Communication
Teaching Math: A Video Library, K–4; Tape 21

Concepts of Whole Number Operations
Teaching Math: A Video Library, K–4; Tape 4

Whole Number Computation
Teaching Math: A Video Library, K–4; Tape 7

Fraction Tracks and Hexominoes
Teaching Math: A Video Library, 5–8; Tape 1

Geometry and Spatial Sense
Teaching Math: A Video Library, K–4; Tape 8

Acknowledgments

We appreciate the thoughtful comments and suggestions made by the reviewers: Anna O. Graeber, University of Maryland; Anne Madsen, University of New Mexico; and Ann S. Massey, Indiana University of Pennsylvania. Further, we are grateful for the insights of the reviewers of the Canadian version: Catherine Ebbs, University of Windsor; Douglas Edge, University of Western Ontario; John Grant McLoughlin, Okanagan College; Helen Horsman, University of Saskatchewan; Wilfred L. Innerd, University of Windsor; Werner Liedtke, University of Victoria; Joan McDuff, Queen's University; Howard Riggs, McGill University; Daiyo Sawada, University of Alberta; and Thomas Schroeder, State University of New York at Buffalo. Their discerning comments became the guidelines used to improve the organization of this text and the applications included.

In addition, we received invaluable suggestions and encouragement from colleagues and students at San Diego State University, numerous teachers in San Diego City Schools, and the students, teachers, and administrators at Rosa Parks Elementary School. Thank you, all.

G. Cathcart

Y. Pothier

J. Vance

N. Bezuk

○ Discover the Companion Website Accompanying This Book

The Prentice Hall Companion Website: A Virtual Learning Environment

Technology is a constantly growing and changing aspect of our field that is creating a need for content and resources. To address this emerging need, Prentice Hall has developed an online learning environment for students and professors alike—Companion Websites—to support our textbooks.

In creating a Companion Website, our goal is to build on and enhance what the textbook already offers. For this reason, the content for each user-friendly website is organized by chapter and provides the professor and student with a variety of meaningful resources. Common features of a Companion Website include:

For the Professor—

Every Companion Website integrates **Syllabus Manager™,** an online syllabus creation and management utility.

- **Syllabus Manager™** provides you, the instructor, with an easy, step-by-step process to create and revise syllabi, with direct links into Companion Website and other online content without having to learn HTML.
- Students may logon to your syllabus during any study session. All they need to know is the web address for the Companion Website and the password you've assigned to your syllabus.
- After you have created a syllabus using **Syllabus Manager™,** students may enter the syllabus for their course section from any point in the Companion Website.
- Class dates are highlighted in white and assignment due dates appear in blue. Clicking on a date, the student is shown the list of activities for the assignment. The activities for each assignment are linked directly to actual content, saving time for students.
- Adding assignments consists of clicking on the desired due date, then filling in the details of the assignment—name of the assignment, instructions, and whether or not it is a one-time or repeating assignment.

- In addition, links to other activities can be created easily. If the activity is online, a URL can be entered in the space provided, and it will be linked automatically in the final syllabus.
- Your completed syllabus is hosted on our servers, allowing convenient updates from any computer on the Internet. Changes you make to your syllabus are immediately available to your students at their next logon.

For the Student—

- **Chapter Objectives**—outline key concepts from the text
- **Interactive Self-quizzes**—complete with hints and automatic grading that provide immediate feedback for students

After students submit their answers for the interactive self-quizzes, the Companion Website **Results Reporter** computes a percentage grade, provides a graphic representation of how many questions were answered correctly and incorrectly, and gives a question-by-question analysis of the quiz. Students are given the option to send their quiz to up to four e-mail addresses (professor, teaching assistant, study partner, etc.).

- **Message Board**—serves as a virtual bulletin board to post—or respond to—questions or comments to/from a national audience
- **Net Searches**—offer links by key terms from each chapter to related Internet content
- **Web Destinations**—links to www sites that relate to chapter content

To take advantage of these and other resources, please visit the Companion Website for *Learning Mathematics in Elementary and Middle Schools* at: www.prenhall.com/cathcart

◦ CONTENTS

CHAPTER 10 Developing Fraction Concepts   199

CHAPTER 11 Developing Fraction Computation   224

CHAPTER 1

Teaching Mathematics: Influences and Directions

Key Concepts

○ **National and state standards**

○ **National and international assessment**

Focus Questions

When you have finished studying this chapter, you should be able to answer these questions:

1. What are some of the factors that influence mathematics teaching?

2. Which four standards are common to the NCTM Curriculum and Evaluation Standards?

3. Why are national and global assessments such as NAEP and TIMSS important to mathematics curriculum development?

4. How will the five "Goals for all Students" in the NCTM Curriculum and Evaluation Standards influence future mathematics teaching?

Mathematics permeates all facets of our lives. Jennifer organizes her collection of baseball cards into a five-by-eight array and wonders how many cards she has. Marco counts his change to be sure he received the correct amount after buying his brother a birthday present. Dad mentally calculates 15 percent of the family's restaurant bill and adds that on as gratuity. Elementary-school children gather data on the weather for a week, exchange their data with other schools around the world via telecommunications, and graph this information in order to discuss and write about similarities and differences.

Often the mathematics in real-life situations is not recognized until after one stops and reflects. Children need help in recognizing that mathematics is all around them. They need the right kind of experiences in order to appreciate the fact that mathematics is a common human activity and that it is important to their present and future well being.

Teaching mathematics is both a challenging and stimulating endeavor because there are significant changes taking place in mathematics education. New insights, new materials, and, of course, children who are growing up in a very different kind of society, dictate a different approach to the teaching of mathematics. This chapter is about the various factors that influence the principles, practices, and future direction of mathematics and mathematics instruction. ○

"More than ever before, Americans need to think for a living; more than ever before they need to think mathematically."

Mathematical Sciences Education Board and
National Research Council, 1990, p. 3

INFLUENCES ON MATHEMATICS EDUCATION

Many factors and movements have influenced what and how mathematics is taught. It is not important for teachers to be experts on these influences, but it is necessary for teachers to have an awareness of them in order to better understand the current state of the art and to put future directions into perspective. The following sections address some of the major influences. Although these influences are not exhaustive, they will be discussed in the context of eight broad categories: psychological, professional, technological, language, societal and research, learner, and the teacher.

Psychological Influences

Theories about how children learn have ranged from the mental discipline theory prominent in the late nineteenth century to the current constructivist point of view (see Chapter 2). Under the former, children were given many lengthy and often complex problems, particularly computations, because this kind of exercise "strengthened" the mind. The constructivist view believes that children "construct" their own understanding of mathematical ideas by means of mental activity and/or through interacting with physical models of the ideas. For example, given a set of blocks that represent our place value numeration system, children may initially build roads and towers, but will, with appropriate suggestions from the teacher, soon begin to structure their play by organizing the blocks by size, resulting in a representation of numbers. The teacher's role is to provide appropriate activities and experiences rather than complex problems.

How children learn mathematics will be examined in more depth in Chapter 2. The purpose of introducing it here is to include learning theories as one of the major influences on what and how mathematics is taught.

Professional Influences

Professional organizations have had a significant influence on mathematics in the schools. In the 1970s, the "Back-to-the-Basics" movement stressed the "three Rs"—reading, writing, and arithmetic (Morgan & Robinson, 1976). In mathematics this often meant a heavier emphasis on addition, subtraction, multiplication, and division of whole numbers and fractions and virtual omission of other important topics. The emphasis was on skills needed for survival in a nontechnological age.

In 1977, the National Council of Supervisors of Mathematics (NCSM) published a reaction to the Back-to-the-Basics movement. The Council agreed that computational skills were important but they identified ten basic skill areas with problem solving as the principal area. Also in 1977 the National Council of Teachers of Mathe-

matics (NCTM) published a companion statement that included the following words:

> "In a total mathematics program, students need more than arithmetic skill and understanding. They need to develop geometric intuition as an aid to problem solving. They must be able to interpret data. Without these and many other mathematical understandings, citizens are not mathematically functional. Yes, let us stress basics, but let us stress them in the context of total mathematics instruction"
>
> (NCTM, 1977, p. 18).

Later (1988) the NCSM updated its 1977 statement. The new statement, entitled *Essential Mathematics for the 21st Century,* contained twelve components, including problem solving, communicating mathematical ideas, mathematical reasoning, applying mathematics to everyday situations, alertness to the reasonableness of results, estimation, appropriate computational skills, algebraic thinking, measurement, geometry, statistics, and probability. In addition to these twelve components, the NCSM paper discussed the importance of the learning climate, technology, and evaluation in the mathematics program.

The NCTM also developed a statement, entitled *An Agenda for Action,* that would provide direction for mathematics education in the 1980s. The Agenda contained eight major recommendations, each with numerous sub-recommendations. The first recommendation was that "problem solving be the focus of school mathematics in the 1980s" (NCTM, 1980, p. 1). Note that the emphasis from both of these organizations was on problem solving. As a result of these recommendations, curriculum developers included more problem-solving activities in their materials.

Later in the 1980s, the National Council of Teachers of Mathematics, in planning for the 1990s, acknowledged that much criticism had been leveled at school mathematics during that decade. International studies showed that students in the United States did not fare very well on tests of mathematics proficiency compared to students in some other countries (Travers & McKnight, 1984; Lapointe, Mead, & Phillips, 1989). In an effort to improve this situation, NCTM developed a set of standards for school mathematics, published in 1989, entitled *Curriculum and Evaluation Standards for School Mathematics.* (Hereafter, this document will be referred to as the Curriculum Standards.) The Curriculum Standards describes criteria for a quality mathematics curriculum from kindergarten through the twelfth grade, including what students should learn and strategies for teaching the recommended material. Tables 1-1 and 1-2 list the standards for Grades K–4 and for Grades 5–8, and Tables 1-3 and 1-4 present a summary of the shift in content and emphasis recommended in the Curriculum Standards.

TABLE 1-1
NCTM STANDARDS—GRADES K–4
Mathematics as PROBLEM SOLVING
Mathematics as COMMUNICATION
Mathematics as REASONING
Mathematics as CONNECTIONS
Estimation
Number Sense and Numeration
Concepts of Whole Number Operations
Whole Number Computation
Geometry and Spatial Sense
Measurement
Statistics and Probability
Patterns and Relationships

TABLE 1-2
NCTM STANDARDS—GRADES 5–8
Mathematics as PROBLEM SOLVING
Mathematics as COMMUNICATION
Mathematics as REASONING
Mathematics as CONNECTIONS
Number and Number Relations
Number Systems and Number Theory
Computation and Estimation
Patterns, Relations, and Functions
Algebra
Statistics
Probability
Geometry
Measurement

The NCTM recognized that teaching was another important influence on students' learning, but teaching was not included in the Curriculum Standards. So the NCTM subsequently produced a companion document: *Professional Standards for Teaching Mathematics* (hereafter referred to as the Professional Standards) (NCTM, 1991). This document outlined six standards for teaching mathematics, eight standards for the evaluation of the teaching of mathematics, six standards for the professional development of teachers of mathematics, and four standards for the support and development of mathematics teachers and teaching.

STANDARDS LINK 1-1
Woven into the fabric of the *Professional Standards for Teaching Mathematics* are five major shifts in the environment of mathematics classrooms. . . . We need to shift:

- toward classrooms as mathematical communities—away from classrooms as simply a collection of individuals;
- toward logic and mathematical evidence as verification—away from the teacher as the sole authority for right answers;
- toward mathematical reasoning—away from merely memorizing procedures;
- toward conjecturing, inventing, and problem solving—away from an emphasis on mechanistic answer finding;
- toward connecting mathematics, its ideas, and its applications—away from treating mathematics as a body of isolated concepts and procedures. (NCTM, 1991, p. 3)

A belief that "new assessment strategies and practices need to be developed that will enable teachers and others to assess students' performance in a manner that reflects the NCTM's reform vision for school mathematics" (NCTM, 1995, p. 1) prompted the NCTM to develop and publish in 1995 a third set of standards, *Assessment Standards for School Mathematics* (hereafter referred to as the Assessment Standards). This document outlines six mathematics assessment standards and then discusses their use for purposes such as monitoring students' progress, making instructional decisions, evaluating students' achievement, and assessing programs, and will be discussed in detail in Chapter 4.

Technological Influences

Modern school mathematics programs include calculator and computer activities. Many children have access to both calculators and computers at home. Indeed, the students in your classroom will graduate from high school after the turn of the millennium into a society that is technologically very different from what we know today (Corelli, 1989; McKay, 1989). Teachers must prepare them to succeed in an electronic environment.

The school mathematics curriculum will continue to be influenced by three major developments: the calculator, the computer, and interactive multimedia, including Internet access.

Calculators In the Agenda for Action (NCTM, 1980), the council recommended that "mathematics take full advantage of the power of calculators and computers at all grade levels" (p. 1). The NCTM followed this recommendation with a published position statement in

TABLE 1-3

SUMMARY OF CHANGES IN CONTENT AND EMPHASIS IN K–4 MATHEMATICS

INCREASED ATTENTION	DECREASED ATTENTION
Number	**Number**
• Number sense	• Early attention to reading, writing, and ordering numbers symbolically
• Place-value concepts	
• Meaning of fractions and decimals	
• Estimation of quantities	
Operations and Computation	**Operations and Computation**
• Meaning of operations	• Complex paper-and-pencil computations
• Operation sense	• Isolated treatment of paper-and-pencil computations
• Mental computation	• Addition and subtraction without renaming
• Estimation and the reasonableness of answers	• Isolated treatment of division facts
• Selection of an appropriate computational method	• Long division
• Use of calculators for complex computation	• Long division without remainders
• Thinking strategies for basic facts	• Paper-and-pencil fraction computation
	• Use of rounding to estimate
Geometry and Measurement	**Geometry and Measurement**
• Properties of geometric figures	• Primary focus on naming geometric figures
• Geometric relationships	• Memorization of equivalencies between units of measurement
• Spatial sense	
• Process of measuring	
• Concepts related to units of measurement	
• Actual measuring	
• Estimation of measurements	
• Use of measurement and geometry ideas throughout the curriculum	
Probability and Statistics	**Probability and Statistics**
• Collection and organization of data	
• Exploration of chance	
Patterns and Relationships	**Patterns and Relationships**
• Pattern recognition and description	
• Use of variables to express relationships	
Problem Solving	**Problem Solving**
• Word problems with a variety of structures	• Use of clue words to determine which operation to use
• Use of everyday problems	
• Applications	
• Study of patterns and relationships	
• Problem-solving strategies	
Instructional Practices	**Instructional Practices**
• Use of manipulative materials	• Rote practice
• Cooperative work	• Rote memorization of rules
• Discussion of mathematics	• One answer and one method
• Questioning	• Use of worksheets
• Justification of thinking	• Written practice
• Writing about mathematics	• Teaching by telling
• Problem-solving approach to instruction	
• Content integration	
• Use of calculators and computers	

Source: National Council of Teachers of Mathematics (1989).

1986 on the use of calculators in the mathematics classroom; in 1991 this statement was updated. This statement recommends that all students use calculators to explore and experiment with mathematical ideas, to develop and reinforce skills, to focus on problem-solving processes rather than the associated computation, to perform tedious computations, and to gain access to more advanced mathematical ideas (NCTM, February 1991).

There is widespread support from mathematics educators for the use of calculators by students in classrooms

TABLE 1-4

SUMMARY OF CHANGES IN CONTENT AND EMPHASIS IN 5–8 MATHEMATICS

INCREASED ATTENTION	DECREASED ATTENTION
Problem Solving • Pursuing open-ended problems and extended problem-solving projects • Investigating and formulating questions from problem situations • Representing situations verbally, numerically, graphically, geometrically, or symbolically	**Problem Solving** • Practicing routine, one-step problems • Practicing problems categorized by types (e.g., coin problems, age problems)
Communication • Discussing, writing, reading, and listening to mathematical ideas	**Communication** • Doing fill-in-the-blank worksheets • Answering questions that require only yes, no, or a number as responses
Reasoning • Reasoning in spatial contexts • Reasoning with proportions • Reasoning from graphs • Reasoning inductively and deductively	**Reasoning** • Relying on outside authority (teacher or an answer key)
Connections • Connecting mathematics to other subjects and to the world outside the classroom • Connecting topics within mathematics • Applying mathematics	**Connections** • Learning isolated topics • Developing skills out of context
Number/Operations/Computation • Developing number sense • Developing operation sense • Creating algorithms and procedures • Using estimation both in solving problems and in checking the reasonableness of results • Exploring relationships among representations of, and operations on, whole numbers, fractions, decimals, integers, and rational numbers • Developing an understanding of ratio, proportion, and percent	**Number/Operations/Computation** • Memorizing rules and algorithms • Practicing tedious paper-and-pencil computations • Finding exact forms of answers • Memorizing procedures, such as cross-multiplication, without understanding • Practicing rounding numbers out of context
Patterns and Functions • Identifying and using functional relationships • Developing and using tables, graphs, and rules to describe situations • Interpreting among different mathematical representations	**Patterns and Functions** • Topics seldom in the current curriculum
Algebra • Developing an understanding of variables, expressions, and equations • Using a variety of methods to solve linear equations and informally investigate inequalities and nonlinear equations	**Algebra** • Manipulating symbols • Memorizing procedures and drilling on equation solving
Statistics • Using statistical methods to describe, analyze, evaluate, and make decisions	**Statistics** • Memorizing formulas
Probability • Creating experimental and theoretical models of situations involving probabilities	**Probability** • Memorizing formulas
Geometry • Developing an understanding of geometric objects and relationships • Using geometry in solving problems	**Geometry** • Memorizing geometric vocabulary • Memorizing facts and relationships

continued

TABLE 1-4

SUMMARY OF CHANGES IN CONTENT AND EMPHASIS IN 5–8 MATHEMATICS *(CONTINUED)*

INCREASED ATTENTION	DECREASED ATTENTION
Measurement • Estimating and using measurement to solve problems	*Measurement* • Memorizing and manipulating formulas • Converting within and between measurement systems
Instructional Practices • Actively involving students individually and in groups in exploring, conjecturing, analyzing, and applying mathematics in both a mathematical and a real-world context • Using appropriate technology for computation and exploration • Using concrete materials • Being a facilitator of learning • Assessing learning as an integral part of instruction	*Instructional Practices* • Teaching computations out of context • Drilling on paper-and-pencil algorithms • Teaching topics in isolation • Stressing memorization • Being the dispenser of knowledge • Testing for the sole purpose of assigning grades

Source: National Council of Teachers of Mathematics (1989).

(NCTM, 1981; Reys & Reys, 1987). But in spite of this support and easy access, calculators are not being optimally used in classrooms. In part, this may be due to parental, perhaps even teacher, fears that children will become dependent on the calculator, which, in turn, may have a negative effect on learning basic computational procedures and/or reduce the need to think. Research (e.g., Hembree & Dessart, 1986) has demonstrated that this is not the case; in fact, the opposite seems to be true.

Computers In 1987, the NCTM also published a position statement on computers in learning and teaching mathematics, which was revised in 1994 to include technology rather than only computers. This council stated that technology tools are integral to learning and teaching mathematics and recommended that technology should be used to enhance mathematics programs at all levels (NCTM, 1995).

When computers began to appear in schools in the early 1980s, programming was the major activity. Today, however, the computer is used in many other interesting ways. Indeed, the major thrust is to integrate the computer into the curriculum, to use it as a learning tool just as one would use counters, geometric shapes, or a calculator.

Both the quality and quantity of educational software have improved. It is now possible to select high-quality practice programs that are appropriate for the needs of specific students. Further, some software provides assistance or advice to users to help them understand the concepts they are practicing.

Problem solving and higher-order thinking skills also can be developed using the computer as a tool. Simple ordering, classifying, patterning, and related problems have been designed for younger students. *Millie's Math House* (Edmark, 1993), for example, contains six modules that provide experiences with these processes. Programs in-

volving estimation, guess and test, and other problem-solving heuristics can be used with older children. Some mathematics problems can be solved with the use of computerized spreadsheets.

Simulations are another way the computer can be used to facilitate teaching and learning. Several popular programs exist that simulate the operation of a small business. Children can learn how to control variables to maximize profit (Friel, 1983). At a different level, students might program the computer to simulate the shaking of two die and the recording of the sum, say 10,000 times. When you do that with real dice (the best way to introduce the concept) you toss the dice only a few times. Yet we know the laws of probability are based on "large" numbers. The computer, therefore, should be able to generate a better estimate.

Further, there are many good educational games (note the adjective *educational*) that involve strategy. These can be used to develop logical thinking skills.

Obviously the computer can be used in many other ways as well, including generating mathematical materials that can be given to students or having students use the word processor to write about what they have learned in mathematics or to write a report on a famous mathematician whom they have researched. It would also be interesting to develop a database on famous mathematicians or on characteristics of class members (Browning & Channell, 1992).

Interactive multimedia Interactive multimedia is a technology based on a convergence of computer technology and systems such as CD-ROM. Text, sound, graphics, photographs, motion pictures, and animation can be incorporated into a learning package. Thousands of graphic images, film sequences, and text blocks can be stored on a CD-ROM. These can be randomly and almost instantly accessed by computer control. A child could manipulate mathematical images by responding to questions on a computer screen or by means of the computer mouse. While this is not a replacement for doing an activity concretely, it could certainly be a powerful learning device at the iconic level. Certainly, the integration of available high technology will have a powerful influence on what and how mathematics is taught in the twenty-first century.

The Internet is fast becoming a resource for teaching. Lesson plans, classroom activities, and much more can be accessed via the Internet. You might start collecting these resources by visiting the home page of your local school board, university, or state government. The NCTM has, among other features, some student-ready activity sheets on their site at http://www.nctm.org. Numerous other excellent sites are available. Some excellent sites include the Eisenhower National Clearinghouse (http://www.enc.org) and Teachers' Net (http://teachers.net).

Societal Influences

State government Each state government is a major determinant of the curriculum in that state, developing curriculum standards or frameworks that guide the teaching of mathematics within the state. Some states also have a statewide textbook adoption process, by which a list of textbooks that state funds may be used to purchase is developed. Many states also mandate statewide testing based on these standards. It is essential for teachers to become familiar with the curriculum guidelines in their state.

School districts Although many states have curriculum standards in place, many school districts develop their own curriculum standards. These local standards usually are based on the state and national standards. Teachers must be aware of the curriculum standards for their school district as well as for their state.

Lobby groups Sometimes, lobby groups, and even individual parents, can influence curriculum decision makers at the national, state, or local level. For example, educators may form a lobby group in an attempt to influence curriculum on pedagogical grounds. At other times, business or industry might lobby for changes to make mathematics more application oriented. Lobby groups have been quite effective in promoting change.

Bandwagons Educators sometimes rally around some new proposal or device believing that it will be a remedy for certain problems. Many of these "new" ideas are sound and do result in positive changes; others are just bandwagons, but they do influence schools and the curriculum, at least temporarily. Unfortunately, bandwagons often are not recognized as such until after the wheels have fallen off.

For example, one curriculum innovation that might be considered a "bandwagon" was the individualized instruction movement of the 1970s. This movement was based on the idea that children were unique individuals and, as such, learned best independently and individually. In classrooms organized around this philosophy, each child had a learning contract and often spent most of the time working individually, sometimes in workbooks that were self-correcting. Unfortunately, this philosophy of learning overlooked the fact that children are also social beings who can and need to learn from each other as well as alone.

Influences of Research and Assessments

Research We are sometimes cynical about the ability of educational research to affect the teaching-learning process. Any one piece of research may have limited application or generalizability. However, when taken collectively, research can help us make decisions about what to teach, and when and how to teach it.

One good example of research affecting school mathematics programs was William Brownell's research in the 1940s on subtraction algorithms (Brownell, 1947; Brownell & Moser, 1949). Prior to his work, the equal addition algorithm was widely used in North America. After his research, schools gradually switched to the decomposition algorithm, commonly known as the "borrowing" method, which is widely used in this country. Algorithms will be discussed in Chapter 9.

It is difficult for a busy teacher to keep up with significant research findings. Strategies that help are reading journals such as *Teaching Children Mathematics* (formerly the *Arithmetic Teacher*) and *Mathematics Teaching in the Middle School* and attending conferences, inservice workshops, and university courses. For example, Suydam (1984) concluded that "lessons using manipulative materials have a higher probability of producing greater mathematics achievement than do lessons in which such materials are not used" (p. 27).

Several books include summaries of research with implications for classroom practice. Teachers may be interested in further investigating these classroom practices as part of their own action research projects. Jensen (1993) and Owens (1993) are examples of very readable books that relate research to classroom practice.

In many respects, the good and creative teacher is a researcher engaged in a variety of "action research" projects. Action research is a teacher's ongoing formal evaluation of his or her own use of teaching strategies, student activities, classroom organization, resource selection, and other applications of learning theory. We encourage teachers to actively reflect and self-evaluate what they do, what they use, and what happens in the classroom as a result. Such activities contribute to professional and personal growth, and to the quality of mathematics instruction.

TIMSS The Third International Mathematics and Science Study (TIMSS) examined the mathematics and science achievement of students at five grade levels in more than 40 countries. TIMSS reported that the mathematics performance of U.S. eighth graders was close to that of other major industrialized nations such as Canada, England, and Germany, but ranked well below the average of the 41 countries participating in TIMSS graders (Mullis, 1997; U.S. Department of Education, 1996). The U.S. fourth graders' performance was better, scoring above the international average (U.S. Department of Education, 1997).

NAEP The National Assessment of Educational Progress (NAEP) is a nationwide assessment of mathematics achievement conducted over time. The most recent NAEP study for which data are available was conducted in 1992 (Kenney & Silver, 1997) and is referred to as the Sixth Mathematics Assessment. This assessment was given to a sample of U.S. students nationwide at grades four and eight. The framework for the sixth NAEP assessment evaluated conceptual understanding, procedural understanding, and problem solving across the mathematics content areas of numbers and operations, measurement, geometry, data analysis, statistics and probability, and algebra and functions. This assessment showed that "students continue to maintain or improve their mastery of basic objectives for mathematics education" (Dossey & Mullis, 1997, p. 31). But it was also noted that there still is much to be done to help students nationally to enhance and expand their basic understandings of mathematics concepts.

Learner Influences

Language issues Language and its level of development in a child is another factor that influences the nature of the mathematics program and how it is taught. Language is a part of the thinking process through which problems are solved, relationships are discovered, and ideas are formulated. The "new math" of the 1950s and 1960s emphasized strict use of precise mathematical terms. Admittedly, the language of mathematics is precise, and terms often have very specialized meanings. For example, the expression "fairly small" may be adequate in some settings, but if you were telling mission control how much rocket fuel was stored in and present for launching the shuttle, it is a totally inadequate expression of quantity. However, even in mathematics there is room for children's own language. Their expressions will develop into more precise language as concepts develop.

Many children in elementary and middle schools today are English language learners, whose first language is a language other than English. Teachers must be careful *not* to confuse limited ability to communicate in English with limited potential for learning mathematics. There are many teaching strategies available, such as

sheltered instruction, ESL (English as a Second Language), and SDAIE (Specially Designed Academic Instruction in English) to help children learn English as they learn mathematics. Strategies that many good teachers use to help all children learn mathematics, such as cooperative groups, manipulative materials, and visuals, are especially helpful for English language learners as well.

The language used to convey a mathematical idea has a bearing on the child's understanding of the concept. For example, some children do not understand the term "perimeter." If you talked about the "distance around" or if you drew a diagram and asked how much fencing would be needed to enclose the shape, many more would understand and be able to successfully respond to the question. Likewise, the introduction of terms such as *commutative, associative,* and *distributive* serves no useful purpose if children have not already formed generalizations from repeated experiences illustrating these properties.

Another language-related factor of which you should be aware is children's ability to use mathematics vocabulary but not really understand the concepts. For example, most children can talk about a triangle, but there are many who think that a figure is not a triangle unless it is equilateral, or they might say that the following figure below is a triangle. Others might argue that the figure at right is not a triangle because one side is not horizontal or parallel to the bottom of the page.

Children's misconceptions may be due to the visual images presented to them. Are the triangles drawn by the teacher always equilateral in appearance? Teachers must be cognizant of their own teaching behaviors.

Gender issues There is some evidence that suggests that, beginning in late elementary school, some differences in the mathematics performance of boys and girls become noticeable. It is beyond the scope of this book to provide a detailed analysis of gender differences and their possible causes, however, interested readers can refer to Meyer and Fennema (1992) for a very readable discussion of this issue. The following list presents observations that teachers should carefully consider.

Some Facts

- Girls have lower enrollment rates in advanced Grade 12 and postsecondary mathematics and science courses. This results in limited career choices for women.

- Girls have less confidence in their mathematical competence, even when they have equal ability. Girls (and their parents) are more likely to attribute their success to hard work, while boys attribute it to their ability.

- Although the gap is narrowing, there are differences in performance at different levels and on different topics. Boys tend to score higher on higher-level thinking tasks, and girls on facts and computation items (Hyde, Fennema, & Lamon, 1990; Meyer, 1989). Male superiority seems to increase throughout the grades and as the difficulty level of the material increases.

The Causes

- Although boys tend to score higher on spatial visualization tasks, there is no conclusive evidence that genetic factors cause the observed differences.
- The above point notwithstanding, some internal factors, such as affective considerations (motivation, interest, etc.) could be at play.
- Societal and familial expectations and perceptions (i.e., mathematics is a male domain) are thought to be major factors. External factors may also include increased access to technology for males.
- Differential treatment of boys and girls in the classroom has been documented and may contribute to differences in performance. Teachers tend to interact more with boys than girls (calling on them more often and giving them more criticism and praise) and have higher achievement expectations for boys.

What Can Teachers Do?

Perhaps more than anyone else, it is teachers who can help girls achieve equity in mathematics. Teachers should:

- Increase their interactions with girls on high-cognitive-level mathematics activities, encourage them to engage in independent learning, assure that they attend to their tasks, and expect them to be successful.
- Place more emphasis on cooperative mathematics activities (which increase girls' achievement) and less emphasis on competitive activities.
- Provide girls with opportunities to work in same-gender groups of students, rather than always using mixed-gender groups.

Teacher Influences

The influences identified above imply that the next decade should be a very exciting time in which to be teaching mathematics in elementary and middle schools. However, we haven't mentioned the most important influence on what mathematics children learn and on how that learning is constructed: an enthusiastic, understanding, and knowledgeable teacher. The assertion that children should construct their own mathematical knowledge is not to suggest that the teacher should sit back and wait for it to happen. Rather, the teacher must actively observe and listen to children as they engage in, and talk about, their mathematical explorations. She or he must be skilled in detecting germs of mathematical concepts and in providing experiences that will enable those germs to grow into mature understandings.

DIRECTIONS IN MATHEMATICS EDUCATION

What specific changes have occurred as a result of the preceding influences? There are many! Some were identified in the previous sections; others will be described below.

Looking into the future is difficult. It seems reasonable, however, to predict that problem solving, communication, logical reasoning, and connections within mathematics—and between mathematics and other curricular areas—will continue to be emphasized. Further, equity with regard to achievement, the use of technology, computation, and estimation will be pursued. Finally, the representation of mathematical ideas and strategies for assessment will continue to play important roles in mathematics teaching and learning. At the same time, the role of concrete models will not diminish, and the realigned view of computation will persist as technology becomes even more powerful and pervasive.

The Annenberg/CPB Math and Science Collection

VIDEO LINK 1-1
Communication

Brief Summary: Preview the "Communication" video and observe the teachers' and students' behaviors in each of the different mathematics classes depicted. Look to find answers to the following questions:

1. How do the classes and teachers in the "Communication" video compare with the mathematics classrooms and teachers you experienced in elementary school?
2. Students in mathematics class traditionally have worked silently and individually with paper and pencils doing long problem sets. What activities were the students in the video doing? What do you think they were learning? What does it mean to "do mathematics"?
3. How are the children in the video communicating about mathematics?

Video Source. Teaching Math: A Video Library, K–4; Tape 21 from The Annenberg/CPB Math and Science Collection.

Problem Solving

Problem solving has always been an important part of a mathematics program. Since the late 1970s, however, it has received increased emphasis and likely will continue to be emphasized. This is in keeping with previously mentioned recommendations from both the NCTM and the NCSM. The increased emphasis on problem solving is evident in modern school texts and government curriculum guides, which now include many good problem-solving activities. This focus on problem-solving will continue, but will take on a different form as mathematics programs move toward developing mathematics from real-world settings. For example, children may be working on a stamp collection. The problem setting may be how to display the collection, which will probably lead children to explore an array. Multiplication problems arise when the children want to know how many stamps they have displayed in a particular array.

Researchers have been actively trying to document the characteristics of good problem solvers. Likewise, teachers have been experimenting with strategies (often called heuristics) that develop problem-solving skills in children. Problem solving will be discussed in more detail in Chapter 3.

 STANDARDS LINK 1-2
Mathematics as Problem Solving

In grades K–4, the study of mathematics should emphasize problem solving so that students can:

- use problem-solving approaches to investigate and understand mathematical content;
- formulate problems from everyday and mathematical situations;
- develop and apply strategies to solve a wide variety of problems;
- verify and interpret results with respect to the original problem;
- acquire confidence in using mathematics meaningfully. (NCTM, 1989, p. 23)

 STANDARDS LINK 1-3
Standard 1: Mathematics as Problem Solving

In grades 5–8, the mathematics curriculum should include numerous and varied experiences with problem solving as a method of inquiry and application so that students can:

- use problem-solving approaches to investigate and understand mathematical content;
- formulate problems from situations within and outside mathematics;
- develop and apply a variety of strategies to solve problems, with emphasis on multistep and nonroutine problems;
- verify and interpret results with respect to the original problem situation;
- generalize solutions and strategies to new problem situations;
- acquire confidence in using mathematics meaningfully. (NCTM, 1989, p. 75)

Communication

A major factor in shaping mathematics programs and teaching in the next decade concerns mathematics as communication. Children need an opportunity to reflect upon and explain or justify their ideas and solutions both orally and in writing. There are two aspects to mathematical communication. First, mathematics is a language. Like English, Spanish, or any other language, mathematics has words (symbols), and semantic and syntactical rules; meaning is conveyed through mathematical symbols and their associated rules. A second aspect of mathematical communication involves the use of language within mathematics. This can be a powerful determinant of what is learned and how it is learned.

McKenzie (1990) draws a parallel (and highlights some differences) between reading for meaning and solving a mathematics problem with meaning. Both processes require the use of prior knowledge. Indeed, in both

Source: M. Cappo & G. Osterman (1991). Teach students to communicate mathematically. *The Computing Teacher* (now *Learning & Leading with Technology*), *18*(5), 34–39 ©1991. International Society for Technology in Education, (800) 336-5191, *cust_svc@iste.org, www.iste.org.* Reprinted with permission.

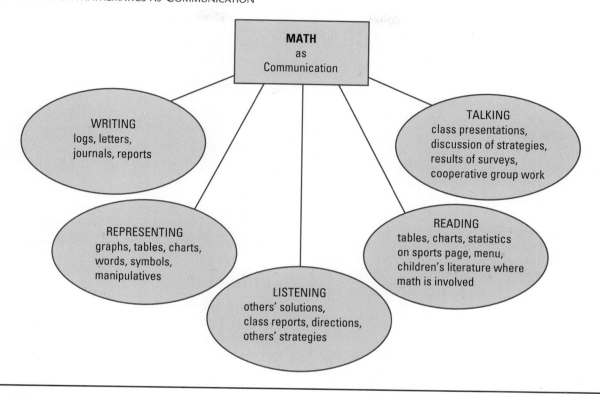

FIGURE 1-1

COMPONENTS OF MATHEMATICS AS COMMUNICATION

processes children are continually predicting, sampling, confirming, self-correcting, and reprocessing—further evidence that reading is not an isolated subject to be taught at a particular time of day. Rather, reading for meaning is a process that must permeate all subject areas.

Talking, reading, writing, listening, and representing are important components of communication in mathematics. Children need to engage in all of these. Figure 1-1 suggests a variety of activities for each that serve to reinforce their roles in mathematical communication. In addition, asking thought-provoking questions will encourage quality communication. Table 1-6 suggests some categories of questions teachers should ask.

TABLE 1-6

QUESTIONS TO STIMULATE COMMUNICATION

CATEGORY	EXAMPLE
Classifying	How are these shapes alike? How are they different?
Hypothesizing	What if . . .? What could be true here?
Specializing	Can you give a specific example of how this works?
Generalizing	Can you see a pattern? Describe it.
Convincing	How do you know you are right?
Analyzing	Is this diagram correct? What is this all about?

STANDARDS LINK 1-4
Standard 2: Mathematics as Communication

In grades K–4, the study of mathematics should include numerous opportunities for communication so that students can:

- relate physical materials, pictures, and diagrams to mathematical ideas;
- reflect on and clarify their thinking about mathematical ideas and situations;
- relate their everyday language to mathematical language and symbols;
- realize that representing, discussing, reading, writing, and listening to mathematics are a vital part of learning and using mathematics. (NCTM, 1989, p. 26)

Logical Reasoning

Mathematics programs often have been criticized for their emphasis on memorization of basic facts, rules, and principles. Today, however, more emphasis is being placed on mathematical reasoning and other higher-order thinking skills such as application, analysis, synthesis, and evaluation. These skills often are included in problem-solving activities. Problems such as the following help children develop logical thinking skills:

Sarah is younger than Alyssa. She is also older and shorter than Patrick. Alyssa is taller and younger than Juan. Juan is taller than Patrick.

1. Arrange the four people by age.
2. Arrange the four people by height.

Connections

In the past, mathematics was often considered a subject unto itself. Frequently, it was broken down internally into many unrelated parts. In the future, however, you will find mathematics integrated throughout the curriculum and punctuated by real-world applications.

Integration with other school subjects
When children recognize that mathematics can be used in other subject areas, it becomes more relevant to them. For example, graphing is a skill that students can apply to problems in social studies and science. In art class, geometric concepts such as slides, flips, and turns can be applied to create a variety of interesting designs. And finally, as a language-learning assignment, children can write about the way they solved a problem, how they feel about the mathematics they are doing, or about successes or difficulties they experience in understanding mathematics.

Integration with real-world settings In the real world, people solve mathematics problems that arise from a particular setting. Pilots use mathematics for navigational problem solving, firefighters apply measurement concepts and processes, collectors employ mathematics when they design displays, and so on. The 1995 yearbook of the National Council of Teachers of Mathematics, *Connecting Mathematics Across the Curriculum*, focuses on mathematics in the real world.

Mathematics is *holistic* in the sense that integrative threads that connect other content areas in the curriculum will be explicitly identified so that children can "see" the connections. Some connections are mentioned in subsequent chapters. One example, a connection between elementary and secondary levels, is illustrated on page 13. A simple number, 7425, familiar to elementary school children, is written in expanded form and, through a series of generalizations, transformed into a polynomial, familiar to secondary school students.

$$7425$$

$$7 \times 1000 + 4 \times 100 + 2 \times 10 + 5$$

$$7 \times x^3 + 4 \times x^2 + 2 \times x + 5$$

$$7x^3 + 4x^2 + 2x + 5$$

$$ax^3 + bx^2 + cx + d$$

 STANDARDS LINK 1-8
Standard 4: Mathematical Connections

In grades K–4, the study of mathematics should include opportunities to make connections so that students can:

- link conceptual and procedural knowledge;
- relate various representations of concepts or procedures to one another;
- recognize relationships among different topics in mathematics;
- use mathematics in other curriculum areas;
- use mathematics in their daily lives. (NCTM, 1989, p. 32)

 STANDARDS LINK 1-9
Standard 4: Mathematical Connections

In grades 5–8, the mathematics curriculum should include the investigation of mathematical connections so that students can:

- see mathematics as an integrated whole;
- explore problems and describe results using graphical, numerical, physical, algebraic, and verbal mathematical models or representations;
- use a mathematical idea to further their understanding of other mathematical ideas;
- apply mathematical thinking and modeling to solve problems that arise in other disciplines, such as art, music, psychology, science, and business;
- value the role of mathematics in our culture and society. (NCTM, 1989, p. 84)

Equity

An achievement gap in mathematics has existed for far too long. In the past, achievement gaps based on gender, race, ethnicity, culture, native language, and income have been noted. The gender gap has begun to narrow in recent years, but other gaps continue to exist. To develop equity in a mathematics program the NCTM Curriculum Standards include five NCTM Goals to apply to *all* students:

- They learn to VALUE mathematics.
- They become CONFIDENT in their ability to do mathematics.
- They become mathematical PROBLEM SOLVERS.
- They learn to COMMUNICATE mathematically.
- They learn to REASON mathematically.

It is important for all teachers to have high expectations for each student and to work toward assuring the learning of every student.

Technology

We believe that the use of calculators and other technologies will increase. This prediction stems from the following reasons:

- Calculators and other forms of technology continue to be used extensively in the home and office.
- The cost of calculators and other forms of technology continues to decrease while their power and functions continue to increase.
- Curriculum documents increasingly encourage the use of calculators and other forms of technology.
- Some tests currently available allow and even encourage calculator use.

Computation

In the past, there has been a heavy emphasis on computation and computational procedures in elementary schools. But according to the Mathematical Sciences Education Board and National Research Council (1989, p. 5), "Mathematics today involves far more than calculation; clarification of the problem, deduction of consequences, formulation of alternatives, and development of appropriate tools are as much a part of the modern mathematician's craft as are solving equations or providing answers."

Today, while the need for children to learn computational algorithms is acknowledged, the focus is on less complex calculations. More complex computations (e.g., three-digit multiplier) are more realistically done on a calculator than with paper and pencil. Furthermore, the emphasis today is on algorithmic knowledge growing out of real problems that require their use, rather than computation for computation's sake. The focus will continue to be on the choices students have. That is, is an estimate sufficient? If not, is mental computation feasible? Can this be done easily with pencil and paper or should a calculator be used? Figure 1-2, adapted from the Curriculum Standards, reflects this philosophy.

Estimation and Mental Computation

Today more emphasis is being placed on estimation (approximate computation or measure) and mental arithmetic (exact computation without any aids). The Curriculum Standards, while isolating estimation as a specific standard, also refer to its value in many of the other standards. Mental arithmetic was a significant component in mathematics teaching in the early part of the twentieth century, partly influenced by the mental discipline theory. During the intervening decades it fell into some disfavor; however, today mental arithmetic is being advocated for its utilitarian value and for its contribution to the development of number and operation sense.

The renewed emphasis on estimation and mental computation can be traced, at least in part, to the advent of the calculator. The calculator will display a result when keys are pressed, but were the correct keys pressed? Were they pressed in the right sequence? An estimate will tell you whether your answer is reasonable. (Estimation and mental computation will be discussed more fully in Chapter 9.)

Representation of Mathematical Ideas

Much in mathematics is abstract, and making it meaningful to children has been a continuing challenge for teachers. In the past, mathematics was taught at an abstract level, even in elementary school where children are not yet fully able to make the kinds of abstractions expected for understanding. Since we know now that children learn in different ways, it makes sense to represent mathematical concepts in different ways as well. There is considerable emphasis on representing mathematical ideas with concrete materials: blocks, counters, and many other physical apparatuses that children can manipulate have been used to embody mathematical ideas. This emphasis will continue, but currently there is a shift to a more multi-representational approach that includes spoken language, concrete objects, pictures, real-life situations, and written symbols. Observing and making relationships within and among these representations helps children develop understanding (Behr, Lesh, Post, & Silver, 1983; Hiebert, 1990).

Assessment

The nature of assessment and strategies for assessing student learning are changing markedly. This topic is discussed in depth in Chapter 4. We mention it here, how-

---

FIGURE 1-2

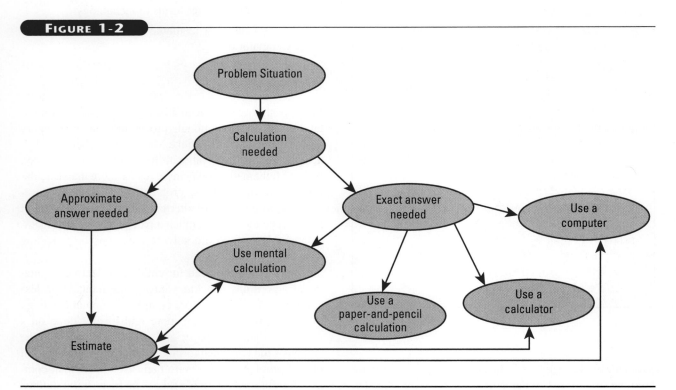

Source: Redrawn from National Council of Teachers of Mathematics (1989).

ever, because it is another area in which significant change is occurring.

The Curriculum Standards addressed evaluation as well as the mathematics curriculum. A program and teaching style that is congruent with the change in emphases recommended in the Curriculum Standards must reflect a concomitant change in evaluation methods. That is, we must assess what students know and how they think about mathematics. The Assessment Standards "expand on and complement, not replace, the NCTM Evaluation Standards" (NCTM, 1995, p. 1). Assessment continues to be an important part of a good mathematics program.

CONCLUSION

In this chapter we have documented a number of factors that have influenced the course of mathematics education in schools. These factors have changed and will continue to change both the mathematics curriculum and how mathematical ideas are taught.

Sometimes influences pull in opposite directions, making it difficult to maintain a balance. Years ago, Vincent Glennon (1963) argued for a balance in school mathematics among three needs: the needs of the child, the needs of society, and the needs of the subject. He diagrammed it as shown in Figure 1-3.

Glennon's argument for a balance still is valid today. If we overemphasize the computation component of mathematics, for example, we may tend to neglect its application in society and also the needs of the child, resulting in an imbalance.

The suggestions and activities in the remaining chapters of this book will enable you to devise a mathematics program for your students that develops mathematical ideas in a nontrivial way, makes applications to society apparent, and carefully considers the needs of the child,

making allowances for differences in background, learning style, and motivation to learn mathematics. Throughout the instructional process, the teacher is the most important factor in determining the strength of the mathematics program. Your challenge as a future teacher is to learn as much as you can about how to help children learn mathematics.

For Your Journal

When you have finished studying this chapter, reflect on these questions in your math journal:

1. Write a mathematics autobiography. Tell about your past study of mathematics and your success in it. Describe your feelings about mathematics at the elementary level and at higher levels. Identify any experiences or mentors you have had in learning mathematics (include factors/persons who were influential in your desire/lack of desire to teach mathematics). Describe your view of yourself as a future elementary mathematics teacher. The following prompts may help your thinking:
   - Write about your triumphs and disasters.
   - What do you like about learning math? What do you not like?
   - What is your first (or strongest) memory of learning or doing math?
   - What teacher(s) had a strong impact on your mathematics learning and/or attitude? How?
   - Identify an experience that affected your attitude about mathematics.
   - Did your attitude toward math affect your career decision? How?
   - Have you ever been embarrassed, humiliated, or especially proud of your mathematics ability?
   - How do you think your attitude about math will affect your teaching of math?

For Your Portfolio

When you finish studying this chapter, complete these activities to include in your professional portfolio:

1. Browse through issues of *Teaching Children Mathematics* and *Mathematics Teaching in the Middle School.* Begin collecting articles you find interesting and useful.

2. Interview elementary- or middle-school children. Ask them what they like and don't like about mathematics class. Describe what you as a teacher might do to change any negative attitudes they have.

3. Consult a copy of your state or local mathematics standards. Compare them with the NCTM *Curriculum Standards.*

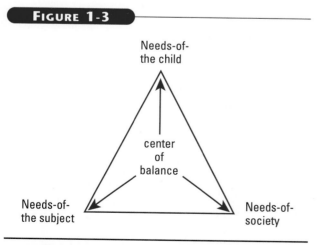

FIGURE 1-3

Needs-of-the child

center of balance

Needs-of-the subject

Needs-of-society

Source: Adapted from Glennon, V.J. (1963). "Some Perspectives in Education," *Enrichment Mathematics for the Grades,* NCTM's 27th Yearbook.

Resources for Teachers

Children's Book

Scieszka, J., & Smith, L. (1995). *Math Curse*. New York, NY: Penguin Group.

Books on Increasing Equity in Learning Mathematics

Downie, D., Slesnick, T., & Stenmark, J. (1981) *Math for girls and other problem solvers*. Berkeley, CA: Lawrence Hall of Science.

Krause, M. (1983). *Multicultural mathematics materials*. Reston, VA: National Council of Teachers of Mathematics.

Skolnick, J., Langbort, C., & Day, L. (1982). *How to encourage girls in math and science*. Palo Alto, CA: Dale Seymour Publications.

Stenmark, J., Thompson, V., & Cossey, R. (1986). *Family math*. Berkeley, CA: Regents, University of California.

Stenmark, J., Thompson, V., & Cossey, R. (1987). *Mathematica para la familia*. Berkeley, CA: Regents, University of California.

Links to the Internet

National Council of Teachers of Mathematics

http://www.nctm.org

Contains information about the NCTM Standards and other publications, as well as news releases related to mathematics teaching and learning.

Math Forum

http://forum.swarthmore.edu/

Contains a Student Center, Teachers' Place, Research Division, and section for parents and citizens. Also includes "Ask Dr. Math," where you can ask questions about K–12 mathematics.

Eisenhower National Clearinghouse

http://www.enc.org

Contains mathematics and science standards, international comparisons such as the TIMSS data, and resources for teachers, including a large set of math and science Internet sites and classroom activities.

Teachers' Net

http://teachers.net

Contains many different types of resources for teachers, including curriculum resources, lesson plans, chatboards, and mailrings.

Millie's Math House

http://204.200.238.31/prod/house/millie/quotes.html (awards)

Contains information about the topics included in "Millie's Math House," and a list of awards it has won.

http://tcp.ca/Dec94/ChildrenSoftware.html

Contains a review of "Millie's Math House," entitled "Learning and Having Fun: Guide to Children's Software" by Pedro Arrais.

the same amount of clay in both or if one has more than the other. Because some students are not yet ready to grasp the notion of the conservation of matter, this may cause some disequilibrium in the child's thinking. To convince herself or himself, the child may restore the ball to its original shape and announce that both balls have the same amount of clay. This ability to reverse a transformation leads to a state of equilibrium in which the child knows that the transformation did not change the amount of clay.

Teachers do not have much control over maturation but they can play a significant role in experience and social transmission and, to some extent, in producing equilibration through the quantity and quality of experiences they provide children.

Implications. Most children in the elementary grades are in what Piaget called the *concrete operations stage.* This means that elementary schoolchildren will learn mathematical concepts by manipulating materials and observing what happens. A teacher must provide the kind of concrete experiences that will facilitate learning. Even for the middle school, experience and research suggest that children are not yet able to think about many concepts at a formal level and, in fact, still need concrete representations. Visual learners may continue to find such models helpful throughout their educational careers.

Piaget's *conservation* tasks provide us with some ingenious methods for assessing readiness for certain concepts. Conservation involves recognizing that an invariant transformation does not change the property in question. For example, a row of 10 counters still contains 10 counters when spread out or pushed together. "Spreading out" and "pushing together" are invariant transformations with respect to number. (A number conservation task is described in Chapter 5 and several measurement conservation tasks are described in Chapter 15.)

Piaget's work can also provide direction for sequencing the curriculum. For example, children seem to conserve number early in the concrete operational stage while mass and volume are not conserved until the end of this stage. These findings suggest that formal measurement of area and volume would appropriately be delayed until intermediate grades.

Piaget's observations on knowledge development suggest a learning environment that allows the elementary and middle school child to explore ideas. In mathematics learning, this is most effectively done with the aid of concrete manipulative materials.

Zoltan Dienes   Zoltan Dienes developed a theory of mathematics learning that includes the dynamic, perceptual variability, mathematical variability, and constructivity principles.

FIGURE 2-2

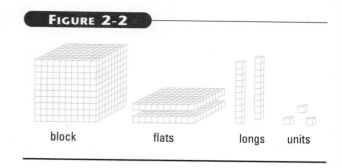

block   flats   longs   units

The *dynamic principle* is a three-phase process. The first is a *preliminary,* or *play* phase, in which activities are relatively unstructured. The teacher would, however, provide the kinds of materials out of which the structure of a mathematical concept can be developed. For example, children might be given a set of Dienes's Base-Ten Multibase Arithmetic Blocks (MAB) as shown in Figure 2-2. (In subsequent chapters these blocks will be referred to simply as base-ten blocks.) Initially children will build towers, bridges, and other creative objects. Children are very good at making up rules for their play. (You can hear them doing this when you are on playground supervision.) Soon they will start to develop some rules for using the blocks. For example, you have to "use the least number of pieces" when you build a road. This leads to the next phase of the dynamic principle, *structured play* or games. The above rule leads to the notion of trading ten short units for one long unit. Students thus become aware of the relationships among the blocks.

The third component of the dynamic principle involves an *explicit representation* of some mathematical concept. For example, children can use their understanding of the relationship among the blocks developed in Phase 2 to represent base-ten numbers, say 213, as shown here.

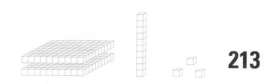

213

Dienes diagrams this process cyclically (Figure 2-3). Actually it is both cyclical and spiral in the sense that the final or more abstract phase can serve as the play stage for a higher-level related concept. For example, the representation of specific numbers can be a play activity in which children represent more than one number and then later, in the more structured phase, combine these to demonstrate addition.

The perceptual variability principle, (also known as the multiple embodiment principle), says that learning a

FIGURE 2-3

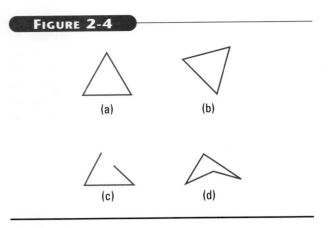

Application of abstraction forms play stage for higher level of a concept → Play → Structuring to form a concept or abstraction → Abstraction

FIGURE 2-4

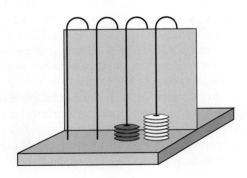

(a) (b)

(c) (d)

concept is facilitated when children can "see" the concept in a variety of forms or embodiments. This allows the child to abstract the common or relevant properties of the concept from various representations. Again consider the representation of a base-ten number as an example of the perceptual variability principle. Initially children could bundle popsicle sticks, putting groups of 10 together with rubber bands. Later they could use the base-ten blocks to represent, say, 47 as shown at the bottom of the page.

At a more abstract level, 47 could be shown on an abacus. In each case the number represented is the same but each representation is "perceptually" different.

Like the perceptual variability principle, the *mathematical variability principle* suggests that children be exposed to a variety of variables so that essential ones become evident by their presence in all examples. The difference is that for mathematical variability, mathematical variables are changed rather than perceptual ones.

Again using the base ten blocks you could focus on the concept of "grouping" in numeration. What is important is the process of grouping and not the number of objects in a group. So a teacher might use a base-three version of the MAB, then a base-five version, and so on.

In teaching the concept of "triangle," a teacher should employ different triangles in different orientations. Many young children will agree that the shape in Figure 2-4(a) is a triangle, but they may not acknowledge that the shape in Figure 2-4(b) is a triangle. Children need many examples of triangles so that they can abstract the essential mathematical variables from the irrelevant ones. Non-examples of a concept may be included in the mathematical variability principle. However, children need to know that an instance is a non-example. Using the triangle concept, figures or designs such as those in Figure 2-4(c) and (d) could be identified as non-examples to help children focus on the relevant mathematical variables.

The *constructivity principle* suggests that children be allowed to build up (construct) their own knowledge from their own experiences. Analysis will come later. Dienes argues that something has to exist before it can be analyzed.

Implications. Dienes's theory, like Piaget's, underlines the importance of an active learning environment in which children are actively involved with a concrete

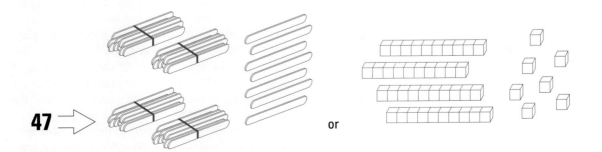

47 ⟹ or

representation of a mathematical concept in order to build up their understanding of the concept. The work of Dienes makes somewhat more explicit the need for teachers to be aware of individual learning rates and styles. One embodiment of a concept may make sense to one student, but a different embodiment may be needed to help another student understand.

VIDEO LINK 2-1
Communication

Brief Summary: The "Communication" video shows excerpts of several different mathematics classes.

1. How did the teachers accommodate students' different learning styles?
2. How do these lessons illustrate the principles of constructivism?
3. What is the role of a teacher in a constructivist classroom?

Video Source. Teaching Math: A Video Library, K–4; Tape 21 from The Annenberg/CPB Math and Science Collection.

BASIC PRINCIPLES REVIEWED

From the work of Piaget, Dienes, and many others, a number of basic principles can be derived. The following four guidelines, while not exhaustive, are important. For a more exhaustive listing and for more elaboration the reader should consult a recent text on learning theory.

STANDARDS LINK 2-1

In grades K–4, the study of mathematics should include numerous opportunities for communication so that students can:

- relate physical materials, pictures, and diagrams to mathematical ideas;
- reflect on and clarify their thinking about mathematical ideas and situations;
- relate their everyday language to mathematical language and symbols;
- realize that representing, discussing, reading, writing, and listening to mathematics are a vital part of learning and using mathematics. (NCTM, 1989, p. 26)

Begin with Concrete Representation

Children seem to learn best when learning begins with a concrete representation of a mathematical concept. In fact, it is best to provide children with *multiple embodiments* of the concept. To provide multiple embodiments the use of *manipulative materials* is essential in all mathematics classrooms. This does not mean that concrete manipulatives should be used exclusively. Other forms of representation are also important, including mental images and computer images (Clements & McMillen, 1996).

When building an understanding of the addition algorithm, children should set out bundles of popsicle sticks (or equivalent objects) and manipulate these to represent the process of addition (Figure 2-5). The use of different manipulatives at different times helps children to abstract the essence of the concept as well as to lend variety to the mathematics program.

Manipulatives do not guarantee success. A teacher must take steps to promote success when planning a lesson that includes manipulatives. Ross and Kurtz (1993) suggest:

When planning such a lesson, the teacher should be certain that

FIGURE 2-5

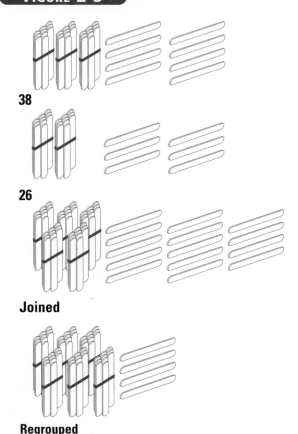

38

26

Joined

Regrouped

1. manipulatives have been chosen to support the lesson's objectives;

2. significant plans have been made to orient students to the manipulatives and corresponding classroom procedures;

3. the lesson involves the active participation of each student; and

4. the lesson plan includes procedures for evaluation that reflect an emphasis on the development of reasoning skills (p. 256).

Develop Understanding

Understanding is a term that is often used somewhat synonymously with meaningfulness. Structuring activities and experiences that will enable children to build understanding is the essence of teaching. Beyond the level of straight recall or recognition, children can exhibit understanding through at least four higher-level cognitive processes. These processes are application, noting relationships, transformation, and transfer. *Application* involves using concepts in related but somewhat different problems. If children can identify and state *relationships* among concepts, they likely have a meaningful understanding of those concepts. Being able to relate multiplication to addition is one example of this level of understanding.

$$4 \times 5 \quad \rightarrow \quad 5 + 5 + 5 + 5$$

Transformation involves taking a problem or idea in one form and representing it in another form. Restating ideas in other words, constructing a graph, or drawing a diagram to illustrate a concept would be examples of transformation. *Transfer* involves using an idea or concept in a context different from that in which it was learned; an extremely important process in a rapidly changing society.

One way to help children develop understanding is for teachers to carefully select the *modes of representation* they use in instruction. Mathematics concepts may be represented in many different ways, called *modes of representation* (Behr, Lesh, Post, & Silver, 1983). These five modes include real-world situations, manipulative models, pictures, oral language, and written symbols (see Figure 2-6). For example, the concept of five might be represented with 5 fingers (real-world situation), with five Unifix cubes (manipulative model), with a picture of 5 flowers (pictures), by saying the word "five" (oral language), and by writing the word "five" or the symbol "5" (written symbols). See Figure 2-6.

Using the example above of the concept of five, a teacher might ask a child who has displayed five fingers if he or she could show the same number in another way, such as by drawing a picture of five objects or picking up a group of five blocks. This is called translations. Translations refer to asking children to represent a concept in more than one mode and is indicated by the arrows in Figure 2-6.

Why is this concept important? Research shows that instruction in which children are encouraged to make

---

FIGURE 2-6

Modes of Representation

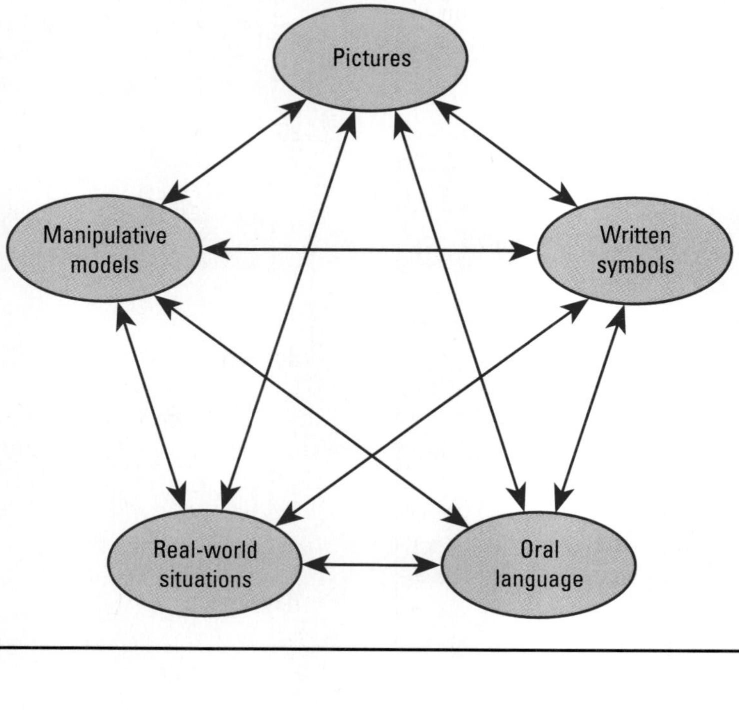

translations between modes of representation enhances students' understanding. Thus, good teachers ensure that their lessons include a variety of modes of representation and opportunities for children to make translations between modes.

The Annenberg/CPB Math and Science Collection

VIDEO LINK 2-2
Communication

Brief Summary: In the "Communication" video, Leland Clarke conducts a lesson with his kindergarten students in which numbers are represented in many different ways. For example, the number six is represented with a word (six), a numeral (6), a picture (six daisies), and actual students (6 students wearing hats to represent flowers).

1. Why did the teacher represent the number six in more than one way?
2. What other modes of representation could have been used?

Video Source. Teaching Math: A Video Library, K–4; Tape 21 from The Annenberg/CPB Math and Science Collection.

Hiebert (1990) states that "Meaning or understanding in mathematics comes from building or recognizing relationships either *between* representations or *within* representations" (p. 32).

STANDARDS LINK 2-2
Representing is an important way of communicating mathematical ideas at all levels, but especially so in grades K–4. Representing involves translating a problem or an idea into a new form. Translations of this type often are used by adults and children as they converse with others. Children might draw diagrams, for example, to express an idea or viewpoint in an alternative format that could be more comprehensible to the listener. The act of representing encourages children to focus on the essential characteristics of a situation. Representing includes the translation of a diagram or physical model into symbols or words. (NCTM, 1989, p. 27)

Building relationships *between* representations occurs, for example, when a child listens (spoken language) to a problem, represents and manipulates it with blocks (concrete objects), and then writes a response on paper (written symbols).

The Annenberg/CPB Math and Science Collection

VIDEO LINK 2-3
Communication

Brief Summary: The "Communication" video shows excerpts of several different mathematics classes in which students were communicating in many different ways.

Early in this video, DeAnn Huinker used the phrase "the power in using multiple representations." What do you think she meant by this?

Video Source. Teaching Math: A Video Library, K–4; Tape 21 from The Annenberg/CPB Math and Science Collection.

Building relationships *within* representations often involves recognizing patterns within the representation. Hiebert (1990) uses the base-ten blocks in a decimal context as an example. In this setting children can recognize the "pattern of *repeated* partitioning by 10 and the corresponding decrease in the size of the blocks" (p. 33), which could go on forever if the blocks could be cut finely enough.

Reflection enhances understanding or meaningfulness of a concept. Reflection is often needed to observe patterns within a representational system. The teacher or students can encourage reflection by asking appropriate questions or by challenging each other's observations. Note again the importance of communication.

Understanding of new concepts is more likely to occur when children understand prerequisite concepts than when they have only a superficial understanding or when they have learned previous skills and concepts by rote. Just as we would not consider building a house without proper footings, so children cannot build mathematical structures without meaningful prerequisite learnings. For example, children who do not have a good understanding of the place-value concept often have considerable difficulty ordering decimal fractions. They often order on the basis of the number of digits (see Chapter 12).

STANDARDS LINK 2-3
Communication plays an important role in helping children construct links between their informal, intuitive notions and the abstract language and symbolism of mathematics; it also plays a key role in helping children make important connections among physical, pictorial, graphic, symbolic, verbal, and mental representations of mathematical ideas. (NCTM, 1989, p. 26)

Van de Walle (1994) points out that understanding is demonstrated when connections are formed between procedural knowledge and conceptual knowledge. *Procedural knowledge* is a knowledge of the symbolism used to represent mathematical ideas and the rules and procedures used to perform a mathematical task. *Conceptual knowledge* consists of relationships that connect a number of mathematical ideas or concepts. [For example, in Chapter 7 we will see that the concepts of addition and subtraction are related (knowing $6 + 5 = 11$ helps one think about $11 - 5 = 6$).] This conceptual knowledge greatly facilitates acquisition of the procedural knowledge of addition and subtraction computation. An example that nicely illustrates the difference between knowing "how" and knowing "why" involves division of common fractions. Recalling and applying the rule "invert and multiply" is procedural knowledge; being able to explain or justify why it works is conceptual knowledge. Being able to see or make connections between conceptual knowledge and procedural knowledge is what Skemp (1989) calls *relational understanding* (Figure 2-7).

Encourage Communication

Communication plays an important role in children's mathematics learning. It "forces" children to think through a concept, often resulting in more refined understanding. Highlighted in the NCTM standards, communicating in mathematics means encouraging students to engage in interactive conversations as they work through mathematical processes. Student interactions can help students clarify what they do or do not understand about mathematical concepts or processes. According to Stigler (1988), Japanese teachers spend more time than do most American teachers encouraging students to communicate verbally about mathematics concepts and procedures. It is time for American teachers to capitalize on opportunities to get students talking about mathematics.

STANDARDS LINK 2-4
Young children learn language through verbal communication; it is important, therefore, to provide opportunities for them to "talk mathematics." Interacting with classmates helps children construct knowledge, learn other ways to think about ideas, and clarify their own thinking. (NCTM, 1989, p. 26)

Problems and models provide many opportunities for communicating about mathematics. In addition, talking and writing about mathematics helps children solidify their understanding of mathematics.

Communication in the mathematics classroom can take many forms. It can be oral or written. It can be from

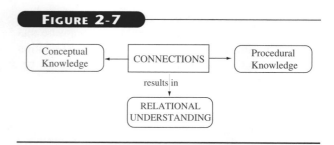

FIGURE 2-7

student to student or between a student and his or her teacher. It can be a report, a story, a word problem for other students to solve, a description of how a student solved a problem, or an entry in a math journal. While keeping a journal is generally associated with the language arts discipline, a math journal can be used to reinforce a child's understanding of mathematical concepts.

A math journal serves many purposes. It offers an opportunity for children to think about and write about the mathematics concepts they are learning. Further, it provides the teacher with an excellent assessment tool. Journals should be a regular part of mathematics class activities, and can also be included routinely as part of homework assignments.

Math journal prompts might include the following:

I think the answer is . . . .
I solved the problem by . . . .
Another way to solve the problem would be . . . .
I still have a question about . . . .
The thing I liked most was . . . .

STANDARDS LINK 2-5
Having students keep journals in mathematics class is another way to facilitate communication and give them an opportunity to reflect on their learning. A journal can be a form of free expression about the mathematics studied, or children can be asked to respond to directions such as these: Tell me what you thought were the hardest and easiest parts of today's lesson and why. (NCTM, 1989, p. 28)

Communication in the mathematics classroom provides teachers with valuable insights into children's understanding, which helps teachers plan further instructions.

Make Connections

When children build connections between mathematical ideas and other topics, mathematics becomes more meaningful and understanding is enhanced. Using a thematic approach is one way to provide integration because it can address not only basic skills but also more open-ended and higher-level objectives. Individual interests and other individual differences may be more easily accommodated in a thematic unit. The cooperative learning approach lends itself to thematic units.

Thematic units also provide opportunity to connect mathematics to real life through field trips and related activities. For example, children might go to a nearby shopping mall (with permission from the administration) to observe geometric shapes in the mall decor, observe slides, flips, and turns in shop logos, calculate the total cost for each member of their small group to purchase a particular snack at one of the food outlets, and so on.

Even without a thematic approach, however, many opportunities to integrate mathematics with other subjects are encountered daily. For example, an art teacher might reinforce one-to-one correspondence by having one child distribute one paint brush to every child. In physical education, children might measure distance and time, count when skipping, and keep track of scores and other statistics in games. Social studies and science offer many opportunities for creating and interpreting graphs. Serendipitous opportunities need to be seized and discussed so that children "see" the connection of mathematics to their in-school and out-of-school experiences.

Connections are not automatic. Teachers must provide experiences in which the connections are "obvious" or at least where they can be made explicit as described in the previous paragraph. This will encourage children to look for other connections and eventually recognize the pervasive nature of mathematics in the world around them.

STANDARDS LINK 2-6

In grades K–4, the study of mathematics should include opportunities to make connections so that students can:

- link conceptual and procedural knowledge;
- relate various representations of concepts or procedures to one another;
- recognize relationships among different topics in mathematics;
- use mathematics in other curriculum areas;
- use mathematics in their daily lives. (NCTM, 1989, p. 32)

Take Time to Motivate Students

Motivation fuels mathematical learning. If children are motivated, they attend to instruction, strive for meaning, and persevere when difficulties arise. Competent teachers, effective instructional models, and thought-provoking activities guide the process, but children must first be motivated to learn mathematics (Holmes, 1990, p. 101).

Motivation in a student is his or her willingness to give attention, time, energy, and perseverance to learning. It is the willingness to accept the challenge to understand a concept or solve a problem. Motivation also is associated with the belief that one can succeed. Almost all students begin kindergarten with this belief. As the years pass, some lose faith in their ability, especially in mathematics. Thus, the level of motivation is one of many ways in which students within the classroom differ.

While motivation is largely internal to each child, there are strategies a teacher can employ to increase motivation. On a general level, individuals become motivated when the concepts being learned are meaningful and when they experience satisfaction, success, and recognition. Communication and meaningful opportunities for students to engage in mathematics conversations about real-world problems can be very motivating, in addition to enhancing students' understanding of mathematics concepts. Give children meaningful tasks and assignments at which they can be successful, then recognize their achievements.

More specifically, there are differences in what motivates children. So-called academically inclined children are motivated by achievement. Special challenges such as puzzles, nonroutine problems, and strategy games will capture their attention and increase motivation. Other children experience increased motivation when they can see the utilitarian value of what they are learning. Application or real-world type activities should be designed for these students. This does not imply that certain children are given one type of experience exclusively. All children should experience different types of activities, however some may simply opt for a larger dose of one type than another. Variety in activities helps to enhance motivation.

In the literature on the subject, motivation has often been categorized as *extrinsic* (grades, stars, etc.) or *intrinsic* (internal interest and desire to learn). Both should be considered, although intrinsic motivation seems to be more congruent with the theory that children build their own mathematical understanding.

Attitudes   Attitudes are an important part of motivation. Children who feel good about mathematics and their ability to do mathematics will normally be motivated to learn. On the other hand, children who have negative attitudes about mathematics or their ability in mathematics often exhibit disinterest. Given that there is a positive correlation between attitude and achievement in mathematics, it is important for the teacher to provide experiences and the kind of environment that will foster positive attitudes. Minimal stress, emphasis on meaning and understanding rather than memorization, success experiences, meaningful use of manipulatives, relating mathematics to the real world, and meaningful cooperative group work are some generalized guidelines for fostering the development of positive attitudes regarding mathematics.

It is essential to add that the teacher's attitude toward mathematics also is influential in forming children's attitudes. The teacher needs to be positive and show enthusiasm for, and interest in, mathematics.

Provide Opportunities for Practice

The belief that mathematics needs to be meaningful and the idea that children construct their own mathematical knowledge do not rule out the need for practice. Practice contributes significantly to making routine procedures automatic. This results in more efficient execution of a procedure and, thus, to the expenditure of less mental effort (Hiebert, 1990). Expending as little mental effort as possible on a routine procedure is important because it allows one to give more effort to a more complex task of which the routine is only a part. If a person has to devote too much effort to the routine task, attention to the major task may be lost.

Practice does not have to be dull and boring, though. Games, puzzles, riddles, little surprises, novel algorithms, novel formats, calculators, and computers all are useful ways of providing practice. Of course, this is not to say that worksheets, flash cards, and other traditional means of providing practice should not be used. The difference is in the purpose: thinking versus rote memorization. The following guidelines may be helpful in selecting activities for practice purposes. Teachers must recognize, however, that any one activity may not meet all of the guidelines.

Practice activities should

- be based on a well-defined cognitive objective. They should not be "busy work."
- be self-motivating and fun.
- make use of the concept or procedure being reinforced in a new and interesting form.
- be self-checking. That is, children should know when they have done it correctly.
- be adaptable for use with the whole class, a small group, or an individual student.
- provide for extension of knowledge. Further exploration of an idea should be stimulated.

Games Children enjoy playing games. They are certainly self-motivating and fun and, in fact, meet most of the above guidelines for practice activities. The public market as well as school supply companies offer many games that may meet specific mathematics objectives. More importantly, teachers can create and/or adapt games that are appropriate for the curricular objectives.

FIGURE 2-8

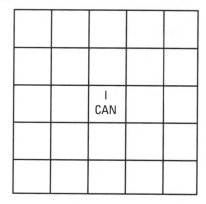

For example, a teacher might create a template (Figure 2-8) for a bingo-like game. By changing what goes in the cells and the nature of the calling cards, bingo-type games can be created to reinforce many different mathematical ideas and procedures. (If templates are created with a word processor, changes can be made quickly and easily.) Note the use of "I can" in the conventional "Free" space. Messages such as this can help to enhance a child's self-concept with respect to mathematics.

Puzzles and riddles Various forms of puzzles and riddles can be used to provide interesting, often self-checking practice. Puzzles can range from simple join-the-dot pictures to complex pattern recognition. Magic squares could also be included in this category. The sample puzzle in Figure 2-9 involves placing only numbers from 1 through 14, 3 in each circle, so that the sum in each circle is 21. No number may be used more than once. Note that 3, 6, 7, 10, and 12 have been placed as starters.

Riddles are closely related to puzzles. Many school libraries contain books with riddles of the type, "What fish do you see at night?" It takes only a few minutes to turn these into interesting and useful practice exercises. (An example of how this can be done appears in Chapter 6.)

FIGURE 2-9

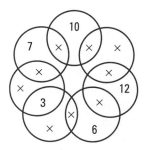

Surprises There are many little "surprises" in mathematics that can be used as warm-up activities at the beginning of a class. For example, a teacher might give the following instructions:

- Write a three-digit number in which the first and third digits are different by at least 2.
- Reverse the digits to create a second number. Subtract the smaller number from the larger.
- Reverse the digits in the difference and add to the difference.
- Did you get 1089?

$$
\begin{array}{r}
591 \\
195 \\
\hline
396 \\
693 \\
\hline
1089
\end{array}
$$

A challenge such as "Do you think this will work for all three-digit numbers" will motivate children to do more of these problems. In the process, they will get a great deal of practice with addition and subtraction—and the teacher didn't have to photocopy a worksheet. This could also be turned into a problem-solving activity by asking children to explain why this process works.

Different algorithms An *algorithm* is a routine process used to obtain a certain result. For example, most of us use an algorithm for tying our shoes—an algorithm that we've performed so many times it has become a mindless task. A mathematics algorithm is a process used again and again to find an answer to a mathematics problem. In this country we have standard algorithms for addition, subtraction, multiplication, and division tasks.

Demonstrating a novel (different) algorithm serves two purposes. First, it reinforces the fact that algorithms are human inventions. Secondly, a novel algorithm can stimulate practice with the conventional algorithm because once students have obtained a result with the new algorithm, they will verify the result by redoing the computation in the conventional way. Again, self-motivating practice is provided without the use of a worksheet. (The *lattice* method of multiplication described in Chapter 9 is one possible alternative algorithm that would serve this purpose.) As an *extension,* a teacher might challenge students to reflect on the algorithm they just completed and try to relate it to the conventional algorithm.

Novel formats Doing the "usual" thing in a different format can also be a means of providing self-motivating practice. For example, if some children are having difficulty with addition and subtraction facts involving 7, the teacher might challenge them to use only the numbers 1, 3, 5, and 7 (in any order) with addition and subtraction to generate consecutive results from say 5 through 14. For

example, 14 is the result of $3 + 5 + 7 - 1$. (Restrictions like these may make some results impossible.) Children will try many combinations and in the process they practice the basic facts involving 7 (Several activities such as this are suggested in Chapter 8.) Children could use the calculator for this activity by pretending the 0, 2, 4, 6, 8, and 9 keys are broken.

The calculator as a practice tool The calculator can be used to provide practice with concepts as simple as counting, for estimation, and for more complex calculations. Even children in the primary grades can use the built-in constant feature (now standard in almost all inexpensive calculators) to verify a counting sequence starting at any number, to count on, to count back, and to skip count. (Chapter 5 elaborates on how this can be done.) Activity 2-1 is an example of a calculator activity providing practice with the concept of numeration.

Personal computers Personal computers are widely used to provide practice. During the last few years the quality and quantity of practice courseware has improved markedly. Most allow a considerable number of options to be controlled by the teacher so that a program can be tailor-made for the individual needs of students. Many programs also keep track of responses so the teacher can analyze student performance later. Students are also given feedback on their responses and a summary at the end. The teacher must carefully review each software program to anticipate any difficulty children might have with data entry, screen displays, etc., and to evaluate the quality of the activity and how it relates to the curriculum. The teacher also needs to know precisely what the program will do so that appropriate options can be set and to decide which children could benefit from

---

✳ ACTIVITY 2-1

PLACE VALUE ON THE CALCULATOR

MATERIALS:
Calculators

PROCEDURE:
1. Player A announces a number that all other participants enter into their calculator. (For example, Player A selects the number 972.)

2. Player A then announces which digit in the chosen number is to be changed to zero without changing any of the other digits. (For example, Player A wants the 7 in 972 to be changed to a zero—so the calculator would display the number 902.)

3. All remaining players attempt to change the given digit to zero by doing only one subtraction. (The correct answer in this example would be to subtract 70, because $972 - 70 = 902$.)

interacting with it. Many organizations and school districts provide a list of recommended software that has been carefully evaluated.

THINKING ABOUT TEACHING

Teaching mathematics requires thinking about three things: how children learn, the teaching process, and what to teach. The first has already been discussed; the latter two are the focus of this section.

The teaching act is a three-phase process: what the teacher does before the lesson, what the teacher does during the lesson, and what the teacher does after the lesson. This is not a totally linear process. Each phase provides input and/or feedback for the others.

Pre-Teaching Activities

Before teaching a lesson, the teacher must be cognizant of the nature of the children, diagnose what they already know, decide on an appropriate approach that will make the content meaningful, and then plan the instructional sequence and activities in more detail.

Pre-planning considerations

Child considerations. A teacher must be cognizant of the child when planning mathematics experiences. Each child is an individual who comes to the classroom with unique needs, interests, attitudes, background, and motivation to learn mathematics.

Mathematical ideas generally are not learned as the result of one lesson. Teachers need to be patient with the process and with children because the understanding is slower to develop for some children and for some concepts than for others.

Activity involvement of the children needs to take many forms: physical as well as mental, verbal as well as written. A teacher should plan for activities that foster, perhaps at different times, all of these forms of involvement. Because success is a powerful motivator, plan learning activities in which children will be successful. This does not necessarily mean that the activity is to be easy, however. If work is too easy, children lose motivation. Plan activities to be challenging, but within the range of a child's ability to complete.

Mathematics anxiety (mathophobia) is a fear of mathematics. There is evidence that mathematics anxiety often starts in elementary school, although the symptoms often are not evident until years later. Kennedy and Tipps (1991) list five teacher practices that contribute to mathematics anxiety. These are: an emphasis on memorization, an emphasis on speed, an emphasis on doing one's own work, authoritarian teaching, and lack of variety in the

teaching-learning process. Mathematics anxiety can be lessened or eliminated by avoiding the practices cited by Kennedy and Tipps and by incorporating meaningful, active, and success-oriented activities.

Social factors can contribute to an individual's attitude and motivation to learn mathematics. Placing students in nonthreatening cooperative groups can improve a child's self-concept, raise achievement, and increase motivation for learning. Group work is as important in mathematics as it is in social studies, science, or any other school subject.

Social considerations may also include factors such as the child's home situation and hours of sleep the night before. A tense home situation can reduce a child's attentiveness and desire to learn. Furthermore, if an elementary schoolchild was awake until midnight the night before a test, the child's performance will likely be below expectation.

The teacher significantly influences the social situation within the classroom. Factors such as a child's home situation or sleep patterns, however, cannot be controlled by the teacher. Thus, accountability for learning rests with the parents, the child, and the teacher.

Myths about learning mathematics. According to Ginsburg and Baron (1993), there are five myths about learning mathematics. It is important that all teachers are aware of the fallacy of these myths, so they can plan appropriate instruction.

Myth #1: Some children cannot learn math. There is no reason all children cannot learn math, provided that they have good mathematics instruction. It is a challenge to every teacher to expect that all children will succeed in mathematics, and to use a variety of instructional strategies to help them do so.

Myth #2: Boys learn math better than girls. In fact, at the elementary level, there are often few differences in mathematics achievement based on gender. Frequently, differences that do occur begin appearing in middle school and junior high school and seem to be due more to cultural influences. One difference between boys and girls that has been documented, however, is that girls sometimes have slightly weaker spatial visualization ability. This points to the importance of teachers providing opportunities for all children, girls as well as boys, to develop their spatial abilities through hands-on activities in geometry and other topics.

Myth #3: Poor children and children from underrepresented groups cannot learn math. There are many success stories pointing to the fallacy of this myth. The key components of programs that are successful for poor children and children from underrepresented groups include motivation, high expectations, role models, appropriate teaching, and real-world applications.

Myth #4: American children have less mathematical ability than Asian children. Differences in mathematics achievement emerge between American and Asian children after a year or two of schooling. However, these differences seem not to be related to ability but instead due to differences in teaching and in expectations. For example, a common American notion is that "you're either good at math or you're not, and if you're not good at math, there's nothing you can do about it." We must change our expectations to believe that *all* children can learn mathematics, given good teaching.

Myth #5: Mathematics learning disabilities are common. There are many cases in which children do not seem to learn mathematics. But as illustrated by the previous myths about learning mathematics, usually this lack of achievement is not due to learning disabilities but instead to a lack of motivation and appropriate teaching.

Clearly, good math teaching is critical. A teacher who is motivated and knowledgeable can help any child to understand and achieve success in mathematics.

Diagnosing. Mathematics teachers are responsible for learning what mathematics knowledge students have already built, and on the basis of this, making decisions about current and future mathematical concepts children might be ready to learn. Only when we have learned the nature of the mathematical knowledge children have acquired can we plan appropriate learning activities that will meaningfully expand students' knowledge.

Other pre-planning decisions. Other preplanning activities include making decisions about broad goals, what content to include and what to exclude from a unit or lesson, and the nature of the most appropriate student activities (hands on, discussion, computer based, long-term project, etc.).

Planning

The unit. Decisions and observations made in the preplanning stage lead naturally into unit planning. The unit plan generally expands on one curriculum topic and including lesson plans and teaching strategies for a few days or a few weeks. The unit plan might consist of a series of headings such as:

1. Goals
2. Prerequisites
3. Sequence of new skills to be introduced
4. Developmental activities
5. Practice activities
6. Application of new skills
7. Problem solving
8. Enrichment activities
9. Evaluation of student learning

Another strategy for developing a unit plan is a *concept map*. A concept map is a schematic organization of your ideas about a particular topic so that relationships among various subtopics are visually displayed (Morine-Dershimer, 1990). A concept map for a unit on multiplication of a two-digit number by a one-digit number has been *started* in Figure 2-10. As you read more about specific

FIGURE 2-10

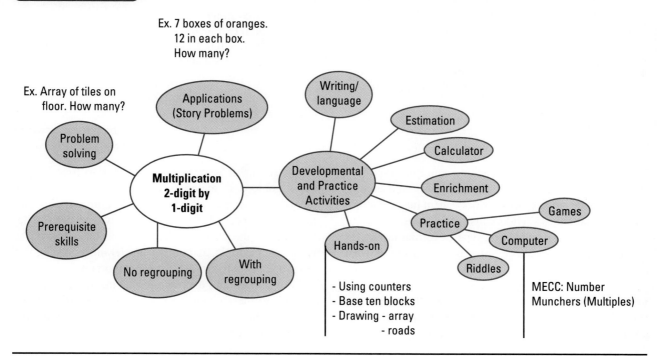

BOX 2-1

Sample Lesson Plan
Commutative Property of Addition for Grade 1

Objectives:

- Given concrete materials, children will demonstrate the commutative property of addition with sums less than 10.
- Given an addition sentence, children will write the commutative form.

Materials:

- Two clothes hangers with two distinct sets of clothes pins clipped onto the bottom wire. For example, one will have 2 pins adjacent to each other, a distinct space, and then 4 pins close together to show sets of 2 and 4. The other hanger will show 4 pins, a space, and then 2 pins.
- Counters

Procedure:

1. Tell a motivational story about two children who were given money on different days. Trish was given 2 dimes on Saturday and 4 dimes on Sunday. Josh was given 4 dimes on Saturday and 2 on Sunday. Ask, who do you think had the most dimes? Why? Allow discussion.
2. Show the hanger with the 2–4 arrangement and ask the children to talk about the display. (2 and 4 is 6.) Produce the second hanger so both are visible to students and elicit discussion about what is the same and what is different about the clothes pins.
3. Children work in pairs with counters. One makes two arrangements of two sets (similar to the two hangers) and the other child verifies that, when joined, both arrangements have the same number of counters. Change roles. Repeat several times.
4. Repeat procedure 3. This time the children record on paper the two arrangements with the results when combined (addition sentences).

Closure:

Use one hanger with a different arrangement of pins and ask the children to orally give you two addition sentences for the arrangements. Then ask the children:

- how they could prove that the two sentences are correct.
- to articulate what is happening (the "order" property).
- if they think the order property holds true for all addition sentences with two numbers.

Evaluation:

- Could students successfully translate the concrete models to abstract arithmetic sentences?
- Which particular students need more help?

Extension: (if time, or as an out-of-class challenge)

Use the numbers 3, 5, and 8. How many *different* addition sentences can you write?

Individualized Assessment Task: (to be done at at later time)

Show the child a card on which is written 2 + 5 and 5 + 2. Ask:

- "Read each of these." *(2 plus 5; 5 plus 2)*
- "Are they the same or different?" *(different story; same answer)*
- "Explain how you know they are the same." *(uses counters and switches the two groups)*
- "If you didn't know the answer and were going to figure it out, which form would you use?" *5 + 2 is faster because there is less counting on)*

---

instructional strategies for teaching multiplication, you could add to this concept map. Bartels (1995) and Hanselman (1996) describe other uses of concept maps and provide some examples of child-constructed maps.

A teacher will decide what type of format to use for unit planning. The process, rather than the form, is what is important.

Lesson plans. Lesson plans translate the yearly and unit plans into daily activities and experiences for the children. As with unit plans, many special formats have

been developed. Some consist of as few as four components—objective, materials, procedures, and evaluation (Morine-Dershimer, 1990)—to much more complex outlines (Orlich et al., 1990). The format will, in part, be determined by the preferred teaching style, the nature of the activities, the topic, and other considerations. Again, it is the process, not the format, that is important.

Box 2-1 contains a simple-format sample lesson plan to develop the commutative property of addition based on the clothes hanger suggestion in Chapter 8. Note that the answer to the extension question is 4.

Process of Teaching

There are many different models or styles of teaching. At a very simplistic level these have sometimes been described as being along a continuum from "pure telling" to "pure discovery" (Riedesel, 1990). No teacher operates at only one location along this continuum. An individual teacher normally has a region or range along the continuum in which she or he feels most "comfortable." Many of the decisions made in the pre-planning stage will influence the teaching style for a particular lesson.

Models for teaching mathematics A teacher with a constructivist theory of learning will likely employ a *developmental* model of teaching in which children actively engage in inquiry and investigations. Even then there are times when an explanatory approach with the whole class is appropriate.

Riedesel (1990) identifies four aspects in which the "developmental" approach is different from the "telling" approach.

1. The developmental approach emphasizes *active* learning as opposed to waiting for the teacher to explain.

2. The developmental approach builds new knowledge on experience. Therefore, it is socially relevant. The explanatory approach tends to build dependence on the teacher or a textbook.

3. Developmental approaches stress student thinking. Therefore, the classroom is student centered. In an explanatory environment children tend to wait to see what the teacher thinks.

4. The developmental approach emphasizes a "search for relationships and patterns and leads to an understanding of mathematical structure" (p. 12).

A *diagnostic* model places assessing students' current level of mathematical understanding at the core of the teaching process. That knowledge is then used to structure learning activities that will help the child build onto existing mathematical knowledge. A diagnostic model developed by Ashlock, Johnson, Wilson, and Jones (1983) suggested a sequence of five types of lessons arising from a diagnostic core.

1. Initiating—provides experiences with the new concept to be learned.

2. Abstracting—focuses on the attributes of the new concept to develop understanding.

3. Schematizing—focuses on interrelationships between the new concept and previously learned concepts.

4. Consolidating—provides practice to sharpen and clarify the new concept.

5. Transferring—problem-solving activities that show application of the new concept to new settings.

Earlier we referred to the claim of Behr et al. (1983) that meaning in mathematics results from building or recognizing relationships *between* or *within* representations. Building relationships between representations leads to a type of *translation* model for teaching. A teacher might state a problem (spoken language) and ask the children to represent (translate) it using concrete materials. At other times pictures may be used to represent the idea. Later, translations or connections will be made between verbal, concrete, pictorial, and symbolic representations (Sawada, 1985). The translation model may be observed most often in lessons involving the operations. These ideas are summarized in Figure 2-11. The reader should be able to write descriptions in the empty cells.

Children build mathematical knowledge when they explore and experiment with ideas, processes, or data. The *investigative* model focuses on experimentation as well as inquiry. A possible sequence of steps in such a lesson might be as follows:

- Structure a problem or make a statement that stimulates investigation
- Children do something
  - experiment, collect data
- Record or summarize data
  - discuss and decide on appropriate form (table, graph, chart, etc.)
- Analyze or interpret the data
  - look for patterns, relationships, etc.
  - describe the pattern (oral and/or written)
- Make a generalization or hypothesis
  - test with other data
- Respond to initial problem or statement
  - write a report on the experiment/project
- Extend generalization to other problems, settings, or applications

The above steps are not to be interpreted rigidly. They are fluid and flexible, and will need to be adapted or modified for different problems and experiments. The emphasis is on exploration, experimentation, interpretation, hypothesizing, and generalizing. The investigative model fits well into a cooperative learning approach.

These models of teaching mathematics are not exclusive. That is, a good teacher adapts a model based on her or his physical setting, the nature of the students and their individual differences, the mathematical topic, and her or his philosophy of teaching.

FIGURE 2-11

Teacher Moves

		Concrete	Pictorial	Symbolic	Oral
Child's Response	**Concrete**	Teacher shows concrete representation; child manipulates concrete objects	Teacher shows picture; child manipulates concrete objects	Teacher writes; child manipulates concrete objects	Teacher talks; child manipulates concrete objects
	Pictorial	Teacher shows concrete representation; child chooses or draws picture	P⟶P	S⟶P	O⟶P
	Symbolic	Teacher shows concrete representation; child writes symbols	P⟶S	S⟶S	O⟶S
	Oral	Teacher shows concrete representation; child discusses/ talks	P⟶O	S⟶O	O⟶O

Role of communication revisited. Earlier in this chapter, we stated that communication about mathematics significantly influences the mathematics curriculum and the learning of mathematics.

Communication also is an important factor in daily teaching activities and so it deserves additional comment here. The *Curriculum Standards* state that

> Young children learn language through verbal communication; it is important, therefore, to provide opportunities for them to "talk mathematics." Interacting with classmates helps children construct knowledge . . . . Writing about mathematics . . . also helps students clarify their thinking . . . . Reading children's literature

about mathematics . . . needs more emphasis (p. 26).

Why are communication skills important in mathematics? Primarily because they help children clarify their thinking and sharpen their understanding of concepts and procedures. Representing an idea or problem in a different form, talking about a concept or algorithm, listening to explanations by others, writing a definition in our own words, and reading textual material all contribute to an individual's building mathematical understandings.

Reuille-Irons and Irons (1989) state that

> Children's knowledge and excitement about mathematics grow if situations are provided to

encourage discussion about their learning. This allows children to extend their own strategies and build new ones. It is important to plan learning experiences that will foster exploration and investigation. These activities will promote the use of language that can be gradually extended to more sophisticated ideas that might be associated with the important mathematical concepts (p. 86).

Thus, Reuille-Irons and Irons have identified four sequential stages in which the development of language in mathematics can occur. These are

1. *Child's language.* The natural language of the child.
2. *Material language.* This is language that might be associated naturally with a specific representation of a mathematical idea. "Cover up" might be an example of a material-specific expression if pictures were being used to represent a subtractive situation.
3. *Mathematical language.* This involves using a word or short phrase for the mathematical operation.

    8 apples "put with" 2 apples

    Start with 3, "add" 5
4. *Symbolic language.* The words or phrases from stage three are now converted to symbols.

Within each stage, Reuille-Irons and Irons recommend language experiences that move from modeling aloud to creating to sharing.

The major purpose of writing in mathematics is that it "forces" one to think through a concept or process, resulting in a honing of one's understanding.

McIntosh (1991) suggests four useful forms of writing. In learning logs children can reflect on what they are doing and learning. Journals are similar but often less formal and may, therefore, be more communicative than logs. They may also provide more insight into a child's feelings about mathematics than logs. In expository writing children explain an idea or process. For example, a child may explain to an alien how she or he does multiplication. Creative writing gives children a chance to use abilities not often a part of school mathematics. Children may write poems about mathematical ideas or stories about concepts, mathematicians, etc. Here are some examples:

• Write a story about 6
• Write a story about a reflection (flip).
• Write a poem about addition.

If understanding is sharpened through writing, achievement should improve as well. Evans (1984) asked her Grade 5 children to engage in three kinds of writing;

explanations, definitions, and troubleshooting (describe an error and tell why it was made). Her students made much larger gains in achievement than a control class in which no writing was done other than what was required to answer questions, exercises, and problems. Other writers (Azzolino, 1990; Burton, 1985; Davidson & Pearce, 1988; Fennell & Ammon, 1985; Thompson, 1990) have provided rationales and suggested strategies for incorporating writing into the mathematics class.

The Annenberg/CPB Math and Science Collection

VIDEO LINK 2-4
Communication

Brief Summary: The "Communication" video shows excerpts of several different mathematics classes in which students were communicating in a variety of ways.

1. This video showed several groups of students working together on tasks. Describe advantages and disadvantages of groupwork in the mathematics classroom.
2. Describe some ways a mathematics lesson may be structured.
3. Describe ways of organizing the classroom for mathematics instruction.
4. Describe ways children can communicate about mathematics.
5. Describe the possible roles of a teacher when teaching mathematics.

Video Source. Teaching Math: A Video Library, K–4; Tape 21 from The Annenberg/CPB Math and Science Collection.

Post-Teaching Activities

The teacher's primary responsibilities in the post-teaching phase include the ongoing activities of evaluation and reflection. Evaluation is the process of gathering information and using it to make judgments that, in turn, are used to make decisions. A teacher should evaluate the lesson and his or her teaching, reflect on the teaching strategies used, and assess student learning. (Assessment of student learning will be discussed in Chapter 4.)

Evaluation of teaching According to NCTM (1991), the goal of evaluating mathematics teaching is to "improve teaching and enhance professional growth" (p. 72). Evaluation should be ongoing and linked to professional development. Teachers should have opportunities to analyze their own teaching and discuss their teaching with colleagues and supervisors. Evaluation should

BOX 2-2
Creating Mathematical Environments

Does the learning environment foster the development of all students' mathematical power?

Teaching Mathematical Concepts, Procedures, and Connections

Does the teacher have a sound knowledge of the mathematical concepts and have students been given tasks that promote their understanding of those concepts? Has the teacher engaged students in tasks and discussions that will enable them to see and use connections within mathematics and with other disciplines?

Teaching Mathematics as Problem Solving, Reasoning, and Communication

Did the teacher model different aspects of problem solving and engage students in activities and discussions related to a variety of aspects of problem solving? Did the teacher model mathematics as communication, monitor students' mathematical language, and provide opportunities for students to engage in a variety of communication forms? Did the teacher emphasize reasoning processes and provide opportunities for students to reason mathematically?

Promoting Mathematical Disposition

Assessment of a teacher's fostering of students' mathematical dispositions should provide evidence that the teacher—

- models a disposition to do mathematics;
- demonstrates the value of mathematics as a way of thinking and its application in other disciplines and in society;
- promotes students' confidence, flexibility, perseverance, curiosity, and inventiveness in doing mathematics through the use of appropriate tasks and by engaging students in mathematical discourse (p. 104).

Assessing Students' Understanding of Mathematics

Did the teacher use a variety of appropriate assessment methods? Were these methods congruent with the level and background of the children and with the way in which the concepts were taught? Were the results analyzed for reporting purposes and for modification of future instruction?

be based on the teacher's goals and expectations for students, the teacher's plans, and evidence of students' learning and understanding.

The NCTM (1991) Professional Teaching Standards lists many components of the evaluation of teaching. In general, the evaluation of teaching should focus on the teacher's ability to (1) teach concepts, procedures, and connections; (2) promote mathematical problem solving, reasoning, and connections; (3) foster students' mathematical dispositions; (4) assess students' understanding of mathematics; and (5) create a learning environment that promotes the development of each child's mathematical power.

Reflection on teaching   It is critical that a teacher spend time reflecting on her or his instruction (Hat, Schultz, Najee-ullah, & Nash, 1992). This includes the general approach to teaching and the type of learning activities developed for the students as well as the more overt teaching strategies. Such reflection results in professional growth. Self-evaluation of teaching practices and effectiveness is strongly encouraged in the *Professional Standards*. Specific standards directly related to evaluation of teaching are presented in Box 2-2.

THINKING ABOUT THE CURRICULUM

The mathematics curriculum can be thought about at two levels: first, as the mathematics concepts, procedures, and processes the child is exposed to; second, especially as it is experienced by the child, as all the activities and tasks the student engages in that are designed to help her or him build some mathematical understanding. The beginning teacher is initially more concerned about what to teach; the more experienced teacher is probably more interested in the kinds of activities that help develop the concepts. Every teacher, however, needs to be concerned with both.

The Mathematics

A teacher needs to know what mathematics knowledge the children have at the start of the school year, what concepts they are expected to learn during the year, and where these concepts will lead. This information may be obtained by assessing children's understanding (see Chapter 4) and by examining the district and state grade-level standards, the textbook and curriculum guide used in the school district, and the end-of-year assessment that students are required to complete.

The teacher must assess what mathematical understandings her or his children actually possess and then adapt the stated curriculum so that students understand prerequisite skills and concepts before attempting to build new ones.

The Activities

The real curriculum consists of much more than the concepts listed in a mathematics curriculum guide or state or district standards. It is the total of all the mathematics-related experiences a child has, both in and out of school. These experiences include playing counting games at recess, going to the store to purchase something after school, and the activities designed by the teacher. All such experiences contribute to a child's construction of mathematics knowledge.

When selecting or developing mathematics activities for children, it is important that the teacher keep in mind the standards that the children are expected to meet, in order to clearly write objectives for each lesson and goals for each unit.

CONCLUSION

The importance of meaning or understanding in learning mathematics cannot be overemphasized. The model below may help focus the picture. It shows meaning as a function of the child's exploration, often, but not exclusively, with concrete models, construction, and communication—all active, not passive, processes.

Teaching mathematics requires hard work. A teacher's task is to create and help children create for themselves representations of mathematical ideas that will enable the child to build a significant mathematical knowledge structure. To do this effectively teachers must be

- cognizant of how children learn mathematics;
- familiar with the mathematics included in the curriculum;
- able to design strategies and activities that will help children learn the concepts meaningfully;
- able to assess the level of development of the concept in children

A child's attitude toward mathematics must also be assessed and the information used to plan activities that will generate a positive attitude.

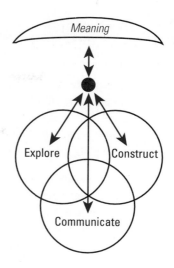

For Your Journal

When you have finished studying this chapter, reflect on these questions in your math journal:

1. Imagine you are an elementary teacher and another teacher in your school asks why you let children choose from a variety of materials when solving problems. How will you respond?

2. Imagine you are an elementary teacher and the parents of one of your students feel that their child is spending too much time talking and writing in math class. How will you respond?

3. Explain the five different modes in which a mathematics concept may be represented, and give an example of each for a concept of your choice.

For Your Portfolio

When you have finished studying this chapter, complete these activities to include in your professional portfolio:

1. Write a lesson plan for a concept of your choice. Include at least two different modes of representation in this lesson, and describe the translations that take place during the lesson.

2. Write a lesson plan that develops conceptual knowledge for a concept of your choice.

3. Write a lesson plan that includes several forms of communication.

Resources for Teachers

Books on Implementing Cooperative Learning

Erickson, T. (1989). *Getting it together: Equals.* Berkeley, CA: Regents of the University of California.

Fraser, S. (1982). *SPACES: Solving problems of access to careers in engineering and science.* Palo Alto, CA: Dale Seymour Publications.

Books on Preventing Math Anxiety

Martinez, J., & Martinez, N. (1996). *Math without fear.* Needham Heights, MA: Allyn & Bacon.

Tobia, S. (1978). *Overcoming math anxiety.* Boston, MA: Houghton Mifflin Company.

Books on Using Children's Literature

Bresser, R. (1995). *Math and literature, Grades 4–6.* Sausalito, CA: Math Solutions Publications.

Burns, M. (1992). *Math and literature, K–3, book one.* Sausalito, CA: Math Solutions Publications.

California Department of Education. (1993). *Literature for science and mathematics.* Sacramento, CA: California Department of Education.

Kruse, G., & Horning, K. (1991). *Multicultural literature for children and young adults.* Madison, WI: Wisconsin Department of Public Instruction.

Sheffield, S. (1995). *Math and literature, K–3, book two.* Sausalito, CA: Math Solutions Publications.

Thiessen, D., Matthias, M., & Smith, J. (1998). *The wonderful world of mathematics.* Reston, VA: National Council of Teachers of Mathematics.

Welchman-Tischler, R. (1992). *How to use children's literature to teach mathematics.* Reston, VA: National Council of Teachers of Mathematics.

Links to the Internet

Search Engines for Lesson Plans

http://www.altavista.com

http://www.hotbot.com

http://www.lycos.com

http://www.netscape.com

http://www.yahoo.com

Search engines are sites on the Internet where visitors can enter key words and find resources on the Internet. Visit any of the sites above and type "math lesson plans." You will receive a list of many sites containing math lesson plans. The following are a few of those sites:

AskERIC Lesson Plans

http://ericir.syr.edu/Virtual/Lessons/

Contains more than 1,000 lesson plans.

Eisenhower National Clearinghouse

http://www.enc.org/classroom/index.htm

Contains links to mathematics lessons.

ProTeacher

http://www.proteacher.com

Contains lesson plans and education news.

The Teachers' Plan-It

http://www.erols.com/akbarq/index.html

Contains lesson plans and links to educational websites.

TeachWeb

http://www.teachweb.net

Contains lesson plans and other useful resources for teachers.

CHAPTER 3

Developing Mathematical Thinking and Problem-Solving Ability

Focus Questions

When you have finished studying this chapter, you should be able to answer these questions:

1. What is a problem?
2. How do the various types of problems differ?
3. What are examples of several different types of problems?
4. What are the four steps involved in the problem-solving process?
5. How do the components of a problem-solving instructional program help teachers plan for instruction?

"A teacher of mathematics has a great opportunity. If he fills his allotted time with drilling his students in routine operations he kills their interest, hampers their intellectual development, and misuses his opportunity. But if he challenges the curiosity of his students by setting them problems proportionate to their knowledge, and helps them to solve their problems with stimulating questions, he may give them a taste for, and some means of independent thinking" (Polya, 1957, p. v).

Problem solving is a daily activity for most people. A student considers the most efficient route to the university from a number of alternatives. A homemaker examines the contents of the cupboard, wondering what to prepare for dinner. A ten-year-old wants to buy an ice cream bar at the local store. She knows she has several coins in her pocket and she remembers that she has at least two quarters. Before approaching the cashier, she wonders if it is possible that she does not have enough money to buy the $0.75 ice cream bar.

The past two decades have witnessed a resurgence of interest in problem solving as an integral part of the mathematics curriculum. Although problem solving has always been a part of mathematics programs, during the 1980s the National Council of Teachers of Mathematics (NCTM) and other influential groups promoted problem solving as a significant component of mathematics programs. More recently, the NCTM has reiterated the importance of problem solving in mathematics learning by designating "Mathematics as Problem Solving" as the first standard for all levels in the *Curriculum Standards* (NCTM, 1989). The Council recommends a "comprehensive and rich approach to problem solving in a classroom climate that encourages and supports problem-solving efforts" (NCTM, 1989, p. 23). *This focus on problem solving may be interpreted as a shift from a concern with algorithms or fixed content to mathematical thinking and inquiry.*

This chapter is about teaching-learning considerations for engaging students in solving problems so that they will develop mathematical thinking and learn mathematics via problem solving. It is also about teaching students how to solve problems. Different strategies that students should learn to enable them to devise solution plans are discussed. Problem examples with some solution processes also are provided. ○

STANDARDS LINK 3-1
In grades K–4, the study of mathematics should emphasize problem solving so that students can:

- use problem-solving approaches to investigate and understand mathematical content;
- formulate problems from everyday and mathematical situations;
- develop and apply strategies to solve a wide variety of problems;
- verify and interpret results with respect to the original problem;
- acquire confidence in using mathematics meaningfully. (NCTM, 1989, p. 23)

STANDARDS LINK 3-2
In grades 5–8, the mathematics curriculum should include numerous and varied experiences with problem solving as a method of inquiry and application so that students can:

- use problem-solving approaches to investigate and understand mathematical content;
- formulate problems from situations within and outside mathematics;
- develop and apply a variety of strategies to solve problems, with emphasis on multi-step and non-routine problems;
- verify and interpret results with respect to the original problem situation;
- generalize solutions and strategies to new problem situations;
- acquire confidence in using mathematics meaningfully. (NCTM, 1989, p. 75)

MATHEMATICAL CONSIDERATIONS

The science of mathematics was born from people's efforts to understand their environment. The process of solving environmental problems led to the discovery of mathematical facts, which in turn enabled the resolution of other problems. It is through the process of problem solving that students can experience the power and usefulness of mathematics. When the problems that students are asked to solve are meaningful and interesting, they will wholeheartedly engage in problem-solving activities.

What Is a Problem?

STANDARDS LINK 3-3
Problem solving is the process by which students experience the power and usefulness of mathematics in the world around them. (NCTM, 1989, p. 75)

Charles and Lester (1982) define a mathematical problem as a task for which:

1. The person confronting it *wants* or *needs* to find a solution.

2. The person has *no readily available procedure* for finding the solution.

3. The person must *make an attempt* to find a solution (p. 5).

From this definition, one would conclude that the traditional story problems found at the end of textbook chapters do not qualify as bona fide problems. Generally, there is no evidence that students want to work at this type of problem. Usually, students quickly glance at the problem to note word clues *(altogether, left, times)*, then immediately apply some operation to the data to arrive at an answer. Solving this type of problem hardly serves to develop one's mathematical thinking. Thus, other kinds of problems must be included in mathematics programs if students are to develop their thinking processes.

Students must be presented with some interesting and challenging problems so that they will gain experience in analyzing information and in proposing and testing hypotheses. It is essential that they be given the opportunity to develop insights into mathematical relationships.

Types of Problems

Mathematics programs include different types of problems: process problems, translation problems, application problems, and puzzles.

Process problems
Problem 3-1: Air Show
At an air show, 8 skydivers were released from a plane. Each skydiver was connected to each of the other skydivers with a separate piece of ribbon. How many pieces of ribbon were used in the skydiving act?

Problem 3-2: Dividing Up the Land
A town has a square piece of land to use as a recreation park. The recreation officer wants to divide the land into as many areas as possible using four straight lines. The areas can be of different sizes. What is the greatest possible

number of areas that can be obtained with four straight lines?

Process problems are a type of mathematics problem that requires solution processes other than computational procedures. These kinds of problems are important because of the processes used in solving them.

According to Polya (1949, p. 1) "to solve a problem is to find a way where no way is known off-hand, to find a way out of a difficulty, to find a way around an obstacle, to attain a desired end, that is not immediately attainable, by appropriate means."

From this definition, it is clear that problem solving involves higher-order thinking. It forces students to think creatively and innovatively, finding a new way to solve a problem.

When attempting to solve a process problem, one uses available knowledge and employs certain strategies to devise a solution. When one is engaged in solving a process problem, usually the conditions for a true mathematics problem (according to Charles & Lester, 1982) are met.

Prior to the 1980s, process problems were not found in mathematics textbooks for the elementary grades. At present, process problems form an integral part of mathematics programs and one can expect that their importance will increase.

 A Solution to the Air Show Problem

Skydiver 1 (S1) is connected to 7 skydivers.
Each skydiver is connected to 7 other skydivers.

$$8 \times 7 = 56$$

But, it takes one ribbon to connect S1 to S2 and S2 to S1. Therefore, the total number of ribbons used is 56/2 = 28. Twenty-eight ribbons are needed.

Other strategies that could be used to solve this problem are construct a diagram, model the situation, and solve a simpler problem. These strategies are discussed on pages 46–49. Try them.

Although process problems are regarded as an important component of a mathematics program, there are other types of problems that should not be neglected entirely. These are the kinds of problems that have traditionally been a part of programs, namely, translation and application problems.

Translation problems
Problem 3-3: Seating Capacity
A school auditorium can seat 648 people in 18 equal rows. How many seats are there in each row?

Problem 3-4: Jogging Rate
Ryan jogged 2 miles in 15 minutes. At this rate, how long would it take him to jog 26 miles?

Translation problems include the one- and two-step story problems typically found in textbooks. These problems can be a medium for students to develop understanding of the basic operations or to construct their own computational algorithms. Approached in this way, story problems can help students grow in their knowledge of mathematics and enhance mathematical thinking. However, if story problems are presented to students after they have learned how to compute, then the problems are mere practice exercises and they do not help to develop problem-solving ability.

Application problems
Problem 3-5: Electricity Costs
How much does the school board pay for the electricity used in your school in a school year? What is the monthly average cost?

Computation is generally the solution process used to solve application problems. Once the required data has been gathered and a decision has been made about a solution process, a calculator can lessen the time needed to arrive at an answer. Solving applied problems that are of interest to children can enhance their appreciation of mathematics.

Puzzles
Problem 3-6: Nine-Dot Puzzle
Can you join all nine dots using four straight lines without lifting your pencil off the paper?

Problem 3-7: Four Congruent Parts
Can you partition the figure in four congruent parts?

Although solving puzzles may not require any mathematical knowledge, they are classified as a type of mathematical problem (Charles & Lester, 1982) and are included in school programs. It is often difficult to identify what strategy to use to solve a given puzzle. Usually, mathematical processes such as visualization, analysis, conjecturing, and testing are involved.

Solutions to Problems 3-6 and 3-7

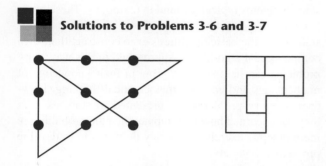

Ask Students to Write Problems

> **STANDARDS LINK 3-4**
>
> A vital component of problem-solving instruction is having children formulate problems themselves. Children can write variations for problems previously explored, word problems that correspond to a number sentence, or a question that can be answered by investigating data in a menu, advertisement, or chart. (NCTM, 1989, pp. 24–25)

One way to help students become comfortable with problems and the problem-solving process problems is to have students write problems. Through such experiences, students develop critical thinking, learn to collect and organize data (Fennell & Ammon, 1985), and learn how to express ideas in a clear and succinct manner.

A teacher can collect newspaper clippings, restaurant menus, sale flyers from local businesses, statistics from government departments, etc., and make these available to students to use when writing problems.

Another type of problem-writing activity is to ask students to write a problem for a given mathematical sentence. Some examples are given below.

1. Write a problem that fits the number sentence $46 + 17 = 63$.

2. Write a problem that fits the number sentence $35 - 28 = 7$ and that asks the question "How many more . . .?"

3. Write a multiplication story problem for the array.

```
· · · · · · · · · ·
· · · · · · · · · ·
· · · · · · · · · ·
· · · · · · · · · ·
```

4. Write a division story problem that asks to solve 138 divided by 6.

5. Write a word problem in which one has to first add, then subtract to answer the question.

> **VIDEO LINK 3-1**
> **Concepts of Whole Number Operations**
>
> Brief Summary: In the "Amazing Equations" segment, Flo Pearson asks her first- and second-grade students to compose and share word problems that have 20 as the solution.
>
> 1. Describe the differences between students writing problems to solve versus students solving teacher's problems.
> 2. Describe the role of language and other representations in problem solving in this lesson.
>
> *Video Source.* Teaching Math: A Video Library, K–4; Tape 7 from The Annenberg/CPB Math and Science Collection.

The writing process. When students are asked to write problems, a teacher may direct them through a process similar to writing stories. That is, there can be a prewriting stage followed by the writing, conferencing, and revising stages. Final stages can be publication and follow-up (Ford, 1990).

The prewriting stage is a time to create or examine a set of data and to think of a story to "flesh out" the data. When a problem has been written, it should be shared with other students. Conferencing about the problem can assist one in clarifying expressed ideas. When other students cannot understand a problem, then the writer must revise it until ideas are clearly expressed. Students may find that in some problems, there is missing data, extraneous information, or that the question does not fit the data. Such feedback helps one to revise the problem so that it is comprehensible and acceptable (Ford, 1990).

Students can "publish" their problems on paper to place in a binder or on cards for easy access. Follow-up activities include having a class discuss some problems in order to highlight particular types, or having students solve each others' problems. A successful experience of reading and solving a problem written by a classmate may augment a student's interest in learning mathematics.

Posing problems The activity of posing problems is different from that of writing problems as described above. Problem posing usually refers to the process of changing an existing problem into a new one by modifying the *knowns, unknowns,* or the *restrictions* placed on the answer (Moses, Bjork, & Goldenberg, 1990).

A trusting and supportive relationship between teacher and students will set the stage for both teacher and students to pose interesting problems. Mathematics classes should also be "alive" with students actively participating by questioning, conjecturing, and eagerly testing possibilities for solutions. In such a classroom climate, a teacher can easily encourage students to "study" given problems in order to see how they might be modified to create new and possibly more interesting and challenging problems. That is, students become problem posers by generating new problems.

Teachers are encouraged to initiate problem-posing activities with students by

> modelling the process personally by wondering openly *with* the students, fostering the free exchange of ideas and actively encouraging collaboration among students, honoring students' spontaneous what-ifs and conjectures, and being as interested in *how* students thought about a problem as in *what* they came up with. (Moses, Bjork, & Goldenberg, 1990, p. 86.)

Moses, Bjork, and Goldenberg (1990) offer four principles for guiding students to engage in posing problems. The four principles are:

1. Have students learn to focus their attention on *known, unknown,* and *restrictions.* Then consider the following questions: What if different things were known and unknown? What if the restrictions were changed?
2. Begin with a comfortable mathematics topic.
3. Encourage students to use ambiguity to create new questions and problems.
4. Teach the idea of domain from the earliest grades, encouraging children to "play the same (mathematical) game with a different set of pieces" (pp. 83–86).

The process of problem posing can contribute considerably to enriching mathematics classes by actively engaging students in constructing mathematics for themselves.

THE PROBLEM-SOLVING PROCESS

George Polya's (1957) four phases of problem solving have become the framework often recommended for teaching problem solving. These phases include:

- understanding the problem
- devising a plan to solve the problem
- implementing a solution plan
- reflecting on the problem

Understanding the Problem

This first phase of the problem-solving process is important, although some students do not see it as such. Students who do not try to understand the problem look for word clues or quickly decide on an operation to apply to the data. Rather, this first phase of problem solving should be given attention so that students will come to see the need for understanding a problem.

Understanding a problem is more than a matter of reading comprehension. It consists of apprehending the goal being sought, differentiating between required information and extraneous information, and detecting missing information. It also involves checking for assumptions regarding the given conditions.

Provide time for students to familiarize themselves with a problem. Familiarization can happen by rereading the problem in an effort to visualize the situation. Students can be encouraged to "see in your mind the problem situation" and "tell the problem story to yourself." Students can also be asked to tell the problem story to the class in their own words. The intent here is to have students verbalize the problem clearly and succinctly, giving all necessary information to solve the problem. Questions to ask students include:

- How would you tell the problem story?
- Can someone describe the problem another way?
- Did _____ give all the important information?
- Is there something that needs to be added to what _____ said?
- Could some information that _____ gave have been left out?
- What will you know when you have solved the problem?

When students understand a problem, they are more likely to accept the problem and devote themselves to finding a solution.

Devising a Plan to Solve the Problem

Allow time for students to reflect upon possible solution processes. Students can be invited to share possible solution strategies with one or two classmates. A group of students working together may discuss possible solution strategies. A student would tell the group why she or he thinks a particular strategy is an appropriate one for a given problem. The group may then decide to try a common strategy or have each member try a different strategy.

For a potentially difficult problem, the class as a whole can be invited to discuss solution strategies. This sharing can provide ideas for students who are stumped as to how to begin without removing the challenge to develop a solution process.

Whenever appropriate, encourage students to make an estimate about the quantity, measure, or magnitude of the solution before proceeding to implement a solution plan. The estimate can be revised as they progress through the solution process and recorded as first estimate, second estimate, etc. Making estimates requires that students reflect on what is happening and "think ahead," which can assist them in "seeing" a solution pattern without having to work through all the cases of the problem.

Implementing a Solution Plan

When students have personally decided on a plan, they begin to implement it to find a solution. Students should be allowed and encouraged to use their own ingenuity to develop a solution plan. Figure 3-1 (Pothier, 1992; p. 12) depicts three different tables Grade 5 students constructed to solve the same problem. The freedom to select and develop solution processes is favored by students over having to follow uniform procedures.

Students should be encouraged to solve problems in different ways and to discuss the different solution processes. For example, elementary students could solve the Barnyard problem (Figure 3-2) by drawing a picture, through trial and error, and by constructing a table and considering all possibilities. Middle school students could possibly solve the problem algebraically.

In addition, suggest that students develop their solution process in detail, not erasing "mistakes" or partial solutions. By commenting on the different approaches, teachers can assist students to realize that processes that didn't work can be informative in subsequent problem-solving activities. The analogy can be made to a scientist performing numerous experiments in an effort to discover, for example, a cure for a disease. A scientist does not destroy unsuccessful experimental results but keeps the data to inform further research efforts. Likewise, when students are trying to solve a problem, comparisons can be made with previous attempts to solve a somewhat similar problem. Recorded problem-solving attempts can also serve to provide insights into a student's thinking and assist a teacher in evaluation.

When engaging in problem-solving activities, students should not expect to find a solution to every problem they attempt to solve. The activity of problem solving, that is, the attempt, is more important than the solution.

Reflecting on the Problem

A teacher should advise a child that a solution process should be checked after a solution has been reached or while working through a solution strategy. For example, pausing to reflect on one's approach to solving a problem may lead one to abort a plan and seek another solution strategy.

Upon the completion of a solution, students should be encouraged to *look back* to the problem to see if the conditions of the problem have been met. Were wrong assumptions made? Has the problem question been answered? Is the answer unique or are there others?

At this stage, students should also reflect on the solution process and think of other appropriate solution strategies. One might notice how the problem could have been solved not only by a different approach but through a more efficient process.

Students should also be encouraged to *look forward* for ways of extending a problem. Asking the question "What if . . .?" is a good approach to modifying a problem. Changing one aspect of a problem such as the setting, the conditions, or the data and then attempting to solve the new problem can lead to insightful learning. It is also worthwhile to ask how the problem is similar to or different from other familiar problems.

Students should "feel right" about their solution before declaring that they have solved the problem. Therefore, this final step in the problem-solving process should not be quickly dismissed but should lead students to be ready to "defend" their solution when called upon to do so.

PROBLEM-SOLVING STRATEGIES

Learning a number of problem-solving strategies is an asset for problem solving (Suydam, 1984). Although students should be encouraged to devise their own approach to solving a problem, a teacher can at a given time highlight a particular strategy and lead the students in a class discussion and application of the strategy. In time, students will acquire a repertoire of different strategies to draw upon when faced with a problem.

A number of problem-solving strategies are described below. Two examples of a problem that can be solved using each strategy are included. Some possible solutions are provided.

STANDARDS LINK 3-5
A major goal of problem-solving instruction is to enable children to develop and apply strategies to solve problems. Strategies include using manipulative materials, using trial and error, making an organized list or table, drawing a diagram, looking for a pattern, and acting out a problem. (NCTM, 1989, p. 24)

FIGURE 3-1

Problem:

Josh has 3 pairs of pants, 4 sweaters, and 2 pairs of shoes. How many different pant-sweater-shoes combinations can Josh choose from to wear to school on Monday?

Solution 1   (Paula, Grade 5)

SWEATERS				PANTS			SHOES		SWEATERS				PANTS			SHOES	
O	Y	B	W	B	B	A	B	G	O	Y	B	W	B	B	A	B	G
X				X			X		X				X				X
X					X		X		X					X			X
X						X	X		X						X		X
	X			X			X			X			X				X
	X				X		X			X				X			X
	X					X	X			X					X		X
		X		X			X				X		X				X
		X			X		X				X			X			X
		X				X	X				X				X		X
			X	X			X					X	X				X
			X		X		X					X		X			X
			X			X	X					X			X		X

24 Combinations

Solution 2   (Mark, Grade 5)

P	S	SH	
Jeans	Fluorescent	Reeboks	Vision Streetwear
Joggers	Rockshirt	Reeboks	Vision Streetwear
Acid Washed	White	Vision Streetwear	Reeboks
Jeans	Trappers	Vision Streetwear	Reeboks
Jeans	Rockshirt	Reeboks	Vision Streetwear
Jeans	White	Vision Streetwear	Reeboks
Joggers	Trappers	Reeboks	Vision Streetwear
Joggers	Fluorescent	Vision Streetwear	Reeboks
Joggers	White	Reeboks	Vision Streetwear
Acid Washed	Trappers	Vision Streetwear	Reeboks
Acid Washed	Rockshirt	Reeboks	Vision Streetwear
Acid Washed	Fluorescent	Vision Streetwear	Reeboks

24 combinations

Solution 3   (Carl, Grade 5)

PANTS	SWEATERS	SHOES	NO. OF WAYS
1	1	1	1
1	2	1	2
1	3	1	3
1	4	1	4
1	1	2	5
1	2	2	6
1	3	2	7
1	4	2	8

Think: Since there were 3 pants and each had 8 different ways you get 24 different ways to dress.

Source: Pothier, Y. (1992). "Writing to Communicate Mathematics." In Daiyo Sawada (ed.), *Communication in the Mathematics Classroom.* Edmonton, AB: Mathematics Council of the Alberta Teacher's Association.

FIGURE 3-2

THE BARNYARD PROBLEM

Jill counted 20 pigs and chickens in the barnyard. Jack counted a total of 54 legs for the 20 animals. How many pigs and chickens were there?

a) Draw a diagram

2 legs each. This is 40 legs. Need 14 more. I'll add 2 to 7 animals.
Answer: There are 7 pigs and 13 chickens.

b) Trial and error

10 pigs and 10 chickens	$40 + 20 = 60$	Too many legs.
8 pigs and 12 chickens	$32 + 24 = 56$	Still too many.
6 pigs and 14 chickens	$24 + 28 = 52$	Not enough.
7 pigs and 13 chickens	$28 + 26 = 54$	That's it!

Answer: There are 7 pigs and 13 chickens.

c) Consider all possibilities

Pigs	Chickens	Legs	Total
1	19	$4 + 38$	42
2	18	$8 + 36$	44
3	17	$12 + 34$	46
4	16	$16 + 32$	48
5	15	$20 + 30$	50
6	14	$24 + 28$	52
7	13	$28 + 26$	54
8	12	$32 + 24$	56
9	11	$36 + 22$	58

Answer: There are 7 pigs and 13 chickens.

d) Solve algebraically

Let x = the chickens
Let y = the pigs

Solve for y

$2x + 4y = 54$
$2x + 2y = 40$
$\overline{ 2y = 14}$
$y = 7$

Solve for x

$x + y = 20$
$x + 7 = 20$
$x = 20 - 7$
$x = 13$

$x + y = 20$
$2x + 4y = 54$

Check

$x + y = 20$
$13 + 7 = 20$

$2x + 4y = 54$
$2(13) + 4(7) = 54$
$26 + 28 = 54$

Answer: There are 7 pigs and 13 chickens.

Dramatize or Model the Situation and Solution Process

Problem 3-8: The Class Reunion

Twelve people came to celebrate their ten-year high school reunion. Each person shook hands once with all the other persons. How many handshakes were exchanged at the reunion?

Problem 3-9: Karla's Farewell Party

Karla is moving to another state and her best friend has organized a farewell party for her. The people arrive at the house in the following manner: The first time the doorbell rings, Karla, as the first guest, enters. On each successive ring a group enters that has two more people than the group that entered on the previous ring. How many guests will have arrived after the twelfth ring?

Dramatization is a powerful medium to demonstrate understanding of a problem situation and can also lead one to "see" a solution. The "Class Reunion" and "Karla's Farewell Party" are examples of problems that children enjoy acting out.

Rather than participate in a dramatization, children may prefer to model the problem situation. For example, children could use objects to represent guests at Karla's party, and to keep track of the separate groups arriving at the party.

Solution to the Class Reunion Problem

In acting out this problem, groups of twelve students could be formed. (The problem could be solved for a smaller group of people to accommodate all the students.)

In a dramatization, each student would shake hands with each of the other people in the group. The realization that there is only one handshake when, for example, Sue shakes hands with Tom and Tom shakes hands with Sue, will assist students in arriving at a solution.

The discussion could be the following:

There are twelve of us. Each one has shaken hands with eleven other persons. That means 12 × 11 or 132 hand-shakes have taken place. But, there were really only half that number because when two people shake hands, there is only one handshake and not two. Therefore, when twelve people shake hands with each other, there are 66 handshakes.

Draw a Picture or Diagram

Drawing a picture is a favored strategy of many problem solvers. Some people draw a picture to help them visualize the situation and, when they understand the problem, they use another strategy to solve it.

Young children like to draw and usually enjoy developing a solution process to problems by using pictures. This strategy can be time consuming, as children may want to draw objects in great detail. In time, they will realize that representational diagrams are all that are required in problem solving.

Problem 3-10: The Cycle Problem

Kyle and Jason watched the children's bicycle and tricycle parade during the summer festival. They agreed to keep count of the number of cycles and the number of wheels as the children's parade passed by. At the end of the parade, Kyle declared he had counted 17 cycles and Jason said he had counted 43 wheels. How many bicycles and tricycles were in the parade?

Problem 3-11: The Barnyard Problem

Jill counted 20 pigs and chickens in the farmyard. Jack counted a total of 54 legs for the 20 animals. How many pigs and chickens were there? See Figure 3-2.

Solution to the Cycle Problem

There were 17 cycles in the parade.

Altogether there were 43 wheels.

Begin by drawing all the cycles with two wheels each. Seventeen cycles with two wheels each make 34 wheels. Nine wheels are missing. Draw them on the cycles.

There were 8 bicycles and 9 tricycles in the parade.

If students have solved the Barnyard problem, they should notice the similarity between the two problems.

Construct a Table or Chart

Constructing a table involves identifying appropriate labels to keep track of pertinent data as one works through a solution process. Some students may be able to set up a table with proper headings but may not be able to systematically list the data to assist them in arriving at a solution. Therefore, provide time for students to practice making organized lists of data. The three solutions in Figure 3-1 show how differently each child organized the data concerning clothing combinations.

Problem 3-12: Clear Pond

Today one blade of grass took root in Clear Pond. Every day the grass population doubles—that is, tomorrow there will be two blades of grass, the next day, four blades, and so on. On the tenth day, how many blades of grass are in the pond? If the capacity of the pond is one million blades of grass, on what day will it be filled? Estimate first and then figure it out.

Video Link 3-2
Communication

Brief Summary: In the "Communication" video, teacher Kirstin Gregory asks her first-grade students to solve the following problem: How many vehicles could be in a parking lot if the total number of wheels is 24? Ms. Gregory tells her students that they may use any combinations of vehicles, and any materials they'd like to help them solve the problem.

1. What different materials did the students use?
2. What strategies did the students use to solve the problem?
3. How did working with a partner help students solve the problem?

Video Source. Teaching Math: A Video Library, K–4; Tape 21 from The Annenberg/CPB Math and Science Collection.

Problem 3-13: The Garden Fence
A gardener has 60 feet of fence to keep animals out of the garden. What is the largest area of garden that this fence will enclose?

 Solution to the Clear Pond Problem

On day one, there is one blade of grass.
Each day, the number doubles.
Setting up a table will help to keep the data organized.
The table headings will be Days and Blades of Grass.
I'll use my calculator to obtain the products.

Days	Blades of Grass
1	1
2	2
3	4
.	.
.	.
.	.
20	524,288
21	1,048,576

Using a calculator, I quickly arrive at day 20 with 524,288 blades of grass. Doubling this amount gives more than a million.
Clear Pond will be filled to capacity on day 21.

Find a Pattern

An efficient way to solve some problems is by recording data in a table and then looking for a pattern.

When students observe data in a table, they should be encouraged to look for a pattern that will enable them to make a prediction about unknown data. Detecting a pattern can abbreviate a solution process considerably.

The Streamer Problem was presented to one combined class of fifth- and sixth-graders. The students first suggested that "acting it out" would be a good way to begin. Students were provided with "streamers" and they formed groups of six so that they could model a "five-sided" and then a "six-sided room." The students then returned to their desks to record what they had observed and continued to solve the problem.

One sixth-grade student's work is presented in Figure 3-3 (Pothier, 1992; p. 12). Although Jennifer began by drawing diagrams, she decided that organizing the data in a table would help her find a pattern.

Problem 3-14: The Streamer Problem
Imagine that you have been hired to decorate a room with streamers. The streamers are to be attached at the ceiling in such a way that all opposite corners of the room will be connected. How many streamers are needed to decorate a 10-sided room?

Problem 3-15: The Patio Walk Problem
Suppose you have concrete tiles 2 feet by 1 foot in size and you wish to use them to construct a patio walk that is 2 feet wide. Three sample patio walks that could be constructed with 6 blocks are pictured here.

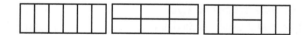

But there are other possibilities. How many different patio walks is it possible to build with eight blocks?

Solve a Simpler Problem

Changing a given problem to a simpler problem can be helpful in visualizing the situation and in determining what procedure to use. Sometimes, beginning with the simplest case and progressing systematically to more difficult cases can yield a pattern that quickly leads to a solution.

Problem 3-16: The Checkerboard Problem
How many squares (of different sizes) are there on an 8-by-8 checkerboard?

FIGURE 3-3

THE STREAMER PROBLEM

(Jennifer, Grade 6)

Situation: Decorating a room with streamers. Streamers are needed to connect all opposite corners.

Question: How many streamers are needed to decorate a 10-sided room?

1. -5 streamers
   -walls form a pentagon
   -we made a pentagon

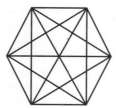

2. -9 streamers
   -walls form a hexagon
   -we made a hexagon with the streamers

Table:

Walls	4	5	6	7	8	9	10
Streamers	2	5	9	14	20	27	35

(differences: 3, 4, 5, 6, 7, 8, 9)

I felt proud of myself for having discovered the pattern.

Source: Pothier, Y. (1992). "Writing to Communicate Mathematics." In Daiyo Sawada (ed.). *Communication in the Mathematics Classroom.* Edmonton, AB: Mathematics Council of the Alberta Teachers' Association.

Problem 3-17: Connecting Points

A circle has 25 points marked on it. How many straight lines will there be when each of the points is connected to each of the other points on the circle?

 A Solution to the Checkerboard Problem

I'll probably get confused as I count the squares on an 8-by-8 checkerboard, so I'll begin with a smaller board. This should help me find all the squares on an 8-by-8 checkerboard.

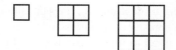

Number of Squares per Size

	1 × 1	2 × 2	3 × 3	4 × 4	. . .	Total
1 × 1	1					1
2 × 2	4	1				5
3 × 3	9	4	1			14
4 × 4	16	9	4	1		30
5 × 5	25	16	9	. . .	. . .	

. . .

I notice that the number of squares on each different-sized checkerboard is the sum of the square number that is the area of the board and the other smaller square numbers. For example, a 4-by-4 checkerboard has 16 + 9 + 4 + 1 total squares. A 5-by-5 checkerboard has 25 + 16 + 9 + 4 + 1 squares. Therefore, an 8-by-8 checkerboard will have 64 + 49 + 36 + 25 + 16 + 9 + 4 + 1 squares or 204 squares.

Beginning with a simpler case helped me notice a pattern in the table. This enabled me to arrive at the answer quickly.

Guess and Check

For some problems, one first thinks through the problem situation to make a guess, and then proceeds to check its accuracy. If the guess is not correct, one uses the knowledge obtained from the guess-and-checking process to make another more "educated" guess or change to a different strategy to solve the problem. Although solutions can be obtained through guessing and then checking, the procedure usually is not an efficient one. Use this strategy to solve problems 3-18 and 3-19.

Problem 3-18: Balanced Triangle

Place the digits 1, 2, 3, 4, 5, and 6 in the circles, using each digit only once, so that the 3 numbers on each arm of the triangle add up to 12.

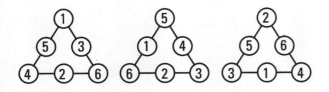

Problem 3-19: Multiples of Five

Find 6 consecutive multiples of 5 that, when added, make a sum of 345.

 A Solution to the Balanced Triangle

I've made several guesses without any luck.

I'll try putting the smallest numbers in the vertices. This doesn't work either. But they all equal 9! I've found one solution!

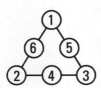

I'll try the largest numbers in the vertices. Yes, I've found a solution for 12.

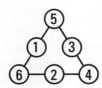

An organized list of all the possibilities of sums of 12 is another strategy one could use to solve the problem. The numbers that are used twice go in the vertices.

Sum of 12

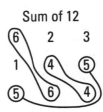

Working Backwards

In reading the "Rock Star Pictures" and "Apple Orchard" problems you will notice that they describe a series of actions or events. Problems of this type are best resolved by beginning at the end state and working backward until a solution has been reached.

Problem 3-20: Rock Star Pictures

Shane gave one-half of his rock star pictures to Samantha, then gave 6 pictures to Darryl and had 12 left. How many rock star pictures did Shane have before he gave any away?

Problem 3-21: Apple Orchard

The owner hired 3 watchmen to guard his apple orchard, but a stranger got in and stole some apples. On the way out, the stranger met each watchman, one at a time. To each he gave half of the apples he had then, plus 2 more besides. He escaped with one apple. How many apples did he pick and attempt to steal?

Elementary students find this type of problem difficult to understand and solve. They have to learn that working backward not only means beginning at the end and working one's way through the steps backward but also that the operations in the problem must be reversed. One way to have students practice reverse operations is to describe a route from Place *A* to Place *B* and then have them tell how to get from *B* to *A*. They will realize that all the right turns become left turns and vice versa.

In arithmetic situations, one can ask, what is the opposite of giving away $10.00? (receiving $10.00); the opposite of halving 6 (doubling 6); the opposite of 3 times 6 (1/3 of 6). When students understand reverse operations, they can be asked to find solutions to problems that can be solved by working backward.

 **A Solution to the Rock Star Pictures Problem**

Shane gave half his pictures to Samantha and 6 to Darryl.

He then had 12 pictures left.

I need to find out how many pictures he had to begin with so I'll work backward.

12 pictures. Add the 6 given to Darryl. 18 pictures. Double 18 because half were given to Samantha. 36 pictures.

Shane had 36 pictures.

Consider All Possibilities

Problem 3-22: Buying Stamps
Katherine's mother sent her to the post office to purchase some stamps. When Katherine arrived at the post office she remembered that she was to buy 18 stamps, which her mother had figured out would cost $4.90. Can you help Katherine find out how many 20-cent and 33-cent stamps her mother wants?

Problem 3-23: Police Vehicles
A city's police department has 15 cars and motorcycles. The total number of wheels on the cars and motorcycles is 42. How many police cars does the police department have?

Some problems involve the consideration of data in different combinations to find a right combination. A strategy used in such instances is to consider all possibilities so that the right combination(s) is (are) found. Making a table and systematically considering all possibilities is an efficient way to resolve such problems.

 A Solution to the Police Vehicles Problem

Information: 15 vehicles. 42 wheels in all.

I'll set up a table and list all the combinations of 15 until I find one that gives 42 wheels.

Motorcycles	Cars	Vehicles	Wheels
15	0	15	30 + 0 = 30
14	1	15	28 + 4 = 32
13	2	15	26 + 8 = 34
12	3	15	24 + 12 = 36

The total goes up by 2.

9	6	15	18 + 24 = 42

There are 9 motorcycles and 6 cars in the police fleet.

Logical Reasoning

Problem 3-24: Partners
Mona, Rita, and Sandra are married to Allan, Fred, and John, but (a) Sandra does not like John, (b) Rita is married to John's brother, and (c) Allan is married to Rita's sister. Who is married to whom?

Problem 3-25: Ranking by Age
Peter is twice as old as Ann will be when Sarah is as old as Peter is now. Can you tell who is the youngest, next youngest, and the oldest?

The development of logical reasoning is often stated as a requirement for the successful learning of mathematics. When students state that they solved a problem by "thinking it through," they should be encouraged to reflect on how they did it and to share the thinking steps they followed. Such sharing can assist other students to develop logical thought processes. Problems encountered in everyday life often require logical thinking to arrive at a suitable decision.

 A Solution to the Partners Problem

Setting up a grid will help to organize the information.

	Mona	Rita	Sandra
Allan		x	
John		x	x
Fred			

Because of the information given, I can mark several x's on the chart. Studying the chart, I find that John must be married to Mona, and Rita must be married to Fred. That leaves Sandra and Allan as partners.

Change Your Point of View

Problem 3-26: Planting Tomatoes
Mrs. Andrews planted 10 tomato plants in 5 rows of 4 plants each. How did she do this?

Problem 3-27: Looking for Squares
Find a square with an area of five square units on the grid.

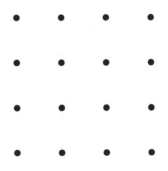

Have you ever met with failure at solving a problem because of the perspective you took in attempting a solution?

Often, by taking a certain perspective, we set limits to the considerations of possible solutions. For example, in the nine-dot puzzle (Problem 3-7), many people establish the perimeter of the square formed by the dots as the boundary for constructing lines. However, to solve the problem, three lines must be extended beyond the dots.

 A Solution to the Planting Problem

Trial and error is the only way that I can see to solve this problem.

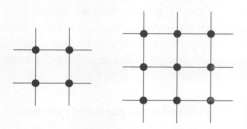

I've tried parallel lines without success.

Oh, what about lines intersecting at vertices?

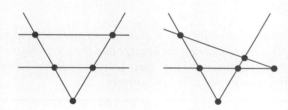

I'm getting only 3 plants per row. But I need another row.

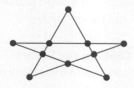

That's it. It looks like a five-point star. I can see how 12 plants could be planted in 6 rows of 4 plants each. Can you? What about 19 plants in 9 straight rows with 5 plants in each row?

Write an Open Sentence

Problem 3-28: Fruit Problem

Elaine bought 5 peaches and 3 apples. She figures out that she would have to pay 8 cents more if she bought 3

peaches and 5 apples. What is the difference between the price of 1 peach and 1 apple?

Problem 3-29: Rectangle Size

Find the dimensions of a rectangle whose perimeter is 26 cm and whose area is 36 cm^2.

Some problems presented to elementary students can be solved by writing an open sentence and then solving it. For example, the Barnyard Problem (see Figure 3-2) can be solved by writing equations and solving first for one variable and then the other. Junior high students will learn how to write mathematical sentences for word expressions such as "twice as old" ($2x$), "3 times as many plus 6" ($3x + 6$), and then use algebraic skills to solve problems.

 A Solution to the Fruit Problem

p = *peaches*   a = *apples*
5p + 3a = 3p + 5a + 8
2p − 2a = 8
p − a = 4

The difference between the price of a peach and an apple is 4 cents.

PLANNING FOR INSTRUCTION

There are several important components of a problem-solving instructional process (Charles & Lester, 1982): selecting appropriate tasks and materials, identifying sources of problems, clarifying the teacher's role, organizing and implementing instruction, and changing the difficulty of problems. Identifying the essential elements that make up these components can assist teachers in planning effective instruction about problem solving.

Selecting Appropriate Tasks and Materials

Good instruction on problem solving not only uses a variety of types of problems (Kroll & Miller, 1993), but also considers that problems:

* should be motivating
* sometimes contain missing, extraneous, or contradictory information
* invite the use of calculators, computers, and other technology

- engage students in activities that use a variety of problem-solving strategies
- involve students in activities that promote communication about mathematical thinking

Problems that are motivating Students are more interested in solving problems about things they are interested in, problems that are based in realistic, familiar settings, and problems that they or other students have written.

Problems with missing, extraneous, or contradictory information Motivating, realistic problems often contain irrelevant or incomplete information and are not well-structured. Because students need practice in solving such problems, instruction should include discussions on organizing the information problems provide and eliminating or ignoring extraneous information.

Problems that encourage the use of calculators, computers, and other technology Calculator usage stimulates students to think more about their approaches to problem solving and permits them to solve more realistic problems.

> **STANDARDS LINK 3-6**
> Computers and calculators are powerful problem-solving tools. The power to compute rapidly, to graph a relationship instantly, and to systematically change one variable and observe what happens to other related variables can help students become independent doers of mathematics. (NCTM, 1989, p. 75)

Activities that require the use of a variety of problem-solving strategies Students who can use a variety of problem-solving strategies are better able to deal with unfamiliar problem situations. And students who use strategies such as making a diagram or solving a simpler problem are able to more flexibly select another strategy when their first strategy does not work.

Activities that promote communication about mathematical thinking Students need to be able to explain how they solved a problem. Such explanations are important in refining their own understanding and communicating their understanding to others. Asking students to write word problems, to solve problems written by other students, and to look for errors in the problems or explanations of other students helps to develop mathematical communication skills.

> **STANDARDS LINK 3-7**
> When problem solving becomes an integral part of classroom instruction and children experience success in solving problems, they gain confidence in doing mathematics and develop persevering and inquiring minds. They also grow in their ability to communicate mathematically and use higher-level thinking processes. (NCTM, 1989, p. 23)

Sources of Problems

Problems arising from mathematics itself can be about the following:

- Number theory: Are there more prime numbers from 100 to 200 than there are from 1 to 100? How can I find the greatest common factor of three numbers? Sixty-four is both a square number and a cube. What is the next number greater than 64 that has this property?
- Properties of number systems: Is there a multiplicative identity element for fractions? Does the commutative property hold true for integers? For which operations?
- Arithmetic: Is there another algorithm for subtracting whole numbers? How can I subtract $4\frac{4}{5}$ from $6\frac{2}{5}$?

Projects about the school environment can be related to the school store, a school fund-raising project, a paper-conservation endeavor, or other project. Students can gather data from a number of community service organizations, public places, or businesses and use the data to pose and solve problem questions. Here are some examples:

- Airport: Gather data about air traffic, passenger capacity or certain airplanes, baggage capacity, flight schedules, or ticket prices.
- City Park: Obtain data on the number of trees, area for flower beds, types of flowers, or maintenance costs.
- Bridge: Obtain data about daily traffic, income from bridge tolls, maintenance costs, etc.
- Orchard: Gather data on the area of an orchard, the number of fruit trees, average harvest per tree, selling price of fruit, or anticipated profits.
- Public Transportation System: Obtain information on a city's fleet of buses, operating costs per month, and the average number of passengers on a particular route per day.

Some mathematical problems can be found in math journals or other publications and on the Internet. The "Resources for Teachers" and "Links to the Internet" that appear at the end of the chapter offer some specific examples.

The Teacher's Role

The teacher plays an important role in problem-solving instruction. This role includes sequential activities that identify what a teacher does before students begin to solve a problem, while students are solving a problem, and after students solve the problem.

Before students begin to solve the problem

Teachers initiate the lesson by posing a problem to students. Problems can be presented to students orally or in written form. When presented orally, a teacher can employ a story format such as "Suppose you were asked to . . ." or "There once was . . . How would you have solved the problem?" or "What would happen if . . .?" In another format, a teacher can relate the problem orally and write key information on the board. A third way is to have students read the problem. Then, the problem can be written on the board, on an overhead transparency, or on a paper with a copy provided for each student. In the latter case, students can glue the piece of paper on a notebook page or in their math journal and develop a solution plan there. In this way, a record of the problem is kept with the student's work.

Before asking students to solve the problem, effective teachers ensure that students understand it. This means asking students to identify what is being asked in the problem, discussing any terms that might be unclear, brainstorming possible solution strategies, and clarifying the task at hand. Finally, a teacher should ask students to devise a plan or select a strategy for solving the problem.

While students are solving the problem

While students are working on the problem, the teacher should circulate among them, observing and questioning individuals or students working in groups about the strategies they are using, what they are finding, and what it means. Further, teachers should ask students questions to help them clarify the direction in which their solution process is taking them. Teachers should provide hints to students who are stuck and encourage students who are finished to solve the problem in a different way or to solve an extension of the problem. The essential goal for teachers is to consistently ensure that students are answering the question the problem asks.

After students solve the problem

After students are finished working on a problem, the teacher must encourage them to reflect on their solutions and the problem-solving processes they used. Usually this can be done through a whole-class discussion. Most valuable is to emphasize the process as well as the answer and to encourage all students to participate in this discussion. Getting students to communicate their ideas through words and diagrams and with manipulative materials can keep students engaged. It can also ensure teachers that they have done their job well if students offer high-level responses.

The Annenberg/CPB Math and Science Collection

VIDEO LINK 3-3
Geometry and Spatial Sense

Brief Summary: In the "Shapes from Squares" segment, Marco Ramirez asks his second- and third-grade students to find all the different shapes they can make by folding a piece of paper that has been prefolded in a few places, without making additional folds.

1. Describe the teacher's role before, during, and after problem solving.
2. What were students' responsibilities while working in small groups?
3. Describe the teacher's questioning of students working in small groups. What impact did his questioning have on students' understanding?

Video Source. Teaching Math: A Video Library, K–4; Tape 8 from The Annenberg/CPB Math and Science Collection.

The Annenberg/CPB Math and Science Collection

VIDEO LINK 3-4
Geometry and Spatial Sense

Brief Summary: In the "Hexominoes" video, Nan Sepeda's fifth-grade class is learning about hexominoes—shapes made up of six squares. Ms. Sepeda asks her students first to create their own set of hexominoes from grid paper, and then to sort their hexominoes based on characteristics of their choice.

1. Describe the teacher's role before, during, and after problem solving.
2. What were students' responsibilities while working in small groups?
3. Describe the teacher's questioning of students working in small groups.
4. Suppose you were the teacher and wanted this lesson to be less exploratory. What changes would you make? What might you plan as a follow-up lesson to the video lesson?

Video Source. Teaching Math: A Video Library, K–4; Tape 8 from The Annenberg/CPB Math and Science Collection.

Organizing and Implementing Instruction

Establishing an effective problem-solving program requires examining factors related to organization and implementation. These factors include providing students a classroom climate that is conducive to learning, grouping students to facilitate interactive learning, allocating appropriate instructional time, and planning for student assessment.

Classroom climate A classroom that promotes problem solving is open and supportive, encouraging students to try different solution strategies and endorsing students' efforts. Such a supportive environment encourages students to take risks and to defend their solutions. The teacher should encourage students to persevere in their problem solving and to respect each other's efforts.

Grouping students A classroom that promotes problem solving includes individual, small-group, and whole-class problem solving experiences. Each of these formats helps students develop distinct and important types of problem-solving skills. Small-group work is particularly useful in that it provides opportunities for all students to interact, share, and discuss solution strategies.

STANDARDS LINK 3-8

Students should frequently work together in small groups to solve problems. They can discuss strategies and solutions, ask questions, examine consequences and alternatives, and reflect on the process and how it relates to prior problems. Students must verify results, interpret solutions, and question whether a solution makes sense. They should verify their own thinking rather than depend on the teacher to tell them whether they are right or wrong. Such experiences develop students' confidence in using mathematics. (NCTM, 1989, p. 76–77)

Allocating time A classroom that promotes an adequate allocation of instructional time for problem solving, on a regular basis, is integral to learning mathematics. Problem solving should be an integral part of mathematics instruction, not an add-on, "Fridays only" topic.

Student assessment A classroom that promotes problem solving includes assessment of students' understanding, problem-solving skills, and strategy usage. Chapter 4 discusses assessment in greater detail.

Changing the Difficulty of Problems

Remember the discussion at the beginning of this chapter on types of problems? We know much about which problems are easier than others to solve and ways to set problems up to make them easier or harder. For example, the wording of a problem can affect the difficulty level of a problem. Because teachers can control how easy or difficult problems can be and thus meet individual student needs, it is a good time to discuss the factors involved in adapting problems. These factors include problem context and problem mechanics or structure.

Problem context The context of a problem is the nonmathematical setting in which it is placed. For example, a problem about two children sharing six cookies is different from a problem about two aliens sharing six mega-blasters because of the setting or context of the problem. Different contexts can include abstract (using symbolic or intangible elements), concrete (involving a real situation or objects), factual (describing an actual situation), hypothetical (describing possible situations), and personalized (using the solver's own interests and characteristics in the problem) (Hembree & March, 1993). Problems involving concrete, factual, or personalized settings are easier for children to solve than are hypothetical or abstract problems.

Problem structure A problem's structure consists of several aspects related to how problem data is presented. These aspects include problem length, readability, whether the problem includes action (e.g., "Tom *gave* Maria 2 more cookies"), the order in which data are presented, the inclusion of extraneous data, and the use of familiar versus unfamiliar terms. The difficulty of each of these aspects is as might be expected. More difficult problems might include any of these factors: longer, more difficult readability, lack of action, presence of extraneous data or information, and unfamiliar terms.

Classroom implications Teachers must be aware of factors that affect problem difficulty in order to systematically vary those factors to help children become better problem solvers. A common way to sequence problem-solving instruction is to begin with problems involving action and reasonably sized numbers in concrete or personalized settings, later progressing to more complicated problems by varying the factors described above.

This is not to say, however, that teachers always must pose easy problems, realistic, real-world problems encountered in everyday situations usually are not clean, tidy, or clearly stated. Children need to learn how to solve such problems. When planning instruction, teachers must

BOX 3-1
Types of Problem Contexts

Abstract Setting

A certain number is 5 more than 7. What is the number?

Concrete Setting

Matt has 7 baseball cards. Peter has 5 more baseball cards than Matt has. How many baseball cards does Peter have?

Hypothetical Setting

Peter has some baseball cards. If Peter has 5 more baseball cards than Matt has, and Matt has 7 baseball cards, how many baseball cards does Peter have?

Personalized Setting

{Insert Child A's name here} has 7 {insert relevant item here}. {Insert Child B's name here} has 5 more {insert relevant item here} than {Insert Child A's name here} has. How many {insert relevant item here} does {insert Child B's name here} have?

---

find a balance between supporting children's learning and challenging children to solve realistic problems. Teachers must systematically vary problem structure and format to help children learn strategies and develop confidence that will help them solve more complicated problems.

> **STANDARDS LINK 3-9**
> Real-world problems are not ready-made exercises with easily processed procedures and numbers. Situations that allow students to experience problems with "messy" numbers or too much or not enough information or that have multiple solutions, each with different consequences, will better prepare them to solve problems they are likely to encounter in their daily lives. (NCTM, 1989, p. 76)

Other Factors Contributing to Students' Difficulties in Problem Solving

From their review of the research literature, Kroll and Miller (1993) have identified major factors that contribute to middle school students' difficulties in problem solving. These are: knowledge, beliefs and affective factors, control, and sociocultural factors. All teachers should address each of these areas during instruction. In particular, the elementary grades should be viewed as a time of "preparation for good problem solving" (Hembree & Marsh, 1993, p. 166).

Knowledge factors Beginning in the elementary grades and throughout the middle school grades, students should have ample experience in problem solving so that they can come to recognize structurally similar problems

(schema knowledge) and learn varied strategies to solve process problems (strategic knowledge) (Kroll & Miller, 1993). Thus, building prior knowledge required for successful problem solving includes making teachers accountable for developing algorithmic, linguistic, conceptual, and schema and strategic knowledge. As a teacher you must not only enable students to read problems and compute accurately but also help students come to understand problems so that they can make a wise choice on what operation or strategy to use to develop a solution. Choosing a solution process should emerge from a clear understanding of a problem, rather than be dependent upon word clues or other unreliable strategies.

Beliefs and affective factors Success in problem solving is adversely affected by a lack of confidence in one's own ability to create solutions to problems. Teachers who have a narrow view "that there is only one right way to solve a problem" can prevent students from experiencing the joy of truly "doing" mathematics.

Control Kroll and Miller (1993) mention the need for students to be able to monitor their own thinking when engaged in problem solving. Research shows that students do not spend sufficient time reflecting on their thinking process or on their approaches to problem solving. Can you understand then the need for a teacher to engage students in reflection on their own thinking processes?

Sociocultural factors Students' out-of-school experiences are varied, therefore, they develop their own problem-solving strategies. However, students are unable to use their "natural" problem-solving abilities in school mathematics, although they serve them well in out-of-school situations (Kroll & Miller, 1993). As was stated earlier in this chapter, the classroom atmosphere is important in mathematics learning as it can positively or negatively affect students' achievement. Teachers must keep in mind that they control the environment and context of students experiences. This is an awesome responsibility but one that separates good instruction from poor student experiences.

A Case to Consider the Students

A problem-solving teaching project with fourth-, fifth-, and sixth-grade children revealed that students valued certain instructional practices when engaged in problem solving (Pothier & Sawada, 1990). Some of the favored characteristics of the teaching-learning situation expressed by the students are: time to complete a problem, freedom to choose a solution strategy, receiving personal attention, and an understanding teacher.

- Students need time to work through a problem; they do not want to be rushed to complete a set of problems. When relieved of the pressure to complete work, students feel free to explore solution possibilities.
- Students appreciate the freedom to personally select and develop a solution strategy rather than follow a uniform procedure. This provides them with the opportunity to transform a problem into something personal, and it becomes an enjoyable task.
- Students appreciate receiving personal attention when engaged in problem solving. This attention can be in the form of a teacher's asking questions to direct their thinking, offering hints regarding solution procedures, or merely listening to a fellow student talk about what she or he is doing.
- Students value an understanding teacher. When a trusting relationship is established, students will readily request assistance knowing that, as one student expressed it, "it's all right if you don't know how to do it." They will take risks in tackling problems that they might not otherwise attempt, an important component in a mathematics classroom.

A nonthreatening and supportive classroom atmosphere is effective in promoting students' progress in developing their problem-solving abilities.

Benefits of Using a Problem-Solving Approach to Mathematics Instruction

A teacher who decides to approach all mathematics work from a problem-solving point of view has students solve computation problems, work at geometry and measurement activities, and approach number theory investigations from a problem-solving perspective. Process problems that relate to the different mathematics topics are an important part of this kind of program. Students learn problem-solving strategies that enable them to gain insights into mathematical connections and understand that problems are the context for learning concepts and skills. That is, students learn mathematics via problem solving. Such a program promotes students' mathematics understanding and achievement.

> **STANDARDS LINK 3-10**
> Classrooms with a problem-solving orientation are permeated by thought-provoking questions, speculations, investigations, and explorations; in this environment, the teacher's primary goal is to promote a problem-solving approach to the learning of all mathematics content. (NCTM, 1989, p. 23)

Another benefit of a problem-solving approach to mathematics teaching is that it supports students with different learning styles. According to Moser (1992), "an orientation toward problem solving can accommodate individual differences, especially if the philosophy is adopted that there is more than one way to solve most problems" (p. 131). A classroom in which problem solving is the central feature of the mathematics instruction and in which more than one way to solve a problem is not merely tolerated but is valued is an environment that promotes the learning of all children.

CONCLUSION

In this chapter, current thinking about problem solving as an integral part of mathematics programs has been presented. This vision is for students to learn mathematics through problem solving and teachers to teach in a way that allows students to learn how to solve problems. Such a mathematics program should include different types of problems with more emphasis placed on process problems.

It is not only appropriate but also imperative for teachers to provide instruction in problem-solving strategies to enable students to develop a resource of processes to use when engaged in problem solving. The instructional goal then is to ensure that by the end of middle school, students should have developed confidence and some flexibility in using different problem-solving strategies.

For Your Journal

When you have finished studying this chapter, reflect on these questions in your math journal:

1. Choose three different problems from the chapter and solve them. Describe the solution strategies you used.

2. Imagine you are an elementary teacher and one of your students expresses frustration about solving problems, asking you to "just tell me how to do it." How will you respond?

3. Describe how you would establish a classroom environment conducive to problem solving.

For Your Portfolio

When you have finished studying this chapter, complete these activities to include in your professional portfolio:

1. Begin a collection of process problems.

2. Write a lesson plan for a problem-solving lesson focusing on teaching students to use a solution strategy of your choice. Include the questions you would ask.

3. Visit a classroom and observe the solution strategies used by children. Describe these strategies and the follow-up lessons you might plan if you were the teacher in that classroom.

Resources for Teachers

Books on Problem Solving

Baroody, A. (1993). *Problem solving, reasoning, and communicating: Helping children think mathematically.* New York: Macmillan Publishing Company.

Charles, R., Lester, F., & O'Daffer, P. (1987). *How to evaluate progress in problem solving.* Reston, VA: National Council of Teachers of Mathematics.

O'Daffer, P. G. (1988). *Problem solving: Tips for teachers.* Reston, VA: National Council of Teachers of Mathematics.

Reys, B. (1982). *Elementary school mathematics: What parents should know about problem solving.* Reston, VA: National Council of Teachers of Mathematics.

Links to the Internet

Problems of the Week
http://forum.swarthmore.edu/elempow/

Contains a weekly "Problem of the Week" as well as a mechanism to submit solutions electronically. Past Problems of the Week and solutions are also available.

MathWorld Interactive
http://forum.swarthmore.edu/mathworld/

Contains challenges, activities, and puzzles for students to solve individually or in groups and a way to submit solutions electronically. Particular emphases include open-ended problems and communicating mathematically.

Education Place's BrainTeasers
http://www.eduplace.com/math/brain/

Contains math puzzles for grades 3–7, with solution hints.

Teacher TidBytes' Problem-Solving Resource Sites
http://www.teachertidbytes.com/Teacher_WebResources/ProblemSolving.html

Contains many links to problem-solving resources on the Internet.

CHAPTER 4

Assessing Mathematics Understanding

Assessment in mathematics no longer refers only to a student's score on a test. Instead, assessment involves a more holistic view of each child's understanding, skill, and attitude about mathematics. Assessment communicates to students what we believe is important for them to know and be able to do. It is essential that assessment matches the mathematics curriculum and the instructional strategies in use. This chapter discusses recommendations and methods for assessing students' understanding of mathematics. ○

Key Concepts

- NCTM Assessment Standards
- Purposes of assessment
- Types of assessment
- Performance assessment
- Portfolio assessment

Focus Questions

When you have finished studying this chapter, you should be able to answer these questions:

1. What are the purposes of assessment?

2. What are the different types of assessment, and what are the benefits of each type?

3. What are the advantages of using performance assessment? Of using portfolio assessment?

"In order to develop mathematical power in all *students, assessment needs to support the continued mathematics learning of each student. This is the central goal of school mathematics."*

(NCTM, 1995, p. 6)

THE ASSESSMENT STANDARDS

In 1995 the National Council of Teachers of Mathematics (NCTM) published the *Assessment Standards for School Mathematics*. Completing the trilogy of standards developed by NCTM, these assessment standards describe new assessment strategies and practices that "enable teachers and others to assess students' performance in a manner that reflects the NCTM's reform vision for school mathematics" (NCTM, 1995, p. 1). For the purposes of this text we will refer to the *NCTM Assessment Standards for School Mathematics* as the Assessment Standards.

> **STANDARDS LINK 4-1**
> Instead of assuming that the purpose of assessment is to rank students on a particular trait, the new approach assumes that high public expectations can be set that every student can strive for and achieve, that different performances can and will meet agreed-on expectations, and that teachers can be fair and consistent judges of diverse student performances. (NCTM, 1995, p. 1)

The Assessment Standards complement the recommendations of the Curriculum and Evaluation Standards (NCTM, 1989), which propose the following:

- student assessment be aligned with, and integral to instruction;
- multiple sources of assessment information be used;
- assessment methods be appropriate for their purposes;
- all aspects of mathematical knowledge and its connections be assessed;
- instruction and curriculum be considered equally in judging the quality of a program. (NCTM, 1989, as cited in NCTM, 1995, pp. 1–2)

The Assessment Standards describe five shifts that are needed to attain the vision of the Curriculum Standards (see Table 4-1). These shifts clearly characterize the recommended changes in mathematics teaching, learning, and assessment.

What Is Assessment?

Assessment is "the process of gathering evidence about a student's knowledge of, ability to use, and disposition toward, mathematics and of making inferences from that evidence for a variety of purposes" (NCTM, 1995, p. 3).

> **STANDARDS LINK 4-2**
> Assessment should be a means of fostering growth toward high expectations. To do otherwise represents a waste of human potential. (NCTM, 1995, p. 1)

The Assessment Standards include six standards to guide mathematics assessment and focus on six important areas: mathematics, learning, equity, openness, inferences, and coherence. These six standards set the criteria for determining the quality of mathematics assessments, and ultimately the quality of instruction.

The **mathematics standard** states that "assessment should reflect the mathematics that all students need to know and be able to do" (NCTM, 1995, p. 11). This means that teachers must make sure to assess students' understanding of the mathematics concepts and procedures that current recommendations, such as the NCTM Curriculum Standards, say that students should know.

The **learning standard** states that "assessment should enhance mathematics learning" (NCTM, 1995, p. 13). That is, good assessments are those that not only assess students' understanding, but also encourage and support further growth in that understanding.

The **equity standard** states that "assessment should promote equity" (NCTM, 1995, p. 15). Equity in this

---

TABLE 4-1

RECOMMENDED SHIFTS IN MATHEMATICS INSTRUCTION

A SHIFT IN:	TOWARD:	AWAY FROM:
• Content	• A rich variety of mathematical topics and problem situations	• Just arithmetic
• Learning	• Investigating problems	• Memorizing and repeating
• Teaching	• Questioning and listening	• Telling
• Evaluation	• Evidence from several sources	• A single test judged externally
• Expectation	• Using concepts and procedures to solve problems	• Just mastering isolated concepts and procedures

Note: Adapted from *Assessment Standards for School Mathematics* (pp. 2–3), by National Council of Teachers of Mathematics, 1995, Reston, VA: National Council of Teachers of Mathematics. Copyright 1995 by the National Council of Teachers of Mathematics.

context means that all students are successful in math. Thus, assessments should take into account differences among students to support the learning of all students. This can be done, for example, by permitting different modes of responses to an assessment.

The **openness standard** states that "assessment should be an open process" (NCTM, 1995, p. 17). An open process includes informing the public about the process, involving teaching professionals, and being accepting of review and change.

The **inferences standard** states that "assessment should promote valid inferences about mathematics learning" (NCTM, 1995, p. 19). Valid inferences are those based on relevant evidence, which could include evidence from multiple sources, such as tests, teacher observations, and portfolios.

The **coherence standard** states that "assessment should be a coherent process" (NCTM, 1995, p. 21). Specifically, the assessment process must (1) be complete and sensible, (2) match the purposes for which it is being conducted, and (3) be consistent with curriculum and instruction that have been implemented.

Purposes of Assessment

According to the Curriculum Standards, assessment may be used for several purposes, including diagnosis, instructional feedback, grading, generalized mathematical achievement, and program evaluation. Done well, assessment helps students and parents realize what students have learned and what they still need to learn. It also allows teachers to understand what their students know so they may plan appropriate instruction.

Similarly, the Assessment Standards identifies four purposes for assessment: monitoring students' progress, making instructional decisions, evaluating students' achievement, and evaluating programs. A description of each of these purposes follows.

- *Monitoring students' progress* toward learning goals is a continuous process that includes setting high expectations and collecting evidence about students' understanding and progress.

- *Making instructional decisions* refers to teachers using evidence of students' understanding to modify instruction to better meet students' needs and to lead to increased learning.

- *Evaluating students' achievement* must be done at regular intervals and includes collecting evidence, summarizing it, and reporting it. This serves both to inform parents and to assure that important milestones are attained.

- *Evaluating programs* must be done by collecting evidence about students' learning to assure that all students are learning.

Each of these four purposes of assessment is an important link in improving teaching and learning. For example, in monitoring a student's progress a teacher can recognize increased student growth or a lack of growth. Thus, assessment can then affect instructional decision making and lead to improved instruction. Also, because evaluating a student's achievement is a part of effective instruction, assessment records are accumulated to reflect a student's accomplishments or underscore a need for an evaluation to determine the appropriateness of giving special learning support services to the student. Further, evaluating the mathematics program itself can lead to a decision to make program modifications. Each of these assessment purposes provides teachers with information to benefit student learning. The use of any one of them, however, requires several phases of planning.

Phases of Assessment

There are generally four parts or phases of assessment: planning what kind of assessment tool to use, gathering evidence through its use, interpreting that evidence, and applying the results to measure growth or determine the need for change. These phases are interconnected, though not necessarily sequential. It often is helpful, however, to keep these phases in mind to aid decision making related to assessment choices.

When planning assessment, think about the purpose of the assessment, the methods you will use to collect and interpret evidence, the criteria you will use to judge performance, and the format you will use to summarize findings. For example, do you intend to use the results of the assessment primarily to decide how to plan tomorrow's math lesson? Or will the results be used to help parents understand their child's strengths and areas needing growth?

When gathering evidence, consider the activities, tasks, and procedures you will use to involve students. For example, might your students choose to respond in different ways, such as by using manipulative materials, drawing a picture, or writing a description, to convey their understanding of a concept?

When interpreting evidence, think about how you will determine understanding and the criteria you will use to analyze the evidence. For example, how do you hope your students will respond to a question? What other responses are acceptable to demonstrate understanding?

When using results from assessment, consider how the results will be reported, and decide how the results will affect future instructional decisions. For example, will you share the results with parents on written report cards or orally during parent-teacher conferences? How will you use students' understandings to plan instruction for the next lesson or the next unit or to reteach particular concepts?

ASSESSMENT CHOICES

The purpose of the information teachers gather from assessment dictates the nature of its use. For example, generalized mathematics achievement can best be assessed with standardized testing instruments. Standardized testing also is useful to indicate how well the class is doing as a whole and the effectiveness of instruction or instructional programs. Individual diagnosis, however, is better done through a variety of other means including observation, interviews and oral questioning, performance tasks, and a collection of students' work over time (as in the maintaining of portfolios). Through any of these means a teacher can assess his or her students' understanding of mathematical concepts, as well as computational ability, problem-solving ability, thinking processes and solution strategies, attitudes, and oral and written communication skills.

Achievement Tests

Tests probably are the first measurement tools that come to mind when considering evaluating student progress. An achievement test generally falls into one of two categories, standardized or teacher-made.

Standardized tests Most standardized achievement tests are norm-referenced tests because their purpose is to compare a student's level of performance to the performance of a large number of similar students. The norming population usually represents a cross-section of children in a school system, a state, or even a nation. Standardized tests usually are administered on the mandate of a school district or state official and often are given at incremental levels such as second grade, fourth grade, and so on. Some states and local school districts have expended considerable time, effort, and money to design tests that would be valid for the state or local objectives at different levels. Widely used standardized tests include the Stanford Achievement Test and the Iowa Test of Basic Skills.

Teacher-made tests Teacher-made tests are criterion-referenced tests because they measure knowledge of specific objectives. A chapter test in a textbook often does not reflect all of the objectives a teacher covered, so the teacher may devise her or his own test to assess student progress in understanding material in the chapter. Teacher-made tests often are given as pretests as well as posttests. Pretests are important to help a teacher plan instruction based on class needs. In designing a test, the teacher should do the following:

- List all the objectives to be measured.
- List the thought processes students may need to answer test questions.

- Design test items that will match both the objectives to be measured and the critical thinking processes involved.

Further, it is necessary to edit all items carefully to eliminate ambiguity. The teacher should do the following:

- Prepare the test in an attractive and clear format.
- Analyze the results, examining how children responded to each item.

Indeed, it is important that teachers go beyond simply calculating a score to examine each child's response to each item. Use these results to determine instructional needs. For example, if many children made errors on the items that you intended as problem-solving items, then you need to provide more experiences with problem-solving and solution strategies.

Diagnostic tests Achievement tests usually do not provide the kind of details that allow a teacher to describe strengths and/or weaknesses of a particular student. A diagnostic test provides such information, however. Diagnostic tests help teachers understand which parts of a concept students have mastered as well as the topics on which students need more learning experiences.

Although commercial diagnostic tests exist, it is better for teachers to design their own because they interact with the children daily and can use their knowledge of their students to develop appropriate tasks and interpret the responses. Observation and interviews described in the next section are other ways to gather diagnostic data.

Individualizing Assessment

Individual diagnosis of students' understanding of mathematical concepts, computational ability, problem-solving ability, thinking processes and solution strategies, attitudes, and oral and written communication skills are best made through a variety of means. These means include observation, conferences and interviews, performance tasks, and collecting students' work over time in portfolios.

Observations Observations involve systematically examining students' behavior. They are a powerful way to learn more about what students know and are able to do.

Observations are most effective when a teacher concentrates on a few students each day and systematically observes specific aspects such as solution strategies used, types of problems solved, level of skill or concept development, and so on. Teachers can record observation data by keeping anecdotal records that include written notes describing students' behaviors.

Checklists are another good way to organize data collected via observations. For example, in order to plan instruction a teacher might be interested in assessing the counting strategies students use to solve addition problems. The teacher could use a checklist to keep track of which students are using the "counting on from the first addend" strategy and which are using the "counting on from the larger addend" strategy. The checklist should contain the names of all the students in the class, with columns listing the date on which the teacher observed each student using each strategy and the particular problem on which the strategy was used. Table 4-2 shows part of a sample observation checklist a teacher used to organize these data. Notice that the teacher completed this table over a period of several months. This checklist shows students' progress over time in using the two counting strategies observed.

Conferences and interviews At times a teacher may want to schedule an interview with a child, but most often interviews will occur spontaneously. A planned interview would be more likely to occur when a student does one of the following:

- reveals a special interest or expertise in a particular topic (the teacher may help the student plan some additional work, culminating with a report or demonstration to the class);
- demonstrates unusual insight or an unusual algorithm;
- transfers into the class from another school; or
- demonstrates a particularly negative attitude.

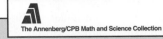

VIDEO LINK 4-1
Whole Number Computation

Brief Summary: In "Amazing Equations," teacher Flo Pearson's first- and second-graders are writing "Problems of the Day," in which the answer to each problem is 20—the date on which the video was filmed.

1. What did Ms. Pearson learn about her students' understanding of addition and subtraction concepts and symbols by observing her students during this lesson?
2. How did the teacher's questioning during her observations help her assess students' understanding?

Video Source. Teaching Math: A Video Library, K–4; Tape 7 from The Annenberg/CPB Math and Science Collection.

Interviews also may be planned when the teacher wants to assess the level of development of a concept. This could involve asking children to solve an addition word problem or to show three different representations of 3 times 6, for example. Teachers can learn much about their students' mathematical thinking through such interviews.

Spontaneous interviews usually occur as a teacher watches children work. "Tell me how you did that" and "Here is another problem—think aloud as you work it out" are the kinds of questions or statements a teacher might make in these more unstructured interviews. Giving a few words of encouragement may also be classified as a spontaneous interview.

TABLE 4-2

PART OF A SAMPLE OBSERVATION CHECKLIST FOR STUDENTS' USE OF COUNTING STRATEGIES

STUDENT'S NAME	DATE/PROBLEM APPLICATION	
	Counting on From First Addend	Counting on From Larger Addend
Andrew	10/23 2 + 5 =	1/15 3 + 9 =
Anton	9/22 3 + 4 =	12/2 2 + 9 =
Crystal	10/23 6 + 3 =	11/15 4 + 7 =
Gabriella	1/22 3 + 6 =	
Heather	9/22 3 + 4 =	10/23 3 + 8 =
Juan	9/22 3 + 4 =	11/15 4 + 7 =

VIDEO LINK 4-2
Concepts of Whole Number Operations

Brief Summary: In "Choose a Method," teacher Mary Holden's fourth- and fifth-graders solve problems in different ways: with base-ten blocks, mental math, paper and pencil, or calculators. Ms. Holden asks students to first estimate and then find the exact value of an arrangement of blocks.

1. What did Ms. Holden learn about her students' understanding of computation and of estimation from this lesson?
2. How did the teacher's questioning help her assess students' understanding?

Video Source. Teaching Math: A Video Library, K–4; Tape 4 from The Annenberg/CPB Math and Science Collection.

Interviews with parents often reveal information and background that is helpful in understanding their child. For example, previous attitude-forming experiences (positive and negative), experiences that contribute to the student's mathematical knowledge, experiences with computers, parental attitudes toward mathematics, and so on often are useful in helping assess a student's progress or lack of progress. Some schools encourage interviews in which both the child and his or her parents are present.

Performance assessment Performance assessment in mathematics involves "presenting students with a mathematical task, project, or investigation, then observing, interviewing, and looking at their products to assess what they actually know and can do" (Stenmark, 1991, p. 13). Performance assessment can include evaluation of students' daily work, observations, conferences, and interviews.

STANDARDS LINK 4-3

To demonstrate real growth in mathematical power, students need to demonstrate their ability to do major pieces of work that are more elaborate and time-consuming than just short exercises, sets of word problems, and chapter tests. Performance tasks, projects, and portfolios are some examples of more complex instructional and assessment activities. (NCTM, 1995, p. 36)

While engaged in a performance assessment, children demonstrate "their ability to use the skills they have learned and the conceptual understanding they have developed in the context of a real-life application or complex problem" (Collison, 1992). Collison uses the analogy of a driving test to describe processes involved in, and characteristics of, a mathematical performance assessment.

Performance assessment presents students with an opportunity to demonstrate their understanding rather than just their speed and accuracy. It provides teachers with more detailed information about students' thinking, solution processes, misconceptions, and errors.

Performance assessment can also be a part of daily lessons. For example, at the start of a lesson teachers can ask their students to do a "quick write" of everything they know about the topic of the lesson. For example, during a lesson on fractions the teacher could ask students to write everything they know about the fraction one-half. At the end of the lesson, the teacher asks the students to add anything they'd like to their "quick write." Reviewing these writing samples may be helpful in assessing students' understanding. "Quick writes" provide feedback to

the teacher and the student about what he or she knows at the beginning of the lesson and what the student learned from the lesson.

Examples of performance tasks. Performance tests may include an elaborate problem-solving activity or an activity as simple as asking a child to set out counters in an array to illustrate a particular multiplication problem. Indeed, concrete materials often are part of the assessment. Performance assessment frequently is done with individuals or small groups. Table 4-3 includes some examples of performance assessment tasks.

Materials designed for instruction can be quickly modified for use as a performance assessment by modifying the final question and changing the way it is administered. The key to an effective performance task is to require students to provide *explanations* rather than *products*.

For example, consider a basic activity in which students are asked to use a manipulative material, such as base-ten blocks, to represent a list of numbers. Figure 4-1, which shows possible student responses, is an example. This task can easily be modified to focus on students' thinking by asking them to represent one number, say 37,

---

TABLE 4-3

SAMPLE PERFORMANCE ASSESSMENT TASKS

Fractions: Ask third-grade students who are learning about fractions to show you with manipulatives how they would divide different items, such as 5 candy bars, 10 pencils, or 11 comic books, among 4 students.

Place Value: Have students explain how they would teach a younger sibling to understand the meaning of tens and ones in place value.

Long Division: Give each group of students a different division problem. Ask each group to make a poster to share with the class that explains the methods they used in solving their problem.

Organizing and Displaying Data: Ask a group of students to find and demonstrate the value of *pi* by measuring the diameter and circumference of different circles, expressing the ratios, and finding decimal equivalents on a calculator. Allow the students to choose a way to explain and display their findings.

Data Collection: Your group's task is (1) to identify an interesting question that may be answered by collecting data, (2) to develop a plan for investigating this question, and (3) to prepare an oral report, with overheads or other displays, for the class. Here is a sample question: "How many bicycles are there within two miles of this school?" Your group's planning report is due in three days. Please keep a daily log of your work. Final reports will be due two weeks from today.

Source: From Stenmark, J. K. (Ed.) (1991) *Mathematics Assessment: Myths, Models, Good Questions, and Practical Suggestions* (pp. 14–15), Reston, VA: National Council of Teachers of Mathematics. Copyright 1991 by the National Council of Teachers of Mathematics.

FIGURE 4-1

CHANGING A LEARNING ACTIVITY TO A PERFORMANCE ASSESSMENT TASK

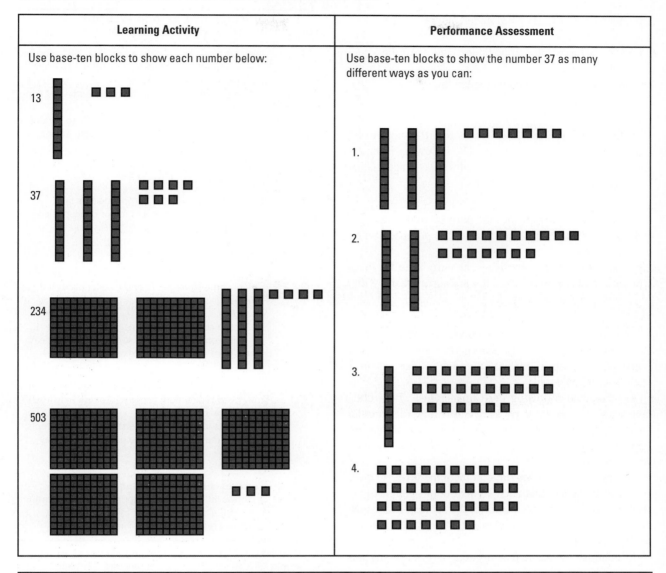

Learning Activity	Performance Assessment
Use base-ten blocks to show each number below:	Use base-ten blocks to show the number 37 as many different ways as you can:

in as many different ways as possible and to explain *why* they are the same. A student who understands that 37 is the same as $27 + 10$, for example, shows that he or she understands equivalent representations and is able to think flexibly about the concept of place value.

What makes a good performance assessment task? According to Stenmark (1991), quality performance assessment tasks include several characteristics: they are *essential* (consistent with the core curriculum), *authentic* (uses appropriate mathematics processes), *rich* (has many possibilities), *engaging* (thought-provoking), *active* (students interact with other students), *feasible* (can be done in time available), *equitable* (accessible to students with different learning styles), and *open* (can be solved with more than one solution strategy).

Using rubrics to score performance tasks. Performance tasks give teachers a great deal of information to use in evaluating students' mathematics understanding. Sometimes teachers choose to quantify students' performance on a performance task. One way of doing this is by using a structure or scoring system known as a rubric. A rubric is a scale, often ranging between two to six points, that is used to holistically score a student's work.

Teachers might begin by using a two-point rubric, sorting students' work into two piles based on whether or not the students' work demonstrates understanding. This somewhat crude analysis provides some information about students' performance, but teachers often need more detailed information and thus move to a three-point scale.

A three-point rubric includes three levels, which might be differentiated as follows:

3 points   demonstrates good understanding of the concept

2 points   demonstrates some understanding of the concept

1 point   demonstrates no understanding of the concept

A four-point rubric allows for more differences to be noted among the students' work. The following is an example of a four-point rubric (California Mathematics Council, 1996):

4 points   fully accomplishes the purpose of the task

3 points   substantially accomplishes the purpose of the task

2 points   partially accomplishes the purpose of the task

1 point   little or no progress toward accomplishing the purpose of the task

Table 4-4 shows a six-point rubric developed by the California Department of Education (Pandey, 1991). This rubric can be used to evaluate a variety of performance tasks with much detail.

Consider the following performance task: Four children want to share three cookies. Show how to share the cookies, and explain how you know each person has the same amount. Box 4-1 shows the work of three students who performed this task.

Notice that Andy does not complete the task. He does not seem to realize that each student could get part of a cookie. Using a four-point rubric, the score for his solution would be a "1." He makes little or no progress toward accomplishing the task.

In contrast, Becky makes a good start at solving the problem. She understands that each child will get part of a cookie and cuts each cookie into fourths. But she does not explain how much of a cookie each child gets in all. Using a four-point rubric, the score for her solution would be a "3." She substantially accomplishes the purpose of the task.

Chantal solves the problem completely. She cuts the cookie so that each child gets the same amount, and she uses fraction language to identify the total amount each child receives. Using a four-point rubric, the score for her solution would be a "4." In other words, she fully accomplishes the purpose of the task.

Students, too, can use rubrics to assess their own work and that of other students. One benefit is that students come to understand why their work received the score that it did. But more importantly, using rubrics helps students recognize that developing an understanding of a concept occurs on different levels. Thus their goal is to

TABLE 4-4

PERFORMANCE STANDARDS FOR STUDENT WORK

LEVEL	STANDARD TO BE ACHIEVED FOR PERFORMANCE AT SPECIFIED LEVEL

6	Fully achieves the purpose of the task, while insightfully interpreting, extending beyond the task, or raising provocative questions.
	    Demonstrates an in-depth understanding of concepts and content.
	    Communicates effectively and clearly to various audiences, using dynamic and diverse means.

5	Accomplishes the purposes of the task.
	    Shows clear understanding of concepts.
	    Communicates effectively.

4	Substantially completes purposes of the task.
	    Displays understanding of major concepts, even though some less important ideas may be missing.
	    Communicates successfully.

3	Purpose of the task not fully achieved; needs elaboration; some strategies may be ineffectual or not appropriate; assumptions about the purposes may be flawed.
	    Gaps in conceptual understanding are evident.
	    Limits communication to some important ideas; results may be incomplete or not clearly presented.

2	Important purposes of the task not achieved; work may need redirection; approach to task may lead away from its completion.
	    Presents fragmented understanding of concepts; results may be incomplete or arguments may be weak.
	    Attempts communication.

1	Purposes of the task not accomplished.
	    Shows little evidence of appropriate reasoning.
	    Does not successfully communicate relevant ideas; presents extraneous information.

Source: From Pandey, T. (1991) *A Sampler of Mathematics Assessment.* Sacramento, CA: California Department of Education. Copyright 1991 by the California Department of Education.

try to continue to enhance their understanding of mathematical tasks.

Portfolio assessment A portfolio is a collection of selected student work (Crowley, 1993). It provides an opportunity for a student to showcase her or his work and growth in mathematics over a period of time, such as a school year. The use of portfolios promotes student self-assessment, "encourages students to communicate their understandings of mathematics with a high level of proficiency, and emphasizes the role of the student as the active mathematician and the teacher as the guide" (Lambdin & Walker, 1994, p. 318).

Portfolios can provide students, teachers, and parents with much more detail about a student's performance in

BOX 4-1

A Cookie-Sharing Performance Task

Name: _Andy_

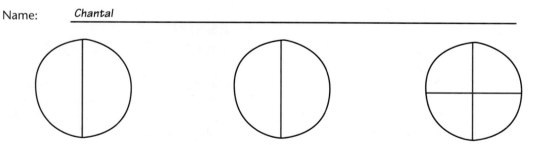

"There's not enough cookies for four kids to share."

Name: _Becky_

"Each kid would get one-fourth of each cookie."

Name: _Chantal_

"Each kid would get one-half of a cookie and one-fourth of another cookie. They'd get three-fourths altogether."

and understanding of mathematics than a letter grade offers. Further, portfolios are useful for supporting points of discussion in parent-teacher conferences.

What should be included? Portfolios may include a student's daily work, written descriptions of investigations, solved and unsolved problems, excerpts from his or her math journal, group reports, problems that he or she wrote, illustrations, photographs of the student's mathe-

matics projects, and videotapes of his or her mathematics presentations or projects.

One method is to have two portfolios: a working portfolio and a permanent portfolio. Students can use the working portfolio over time to collect materials they might want to keep in their permanent portfolios. At the end of a designated period of time, or as the grading period nears its end, students can reevaluate their work in their working portfolios and decide which entries to move to their permanent portfolios. A student may ask for help in selecting items to move to his or her permanent portfolio. To ensure that the portfolio reflects a range of work assignments, teachers often specify that students must include at least one example of a variety of types of activities, such as journal entries, investigations, nonroutine problems, projects, application problems, and group work.

Further, teachers can require that students write a brief description for each portfolio entry, explaining their selections and what they demonstrate about their understanding. A description such as this should then be attached to the appropriate entry. Some teachers also ask that each student select another student to conduct a written review or peer-evaluation of his or her portfolio, as well as complete a personal review for self-assessment.

Evaluating portfolios. There are several criteria that may be used for evaluating portfolios. One is to evaluate students' characteristics such as problem-solving skills, ability to make mathematical connections, ability to communicate mathematically, and attitudes toward mathematics and self (Crowley, 1993).

Another set of portfolio evaluation criteria (Stenmark, 1991) includes the following:

1. Understands the problem or task
2. Uses a variety of strategies
3. Uses models, technology, and other resources
4. Interprets results
5. Solves problems in a cooperative group
6. Relates mathematics to other subjects and the real world
7. Uses appropriate mathematics language and symbols
8. Shows evidence of self-assessment and self-correction of work

Before initiating the use of portfolios, it is wise to determine which criteria are most important and to develop these in a portfolio evaluation plan.

Student self-assessment This technique helps students reflect critically on their own work and reasoning. It also encourages students to take responsibility for their learning and to think independently. This personal assessment may be open-ended or it may include responses to a questionnaire. Likewise, it may be something students write about in their math journals. A sample prompt might be, "Tell me everything you know about multiplication. What else would you like to know about multiplication? Are you good at doing multiplication? Why or why not? Is there anything about multiplication you'd like to do better?"

STANDARDS LINK 4-4
Students learn to share responsibility for the assessment process as they come to understand and make judgments about the quality of their own work. (NCTM, 1995, p. 39)

The Annenberg/CPB Math and Science Collection

VIDEO LINK 4-3
Geometry and Spatial Sense

Brief Summary: In "Shapes from Squares," teacher Marco Ramirez's second- and third-graders are making different shapes from paper that has already been folded.

1. What types of assessment does Mr. Ramirez include in this lesson?
2. What did Mr. Ramirez learn about his students' understanding of geometry concepts and language from this lesson?
3. How does Mr. Ramirez use questioning to learn more about his students' understanding and to help them extend their understanding?

Video Source. Teaching Math: A Video Library, K–4; Tape 8 from The Annenberg/CPB Math and Science Collection.

ASSESSING ATTITUDES TOWARD MATHEMATICS

Success in mathematics often is correlated positively with favorable attitudes toward mathematics. It is important that teachers assess students' attitudes toward mathematics at the beginning of and throughout the school year. There are a number of ways to assess children's feelings toward mathematics. A Likert-type attitude scale is the most common. In this type of scale the student responds to statements such as "I am happier in mathematics class than in any other class" on a five-point scale labeled in a range from strongly disagree to strongly agree. For students in the primary grades, the statements can be simplified and the choices reduced to three faces, as in Figure 4-2. The happy face is a positive response, the sad face is negative, and the middle face is neutral.

The semantic-differential approach to assessing attitudes consists of devising pairs of opposites, for example "Easy" and "Hard" (or "Difficult," depending on the level of the students). The student marks a point on

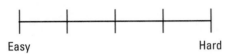

FIGURE 4-2

a five-point scale to indicate which word most closely represents her or his feelings. A typical presentation format is shown below:

Easy   Hard

A mark on the left above "Easy" usually is assigned a value of 1, while a mark on the right above "Hard" usually is assigned a value of 5, with corresponding values falling in between. The greater the total score, the more positive the attitude toward mathematics.

In addition, sentence completion can be used to assess attitudes. Give students the beginning of a sentence and ask them to complete the sentence. For example,

Mathematics is important because _____.
Compared to other subjects, mathematics is _____.

Results are not easily quantifiable but often reveal very important insights into how a child feels about mathematics.

Finally, daily routine observations also yield important clues about a child's attitude toward mathematics. Half-muttered statements, the level of enthusiasm, the degree of perseverance, and other behaviors are indications of a student's like or dislike of mathematics.

CONCLUSION

Assessment is an integral part of mathematics teaching and learning, providing information about children's growth and development in conceptual understanding. Many types of assessment are available to teachers; each type plays an important role in evaluating and maximizing students' learning. The type of assessment a teacher chooses to use is dependent on the purpose for the assessment.

For Your Journal

When you have finished studying this chapter, reflect on these questions in your math journal:

1. Visit an elementary or middle-school classroom and interview a teacher. How does he or she assess students' mathematics understanding and achievement? Characterize the assessment according to the types discussed in this chapter.

2. Visit a classroom and ask for samples of the written work of at least two students in mathematics. How would you assess the students' understanding based on that written work?

3. Interview a teacher who uses either performance tasks or portfolios as part of his or her mathematics assessment plan. How does the teacher employ performance tasks or portfolios in assessing his or her students?

For Your Portfolio

When you have finished studying this chapter, complete these activities to include in your professional portfolio:

1. Develop a performance task to assess understanding of a concept of your choice.

2. Analyze a chapter in an elementary mathematics textbook and the corresponding assessment. What would that assessment tell you about students' understanding?

Resources for Teachers

Books on Assessment

Bryant, D., & Driscoll, M. (1998). *Exploring classroom assessment in mathematics.* Reston, VA: National Council of Teachers of Mathematics.

Lambdin, D. V., Kehle, P. E., & Preston, R. V. (Eds.). (1996). *Emphasis on assessment: Readings from NCTM's school-based journals.* Reston, VA: National Council of Teachers of Mathematics.

Stenmark, J. K. (Ed.). (1991). *Mathematics assessment: Myths, models, good questions, and practical suggestions.* Reston, VA: National Council of Teachers of Mathematics.

Links to the Internet

Assessment Resources

http://score.kings.k12.ca.us/assess.html

Contains links to mathematics assessment resources.

Balanced Assessment in Mathematics
http://edetcl.harvard.edu/ba/

Contains sample mathematics assessment tasks for elementary and secondary grades.

Assessment in Mathematics Teaching
http://forum.swarthmore.edu/mathed/assessment.html

Contains links to publications and presentations about mathematics assessment.

Performance Assessment and Authentic Instruction
http://www.interactiveclassroom.com/assess.html

Contains links to articles about assessment topics, including creating rubrics and journal writing.

CHAPTER 5

Developing Number Concepts

- Pre-number activities
- Types of Counting
- Ways to Represent Numbers
- Number Relationships

When you have finished studying this chapter, you should be able to answer these questions:

1. What types of pre-number activities must children engage in to develop understanding of number concepts?

2. What types of counting abilities are necessary for children to develop?

3. What are several of the ways in which children must be able to represent numbers?

4. What types of number relationships are essential for children to understand?

You have likely observed a child respond to the question "How old are you?" by proudly but shyly holding up the accurate or inaccurate number of fingers. You may also have heard a young child respond, one–two–three–five–ten, when asked to count a set of five objects. Mastering the number names and learning to count are early formal mathematics milestones of children. Such capabilities, however, can be mere mimic or rote memorization and usually occur before an understanding of numbers.

This chapter discusses important concepts that relate to the development of number understanding. Numerous and varied experiences are described to demonstrate how to enhance young children's construction of number relationships. ○

STANDARDS LINK 5-1

In grades K–4, the mathematics curriculum should include whole number concepts and skills so that students can

- construct number meanings through real-world experiences and the use of physical materials;
- understand our numeration system by relating counting, grouping, and place-value concepts;
- develop number sense;
- interpret the multiple uses of numbers encountered in the real world. (NCTM, 1989, p. 38)

The Annenberg/CPB Math and Science Collection

VIDEO LINK 5-1
Concepts of Whole Number Operations

Brief Summary: In "Cubes and Containers," Janice Sette-Lund's kindergarten students are sorting Unifix cubes by color and placing them into containers.

1. Near the beginning of this segment, Ms. Sette-Lund asks students how they might sort the Unifix cubes. What were some of the different ways students suggested? How did the teacher respond when a child suggested a way that would not work?
2. One group decided they needed more than 10 containers to complete the sorting. Why did they decide this? How did Ms. Sette-Lund handle this situation?

Video Source. Teaching Math: A Video Library, K–4; Tape 4 from The Annenberg/CPB Math and Science Collection.

THE FOUNDATIONS OF NUMBER

Counting activities, comparing sets, learning the sequence of number names and the numerals to represent one-digit numbers have traditionally formed an important part of kindergarten and Grade 1 mathematics programs. This is because it is believed that such activities help a child develop an understanding of number concepts.

Other activities that also enhance the development of number concepts are classifying, seriating, and patterning (Piaget, 1965). As with counting, by the time children enter kindergarten, they will have had experiences in these processes in their preschool activities, whether during their play or through interactions with adults. At school, teachers should plan activities for children so that these processes will eventually extend to number classification, ordering, and patterning.

Understanding numbers resides in the recognition and knowledge of number relationships (Van de Walle, 1994). Knowing the number 5 means more than being able to rationally count a set of 5. It is knowing this number in relationship to other numbers. For example, 5 is one less than 6, 5 is one more than 4, and 5 is 3 plus 2. Developing number relationships is at the heart of Kindergarten and Grade 1 mathematics learning.

Pre-Number Activities

Classification   The process of classifying or sorting a collection of objects involves focusing on an attribute or characteristic of the objects and subsequently grouping them accordingly. For example, given a collection of books, they could be sorted according to the characteristic "stories about animals."

Connecting with science and social studies. Classification is a topic that lends itself nicely to integrating mathematics with other subject areas such as science and social studies.

For science and social studies projects, teachers often take children on outings—trips to the zoo, nature walks, or visits to local establishments such as a grocery store, a department store, a bank, a factory, or a post office. During an outdoor excursion, children can be asked to gather a small collection of objects. Upon their return to the classroom, a science lesson might focus on the characteristic "growing" and the objects collected can be classified in sets of "things that grow" (e.g., leaves, moss, mushrooms, twigs) and "things that do not grow" (e.g., stones, metal, paper). While at a grocery store, children might be asked to observe how food displays are organized (fruits in one section, vegetables in another, meats in another, etc.); at a department store, they could observe the furniture area (bedroom furniture together, living room furniture together in another area, etc.), or how shoes are displayed (children's shoes in one area, women's and men's in other separate areas).

If it is not feasible to go on class field trips, children could be encouraged to notice how objects are classified during family outings or in their home. For example, children can examine kitchen cupboards, clothes closets, linen cupboards, etc., to see how objects are organized. Provide time for the children to report their findings to the class.

Other classification activities.   In class, the children themselves can be the objects for classification activities. Attributes that can be considered for classification include wearing glasses and not wearing glasses, wearing something red and wearing something green, wearing a buttoned blouse or shirt and wearing a t-shirt. Depending on the classification category, not all children in a class may be able to participate in a particular activity. The class should discuss this so children will know why they "do not belong" in either category being classified. Sometimes, all children can participate if two categories are specified as, for example, children wearing footwear with laces and without laces. It is also possible to select more than two classification categories.

Commercial classification sets. A commercial set of Attribute Logic Blocks lends itself to numerous classification activities of varying sophistication. The set consists of plastic blocks in five shapes (triangle, square, rectangle, hexagon, and circle), two different sizes (large and small), two thicknesses (thin, thick), and three colors (yellow, red, and blue) for a total of 60 pieces. The set is structured, that is, there is only one block for every possible combination of values for the attributes. For example, there is only one large, thin, red circle. If purchasing a set of Attribute Logic Blocks is problematic, try making a set from felt. The felt shapes can be placed on flannel- or felt-covered boards for display.

In a lesson observing attributes children may first focus on color. Through maturation and experience, children are able to concentrate on other perceptual characteristics and eventually can classify sets according to abstract attributes such as number.

Class conversation. When all the children have had an opportunity to sort a particular set of materials, a teacher could gather the children on a mat for a class conversation. An opening remark by the teacher might be, "Did you notice many differences in the things you've been sorting? Let's see what differences you noticed. Becky, would you begin, please?" As children voice their observations, the teacher could note these on cards to attach to the bulletin board. Sometime during the day or week, each child can affix objects to the bulletin board or gather them into a group under their proper characteristic.

Class conversations can take place following any mathematical activity to provide an opportunity for children to talk about the mathematics they are doing. Such dialogue enhances the development of mathematical understanding (Baker & Baker, 1990).

The following six activities describe classification experiences using unstructured materials, while activities with commercial attribute blocks are described in Activities 5-1 and 5-2.

1. Classifying
   - Ask a small group of children to stand side by side in front of the others.
   - Then ask the class, "Can you tell why these girls and boys belong together?" (The teacher decides on an attribute.)

✳ ACTIVITY 5-1

GUESS WHICH BLOCK I HAVE?

MATERIALS:
a set of attribute blocks for each child and the teacher

PROCEDURE:
1. Have the children select one block from their set. The teacher does the same without showing his or her block to the children.
2. A child asks the teacher a question about the chosen block. Example: "Is your block red?" If the teacher's block is not red, the teacher answers "No, my block is not red." The children who had chosen a red block must change their block for a non-red block.
3. The questioning continues until the teacher's block has been identified. By this time, every child should have in her or his hand a block that is the same as that of the teacher.
4. Have a child identify the block by naming attributes.
   Example: "The block is a large, thin, blue triangle."
5. Repeat procedures with another block. Students could guess the block selected by a student rather than by the teacher.

2. Classifying
   - Choose three children who are wearing something blue and one who is not.
   - Ask the class, "Who doesn't belong in this group?" "Why not?"
   - Choose someone to replace the child who does belong in this group, based on the chosen attribute.

3. Classifying
   - Provide children with a collection of buttons, seeds, or other objects that have easily distinguishable attributes.
   - Ask them to group the objects in ways they are the same.
   - Have them tell or write about the groupings they made.

Over a period of class days, provide students with lots of opportunities to classify objects, beginning with concrete items and moving to semi-concrete objects such as pictures of objects.

4. Describing properties
   - Have all students stand beside their chairs and ask a child to volunteer to stand where all can see her or him.
   - Have students, in turn, tell something about the volunteer. Example: "Jeremy has brown hair."

✳ ACTIVITY 5-2

BUILDING TRAINS

MATERIALS:
a set of attribute blocks for each child

PREPARATION:
Make an "engine" for each child as pictured below.

(The side of the square is 8 cm.)

PROCEDURE:
1. Direct the children to select a block and place it on their engine.

2. The children are then to select other blocks, in turn, to be the "cars" that the engine has to pull. Each car has to be different from the preceding car in only one way.

3. When the trains are 6 to 8 cars long, children should check each other's train to see if the rule was followed for each car.

VARIATIONS:
Trains can be made with cars that are different in more than one way; in at least two ways.

- As the teacher writes "brown hair" on the board, all children who have a different hair color should sit down. Other statements could refer to clothing and jewelry worn or other known facts about the person (e.g., Jeremy takes music lessons).
- Students continue to name properties of the volunteer until he or she is the only student left standing.

5. What can we sort?
- Ask the class to think of some collections they could classify.
- When a list has been generated, have children, on different days, select one of the collections named and think of ways to classify the collection.
- Children should record their ideas, as these will be used at another time.

6. How can we sort this collection?
- Using one of the collections identified by the children (previous activity), have them share their ideas

about possible ways to sort the objects. If it is feasible to gather a set of the objects, do so for only one day, because some children may need to have the objects visible in order to think of characteristics.
- The particular set of objects gathered should then be classified.

Seriation *Seriation* is the process of focusing on an attribute and then ordering a set of objects according to that attribute. For example, given a set of crayons, children could be asked to order them according to length. The Cuisenaire Rods are a commercial set consisting of ten rods, each of a different color, that can be ordered by length.

Prior to asking children to order a set of three or more objects, a teacher would have them compare two objects in order to recognize different attributes and learn comparative terms. For example, children should be able to examine two objects and make such statements as the following:

This ruler is longer than that ruler.
This tower is shorter than that tower.
The red paper is larger than the green paper.
The tub of beans is heavier than the tub of macaroni.

When children are able to make these kinds of comparisons, they can be asked to order larger sets according to various attributes.

In seriating or ordering activities, a teacher should vary the number of objects to be ordered as some children are successful in seriating seven or fewer items but not with sets of ten or more. Objects can be ordered, for example, according to mass, shade of color, length, size, height, or thickness.

Objects that can be seriated include the following:

Attribute	Objects to be Ordered
length	sets of pencils, nails, pieces of rope or yarn
size	mittens, socks, containers, jars
capacity	measuring spoons, jars, boxes
mass	small vials of sugar, flour, rice, beans, etc.
height	students, potted plant seedlings

Teachers can construct sets of objects that vary in length, height, or size according to a fixed ratio such as, for example, strips of cardboard, cylinders cut from paper towel rolls, rectangles and other regular shapes, and outlines of houses or other objects. Pairs of objects of different lengths such as, for example, vases and flowers, dolls and hats, or bats and balls can be constructed and used for double seriation activities. See Activity 5-3.

Through classification and seriation activities, a teacher will be able to observe how children's observation skills, logical reasoning ability, and problem-solving strategies are developing.

✳ ACTIVITY 5-3

DOUBLE SERIATION

MATERIALS:
a set of 8 to 12 similar paper balls and bats, each bat differs in length by 1 cm and each ball is proportionally larger

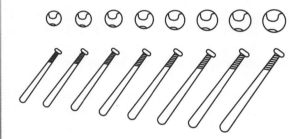

PROCEDURE:
1. First ask a child to order the balls from smallest to largest. You may place the smallest and the largest ball in place.
2. Next, ask the child to match each bat with the ball to which it belongs. Again, match the first and the last bat.

VARIATION:
After the child has ordered the balls only, point to one bat from the set and ask the child to find the ball to which it belongs.

Patterns The recognition of patterns is a basic skill that enhances the development of mathematics concepts. Prior to recognizing number patterns, children should become familiar with concrete patterns. Varied kinds of patterns such as A B A B A B . . . and A B B A B B . . . can be clapped, tapped, danced, walked, jumped, or otherwise acted out. Patterns can also be sung, read, or recited.

Patterns can be constructed, for example, with colored beads on a string, or made with gummed shapes on paper. Other materials include a pegboard and colored pegs, Unifix cubes and multi-link cubes of various colors, and pattern blocks. The following two activities serve as examples.

1. Creating Patterns
   • Provide children with buttons in two colors and a piece of 2 cm grid paper.
   • Invite students to create patterns by placing the buttons on the grid paper.
   • Have students describe the pattern they made.

2. Creating Patterns
   • Provide children with Unifix cubes in two colors.
   • Ask students to construct a pattern by interlocking the cubes a certain way.
   • Have students describe their pattern.

Eventually, children will recognize simple number patterns such as "counting by one," "adding one," or "counting by twos" to generate number series. Upper elementary students will learn that *looking for a number pattern* is a useful problem-solving strategy.

Classification, seriation, and patterning skills can be learned from storybooks. Examples of good storybooks to read to or with a class include *I Was Walking Down the Road* (Barchas, 1975), *Nancy No-size* (Hoffman, 1990), *Have You Seen Birds?* (Oppenheim & Reid, 1986), *I Love Spiders* (Parker, 1988), *Who Said Red?* (Serfoza, 1988), and *Red is Best* (Stinson, 1982).

The next step with patterning is to encourage students to translate patterns from one medium to another. For example, an extension or follow-up task to "Creating Patterns" (shown above) is as follows: Ask students to represent the pattern they showed with the Unifix cubes in another way—by using another manipulative, such as buttons, or by using letters, such as A and B, for example. Activities of this sort *help students abstract the key features of patterns.*

One-to-one correspondence Prior to counting capabilities, children can compare sets by using a one-to-one correspondence strategy. For example, children can be asked to find out if there are enough books or pencils for each child in a group. Children can be given a set of miniature dolls, a set of cars, small raisin boxes or other small objects and asked to record in some way (tallies or circles, for example) "how many" objects they have. There should be one tally or mark per object. Children should be aware that the diagram (tallies) shows how many objects there are in the set.

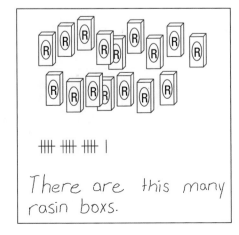

Children need to learn the meaning of comparative terms such as "more than," "fewer than," "the same number as," and "as many as." These terms should be used when comparing sets. As children learn to count objects in sets, they will compare and order sets according to the number of objects in each.

1. Comparing Groups
   • Direct children to stand in groups of two, three, and four.
   • Ask the children to make a statement to compare one group with another. ("This group has one more than that one. This group has one fewer than that one.")

2. Comparing Collections
   • Show students collections of small objects on three plates, each plate with a different number of objects.
   • Ask them to compare the collections.
   • Change the size of the collections and have children compare the sets again.

3. One-to-one Correspondence
   • Provide a child with a set of Valentine's Day cards and envelopes.
   • Ask the child to find out if there are enough envelopes for the cards.
   • Have the child make a statement about the situation. ("There are more cards than envelopes.")

Other sets could be cups and saucers, pencils and paper, books and children, paint jars and brushes.

4. Comparing Collections
   • Place 6 small objects, all the same, on each of 3 paper plates and 7 objects on another plate.
   • Ask students, "Which set does not belong?" "Can you make it belong?"

5. Comparing Pictured Sets
   • Prepare a set of six cards with stickers on them. Each card except one has the same number of stickers on it. One card has one more or fewer.
   • Ask a child, "Which card is different?" "How is it different?"

Examples:

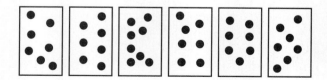

6. Comparing Pictured Sets
   • Show students a set of six cards with 2, 3, 3, 4, 4, and 5 dots on them.

• Ask students, in turn, to select two cards and make a comparative statement: "This card has as many dots as this one"; "This card has more dots than this one"; "This card has one fewer dot than this one."

Classifying according to number. In one-to-one correspondence activities, close attention should be paid to the comparative language used by children. When children use expressions such as "as many books as children," the expression "as many as" can be used to classify sets. Such sets have the same number. *Number then is a property of sets that is independent of attributes such as color, shape, size, and arrangement.* Further, the objects within a set do not have to be uniform.

Conservation of number The ability to conserve number quantities under varied configurations marks a certain mental maturity. Piaget has identified the age of 6–7 years as the time when a child is successful at number conservation tasks, but not all children attain the capability at that age. A teacher should become knowledgeable of students' conservation abilities so that they are not expected to complete number exercises beyond their cognitive level (Marchand, Bye, Harrison, & Schroeder, 1985). For example, a child who cannot yet conserve large numbers will have difficulty making sense of number groupings. Conservation of large numbers can be assessed by having a child count two sets of the same objects, for example, Unifix cubes. One set of, say 32 cubes, is left spread out on the table while the other set is placed in small transparent plastic glasses in groups of 10. The child is subsequently asked to compare the sets.

NUMBER MEANINGS

As children use numbers in their daily lives, they will come to differentiate between three uses of numbers: cardinal, ordinal, and nominal.

> **STANDARDS LINK 5-2**
> Children must understand numbers if they are to make sense of the ways numbers are used in their everyday world. They need to use numbers to quantify, to identify location, to identify a specific object in a collection, to name, and to measure. (NCTM, 1989, p. 38)

Cardinal Use of Numbers

"Cardinal" numbers are used to designate the quantity of a set. The *cardinal* aspect of number is the idea that whenever a set is counted the last number named is the total number of objects in the set. For example, a child who is asked to count the pieces of chalk on the board ledge and states, after counting to seven, that *there are seven pieces of chalk on the ledge,* is using the cardinal aspect of number.

Ordinal Use of Numbers

"Ordinal" means *order;* ordinal numbers are used to de-note the order of an object. In their play, children will of-ten make statements such as the following: "Michelle fin-ished *first*" or "Marc came in *third.*" Other times, children will hear expressions such as "This is the *fifth* time the phone has rung since dinner" or "Christmas is on the *twenty-fifth* day of December." The use of num-bers such as first, second, third, etc. is an *ordinal* use of number.

Nominal Use of Numbers

"Nominal" means *name;* nominal numbers are used to name objects. A third use of number is for a *nominal* pur-pose, that is, numbers are used to identify objects. Num-bers are used in a nominal sense, for example, to identify a house on a street, a postal code, a license plate, floors and rooms in large buildings, or a team player.

1. Number Walk
   * Take children on a "number walk" along a city block.
   * Have them look for numerals and jot them down and where they saw them.
   * Back in class, discuss what "numbers" they saw. Ask, "What did the number tell?" (how many; iden-tified something) "Did you notice a pattern?"
2. Different Uses of Numbers
   * Have children bring to class newspaper or magazine clippings that depict numbers used in a cardinal, an ordinal, and a nominal sense.
   * Discuss the different uses of numbers.
   * The pictures can subsequently be affixed to a bul-letin board under appropriate headings.

COUNTING

Discrete and Continuous Quantities

As children engage in counting objects in their environ-ment, they will come to realize that counting is not ap-propriate for some objects. For example, one does not count the amount of water in the bathtub or the amount of cake on a plate. In time, children will be able to discrimi-nate between discrete and continuous quantities.

Discrete objects are those that can be counted to find out "how many" there are in the group. For example, one can ask: "How many people are in your family?" "How many books do you own?" *Continuous quantities,* on the other hand, measure "how much." Examples are: "How much milk did you drink?" "How long did it take you to tidy your room?" Measurements can be of length, area, volume, temperature, mass, or time.

Rote Counting

Rote counting is simply the reciting of the number name sequence in proper order. Some children learn the num-ber sequence to twenty and beyond, even up to one hun-dred, without being able to count a set of objects less than twenty. Some children who know the number name se-quence make counting errors by counting objects in a set more than once, or not counting others. That is, they do not establish a one-to-one correspondence between num-ber names and objects.

Rational Counting

According to Gelman and Gallistel (1978), children who are rational counters possess the following five capabil-ities:

1. They realize that any collection of real or imagined objects can be counted.
2. They know that counting numbers are arranged in a sequence that does not change.
3. They know that, when objects are counted, these are counted in such a way that one and only one number is used as each object is counted.
4. They know that the order in which objects are counted is irrelevant. The count number is the same regardless of the order.
5. They know that the last number named represents the total number of objects in the set.

To test the last capability, after a child has counted a set of eight objects, for example, blocks, ask the child to show you eight blocks. Does the child point to the last block counted or to the set of eight blocks?

Children should have ample opportunities to count ob-jects. Sets arranged in linear fashion such as beads on a string or a row of blocks are easier to count than a set of objects in scatter formation. Some children may need to be shown how to organize objects when counting to avoid making errors. They can be told to move the ob-jects to the side as each one is counted.

For sets of twenty or more, children can be asked to count the objects twice to see if they arrive at the same number. If not, a third count should corroborate with one of the first two totals.

1. Oral Counting
   • Say to a child, "Count for me."
   • Allow the child to continue counting until she or he makes several errors in the number sequence.
2. Counting Objects
   • Place some unifix cubes before a child seated at a table.
   • Say, "Count the cubes."
   • Allow the child to continue counting until you notice several errors.

You may want to record what type of errors the child made: Were they number sequence errors? Did the child skip cubes? Did the child count a cube more than once?

3. How many do you see?
   • If there is a window in the classroom that faces a street, have a child count vehicles as they pass by during several minutes.
   • Looking out the window, have children count how many buildings they see; how many trees they see.
   • Ask some children to walk down the hallway and count the doors they see. Then, have children walk down the stairs and count the steps.
   • During recess, ask the children to count the windows on one side of the school; count how many cars they see in the parking lot.
4. Counting Objects
   • Place objects on plates or in boxes, plastic tubs, or jars.
   • Have children count to find out how many objects there are in each container.

Children can record their work. ("I counted twelve buttons." "I counted fifteen sticks.")

When children know the number name sequence to at least twenty and can count objects, they can be engaged in more sophisticated counting activities.

Counting All, Counting On

Children use different counting procedures when quantifying sets. For example, suppose a child counts six apples in a basket and then five apples are placed beside the basket and the child is asked to find how many apples there are in all. A child might say "six" then continue to count "seven, eight, nine, ten, eleven" and state that there are eleven apples in all. This is a *counting-on* strategy.

Another possibility is to begin counting at one and re-count the six apples in the basket and continue counting until eleven has been reached. This latter strategy is called *counting all*.

✳ ACTIVITY 5-4

COUNTING ON

MATERIALS:
Purse or similar container and approximately 20 pennies or other counters

PROCEDURE:
1. Say: There are seven pennies in the purse. Count to find out how many there are altogether.
2. If the child wants to count the pennies in the purse, allow her or him to do so. When the child has counted the twelve pennies, tell the child that another way to count the pennies is to begin at seven and continue to count on.
3. Have the child count several collections as above by first counting all, then counting on.

A teacher should observe how children count sets. For those who always count all the objects, a teacher should demonstrate a counting-on method. See Activity 5-4 for a sample task. Children could use a counting-on and then a counting-all strategy to prove that they produce the same count. Children will eventually see that the counting-on strategy is the quicker way to count. To facilitate this, a teacher might say, "I have six pennies in my hand and these (seven on the table) are left. Count to find how many pennies in all."

When children are able to count on to find the number of objects in given sets, they can be asked to count on from a given number as shown on the cards in Figure 5-1 to find how many in all.

Counting Back

Some children who are proficient counters are unable to *count backward*. An introduction to counting backward can be to ask "What number is one less than 9?" When the child responds, say, "Tell what number is one fewer than 8." Continue in this manner for several more numbers. Then ask the child to write or recite the numbers, counting backward from 9 to 0 thinking of "one fewer than" the last number named. In time, counting backward activities should include bridging decades

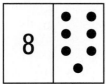

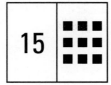

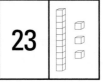

Chapter 5 Developing Number Concepts **79**

FIGURE 5-1

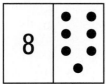
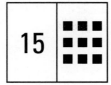
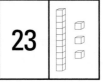

(32, 31, 30, 29, . . .) and eventually centuries (202, 201, 200, 199, . . .).

Skip Counting

Skip counting refers to counting by multiples of a certain number. For example, "skip counting by five" means to count "five, ten, fifteen, twenty" and so on. Skip counting lays the foundation for understanding the concept of multiplication. It usually is introduced in Grade 1, with students first learning to skip count by two, five, and ten.

Skip counting can be taught conceptually by counting groups of objects. For example, skip counting by two can be introduced by counting all the feet in the class. All the

children could stand in a line, and the teacher could move along the line, pointing to each set of two feet and encouraging the class to skip count together by two.

Later work on skip counting can also be based on patterns. A Grade 1 child was asked what he could say about the number series 2, 4, 6, 8, ... He quickly responded, "They're even numbers and it's counting by twos." And what about the numbers 1, 3, 5, 7, . . . ? "They're odd," he responded. The teacher asked, "This is counting by what?" "By threes. No. I don't know."

In later grades, when children do some skip counting activities, they should begin counting with different numbers. For example, when counting by tens, have children begin with any single digit number (e.g., 2, 12, 22, 32, . . .; 6, 16, 26, 36, 46, . . .).

A calculator can assist a child in naming the counting numbers or "skip counting" sequences. Calculators that have an automatic constant for addition or multiplication are particularly useful for this. For calculators with an automatic constant for addition, a key stroke sequence to count by 5 beginning at 4 would be $4 + 5 = = = =$.

Counting backward can also be done on a calculator with the following keystroke sequence for counting by threes beginning with 30: $30 - 3 = = = = $. Some calculators have the constant number registered before the

✹ ACTIVITY 5-5

COUNTING BACK

PROCEDURE:
Count backward from 22 to 16

- from 33 to 25
- from 62 to 57
- from 112 to 97
- from 152 to 137.

✹ ACTIVITY 5-6

WRITING COUNTING NUMBERS IN REVERSE

MATERIALS:
pencil and paper

PROCEDURE:
Write the numerals from 24 to 14

- from 56 to 35
- from 81 to 68
- from 105 to 95.

✹ ACTIVITY 5-7

COUNTING BY TENS

PROCEDURE:
Count by tens. Begin with

10	___	___	___	___
	___	___	___	___
3	___	___	___	___
	___	___	___	___
8	___	___	___	___
	___	___	___	___
12	___	___	___	___
	___	___	___	___

☀ ACTIVITY 5-8

COUNTING BY FIVES

MATERIALS:
pencil and paper

PROCEDURE:
Write ten numbers counting by fives.
Begin with 5; 6; 4; 1.

☀ ACTIVITY 5-9

COUNTING BACKWARD BY TENS AND FIVES

MATERIALS:
pencil and paper

PROCEDURE:
1. Write the numbers, counting by tens
   - from 60 to 10
   - from 120 to 50.

2. Write the numbers, counting by fives
   - from 45 to 20
   - from 110 to 75.

operation sign in the keystroke sequence rather than the number following it. When using a calculator to develop number sequences, children should be encouraged to "say the number first, then press the equal key and check the display to see if you said the right number." This procedure provides instant feedback and children can practice by themselves.

Simple computer programs can be written to "make the computer count." Computer or calculator printouts of number sequences can be helpful to children when studying number patterns.

REPRESENTING NUMBERS

How can the abstract idea of number be modeled so that children will come to know numbers and their properties? An approach has been to use concrete materials and pictures quite extensively in the early grades.

While children are engaged in counting activities, attention should be given to developing number-related ideas of equality, more than, fewer than, combining groups, and separating groups. The symbolic form of these operations or relations should only be used to record some meaningful action. The mathematical symbols $=$, $+$, and $-$ are usually introduced in the latter part of Grade 1 or early Grade 2, and the symbols $<$ and $>$ in Grade 2 or Grade 3.

◩ STANDARDS LINK 5-3

Children come to understand number meanings gradually. To encourage these understandings, teachers can offer classroom experiences in which students first manipulate physical objects and then use their own language to explain their thinking. This active involvement in, and expression of, physical manipulations encourages children to reflect on their actions and to construct their own number meanings. (NCTM, 1989, p. 38)

Concrete Models

Concrete materials are readily available for use in number development activities. Most primary classrooms are well equipped with boxes or buckets of small discrete objects for the children to use in counting activities. Some that I have seen include collections of acorns, small fir tree cones, toothpaste tube caps, square ceramic tiles,

☀ ACTIVITY 5-10

MAKING SETS

MATERIALS:
nine paper plates and small objects for each child

PROCEDURE:
Make sets of all the counting numbers to nine.

☀ ACTIVITY 5-11

SHOWING NUMBERS ONE TO NINE

MATERIALS:
toothpicks, glue stick, and a piece of cardboard

PROCEDURE:
Glue toothpicks on the cardboard to show the numbers from one to nine.

☀ ACTIVITY 5-12

SHOWING NUMBERS TO NINE

MATERIALS:
Unifix cubes

PROCEDURE:
Use the cubes to construct rods to show numbers to nine.

✳ ACTIVITY 5-13

COUNTING OBJECTS AND WRITING NUMERALS

MATERIALS:
a collection of buttons or other small objects. The size of the collection can be between twenty to fifty objects.

PROCEDURE:
1. Count the number of objects you have and record the amount in a statement. ("I counted twenty-six buttons." "There are thirty-two blocks in the box.")

2. Now recount the amount, checking for accuracy.

3. If the count number is not the same, the collection should be counted a third time.

VARIATION:
One child could count a collection and then another child could count the collection. The children then check their count numbers with each other.

and buttons. Besides using such materials at their desks, children can be asked to find out how many crayons are in a box, how many books are on a shelf, how many children have brought their lunches, how many rooms are on one floor of the school, etc.

In another counting activity, square tiles can be used to model numbers in geometric patterns. For example, children can be asked to make "number rectangles" as pictured in Activity 5-15. From this activity, the ideas of even and odd numbers can be discussed as well as what

✳ ACTIVITY 5-14

COUNTING AND WRITING NUMERALS

MATERIALS:
objects in the room

PROCEDURE:
Count three sets of objects in the room and write statements about your findings.

POSSIBLE EXAMPLES:
There are twelve books on the top shelf.
There are twenty-six desks in the room.
There are thirty chairs in the classroom.

VARIATION:
The children could count three sets of objects at home and write statements about their findings. For example: there are ten pairs of shoes in the closet; there are twenty-four spoons in the drawer; I have sixteen books in my room.

✳ ACTIVITY 5-15

NUMBER RECTANGLES

MATERIALS:
square tiles

PROCEDURE:
1. Show numbers with the tiles in the manner above.

2. Which numbers form rectangles? What can you say about them?

3. Try joining pairs of even and odd numbers. What do you notice?

4. Join two odd numbers. What do you notice?

5. Join two even numbers. What do you notice?

happens when one combines two even numbers, two odd numbers, or an even and an odd number.

Square tiles also can be used to model square numbers by constructing squares and the triangular numbers by making staircases.

The base-ten blocks are used by children when they understand grouping, particularly a group of ten. See Figure 5-2 and Blackline Master 1 at the end of the book.

Pictorial and Graphic Representation of Numbers

In general, children enjoy drawing. This capability can be the medium used to record the results of their number-related explorations.

Children can be asked to draw pairs of sets with different numbers of objects and to indicate which set has more objects and/or which set has the greater number. Provided with graph paper, they can draw the "number rectangles" they constructed with tiles.

Children can attempt to draw pictures of base-ten blocks or be provided with rubber stamps of the blocks. Later, a graphic representation can be made by using a dot for ones, a line for tens, and a square for hundreds as shown in Figure 5-3.

FIGURE 5-2

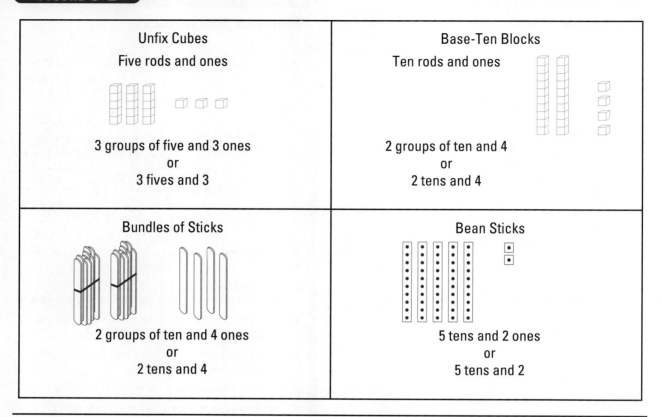

Unfix Cubes	Base-Ten Blocks
Five rods and ones	Ten rods and ones
3 groups of five and 3 ones or 3 fives and 3	2 groups of ten and 4 or 2 tens and 4
Bundles of Sticks	Bean Sticks
2 groups of ten and 4 ones or 2 tens and 4	5 tens and 2 ones or 5 tens and 2

Symbolic Representation of Numbers

STANDARDS LINK 5-4
For children to use both single-digit and multi-digit number ideas fluently, written symbols should be linked to physical models and oral names. (NCTM, 1989, p. 39)

Kindergarten number activities have children counting sets, constructing sets concretely and pictorially, and matching sets with number names and numerals. What is important for children to internalize are number relationships—not how to write numerals or recognize number symbols. Thus, children should be encouraged to talk about their number work and to record what they do in their own way. Work with number symbols should not appear to be of prime importance and can be delayed for some time.

FIGURE 5-3

GROUPS OF TENS AND ONES

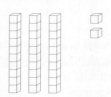

(a) Rubber stamp of base-ten blocks

(b) Graphic representation of base-ten blocks

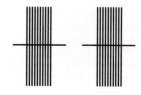

(c) Graphic representation of stick bundles

FIGURE 5-4

Number Cards

one	two	three	four	five	six	seven	eight	nine

Numeral Cards

1	2	3	4	5	6	7	8	9

Sets

Bundles of sticks

Marbles in bags

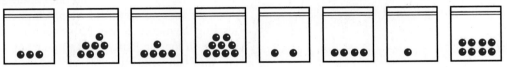

Pictures of sets

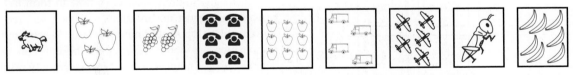

Pattern Dot Cards

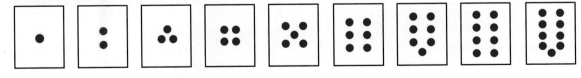

Dot Cards

A teacher can introduce an activity in one of four ways: concretely, pictorially, symbolically, or orally, using number words. Likewise, children can be asked to respond in any of the four ways. An effective teaching or assessment strategy is to present a task in one mode and have the students respond in a different mode (Figure 2-10, Chapter 2). Flexibility in transferring from one mode to another is indicative of some understanding. Some materials for number work are shown in Figure 5-4. The following four activities are appropriate for learning to match numerals with number words and quantities.

1. Ordering Numerals
    *   Cut out some magazine or newspaper pictures that show a large numeral.
    *   Have students order the pictures according to the numeral on them.
2. Matching Sets With Numerals
    *   Prepare a set of numbered garages and a set of cars with dots on them (e.g., one dot on a car, two dots on another, etc.)
    *   Direct a child to match the cars with the garages.
3. Matching Numerals, Number Names, and Picture Cards
    *   Prepare three sets of cards; one with number names, one with numerals, and one with pictures.
    *   Have a child match the picture cards with its number name and numeral.

Sample cards:

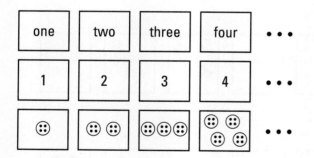

4. Writing Numerals to Match Sets
    *   Prepare a set of cards with pictures on them.
    *   Ask a child to count the pictures on a card and then write the appropriate numeral on a piece of paper to go with the card.

Numerals

Just as individuals develop their own handwriting style, children also develop their own way of forming numerals. For some numerals there is more than one acceptable

form (e.g., 4 and ⁴, 2 and ², 9 and ⁹). Teachers usually present young children with one numerical form for each number. However, children will likely see other forms for numerals, as, for example, on a calculator display. A poster depicting acceptable numerals may help children recognize and write different forms.

Teachers should observe children as they form numerals either when copying them or when writing them from memory. Devote some time to practice forming numerals so that children can internalize an efficient way of writing each numeral. A recommended stroke sequence is presented here (Baratta-Lorton, 1987).

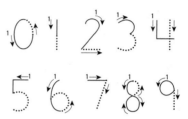

The first stroke (solid line) for each numeral is made in a downward (straight or curved) or horizontal motion. Only the second stroke (dotted line) in the zero, six, and the eight have an upward motion. Children can practice forming the numerals with their fingers on their desks, in the air, in the sandbox, in shaving cream, or in a water tub; they can write numerals on the board, on individual slates or blackboards, with crayons, and in their notebooks with pencils.

Although children must learn how to form numerals, this activity must not interfere with or take precedence over the development of number sense. When number relationships are being developed, children can use numeral cards or number words to show activity results.

NUMBER RELATIONSHIPS

The development of number sense is an important objective of the K–4 curriculum. Possessing number sense implies in part having well-understood number meanings and having developed multiple relationships among numbers (NCTM, 1989, p. 38). Number relationships cannot be taught directly but must be constructed by children through their own mental activity (Hughes, 1986; Kamii & Joseph, 1988; Van de Walle, 1994). Children need to engage in number explorations so that number relationships can be discovered. Invite them to verbalize number relationships and, when they are capable, to write about them.

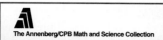

VIDEO LINK 5-2
Concepts of Whole Number Operations

Brief Summary: In part 2 of "Cubes and Containers," Janice Sette-Lund has each student choose a chip on which a numeral has been written and make a train of Unifix cubes corresponding to the numeral on the chip.

1. What types of number relationships does the teacher include in this discussion?

2. What might a teacher learn about the children's understandings of number concepts and number relationships by their work on these problems and their descriptions of their thinking?

Video Source. Teaching Math: A Video Library, K–4; Tape 4 from The Annenberg/CPB Math and Science Collection.

Order Relations

Given several sets of varied numerical size, children should be able to order them from smallest to largest.

Examples of sets to be ordered are

- A set of five plates, each with a different number of small objects.
- Vases (paper cups) each with a different number of paper flowers.
- Bags of marbles.
- Boxes of crayons (8, 16, 24, 36 crayons).
- Sets represented on cards as shown in Figure 5-5.
- Discs on vertical rods as shown in Figure 5-6.

FIGURE 5-6

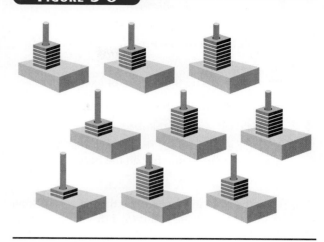

More Than, Fewer Than

When children compare sets by counting, number relation questions to ask include: Which set has more? How many more? Which set has fewer? How many fewer? Does this set have as many as that set?

Sets with a small number of objects are easily identified as "more than" or "fewer than" another set. However, the comparative task becomes more challenging when the sets are more than ten and when the objects are arranged in scatter formation. See Figure 5-7. The strategy used may be one-to-one matching, pattern identification, or counting.

One Greater Than, One Less Than

"One greater" and "one less" relationships can be practiced by showing different sized sets and having children tell the number that is one more than and one less than each set. When numerals are known, they can be written

FIGURE 5-5

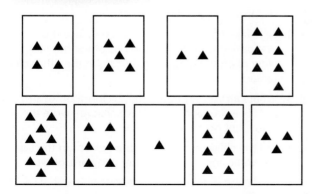

FIGURE 5-7

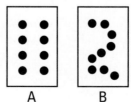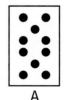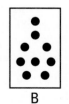

A B A B

Are there more or fewer dots in Set A than in Set B?

✳ ACTIVITY 5-16

ONE GREATER AND ONE LESS RELATIONSHIPS

PROCEDURE:

1. Write numerals on the board. For example:

   6 3 9 5 2 8 4 1 7

2. Have a child read the numbers.

3. Then have the child say the number that is one greater than each number on the board

   (7, 4, 10, . . .).

4. Have the child say the number that is one less than each number on the board (5, 2, 8, . . .).

✳ FIGURE 5-8

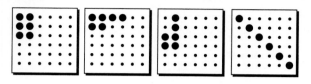

What can you say about six? *(Six is two and two and two. Six is four and two. Six is two and four. Six is six ones.)*

in random order on the board and students can be asked to name the number that is one greater (also, one less) than the numeral they see (Activity 5-16).

Part–Part–Whole Relationships

Children should have experiences in concretely showing numbers in different ways. For example, children could be asked to show six blocks in different ways on a 2 cm square grid. The patterns could be reproduced on a large chart to form the focus of a class discussion. Number patterns can also be shown with pegs on a pegboard. See Figure 5-8.

Finding "two parts" of numbers on a "two-part mat" is another good activity for developing number relationships. See Activity 5-17.

The "family" of combinations for a given number can be easily constructed with Unifix cubes in two colors

The Annenberg/CPB Math and Science Collection

VIDEO LINK 5-3
Concepts of Whole Number Operations

Brief Summary: In "Domino Math," teacher Alma Wright's first- and second-grade students use dominoes to find various combinations of numbers equal to a given sum.

1. How does this activity help strengthen students' understanding of number concepts?

2. What factors did the teacher consider when forming the small groups of students?

Video Source. Teaching Math: A Video Library, K–4; Tape 4 from The Annenberg/CPB Math and Science Collection.

✳ ACTIVITY 5-17

SHOWING TWO PARTS OF SIX

MATERIALS:

two-part mat as pictured and six small objects (buttons, chips, or centimetre cubes)

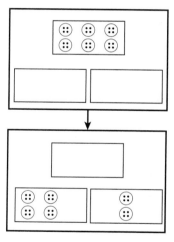

PROCEDURE:

1. Direct the children to place the six objects in the rectangle at the top of the mat.

2. Say: Take some of the buttons and place them in one of the rectangles at the bottom of the mat. Now place the remaining buttons in the other rectangle.

3. What can you say about six? Elicit responses such as "Six is four and two." Have children write the statement on a piece of paper.

4. Tell the children to replace the buttons in the top rectangle and to find another two parts of six.

5. Challenge them to find as many two parts of six as they can, recording each one on their paper.

(Activity 5-18). When children are constructing two parts of numbers, the idea of the combination "zero and a number" may arise. If it has not been done earlier, a discussion on the meaning of the number zero should take place.

Tell children that the number zero tells "how many" when a group or set has no members. For example, ask them, "How many live horses are in the room?" (Zero.) You and the class may decide that when making two parts of numbers, say five, the combinations "0 and 5" and "5 and 0" are entirely appropriate, as exemplified in Activity 5-18.

As children make concrete representations of numbers, they will begin to use the language of addition and subtraction. Statements to be encouraged include: "six blocks is four blocks and two blocks"; "seven robots is the same as five robots and two robots"; "three keys and four keys are seven keys." Some children have difficulty

understanding questions such as "How many are four and five?" Changing the question to "How many pencils are four pencils and five pencils?" is easier for children to understand (Hughes, 1986). Thus, it is recommended that early work with part-part-whole number relationships should be with and about physical objects.

As children work at constructing parts of numbers (seven is four and three), comparing the whole to its parts (Is eight the same as three and five?), or finding a missing part (Four is one part of six. What is the other part?), observe them to find out if they have developed the logic of considering the whole and its parts simultaneously. The logic of number addition requires that the parts be considered in relation to each other and that both parts be considered in relation to the whole (the sum). In the absence of these logical ideas, a child solves part-part-whole problems perceptually (Labinowicz, 1980). A task to assess a child's logical ability to compare a whole and its parts is presented in Activity 5-19 (Labinowicz, 1980, p. 106).

Research has shown that children can complete addition statements such as $1 + 7 =$ _____ symbolically and not be successful at similar problems logically (Labinowicz, 1980). Therefore, it is important that children, particularly in the primary grades, explore concrete representations of numbers in order to construct logical number relationships.

Relationship to five and ten One part-part-whole relationship that is particularly important is the relationship of numbers to five and ten. This relationship will be especially useful when children begin learning number facts. For example, if a child knows that 6 is one more than 5, that will help the child reason that $6 + 3$ must be one more than $5 + 3$, so if $5 + 3 = 8$, then $6 + 3$ must be one more than 8, or 9.

One way to help children understand the relationship of numbers to five and ten is to use the ten-frame (Wirtz, 1974). The ten-frame consists of a two-by-five array of squares in which dots are placed to represent numbers

---

✳ ACTIVITY 5-18

TWO PARTS OF SIX WITH UNIFIX CUBES

MATERIALS:
fifteen Unifix cubes in each of two colors

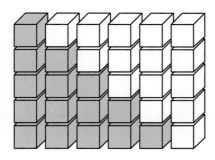

PROCEDURE:
1. Ask the children to make rods to show two parts of six using cubes in two colors.

2. If children suggest "six and zero" as two parts of six, provide additional cubes so a rod of each color can be made.

3. Direct the children to arrange their rods in a pattern as pictured.

4. Say: "Look at your rods and read the two parts of six in order" (Zero and six, one and five, two and four, etc.).

5. Invite the children to close their eyes and try to say to themselves the two parts of six. Tell them to open their eyes to look if they get mixed up and to begin again.

✳ ACTIVITY 5-19

NUMBER ADDITION LOGICAL TASK

PROCEDURE:
Teacher: "I'm going to give you some cookies." (Place eight cookies before the child.) "Today you can have four cookies in the morning and four cookies in the afternoon." (Arrange the cookies in groups of four.)

"Tomorrow you can have one cookie in the morning and seven cookies in the afternoon." (Rearrange the cookies in groups of one and seven.) "Will you have more cookies on one of the days or will you have the same number on both days?"

(see Blackline Master 2). One rule of working with the ten-frame is that the top row of squares must be filled with dots before any dots are placed in the second row. When the top row is filled, there are five dots in the ten-frame. When both rows are filled, there are ten dots.

Ten-frames can be made on plain white paper or construction paper. Dots to represent the numbers can be bingo chips, buttons, or stick-on dots, which can easily be removed from paper that has been laminated.

It is important to discuss the relationships students observe in a ten-frame. For example, when the number seven is represented in the ten-frame, as in Figure 5-9, the top row is filled and there are two dots in the bottom row. This shows that seven is two more than five.

Using action language The formal language of addition and subtraction should be delayed until children are able to perform mental actions on numbers. For example, children may not understand the meaning of "five add three" or "eight subtract five." While working with concrete materials, the language expressing actions is more appropriately used (Skemp, 1989). For example, after an addend has been identified, one could say about the second addend, "I am giving you three more . . . ," "If you put three more . . . ," or "three more arrived . . ."; for subtraction, the expressions "take away four . . . ,"

"gave away four . . . ," or "four were removed . . ." could be used. In time, children will be able to, for example, partition a set of nine objects and state: "Nine is six and three" or "five add four is nine."

Number relationships can also be developed through the use of patterned cards. Activities with patterned cards as described below help children learn the combinations of numbers.

1. Two parts of a Number
   • Prepare patterned cards for a selected number, say, six. Sets of cards as pictured in Figure 5-10 (a)–(d) can be used.
   • Children are told that a set of cards shows two-parts of six.
   • Each card is shown, in turn, for a brief moment.
   • Ask: What two parts of six did you see?

FIGURE 5-10

(a) Cards with bow tie stickers

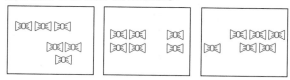

(b) Dot cards

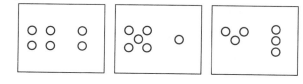

(c) Dot cards in two colors, rectangular format

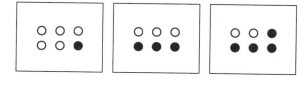

(d) Domino cards

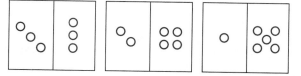

(e) Cards with one part missing

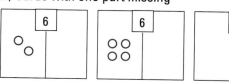

FIGURE 5-9

TEN-FRAMES

[Ten-frame diagrams showing dots representing numbers 1 through 10]

2. Two parts of a Number
- Prepare a set of patterned number cards for two or three consecutive numbers (e.g., 4, 5, and 6).
- Show each card, in turn, for a brief moment.
- Ask: How many objects did you see? What two parts of the number did you see?

Finding the "missing part" of a number helps children learn subtraction facts.

3. Finding the Missing Part
- Prepare number cards showing a number and one part of the number (Figure 5-10e).
- Show a card for a moment and ask children to give the *missing part*.

The number activities described above can be used for a few minutes of mental arithmetic at the beginning of a mathematics period two or three times a week. By the end of Grade 1, children should have learned the basic facts for single digit numbers.

Bi-Directional Relationship of an Equation

Research has shown that children in Grade 3 do not accept as correct equations in the following forms: 6 = 4 + 2, 4 + 5 = 5 + 4, 3 + 6 = 6 + 3, and 5 = 5 (Labinowicz, 1985). This attests to their narrow understanding of the equal sign. To some, the sign means that you "put the answer after it" and operation signs do not belong on the right of an equal sign.

Before the equality or operation symbols are introduced, the language of equality statements should be developed. Thus, when developing the part-part-whole relationships, statements such as the following should be verbalized and written by the children:

9 is 4 and 5
4 and 5 is the same number as 5 and 4
6 and 3 is the same number as 4 and 5
9 is the same number as 9 and 0
9 is the same number as 9.

As children eventually replace the operation and relation words with symbols, it should be easy to accept varied forms of equations. Thus, "9 is 4 and 5" can be stated as "9 equals 4 plus 5" and is symbolized as 9 = 4 + 5. The number sentence "4 and 5 is the same as 5 and 4" can be stated as "4 plus 5 equals 5 plus 4" and is written symbolically as 4 + 5 = 5 + 4. The focus should be on the correctness of the relationship expressed rather than on the form of the equation. This is different than asking children to "find the answer" to a question such as "What are 4 and 5?" or "4 plus 5 equals what?" Such questions cause children to focus on "the answer" which they record after the "equal sign." There is no opportunity to

develop an understanding of the meaning of the equality symbol.

A math balance is a good instrument to use in exploring equality statements (Activities 5-20 to 5-22). Students can be asked what they notice on the balance when

✳ ACTIVITY 5-20
WORKING WITH A MATH BALANCE

MATERIALS:
math balance

PROCEDURE:
1. Place some weights on each side of the math balance to make it balance.
2. Record your work.

EXAMPLES:
4 and 2 balance with 1 and 5; 8 balances with 4 and 4; 10 balances with 2 and 2 and 6.

✳ ACTIVITY 5-21
MAKING BALANCING LOADS WITH TEN

MATERIALS:
math balance

PROCEDURE:
1. Place a weight on ten on the left side of the balance.
2. Balance the load by placing weights on two numbers on the right side.
3. How many different balancing loads for ten can you make?
4. Record your work.

✳ ACTIVITY 5-22
MAKING BALANCING LOADS

MATERIALS:
math balance

PROCEDURE:
1. Show 3 plus 4 on the left side of the balance.
2. Now make a balancing load by placing weights on two numbers on the other side.
3. How many different ways can you do this? Record your work.
4. Repeat this activity by placing two other numbers on the left-hand side of the balance.

the numbers are not equal (the *greater* number is *lower*, not higher, on the balance).

✳ ACTIVITY 5-23

FINDING THE SUM OF "DOUBLES"

MATERIALS:
math balance

PROCEDURE:

1. Put two weights on hook 4 on the left-hand side.
2. Balance the load by placing a weight on one hook on the other side.
3. Write the number sentence that is represented on the balance.
4. Put two weights on another hook and make a balancing load as before.
5. Do this three more times.
6. Write the number sentences that are represented on the balance.

ESTIMATION

The meaning of the term *estimate* can be developed by referring to the word *about*. Questions such as "About how many apples are in the box?" and "About how many books are on the shelf?" can be used to develop understanding of estimation.

STANDARDS LINK 5-5

Number sense is an intuition about numbers that is drawn from all the varied meanings of number. It has five components:

1. Developing number meanings, including the cardinal and ordinal meanings of numbers.
2. Exploring number relationships with manipulatives.
3. Understanding the relative magnitudes of numbers.
4. Developing intuitions about the relative effect of operating on numbers.
5. Developing referents for measures of common objects and situations in their environment. (NCTM, 1989, p. 39–40)

Estimates are approximations rather than exact quantities. Referring to the question "About how many apples are in the box?" explain to children that, for example, "twelve" is the exact number of apples in the box but that "ten" is a good estimate.

When giving estimates, it is important that "good estimates" be identified. Children should be told that, within the range of acceptable estimates, the exact answer is no better than any of the other amounts (NCTM, 1989).

During the first years in school, children should be asked to estimate small quantities and progress to larger amounts as they demonstrate success. Also, ask children to tell how they arrived at their estimates. Estimating strategies should be discussed so children can learn from each other. Estimation activities with numbers less than twenty are described below.

1. Estimating Quantities
   * Place a collection of twelve objects on a table.
   * With the objects covered, gather the children around the table.
   * Uncover the objects for a moment and then have the children make an estimate of the number of objects displayed.

2. Estimating Quantities
   * Place twelve or fifteen objects on an overhead projector.
   * Turn on the machine briefly, then have the children estimate the number of objects that are on the projector.

3. Estimating Quantities
   * Find a large picture with fifteen to twenty objects pictured. These could be animals, fruit, cars, or other appropriate objects.
   * Show the picture to the children and have them estimate the quantity.

4. How Many Jelly Beans?
   * Fill a small jar with jelly beans.
   * Ask children to estimate how many jelly beans are in the jar.

Other materials for estimating "large" quantities include:

* Unshelled walnuts or peanuts in a clear plastic bag.
* Unifix cubes in a transparent tub.
* Pennies in a jar.

Children can be taught to look for groups of five to help them make estimates of quantities over ten. As the quantities are increased, ten and twenty should be given as important benchmarks in making estimates.

The size of the objects must be taken into consideration when making estimates. Thus, when estimating concrete quantities, estimation interacts with number sense and spatial sense to help children develop an awareness of reasonable results (NCTM, 1989). Specific estimation strategies will be developed when students begin to compute with large numbers.

CONCLUSION

The focus of this chapter has been to present foundational concepts related to the development of number. The principal idea to bear in mind when planning number activities for children is the importance of developing number relationships. This is a significant change from the traditional count, read, and write number program. The activities described are useful in helping children construct number relationships to facilitate mental operations with numbers.

For Your Journal

When you have finished studying this chapter, reflect on these questions in your math journal:

1. Why is it important for children to be able to represent numbers in more than one way?

2. How might a child's understanding of number help her or him begin to develop some beginning mental computation skills?

For Your Portfolio

When you have finished studying this chapter, complete these activities to include in your professional portfolio:

1. Write a lesson plan to help rote counters become rational counters.

2. Write a lesson plan to introduce the relationship of numbers to five and ten.

3. Write a lesson plan in which students are asked to represent numbers in more than one way.

Resources for Teachers

Children's Books

Feelings, M. (1972). *Moja Means One: Swahili Counting Book*. New York, NY: Pied Piper Printing.

Giganti, P. (1988). *How Many Snails? A Counting Book*. New York, NY: Greenwillow Books.

Jernigan, G. (1988). *One Green Mesquite Tree*. Tuscon, AZ: Harbinger House, Inc.

Books on Number Concepts and Number Sense

Baratta-Lorton, M. (1976). *Mathematics Their Way*. Menlo Park, CA: Addison-Wesley Publishing Company.

Burton, G. M. (1993). *Number Sense and Operations: Curriculum Evaluation Standards for School Mathematics Addenda Series Grade K–6*. Reston, VA: National Council of Teachers of Mathematics.

Reys, B. (1991). *Developing Number Sense: Curriculum Evaluation Standards for School Mathematics Addenda Series Grade 5–8*. Reston, VA: National Council of Teachers of Mathematics.

Richardson, K. (1984). *Developing Number Concepts Using Unifix Cubes*. USA: Addison-Wesley Innovative Division.

Richardson, K. (1999). *Developing Number Concepts, Book 1: Counting, Comparing, and Patterns*. White Plains, NY: Dale Seymour Publications.

Ward, S. (1995). *Constructing Ideas About Counting, Grades 3–6*. Mountain View, CA: Creative Publications.

Links to the Internet

Ask Dr. Math (About numbers)

http://forum.swarthmore.edu/dr.math/tocs/about.numbers.elem.html

Contains a list of interesting questions about number concepts and answers given by Dr. Math.

Explorer: General Whole Numbers

http://explorer.scrtec.org/explorer/explorer-db/browse/static/Mathematics/browse/f15.html

Contains many lessons on and lists of other resources for number concepts.

CHAPTER 6

Developing Understanding of Numeration

- Types and examples of base-ten models
  - Proportional and nonproportional models
- Grouping by tens
  - Equivalent representations

Focus Questions

When you have finished studying this chapter, you should be able to answer these questions:

1. Why is our number system called a "place value" system?

2. What is an example of a proportional base-ten model? a nonproportional base-ten model? How do these models differ?

3. What are "equivalent representations"?

Which of the following are representations of twenty-five?

XXV	37 − 12
5^2	17 + 8
∩∩IIIII	25

They all are! To progress in mathematics, a system for recording quantities is required. A numeration system is a system that enables one to record and thereby communicate one's ideas about number. To comprehend why the numerals 10 and 100 represent numbers ten and one hundred respectively, and why the two symbols 2 and 5 can be combined to communicate twenty-five, one needs to understand the structure of our numeration system.

A knowledge about number relationships also is required to progress in mathematics, that is, students must develop number sense. Children with number sense, in part, understand the meaning of numbers, have developed number relationships, and can recognize the relative size of numbers (NCTM, 1989, p. 38).

This chapter presents guidelines and activities for helping children develop number sense in concert with an understanding of multi-digit numbers within the Hindu-Arabic system of numeration. ○

STANDARDS LINK 6-1

In grades K–4, the mathematics curriculum should include whole number concepts and skills so that students can

- construct number meanings through real-world experiences and the use of physical materials;
- understand our numeration system by relating counting, grouping, and place-value concepts;
- develop number sense;
- interpret the multiple uses of numbers encountered in the real world. (NCTM, 1989, p. 38)

NUMERATION

Historically, people developed the idea of number before a system of numeration. As symbols were assigned to quantities of one and successive increments of one, people likely became concerned over the potentially large number of different symbols to be created. To limit the number of symbols, rules for using a basic set of symbols were devised. In the case of the Hindu-Arabic numeration system, rules were refined over centuries until the system we know today was in place. Having established a numeration system for recording whole numbers, other number systems such as fractions, decimals, and integers were developed in order to solve particular problems.

Number Systems

A *number system* is characterized by a set (infinite) of elements called numbers, basic operations to perform on those numbers, and some generalizations or principles that hold true for a particular number system. (The operations on whole numbers, fractions, decimals, and integers will be the focus of subsequent chapters.)

Numeration Systems

A *numeration system* can be characterized as consisting of a finite set of symbols for certain numbers together with a set of rules governing the use of the symbols. The set of numbers represented by particular symbols are known as the digits of the system. The digits of four different numeration systems are presented in Figure 6-1. Within each system, combinations of the digits represent larger numbers and are interpreted according to established rules.

Historical recordings reveal that different civilizations developed numeration systems to meet their needs. Each system was characterized by its own particular set of symbols and rules. In time, the Western world adapted aspects of a numeration system used by the Hindus and one developed by the Arabs, thus the name *Hindu-Arabic* numeration system.

HINDU-ARABIC NUMERATION SYSTEM

An understanding of the Hindu-Arabic numeration system is a prime goal of elementary mathematics programs. Students begin to learn the particular characteristics of the system by constructing numbers concretely in groups of tens and ones and in describing what they have done. For example, a child who says that with 26 buttons, she was able to make two groups of ten and had six left will later be able to describe 26 as two tens and six. The Hindu-Arabic numeration system can be described by the following five characteristics: base-ten; positional or place value; multiplicative principle; additive principle; and zero as a placeholder.

Base-Ten

The base of a system is the number of objects used in the grouping process. Our system is a base-ten system, that is, ten is the number that designates a first grouping.

FIGURE 6-1

System	Digits of the System
Hindu–Arabic	0, 1, 2, 3, 4, 5, 6, 7, 8, 9
Romans	I, V, X, L, C, D, M
Mayans	•, —
Egyptians	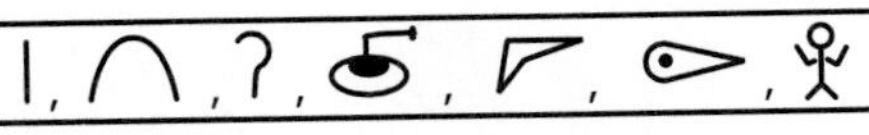

Therefore, there is no special symbol for ten; the largest number having a symbol is nine, the number that precedes the grouping size. With zero, there are ten digits in the system. A base-five system would have five symbols: four for the numbers one to four and zero. Knowing this makes it easy to write numbers in different bases.

Positional or Place Value

If the number of digits in a numeration system is limited, then it follows that digits will need to be repeated in expressing larger numbers. In a place value system, a digit takes on a value determined by the place it occupies in a number. The unit digits occupy the place furthest to the right in a multi-digit numeral. Because ten is the size of the initial grouping, ten is the value of the place to the immediate left of the "ones" place. Thus, we can say that the second place (to the left) in a numeral is the "tens" place. The numeral 10, therefore, designates "one group of ten and zero ones." One more than nine groups of ten and nine (99) requires a regrouping to show "one group of ten groups of ten" and is represented by the numeral 100. The third place in a numeral, therefore, has the value of "ten groups of ten" or "ten times ten" and is named "hundred." The symbolization system is extended to the left by designating place values for successively larger groups of ten. In a base-five system, places would take on the values of successive groups of five. Figure 6-2 depicts place values for bases ten and five.

To summarize, the *place value principle* enables one to distinguish between the face value of a digit (e.g., 5 as five) and its value because of its particular position in a numeral (e.g., the digit 5 has the value of fifty in 52 and five hundred in 534).

Multiplicative Principle

Multiplication is employed in decoding the value of each digit in a numeral. For example, in the base-ten numeral 333, each 3 has a different quantitative value: the 3 on the left has the value of 3 times one hundred, the 3 in the center has the value of 3 times ten, and the 3 on the right has the value of 3 times one. In a base-five system, each digit in the numeral 333 also has a different value: The 3 furthest to the left has the value of 3 times twenty-five, the 3 in the center has the value of 3 times five, and the 3 furthest to the right has the value of 3 times one.

When children first decode numbers, they are not likely to use the multiplicative term "times"; rather, they

---

FIGURE 6-2

BASE-TEN

Places	base^5	base^4	base^3	base^2	base^1	base^0
Base Power	10^5	10^4	10^3	10^2	10^1	10^0
Place Names	hundred thousand	ten thousand	one thousand	hundred	ten	one
Place Value (base-ten)	100 000	10 000	1000	100	10	1

BASE-FIVE

Places	base^4	base^3	base^2	base^1	base^0
Base Power					
In base-ten numerals	5^4	5^3	5^2	5^1	5^0
In base-five numerals	10^4	10^3	10^2	10^1	10^0
Place Value					
Base-ten names	six hundred twenty-five	one hundred twenty-five	twenty-five	five	one
Base-ten numerals	625	125	25	5	1
Base-five numerals	10 000	1000	100	10	1

talk about "groups." For example, the two in 28 is explained as "two groups of ten" or "two tens."

Additive Principle

In the Hindu-Arabic system, the additive principle means that numbers are the sum of the products of each digit and its place value in a numeral. For example,

$$765 = (7 \times 100) + (6 \times 10) + (5 \times 1)$$
$$= \quad 700 \quad + \quad 60 \quad + \quad 5$$
$$= \quad 765$$

In numeration systems without a multiplicative principle, the value of a number is determined by the sum of the digits in a numeral. For example, in Roman numeration the number represented by XXVII is determined by adding ten + ten + five + one + one to make twenty-seven.

When the multiplication operation has been learned, students can describe numbers as, for example, 36 means "3 times 10 plus 6" or write them in symbolic form as "$(3 \times 10) + 6$."

Zero as a Placeholder

The genius of our numeration system lies in the combined characteristics of place value and a placeholder numeral, that is, a symbol for the number zero.

Although zero is first introduced as a number, students can be asked to do numeration activities that have them specifically think of zero as a placeholder. For example, the teacher says:

- I have 8 hundreds and 3 tens. What's my number? (Students write the number on paper; then one student writes the number on the board. Students check their work.)
- I have 3 hundreds and 6 ones. What's my number?
- I have 1 thousand, 4 tens, and 9 ones. What's my number?
- I have 5 ones and 9 hundreds. What's my number?

A discussion should follow stimulated by a question such as "Why is a zero needed in each number?"

Each of the characteristics described above comes into play when interpreting a multi-digit numeral in Hindu-Arabic numeration. In learning our base-ten system, students should come to realize that the choice of base in a numeration system is arbitrary, as are the number names and symbols we use. Writing numbers in a different base within the structure of our numeration system can help students learn the different characteristics of the system. Also, the structure of the Hindu-Arabic system can be learned via a base other than ten. The popular Chip Trading activities (described in this chapter) encourage this approach.

UNDERSTANDING PLACE VALUE

The foundation for developing place value concepts lies in *grouping activities.* Thus, Grade 1 students should engage in grouping activities and counting activities with sets of objects greater than 9.

> **STANDARDS LINK 6-2**
> . . . symbolic tasks with numbers should not be presented in isolation and should not be emphasized until the numerals have been carefully linked to concrete materials and children understand the major concepts. (NCTM, 1989, p. 38)

Grouping

When children know the numbers zero through nine and can identify and write their respective numerals, they can be engaged in grouping activities. Grouping activities can vary by:

- the materials used,
- the size of the groups,
- the number of groups formed, and
- the manner of recording.

Six activities involving grouping that are appropriate for Grade 1 children are described below.

1. Making Groups of Airplanes
   - Each student will need a set of centimeter cubes and pieces of black construction paper (about 5 cm by 12 cm). The teacher will need 15 small toy airplanes and pieces of black construction paper.

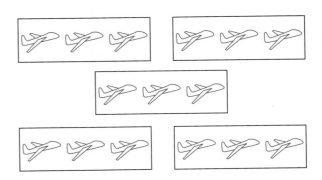

- With the students gathered in an appropriate place in the room, the teacher explains that the airplanes are to be placed on the runways (black paper) with the same number of airplanes on each runway. (The groups are made by the children or the teacher.)
- The children should verbalize what they did. For example, "We have made groups of three." "There are five groups of three airplanes."
- The above procedures are repeated with another set of airplanes and different-sized groups are constructed. Again, students should verbalize the groupings.
- Students can then be directed to go to their seats and, pretending the centimeter cubes are airplanes, make groups of four airplanes on each runway. Have students verbalize what they have done. For example, "I made three groups of four airplanes."
- Students may be asked to draw a picture and then write about what they have done. For example, "I made 6 groups of 4 airplanes."

2. Making Groups of Buttons

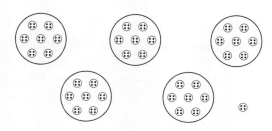

- Each student will need a set of 36 buttons and 10 small plates.
- Direct the children to choose a number and to make groups of that size on each plate.
- Have students verbalize what they have done. For example, "I made five groups of seven and have one button left."

3. Making Groups of Unifix Cubes
- Each student will need 50 Unifix cubes.

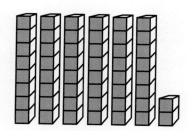

- Direct students to choose a number and to make towers of that size with the cubes.

- Have students verbalize what they have done. For example, "I made six towers that are eight blocks high. I have two blocks left."

4. Counting in Groups of Six

- Have numerous popsicle sticks and elastic bands available.
- Provide each student with twenty-nine sticks and direct them to put the sticks in bundles of six. After the bundles have been made, have students count as follows:

One bundle of six,

One bundle of six and one,

One bundle of six and two,

- •
- •
- •

Two bundles of six,

Two bundles of six and one, etc.

- Repeat the above procedure with different-sized bundles.

5. Counting How Many from Groups
- Each student will need approximately thirty-five small objects to count.

- Say, "Two groups of seven birds and three more birds landed in the school yard. Let's find out how many birds came."
- Have children model the groups with the materials provided, then count to determine the number seventeen.
- Repeat with five groups of four birds and two birds; three groups of nine birds and four birds; three groups of ten birds and three birds.

6. Making Groups and Recording
- Each student will need a set of small objects (between thirty and fifty), pencils and paper, and several

small plastic or paper plates. Children need not have the same number of counters.

- Have children first count how many objects they have and then record the number on their paper. A second counting can serve to verify the count.
- Tell the children to decide on a group size and to make as many groups of that size as they can with their materials. Children then record what they have done.
- The children then select another number as a group size and, using the same materials, make as many groups as they can. Recording follows.
- Children could then select a different number of counters and repeat the above steps.

In grouping activities, the group sizes usually are numbers between two and nine but larger-sized groups can be formed. A Grade 1 class was given 28 Unifix cubes to place in groups as described in the sixth activity above. While most students chose to make groups of sizes 2 to 9, several made groups of 10, 15, and 25. Melissa, after having made groups of 6, 2, and 5, decided to make groups of 1 and was surprised to discover upon counting all the groups she had made that she had 28 groups of one. (She knew she had 28 cubes but she had to recount them to find out how many groups of one there were!) In the same class, Jonathan decided to make groups of zero using the 8 plates he had on his desk. His written record of this activity was: "I made 8 groups of 0 and 28 (left)." From this experience, one learns not to be too prescriptive when assigning tasks to students. Left to their own decisions, children will conduct experiments that are meaningful to them.

Communicating Mathematics

In early grouping activities, children can be requested to "tell what you have done." Statements such as "I made four groups of three airplanes" and "I made five groups of four buttons and had two left" should be encouraged. When first recording on paper, a form such as the one in Figure 6-3 can be prepared. In time, the recording can be in the form of a table as depicted in Figure 6-4. A sample of a child's work is presented in Figure 6-5.

FIGURE 6-4

a) Groups of Five	Number Left		b) Number in Group\n\nEIGHT	Ones
4	2		5	2

Grouping by Tens

When engaged in making groups of ten, the grouping and recording can progress from "5 groups of ten and 3" to "1 group of ten and 0." Recording the latter statement in a table similar to that in Figure 6-4 will be an easy link to the numeral 10. Thereafter, when a child hears that "when writing numbers, we show groups of ten and ones" she or he should understand that in 25 there are "2 groups of ten and 5 ones" or "2 tens and 5." Children must come to realize that it is the 1 in 10 that indicates ten and the 0 indicates that it is an even group of ten, whereas the numeral 11 indicates 1 group of ten and 1 more.

Children who have engaged in grouping activities as described above will likely know that when you have 1 group of ten and 9, 1 more will result in 2 groups of ten and is recorded as 20. Thus, the system of numerals could theoretically be developed by children without knowledge of number names. Usually, the reverse is the case. Children learn the sequence of number names and are told that, for example, fifteen means "one ten and five ones." This can be confusing to children and the basis for the erroneous symbolization of teen numbers as 101, 102, 103, ... This type of error is more commonly made when writing numbers beyond one hundred (e.g., 1001 for one hundred one; 1002 for one hundred two, etc.), demonstrating a lack of understanding of place value.

An unhurried introduction to grouping experiences can enhance the development of place value understanding. When involved in grouping activities, it is important that children not only construct groups but also describe what they have done before they are given an explanation of two-digit numerals.

FIGURE 6-3

Name: _____

I had _____ buttons.

I made _____ groups of _____ buttons and _____ .

I made _____ groups of _____ buttons and _____ .

I made _____ groups of _____ buttons and _____ .

FIGURE 6-5

I counted 38 squares.
I made 7 groups of 5 and had 3 left.
I made nine groups of 4 and had two left.
I made 3 groups of ten and had 8 left.
I made five groups of seven and had 3 left.
I made six groups of six and had 2 left.

Margie, Grade One

Equivalent representations   One important component of developing place value understanding is the notion of equivalent representations. **Equivalent representations** refers to the fact that a number can be represented in many different ways, all of which are equivalent to the same number, but which may look different.

For example, the number 32 can be represented in a variety of ways using groups of ten: as three groups of ten and two singles, as two groups of ten and 12 singles, as one group of ten and 22 singles, and as zero groups of ten and 32 singles (see Figure 6-6). Children need to understand that each of these representations is equivalent, because each represents the number 32. Children who are able to think flexibly and recognize these equivalent groupings will be better able to regroup and rename two-digit numbers, which will assist them later in computation work.

Place Value

As groups of ten become the dominant grouping activities, students will work with proportional and non-proportional materials to represent numbers. *Proportional* materials should be used first because the representative piece for ten is actually ten times the size of the piece that represents one (see Figure 6-7). Examples of proportional materials are

- pre-bundled sticks in singles, groups of ten, and groups of hundred;
- base-ten blocks in which a "rod" is constructed of ten "units" and a "square" is made up of ten rods or 100 units;
- meter, decimeter, and centimeter sticks.

Within the set of proportional models there are variations in the level of abstraction. Counters such as beans or buttons are the most concrete. Ten of these can be put into a cup to represent the number 10. A one-to-one correspondence exists between the material and the number being represented. Popsicle sticks or connecting cubes such as Unifix cubes are only slightly more abstract in that groups of 10 can be easily formed to create a one-to-

ten relationship. The bundles or rods, however, can be taken apart easily for verification. Beansticks or base-ten

FIGURE 6-6

EQUIVALENT REPRESENTATIONS OF 32 OBJECTS

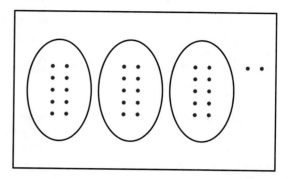

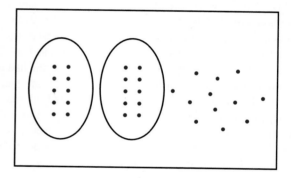

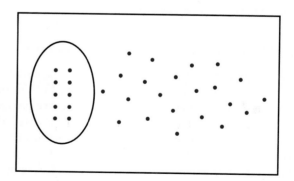

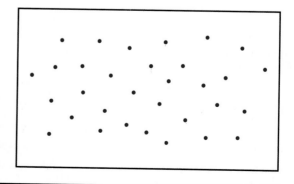

FIGURE 6-7

EXAMPLES OF PROPORTIONAL BASE-TEN MATERIALS

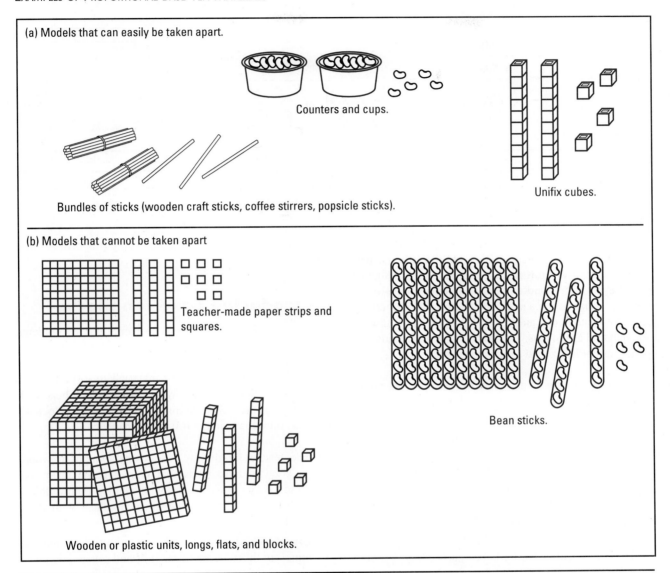

(a) Models that can easily be taken apart.

Counters and cups.

Bundles of sticks (wooden craft sticks, coffee stirrers, popsicle sticks).

Unifix cubes.

(b) Models that cannot be taken apart

Teacher-made paper strips and squares.

Bean sticks.

Wooden or plastic units, longs, flats, and blocks.

blocks represent one more step toward abstraction. Here the groupings are permanent but verification still is possible through matching or counting because one-to-one correspondence still exists. Unscored base-ten blocks require more abstraction on the part of the child and could serve as a transition to nonproportional materials. The unscored blocks maintain the one-to-ten proportion but there is no longer visual one-to-one correspondence.

In *nonproportional materials,* the same object is sometimes used to represent ones, tens, and hundreds (see Figure 6-8). Some nonproportional materials are challenging because they necessitate a focus on the position, color, size, or value of objects. For example, when using centimeter cubes on a place value mat, attention must be on the position of a cube to determine its value

rather than on a visible "group of ten" or "group of hundred." When using colored chips on a place value mat (Chip Trading materials), position and color must be considered. Size may have to be considered depending on the materials selected to represent different amounts. When coins (dollars, dimes, and pennies) are used, one must take into consideration the value of each coin. Examples of nonproportional materials are place value mats and chips, an abacus, pocket charts, and money.

Developing Two-Digit Numbers

When beginning to develop the meaning of two-digit numbers, it is preferable to use unstructured materials such as loose popsicle sticks or interlocking blocks and

EXAMPLES OF NONPROPORTIONAL BASE-TEN MATERIALS

have the children construct the groupings themselves. At some time in the primary grades, children should have the experience of constructing numbers in this manner even beyond one hundred. Bundling ten bundles of ten sticks or constructing a square with ten rods of interlocking Unifix cubes will aid in developing understanding of one hundred as ten tens. The following representative experiences could be used for this purpose.

- Have children use Unifix cubes to show two-digit numbers as, for example, 36, by constructing three rods of ten cubes and six singles.

- Multilink cubes are used in the same manner as Unifix cubes to make groups of ten. For one hundred, ten rods are interlocked to make a square.

- Children can place elastic bands around groups of ten popsicle sticks and use the bundles and single sticks to show two-digit numbers. For three-digit numbers, ten bundles of ten are grouped together.

- Using interlocking Unifix cubes each child in a class can have the experience of constructing a hundred square to use with rods of ten and singles to show three-digit numbers. (Unifix cubes are readily available in large quantities.)

Although the main focus of the activities is the development of the meaning of two-digit numbers, some children will be interested in knowing how to represent hundreds with the materials. It can be explained that another grouping is made and that this grouping consists of "ten groups of ten."

As children model numbers with bundles or groups of ten they have constructed, ask them to describe the numbers. One Grade 2 student's work is presented in Figure 6-9.

When it is determined that students know the meaning of two-digit numbers, that is, they can show, for example, that 48 means 4 tens and 8 ones, word problems with two-digit numbers can be solved using proportional materials.

Introducing Base-Ten Blocks

A teacher could present word problems and ask students to solve them using the rods of ten and singles they have constructed with Unifix cubes.

When students can use the materials to solve addition and subtraction problems with two-digit numbers with regrouping, the rods and units from the base-ten block set can be introduced in the following manner:

- The teacher might say, "Someone thought it would be good to make rods that do not come apart like these (show rods) to use with singles (show units). Let's see how we can represent numbers with these blocks."

- Give the children some rods and units and ask them to represent thirty-seven (three rods and seven units).

Meaning of Numbers

Task: Use the popsicle sticks to represent numbers. Write how you modeled each number.

Wendy's work.

52	5 bundles of ten and 2 singles
47	4 tens and 7 singles
29	2 groups of ten and 9 ones
40	4 groups of ten
7	7 singles and 0 bundles

Note: Wendy used varied expressions in this exercise. It is wise to encourage students to describe events in different ways.

✷ ACTIVITY 6-1

MODELING TWO-DIGIT NUMBERS

MATERIALS:
base-ten blocks (rods and units)

PROCEDURE:
1. Represent the number 42 with the blocks.
2. Show 42 another way.
3. How many different ways can you show 42 with the blocks?
4. Draw a picture or write about what you did.

- Ask the children if they can represent the number another way. When someone suggests exchanging a rod for ten units, direct students to do this. Have students determine that two rods and seventeen units are also thirty-seven.

- The teacher may want students to exchange another rod to determine that one rod and 27 units also represent 37. The next move would be to exchange the last rod to obtain all singles. Note that these all are equivalent representations.

After the children have completed an activity similar to Activity 6-1, the teacher might stimulate discussion by asking, "What is the simplest way to represent 42 with the blocks?" (Figure 6-10)

On other occasions, the teacher could show children pictures of base-ten blocks and ask the children to write the numeral for each picture.

To solve addition and subtraction problems with the base-ten blocks, children *exchange* a rod for ten units rather than "take apart" a rod as they did with rods made from Unifix cubes. (Solving addition and subtraction problems with base-ten blocks is discussed in detail in Chapter 9.)

✷ ACTIVITY 6-2

FROM NUMERAL CARDS TO BLOCKS

MATERIALS:
base-ten blocks

PROCEDURE:
Use the blocks to show each number.

38		18

	62		51

Using Place Value Mats

A caution is offered when using proportional materials to model numbers on a place value mat. For example, when using base-ten blocks, if ten unit blocks are replaced on a place value mat with a "rod" (ten units) in a column labeled "tens," then a misleading notion about place value can develop because the value of a rod in the tens column is one hundred. Whenever the expectation is that children will replace ten unit blocks with a "rod" to represent a two-digit number, then an organizational mat (without column headings) should be used rather than a place value mat (with headings) (Figure 6-11).

If one is to be consistent with numeral representation, more than nine units should not be placed in any of the columns on a place value mat. Teachers should note that some commercial abacuses have nine discs per column while some have ten. There are others that have eighteen discs per column in order to show intermediate steps in algorithms.

FIGURE 6-10

Modeling 42 with Base-Ten Blocks

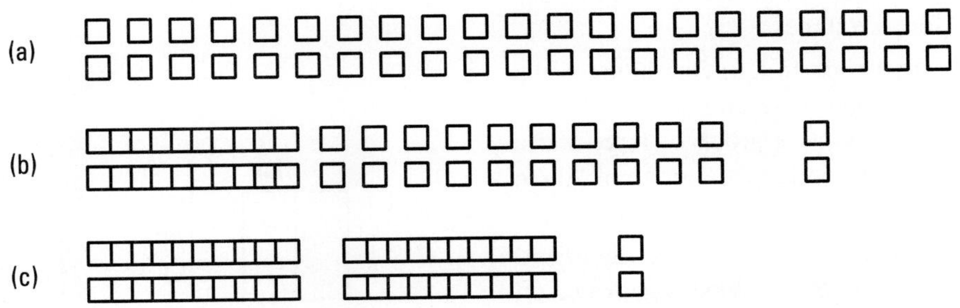

FIGURE 6-11

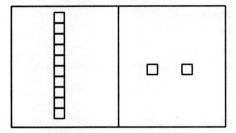

ORGANIZATIONAL MAT

1 rod and 2 units show 12
or
1 ten and 2 are 12

PLACE VALUE MAT

tens	ones

1 ten and 2 are 12

tens	ones

10 tens and 2 are 102

Changing ten unit blocks for a tens rod, or ten sticks for a bundle of ten sticks, is a concrete representation of numbers. Representing the number 12 on a place value mat with one chip or a unit cube in the tens column and two chips or unit cubes in the units column is a more abstract representation of numbers. The introduction of a place value mat signifies a move from the concrete type of modeling to the semi-abstract type.

Introducing Nonproportional Materials

One way to introduce nonproportional place value materials to students is to have them play trading games. These can be played with unit blocks from the base-ten set, a die, and mats. The procedures for playing with a three-column mat and unit blocks are as follows:

• Students in groups of three or four decide on a number to be the maximum number of blocks allowed in one column, say two (for base three).

• Columns are used from right to left. One block in the column furthest to the right represents one, a block in the second column represents a group of three and a block in the third column represents a group of "three groups of three," or nine.

• Students toss the die in turn and place in the right-hand column on their mat the number of blocks indicated on

the die. Whenever a group of three is obtained, the group is exchanged for a single block in the next column.

• The winner is the first to obtain one block in the left-hand column.

A sample game with two as the maximum number of blocks per column might proceed as follows:

• Jan tosses the die and gets a five. She counts five blocks from the cache, notices a group of three which she represents on her mat with a block in the second column (two blocks are returned to the cache) and places two blocks on the mat in the first column.

• Timmy tosses the die and gets a six. He counts six blocks, notices two groups of three, and places two blocks in the second column.

GAME

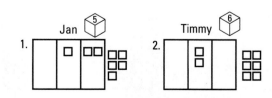

• The game continues until one student has one block in the third column.

Materials from the Chip Trading Kit could also be used. The game procedures are similar to those described above except that color is a factor: yellow chips have a value of one, blue chips represent the group size, green chips represent "groups of groups" or square numbers, and red chips represent the next place value in the particular system chosen, the cubic numbers. A sample game with two players using four (for base five) as the maximum number of chips allowed per column might proceed as outlined below. The goal is to accumulate two red chips.

• Mike tosses the die and gets a four. He counts four yellow chips and places them on the first column (headed yellow) on his mat.

• Linda tosses the die and gets a six. She counts six yellow chips, notices a group of five and exchanges these for a blue chip. She completes her move by placing the blue chip in the second column (headed blue) and the remaining yellow chip in the first column.

• Mike tosses again and gets a six. He counts out six yellow chips, notices a group of five and exchanges them for a blue chip; then, he notices that he has another

group of five with the one chip remaining and the four yellow chips on his mat from the first play. He exchanges this set of five for another blue chip which he places in the second column.

• Linda tosses and gets . . . .

The trading games can be played in a backward manner, that is, beginning with blocks or chips on the mat. When a die is tossed, exchanges are made in order to "subtract" an amount from that shown on the mat. Figure 6-12 illustrates the beginning of a sample game in which the trading rate is three. Games can be lengthened by changing the starting position. For example, the game can begin with players having one cube in each column on the mat.

Trading games can be extended to include experiences like the following:

• Provide students with 38 counters and a place value mat with 4 columns.

• Have them make groups of five, model the number on a place value mat, and then write the numeral in base five (123). (The procedure should be to count groups of 5, then see if there are *at least* 5 groups of 5, and represent them with one counter in the third column on a mat, then count the remaining groups of 5 and represent

---

FIGURE 6-12

BACKWARD TRADING GAME

MATERIALS:
unit cubes from base-ten set

PROCEDURE:
Sample game for two (Trading rate is three.)

1. Starting position for both players.

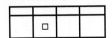

2. Player 1 tosses the die and gets a two. The exchanges are as follows:

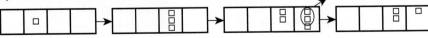

3. Player 2 tosses a three. The exchanges are:

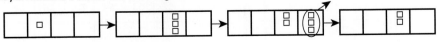

4. Player 1 tosses a five. Exchanges are:

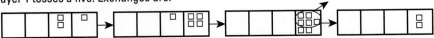

them with two counters on the appropriate column on the mat, and lastly the 3.)

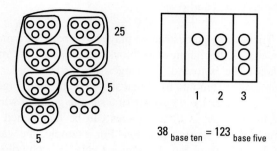

$$38_{\text{base ten}} = 123_{\text{base five}}$$

- Repeat the procedure for other bases.

The ease with which students are able to represent quantities on a place value mat in different bases will enhance their understanding of base-ten numeration. Using base five or a smaller base, it is possible for students to carry out regroupings to four and five place values and still be dealing with three-digit numbers.

An abacus is another nonproportional device that is found in many classrooms. Place value ideas are reinforced when counting on an abacus. The counting process for abacuses with ten and those with nine counters per column is different. With an abacus with ten counters per column, children must exchange one ten for ten units and one hundred for ten tens, etc. If the abacus has nine counters per column, counting proceeds to nine, then as one counter in the second column is brought forward for ten, the nine counters are flipped back; similarly as one hundred is counted, the nine tens and nine are flipped back.

The relationship between dimes and pennies and between decimeter and centimeter strips also can help children develop an understanding of numeration concepts. Give children some dimes and pennies and ask them to show different amounts with them such as 46¢, 72¢, and 36¢. Solving problems involving money transactions will provide additional trading experiences. For example:

Jack paid 68¢ for Tom's lunch at school one day. Tom promised to return the money to Jack. What coins will Jack give Tom for change left from a dollar?

Once children have learned the relationship between a decimeter and a centimeter, they can record measurement of 82 cm as 8 dm and 2 cm. This reinforces the "exchange for ten" principle.

Using Hundreds Charts

Hundreds charts are 10×10 charts with numbers written in order. Some hundreds charts contain the numbers 0 through 99; others contain the numbers 1 through 100 (see Figure 6-13 and Blackline Masters 3 and 4). Teachers

---

FIGURE 6-13

HUNDREDS CHARTS

0	1	2	3	4	5	6	7	8	9
10	11	12	13	14	15	16	17	18	19
20	21	22	23	24	25	26	27	28	29
30	31	32	33	34	35	36	37	38	39
40	41	42	43	44	45	46	47	48	49
50	51	52	53	54	55	56	57	58	59
60	61	62	63	64	65	66	67	68	69
70	71	72	73	74	75	76	77	78	79
80	81	82	83	84	85	86	87	88	89
90	91	92	93	94	95	96	97	98	99

1	2	3	4	5	6	7	8	9	10
11	12	13	14	15	16	17	18	19	20
21	22	23	24	25	26	27	28	29	30
31	32	33	34	35	36	37	38	39	40
41	42	43	44	45	46	47	48	49	50
51	52	53	54	55	56	57	58	59	60
61	62	63	64	65	66	67	68	69	70
71	72	73	74	75	76	77	78	79	80
81	82	83	84	85	86	87	88	89	90
91	92	93	94	95	96	97	98	99	100

should have a large hundreds chart that all children in the classroom can see from their desks. This can be done by enlarging or making an overhead transparency of a hundreds chart. Also, each child or pair of children should have an individual hundreds chart readily accessible.

Hundreds charts help children understand place value and patterns. For example, consider the following activities:

- Put a marker on 37. Put another marker on the number that is 10 more than 37. Now put another marker on the number that is 10 less than 37. What patterns do you notice about those three numbers?

- Put a marker on 21. How would you use the hundreds chart to find a number that is 35 more than 21? (For example, you could count 5 spaces to the right, which is 5 more than 21), and count down 3 rows (which is 30 more).

Activities and questions such as these help children think about numbers as groups of tens and ones.

Assessing Place Value Knowledge

STANDARDS LINK 6-3
A variety of place-value tasks that assess children's thinking can be used to identify those numbers that have meaning to individual students; traditional numeration tasks are not good indicators of children's understanding. (NCTM, 1989, p. 38)

Nonproportional materials can be used to assess place value understanding. Questions to ask include:

- Given a place value mat and a single counter placed in the tens column, ask the student to *remove six.*

- Ask the student to *show twenty-four* on the mat and then, to *add eight.*

- If students have been playing trading games using different trading values, place two chips in the second column on an unlabeled place value mat and ask: "If the trading rate is five, what is the value of the chips on your mat?" A student may wish to "trade backward" to answer the question. Ask similar questions with other trading rates.

Flexibility in figuring out the value of varied representations in different "bases" is evidence of place value understanding.

Another assessment task is to begin by asking a child to read a numeral as, for example, 36. Next, the child is asked to count that many robots. Observe the child as he or she counts the robots (does the child move the robots? group them in twos, fives, or tens?). Pointing to the "6" in 36, the teacher asks: "Does this part of the 36 have anything to do with how many robots you have?" The question is repeated, this time pointing to the "3" in 36. A child who understands the meaning of 36 will match six robots with the "6" and thirty with the "3" (NCTM, 1989, p. 38).

What Research Says About Place Value Learning

There is evidence from research that elementary school children do not understand our numeration system, specifically place value (Kamii & Joseph, 1988; Ross, 1986, 1989; Smith, 1973). One is surprised at Kamii and Joseph's findings that third and fourth graders were unable to respond correctly to a tens place value question. Kamii and Joseph report that, generally, no Grade 1 student gives the expected response that in the numeral 16, "1 means ten" and that approximately only 33 percent of third graders and 50 percent of fourth graders are able to respond appropriately (Figure 6-14). Kamii and Joseph conclude that Grade 1 children are unlikely to understand place value; rather, they understand 16 as sixteen ones and not as 1 ten and 6 ones. This statement corroborates the studies by Ross (1986, 1989).

There are, however, others who believe that with carefully planned experiences of counting and grouping by tens and ones, Grade 1 children can learn place value to some significant level of performance (Payne, 1988). It is recommended that teachers have Grade 1 students engage in grouping activities as foundational experiences for place value development. Generally, Grade 2 students are expected to develop understanding of two-digit numbers and Grade 3 students work with numbers greater than ninety-nine.

Stages in Place Value Development

Ross (1989) proposes a five-stage development of place value understanding. At Stage One, students associate two-digit numerals with the quantity they represent. For example, 28 means the whole amount. At Stage Two, students can identify the positional names but do not necessarily know what each digit represents. For example, in 54, a child may state that there are 4 ones and 5 tens. This is mere verbal knowledge based on positional labels. At Stage Three, students can identify the face value of digits in a numeral as, for example, in 34, the 3 means "3 tens" and the 4 means "4 ones." The value of each digit is not necessarily known, that is, "3 tens" meaning thirty. Success in representing numerals with base-ten blocks could merely signify a Stage Three performance. With the Chip

FIGURE 6-14

Place Value Task

Show the numeral 16 on a card.

Ask: What does this part (circle the 6 in 16) mean?
Could you show me with the chips what this part means?

Have the child show (count out) the appropriate number of chips.

Ask: What about this part (circle the one in 16)?
Show me with the chips what this part means.

16

Source: Adapted from "Teaching Place Value and Double-Column Addition," by C. Kamii and L. Joseph, 1988, *Arithmetic Teacher, 35*, p. 48.

Trading materials, a particular color is used to represent tens and another color for ones. Ross describes Stage Four as a transitional stage when true understanding of place value is constructed. Children progress from unreliable task performance to the point at which they know that the tens digit represents quantities of ten units and they can coordinate the part-whole relationships within two-digit numbers. Stage Five is the level of understanding the structure of our numeration system. The child knows that digits in a two digit numeral represent a partitioning of the whole quantity into tens and ones and that the number represented is the sum of the parts (Ross, 1989).

Knowledge of place value has great implications for success in arithmetic tasks as will be seen, in part, in Chapter 9. Therefore, care should be taken that students develop a meaningful understanding of numbers.

THREE-DIGIT NUMBERS

When it is determined that children understand two-digit numbers, the progression to three-digit numbers should be a smooth one. Three-digit numbers can be introduced by an activity such as Activity 6-3. Significant learning occurs as the teacher questions the children during and after the activity. Ask the children about the meaning of each digit in the numeral produced. Explain that when representing numbers, ten items make a new group. Ten

ones are grouped to make a ten and ten groups of ten are grouped to make a hundred.

Students should be told that a hundred also can be represented with a group of a hundred singles, but that groups of tens make it easier to solve problems using the materials. The language corresponding to groupings of hundreds, tens, and ones should ensue. For example, the teacher could write on the chalkboard (or say) a numeral like 134 and ask the children to model it with bundles of ten sticks and singles. Have them identify the "hundred," the "thirty," and the "four." Tell them that the ten groups of ten for hundred can be bundled together for easy counting.

Discussion after completing the modeling might be focused through questions such as:

1. What is the value of the third place in a numeral?
2. How can we describe the value when using bundles of sticks?

(The third place value in a numeral is ten bundles of ten. One hundred is "one bundle of ten bundles of ten," two hundred is "two bundles of ten bundles of ten," etc.)

The same activity could be done with base-ten blocks. These usually are available in large quantities so that each child in a class can have the experience of putting together ten rods of ten to make a hundred square. Three-digit numbers can be modeled using squares, rods of ten, and units. Discussion questions similar to the two above could be used for number work with base-ten blocks.

If children have been constructing different-sized groups, they can be asked to construct, for example, three rods of three, four rods of four, and five rods of five. They will notice that each set can be put together to form a square. Thus, the pattern is, regardless of the group size, singles, rods, and squares. A "game" devised by Skemp (1989) helps children develop mental pictures for numbers and also the language for number relationships. The procedure is described for base-three in Activity 6-4. It is easily adapted for other groupings.

✳ ACTIVITY 6-3

THREE-DIGIT NUMBERS

MATERIALS:
at least 125 popsicle sticks for each child

PROCEDURE:
1. Make as many groups of ten as you can.
2. Write a numeral for your groups.

✳ ACTIVITY 6-4

WORKING IN BASE THREE (AN ACTIVITY FOR 3 OR 4 PLAYERS)

MATERIALS:
- 25 interlocking cubes for each child
- 2 dice (red and white) for each group of children
- game card as pictured

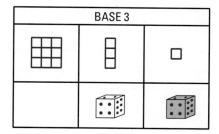

PROCEDURE:
1. One child throws the dice and places the red one in the first column and the white one in the second column.
2. Each child makes sets according to the numbers on the dice. When appropriate, they construct rods and squares. Children check their work to see if they all agree.
3. Procedures are repeated with children taking turns tossing the dice.

Have children tell what they did. Listen for expressions such as "three rods," "three squares," "three groups of three," "three threes," and "one three." A class of second graders played the base-ten game. Afterward, students made the following statements about the values:

Ten rods have one hundred ones.

One square is one hundred.

One square has ten rods.

Ten squares make one cube.

One cube is one thousand.

One cube has one hundred rods.

Number Meanings: Oral Expressions

Students should learn to describe three-digit numbers in several ways. For example, 125 can be described as:

- 125 items is 1 group of ten groups of ten plus 2 groups of ten plus 5.
- 125 is ten tens plus 2 tens plus 5.
- 125 is twelve tens and 5.
- 125 means one hundred plus twenty plus five.

The number is read "one hundred twenty-five."

When focusing on place value notation, the numeral 100 represents one group of hundred, zero tens, and zero ones. However, children should think of one hundred as ten groups of ten and as one hundred ones.

DEVELOPING NUMBER RELATIONSHIPS

The Annenberg/CPB Math and Science Collection

VIDEO LINK 6-1
Whole Number Computation

Brief Summary: In "Choose a Method," teacher Mary Holden's fourth-grade students are using different computational methods to solve problems. One method they use is base-ten blocks.

1. Why do you think Ms. Holden begins the lesson with children exploring the blocks?
2. What different types of reasoning do the students use to estimate the value of different structures built with blocks?
3. How and why does the teacher relate money to the value of the blocks?
4. What role do the base-ten blocks play in supporting students' understanding of computation?

Video Source. Teaching Math: A Video Library, K–4; Tape 7 from The Annenberg/CPB Math and Science Collection.

Building on knowledge of single digit numbers, children are encouraged to develop mental computation strategies with two-digit numbers. Activities 6-5 and 6-6 are appropriate for developing number relationships. Instructions for these activities should be given orally and repeated several times using different number series.

Note that in the last exercise in Activity 6-6, the child counts from 58 to 60, then to 64. A worksheet could be prepared as presented in Figure 6-15.

A similar activity could be done using a hundred chart for each student and instructions such as the following:

- Begin with 16 and count up to 38. (16, 26, 36, 37, 38)
- Record what you did. (16 + 10 + 10 + 2 = 38)
- Repeat with other numbers.

✳ ACTIVITY 6-5

COUNTING ON—BASE-TEN BLOCKS

MATERIALS:
base-ten blocks

PROCEDURE:

1. Show 64 with the blocks. (6 tens and 4 units)

2. Now show seventy-four.

3. Tell your partner what you did. (*Added another ten*)

4. Now show eighty-six.

5. Tell your partner what you did. (*Added a ten and two units*)

STANDARDS LINK 6-4

. . . an understanding of place value is crucial for later work with number and computation. (NCTM, 1989, p. 38)

Children enjoy counting beyond a hundred. Give each student an egg carton and 350 to 550 small objects. (Objects can be buttons, cubes, pieces of straws, or match sticks.) Have students count the objects by making groups of ten in each cup (using ten cups). Instruct students to write about the counting procedures they followed. Two students' sample work is presented in Figure 6-16.

Thinking and Writing About Numbers

One way to find out how children think about numbers is to ask them to respond to number questions in writing. The following are sample questions that are appropriate for Grade 2 children.

1. What can you say about the number 25? 45? 90? 100? Write statements about each number.

2. Write the following numerals on the board:

    2, 3, 4, 5, 6, 10, 12, 15, 30

    How many different number sentences can you make?

3. How are these numbers different?

    86 and 806   45 and 450

4. Is the answer more than a hundred? Write about how you found out.

    25 + 55 + 25   67 + 45   22 + 33 + 44

FIGURE 6-15

Worksheet

Name: _____

Begin with	Count up to
16	35
24	49
61	85
72	91
44	70

Mathematics sentence
_____

$16 + 10 + 9 = 35$

$24 + 10 + 10 + 5 = 49$

_____

_____

✳ ACTIVITY 6-6

COUNTING ON—POPSICLE STICKS

MATERIALS:
popsicle sticks in bundles of ten and singles

PROCEDURE:

1. Show 35 with the sticks.

2. Now add sticks to count up to 67.

3. Record what you did. ($35 + 10 + 10 + 10 + 2 = 67$)

4. Show 28. Count up to 64. Record. ($28 + 10 + 10 + 10 + 2 + 4$)

FIGURE 6-16

Counting Beyond a Hundred

I am counting blocks.
I have ten sets of ten so I have 100.
I have another ten sets of ten so I have 200.
I have 240.
I have another ten sets of ten so I have 300 blocks.
I have another ten sets of ten so I have 400.
I have 460!

Michael, Grade Two

I am counting blocks. Now I have 100.
I got 100 from grouping tens.
Now I have 200. I got 200 from grouping more tens.
I now have 300. I got 300 from still grouping tens.
I have ended at 350. I have grouped all these numbers and got 350.

Jenny, Grade Two

Some Grade 2 children's responses to similar problems as in number 4 are presented below:

88 + 15

I knew that 90 + 100 = 100 so I took 2 of the 15 and that made 90 on one hand and 13 on the other so now I just added 13 and it made 103. —Jill, Grade 2

35 + 35 + 35

First I remembered that 3 3s equaled 9. So I knew that three 30s equaled 90, so I added 15, and it left me with 105! —Annie, Grade 2

73 + 37

73 + 37 = 110 because 70 from the 73 and 30 from the 37 = 100 plus 7 and the 3 leftover = 110. —Danny, Grade 2

UNDERSTANDING LARGE NUMBERS

> **STANDARDS LINK 6-5**
> Understanding place value is another critical step in the development of children's comprehension of number concepts. Prior to formal instruction on place value, the meanings children have for larger numbers are typically based on counting by ones and the "one more than" relationship between consecutive numbers. Since place-value meanings grow out of grouping experiences, counting knowledge should be integrated with meanings based on grouping. Children are then able to use and make sense of procedures for comparing, ordering, rounding, and operating with larger numbers. (NCTM, 1989, p. 39)

Number Names

Although children learn the number name sequence fairly early, it is recognized that the words for eleven, twelve, thirteen, etc., to nineteen are more difficult than the decade names, because they do not exhibit a ten grouping in their names. For the decades, a child can connect the "ty" in each number name to be a derivation from the name ten. The teen numbers would have been advantageously named ty-one, ty-two, etc., or ten-one, ten-two, etc. In this respect Japanese children, for example, have a headstart on English-speaking children. The Japanese system of number names follows a logical development employing only the names of the digits plus a name for ten and each successive power of ten. Examining the number names in Table 6-1, one notices how relatively easy it is to progress in naming successive numbers.

TABLE 6-1

JAPANESE NAMES

1—ichi	11—juichi	100—hyaku
2—ni	12—juni	101—hyakuichi
3—san	13—jusan	111—hyakujuichi
4—shi	14—jushi	200—nihyaku
5—go	15—jugo	201—nihyakuichi
6—roku	16—juroku	211—nihyakujuichi
7—shichi	17—jushichi	
8—hachi	18—juhachi	1000—sen
9—kyu	19—jukyu	1997—senkyuhyakukyujushichi
10—ju	20—niju	
	21—nijuichi	

Writing Consecutive Numbers

It is a common practice in school programs to have children write numbers in sequence from 1 to 100. These numbers are often pictured on wall charts or on a hundred board. Usually, the numbers are recorded in ten rows of ten. The task can be made somewhat more challenging by providing students with blank charts featuring fewer or more than ten spaces per row (Figure 6-17).

Elementary students should have the experience of writing numbers in sequence beyond one hundred as counting by tens or hundreds to a thousand does not give them a sense of the size of one thousand. Also, when asked to complete a number sequence, errors in bridging

FIGURE 6-17

1	2	3
4	5	6
7	8	9
10	11	12
13	14	15
16	17	..

1	2	3	4	5	6
7	8	9	10	11	12
13	14	15	16	17	18
19	20	21	22	23	24
25	26	27	28	29	30
31	32	33	..	..	..

1	2	3	4	5	6	7
8	9	10	11	12	13	14
15	16	17	18	19	20	21
22	23	24	25	26	27	28
29	30	31	32	33	34	35
36	37	..	..	..	..	..

decades and centuries are frequently made. A teacher could watch for these difficulties by organizing a group project such as the following:

- Prepare charts for students to write numbers in some organized way. The charts could be strips of poster board with spaces for fifty numbers or they could be twelve by twelve squares for 144 numbers per chart.
- Students can share the work of writing numbers to one thousand by each filling in a part of a chart or charts.
- The charts could be displayed on a bulletin board and used in number activities.

Number Periods

When children understand that each position in a numeral has a value that is ten times as large as the position to its immediate right, they can be introduced to number periods. In multi-digit numbers, each group of three digits forms a number period. When children are learning to write numbers to 999, there is no need to talk about number periods.

It is recommended that the thousand, ten thousand, and hundred thousand place value names be introduced simultaneously because they form one number period. A prominently displayed number periods chart (Figure 6-18) can be the focus for a class discussion. What children need to come to realize is that every number period or group of three digits includes a place value for ones, tens, and hundreds. Therefore, four digits are needed before a new number period is named and a total of seven digits to name yet another number period. Focusing on number periods from the onset of naming thousands would seem to act as a deterrent to falsely naming a five-digit numeral such as 54 623 as 5 million, 4 thousands, etc. It is believed that a number of teaching aids featuring four place values (e.g., a four-column abacus or four-column pocket chart) could unwittingly be a cause of children's errors in reading large numbers. Children using such materials learn the number name sequence one, ten, hundred, thousand without any differentiation of number periods. They also learn that the next new number name after "thousand" is "million." Thus, in reading numbers, some children omit the hundred thousand and ten thousand values.

Using place value materials with three or six place values might alleviate the problem.

When writing numbers, it is the acceptable practice to leave a space (without a comma) between number periods. In a 4-digit number the thousands digit need not be separated from the hundreds digit. Examples: 800 006 070; 34 630 349; 56 458; 2586.

The first two numbers are properly read and written as: eight hundred million, six thousand, seventy; thirty-four million, six hundred thirty thousand, three hundred forty-nine. Note that there is no "and" in the numbers. "And" is reserved to indicate a fractional component of a number.

Magnitude of Numbers

Asking students to compare numbers is one way to assess their understanding of numbers. One task is to write a set of six numbers on individual cards and have the child order the numbers from least to greatest.

Examples:
a. 146   116   106   164   104   140
b. 2105   2015   1520   2520   1250   2555

Ask the child: How can you tell which is larger? A student's response for set (a) above could be:

I first look at the digit in the hundred's place. If they are all the same, then I examine the digit in the ten's place; if these are different, I know that the one with the most tens is the greatest number. When two numbers have the same hundreds and tens, then I compare the ones.

It is possible that students could be learning to list sets of names or other words in alphabetical order at the same time as they are learning to order multi-digit numbers. Certainly, the similarity should be discussed.

Counting to a Thousand and Beyond

Children should engage in at least a few activities that require them to count objects in the hundreds, thousands, ten thousands, and beyond. This is necessary if they are

FIGURE 6-18

MILLIONS			THOUSANDS			ONES		
hundred	ten	one	hundred	ten	one	hundred	ten	one
	1	4	2	0	5	7	3	6

to develop a sense of the magnitude of large numbers. The following activities are helpful in developing the relative size of numbers.

1. Showing a Thousand
   - Provide students with several cards (2 in. by 4 in.) and some toothpicks.
   - Have them count out ten toothpicks and glue them close together and centered on the card. (You may wish to place a piece of cellophane tape across the toothpicks to secure them in place.) The class should prepare enough cards to demonstrate at least a thousand.
   - Take ten cards and attach them to a sufficiently long piece of poster board. Repeat this for each set of ten cards. Ten strips of poster board can be mounted to a bulletin board or wall with additional strips mounted alongside but separate from the set of a thousand. This is for easy identification of a thousand toothpicks.
   - The toothpicks can be the focus of counting activities.

2. Counting Toothpicks
   - Ask students to count different numbers of toothpicks.

   Example: Count 156 toothpicks.
   Possible response: A student might begin counting at one hundred (while pointing to the first strip of a hundred toothpicks), then continue on with "one hundred ten" (pointing to the next group of ten toothpicks), "one hundred twenty, one hundred thirty, one hundred forty, one hundred fifty, one hundred fifty-one, . . . , one hundred fifty-six."

3. Class Project
   - A class project could be to collect bread bag ties or other small objects.
   - When a sufficiently large amount has been collected, students could count the objects, first forming groups of ten, then groups of a hundred, then thousands.

Today, numbers in the millions and billions often are heard in media reports; therefore, children must develop some understanding of large numbers. It seems a reasonable expectation to have students, at least once in their elementary grades, devise a way to represent a million of something. A visual representation of a million dollar signs or other keyboard character can be obtained from a computer printout, although this is not deemed economical to do in terms of computer storage space and time. What may be preferred is to type a page full of dots and photocopy sufficient copies to total a million or part of a million such as one quarter or one half a million. The

---

TABLE 6-2

Number Period Names

ones	billions	quintillions	octillions
thousands	trillions	sextillions	nonillions
millions	quadrillions	septillions	decillions

pages could be mounted on poster board and, following some estimation activity, displayed for some time in the classroom. A teacher may want to organize the "million things" (or part of a million things) by typing 100 characters per piece of paper in a 10-by-10 array. Ten papers of 100 each could then be mounted on a sheet of paper. Thus, the organization of 10, 100, 1000, or 10 000, etc. would be easily recognized.

Another model of one million is to suspend a centimeter cube in a meter cube or skeleton model of a meter cube. It would take a million of the smaller cubes to fill the larger cube.

Hampton-Burnett (1981) suggests the following activity to help children think about the magnitude of a million:

- Ask small groups of students to select an item from nature (a pine needle, blade of grass) or a manufactured one (floor tile, desk, car).
- Describe how to show a million of the item. The report could be presented to their classmates or to another class.

Students should be asked to use large numbers in reporting distances, weights, or other scientific information obtained from an encyclopedia or other source. An example is the mass of the earth expressed in kilograms (600 000 000 000 000 000 000 000). For interest's sake, students may want to learn number period names beyond the familiar billion and trillion. The first twelve number period names are presented in Table 6-2.

EXPANDED NOTATION

As students progress in developing an understanding of numbers and numeration they will learn how to write numbers in expanded notation in several ways. In the primary grades, children are expected to write numbers as the sum of two or more parts.

Example: $63 = 60 + 3$
$$= 6 \text{ tens} + 3$$

In upper elementary grades, numbers will be written in expanded form using the multiplicative property.

Example:
$$785 = (7 \times 100) + (8 \times 10) + 5$$
$$4692 = (4 \times 1000) + (6 \times 100) + (9 \times 10) + 2$$

By Grades 6 or 7, students should be able to use exponential notation.

Example:
$$4692 = (4 \times 10 \times 10 \times 10) + (6 \times 10 \times 10) + (9 \times 10) + 2$$
$$= 4 \times 10^3 + 6 \times 10^2 + 9 \times 10^1 + 2$$

ROUNDING NUMBERS

There are occasions when it is practical to give number approximations. For example, when asking what the population of the United States is, you would not expect an exact number but a response such as 200 million, that is, a number rounded to the nearest million. When completing income tax returns, taxpayers are allowed to round off all amounts reported to the nearest dollar as it is believed that dollar rounding makes for fewer errors. Rounding skills are used frequently in determining estimates for computation questions.

In elementary schools, rules taught for rounding numbers are as follows: When rounding a number to a specified place value, locate the place value and examine the digit to its immediate right (the key digit). If the key digit has a value of 5 or greater, replace all digits to the right of the place value by zeros and increase the place value digit by one; if the key digit has a value less than 5, replace the digits to the right of the place value by zeros. Table 6-3 shows some examples of rounding off.

Students can learn these rules by modeling numbers to be rounded off with base-ten blocks or by drawing number lines to compare numbers between decades, hundreds, etc.

The models children will construct for Activity 6-7 are shown at right. Models for the numbers in Activity 6-8

★ ACTIVITY 6-7

ROUNDING TO NEAREST TEN—CONCRETE MODEL

MATERIALS:
base-ten blocks

TASK:
Round 138 to the nearest ten.

PROCEDURE:
1. Show the number with base-ten blocks.
2. What are the two multiples of ten that are closest to 138?
3. Show these two multiples with the blocks.
4. Examine the three numbers shown. Is 138 closer to 130 or 140?

would be similar. A number line model is used in Activities 6-9 and 6-10.

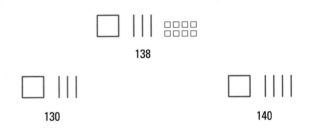

Note that in the activities described, numbers with a five in the determining place value have been omitted.

★ ACTIVITY 6-8

ROUNDING TO NEAREST HUNDRED—CONCRETE MODEL

MATERIALS:
base-ten blocks

TASK:
Round 329 to the nearest hundred.

PROCEDURE:
1. Show the number with base-ten blocks.
2. What are the two multiples of hundred that are closest to 329?
3. Model them with the blocks.
4. Examine the three numbers shown. Is 329 closer to 300 or 400?

TABLE 6-3

ROUNDING NUMBERS

PLACE VALUE	NUMBER	ROUNDED OFF
Nearest ten	543	540
Nearest hundred	629	600
Nearest ten	748	750
Nearest hundred	748*	700
Nearest hundred	5496	5500

*Note that one does not first round off to tens.

✳ ACTIVITY 6-9

ROUNDING TO NEAREST TEN— NUMBER LINE MODEL

MATERIALS:
an eleven-point number line drawn on paper

TASK:
Round 673 to the nearest ten.

PROCEDURE:
1. What are the two multiples of ten closest to 673?

2. Label the end points of the number line with these two multiples.

3. Decide where 673 fits on the number line. Mark it on the number line.

4. 673 rounded to the nearest ten is _____.

This case merits special attention. When students are successful in rounding off numbers according to the rules described above, they should be informed that there are instances when another rule governs the process when the key digit is five. Students could be asked to gather a set of data and then compute the average. See Activity 6-11.

Note that in Set B the numbers ending in 5 in Set A have all been rounded up whereas in Set C the numbers ending in 5 in set A preceded by an even number have been rounded down while those preceded by an odd number have been rounded up. This rule, known as the computer's rule, avoids the possibility of cumulative errors in rounding off and is employed by scientists, statis-

✳ ACTIVITY 6-10

ROUNDING TO NEAREST HUNDRED— NUMBER LINE MODEL

MATERIALS:
an eleven-point number line drawn on paper

TASK:
Round 4567 to the nearest hundred.

PROCEDURE:
1. What are the two multiples of a hundred closest to 4567?

2. Label the end points of the number line with these two multiples.

3. Decide where 4567 fits on the number line. Mark it on the number line.

4. 4567 rounded to the nearest hundred is _____.

✳ ACTIVITY 6-11

EFFECTS OF ROUNDING

MATERIALS:
data collected

PROCEDURE:
1. Study the following sets of numbers for which the average has been calculated.

	Set A	Set B	Set C
	243	240	240
	247	250	250
	245	250	240
	235	240	240
	236	240	240
	231	230	230
	225	230	220
	255	260	260
Average:	239.63	242.5	240

2. Which average is closer to the exact average of Set A? Why?

ticians, and actuaries, among others. Students may notice that when following the computer's rule in rounding off numbers, the retained terminal digit will always be an even number. Students could be asked to determine which rounding off rule their calculator is programmed to use.

ESTIMATING

Good number sense enables one to estimate quantities. Rounding numbers is one way to estimate totals or products. (This estimating strategy along with others is discussed in Chapter 9.)

There are times when one needs to estimate a quantity "at a glance." For example, an approximation of the number of people in attendance at a rally or sports event may be required. Students who have developed good number sense both in physical representations and in understanding number compositions (additive and multiplicative) will feel competent in providing a sensible estimate of the group size.

What strategies could be employed in making such estimates? In a large gathering, one could note a "group of ten" or a "group of twenty" and quickly determine ten or five such groups for the physical size of a "group of hundred." From this number, a look around the arena or other area will enable one to determine "at a glance" an approximate number for the gathering. Whole student body or multiple class gatherings can be occasions when students can practice estimating quantities in the tens and hundreds. Teachers can use different occasions to have students make estimates. Examples include:

- Holiday concert: about how many parents attended the concert?
- Class visit to a museum: about how many samples are in the rock collection? About how many butterflies are in the display?
- Class visit to the public library: about how many science fiction books are there in the children's section? About how many adventure books?

The Annenberg/CPB Math and Science Collection

VIDEO LINK 6-2
Communication

Brief Summary: In the "Communication" video, Brenda Richardson's students are working in groups to estimate how many seeds are in a pumpkin. The students have some difficulty in coming to a consensus. Their discussion includes the following statements by students in the group, labeled Students 1, 2, 3, and 4:

Student 1: "How about 80?"
Student 2: "I say 170."
Student 1: "There's a lot of pulp in the middle."
Student 3: "There's about 80."
Student 4: "One thousand."
Student 2: "Okay, one hundred and eighty."
Student 1: "It's lower than a hundred, I know it!"

1. What understandings do you think these students have about place value and estimation?
2. What follow-up experiences might the teacher plan for upcoming lessons to enhance these children's understandings about place value and estimation?

Video Source. Teaching Math: A Video Library, K–4; Tape 21 from The Annenberg/CPB Math and Science Collection.

Students can be asked to estimate the number of small objects in a jar or clear plastic bag. A child estimating the number of jelly beans in a cylindrical jar might think the following:

There are about twenty jelly beans in one layer and twelve layers altogether. Twenty times ten is 200 and two times twenty is forty, so I estimate that there are about 240 jelly beans in the jar.

Another estimating activity is to scatter a number of centimeter cubes (25 to 35) on an overhead projector and then turn on the projector for a brief moment. Have children tell about how many blocks they saw pictured on the

screen. Other small objects could be placed on a table and students could be directed to look at the objects for a few seconds and then to make an estimate about the number. Children should be encouraged to see "groups of five" or "groups of ten" to help them make quick approximations about the number of objects there are in all. To discourage random guessing, after an estimate has been made, ask: "How did you figure out the amount?" Other children can learn estimating strategies from hearing students' descriptions.

CONSOLIDATING NUMBER SKILLS

Students who have engaged in the kinds of activities described in this chapter accompanied with frequent oral and written expressions of their work should eventually develop an understanding of our numeration system together with number sense. In order to consolidate these ideas, additional experiences may be necessary. Some activities are suggested below.

1. Numeral Cards
   - Write each of the digits 1 to 9 on three cards (27 cards in all).
   - Shuffle the cards.
   - Have a student draw six cards and write the numbers drawn in any order on a chart (Figure 6-19). Zeros are then written in the empty places.
   - Have the child read the number.
   - Fewer or more number cards can be drawn and the chart can be extended to other number periods.

2. Pocket Chart
   - A place value pocket chart showing three or more number periods can be placed on the board ledge.

Thousands			ones		
2		1	1	1	2

- In turn, students put digits on the chart and ask classmates to read the numbers aloud. The aim should be to represent "tricky" numbers to challenge their classmates.

3. Colored Chips
   - Direct students to represent the number 111 on a four-column mat with colored chips (1 yellow, 1 red, and 1 blue).

FIGURE 6-19

BILLIONS			MILLIONS			THOUSANDS			ONES		
hundred	ten	one	hundred	ten	one	hundred	ten	one	hundred	ten	one
				9	1	0	0	4	6	3	4
			4	5	0	2	1	9	0	3	0
	1	4	0	0	2	0	0	0	2	1	8

- Ask them to show the number using only two colors.
- Have them record the two-parts of 111 (see diagram).

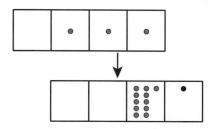

- The task can be repeated with different three-digit numbers.
- With four-digit numbers, have the students represent a number using two or three different colors.
- A base other than 10 can be used for this activity.

4. Calculator
   - Direct students to enter a six-digit number on their calculator and ask them to "wipe out" a specified digit.

   Example: Enter 345 876. Wipe out the digit 8.

   - Students can keep a record of their work as shown (Reys et al., 1984, p. 79).

Enter	Wipe out	Keys pressed	Display
345876	8	− 800	345076

5. Die
   (A set of number cards 0 to 9 could be used in place of a die.)
   - Players try to create the largest possible multi-digit number using the digits generated by repeatedly tossing a die or drawing a card from a set of 0 to 9.
   - As each digit is revealed, players must write it in one of the place value positions and cannot later change a position.

   Example: <u>5</u> <u>4</u> <u>3</u> <u>6</u> <u>2</u>

   - The player making the greatest number is the winner.

6. Counting in a Foreign Language
   - Have students write numbers in sequence in French, Spanish, or another language, assuming the number names are logically developed. For example, in English, a logical development would be: ten, ten-one, ten-two, . . . , ten-nine, two tens, two tens-one, etc.
   - French and Spanish number names are provided below.

	FRENCH	SPANISH
1	un	uno
2	deux	dos
3	trois	tres
4	quatre	cuatro
5	cinq	cinco
6	six	seis
7	sept	siete
8	huit	ocho
9	neuf	nueve
10	dix	diez
100	cent	cien

7. Calendar Activity
   - Have students make a calendar writing the numbers in a base other than ten.
   - Students can be challenged to devise their own number symbols.

✳ ACTIVITY 6-12

STUDYING ANCIENT NUMERATION SYSTEMS

1. Select an ancient numeration system, for example, the Babylonian, Egyptian, Mayan, or Roman, and conduct a study of the system to learn its symbols and the particular rules for using the symbols to represent numbers.

2. Write some large numbers as you think the people would have done.

3. Try to perform the operations of addition and subtraction with the numerals.

4. Try to construct an addition and a multiplication basic fact table for the system.

5. Write about the advantages and disadvantages of the numeration system.

OTHER NUMERATION SYSTEMS

Upper elementary and junior high students can be invited to study ancient numeration systems with a view to developing a better understanding and appreciation of our own. Ideas for such activities are suggested in Activities 6-12 to 6-15. Some information is provided on several numeration systems that could be shared with students as an introduction to further study.

As an extension, students, in groups of four or five, could invent their own numeration system. When completed, their "very own" numeration system can be shared with classmates or other classes in the school. Provide the following suggestions or hints:

• Invent a numeration system with the same characteristics as the Hindu-Arabic system.

• Begin by choosing a base, then create the symbols for the system, giving each single-digit number a name.

✳ ACTIVITY 6-13

MAYAN NUMERALS

MATERIALS:
paper and pencil

PROCEDURE:
1. Write the numerals for the numbers 20 to 50 in Mayan symbolization.

2. At which number would the Mayans require a third place value? Write that number in Mayan symbols.

✳ ACTIVITY 6-14

WRITING ROMAN NUMERALS

MATERIALS:
paper and pencil

PROCEDURE:
1. Write the current year in Roman numerals.

2. Write the year of your birth in Roman numerals.

3. Write in Roman numerals the year that you anticipate seeing on your high school diploma.

4. Write in Roman numerals the year that your school was built.

• In naming multi-digit numbers, try to employ logic so that successively larger numbers can be easily named.

Babylonian Numeration

The Babylonian cuneiform method of recording quantities is among the oldest numeral systems in existence. Although the symbols were mere wedge-shaped imprints on clay tablets, the rules for using those templates to represent numbers were rather complicated. The Babylonians developed (approximately 5000 years ago) a sexidecimal (Base 60) place value system with numbers less than sixty represented in base-ten. The place values and accompanying symbols are shown in Figure 6-20a. Because they had no symbol for zero, their numerals are difficult to interpret as can be seen in Figure 6-20b.

Egyptian Numeration

The Egyptian method of recording quantities can be said to be based on 10 with a symbol for 1, ten, and each successive power of 10. For their number symbols, the Egyptians used a distinct hieroglyphic or picture for each

✳ ACTIVITY 6-15

COMPARISON OF NUMERATION SYSTEMS

MATERIALS:
paper and pencil

PROCEDURE:
1. Write the Mayan numeral for one million.

2. Write the Roman numeral for one million.

3. Write the Egyptian numeral for two million.

4. Which numeral was easiest to write? Why?

FIGURE 6-20

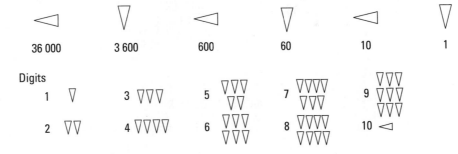

(a) Babylonian symbols

36 000	3 600	600	60	10	1

Digits

1 ▽   3 ▽▽▽   5 ▽▽▽▽▽   7 ▽▽▽▽▽▽▽   9 ▽▽▽▽▽▽▽▽▽

2 ▽▽   4 ▽▽▽▽   6 ▽▽▽▽▽▽   8 ▽▽▽▽▽▽▽▽   10 ◁

(b) Examples of Numerals

◁ ◁ ▽ ▽ ▽ ⟶ ten + ten + three

⟶ 600 + 600 + 60 + 60 + 60

⟶ 2 × 36 000 + 3 × 3600

Source: Bidwell (1967). Used with permission.

power of 10 (Cowle, 1970) (Figure 6-21a), whereas their numerals from 1 to 9 consisted of simple strokes arranged at most in groups of 4 horizontally (Figure 6-21b). An additive rule and the absence of place value rendered the system impractical because symbols had to be repeated the required number of times and could be written in a different order to represent the same number (Figure 6-21c). There was no symbol for zero; therefore, a particular symbol was omitted in a numeral when that multiple of ten was not part of a number (Figure 6-21d).

Mayan Numeration

The Mayans of Central America (before 1000 BC) developed a numeration system in base twenty complete with place value and a symbol for zero. They were a "barefoot people" and their probable early use of fingers and toes to indicate quantity may have influenced their choice of twenty for a number base. Place value notation was in top to bottom manner with the ones in the lower place and each place value separated by a space (Figure 6-22a). The

FIGURE 6-21

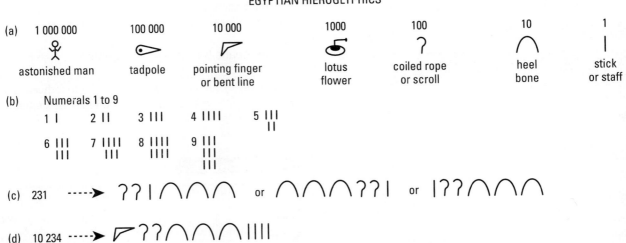

EGYPTIAN HIEROGLYPHICS

(a)

1 000 000	100 000	10 000	1000	100	10	1
astonished man	tadpole	pointing finger or bent line	lotus flower	coiled rope or scroll	heel bone	stick or staff

(b)   Numerals 1 to 9

1 | 2 || 3 ||| 4 |||| 5 |||
||

6 ||| 7 |||| 8 ||||| 9 |||
||| ||| |||| |||
|||

(c) 231 ----▶ ??|∩∩∩   or   ∩∩∩??| or |??∩∩∩

(d) 10 234 ----▶ ▱??∩∩∩∩ ||||

FIGURE 6-22

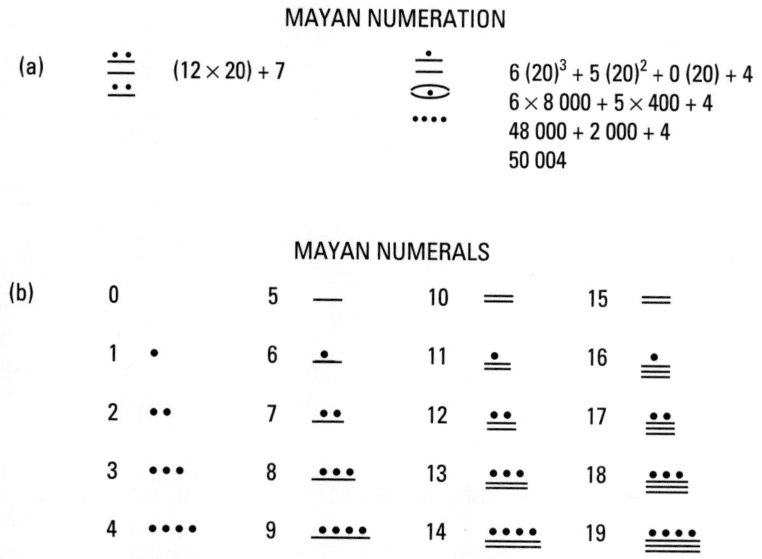

MAYAN NUMERATION

(a) $(12 \times 20) + 7$

$6 (20)^3 + 5 (20)^2 + 0 (20) + 4$
$6 \times 8\,000 + 5 \times 400 + 4$
$48\,000 + 2\,000 + 4$
$50\,004$

MAYAN NUMERALS

(b)
0	5	10	15
1	6	11	16
2	7	12	17
3	8	13	18
4	9	14	19

digits of the system are presented in Figure 6-22b (Bidwell, 1967, p. 764).

The Mayans used only three symbols to represent all numbers: a dot, a bar, and a symbol for zero. The simplicity of the numerals and a vertical place value scheme facilitated the representation of large numbers. The Mayan number names for each place value are presented in Table 6-4 (Bidwell, 1967, p. 764).

Roman Numeration

Although Western Europe and most of Asia chose to merge the numeration systems of the Hindus and Arabs over that of the Romans, Roman numerals were not completely shunned. This is evidenced by their use today on time pieces, tombstones, preface pages and section head-

ings of books, cornerstones of buildings and bridges, degree certificates, and various commemorative events. Because of its continued use, the Roman system is generally included in current mathematics programs.

Similar to the Egyptians, the Romans created a distinct symbol for one, ten, hundred, and thousand. In addition, they created a symbol for numbers that are half of the powers of ten symbolized, that is, five, fifty, and five hundred. Figure 6-23 shows the seven basic Roman numerals and their Hindu-Arabic equivalents.

Chiefly a repetitive and additive system, the advantage over the Egyptian system lies in the simplicity of the symbols and in a subtractive element that reduces the number of digits in a numeral.

The use of position to designate whether a number was to be added or subtracted may have been a historical first step in establishing a system based on digit position in a numeral. Examples of the use of position to determine the value of a digit are the numerals for four and six:

IV means $5 - 1 \rightarrow 4$ VI means $5 + 1 \rightarrow 6$

Only the symbols I, X, and C are used to indicate subtraction to represent certain numbers: I may be subtracted

TABLE 6-4

PLACE VALUE NAMES FOR MAYAN COUNTING SYSTEM

hablat	20^7
alau	20^6
kinchil	20^5
cabal	20^4
pic	20^3
bak	20^2
kal	20^1
hun	1

FIGURE 6-23

	NUMERALS						
Hindu-Arabic	1	5	10	50	100	500	1000
Roman	I	V	X	L	C	D	M

only from V or X; X may be subtracted from L or C; and C may be subtracted from D or M. Multiples of 10 beyond a thousand are symbolized by placing a line over any of the symbols and designates 1000 as a multiplier. Thus, $\overline{X}$ means 10 000 and $\overline{\overline{X}}$ symbolizes 10 000 000.

CONCLUSION

In this chapter, the structural characteristics of our numeration system have been presented together with instructional considerations for developing number meanings and relationships.

A good understanding of numeration is a prerequisite for mental computation and computational estimation with whole numbers. Place value tasks of renaming and regrouping numbers underlie algorithmic procedures for computation. Therefore, students' understanding of numbers and numeration should be assessed before proceeding to the development of computational procedures.

For Your Journal

When you have finished studying this chapter, reflect on these questions in your math journal:

1. How is our number system different from those of the Babylonians, Egyptians, Mayans, and Romans?

2. What does "equivalent representations" mean, and how can it help children understand place value?

3. Imagine that you are a first-grade teacher. You want to begin instruction to help your students understand place value. How might you assess what your students already know? What would you include in that assessment?

For Your Portfolio

When you have finished studying this chapter, complete these activities to include in your professional portfolio:

1. Write a lesson plan to help students understand the concept of grouping tens. Make sure to describe the type of base-ten model you would use.

2. Write a lesson plan to help students understand the concept of equivalent representations.

Resources for Teachers

Children's Books

Friedman, A. (1995). *The King's Commissioners.* New York: Scholastic.

Schwartz, D. (1985). *How Much is a Million?* New York: Scholastic.

Schwartz, D. (1989). *If You Made a Million.* New York: Lothrop, Lee & Shepard Books.

Zimelman, N. (1992). *How the Second Grade Got $8,205.50 to Visit the Statue of Liberty.* Morton Grove, IL: Albert Whitman & Co.

Books on Numeration

Brodie, J. (1995). *Constructing Ideas About Large Numbers.* Mountain View, CA: Creative Publications.

Burns, M. (1994). *Math By All Means: Place Value, Grade 2.* Sausalito, CA: Math Solutions Publications.

Reak, C., Stewart, K., & Walker, K. (1995). *20 Thinking Questions for Base-10 Blocks Grades 3–6.* Mountain View, CA: Creative Publications.

Reak, C., Stewart, K., & Walker, K. (1995). *20 Thinking Questions for Base-10 Blocks Grades 6–8.* Mountain View, CA: Creative Publications.

Richardson, K. (1999). *Developing Number Concepts: Place Value, Multiplication, and Division.* White Plains, NY: Dale Seymour Publications.

Links to the Internet

Ask Dr. Math (place value)

http://forum.swarthmore.edu/dr.math/tocs/placevalue.elem.html

Contains a list of interesting questions about place value and answers given by Dr. Math.

100th Day of School Websites

http://users.aol.com/a100thday/index.html
http://www.siec.k12.in.us/~west/proj/100th/index.html

These websites contain ideas of ways to celebrate the one-hundredth day of school.

CHAPTER 7

Developing Whole Number Operations: Meaning of Operations

Key Concepts

○ **Types of word problems for each operation**

  ○ **Addition and Subtraction: Join, Separate, Part-part-whole, Compare**

  ○ **Multiplication and Division: Equal groups (repeated addition, partitive division, measurement division), Multiplicative comparison, Area and arrays, and Combinations**

○ **Using objects to model problem situations**

Focus Questions

When you have finished studying this chapter, you should be able to do the following:

1. Write a word problem for each type of addition, subtraction, multiplication, and division problem.

2. How could each word problem above be modeled with objects? For each type of word problem, draw a picture to illustrate a model.

3. Explain the difference between partitive and measurement division. How might a child use counters to show 6 ÷ 2 for each interpretation of division?

The NCTM Standards emphasizes the importance of children understanding the meaning of operations, stating that "understanding the fundamental operations of addition, subtraction, multiplication, and division is central to knowing mathematics" (NCTM, 1989, p. 41).

> **STANDARDS LINK 7-1**
> In grades K–4, the mathematics curriculum should include concepts of addition, subtraction, multiplication, and division of whole numbers so that students can
>
> • develop meaning for the operations by modeling and discussing a rich variety of problem situations;
> • relate the mathematics language and symbolism of operations to problem situations and informal language;
> • recognize that a wide variety of problem structures can be represented by a single operation;
> • develop operation sense. (NCTM, 1989, p. 41)

This document goes on to list four key aspects of "developing operation sense," or understanding the operations:

• recognizing real-world settings for each operation;
• developing an awareness of models and properties of each operation;
• recognizing relationships among the operations; and
• understanding the effects of an operation.

Understanding the mathematical operations and their related computational procedures requires that the concepts of the operations be grasped, the basic facts be learned, and computational procedures be developed. This chapter discusses understanding the concepts of the operations. (Learning facts and developing computational procedures will be examined in the following chapters.) ○

INTRODUCE OPERATIONS WITH WORD PROBLEMS

Children begin to construct meaning for mathematical operations before they enter school. Informal, real-life experiences such as sharing cookies or combining collections of cards or marbles help children construct knowledge of mathematical operations. Because these experiences can be translated into word problems and because they are more meaningful to children than symbolic expressions, early instruction on operations should introduce children to addition, subtraction, multiplication, and division by having children solve word problems. Thus, learning about operations should be based on developing meaning and understanding by beginning with real-world settings or problems.

 STANDARDS LINK 7-2
Children should encounter the four basic operations in a wide variety of problem structures. (NCTM, 1989, p. 41)

A Model for Beginning with Word Problems

Young children develop an understanding of operations by solving a variety of word problems. If those problems come from real-world experiences, children can see more personal relevance, which enables them to more easily analyze the problem and its component parts. Real-world problems can come from everyday classroom opportunities such as routine opening activities, classroom events, or even examples from children's literature. In addition, children can help make decisions about sharing and distributing classroom supplies, especially when many-to-one groupings need to be made, which are meaningful contexts for multiplication and division (Kouba & Franklin, 1993). For example, if 10 children get five minutes each to use the computer, how much time will be needed? Teachers can take advantage of these familiar experiences to pose problems and discuss operations. Such rich, comfortable contexts in which mathematical operations are introduced naturally not only help children recognize personal relevance and math connections, but help them judge the reasonableness of their answers.

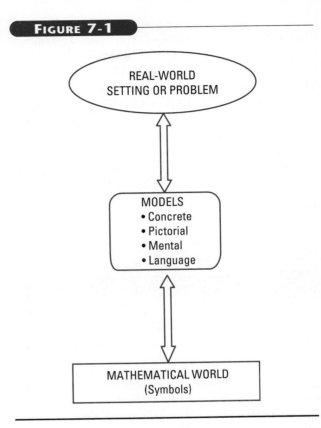

FIGURE 7-1

After introducing a real-world problem, a teacher should then represent or translate it into some model (see Figure 7-1). Initially, this model should be a concrete representation of the setting; later, the teacher can introduce iconic (pictorial) representations. Mental modes and children's natural language skills also can play key roles here in developing conceptual understanding.

Teachers should make different materials available to children to use in modeling problems. They also should encourage children to be creative in their representations of problem situations, whether concretely or pictorially. Further, they should provide ample opportunities for children to discuss and interpret situations presented concretely and pictorially. Once children are able to interpret different types of problems and identify and model the operation needed to solve each one, they can write number sentences to represent solution processes. It is important to remember, however, that children must have an extensive number of experiences with meaningful problem solving before they are introduced to symbolic expressions.

STANDARDS LINK 7-3
Informal experiences with all four operations should begin in kindergarten and continue through grade 4. (NCTM, 1989, p. 41)

STANDARDS LINK 7-4
Children need extensive informal experience with problem situations and language prior to explicit instruction and symbolic work with the operations. (NCTM, 1989, p. 41)

It is worthwhile to note that meanings develop over time and, while they are being developed, there should not be any pressure on children to memorize basic facts. In fact, understanding the meaning of the operations is a critical component of mastering the basic facts. Likewise, working with word problems should be the basis of children's early experiences with operations and must not be delayed until children "know their facts." The most important consideration is for children to connect their real-life experiences and language with the mathematical language and symbolism associated with each operation (Trafton & Zawojewski, 1990).

> ### STANDARDS LINK 7-5
> Instruction should help children connect their intuitions and informal language to operations, including the mathematical language and symbols of each operation. (NCTM, 1989, p. 41)

It also is important to mention now that the "key word" strategy—common translations in word problems of key words such as "*is* means *equal*" and "*of* means *times*"—is purposeless. In fact, teaching children to look for "key words" to solve word problems is ineffective and detrimental (Sowder, 1988). A much better use of instructional time is to help children develop understanding of the meaning of operations.

Encoding and Decoding Word Problems

Once students understand the meaning of a variety of problem situations, children should be asked to both *encode* and *decode* their number sentences. That is, not only should children translate a real-life setting into a model or mathematics sentence (encoding), they should, given a model or mathematics sentence, be able to write a word problem that illustrates that situation. Children should be encouraged to describe and justify their translation. This process is represented in Figure 7-1 by the double-headed arrows that suggest the translation process goes both ways.

For example, a teacher might give students the following problem to solve:

Tom had 7 cookies and gave 3 to Matt. How many cookies does Tom have left?

The teacher could ask the students to solve the problem using counters, or by drawing a picture, and to write a number sentence that matches the problem situation. On another occasion, the teacher could give students a number sentence and ask them to write a word problem that illustrates that number sentence.

Different parts of this generalized, conceptual model, depicted in Figure 7-1, are emphasized at different stages in the three-component process thus mentioned. When developing the concept or meaning of operations, it is most effective for children to focus on the real-world setting, the model for the setting, and the translation of one to the other. Mathematical symbols are not totally ignored but are used only incidentally.

> ### STANDARDS LINK 7-6
> Instruction on the meaning of operations focuses on concepts and relationships rather than on computation. (NCTM, 1989, p. 41)

In summary, research suggests that exposure to a wide range of word problems from the beginning of the school experience significantly improves children's mathematics performance (Stigler, Fuson, Ham, & Kim, 1986). Having children engage in solving word problems before they learn the basic facts enables them to focus on the nature of the problem and to model it to find an unknown answer (Burns, 1991).

> ### STANDARDS LINK 7-7
> Time devoted to conceptual development provides meaning and context to subsequent work on computational skills. (NCTM, 1989, p. 41)

> ### STANDARDS LINK 7-8
> Strong evidence suggests that conceptual approaches to computation instruction result in good achievement, good retention, and a reduction in the amount of time children need to master computational skills. Furthermore, many of the errors children typically make are less prevalent. (NCTM, 1989, p. 44)

UNDERSTANDING ADDITION AND SUBTRACTION

Researchers have identified four types of addition and subtraction problems: **Join, Separate, Part-part-whole,** and **Compare** (Carpenter & Moser, 1982). **Join** and **Separate** problems involve action. **Part-part-whole** and

FIGURE 7-2

THE STRUCTURE OF THE FOUR ADDITION AND SUBTRACTION PROBLEM TYPES

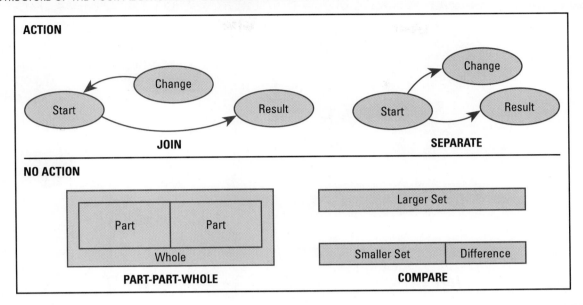

Compare problems do not involve action, but are identified by the relationships of the quantities in the problems. Research shows that this classification system matches the way children think about these problems (Fennema, Carpenter, Levi, Franke, & Empson, 1997).

Types of Addition and Subtraction Word Problems

The four addition and subtraction problems types—Join, Separate, Part-part-whole, and Compare—are distinguished by the presence or absence of action and the types of relationships involved. The basic structure of each of these problem types is illustrated in Figure 7-2.

Examples of each problem type In each of the addition and subtraction problem types, two quantities are given and one is unknown. The examples below use the fact family 4, 7, and 11 to illustrate each problem type.

Join problems. In a *Join problem,* elements are being added or joined to a set. The three quantities involved are the starting amount, the change amount, and the resulting amount. Figure 7-3 contains examples illustrating these three types of Join problems. Box 7-1 shows a sample of a second-grade student's work. Notice that the student wrote a **Join** problem, drew a picture illustrating the problem situation, and wrote a corresponding number sentence.

FIGURE 7-3

EXAMPLES OF JOIN PROBLEMS WITH DIFFERENT UNKNOWN QUANTITIES

TYPE	EXAMPLE	RELATED NUMBER SENTENCE
Join Result Unknown	Peter had 4 cookies. Erika gave him 7 more cookies. How many cookies does Peter have now?	4 + 7 = [ ]
Join Change Unknown	Peter had 4 cookies. Erika gave him some more cookies. Now Peter has 11 cookies. How many cookies did Erika give him?	4 + [ ] = 11
Join Start Unknown	Peter had some cookies. Erika gave him 7 more cookies. Now Peter has 11 cookies. How many cookies did Peter have to start with?	[ ] + 7 = 11

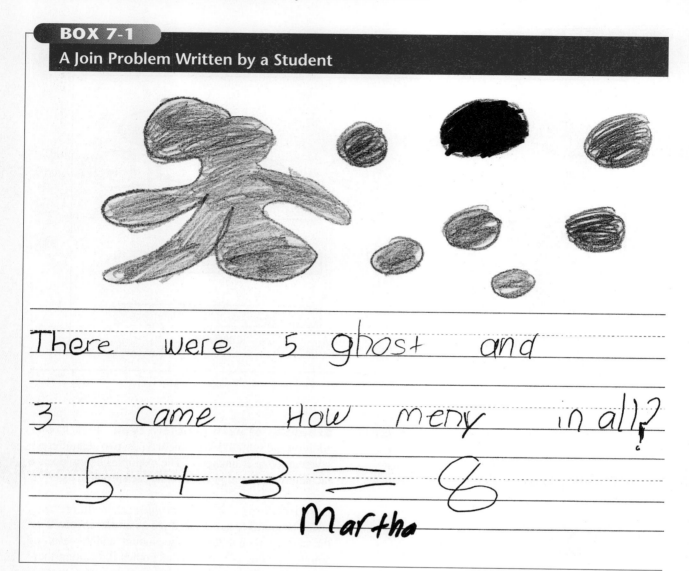

BOX 7-1

A Join Problem Written by a Student

There were 5 ghost and
3 came How meny in all?
5 + 3 = 8
Martha

Separate problems. In a *Separate problem,* elements are being removed from a set. As in Join problems, the three quantities involved are the starting amount, the change amount, and the resulting amount. Figure 7-4 shows examples of these three types of Separate prob-lems. Box 7-2 shows a sample of a second-grade student's work. This student wrote and illustrated a **Separate** problem and wrote a corresponding number sentence. Notice that this student showed that one fish swam away by crossing it out in the picture.

FIGURE 7-4

EXAMPLES OF SEPARATE PROBLEMS

TYPE	EXAMPLE	RELATED NUMBER SENTENCE
Separate Result Unknown	Peter had 11 cookies. He gave 7 cookies to Erika. How many cookies does Peter have now?	11 − 7 = [ ]
Separate Change Unknown	Peter had 11 cookies. He gave some cookies to Erika. Now Peter has 4 cookies. How many cookies did Peter give to Erika?	11 − [ ] = 4
Separate Start Unknown	Peter had some cookies. He gave 7 cookies to Erika. Now Peter has 4 cookies. How many cookies did Peter have to start with?	[ ] − 7 = 4

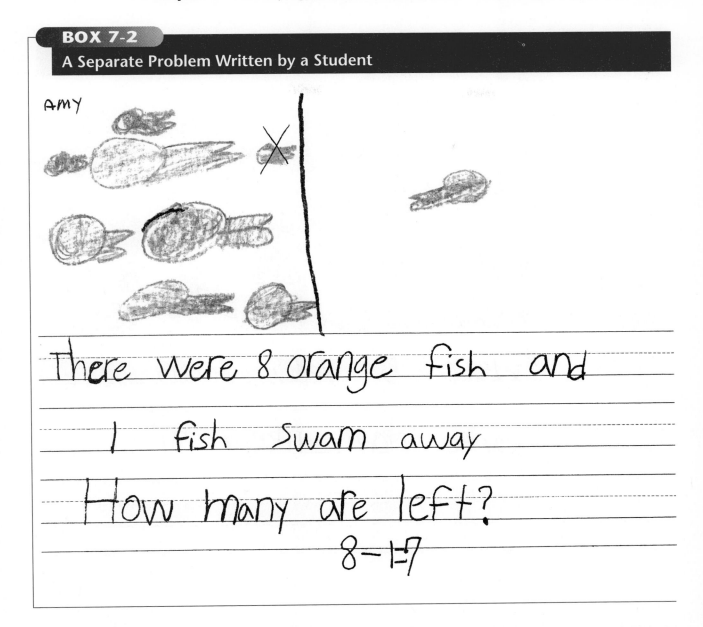

BOX 7-2

A Separate Problem Written by a Student

Part-part-whole problems. In *Part-part-whole problems* there is no action. Instead, they focus on the relationship between a set and its two subsets. The three quantities involved are the two parts and the whole. Unlike Join and Separate problems, there is no change over time. Figure 7-5 contains examples of the two types of Part-part-whole problems. Box 7-3 shows a sample of a second-grade student's work. This student wrote and illustrated a **Part-part-whole** problem. Notice how the use of two different colors of snails clearly shows the two parts of the problem.

Compare problems. There is no action in *Compare problems.* Instead, they involve comparisons between two different sets. The three quantities involved are the two wholes and the difference. Figure 7-6 contains examples of these three types of Compare problems.

These addition and subtraction word problem types result in 11 different kinds of addition and subtraction prob-

lems. Figure 7-7 presents these 11 types in one grid, in order to better examine their similarities and differences.

Using Models to Solve Addition and Subtraction Problems

Direct modeling Addition and subtraction problems can be modeled with many different types of materials, including real-world objects (such as pencils) and manipulative materials (such as poker chips). The term **direct modeling** refers to the process of children using concrete materials to exactly represent the problem as it is written. For example, consider the following Join problem:

Joyce had 3 pencils. Scott gave her 5 more pencils. How many pencils does Joyce have now?

This problem can be solved by having two children (representing Joyce and Scott) directly model or act out

BOX 7-3

A Part-Part-Whole Problem Written by a Student

There were 5 yellow snails and 4 red snails. How many all?

5+4=9

FIGURE 7-5

EXAMPLES OF PART-PART-WHOLE PROBLEMS

TYPE	EXAMPLE
Part-part-whole: Whole Unknown	Peter has some cookies. Four are chocolate chip cookies and 7 are peanut butter cookies. How many cookies does Peter have?
Part-part-whole: Part Unknown	Peter has 11 cookies. Four are chocolate chip cookies and the rest are peanut butter cookies. How many peanut butter cookies does Peter have?

FIGURE 7-6

EXAMPLES OF COMPARE PROBLEMS

TYPE	EXAMPLE
Compare Difference Unknown	Peter has 11 cookies and Erika has 7 cookies. How many more cookies does Peter have than Erika?
Compare Larger Unknown	Erika has 7 cookies. Peter has 4 more cookies than Erika. How many cookies does Peter have?
Compare Smaller Unknown	Peter has 11 cookies. Peter has 4 more cookies than Erika. How many cookies does Erika have?

FIGURE 7-7

ELEVEN ADDITION AND SUBTRACTION PROBLEM TYPES

Join	*Result Unknown* Peter had 4 cookies. Erika gave him 7 more cookies. How many cookies does Peter have now?	*Change Unknown* Peter had 4 cookies. Erika gave him some more cookies. Now Peter has 11 cookies. How many cookies did Erika give him?	*Start Unknown* Peter had some cookies. Erika gave him 7 more cookies. Now Peter has 11 cookies. How many cookies did Peter have to start with?
Separate	*Result Unknown* Peter had 11 cookies. He gave 7 cookies to Erika. How many cookies does Peter have now?	*Change Unknown* Peter had 11 cookies. He gave some cookies to Erika. Now Peter has 4 cookies. How many cookies did Peter give to Erika?	*Start Unknown* Peter had some cookies. He gave 7 cookies to Erika. Now Peter has 4 cookies. How many cookies did Peter have to start with?
Part-Part-Whole	*Whole Unknown* Peter has some cookies. Four are chocolate chip cookies and 7 are peanut butter cookies. How many cookies does Peter have?	*Part Unknown* Peter has 11 cookies. Four are chocolate chip cookies and the rest are peanut butter cookies. How many peanut butter cookies does Peter have?	
Compare	*Difference Unknown* Peter has 11 cookies and Erika has 7 cookies. How many more cookies does Peter have than Erika?	*Larger Unknown* Erika has 7 cookies. Peter has 4 more cookies than Erika. How many cookies does Peter have?	*Smaller Unknown* Peter has 11 cookies. Peter has 4 more cookies than Erika. How many cookies does Erika have?

---

the problem by having one child display 3 pencils and another child give her 5 more pencils. They then can count the number of pencils in the joined sets of pencils now held by Joyce.

Have children use pencils and other classroom materials to create other problems to solve. Ask children to solve those problems and discuss their solutions.

It usually is easier for children to solve a problem by modeling it with the actual objects referred to in the problem, as done in the previous example. Ask children to solve the problem and discuss its solution. Then, after solving a number of problems using the actual objects in the problem for direct modeling, begin to use counters. You should be aware, however, that using a manipulative material such as poker chips to model a problem about pencils is somewhat more abstract and will be a bit more difficult for children to successfully solve.

Problems involving action, such as Join and Separate, are easiest for children to solve by direct modeling. Part-part-whole and Compare problems are more difficult to model, though. Delay introducing these types of problems until children can successfully use direct modeling to solve Join and Separate problems.

Note that diagrams such as in Figure 7-8 sometimes can cause confusion. For example, when asked how many trucks are in set C, a young child may respond that there are none. Some young children do not understand class inclusion, that is, that set A and set B are contained in set C. These children may say that all the trucks are in sets A and B, so there are none in set C. This is one reason concrete objects should be used first in

developing problem-solving skills. When children physically join two sets, the initial sets lose their identity, although they can be reconstructed, and the difficulty sometimes associated with the diagram in Figure 7-8 does not occur.

Modeling Separate problems. Separate problems are fairly easy for children to model. To do so, remove a subset, the subtrahend, from an original set (the total number or minuend), and observe the difference (cardinal number of the remaining subset). Consider the following problem:

Megan had 6 cookies (the minuend). She gave 2 (the subtrahend) to her brother. How many cookies does Megan have left (the difference)?

FIGURE 7-8

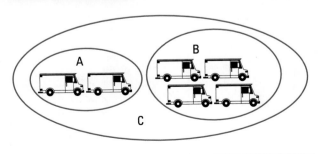

Using counters, children could set out six, physically remove two, then count the four remaining counters. Using a pictorial model, children might place an X through the two cookies given away.

Pictorial models of subtraction are more difficult to use and, at times, can be confusing. A typical textbook picture to illustrate three minus one would show three objects, with one of the objects crossed out. Some children write 2 − 1 because they see groups of two and one.

A better approach would be to show or have children draw a "before" and "after" picture as in Figure 7-9. The pictures show that there were three flowers, one is being "taken away," and the remaining set has two members.

When moving to a more abstract pictorial model, the set being taken away might be circled with an arrow implying it is being removed. Children can easily learn to identify the original set and each subset in such diagrams.

Page (1994) has created a set of sequenced lessons intended to develop an understanding of subtraction as take-away. Integral to these lessons is a chart similar to the one in Figure 7-10 on which children record their subtraction stories.

Modeling part-part-whole and compare problems.

Part-part-whole and Comparison problems necessitate matching two sets through a one-to-one correspondence and noting the number of objects in one set that are unmatched. The real-life setting for this approach to subtraction usually focuses on "how many more" or "how many fewer" there are in one group than another. Figure 7-11 is a pictorial model for the following problem:

Manuel had 6 candies and Keisha had 4 candies. How many more candies did Manuel have then Keisha?

Concretely, children could set out sets of six and four candies or counters to represent candies, place one from one set beside or on top of another from the other set and note the number of unmatched candies.

FIGURE 7-10

	Start With	Take Away	Have Left
1			
2			
3			
4			
5			

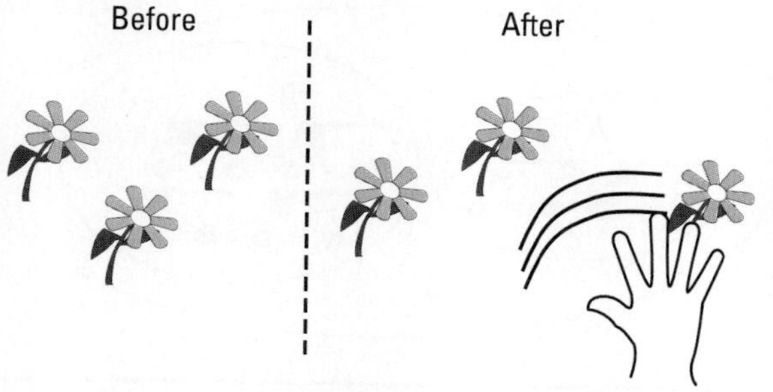

SUBTRACTION RECORDING SHEET

The "how many more (fewer)" setting could be illustrated with the following problem:

Heather has 6¢. A sticker at the flea market costs 15¢. How much more money does Heather need to be able to buy the sticker?

A child might verbalize, "six and how much more makes fifteen?" This language is suggestive of addition, but computationally the problem requires subtraction to solve. The 6¢ is removed from the 15¢ to find out how much money remains to be saved.

The Annenberg/CPB Math and Science Collection

VIDEO LINK 7-1
Communication

Brief Summary: One segment on the "Communication" video shows Leland Clarke's kindergarten class modeling six flowers by having six children wear flower headdresses. After three children put on the flower headdresses, another child says, "we need 3 more flowers" to have six altogether.

1. What interpretation of addition does this situation represent?
2. In what other ways might this problem be modeled?
3. What other word problems could be written based on this flower headdress story?

Video Source. Teaching Math: A Video Library, K–4; Tape 21 from The Annenberg/CPB Math and Science Collection.

Using measurement models Another way to model addition and subtraction problems is by using measurement models. In this approach, lengths, rather than discrete, countable objects, are used to represent the

FIGURE 7-9

Before | After

FIGURE 7-11

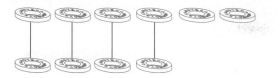

FIGURE 7-12

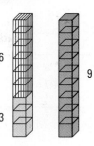

quantities in the problem. Unifix cubes, Cuisenaire rods, and a number line are appropriate and effective ways to communicate different quantities.

Unifix cubes, for example, can be used individually, but, because they interlock, they also can be used as "towers" or "trains" to indicate length. To represent addition, two towers can be constructed separately and then joined. Plastic "boats" or trays that come with the Unifix cubes hold lengths of 1 through 10 cubes. These trays can help children associate a number with a length. Figure 7-12 illustrates using measurement models to solve $3 + 6 = 9$.

Cuisenaire rods are color-coded. The unit rod is white and each of the rods 2 through 10 is a different color. The red rod (2) and the light green rod (3) are joined in the illustration below. The combined length is five unit rods, which is equivalent to the yellow rod. This represents the addition sentence $2 + 3 = 5$. A measurement model such as this one is useful for representing a real-world problem.

red light green

yellow

Addition and subtraction also can be modeled on the number line, which is a semi-concrete device. Children can, however, hop grasshoppers or kangaroos along the number line, making it more concrete. The addition sentence $2 + 7 = 9$ is modeled as a hop of 2 followed by a hop of 7 along the number line. Similarly, Separate problems also can be solved using the number line model. For example, to solve the problem $6 - 2 = n$, a child could begin at six, take a hop backward of two, and note the resulting position on the line.

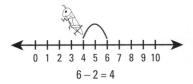

$6 - 2 = 4$

Teachers should note that the number line is a more difficult model for children to understand and should not be the first device used to model an operation. For example, children sometimes want to start at "1" instead of "0" and confuse spaces with points on the line. However, after experiences with other models, the number line should be introduced because it is handy and concise and a common model for representing integers and the operations with integers (Chapter 17). Further, sometimes a more abstract model such as a number line may be used to assess children's ability to transfer from the concrete to a more symbolic representation.

The Annenberg/CPB Math and Science Collection

VIDEO LINK 7-2
Concepts of Whole Number Operations

Brief Summary: In "Amazing Equations," teacher Flo Pearson asks her first- and second-graders to write word problems based on the "number for the day," which is the date (it is April 20, so the number of the day is 20). Students have to write word problems that have an answer of 20.

1. What is the teacher's role in this lesson? What do you think her objectives were for this lesson?
2. What types of problems did the children write? Be specific, using the terminology you learned in this chapter, such as "Separate result unknown" problem.
3. What modes of representation did the teacher and the children use?
4. What were you able to learn about children's understanding by watching and listening to them solve these problems? What lessons might the teacher do next with this class?

Video Source. Teaching Math: A Video Library, K–4; Tape 4 from The Annenberg/CPB Math and Science Collection.

FIGURE 7-13

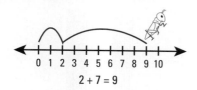

$$2 + 7 = 9$$

Offer children frequent opportunities to translate a measurement model into a real-life problem. For example, given the model in Figure 7-13, a group of children might talk about some settings and decide on the following: To get to school Henry walks 2 blocks north and then 7 blocks west. How many blocks does Henry walk to school?

Writing Number Sentences for Addition and Subtraction

Once children have had many experiences modeling and talking about real-life problems, the teacher should encourage children to write mathematical symbols for problems. Figure 7-14 illustrates this three-step process. Activity 7-1 suggests that the process should also go in the opposite direction, that is, from symbolic expression to expression using a model.

While it is important that children explore addition and subtraction word problems of each type, a teacher must be flexible in accepting the number sentence form in which children write a problem. Ask a child to explain why he or she wrote $a + n = b$ rather than $b - a = n$. Accept the child's explanation if it makes sense. Children's flexibility in selecting alternative number sentences to represent a problem seems to be related to the size of the numbers (Carey, 1991).

The Annenberg/CPB Math and Science Collection

VIDEO LINK 7-3
Concepts of Whole Number Operations

Brief Summary: In "Domino Math," teacher Alma Wright's first- and second-grade students use dominoes to find various combinations of numbers equal to a given sum.

1. How did this lesson help develop children's understanding of addition?
2. How are dominos different from flash cards? How are they similar?
3. What aspects of the lesson provide for students' individual differences?
4. What modes of representation did the teacher and children use?
5. What follow-up lessons might help the children extend their understandings?

Video Source. Teaching Math: A Video Library, K–4; Tape 4 from The Annenberg/CPB Math and Science Collection.

UNDERSTANDING MULTIPLICATION AND DIVISION

Types of Multiplication and Division Word Problems

Researchers have identified several different types of multiplication and division problems (Greer, 1992). These include **Equal groups, Multiplicative comparison, Area** and **Array,** and **Combinations** problems. The

FIGURE 7-14

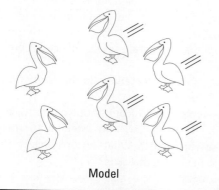

Model

2 plus 4

Semi-abstract model

2 + 4

Symbolic

✳ ACTIVITY 7-1

WRITING A PROBLEM

MATERIALS:
the diagram below

PROCEDURE:

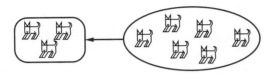

1. In your group discuss some problems that match the picture.

2. Decide on two problems. Write them in your notebook.

Equal groups problem type is by far the most common interpretation in everyday life and in the elementary school mathematics curriculum.

The instruction that teachers give to children must help them connect the different ways of describing multiplication and division to the interpretations and representations that make sense to them (Kouba & Franklin, 1993). Teachers should encourage children to explain relationships and situations in their own words and then help them link their own less formal language with the more formal mathematical language.

Examples of each problem type Multiplication and division problems are fundamentally different from addition and subtraction problems. This is due to the different types of quantities represented in multiplication and division problems. The following sections clarify these differences. The examples below use the fact family 2, 3, 6 to illustrate each problem type.

Equal groups problems. A certain number of equal-sized groups are involved in Equal groups problems. The three numbers in the problem represent the number of groups, the size of the groups, and the total number of objects.

When the total number of objects is unknown, it is a **Multiplication** (or repeated addition) problem. When the size of the groups is unknown, the problem is known as a **Partitive Division** (or fair sharing) problem. And when the number of groups is unknown, the problem is known as a **Measurement Division** (or repeated subtraction) problem. Figure 7-15 contains examples of these three types of Equal groups problems.

In Partitive division problems, the total number of objects is *partitioned* into a specified number of groups. In the Partitive division example in Figure 7-15, 6 oranges are split, or partitioned, into *3 equal groups*. In contrast, in Measurement division problems the total number of objects are *measured out* into groups of a certain size. In the example above, 6 oranges are split into *groups of 3 oranges*. These distinctions will help you remember the names.

Multiplicative comparison problems. The Multiplicative comparison problem type is fairly common. As in the comparison problems discussed previously in the addition and subtraction section of this chapter, Multiplicative comparison problems involve comparing two quantities; however, in this case the comparison is multiplicative rather than additive. The following problem is an example of a multiplicative comparison problem:

Tom has 3 baseball cards. Anton has 2 times as many baseball cards as Tom does. How many baseball cards does Anton have?

FIGURE 7-15

EXAMPLES OF EQUAL GROUPS PROBLEMS

TYPE	EXAMPLE	RELATED NUMBER SENTENCE
Multiplication (repeated addition)	Maria has 2 bags of oranges. There are 3 oranges in each bag. How many oranges does Maria have altogether?	$2 \times 3 = [\ \ ]$
Partitive Division (fair sharing)	Maria has 6 oranges. She put the oranges into 3 bags with the same number of oranges in each bag. How many oranges are in each bag?	$6 \div 3 = [\ \ ]$
Measurement Division (repeated subtraction)	Maria has 6 oranges. She put 3 oranges in each bag. How many bags of oranges did she use?	$6 \div 3 = [\ \ ]$

FIGURE 7-16

EXAMPLES OF MULTIPLICATIVE COMPARISON PROBLEMS

TYPE	EXAMPLE	RELATED NUMBER SENTENCE
Multiplicative comparison	Maria has 3 oranges. Tony has 2 times as many oranges as Maria has. How many oranges does Tony have?	$2 \times 3 = [\ ]$
Multiplicative comparison	Tony has 6 oranges, which is 2 times as many oranges as Maria has. How many oranges does Maria have?	$2 \times [\ ] = 6$ or $6 \div 2 = [\ ]$
Multiplicative comparison	Tony has 6 oranges and Maria has 3 oranges. How many times as many oranges does Tony have than Maria has?	$[\ ] \times 3 = 6$ or $6 \div 3 = [\ ]$

Several types of Multiplicative comparison problems are possible, based on the location and meaning of the unknown, but all share a similar structure. Figure 7-16 contains additional examples of Multiplicative comparison problems.

Area and array problems. Finding the area of a rectangular region or array (arrangement) is the purpose in Area and Array problems. The area of a rectangle can be found by covering the region with unit squares and counting them or by multiplying the length by the width; both methods yield the area in square units. Arrays, in contrast, are rectangular arrangements of discrete, countable objects, such as desks arranged in rows in a classroom. Figure 7-17 contains examples of Area and Array problems.

Combination problems. Also known as Cartesian products, Combination problems involve different combinations that can be made from sets of objects, such as the number of outfits that can be made from 2 shirts and 3 pairs of pants. This type of problem is the most difficult type of multiplication and division problem to model. Figure 7-18 contains examples of Combination problems.

A note on multiplication and division word problems Many of the difficulties children have with multiplication and division relate to the language used. For example, a child might understand "give each child four cookies" but not understand "give four cookies per child."

Initially, children could be encouraged to use "groups of" to indicate joining of a number of equal groups. They would use language such as, "I have three groups of five—that's fifteen." The meanings of other expressions such as "three fives," "three times five," and "three of these fives" should be developed before the symbolic expression $3 * 5 = 15$ is expected to be used. As well, $3 * 5$ should not be read as "3 multiplied by 5" because in this example, 3 is the multiplier and indicates the number of groups.

Be sure to pay particular attention to the meaning of each quantity. Notice that the multiplication problem $2 \times 3 = 6$ can be interpreted as "two groups of 3 objects" or $3 + 3$. This is different than $3 \times 2 = 6$, which means "three groups of 2 objects" or $2 + 2 + 2 = 6$. Even though the total number of objects is the same in both problems, the problems have different meanings. Until children understand the commutative property, verbalizing that 2×3 is the same as 3×2 will confuse many

FIGURE 7-17

EXAMPLES OF AREA AND ARRAY PROBLEMS

TYPE	EXAMPLE	RELATED NUMBER SENTENCE
Multiplication (Area and Array)	The living room floor measures 8 feet by 12 feet. How many square feet of carpeting are needed to cover the floor?	$8 \times 12 = [\ ]$
Division (Area and Array)	72 chairs must be arranged into 8 rows. How many chairs will be in each row?	$72 \div 8 = [\ ]$

FIGURE 7-18

EXAMPLES OF COMBINATION PROBLEMS

TYPE	EXAMPLE	RELATED NUMBER SENTENCE
Combinations	How many different outfits can be made with 2 blouses and 3 pairs of slacks?	$2 \times 3 = [\ \ ]$
Combinations	How many different ice cream cones can be made with 2 kinds of cones and 3 flavors of ice cream?	$2 \times 3 = [\ \ ]$

students. For young children, three groups of two objects is fundamentally different from two groups of three objects. Children think in concrete terms: two children who each get three pieces of candy are luckier than three children who each get two pieces of candy (Anghileri & Johnson, 1992). The fact that the total amount of candy is the same may not be important to the child who is thinking about the lucky children who each got three pieces of candy!

Division with remainders   If children are solving division problems set in meaningful real-world settings, they will encounter some problems that don't have a whole number as the solution. For example, when sharing 5 cookies among 2 people, each person will get 2 cookies, and there will be one left over. Teachers should take advantage of this opportunity for a rich discussion about what to do with the cookie that's left over. Frequently, even young children will suggest that they split the remaining cookie into smaller parts. In this problem, each person will get $2\frac{1}{2}$ cookies.

This type of problem is an excellent introduction to other types of division problems (those whose solution is not a whole number) and to a discussion about what to do with "left overs" when dividing.

The Annenberg/CPB Math and Science Collection

VIDEO LINK 7-4
Communication

Brief Summary: One segment on the "Communication" video shows Steven Levy's fourth-grade class calculating the amount of stain needed to cover all the wooden pencil boxes in the classroom.

1. What interpretation of what operation must students understand to solve this problem?

Video Source. Teaching Math: A Video Library, K–4; Tape 21 from The Annenberg/CPB Math and Science Collection.

Such discussions about realistic problems can be extended to include situations in which it may be appropriate to continue to divide what's left into fractional parts, when the leftovers might just be set aside, and when it may be appropriate to make unequal groups (for example, when 9 children need to ride in 2 cars, it would not be appropriate to cut a child in half or to leave one home, but rather to put 4 children in one car and 5 in the other).

Using Models to Solve Multiplication and Division Problems

As in addition and subtraction, there are many different models that can be used to illustrate relationships posed in multiplication and division problems. The following section describes some of these models.

Modeling equal groups and multiplicative comparison problems   Equal groups problems, such as in the following example, can be modeled using a set model.

Maisha and Peter decided to sell cookies in groups of 3 at their school's bake sale. Mrs. Walsh bought 6 groups. How many cookies did Mrs. Walsh buy?

A set model is illustrated in Figure 7-19, in which six groups of three are assembled. Activities could include the children placing an equal number of cookies or counters on a specified number of plates or putting an equal number of marbles in bags. The mathematics sentence for the representation is $6 \times 3 = n$.

Similarly, measurement division and partitive division problems can be modeled using a set model. Generally, children are introduced to division using a subtractive, or measurement, setting. They are to find the number of groups. The repeated subtraction process for the following problem is symbolically represented in Figure 7-20.

Janice has 12 cookies. She wants to put 3 cookies into each bag. How many bags does she need?

FIGURE 7-19

FIGURE 7-21

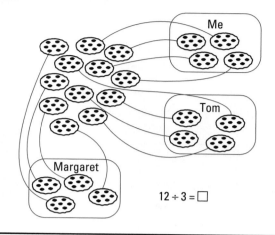

$12 \div 3 = \square$

In a partitioning setting, the total number and the number of equal groups are known. The student is to determine the number in each group. For example:

A father is making lunches for his 3 children. He wants to use 12 cookies and each child is to be served the same number of cookies. How many cookies will each child get?

Children can find the solution by acting out a sharing or "dealing out" process (Figure 7-21). At its most basic level, a child might say "one for me, one for Tom, one for Margaret, one for me, one for Tom, one for Margaret . . . ." Later, children will realize that they can share two or more at a time, thereby making the process more efficient.

Modeling area and array problems   Area and Array problems can be modeled using a row by column representation. Consider the following problem:

Maisha and Peter decided to sell cookies in rows of 3 at their school's bake sale. They put 6 rows of 3 cookies each on one tray. How many cookies were on that tray?

FIGURE 7-20

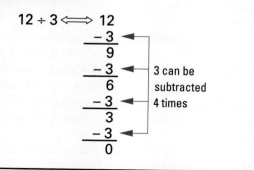

The problem above would be represented by the array shown. By convention the rows represent the number of groups, and the columns represent the number in each group. The array pictured here is a 6-by-3 array, or 6 rows of 3. Encouraging children to construct an array to represent a problem according to convention facilitates group work, class discussion, and assessment.

A teaching aid that helps students model Area and Array problems is the 10-by-10 multiplication array (Blackline Master 5). This array consists of 10 rows of circles with 10 circles in each row. Students use pieces of paper or index cards to frame the circles corresponding to the problem they are solving (and to cover the extra circles not needed for that problem). For example, for the bake sale problem above, with 6 rows of cookies and 3 cookies in each row, students would lay their index cards on the 10-by-10 array so that only a 6-by-3 array of circles was visible. They could then count the number of circles in the 6-by-3 array to find the answer to the problem. The multiplication array saves time by eliminating the need to actually arrange the counters into 6 rows of 3. Note, however, that the multiplication array should be introduced only *after* students are able to construct arrays of counters themselves.

Modeling combination problems Although combination problems are the least used of the four approaches, they can be very helpful in building the concept of multiplication—particularly multiplication with zero. Consider the following example:

Lindsay has a choice of 6 flavors of ice cream and 3 different toppings. How many different kinds of ice cream sundaes could Lindsay have?

Some children have difficulty matching each topping to one flavor and then repeating that for each of the flavors. The use of a six-by-three chart (similar to an array) facilitates understanding this approach (Kouba & Franklin, 1993).

Consider how the problem above about ice cream sundaes would change if there were *zero* flavors of ice cream and 3 toppings. In this situation, no sundaes could be made, illustrating that $0 \times 3 = 0$.

Other models for multiplication

A measurement interpretation. The number line can be used to represent a measurement approach to multiplication. On the number line, equal groups are represented by equal "hops" along the line. As shown, the introductory problem would be represented by six hops or moves, each three units in length.

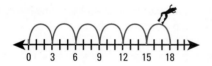

The "crossroads" or network model. A more abstract model is to have the children think of crossroads. The introductory problem could be represented with six roads (lines) running horizontally and three running vertically as shown. The points of intersection represent the product.

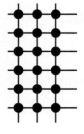

This representation of multiplication is effective in demonstrating multiplication with zero:

*0 * 3 is represented with 0 horizontal lines and 3 vertical lines.*
*3 * 0 is represented with 3 horizontal lines and 0 vertical lines.*

Clearly, there are no intersections, so the product is 0 in both cases.

How would you use the crossroads model to illustrate the sundaes problem if there were 3 kinds of toppings and no ice cream left? Use the model again to show the situation in which any number of ice cream flavors but no toppings are available.

Children should have the freedom to adapt these ideas or invent their own. The important consideration is that children build a sound understanding of the different situations that require multiplication as a solution process.

An instructional sequence for modeling multiplication and division Kouba and Franklin (1993) use the problem "If 8 plates hold 4 cookies each, how many cookies are on all the plates?" to illustrate a sequential development in understanding multiplication:

A child sets out 8 plates, puts 4 cookies (or objects) on each plate, and counts the total number.
A child makes 8 groups of 4 without using separate objects for plates.
A child makes one group of 4 and recounts it 8 times, keeping track of how many groups have been counted by using fingers or another memory device.

"More advanced levels of representation include counting by fours; counting on when they cannot recall the next multiple, for instance, 4, 8, . . . , 9, 10, 11, 12, and so on; adding fours; and using such derived facts as 'Four groups of 4 are 16 and 16 plus 16 is 32.'" (pp. 575–576)

ANOTHER WORD ABOUT NOTATION AND CHILDREN'S LANGUAGE

Children have a natural way of talking about the action involved in the operations. Capturing this natural language and using it in the classroom can help children in understanding whole number operations. Do not rush into using symbolic notation. Instead, make a slow, gradual transition from natural language to symbolic language.

FIGURE 7-22

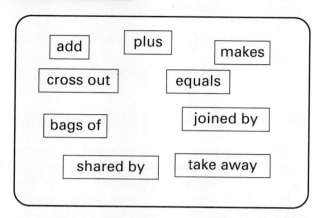

FIGURE 7-24

Listen to the language children use as they talk about problems. They will use phrases such as "ran away" and "joined in" as they describe real-life actions. You also will hear language like "and 3 more," "start with 7 and cross out 4," "3 bags with 2 each," and "12 to be shared by 4." Encourage children to write statements about the problems they are doing and to write number sentences using words rather than mathematics symbols.

To capture this natural language, write key terms or phrases on cards such as those shown in Figure 7-22. The cards created for a specific class will vary with the language used by the children in the class. Also prepare numeral cards with the numbers encountered in the basic facts. Encourage the children to create sentences for problems and for concrete or pictorial models of the operations by using the cards as in Figure 7-23.

Using number and language cards in the classroom can help make the transition from horizontal to vertical notation more natural. Sentences such as those in Figure 7-23 can be arranged in vertical format. Initially, the sen-

tences might be formed as a simple 90-degree rotation of the horizontal sentence (Figure 7-24). Later, the format can be altered to conform more closely to conventional notation. See Figure 7-25.

Over a period of time, introduce the conventional symbols for the different action words. Also introduce the "=" symbol for words such as "makes" and "leaves." Write these conventional symbols on cards as well and have children use them to generate sentences for problems and models in the same way they did with the natural language cards.

Children should understand that the "=" sign means "is the same number as" or "is another name for." Having children write several expressions equivalent to a given expression should facilitate this understanding. For example, give children $5 + 7 = [\quad]$ and ask them to write at least three true expressions (not just one number) in the blank. They may respond with:

$$5 + 7 = 6 + 6 \qquad 5 + 7 = 10 + 2$$
$$5 + 7 = 24 \div 2 \qquad 5 + 7 = 15 - 3$$

Vertical notation could be developed in the same way as it was with the word cards. The arrangement in Figure 7-26 seems to be a natural first step in the transition. The fact that this form is not used in elementary school textbooks does not mean that a teacher could not use it effectively as a transition. The reason the "=" symbol is not used in the vertical format is because this format suggests

FIGURE 7-23

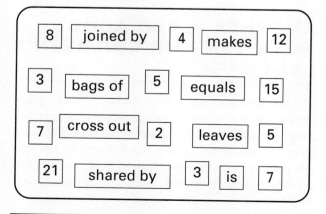

FIGURE 7-25

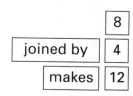

FIGURE 7-26

```
9
-
6
=
3
```

that a standard answer is wanted. The solid line separating the answer from the components of the operation is more appropriate for this more limited response expectation.

Notice that the notation for division is particularly confusing to children. There are three common symbolic representations for division: 6 ÷ 2, 2 "goes into" 6 [*draw in division box*], and 6/2 or 6/2 [*written vertically, as a fraction*]. The last format usually is delayed until children are studying fractions. The first usually is read as "6 divided by 2" and the second as "2 goes into 6," though it should also be read as "6 divided by 2." The second representation is the most common, but also it is the only symbolic representation that should not be read from left to right, as "2 goes into 6." It is important to help children connect the phrase "6 divided by 2" to each of the symbolic forms above.

CONCLUSION

It is critical that children build a sound understanding of whole number operations. Therefore, children should be allowed time to manipulate and assimilate their ideas. Solving word problems of many different types is necessary in order for children to develop this "operation sense." To rush on to "more advanced" work is a mistake that often comes back to haunt both students and teachers.

For Your Journal

When you have finished studying this chapter, reflect on these questions in your math journal:

1. Imagine that you are a first-grade teacher. You want to begin instruction to help your students understand addition and subtraction. What will you do? What problems will you ask students to solve? What materials will you use? What teaching strategies will you employ?

2. Imagine that you are a classroom teacher. A colleague asks why you are spending so much instructional time having children solve word problems rather than drilling them on basic facts. How will you respond?

For Your Portfolio

When you have finished studying this chapter, complete these activities to include in your professional portfolio:

1. Write a lesson plan to help introduce children to the Join type of addition problems.

2. Write a lesson plan to help introduce children to the Equal groups type of multiplication and division problems.

3. Write a lesson plan to help children understand division by zero.

Resources for Teachers

Children's Books

Anno, M., & Anno, M. (1983). *Anno's Mysterious Multiplying Jar.* New York: Philomel Books.

Giganti, P. (1992). *Each Orange Had Eight Slices: A Counting Book.* New York: Greenwillow Books.

Hutchins, P. (1986). *The Doorbell Rang.* New York: Greenwillow Books.

Mahy, M. (1987). *17 Kings and 42 Elephants.* New York: Dial Books for Young Readers.

Mathews, L. (1978). *Bunches and Bunches of Bunnies.* New York: Scholastic.

Neuschwander, C. (1998). *Amanda Bean's Amazing Dream.* New York: Scholastic.

Pinczes, E. (1993). *One Hundred Hungry Ants.* Boston: Houghton Mifflin Company.

Pinczes, E. (1995). *A Remainder of One.* New York: Houghton Mifflin Company.

Books on Whole Number Operations

Brodie, J. (1995). *Constructing Ideas About Multiplication and Division, Grades 3–6.* Mountain View, CA: Creative Publications.

Burns, M. (1991). *Math By All Means: Multiplication Grade 3.* Sausalito, CA: The Math Solution Publications.

Creative Publications. (1994). *The Maharajas' Tasks Investigating Division.* Mountain View, CA: Creative Publications.

Ohanian, S., & Burns, M. (1995). *Math By All Means: Division Grades 3–4.* Sausalito, CA: Math Solutions Publication.

Richardson, K. (1999). *Developing Number Concepts, Book 2: Addition and Subtraction.* White Plains, NY: Dale Seymour Publications.

Richardson, K. (1999). *Developing Number Concepts, Book 3: Place Value, Multiplication and Division.* White Plains, NY: Dale Seymour Publications.

Ward, S. (1995). *Constructing Ideas About Number Combinations.* Mountain View, CA: Creative Publications.

Links to the Internet

ProTeacher: Addition and Subtraction

http://www.proteacher.com/100011.shtml

Contains links to lessons to help children understand and practice addition and subtraction.

ProTeacher: Multiplication and Division

http://www.proteacher.com/100012.shtml

Contains links to lessons to help children understand and practice multiplication and division.

Explorer: Whole Numbers

http://explorer.scrtec.org/explorer/explorer-db/browse/static/Mathematics/browse/f15.html

Contains many lessons on whole number operations.

CHAPTER 8

Developing Whole Number Operations: Mastering the Basic Facts

Focus Questions

When you have finished studying this chapter, you should be able to answer these questions:

1. What are the three components of instruction on basic facts?

2. For each whole number operation, what are some thinking strategies that children can employ? Describe several thinking strategies for each operation.

3. What is the role of consolidating activities for drill and practice? Describe several of these activities.

4. How are games useful in promoting the immediate recall of basic facts?

WHAT ARE BASIC FACTS?

The basic facts for addition and multiplication involve all combinations of single-digit addends and factors. For example, $7 + 9 = 16$ is an addition basic fact, since the two addends, 7 and 9, both are single-digit numbers. Since there are 10 digits, there are 100 combinations for both addition and multiplication.

The basic facts for subtraction are the inverses of the addition facts. Using the example from the previous paragraph, the addition problem $7 + 9 = 16$ may be transformed into two subtraction basic facts: $16 - 7 = 9$ and $16 - 9 = 7$. Consequently, there are 100 basic facts for subtraction.

STANDARDS LINK 8-1

In grades K–4, the mathematics curriculum should develop whole number computation so that students can

- model, explain, and develop reasonable proficiency with basic facts and algorithms;
- use a variety of mental computation and estimation techniques;
- use calculators in appropriate computational situations;
- select and use computation techniques appropriate to specific problems and determine whether the results are reasonable. (NCTM, 1989, p. 44)

Similarly, the basic facts for division are the inverses of the multiplication facts. For example, the multiplication fact $3 \times 8 = 24$ may be transformed into two division basic facts: $24 \div 3 = 8$ and $24 \div 8 = 3$. There are 90 basic facts for division since there are no facts with zero as a divisor. Thus, there are a total of 390 basic facts.

These are basic facts:	These are NOT basic facts:
3 + 9 = 12	4 + 11 = 15
14 − 8 = 6	19 − 9 = 10
7 × 4 = 28	5 × 10 = 50
6 × 0 = 0	46 ÷ 9 = 5 R1
48 ÷ 6 = 8	15 ÷ 0 = undefined
0 ÷ 5 = 0	20 ÷ 10 = 2

Can you determine why each of the number sentences in the second column above is *not* a basic fact? Remember that basic facts consist of addends or factors that are between 0 and 9 inclusive, and the corresponding subtraction and division facts.

In the process of developing number relationships and the meaning of the operations, some basic facts will have been learned already. In fact, many children come to school knowing a number of basic facts. For example, many kindergartners can state that "one and one is two." But in order for children to learn all 390 basic facts, teachers must do more than have students endlessly repeat basic facts with the hope that they will memorize them.

The NCTM (1989) affirms the importance of children developing proficiency with basic facts and algorithms, but cautions against overemphasizing the memorization of facts before understanding is developed, or to the exclusion of other important topics.

STANDARDS LINK 8-2
Premature expectations for students' mastery of computational procedures not only cause poor initial learning and poor retention but also require that large amounts of instructional time be spent on teaching and reteaching basic skills. More important, the instructional focus centers on memorizing facts and rules for carrying out procedures rather than on the thoughtful use of operations and number relationships. (NCTM, 1989, p. 46–47)

In learning the basic facts, children focus less on real-life problems and more on the relationship between models and the symbolic representation of the facts. Children need many opportunities to discuss and to physically translate from model to symbol and vice versa before they can be expected to operate solely at the symbolic level. The approach described in the following section facilitates the learning of basic facts. ○

A THREE-STEP APPROACH TO FACT MASTERY

Many beginning teachers believe all they need to do is have children practice, practice, practice to automatically memorize the basic facts. Practice is important, but it is not effective if other understandings and skills are not already in place.

One very effective method for helping children learn basic facts is the three-step approach (Rathmell, 1978). The three-step approach includes understanding the meaning of the operations, using thinking strategies for fact retrieval, and using consolidating activities for drill and practice. This approach is the best way to help children recall the basic math facts.

STANDARDS LINK 8-3
Children should master the basic facts of arithmetic that are essential components of fluency with paper-and-pencil and mental computation and with estimation. At the same time, however, mastery should not be expected too soon. Children will need many exploratory experiences and the time to identify relationships among numbers and efficient thinking strategies to derive the answers to unknown facts from known facts. (NCTM, 1989, p. 47)

Step 1: Understanding the Meaning of the Operations

As described in Chapter 7, children must understand the meaning of each operation. This understanding lays the foundation for further use of these operations and the development of operation sense. Children who understand the meaning of operations are then able to use thinking strategies to relate facts they've already learned to new facts.

Step 2: Using Thinking Strategies for Fact Retrieval

Thinking strategies are mental strategies that can be used to relate known facts to unknown facts. For example, if a child knows that 2 + 2 = 4, the "one more than" thinking strategy would help him or her determine that the sum of 2 + 3 must be one more than the sum of 2 + 2, or 5.

Thinking strategies help children find the answer to basic facts problems without using concrete materials by "providing structure for organizing facts so that recall is easier" (Rathmell, 1978, p. 18). While many children will "invent" one or more of these thinking strategies on their own (Thornton, 1978), explicit teaching on the use and selection of thinking strategies is necessary. A variety of detailed thinking strategies for each operation follows.

Step 3: Consolidating Activities for Drill and Practice

Consolidating activities provide students with opportunities to practice facts they are learning in order to memorize them. Drill and practice are most effective after students have learned efficient thinking strategies for recalling those basic facts.

ADDITION AND SUBTRACTION FACTS

The one hundred addition facts often are summarized in an addition table as shown in Figure 8-1. To find the sum of 4 and 6, locate the first addend, 4, in the left-hand column, and the other addend, 6, along the top row, or vice versa. The cell in the body of the table that represents the intersection of this row and column contains the sum, 10.

The one hundred subtraction facts can be derived from the addition table as illustrated in Figure 8-1. Locate the minuend (10) opposite the subtrahend (4) in the left-hand column. Read the difference (6) in the top index row.

Obviously the whole table is not given to children initially, since it contains facts they may not have had an op-

portunity to learn. Children normally develop the table during the first and second grades.

All of the joining, separating, and comparing activities described in Chapter 7 can be used to help children learn the basic facts. These activities should now be extended to include more symbolic representation of the facts. Using Cuisenaire rods, activities such as those in Activity 8-1 emphasize the model-symbol interaction. Interlocking Unifix cubes could be used equally as well for this activity.

Thinking Strategies for Addition and Subtraction

Rathmell (1978) described several important thinking strategies that children use when learning addition and subtraction basic facts: counting-on, counting back, one-more or one-less than a known fact, and compensation. In order for thinking strategies to become spontaneous, children need many experiences using them. Teachers should develop one of the strategies, then provide daily opportunities for children to use and verbalize the strategy for several days before introducing another strategy.

Counting on The Counting-on strategy involves starting with the larger addend, counting on the number of the second addend, and noting the ending result. With

FIGURE 8-1

+	0	1	2	3	4	5	6	7	8	9
0	0	1	2	3	4	5	6	7	8	9
1	1	2	3	4	5	6	7	8	9	10
2	2	3	4	5	6	7	8	9	10	11
3	3	4	5	6	7	8	9	10	11	12
4	4	5	6	7	8	9	10	11	12	13
5	5	6	7	8	9	10	11	12	13	14
6	6	7	8	9	10	11	12	13	14	15
7	7	8	9	10	11	12	13	14	15	16
8	8	9	10	11	12	13	14	15	16	17
9	9	10	11	12	13	14	15	16	17	18

✳ ACTIVITY 8-1

NUMBER SENTENCES FOR TRAINS

MATERIALS:
Cuisenaire rods

PROCEDURE:
1. Write number sentences for these trains. Write the sum.

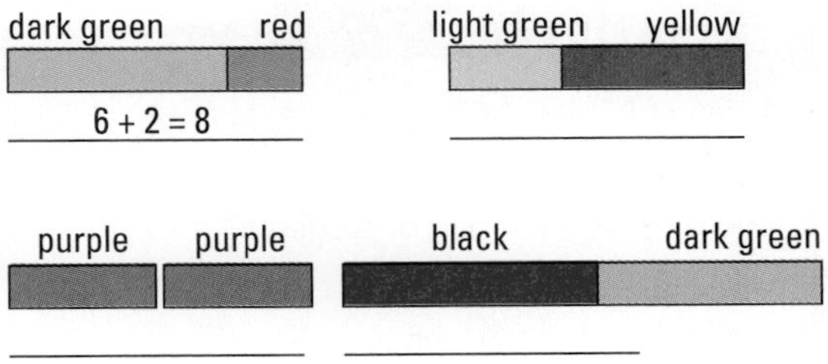

| dark green | red | | light green | yellow |

6 + 2 = 8   _____

| purple | purple | | black | dark green |

_____   _____

2. Make a train for each of the sentences below. Write the sum.

$8 + 5 = \square$ $4 + 0 = \square$ $5 + 7 = \square$
$9 + 1 = \square$

$2 + 5$, the child would start with 5 and count forward two times, saying "six, seven." While counting on is a somewhat "natural" strategy for children, they need specific guidance in starting with the larger addend. Children have a tendency to start with 2 and count on 5 more numbers. This is much more difficult than starting with 5 and counting on 2. An understanding of the commutative property will help with this process. Counting on is most effective when one of the addends is relatively small.

Experiences with counting on could be set up with dice or cards as suggested by Activity 8-2. Cards with larger dots (or another design) may be easier for some children to work with than regular dice.

Counting on in subtraction   Counting on also is a useful strategy in subtraction. It is best used in situations in which the difference is small. Children would begin with the subtrahend and count on to the minuend, noting the number added through counting. For example, to find the answer to $10 - 7$, a child would start at 7 and count forward until she reached 10, saying "eight, nine, ten." The answer is the total number of counts forward—in this example, three.

The number line and the calendar are helpful devices for counting on in subtraction. For example, a child might wonder on Thursday how many days it has been since Monday ($9 - 6$ on the calendar in Figure 8-2). counting on from 6 would give the answer, 3.

Mrs. Weill's hill (Weill, 1978) is an example of a counting-on strategy that she found effective with children who are learning-disabled (see Figure 8-3). It works with minuends greater than 10. For example, consider the problem $16 - 7$. Have the children draw a curve (hill) and underneath place the minuend (16) near the top, the subtrahend (7) near the bottom and the number 10 between them. The children should determine how many steps (count on) from the subtrahend to 10, write that

FIGURE 8-2

Sun	Mon	Tue	Wed	Thur	Fri	Sat
			1	2	3	4
5	6	7	8	9	10	11

number above the hill as shown and then do the same using 10 and the minuend. Now add the two numbers above the curve to get the difference of 9.

Counting back   Counting back is a useful strategy for learning the subtraction facts. This involves counting backward from the minuend by the subtrahend amount. For example, to find the answer to $10 - 2$, a child would start at 10 and count backward two times, saying "nine, eight."

Counting backward is not as easy for children as counting forward. To use this strategy, children need to have experiences with counting backward outside of the context of subtraction. Counting backward on the hundreds chart, the calendar, orally, or by writing the numbers in order from some starting point, say, 18, would be helpful.

With this background, children can then apply the skill to subtraction. Show the child a set of objects and ask her or him to count backward to tell how many are left when, say, 2 are subtracted. Figure 8-4 presents a sample interaction. This strategy is useful when the subtrahend is small.

Another difficulty children encounter with the counting-back strategy is that they also have to count forward to keep track of the number of steps. This can become confusing. Baroody (1984) found that both the number line and a classroom clock, however, are effective aids to help children count backward in subtraction.

✳ ACTIVITY 8-2

COUNTING ON

MATERIALS:
two dice for each pair of students

PROCEDURE:
1. Work with a partner.
2. One person rolls two dice. Beginning with the larger number, count on by the number of dots on the other dice.
3. The other partner writes an addition sentence.
4. Change roles and play the game several more times.

FIGURE 8-3

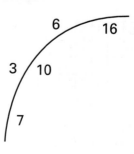

FIGURE 8-4

How many pencils?   (7)
I am going to subtract 2.
Count backward as I do it to tell how many are left.   (7, 6, 5)

ACTIVITY 8-3

COMPENSATION

MATERIALS:
counters

PROCEDURE:
With your counters, show these groups:

Change it into a problem with 10. Draw your new groups.

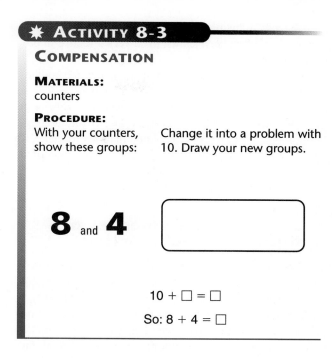

$$10 + \square = \square$$
$$\text{So: } 8 + 4 = \square$$

One more or one less than a known fact

Recognizing an unknown fact to be one more or one less than a known fact is helpful, especially with the harder facts. For example, if a child knows a "doubles fact" such as $4 + 4 = 8$, they can use this knowledge to find the sum $5 + 4$. That is, a child might think "4 plus 4 is 8, and 5 plus 4 is one more, which is 9."

Similarly, if children know that $4 + 4 = 8$, then they can use this strategy to reason that $4 + 3$ must be one *less* than 8, or 7.

The one-more or one-less strategy can be demonstrated through activities such as the following:

Show two groups of 6 objects.

Ask, "How much is 6 plus 6?"

Add one more to one of the groups.

"Now there are 6 plus 7. How many altogether?"

If necessary, say "One more than 12."

Verify that there are 13 objects.

"6 + 6 is 12, so 6 + 7 is one more, or 13."

Compensation The Compensation strategy involves increasing one addend while decreasing the other by the same amount. This can be used for any combination but is especially useful where the sum is greater than 10. For example, $8 + 5$ has the same sum as $10 + 3$. Children can imagine taking 2 away from the 5 (which becomes 3) and giving it to the 8 (which becomes 10) so $8 + 5$ is the same as $10 + 3$, which is 13. These two changes compensate for each other.

The compensation strategy is most useful when it is used with 10, since it is very easy to add a number to 10. Most young children will be able to relate to this because of their experiences with numeration activities. They have already learned, for example, that 17 is one group of 10 and 7 and, conversely, a group of 10 and 7 is 17. In small groups, have the children work on exercises such as the one in Activity 8-3. Encourage the children to talk about the process (that is, what they do in this activity). Later, pencil-and-paper exercises such as the one shown in Activity 8-4 can help children focus on the compensation strategy.

Another type of activity that helps children learn the basic facts involves making all possible combinations of a sum. Using chips with a different color on each side, children take a given number of chips (18 or fewer), shake them, spill them out, and record the two addends determined by the colors showing.

Using thinking strategies to organize instruction Instruction on mastering the basic facts often is organized around the size of the number combinations. Instruction frequently begins with facts with sums up to five (e.g., $1 + 2 = 3$; $2 + 3 = 5$). But research has shown that the size of the numbers is not the only issue to be considered in planning instruction (Baroody, 1984;

ACTIVITY 8-4

WHICH IS EASIER?

PROCEDURE:
Draw a ring around the easier problem in each pair.

$10 + 5 = \square$	$9 + 5 = \square$	$9 + 8 = \square$
$9 + 6 = \square$	$10 + 4 = \square$	$10 + 7 = \square$

Moser, 1992). Instruction that is organized around thinking strategies has been shown to be very effective in promoting mastery of basic facts.

For example, doubles facts and their corresponding subtraction facts, such as $6 + 6 = 12$ and $12 - 6 = 6$, are the easiest to learn, as are the facts with zero (e.g., $6 + 0 = 6$ and $8 - 0 = 8$) and the facts with one (e.g., $6 + 1 = 7$ and $8 - 1 = 7$). Combinations to make 10 (e.g., $3 + 7 = 10$ and $10 - 3 = 7$) and "one more than doubles" facts (e.g., $6 + 7 = 13$ and $13 - 7 = 6$) also are among the easier facts for children to learn.

Mathematical Properties of Addition and Subtraction

Understanding the commutative and associative properties of whole numbers and the identity elements for addition (0) and multiplication (1) contributes significantly to a child's understanding of the operations and his or her ability to master the basic facts. The distributive property will be discussed in the multiplication section of this chapter. An understanding of these properties usually is developed as children model problems. Memorizing the actual words or names of the properties is not critical; what is important is that the child recognizes the properties and is able to use them when working with the operations.

Commutative property   Mathematically, the commutative property states that for all numbers a and b in the system of whole numbers, $a + b = b + a$ and $a \times b = b \times a$. The child might say, "I know that 7 and 8 is 15 so 8 plus 7 must be 15," or "Since 3 times 7 is 21, 7 times 3 must be 21," or more generally, "I can add or multiply the numbers in any order."

Understanding the commutative property reduces the cognitive stress involved in learning the basic facts. Some argue that applying the commutative property reduces the number of facts to be learned from 100 to 55 for each of addition and multiplication. This is true in theory, but a child who learns $3 + 4$ still will model $4 + 3$. It is only after working through a number of problems that the child will recognize that both sums are the same, and will thus construct an understanding of the commutative property.

There are many activities for helping children build an understanding of the commutative property. One strategy that works well is to clip clothespins on a hanger and arrange the clothespins in two distinct sets (Figure 8-5). Ask children to write the mathematics sentence ($3 + 5 = 8$) for the set. Now rotate the hanger 180° horizontally. Ask the children to write the sentence for the set ($5 + 3 = 8$). After several examples of this type, ask the children if they notice anything common in all the examples. Guide them to articulate the commutative property for addition of whole numbers.

FIGURE 8-5

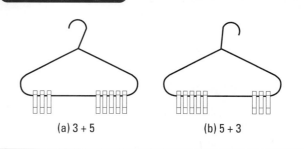

(a) 3 + 5   (b) 5 + 3

When learning a concept, children should also encounter non-examples of the concept. Non-mathematical examples of commutativity and operations in which commutativity does not hold true should be discussed. Activity 8-5 suggests one approach to doing this.

Through activities, children should come to understand that the commutative property does not hold for either subtraction or division. That is, $6 - 2$ is not equal to $2 - 6$, nor is $24 \div 6$ equal to $6 \div 24$.

A clear understanding of where the commutative property can be applied may help reduce the tendency of some children always to subtract the smaller number from the larger and to make other common computational errors.

Associative property   Since both addition and multiplication are binary operations, only two numbers can be joined at a time. The associative property enables one to join more than two sets in sequence.

Mathematically, the associative property states that for all numbers a, b, and c in the system of whole numbers, $(a + b) + c = a + (b + c)$ and $(a \times b) \times c = a \times (b \times c)$. Children's language might include a statement such as, "When adding or multiplying three or more numbers, I can group them any way I like." Children may

✳ ACTIVITY 8-5

COMMUTATIVE AND NON-COMMUTATIVE EXAMPLES

PROCEDURE:
1. Discuss the truthfulness of these statements. Is the result the same?

   • put on right shoe *followed by* left shoe = put on left shoe *followed by* right shoe
   • put on socks *followed by* shoes = put on shoes *followed by* socks

2. Write other examples of commutativity and non-commutativity.

combine the commutative and associative properties and simply say, "It doesn't matter in what order I add or multiply numbers."

The associative property is useful in allowing the combination of "easy numbers" first. Figure 8-6 illustrates two ways in which this can be done. The "doubles" basic facts are easier for many children than some of the other facts. "Near doubles" can be changed into doubles with the use of the associative property as shown in Figure 8-6(a). In Figure 8-6(b), the associative property is used to combine pairs of numbers that are easy to work with.

Identity element   Mathematically, the identity elements 0 (for addition) and 1 (for multiplication) are such that for any *a* in the system of whole numbers, $a + 0 = a$ and $1 \times a = a$. Children might use language such as, "zero added to any number gives you the same number" and "any number multiplied by one gives you the same number."

An understanding of the identity element helps children learn the nineteen addition facts involving zero. When children are solving addition problems, sometimes they will encounter a set of zero elements joined to a set with a non-zero number of objects. These experiences will help them build an understanding of the identity element for addition.

For example, consider the following problem:

Juan had 0 cookies and his mother give him 4 cookies. How many cookies does Juan have now?

This is a very simple situation that students can quickly solve. Teachers can use problems such as this to help students make the generalization that zero added to any number or any number added to zero results in that number. This is what the identity element for addition means.

FIGURE 8-6

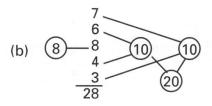

(a) $6 + 7 = 6 + (6 + 1)$
         $= (6 + 6) + 1$
         $= 12 + 1$
         $= 13$

(b)

FIGURE 8-7

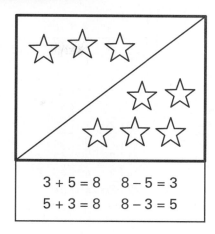

$3 + 5 = 8 \quad 8 - 5 = 3$
$5 + 3 = 8 \quad 8 - 3 = 5$

Fact Families for Addition and Subtraction

The relationship between addition and subtraction allows the basic facts to be organized into "families." Except for the "doubles" (e.g., $4 + 4$), each family consists of four related facts as illustrated for 3, 5, and 8 in Figure 8-7. Organizing facts into families helps children learn them. More particularly, when they know the addition facts, children can more easily remember the related subtraction facts. The ten family (or, in other words, sums that equal ten) is particularly important.

To help children learn fact families, construct a set of cards with a variety of pictorial models similar to the stars in Figure 8-7. In small groups, have the children draw a card, then discuss and write the family of related facts. This activity could easily be converted into a game format.

In programs incorporating the fact families organization, addition and subtraction are taught together. The addition facts for a family normally are learned first, then the subtraction. Children should work with addition facts from several families together, then focus on the corresponding subtraction facts.

MULTIPLICATION AND DIVISION FACTS

The multiplication facts can be summarized in a table format, as shown in Figure 8-8. For example, the basic fact $4 \times 6 = 24$ is found by first locating the two factors, 4 and 6. The product, 24, is found in the cell defined by the intersection of these two factors as shown by the arrows. The two related division facts, $24 \div 4 = 6$ and $24 \div 6 = 4$, also are shown in this figure, with the divisor and quotient (4 and 6) found on the outside of the table and the dividend (24) found in the cell that is the

FIGURE 8-8

X	0	1	2	3	4	5	6	7	8	9
0	0	0	0	0	0	0	0	0	0	0
1	0	1	2	3	4	5	6	7	8	9
2	0	2	4	6	8	10	12	14	16	18
3	0	3	6	9	12	15	18	21	24	27
4	0	4	8	12	16	20	24	28	32	36
5	0	5	10	15	20	25	30	35	40	45
6	0	6	12	18	24	30	36	42	48	54
7	0	7	14	21	28	35	42	49	56	63
8	0	8	16	24	32	40	48	56	64	72
9	0	9	18	27	36	45	54	63	72	81

FIGURE 8-9

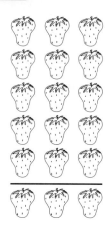

intersection of those two numbers. As in addition and subtraction, this table illustrates the interrelationship between multiplication and division.

Figure 8-8 is a summary table and is not intended for student use in its entirety—at least not until all the facts have been introduced. Children could be asked to complete such a table as they work at learning different facts.

Thinking Strategies for Multiplication and Division

Rathmell (1978) described several thinking strategies that children use when learning multiplication and division basic facts: repeated addition, skip counting, splitting the product into known parts, facts of five, and patterns.

Repeated addition   Using repeated addition, children might say three groups of five is "five plus five plus five." In this example, a child would "repeatedly add" 5 three times.

Skip counting   Skip counting involves counting by the second factor the number of times indicated by the first factor. For example, 3×5 could be found by skip counting in the following way: "5, 10, 15." This method builds on the meaning of multiplication, because counting by five three times corresponds with counting three groups of five. Children use counting by fives to generate the entire "fives" multiplication table.

Skip counting also can be done with a calculator. To skip count by five on most inexpensive nonscientific calculators the student would enter the following keystrokes: 5 + = = . . .

Splitting the product into known parts   This strategy actually includes two strategies: *one more set* and *twice as much as a known fact*. The one-more-set (or group) strategy is very useful, especially for learning the facts in sequence. Each fact in turn can be used to

help learn the next fact for either factor. Given the model in Figure 8-9, the child would verbalize along these lines: "I know that 5 threes is 15, and 1 more group of 3 is 18, so 6×3 must be 18."

To help children learn this strategy, show them 3 groups of 7 objects and ask them to tell (write) a number sentence for the display. Then show one more group of 7 and ask, "If 3 sevens is 21, what will one more group, or 4 sevens be?" This type of activity should take just a few minutes each day. It can be efficiently executed if the teacher prepares a series of folded cards similar to the one shown in Figure 8-10. Some of these cards also could be used for the next strategy (twice-as-much) as well, and a few may be used with the facts-of-five strategy.

Twice-as-much   When at least one of the factors is even, the product may be split into two equal parts. This is referred to as the twice-as-much strategy. The model in

FIGURE 8-10

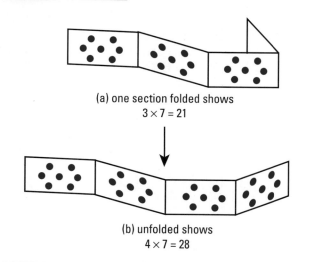

(a) one section folded shows
$3 \times 7 = 21$

(b) unfolded shows
$4 \times 7 = 28$

FIGURE 8-11

Figure 8-11 suggests a thought process such as "2 sixes is 12, 4 sixes is twice as much, that is, 24."

Show children arrays that already are split in half and ask them to write (or orally state) a number sentence for each half and then for the total. Also give the children arrays of 4, 6, and 8, and ask them to split each array in half and write number sentences for each part and the total.

Facts of five Another strategy, facts-of-five, is useful for the "larger" facts. One of the factors must be greater than 5, since this strategy involves breaking one of the factors into a group of 5 and another group. It is assumed that the children already know the facts with 5. Figure 8-12 illustrates this strategy with 7 × 6.

Using this strategy, a child would reason, "I know that 5 sixes is 30 and 2 sixes is 12, so 7 sixes must be 30 + 12, or 42." This strategy is easier to use when the non-partitioned factor is 6 or 8 because 5 × 6 and 5 × 8 are multiples of 10, an easy addend. Otherwise, the first product has a 5 in the ones position. If one of the factors is less than 6, the child would likely use another strategy.

Activities to teach the facts-of-five strategy could be similar to the ideas suggested for the twice-as-much strategy. This time, the children would break the array into a 5-by-*n* array and an *x*-by-*n* array, where *x* is the difference between the factor being partitioned and 5.

Pattern strategy A pattern strategy can be used for many of the facts, but it is most helpful and most often used with the facts involving 9. Expecting children to see patterns is one situation in which the multiplication table could be used prior to the introduction of all the facts. On the multiplication table, children can shade all the multiples for each fact set. For example, shade in all the multiples of 5. Children will observe that all the multiples of 5 end in either a 0 or a 5.

To help children look for patterns, give them several copies of the multiplication table and ask them to shade in multiples for different factors. Multiples of 3 and 9 are shaded in Figure 8-13. Referring to one set of multiples, direct the children to describe a pattern. Then ask them to find and describe another pattern in the table.

Exploring patterns on the multiplication table for the factor 9 shown in Figure 8-14, children will make all or some of the following observations:

> *The sum of the digits for each product, other than zero, always is 9.*
> *The tens digit increases sequentially from 1 to 8.*
> *Where there is a tens digit, it is always one less than the non-nine factor.*
> *Except for the zero fact, the units digits decrease by one from 9 to 1.*

FIGURE 8-12

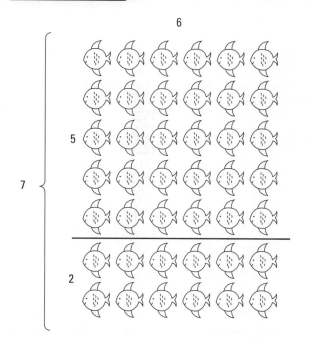

FIGURE 8-13

0	0	0	0	0	0	0	0	0	0
0	1	2	3	4	5	6	7	8	9
0	2	4	6	8	10	12	14	16	18
0	3	6	9	12	15	18	21	24	27
0	4	8	12	16	20	24	28	32	36
0	5	10	15	20	25	30	35	40	45
0	6	12	18	24	30	36	42	48	54
0	7	14	21	28	35	42	49	56	63
0	8	16	24	32	40	48	56	64	72
0	9	18	27	36	45	54	63	72	81

FIGURE 8-14

$$0 \times 9 = 0$$
$$1 \times 9 = 9$$
$$2 \times 9 = 18$$
$$3 \times 9 = 27$$
$$4 \times 9 = 36$$
$$5 \times 9 = 45$$
$$6 \times 9 = 54$$
$$7 \times 9 = 63$$
$$8 \times 9 = 72$$
$$9 \times 9 = 81$$

Another strategy for working with facts of 9 is illustrated in Activity 8-6.

Mathematical Properties of Multiplication

An understanding of mathematical properties contributes to operation sense. In the addition and subtraction section of this chapter, the commutative and associative properties and the identity element for both addition and multiplication were defined and illustrated for addition. This section will illustrate these concepts for multiplication and discuss the distributive property of multiplication over addition.

Commutative property The commutative property of multiplication can be exemplified by gluing or drawing an array of objects on a card. See Figure 8-15(a).

FIGURE 8-15

(a) 4×6

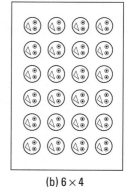

(b) 6×4

Ask the children to write the mathematics sentence for the array ($4 \times 6 = 24$). Now rotate the card 90° as in Figure 8-15(b). Have the children write a sentence for the new arrangement ($6 \times 4 = 24$). Repeat the procedure with several other cards. Ask the children to talk about the different situations, discussing how they are different and what is common to each. Rotating an array on a pegboard or a rectangular region marked off on a geoboard would provide additional illustrations of the same concept.

Associative property Children will find the associative property useful in situations that give rise to fairly large computations such as $26 \times 5 \times 2$. They will recognize that, if they combine 5 and 2 first, the problem becomes very easy compared to trying to do 26×5 first.

✳ ACTIVITY 8-6

FINGER MULTIPLICATION

PROCEDURE:

1. Hold both hands in front of you with the palms facing away from you.

2. To show 2×9, begin counting at the left. Bend the second finger. The finger to the left represents the tens and the fingers to the right of the bent finger represent the ones.

3. Use the finger method to show other multiplication facts of 9.

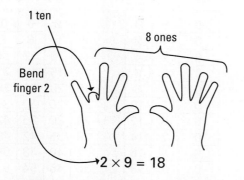

1 ten
Bend finger 2
8 ones
$2 \times 9 = 18$

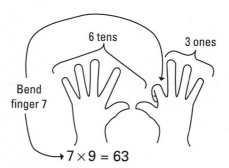

6 tens
3 ones
Bend finger 7
$7 \times 9 = 63$

A three-dimensional model may help children visualize the associative property. Consider the following, for example: $3 \times 2 \times 4 = n$. Will it make a difference if we multiply 3×2 first or 2×4 first?

Beginning first with 3×2, have the children use interlocking cubes to build a 3-by-2 array, which shows 3×2, and then build 3 more arrays to show 4 times (3×2) (using the commutative property). Have the children count the total number of cubes used. The product is 24 [see Figure 8-16(a)].

Next, have the children construct a 2×4 array and then 2 more to show 3 times (2×4). The product still is 24 [see Figure 8-16(b)]. Ask the children to compare the final models.

Distributive property of multiplication over addition Mathematically, the distributive law for multiplication states that for any a, b, and c in the system of whole numbers, $a \times (b + c) = (a \times b) + (a \times c)$ or $a(b + c) = ab + ac$. Also, $(a + b) \times c = (a \times c) + (b \times c)$ or $(a + b)c = ac + bc$. Children will use language such as "6 times 3 plus 2 is the same as 6 times 3 plus 6 times 2." Alternatively, they might say "3 plus 2 times 6 is the same as 3 times 6 plus 2 times 6."

Using the distributive property makes learning some of the more difficult basic facts easier. Consider the following, for example: 8×7 can be thought of as $8 \times (5 + 2)$. Note that 8×5 and 8×2 are easier facts. The products, 40 and 16, can now be added to obtain the product.

In another example, 6×9 can be thought of as $(5 + 1) \times 9$. Note that 5×9 and 1×9 are easier facts. The products, 45 and 9, can be added to obtain the product.

An array of counters is used in Activity 8-7 to help children construct a meaningful understanding of the distributive property. Note also the problem-solving component. Later, children can use this strategy to model the multiplication of a teen number. If the example was 4×13, children could discover among other groupings that $4 \times 13 = (4 \times 10) + (4 \times 3)$. In Chapter 7 this idea is incorporated into the vertical multiplication algorithm.

Identity element An understanding of the identity element helps children learn the nineteen multiplication facts with 1 as one of the factors. Problems that can be modeled by one set, one jump along the number line, a $1 \times n$ or $n \times 1$ array, or intersecting roads with only one road in one direction who help build the notion of one as the multiplication identity.

The role of zero in multiplication For any a in the system of whole numbers, $0 \times a = 0$, or $a \times 0 = 0$. Children will likely say "any number multiplied by zero is zero" and "zero multiplied by any number is zero." This is because zero groups of any number of objects is zero, as is any number of groups of zero objects.

Earlier the crossroads model was suggested as a good model to help children think about $0 \times n$ and $n \times 0$. It is easy for children to see that there are zero intersections when there are zero roads in one direction. Other models for multiplication can be used, but some element of deduction has to be included. For example, the array cannot be used to picture multiplication with zero, but children could be asked to find the pattern in the examples below and then deduce that $0 \times 3 = 0$.

4 rows of 3 is 12
3 rows of 3 is 9
2 rows of 3 is 6
1 row of 3 is 3
0 rows of 3 is 0

FIGURE 8-16

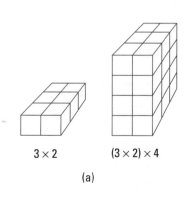

3×2 $(3 \times 2) \times 4$

(a)

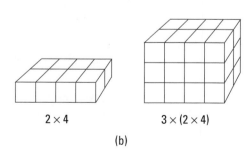

2×4 $3 \times (2 \times 4)$

(b)

✴ ACTIVITY 8-7

DISTRIBUTIVE PROPERTY FROM ARRAYS

MATERIALS:
counters

PROCEDURE:
1. Write a mathematics sentence for this array.

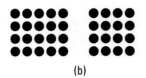

(b)

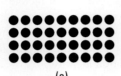

(a)

3. What do you notice about the sentence for array (a) and the two sentences for (b)?

4. Use counters and set out a 4-by-9 array. How many different ways can you separate it into two parts?

5. For each way, complete a sentence such as: $4 \times 9 = (4 \times \underline{\ \ }) + (4 \times \underline{\ \ })$.

2. Write two mathematics sentences, one for each array.

Real-life experiences involving multiplication by zero may seem a bit contrived. For example, "Walter put zero marbles in each of four bags. How many marbles did he use?" Ask the children to make up some of their own examples. Word problems involving multiplication of zero may seem a bit funny to children, but they will help children understand that zero sets of anything or any number of zero sets still is nothing.

A note on division by zero   Division by zero is one of the more confusing issues in mathematics for many adults. Making sense of this concept depends on linking it to concepts that learners already understand. Children can generalize the fact that division by 0 is undefined through observing patterns and relationships such as the following:

$3 \div 0 = n$ $3 = 0 \times n$ *(no number makes this true)*

$2 \div 0 = n$ $2 = 0 \times n$ *(no number makes this true)*

$0 \div 0 = n$ $0 = 0 \times n$ *(any number makes this true)*

$6 \div 2 = n$ $6 - 2 - 2 - 2 = 0$ *(remove three 2s to get 0)*

$6 \div 0 = n$ $6 - 0 - 0 - 0 \ldots$ *(never get to 0 by subtracting 0s)*

These generalizations may be visualized through some semi-contrived problems such as this measurement situation (Watson, 1991):

The ball park is 10 blocks from your home. If you walked 2 blocks each minute, how many minutes would

it take to get to the park? If you walked one block per minute, how long would it take? If you walked zero blocks each minute, how long would it take?

Fact Families for Multiplication and Division

As with addition and subtraction, the multiplication and division facts can be organized into number sentence families. Such organization facilitates learning of the facts. With the exceptions noted below, families have four members. The crossroads diagram (Figure 8-17) can be used to derive the four facts listed below the diagram.

For the "square" facts, there are only two members in the family. The family of facts relating 4, 4, and 16 consists of $4 \times 4 = 16$ and $16 \div 4 = 4$. Where one of the factors is 0, there are only 3 members in the family. For

FIGURE 8-17

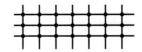

- $3 \times 7 = 21$
- $7 \times 3 = 21$
- $21 \div 7 = 3$
- $21 \div 3 = 7$

example, for 0, 3, 0, the family is comprised of $0 \times 3 = 0$, $3 \times 0 = 0$, and $0 \div 3 = 0$.

When a number sentence contains an unknown to be solved for, there are actually 24 forms the sentence could take for any fact family. This applies to the addition and subtraction families as well. For 3, 7, and 21, some forms including the following:

$$3 \times 7 = n \qquad 7 \times 3 = n$$
$$21 \div 3 = n \qquad 21 \div 7 = n$$
$$n \times 7 = 21 \qquad n \times 3 = 21$$
$$21 \div n = 7 \qquad 21 \div n = 3$$
$$21 = 3 \times n \qquad 21 = 7 \times n$$
$$7 = n \div 3 \qquad 3 = n \div 7$$

The remaining 12 forms are left for the reader to complete. Discussing bi-directional relationships of an equality sentence (sentences in lines 5 and 6 vs. lines 1, 2, 3, and 4 above) will help children build a better understanding of mathematics sentences, number relationships, and the operations.

Children need time and experiences in order to make the concept of fact families a part of their thinking. Activities similar to Activity 8-8 may facilitate the process. For the first part of the activity, the teacher may elect to construct arrays or groups on the overhead projector and have the students write sentences on paper.

✳ ACTIVITY 8-8

FACT FAMILIES

PROCEDURE:

1. For each picture write all the multiplication and division sentences that you can.

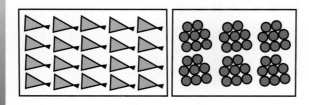

2. For each sentence, write 7 more related sentences (use the same numbers).

$$3 \times 6 = 18 \qquad 35 = 5 \times 7$$

3. Draw a picture to show each family in part 2.

CONSOLIDATING ACTIVITIES FOR DRILL AND PRACTICE

During the process of developing meanings for the operations and learning basic facts, take time periodically to provide consolidation activities. These are intended primarily to improve speed and accuracy, but they also can sharpen understanding and provide another means of assessment for the teacher.

> **STANDARDS LINK 8.5**
> Practice designed to improve speed and accuracy should be used, but only under the right condition; that is, practice with a cluster of facts should be used only after children have developed an efficient way to derive the answers to those facts. (NCTM, 1989, p. 47)

Effective consolidating activities have the following features:

- Activities are short and interesting.
- Activities are organized around sets of facts based on thinking strategies and fact families.
- Activities are self-checking.
- Activities include an approximately equal mix of facts children have and have not yet mastered.
- Each child should understand the goals to which he or she is working and understand his or her progress toward those goals. Each child should have an individual chart showing his or her own goals and progress. There *should not* be a class chart showing individual students' progress or lack thereof. Such charts cause great anxiety to many children, which *reduces,* rather than enhances, their progress.

Effective consolidation of concepts and facts can occur through a variety of brief activities at the beginning of class. Some examples include the following:

Write a set of single digit numbers on the chalkboard in random order. Beside them write a rule such as "add 4."
ADD 4:   3   6   4   9   2   7
Ask specific children to use the rule on each number. Listen for cases in which a child hesitates.

Prepare a set of cards with a single-digit number on each. Say, "Let's think about the number 15." Show a card and have children tell the other part of 15. For example, if you showed the card with 6 on it, children should respond with 9.

Write an expression such as 7 + 8 on the overhead projector. Have children give you the sum and then tell how they know. For example, a child might respond, "15, because I know 7 + 7 is 14, so 7 + 8 is one more." [This type of exercise enables the children (and teacher) to focus on strategies, reasoning, and patterns (Feinberg, 1990) rather than only on the answer.]

In Chapter 2, several categories of activities were suggested for consolidating or practice activities. A sample activity from some of the categories is outlined below to illustrate that these activities do not have to be boring or routine.

Games

Games are a motivational and fun way for children to both develop and maintain mastery of basic facts. To play a bingo-type game, children could be given a copy of the template from Figure 8-18 and asked to randomly fill in the cells with numbers. For addition and subtraction facts, they should use only the numbers 0 through 18. Five of these numbers can be repeated to complete the 24 cells. The teacher or student calls out basic addition and subtraction facts that can be generated from flash cards or randomly by a computer. Otherwise, the game is played similarly to bingo.

The same strategy works for multiplication except that the numbers on the cards should be randomly chosen from the set of possible products. There are 37 acceptable numbers to choose from. This time there need be no repeats.

Another popular game for practicing basic facts is the *24 Game* (Suntex International). The object of the game is to make 24 using all four numbers on a card by adding, subtracting, multiplying, or dividing. For example, one card contains the numbers 1, 5, 7, and 8. One possible solution for this card is the following number sentence: $(8 - 5) \times (1 + 7) = 24$. Several versions of the game are available as well that include addition and subtraction only, factors and multiples, fractions, and exponents.

The Annenberg/CPB Math and Science Collection

VIDEO LINK 8-1
Concepts of Whole Number Operations

Brief Summary: In "Domino Math," teacher Alma Wright's first- and second-grade students use dominoes to find various combinations of numbers equal to a given sum.

1. How could this lesson be modified to provide practice with basic facts?

2. What properties and thinking strategies did the students in this video use?

Video Source. Teaching Math: A Video Library, K–4; Tape 4 from The Annenberg/CPB Math and Science Collection.

Puzzles and Riddles

The sample riddle from Chapter 2—What fish do you see at night?—can be made into a practice exercise. Since the teacher knows the answer, starfish, she or he can assign numerical values to each of the letters in the answer, then make up a question that has that answer. Figure 8-19 is a

FIGURE 8-18

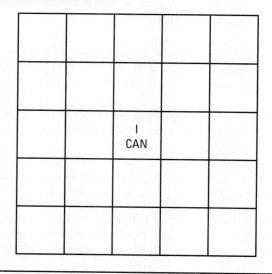

FIGURE 8-19

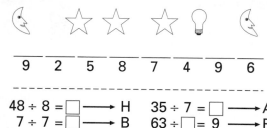

sample riddle sheet that could be given to children for consolidating division facts. Note that a few extra questions are inserted so that children will be less likely to try to simply rearrange the letters into a sensible word. Some children might prefer to create their own riddle practice activities.

Novel Formats

Using formats different from what children have seen is another way to provide interesting consolidation. Create an array of numbers. Figure 8-20 is one example. Ask the children to circle as many pairs as they can of adjacent numbers—which have a specified difference—in a column, row, or diagonal. Two differences of four, for example, have been circled in Figure 8-20.

Computer Software

Computer software needs to be carefully evaluated by the teacher to be sure it provides the kind of practice students need and that it does it in a pedagogically sound way. *Math Blaster* (Davidson and Associates) is a popular, fast-moving, arcade-type game that provides practice with the basic facts for all four operations. The teacher can control the level of difficulty and the teacher or students can generate their own problem sets. The objective is to launch a rocket corresponding to the correct answer to a problem that appears at the top of the screen. The game can be played at five speeds to encourage both accuracy and quick recall.

Millie's Math House (Edmark) has some interesting activities at the conceptual level that younger children would enjoy. Likewise, *KidsMath* (Great Wave Software) and *Treasure MathStorm* (The Learning Company) could be used with older children. Parts of these programs provide practice with basic facts in a game setting. Many other programs also contain good practice activities. See "Links to the Internet" for URLs of these programs and others.

FIGURE 8-20

12	15	11	16
8	4	3	7
9	7	13	10
3	5	9	6

CONCLUSION

This chapter described a three-step approach to mastery of basic facts. This approach includes understanding the meaning of the operations, using thinking strategies for fact retrieval, and using consolidating activities for drill and practice. It is critical that children memorize the basic facts, but that this memorization be based on an understanding of the operations and thinking strategies. Rushing memorization before this understanding is developed is a mistake that often comes back to haunt both students and teachers.

For Your Journal

When you have finished studying this chapter, reflect on these questions in your math journal:

1. Imagine that you are a fifth-grade teacher. You discover at the beginning of the school year that many of your students have not mastered the basic facts. What will you do? What materials will you use? What teaching strategies will you employ?

2. Imagine you are a classroom teacher. The parents of one of your students are concerned about your use of class time to teach teaching strategies, and instead would prefer their child to have much more practice with flash cards. How will you respond?

For Your Portfolio

When you have finished studying this chapter, complete these activities to include in your professional portfolio:

1. Design a non-bingo-type game that could be used to practice some of the basic facts.

2. Using (a) manipulative activities and/or (b) calculator explorations, write a lesson plan to help children understand the concept that division by zero is undefined.

3. Write a lesson plan to help children master one thinking strategy.

Resources for Teachers

Books on Basic Facts

Barson, A. (1992). *Mathematics Games for Fun and Practice*. Menlo Park, CA: Addison-Wesley.

Childs, L., & Choate, L. (1998). *Nimble with Numbers: Grades 3 and 4*. USA: Dale Seymour Publications.

Childs, L., & Choate, L. (1998). *Nimble with Numbers: Grades 4 and 5*. USA: Dale Seymour Publications.

Childs, L., & Choate, L. (1999). *Nimble with Numbers: Grades 5 and 6*. USA: Dale Seymour Publications.

Childs, L., Choate, L., & Jenkins, K. (1999). *Nimble with Numbers: Grades 1 and 2*. USA: Dale Seymour Publications.

Childs, L., Choate, L., & Wickett, M. (1998). *Nimble with Numbers: Grades 2 and 3*. USA: Dale Seymour Publications.

Childs, L., Hill, P., & Choate, L. (1999). *Nimble with Numbers: Grades 6 and 7*. USA: Dale Seymour Publications.

Links to the Internet

A+ Math

http://www.aplusmath.com/

Contains many different practice activities for operations, including games and electronic flash cards.

FunBrain

http://www.funbrain.com/kidscenter.html

Contains several games to practice operations.

Math Blaster

http://www.knowledgeadventure.com/blaster/

Math software to practice basic facts.

Millie's Math House

http://204.200.238.31/prod/house/millie/quotes.html (awards)

Math software to practice basic facts.

Math TreasureStorm (The Learning Company)

http://www.shoptlc.com/searchtlc.asp
http://www.softkey.com/

Math software to practice basic facts.

Estimation and Computational Procedures for Whole Numbers

Key Concepts

- Algorithms
- Mental computation
- Computational estimation
- Alternative algorithms

Focus Questions

When you have finished studying this chapter, you should be able to answer these questions:

1. How is mental computation different from computational estimation? Give an example of each.

2. How do algorithms differ for different operations? Give an example of two algorithms for each operation.

3. Why is it important to link mental computation and computational estimation with paper-and-pencil computation and the use of calculators?

The following shows a child's procedure for subtracting (Cochran, Barson, & Davis, 1970):

$$
\begin{array}{r}
64 \\
-28 \\
\hline
-\ 4 \\
40 \\
\hline
36
\end{array}
$$

A typical textbook might introduce addition with renaming ones as in the example on the following page.

What is *computation?* Computation is finding the *standard representation* for a number. For the child's computation above, 6^2, $46 - 10$, $108 \div 3$, and $30 + 6$ are a few representations for 36 or XXXVI. Only the latter (36 and XXXVI) are *standard representations.*

> **STANDARDS LINK 9-1**
> It is the intent of this standard that computation be viewed not as a goal in itself but as a multifaceted tool for knowing and doing. (NCTM, 1989, p. 97)

A common but somewhat narrow view of computation is that it is a sequence of steps for producing an answer in standard form. These step-by-step procedures are commonly referred to as *algorithms.* This chapter will develop the standard algorithms; but, first, three points need to be emphasized. There is no *one* correct algorithm. Just as we can alter our normal routine for getting ready for work in the morning, so variations in computational procedures can be made. Different computational algorithms are used in different parts of the world, even by different cultures within the same country. For this reason, and because of the mobile nature of our society, teachers should be familiar with some of the more common alternative algorithms.

258 skiers on one hill.
135 skiers on another hill.
How many skiers on both hills?

Add the ones	Add the tens	Add the hundreds
8 + 5 = 13	1 + 5 + 3 = 9	2 + 1 = 3

```
  1
2 5 8        2 5 8        2 5 8
1 3 5        1 3 5        1 3 5
    3          9 3        3 9 3
```

 STANDARDS LINK 9-2

In grades K–4, the mathematics curriculum should develop whole number computation so that students can

- model, explain, and develop reasonable proficiency with basic facts and algorithms;
- use a variety of mental computation and estimation techniques;
- use calculators in appropriate computational situations;
- select and use computation techniques appropriate to specific problems and determine whether the results are reasonable. (NCTM, 1989, p. 44)

 STANDARDS LINK 9-3

In grades 5–8, the mathematics curriculum should develop the concepts underlying computation and estimation in various contexts so that students can

- compute with whole numbers, fractions, decimals, integers, and rational numbers;
- develop, analyze, and explain procedures for computation and techniques for estimation;
- develop, analyze, and explain methods for solving proportions;
- select and use an appropriate method for computing from among mental arithmetic, paper-and-pencil, calculator, and computer methods;
- use computation, estimation, and proportions to solve problems;
- use estimation to check the reasonableness of results. (NCTM, 1989, p. 94)

Children should explore different algorithms for several reasons:

- Alternative algorithms may serve reinforcement, enrichment, and remedial objectives.
- Alternative algorithms provide variety in the mathematics class.
- Alternative algorithms may help children develop more flexible mathematical thinking and "number sense."

- Awareness of different algorithms demonstrates the fact that algorithms are inventions and can change. This needs to be communicated to students so that they will not develop a belief that there is only one way to perform a mathematical computation.

The second point for emphasis is that children can and should be allowed to create and use their own algorithms. The example at the beginning of this chapter is only one instance. Other interesting child-created computational procedures have been documented (Bidwell, 1991; Hamic, 1986; Harel & Behr, 1991; Madell, 1985).

Thirdly, computation is much broader than using just the standard paper-and-pencil algorithms. It also includes estimation, mental computation, and the use of a calculator. Many times all that is needed is an estimate. Strategies for estimating an answer to a computational problem can be quite different from the standard paper-and-pencil procedures. Sometimes an exact answer may be more efficiently calculated using mental procedures than with either a calculator or with paper-and-pencil. Estimation and mental computation often make better use of good number sense and place value concepts than are explicitly employed when using a paper-and-pencil algorithm. ○

COMPUTATIONAL ESTIMATION AND MENTAL ARITHMETIC

Estimation and mental computation play such a pervasive role in out-of-school settings that children must have a wide variety of experiences with the skills. Over 80 percent of out-of-school problem-solving situations involve mental computation and estimation (Reys & Reys, 1986). These processes are often used together, but involve quite different ideas (Atweh, 1982). Mental arithmetic involves computing an *exact answer* without the aid of paper-and-pencil, calculators, or any other device. Estimation has to do with the precision of an answer. Estimation may also employ mental computation but the end result is an approximate answer rather than an exact answer.

> **STANDARDS LINK 9-4**
> The frequent use of calculators, mental computation, and estimation helps children develop a more realistic view of computation and enables them to be more flexible in their selection of computing methods. (NCTM, 1989, p. 45)

Estimation and mental computation skills should be developed along with paper-and-pencil computation because they help children spot unreasonable results. They also contribute to an understanding of the paper-and-pencil procedures and provide a fertile source for computational creativity on the part of students.

Mental Computation

Mental computation has had an up-and-down history with respect to curricular emphasis. Around the turn of the twentieth century, mental computation was advocated as a form of mental discipline. As this theory fell into disfavor the emphasis on mental computation waned. The recent renewal of interest is based on the way in which mental computation can enhance an understanding of numeration, number properties, and operations as well as promote problem solving and flexible thinking (Reys, 1985, Reys & Reys, 1990).

Simple exercises such as those suggested for column addition (see Figure 9-4) could also be used to promote mental arithmetic. "What's My Rule?" (Activity 9-1) is an activity often found in elementary school textbooks. Using it occasionally as a teacher-led or small group activity will promote mental computation.

Strategies for mental computation
Addition and subtraction. A form of the *equal-additions* algorithm is sometimes used to subtract mentally. Given the problem, $725 - 294$, if 6 is added to each number the subtraction becomes easy; $731 - 300 = 431$. Instead of adding 10 as in the algorithm, any convenient number can be used. Children could be taught this strategy and then it could be reinforced occasionally with brief mental exercises.

✳ ACTIVITY 9-1

WHAT'S MY RULE?

PROCEDURE:
1. The leader determines a rule. Example: add 4.
2. The leader
   - asks for a number.
   - applies the rule.
   - announces the result.

   Example: Child says 7, leader responds 11.
3. Repeat Step 2 several times.
4. The leader asks if anyone knows the rule.
5. Others verify or refute the stated rule.
6. If incorrect, repeat steps 2 through 5 until someone discovers the rule.

Mental computation often is done by looking for *compatible numbers*. The examples below indicate two ways children might mentally add 16 + 11 + 24 + 35.

$$16 + 11 + 24 + 35$$
$$40 + 35 = 75$$
$$75 + 11 = 86$$

$$16 + 11 + 24 + 35$$
$$35 + 35 = 70$$
$$70 + 16 = 86$$

Using compatible numbers, older children can mentally compute answers to problems involving both addition and subtraction as shown here.

$$25 - 14 + 63 - 41 + 35$$

$$25 + 35 = 60$$
$$63 - 41 = 22$$
$$82$$

$$82 - 14 = (82 - 12) - 2$$
$$= 70 - 2$$
$$= 68$$

Note that in the last step in the previous example one number was *substituted* for another (14 = 12 − 2). The examples below illustrate this mental process for addition and subtraction.

$$97 + 48 = 97 + (3 + 45)$$
$$= 100 + 45$$
$$= 145$$

$$134 - 56 = 134 - (50 + 6)$$
$$134 - 50 = 84$$
$$84 - 6 = 78$$

Multiplication and division. Before children can become proficient with mental computation, they must master multiplication by powers of 10. That is, they need to be able to mentally compute exercises such as 6×10, 6×100, 6×1000, and 36×100.

Next, children should be able to use multiples of powers of 10. That is, they should be able to mentally compute exercises such as 6×30, 6×400, and 14×2000. In the last two examples, children could think: $6 \times 4 = 24$, so $6 \times 400 = 2400$; $14 \times 2 = 28$, so $14 \times 2000 = 28\,000$.

In front-end estimation, problems such as 50×70 were encountered. The ability to mentally compute exer-cises like this facilitates estimation. A good grasp of place value language will help children recognize that 50×70 is 35 hundreds because tens × tens is hundreds.

Upper elementary and middle school children working with larger numbers will encounter a small problem with computations such as 7000×30 or 21 ten thousands, which normally is thought of as $210\,000$. Children will need some experiences with this dual form in order to become proficient at mental computation. These experiences should be included in the development of computational procedures.

One of the most useful strategies for computing a multiplication exercise mentally is to employ the distributive property. For example, 5×76 can be computed as $(5 \times 70) + (5 \times 6)$. Note that it is best to multiply the tens first to get 350, then add the 30 ones to get 380. This is an illustration of the front-end approach with a second-level adjustment.

While we wouldn't expect elementary or middle school children to mentally compute 34×745 (most of us would have difficulty doing that), some children will, with experience, be able to mentally compute 30×740 by using the distributive property. Steps in their thought process might be:

- "3 tens times 7 hundreds is 21 thousands."
- "3 tens times 4 tens is 12 hundreds."
- "The product is $21\,000 + 1200$ or $22\,200$."

This is equivalent to multiplying 74 by 3 and annexing two zeros.

It is appropriate for children to write down the results but not the actual computations of intermediate steps such as those listed above when the numbers are large. We want to encourage children to compute mentally, not make it difficult.

A *halve-and-double* strategy is another way to facilitate mental computation. For example, 5×18 can be changed to 10×9 by doubling the one factor and halving the other. 10×9 is easy to compute while the product of 5 and 18 is not so obvious. On occasion this process can be repeatedly applied. For example, 25×80 can be changed to 50×40, then 100×20 which is easier.

A type of *substitution* is particularly useful in mental computation when one factor ends in 7, 8, or 9. For example, 6×48 can be thought of as $(6 \times 50) - (6 \times 2)$ or $300 - 12$.

Mental computation of division problems is probably best achieved by thinking of division as the inverse of multiplication. That is, using a basic fact example, $48 \div 6$, children can think, "What times 6 is 48?" This works particularly well when the dividend is a number such as $18\,000$ and the divisor is a single digit. For example,

18 000 ÷ 6 is 3000 because 6 × 3 is 18, so 6 × 3000 is 18 000.

Where the divisor is also a multiple of 10 there are two main approaches children could use to compute mentally. First, children are commonly taught to mentally divide each number by 10. In this case, 240 ÷ 40 becomes 24 ÷ 4, 2400 ÷ 40 is 240 ÷ 4, and so on. These examples are now equivalent to the examples in the preceding paragraph. The second way is to consider only the non-zero digits and then determine the place value of the quotient afterward. For 18 000 ÷ 60, think: "6 × what is 18? 6 × 3 = 18. The 3 must be hundreds because tens (60) × hundreds (300) is thousands (18 000). The quotient is 300." For the most part, computations more complex than these should be done by elementary and middle school children using paper-and-pencil algorithms or calculators, rather than mentally.

Other. Other methods such as the *counting-on* strategy illustrated in Figure 9-1 may be used. The important point is that if children are encouraged to mentally compute, they will develop their own strategies and, in the process, develop good number sense. Children should be asked, on occasion, to explain to the teacher or to the class how they did the computation.

Mental computation often is employed even when a calculator is being used. For example, when adding 350, 785, 256, and 150, individuals with good number sense will mentally combine 350 and 150 and enter 500 into the calculator before entering the other numbers (Sowder, 1990).

Special cases. These are many special situations in which mental computation can be employed. To use these effectively, children must learn the special characteristics and have sufficient experiences that they recognize the characteristics when they show up in a context different from that in which the procedure was demonstrated. For example, the products below can be very quickly written down in one line.

$$
\begin{array}{r} 58 \\ \times 52 \\ \hline 3016 \end{array}
\qquad
\begin{array}{r} 47 \\ \times 43 \\ \hline 2021 \end{array}
\qquad
\begin{array}{r} 36 \\ \times 34 \\ \hline 1224 \end{array}
$$

Did you identify the process and the characteristics that must be present? The process is to multiply the ones digits and record the result. Then multiply one of the tens digits by one more than the other. In the first example, 5 × 6 = 30. The conditions are that the tens digits must be the same and the ones digits must sum to 10. Junior high school students may be able to develop a proof of why this works. Mental computation like this tends to rely too much on rules and should be used as enrichment or as an occasional diversion to provide variety and interest.

Estimation

Researchers have begun to investigate a variety of factors related to computational estimation. Three general cognitive processes seem to be involved (Reys, Bestgen, Rybolt, & Wyatt, 1982; Reys et al., 1991). Reformulation involves altering the numbers to produce a more manageable problem. Rounding is the most obvious example of this process. Translation changes the structure of the problem to a more manageable form. An example would be grouping numbers that are close together and then multiplying by the number of numbers rather than adding to estimate the sum. Compensation adjusts the initial estimate to compensate for obvious errors due to reformulation or translation. If the initial estimate was obtained by rounding all numbers down, then an adjustment could be made to compensate for this in the final estimate.

Strategies for computational estimation
Reys (1986) describes five strategies for computational estimation; front-end, rounding, clustering, compatible numbers, and special numbers. Each of these can be used to some extent by children in the elementary grades, while older children can apply them with greater sophistication.

Front-end strategy. The *front-end* strategy is probably the easiest for younger children to use. This strategy can be introduced when children know some basic facts and the meaning of larger numbers. This strategy focuses

FIGURE 9-1

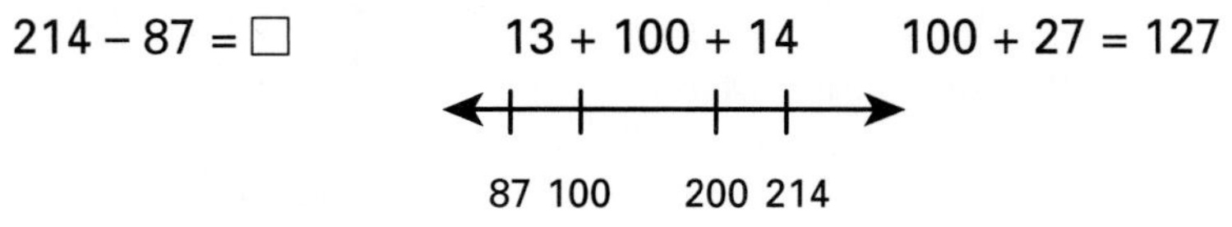

214 − 87 = ☐   13 + 100 + 14   100 + 27 = 127

87 100   200 214

on the left-most or highest place value digits. At the most rudimentary level, children would estimate the sum of 267 + 521 by adding the front-end digits, 2 and 5, estimating 700 for the sum. Later children will look at the remaining digits and adjust their estimate by thinking "67 and 21 is nearly one more hundred so I'll estimate 800."

Given a real-life setting that involved subtracting 254 from 725, younger children could estimate the result by subtracting the front-end digits (7 − 2), getting 500. Middle school children can make adjustments to get a closer estimate. They might reason that another 54 to be subtracted makes the answer closer to 450. Others with good number sense might also consider the additional 25 and decide that 475 is a closer estimate.

For elementary and middle school children, the front-end estimation strategy has one of its most relevant applications in money settings.

Brad wants to buy some school supplies. The items he has picked out cost $1.29, $3.59, and $1.99. About how much will Brad spend?

Since children naturally want to group the dollars first, the front-end strategy is a natural one to use in this setting. Some children will look only at the dollar amounts and estimate about $5. Others will adjust this step because they recognize that 99¢ is almost another dollar and $0.29 + $0.59 is also close to another dollar. They would estimate $5 + $1 + $1 or $7.

The front-end strategy for multiplication involves multiplying the left-most digit in each factor and using zeros in all other positions. A front-end estimate of the product of 6 and 43 would be 6 × 40 or 240. When both numbers have 2 or more digits the number of zeros in the estimate becomes more critical. Children need good place value understanding and good facility with the place value language to become good estimators. For example, the front-end estimate of 76 × 93 is 7 × 9 or 63, but 63 what? Since we are multiplying tens × tens, the result is hundreds, so the estimate will be 6300. Writing (or thinking) 70 × 90 will help children make the association between "hundreds" and the two zeros in the factors.

Children will soon recognize that the front-end approach with whole numbers always results in an estimate that is less than or equal to the actual product. This level of estimation is adequate for most purposes for most elementary school children. Older children will be able to add a second level front-end adjustment to their original estimate.

Since division is performed left-to-right, it is a front-end strategy in itself.

$$6\overline{)2874}$$

In the previous problem, children would first decide the place value column of the first digit in the quotient. This is a 4 and is in the hundreds column, so the first level front-end estimate is 400. Again this is a low estimate and children will develop strategies for adjusting this initial estimate.

Rounding strategy. *Rounding* is a skill that is often introduced in the third or fourth grades, usually in the context of numeration. Computing mentally or with paper-and-pencil with rounded numbers is another frequently used estimation strategy. In the first example above (267 + 521), children might round to the nearest hundred. Their estimate of the sum, then, would be 300 + 500 or 800. In the money problem, children could round to the nearest whole dollar. Their estimate would then be $1 + $4 + $2 or $7. Older children, recognizing whether rounding results in an overestimate or an underestimate, may make an adjustment similar to that used in the front-end approach.

Rounding can be concretized by using a number line; marking multiples of 10, 100, or multiples of whatever place value position one wants to round to; and having children note which of two adjacent multiples a given number is closest to. Bohan and Shawaker (1994) also suggest using stacks of chips for the same purpose.

Rounding also is useful in multiplication. On occasion, rounding actually becomes front-end estimation. For example, in 6 × 43, 43 is rounded to 40 which gives the same factors used with the front-end method.

A practice that often results in a reasonably close estimate is to round one factor up and the other down. For example, 37 × 76 = 2812. Rounding 76 down to 70 and 37 up to 40 produces an estimate of 2800; only 12 off the exact product. On the other hand, rounding to the nearest ten would produce an estimate of 40 × 80 or 3200, a discrepancy of 388.

Clustering strategy. The *clustering* strategy is used when a set of numbers are close to each other in value.

Juan surveyed each room in his school. He prepared this table for his group. About how many students are there in Juan's school?

Room 1	29	Room 5	28
Room 2	32	Room 6	29
Room 3	30	Room 7	31
Room 4	34	Room 8	27

With guidance children can observe that all the numbers are close to 30, so a good estimate would be 8 × 30 or 240. Children who have worked with the concept of "average" will recognize that 30 is an estimate of the average number of children in each room.

Compatible numbers. When using the *compatible numbers* strategy, children adjust the numbers so that they are easier to work with. The compatible numbers strategy is one of the best strategies to use in division. Using compatible numbers involves altering one or both of the divisor and dividend so that they are easy to work with mentally. 13 and 390, 11 and 330, 12 and 3600, and 120 and 3600 all are examples of compatible number pairs. Given a problem 3792 ÷ 14, a child might say: "3792 is close to 3600, 12 will divide evenly into 3600, so I'll estimate 300."

A form of the compatible numbers strategy can be used in addition when there are multiple addends as in the example below.

Six children kept a record of how many minutes of TV they watched on Monday. Altogether, about how many minutes did the children watch TV?

Heather	25	Trevor	60
Roberta	44	Gwen	57
Sam	35	Michael	80

Given the addition exercise above, children could use the compatible numbers strategy to look for groups of 100. They would estimate that together the children watched about 300 minutes of TV.

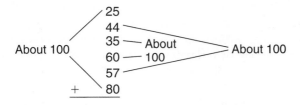

Special numbers. The *special numbers* strategy involves looking for numbers that are close to "special" values that are easy to work with. Clearly, this strategy overlaps with at least the rounding and compatible numbers strategies. Special numbers could be powers of 10. If working with fractions or decimals, special numbers might be $\frac{1}{2}$ or 1. Percentages such as 10 percent could also be considered a special number.

Monica was visiting another state. She discovered the sales tax was 9.4 percent. About how much would this add to the cost of a T-shirt that sold for $19.95?

✳ **ACTIVITY 9-2**

HOW MANY DIGITS?

PROCEDURE:
Tell how many digits are in the answer.

> 609 − 538
> 1215 − 347
> 13 325 − 4467

In solving this problem, children would reason that 9.4 percent is close to 10 percent, $19.95 is close to $20, and estimate 10 percent of $20 or about $2.

Estimation is especially important when calculators are used. A little slip of the finger on the keypad can result in major errors. With an estimate mind-set, children can detect such errors. For example, a child consulting a Christmas catalog to select presents for friends and siblings wants to know the total cost of what she or he has picked out. A child using front-end estimation would estimate $23 plus about $2 more, or about $25 for the amounts listed below. If the calculator display showed 114.4427 the child would immediately conclude that a mistake had been made in entering the data. What error might have been made to get 114.4427?

> $7.99
> 5.25
> 6.19
> <u>5.89</u>

Other activities such as those suggested by Activity 9-2 and Activity 9-3 could be structured to provide experience with estimation and mental computation.

In practice, estimation and mental computation should not be taught in isolation, but incorporated into the teaching of paper-and-pencil computation and other topics. For example, if children are solving the following

---

✳ **ACTIVITY 9-3**

DIFFERENCE OF 50

PROCEDURE:
1. In one minute, find as many pairs of numbers as you can from this list whose difference is 50.

32	9	97	36	62	37	76	58
	64		81		14		39
82	69	93	71	19		85	22
	86	25	121		24	47	

problem, the first question they might ask is, "*About* how many more students attend Rosa Parks School?"

> *There are 826 students enrolled at Rosa Parks Elementary School and 589 students enrolled at Kennedy Elementary School. How many more students are enrolled at Rosa Parks than at Kennedy?*

PAPER-AND-PENCIL COMPUTATION

How are U.S. students doing on paper-and-pencil computation? The sixth National Assessment of Educational Progress (NAEP) assessment noted fairly strong performance of fourth, eighth, and twelfth graders on whole number computation in symbolic and word problems (Kouba, Zawojewski, & Struchens, 1997). Students did best on one-step problems. For example, on a problem involving adding two three-digit numbers with regrouping, 88 percent of the fourth graders and 93 percent of the eighth- and twelfth-grade students were able to choose the correct sum. But only 53 percent of the fourth graders and 84 percent of the eighth graders were able to find the solution to $503 - 207$. Similar trends were noted for multiplication and division.

Results on the NAEP show difficulties with regrouping in subtraction, with interpreting the meaning of remainders in division, on multi-step multiplication and division problems, and in students' ability to justify and explain their work. This points to the need for a continued emphasis on teaching for meaning and on communication in the mathematics classroom.

An Instructional Philosophy

It is important for students to know how to compute with paper and pencil. However, once children can complete with understanding and reasonable skill exercises such as those shown below, nothing new is learned by working with larger numbers or by doing many exercises.

$$
\begin{array}{cccc}
327 & 3207 & 347 & \\
809 & -489 & \times 26 & 18\overline{)1096} \\
\underline{86} & & &
\end{array}
$$

Computational procedures will continue to be an essential component of the elementary school program, but the many hours children currently spend doing long, complex calculations are essentially wasted. Some of the time saved by not having children do tedious paper-and-pencil computation should be added to the time spent developing an understanding of the operations and computational procedures through concrete manipulations and simple

examples such as those above. Time also needs to be allocated for children to explain and write about the procedures they use.

The Annenberg/CPB Math and Science Collection

VIDEO LINK 9-1
Whole Number Computation

Brief Summary: In "This Small House," teacher Bobbie Bateson's second- and third-graders each have only $1.00 to spend to decorate homes they built out of milk cartons.

1. What different methods did students use to calculate the total amount of money they spent?
2. How could the teacher use this activity as an assessment tool?

Video Source. Teaching Math: A Video Library, K–4; Tape 7 from The Annenberg/CPB Math and Science Collection.

A decreased emphasis on paper-and-pencil computation is supported by most mathematics educators. For example, the *Curriculum Standards* (NCTM, 1989) for Grades K–4 state:

> The purpose of computation is to solve problems. Thus, although computation is important in mathematics and in daily life, our technological age requires us to rethink how computation is done today. Almost all complex computation today is done by calculators and computers. In many daily situations, answers are computed mentally or estimates are sufficient, and paper-and-pencil algorithms are useful when the computation is reasonably straightforward. . . . Clearly, paper-and-pencil computation cannot continue to dominate the curriculum or there will be insufficient time for children to learn other, more important mathematics they need now and in the future (p. 44).

The Grades 5 to 8 section of the *Curriculum Standards* contains a similar statement on page 94.

Usiskin (1998) lists several reasons for having algorithms as well as the dangers inherent in all algorithms. Reasons for having algorithms include (1) power, (2) reliability, (3) accuracy, and (4) speed. Dangers include (1) blind acceptance of results, (2) overzealous application of algorithms, (3) a belief that algorithms train the mind, (4) helplessness if the technology for the algorithm is not available. Usiskin notes that paper-and-pencil algorithms and calculator or computer algorithms both require the user to have some equipment.

The instructional model developed in Chapter 7 emphasized connecting the real world and the world of mathematical symbols when learning computational procedures. That is, computation should emerge from the need to solve some problem.

If children have had adequate experiences with concrete and pictorial models when solving simple computational problems, they will understand the concept of the operations and can focus on meaningful procedures to find answers to problems with larger numbers. Our recommended approach is to allow students ample time and opportunity to develop computational procedures for themselves. Initially, problems should be solved with manipulatives. Students should then be encouraged to record *in their own way* the processes they used. Children's *verbal description* of the processes provides them with a connection between the concrete and symbolic procedures (Sawada, 1985; Stanic & McKillip, 1989). Students can then begin to translate their recording into a more symbolic form, but still in their own way. With time the symbolic recording can become more concise, eventually resulting (for most students) in the standard algorithm. As we emphasized earlier, this may be different in different countries or regions of a country.

Prerequisites

Before children can be expected to develop paper-and-pencil computational procedures, they should demonstrate a conceptual understanding of the operations by recognizing different contexts that require the operations to resolve a problem (NCTM, 1989).

Knowledge of *some* basic facts is required before children begin computation with larger numbers. Strategies for knowing the basic facts continue to be developed and practiced as students work at solving problems with larger numbers. Grade 2 students, for example, do not usually know all the basic facts for addition and subtraction but they can still solve some two-digit problems. The final objective, however, for learning paper-and-pencil procedures is to be able to use them efficiently without the use of models. Achievement of this objective does require a mastery of the basic facts.

Children need to have a good understanding of the place value numeration system, as each algorithm is based on principles of the numeration system. In particular, children need to be able to group ones into tens, tens into hundreds, and so on; and they need to be able to break hundreds into tens, tens into ones, and so on.

An understanding of some mathematical properties of whole numbers learned during the concepts and basic facts stages of instruction can help children with computational procedures. In particular, the *commutative law*

FIGURE 9-2

$$
\begin{array}{cc}
40 & 27 \\
\times\,27 & \times\,40 \\
\hline
\text{(a)} & \text{(b)}
\end{array}
$$

and the *distributive property* of multiplication over addition can facilitate computation. For example, the exercise shown in Figure 9-2(a) would be easier to work out if the commutative law was applied as in Figure 9-2(b).

Understanding the distributive property also is prerequisite to efficient algorithm development. An exercise such as 8×37 can be reorganized mentally, or on paper, to $(8 \times 30) + (8 \times 7)$ or $8(30 + 7)$. The extension fact, 8×30, is relatively easy to determine mentally and 8×7 is a known basic fact. The product, then, is the sum of 240 and 56. Notice that expanded notation is included in the use of the distributive property ($37 = 30 + 7$).

Estimation may also be considered a prerequisite. What is prerequisite is an *attitude* of estimation. Children should approach computation with an attitude that estimation is a legitimate mathematical tool.

Other Considerations

Before developing computational procedures there are several related topics that should be considered.

Extension facts Normally students encounter *extension facts* early. These are basic facts in a place value position other than the units position. The thinking runs like this:

- Children know 2 and 5

$$
\begin{array}{cc}
+4 & -2 \\
\hline
6 & 3
\end{array}
$$

  so it is an easy extension to 20 and 50

$$
\begin{array}{cc}
+40 & -20 \\
\hline
60 & 30
\end{array}
$$

- Children know 8 so it is an easy extension to 80

$$
\begin{array}{cc}
\times 6 & \times 6 \\
\hline
48 & 480
\end{array}
$$

- Children know 7 so it is an easy extension to 70

$$
\begin{array}{cc}
+4 & +40 \\
\hline
11 & 110
\end{array}
$$

Computations such as $32 + 5$ and $26 - 4$ usually are also considered extension facts. Since children know

2 and 6 it is an easy extension to 32 and 26

$$
\begin{array}{cccc}
+5 & -4 & +5 & -4 \\
\hline
7 & 2 & 37 & 22
\end{array}
$$

Extension facts should be introduced through some real-life setting such as the one that follows. Children can model this setting as they did the basic facts by setting out a set of three and a set of four longs (tens), joining them and saying, "I have seven tens which is 70."

On the last grade-two field trip there were 30 people on one bus and 40 people on the other bus. How many people went on the field trip?

Extension facts such as 80 + 60 involve an additional grouping step. Children can talk about this as 6 *tens* joined to 8 *tens,* which makes 14 *tens.* From their numeration experiences, they will recognize this as 140.

Money is a very good model (Figure 9-3) for working with extension facts. Most children have had experience adding and subtracting money. They know, for instance, that two dimes and four dimes is 60¢.

Almost all children find the extension facts rather easy if they know the basic facts. If they know the basic facts they can generally mentally compute with the extension facts.

Higher-decade addition *Higher-decade addition* occurs when the sum goes beyond 19 as in combinations such as 17 + 6. The relationship between basic facts, extension facts, and higher-decade addition is shown by the example below. Note that in this example, the extension facts also are higher-decade.

7		
8	7 + 8 = 15	*basic fact*
6	15 + 6 = 21	*higher-decade*
5	21 + 5 = 26	*extension fact*
9	26 + 9 = 35	*higher-decade*
+ 3	35 + 3 = 38	*extension fact*

Children should have sufficient experience with higher-decade addition so that it becomes somewhat au-

tomatic. In addition to adding a set of multidigit numbers, adding a tax to the cost of an item (77¢ + 5¢) is an example of a setting in which higher-decade addition occurs. This is another example of the usefulness of mental computation in daily life.

Column addition *Column addition* refers to the addition of more than two addends can involve basic facts, extension facts, and higher-decade addition. It can be challenging for some students because of the demand on memory. That is, a partial sum must be kept in mind to be added to another addend as illustrated here.

A problem such as the following may provide the motivation younger children need to think about and practice adding a column of digits.

$$
\begin{array}{l}
4 \\
2 \\
+7
\end{array}
\quad
\begin{array}{l}
\text{Child adds } 4 + 2 \\
\text{to get } 6
\end{array}
$$

7 must then be added to 6 (unseen) to get 13

Shelly sorted her marbles by color. She had four red marbles, two green marbles, and seven yellow marbles. How many marbles did Shelly have?

Colored counters could be used to model this situation. Simple exercises such as those in Figure 9-4 could also be used to provide additional experiences in column addition. Children who have difficulty retaining the unseen sum in their memory could be encouraged to record it on paper until they feel comfortable with the process.

Most real-life settings in which column addition is required involve multidigit numbers. Older children could be asked to solve some of these to see if they can be "as accurate as a calculator" or to show what they would do if there was no calculator available and an exact sum was required. In cases in which only an estimate is required,

FIGURE 9-3

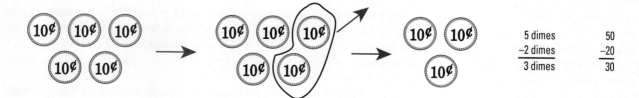

5 dimes	50
−2 dimes	−20
3 dimes	30

FIGURE 9-4

6 7 2 / 1 5 9 / 8 3 4	Find the sum of each row, column, and diagonal. What did you notice?
(triangle of circles)	Place the digits 1, 2, 3, 4, 5, and 6 in the circles so that the sums along the 3 sides of the triangle are the same. What was your sum? Can you place the digits a different way? What is the sum? There are four different sums. Can you find all 4?
(four dice)	Roll 4 dice. What is the sum? Do this 20 times. What was your smallest sum? largest? How many different sums did you get? How many times did you get each sum? Make a graph of this information.

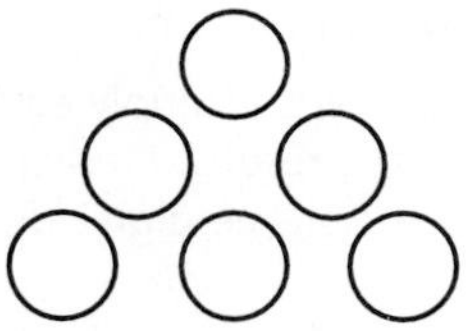

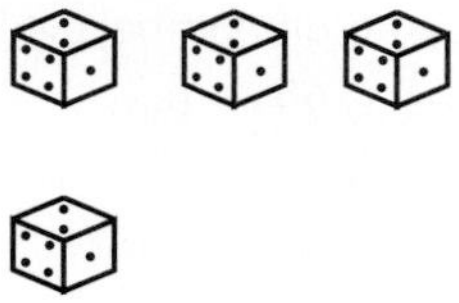

children could put their ability to add multiple single-digit numbers to use by using front-end addition or rounded numbers as shown below.

325	325	300
283	283	300
+738	+738	+700
	3 + 2 + 7 or	3 + 3 + 7 or
	about 1200	about 1300
	using	using numbers
	front-end	rounded to
	estimation	nearest hundred

Types of models Computational procedures can be developed with base-ten blocks. These materials and others such as beansticks and counters are *proportional*. A proportional model maintains the proportion between place value positions. The first work with computation should be with proportional materials such as the base-ten blocks.

Non-proportional materials should be used only when children can easily solve problems with proportional materials. If a child can transfer the execution of a computation from proportional to non-proportional materials, she or he likely has good understanding of the process. Once children have explored both types of materials they will freely move back and forth from proportional to non-proportional materials. The reader is referred to Chapter 6 in which proportional and non-proportional materials were discussed in greater detail.

Language As indicated in Chapter 7, children should continue to use their own language to describe computational processes. Terms such as "joined to" are meaningful to children. For regrouping and renaming, children will want to use other terms: "trade," "group," "break apart," "break a ten," and "make a group."

During work with computation the teacher should use mathematical language associated with each operation so that children will develop more technical language. For example, in the case of subtraction, children should be able to use the terms "subtract," "subtraction," and "difference" meaningfully in a sentence.

In the case of multiplication and division computation, there are a greater number of terms that students *may* eventually learn. In a problem requiring the computation, $27 \times 42 = n$, the *multiplicand* (42) is the number in each group and the *multiplier* (27) is the number of groups. These are often referred to simply as *factors*. When first learning a paper-and-pencil algorithm, children sometimes are encouraged to record all the *partial products* before adding to obtain the *product*. See Figure 9-5.

In a division setting, the total number to be "divided up" (shared) is the *dividend,* the number in each group is the *divisor,* and the resulting number of groups is the *quotient.* (Some problems require the divisor and quotient to exchange meanings.) The number of objects, if any, that cannot be shared equally are referred to as the *remainder.* Children often call these the "leftovers." Some paper-and-pencil algorithms make use of *partial quotients* enroute to obtaining the quotient as shown in Figure 9-6.

FIGURE 9-5

$$27 \times 42 = \square$$

$$
\begin{array}{r}
42 \quad \leftarrow \text{Multiplicand} \\
\times\ 27 \quad \leftarrow \text{Multiplier} \\
\hline
14 \\
280 \\
40 \\
800 \\
\hline
1134 \quad \leftarrow \text{Product}
\end{array}
$$

$\left.\begin{array}{r}14\\280\\40\\800\end{array}\right\} \leftarrow$ Partial products

In normal classroom interaction, the terms *multiplicand, multiplier, partial products,* and *partial quotients,* are not used extensively. Children should be allowed to use informal language for some time rather than be expected to memorize "proper" terminology.

Role of the calculator Checking computation can be done on the calculator. This, however, is a *poor* use of time and of the calculator. The calculator can be used in a more substantive way to help children think about the algorithms, develop estimation skills, and solve computational problems. Activity 9-4 involves finding patterns related to multiplication. Activity 9-5 could be used to help children think about the multiplication and division algorithms, and Activity 9-6 suggests one way the calculator could be used to enhance estimation skills.

Addition

In the past it was common to introduce the addition algorithm with computation that did not require children to regroup. If one begins with realistic problems, some will require renaming, others will not. If children have been doing computation in which no regrouping is involved and then encounter a problem when regrouping is needed (or vice versa), they will notice the difference, grapple with it, and resolve it with proper guidance from the teacher.

Developing the algorithms should take place in three stages: nonstructured concrete manipulations, recording the concrete manipulations, and symbolic representation.

FIGURE 9-6

$$
\begin{array}{r}
42 \quad \leftarrow \text{Quotient} \\
2 \\
40 \\
27\overline{)1138} \quad \leftarrow \text{Dividend} \\
1080 \\
\hline
58 \\
54 \\
\hline
4 \quad \leftarrow \text{Remainder}
\end{array}
$$

Divisor $\diagdown$

$\left.\begin{array}{r}2\\40\end{array}\right) \leftarrow$ Partial quotients

✳ ACTIVITY 9-4

PATTERNS

MATERIALS:
a calculator

PROCEDURE:
1. Choose some two-digit numbers. Use your calculator to multiply each by 99. Record and compare the results. When you think you see a pattern or a relationship use it to predict some other results. Write a statement describing your pattern.

2. Choose only 2 three-digit numbers. Multiply each by 999. Record and examine the results. Predict the results of multiplying 2 other three-digit numbers by 999.

   Write statements that tell how this pattern is

   • the same as the one for two-digit numbers × 99.

   • different from the two-digit × 99 pattern.

Unstructured concrete manipulations Pose a problem such as the following:

On the last grade-three field trip there were 28 children on one bus and 34 children on the other bus. How many children went on the field trip?

If necessary, suggest that students use the base-ten blocks. They will likely first group the tens as shown in Figure 9-7, then combine the ones. Finally they will trade 10 ones for 1 ten to get 6 tens and 2 ones. That is,

FIGURE 9-7

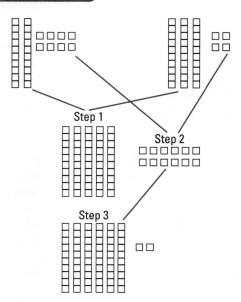

Step 1

Step 2

Step 3

✸ ACTIVITY 9-5

MISSING NUMBERS

MATERIALS:
a calculator

PROCEDURE:

1. Estimate first, then use your calculator to help you find the missing numbers.

$$6\overline{)\square\square\square}^{\;65\ R2} \qquad 7\overline{)2\square3}^{\;\square\square} \qquad \square\square\overline{)3819}^{\;109\ R4}$$

2. Use only 5, 7, 8, and 9 to make

   • the largest possible product

$$\begin{array}{r} \square\square\square \\ \times\ \square \\ \hline \end{array}$$

   • the smallest possible product

$$\begin{array}{r} \square\square\square \\ \times\ \square \\ \hline \end{array}$$

3. Find the missing numbers. All 4 partial products are shown.

$$\begin{array}{r} \square 5 \\ \times\ 3\square \\ \hline \square\square \\ 100 \\ 1\square 0 \\ \square\square\square\square \\ \hline \square\square\square\square \end{array}$$

✸ ACTIVITY 9-6

ESTIMATION

MATERIALS:
calculator

PROCEDURE:
Play with a partner. Each player needs a calculator.

1. Agree on a target number. Circle it.

76		1111		410		309
	107		2345		731	
		96		296		

2. Enter any number into your calculator.

3. Press the X key.

4. Within 5 seconds enter another number that you think will give you a product close to the target number. Then press the = key.

   Example: Target = 107
   Entered: 38 ×
   then   3 =
   Display shows 114

5. The person closest to the target number wins the round.

6. Play 10 rounds.

Repeat the procedure using the ÷ key.

---

children naturally want to group the larger pieces first (Lee, 1991). This left-to-right process is discussed later in this chapter.

Using the blocks (no recording), children can easily extend this process to include numbers in the hundreds provided they have had relevant numeration experiences. In fact, children gain satisfaction from working with larger numbers. They should not do this just for the sake of working with larger numbers but because of a need to solve some relevant real-life problem. This is a good setting in which to encourage estimation. Children could use their previous experience with extension facts and say, "There are at least 20 plus 30 or 50 students on the field trip."

A transition to the recording phase could be made by giving children an adaptation of the organizational mat described in Chapter 6 (Figure 9-8) on which they could do their manipulations. Children may need some initial guidance in how to use each space. The second column in Figure 9-9 illustrates how this mat might be used for the

field trip problem. At this stage children would do only the steps illustrated in the second column.

Place value language. Encourage children to use place value language as they describe their manipulations. For example, "two tens and three tens make five

▇ FIGURE 9-8

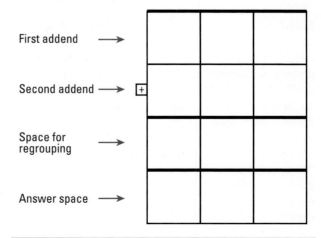

First addend ⟶

Second addend ⟶ +

Space for regrouping ⟶

Answer space ⟶

tens" and "eight ones plus four ones is twelve ones." This will help them to focus on the value of the digits and prepare them for multiplication and division computation in which the use of place value language is more critical.

Recording Once children feel confident using the base-ten blocks to add two numbers, the next step is to begin keeping a record of what was done. This recording will go through a series of refinements and culminate in a concise and efficient symbolic procedure.

Children might begin by using two mats, one for doing the manipulations with the blocks and one for recording. To avoid skipping steps in the recording, children could work in pairs: one recording, the other manipulating. Figure 9-9 illustrates each step in the process and the corresponding record. Note that the series is based on the assumption that children naturally work from left to right (Lee, 1991).

Some educators object to placing *"12"* in the ones column (third row in Figure 9-9). We did it this way because it most accurately reflects *what was done* in the concrete mode—after joining and before regrouping the child does have 12 units. When refinements begin to be made to the recording this step will be eliminated.

Others recommend that once recording begins children should be told to work right-to-left. This adds an additional component to an already big and important step. Allow children to be as natural as possible and match paper-and-pencil work as closely as possible to the steps used in the concrete mode. Working right-to-left may not alter the notation used in the last row of Figure 9-9, only some of the intermediate steps. Furthermore, other activities such as working with money where people almost always group the largest denomination first and proceed to the smallest denomination (Lee, 1991) reinforces left-to-right procedures. In fact, the only reason to add right-to-left is when several multi-digit numbers need to be added. Even here the left-to-right procedure works well but the recording can become a little "messy." But remember, these computations should be done on a calculator.

Symbolic representation Children will begin to develop refinements (shortcuts) to the recording process once they feel comfortable with the basic computational process. To facilitate this, a teacher might make available smaller versions of the organizational mat. Children might initially be shown one on which the words "Hundreds," "Tens," and "Ones" have been printed. Later versions might have just "H," "T," and "O" as headers.

Another early refinement children will make is to "clean up" the notation in the ones column. They will begin to mentally trade the 10 ones for 1 ten before they record the sum. For this step, a child's work might be similar to that shown here.

Later, children may want to remove the regrouping space and record the trade number as shown here. Conventionally the trades are recorded above the first addend. This is not necessary but would not be a difficult step for children to make at this point if a teacher wished to encourage (not require) it.

The place value headings will eventually be removed, producing a notation similar to the one below. Finally, all remaining lines can be dropped, resulting in standard notation. Once children have computed the answer, they often prefer to record it in horizontal fashion

FIGURE 9-9

Problem/Steps	Concrete Representation	Symbolic Representation
28 on first bus 34 on second bus How many?	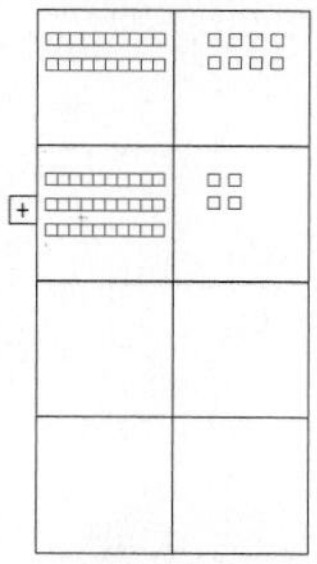	2 8 + 3 4
Join the tens	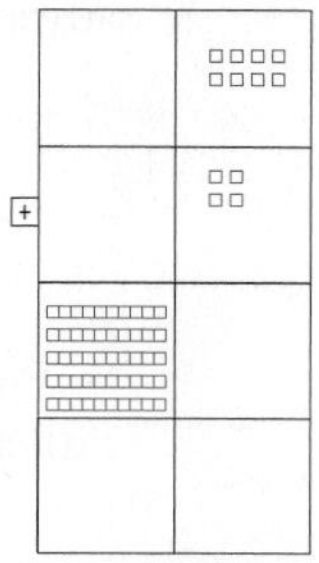	2 8 + 3 4 5
Combine the ones	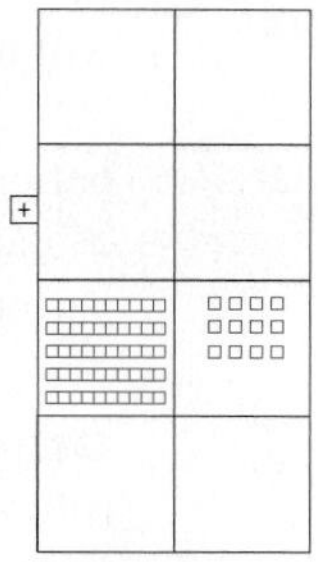	2 8 + 3 4 5 12
Trade ones for a ten	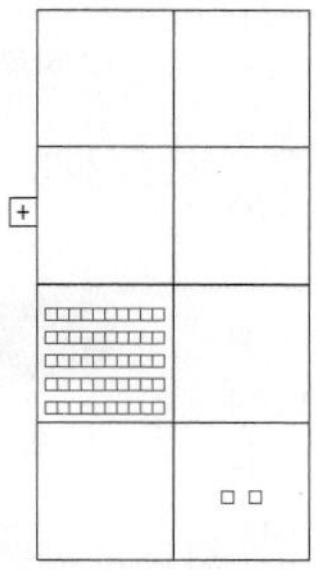	2 8 + 3 4 5¹ 1̶2̶ 2
Represent final answer	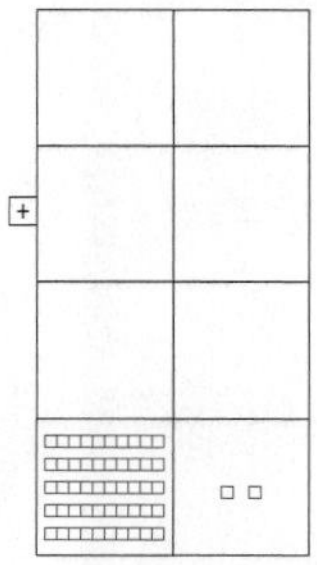	2 8 + 3 4 5¹ 1̶2̶ 6 2

$(28 + 34 = 62)$. This is appropriate for answering the problem that gave rise to the computation.

```
  1
2 | 8
3 | 4
─────
6 | 2
```

Many useful alternatives exist. For example, children might record the partial sums in the appropriate place value columns as shown below.

H	T	O
	2	8
	3	4
	1	2
	5	0
	6	2

This could lead to recording the partial sums in a more symbolic mode before moving to the shorter standard algorithm. See Figure 9-10.

Expanded notation is another type of transitional step. Children might compute the answer to the field trip problem like this:

$$\begin{array}{l} 2 \text{ tens and } 8 \text{ ones} \\ \underline{3 \text{ tens and } 4 \text{ ones}} \\ 5 \text{ tens and } 12 \text{ ones} \\ 6 \text{ tens and } 2 \text{ ones} \\ \qquad 62 \end{array}$$

Whatever approach is encouraged, it is important to remember that children will shorten the steps on their own. Some children need more transitional steps than others and some need to spend longer at some steps than other children. Allow them to discover their own shortcuts. Do not rush children into using the standard algorithm.

When children feel competent in working through computations with two-digit numbers, they should be invited to solve problems with larger numbers. The organizational mat could be extended to four columns (thousands through units).

It is the number and type of regroupings more than the magnitude of the numbers that the teacher needs to be cognizant of. The three problems below are cognitively all the same and could be worked on at the same time. In practice, however, we would not normally expect Grade 2 students to do the last two problems in spite of the fact that they have learned all they need to know in order to do them.

$$\begin{array}{r} 32 \\ + 47 \end{array} \qquad \begin{array}{r} 564 \\ + 231 \end{array} \qquad \begin{array}{r} 8704 \\ + 1263 \end{array}$$

Both of the following problems involve one regrouping. However, trading 10 tens for one hundred is a more advanced process than trading 10 ones for 1 ten.

$$\begin{array}{r} 26 \\ + 47 \end{array} \qquad \begin{array}{r} 146 \\ + 382 \end{array}$$

Problems with two and three regroupings are more difficult for children. Again, the importance of adequate preparation in the form of concrete numeration experiences and addition in a concrete mode must be stressed. Such experiences will minimize the difficulty children will have with multiple regroupings.

Activity 9-7 will stimulate discussion and provide experience with estimation, addition computation, and the calculator. Students should work in a group or with a partner.

Other addition algorithms   The use of algorithms other than the "familiar" ones was advocated earlier in this chapter. There are many algorithms for addition. Two, the left-to-right and low-stress algorithms, are described in the following sections.

FIGURE 9-10

$$\begin{array}{r} 28 \\ + 34 \\ \hline 12 \\ 50 \\ \hline 62 \end{array} \qquad \begin{array}{r} 367 \\ + 85 \\ \hline 12 \\ 140 \\ 300 \\ \hline 452 \end{array}$$

✹ ACTIVITY 9-7

CALCULATOR GAME (ADDITION)

MATERIALS:
calculator for each student

PROCEDURE:
1. One person writes four numbers on paper for all others to see.

2. Without the others seeing, add three of the numbers on your calculator.

3. Write the sum on paper for the others to see.

4. The others decide, by estimation, which one of the four numbers was not used and then check their guesses on their calculators.

5. Take turns doing the activity several more times.

Left-to-right. This algorithm was referred to earlier as the "natural" way for children to add when they use the base-ten blocks. That is, most children will first group the largest place value blocks, then the next highest, and end by grouping the unit blocks (Lee, 1991).

A paper-and-pencil algorithm is very easy to develop for the case in which children regroup, if necessary, each place value as they proceed from left to right. The steps in Figure 9-11 demonstrate this progression for $364 + 287 = 651$.

First add the 3 hundreds and the 2 hundreds and record the 5 in the hundreds column as shown. Now add the 6 tens and 8 tens. Fourteen tens is one hundred and 4 tens so cross out the 5 hundreds and make it 6 hundreds $(5 + 1)$ and record the 4 tens in the tens column. Last, add the units. The 11 units can be regrouped as 1 ten and 1 unit. Cross out the 4 tens and record a 5 $(4 + 1)$ under the 4 in the tens column and the one unit in the units column.

"Oh, but that is messy!" is a common reaction of adults when they first see the above notation. This notation is used initially so that each step in the algorithm is clear and is recorded. After children have had some experience with this procedure they will be able to "clean it up" by using the "peek" method. Using this approach, children would add the first (largest place value) column but before recording the sum would peek at the next column to the right and decide whether regrouping will occur. If there will be regrouping, they add one to their sum and record that. If no regrouping is needed from the next column they will record the initial sum.

Using the second example and beginning in the hundreds column, a child's thinking might be: "3 + 2 is 5. Will I have to regroup the tens? (Child peeks at the tens column to decide.) Yes, so I'll add 1 to 5 making 6. (Child records 6 in the hundreds column.) 6 + 7 is 13. I've already regrouped the 10 tens. Do I have to regroup the ones? No, so I'll record the 3 tens. 2 + 4 is 6. All I need to do is record the 6 ones."

$$
\begin{array}{c}
362 \\
+\ 274 \\
\hline
\end{array}
\quad
\begin{array}{c}
362 \\
+\ 274 \\
\hline
6
\end{array}
\quad
\begin{array}{c}
362 \\
+\ 274 \\
\hline
63
\end{array}
\quad
\begin{array}{c}
362 \\
+\ 274 \\
\hline
636
\end{array}
$$

Low stress. A low-stress algorithm has been devised for all four operations. Its development began in the late 1960s as an alternative approach for children having dif-

ficulty with the conventional algorithms. These algorithms are more fully described in Hutchings (1976).

In the low-stress algorithms, each sum is recorded as you proceed through the numbers to be added. With a column of single digit numbers, the notation would appear as shown below.

$$
\begin{array}{c}
5 \\
{}_1 7\, {}_2 \\
6\, {}_8 \\
{}_1 4\, {}_2 \\
\hline
22
\end{array}
$$

First, $5 + 7$ is added. The 12 is recorded in "half-space" notation, the 2 to the right and below the 7, to indicate ones and the 1 to the left and below the 7 to indicate tens. Then 2 is added to 6 and the 8 recorded in half-space notation. Then the 8 and 4 are added and 12 is written a little below the 4 as shown. The 2 ones also are recorded below the line to indicate the 2 ones in the final sum. Lastly, the ones to the left of the column are counted and the number is recorded in the tens column. Figure 9-12 illustrates the extension of this notation to a column of numbers. A column addition such as this one should be done on the calculator. It is used here only to show the full extension of the low-stress algorithm.

The low-stress algorithm has several advantages over the conventional algorithm. The child uses only basic facts; there is no higher-decade addition. Since all facts and steps are recorded it has significant diagnostic value for the teacher. Consistent errors can be discovered and circled for later discussion with the child.

Subtraction

There are two main types of subtraction algorithms: *decomposition* and *equal additions*. Decomposition, the most commonly used, will be discussed in this section. The equal additions method will be described later as an alternative algorithm. The development in this section will be based on subtraction as "take-away." As with addition, cases in which trading (regrouping) is not required will be subsumed in the general case.

The following development will use the conventional right-to-left approach. The left-to-right procedure will be

---

FIGURE 9-11

$$
\begin{array}{c}
364 \\
+\ 287 \\
\hline
\end{array}
\quad
\begin{array}{c}
364 \\
+\ 287 \\
\hline
5
\end{array}
\quad
\begin{array}{c}
364 \\
+\ 287 \\
\hline
\cancel{5}4 \\
6
\end{array}
\quad
\begin{array}{c}
364 \\
+\ 287 \\
\hline
\cancel{5}41 \\
65
\end{array}
$$

FIGURE 9-12

$$
\begin{array}{r}
{}^2 4_6 \quad {}^2 5_7 \quad 8 \\
2_8 \quad {}_1 3_0 \quad {}_1 7_5 \\
{}_1 5_3 \quad 8_8 \quad 4_9 \\
+\quad 6_9 \quad {}_1 2_0 \quad {}_1 6_5 \\
\hline
1 \quad 9 \quad 0 \quad 5
\end{array}
$$

described as an alternative algorithm. Children should not be required to use any one method. The development of a computational procedure for subtraction will parallel that of addition by using base-ten blocks and the unstructured activities, recording, and symbolic representation phases.

Unstructured concrete manipulations   Pose a problem such as the following:

The clerk in the doughnut shop counted 63 doughnuts on the shelf. A family bought 24 doughnuts. How many doughnuts were left?

Children may want to set out blocks to represent 24 as well as 63. This would be done if the comparison interpretation of subtraction was being used, but not for the take-away approach. The teacher may need to review the basic notion of subtraction as take-away, namely, that there is a known number of objects (63) and that a specified number (24) is to be removed from this group.

When children use only the base-ten blocks (no recording), they experience very little difficulty extending the above process to three-digit numbers provided they have had relevant trading experiences involving hundreds. Of course, these larger numbers need to come from some real-life problem that must be solved.

Encouraging children to estimate an answer will help them verify and feel good about their concrete solution. Children might say, "My answer should be about 40 because I know that 60 minus 20 is 40" (extension fact).

The organizational mat should be modified for subtraction as shown in Figure 9-13. It also provides a transition to the recording phase. In the unstructured activities phase children would simply manipulate the blocks in the spaces provided on the mat as illustrated in the second column in Figure 9-13.

Recording   The development of a paper-and-pencil subtraction algorithm should follow as closely as possible the method used by children when they subtract with base-ten blocks. The strategy recommended for addition could be used here also. That is, use two organizational mats; one child manipulates on one and another child records on the second. Children then change roles. Figure 9-13 illustrates steps a child might use to solve the doughnut problem and the corresponding record.

Two aspects of the development in Figure 9-13 need comment. First, the subtrahend (24) is not represented concretely but recorded in boxes. It needs to be recorded so that children can remember what it is they are removing.

Secondly, the 10 ones were joined to the 3 ones in the first row rather than in a regrouping space as was done in addition. Why? In the concrete mode, the 10 ones were

joined to the group of 3 ones, making 13 ones. Some teachers suggest that children record the subtrahend on a separate piece of paper. This would leave an additional space on the mat for regrouping if desired. The teacher will have to provide some guidance on these matters to ensure that all children understand and can explain the process they use.

Claire found twenty-five candy eggs in her house. She decided to give her young brother eight of the eggs. Then how many candy eggs did Claire have?

Given an organizational mat and base-ten blocks, Grade 2 children tackled the above problem. Aaron's notebook recording (Figure 9-14, top) demonstrated a different solution process than Peter (Figure 9-14, bottom) at the concrete level.

Symbolic representation   After children had some experiences with the translation suggested by Figure 9-13 and can explain the steps in the subtraction procedure, they will begin to make refinements which become more and more symbolic, shorter, and efficient. The sequence of refinements illustrated in Figure 9-15 is one possibility. Many variations on these may be developed. For example, Young (1984) describes a transitional step based on covering all numbers not needed in a specific step of the algorithm. Expanded notation is encouraged by some teachers as a transitional step. The notation

$$
\begin{array}{r}
6 \text{ tens} + 3 \text{ ones} \\
- 2 \text{ tens} + 4 \text{ ones}
\end{array}
\longrightarrow
\begin{array}{r}
5 \text{ tens} + 13 \text{ ones} \\
- 2 \text{ tens} + 4 \text{ ones}
\end{array}
$$

$$
\begin{array}{r}
5 \text{ tens} + 13 \text{ ones} \\
- 2 \text{ tens} + 4 \text{ ones} \\
\hline
3 \text{ tens} + 9 \text{ ones}
\end{array}
\longrightarrow 39
$$

shown illustrates one way the doughnut problem might be recorded and solved using expanded notation.

Since the need to do a particular computation arises from the need to solve some real-life problem, the magnitude of numbers that children need to deal with will vary. As the number of required regroupings increases so does the difficulty level. A teacher, therefore, may want to structure or filter problems so that children can experience success and not become frustrated with problems that they are unable to solve.

The number of regroupings needed provides a guideline. When subtracting up to a three-digit number from a three-digit number, there may be no regrouping or any one of four possible regrouping situations (Figure 9-16). These are tens to ones, hundreds to tens, hundreds to ones, and tens to ones and hundreds to tens.

After children have used proportional materials such as the base-ten blocks, the abacus could be used to

FIGURE 9-13

Problem/Steps	Concrete Representation	Symbolic Representation
63 doughnuts 24 sold How many left?	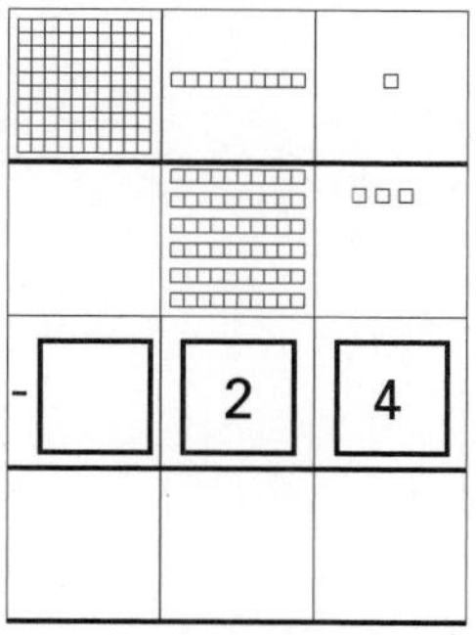 - [ ] 2 4	6 3 - [ ] 2 4
Can't take away 4 ones so exchange 1 ten for 10 ones; leaves 5 tens and makes 13 ones	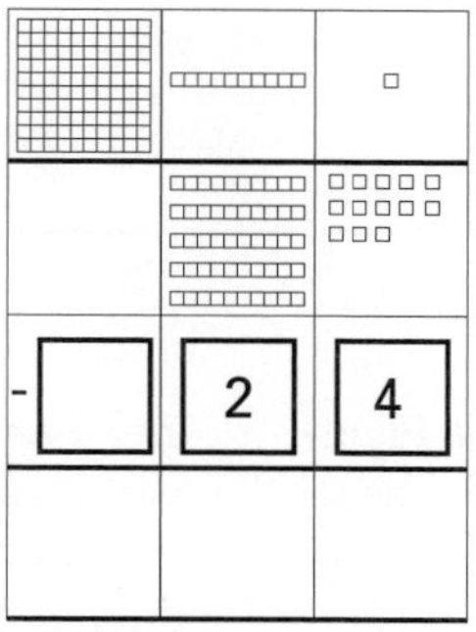 - [ ] 2 4	⁵6̶ ¹3 - [ ] 2 4
Remove 4 ones and record the number of ones left	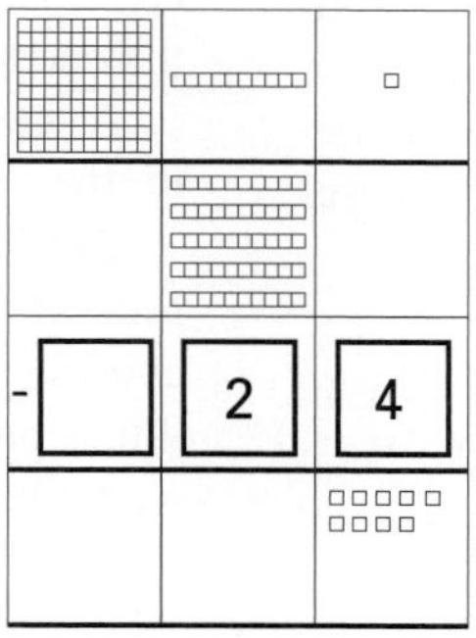 - [ ] 2 4	⁵6̶ ¹3 - [ ] 2 4 9
Take away 2 tens; record number of tens left	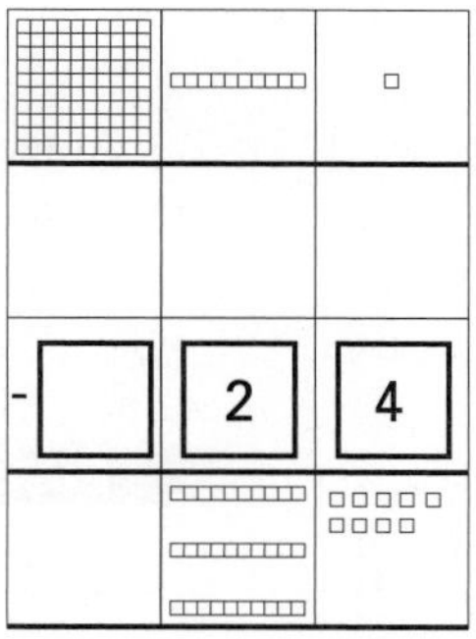 - [ ] 2 4	⁵6̶ ¹3 - [ ] 2 4 3 9

FIGURE 9-14

25
− 8
───
17   Claire has 17 eggs left.

... Aaron, Grade Two

− 25
  8
───
17   She has 17 eggs altogether

... Peter, Grade Two

reinforce the trading process with larger numbers. Figure 9-17 illustrates steps a child might take to compute 1495 − 637 on the abacus proceeding in the traditional right-to-left sequence.

Zeros in the minuend On occasion children encounter problems with one or more zeros in the minuend. The computational procedures involved need careful development. With a 3-digit minuend there are three cases to consider.

Zero in the ones place. Sometimes children want to begin reading the problem below as "5 minus 0." Their grouping and regrouping numeration experiences should enable them to rename 60 as 5 tens and 10 ones.

$$
\begin{array}{r}
760 \\
- \; 345 \\
\end{array}
\longrightarrow
\begin{array}{r}
7\overset{5}{6}\overset{1}{0} \\
- \; 345 \\
\end{array}
$$

Zero in the tens place. One example involves only one regrouping, from hundreds to tens, as required, for example, in 406 − 242. Using the base-ten blocks, children will quickly understand that four hundreds can be renamed as three hundreds plus 10 tens (Figure 9-18). An appropriate paper-and-pencil recording might look like the one to the right in Figure 9-18.

A second example in which regrouping also is needed in the ones position is more difficult. Consider 403 − 246. There are two approaches children might take. Most children will regroup the 4 hundreds as 3 hundreds and 10 tens (first example) and then rename the 10 tens as 9 tens and 13 ones as shown below. This parallels what would be done using base-ten blocks.

$$
\begin{array}{r}
403 \\
- \; 246 \\
\end{array}
\qquad
\begin{array}{r}
\overset{3}{4}\overset{9}{\underset{1}{0}}\overset{1}{3} \\
- \; 246 \\
\end{array}
$$

At the symbolic level, children with good insight into numeration might recognize that the 40 tens can be

FIGURE 9-15

H	T	O
$\overset{5}{\cancel{6}}$	$\overset{1}{3}$	
2	4	
3	9	

use headings

$$
\begin{array}{c|c|}
\overset{5}{\cancel{6}} & \overset{1}{3} \\
\hline
2 & 4 \\
\hline
3 & 9 \\
\end{array}
$$

remove headings

$$
\begin{array}{r}
\overset{5}{\cancel{6}}\,\overset{1}{3} \\
- \; 2\;4 \\
\hline
3\;9 \\
\end{array}
$$

conventional notation

FIGURE 9-16

376	246	325	305	355
− 51	− 29	− 172	− 109	− 186
no regroupings	tens to ones	hundreds to tens (via tens)	hundreds to ones	tens to ones and hundreds to tens

FIGURE 9-17

$1495 - 637 = 858$

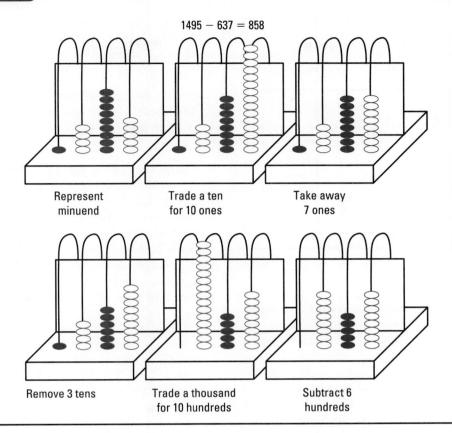

Represent minuend   Trade a ten for 10 ones   Take away 7 ones

Remove 3 tens   Trade a thousand for 10 hundreds   Subtract 6 hundreds

renamed as 39 tens and 10 ones. Children's recording may look like this example.

$$\begin{array}{r} 39 \\ 40\overset{1}{\cancel{3}} \\ -\ 246 \\ \hline \end{array}$$

Zeros in both the tens and ones places. This is the most difficult case. Children should have many experiences using concrete simulations before they move to paper-and-pencil recording. Figure 9-19 illustrates the steps with $400 - 245$.

The same steps are shown symbolically below. Children may include some transitional steps if they need them. As indicated earlier, some children may combine the two renaming steps. That is, they will think of the 40 tens as 39 tens and 10 ones and record it as the second ex-

ample in Case 2 (zero in the tens place). Children with good number sense sometimes mentally compute the answer to this type of problem by saying, "From 245 to 250 is 5, 50 more to 300 is 55, another hundred to 400 is 155."

$$\begin{array}{r} 31 \\ 4\cancel{0}0 \\ -\ 245 \\ \hline \end{array} \qquad \begin{array}{r} 9 \\ 31\ 1 \\ 4\cancel{0}\cancel{0} \\ -\ 245 \\ \hline \end{array}$$

Communication. Children need to talk about the processes they use. For example, a teacher might ask "How is this problem (referring to $403 - 246$) different from this one (referring to $400 - 245$)?" Have children solve each one with the blocks and then ask them to write about what they did to solve each one. Follow this with a class discussion.

FIGURE 9-18

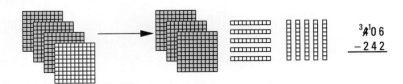

$$\begin{array}{r} 3\ \ 1 \\ \cancel{4}\ \cancel{0}\ 6 \\ -\ 2\ 4\ 2 \\ \hline \end{array}$$

FIGURE 9-19

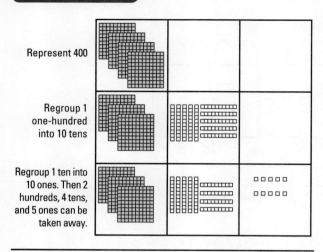

Represent 400

Regroup 1 one-hundred into 10 tens

Regroup 1 ten into 10 ones. Then 2 hundreds, 4 tens, and 5 ones can be taken away.

Interpretations of subtraction and the algorithms Different meanings of subtraction were discussed in Chapter 7. The foregoing development was based on the "take-away" interpretation of subtraction. Matching techniques were used in Chapter 7 to demonstrate comparison situations. This can be done with larger numbers but it does become more cumbersome. Figure 9-20 illustrates the comparison suggested by the following problem.

> *There are 364 children in Roseview Elementary School and 198 in Whitemud Park Elementary School. How many more children go to Roseview than Whitemud Park?*

The difference, 166, is the number represented by the blocks in the upper row not matched to a block in the lower row. The on-paper algorithm is identical to the take-away setting.

The third interpretation revolved around the question "how many more (fewer) are needed?" The following problem is of that type.

> *Les has 84 baseball cards. He wanted to collect 150 cards. How many more does he need to meet his goal?*

The question can be stated as, "What is the difference between 150 and 84?" Concretely, this could be done either by "take-away" or by "comparison."

The above problem could be restated as 84 and how many more make 150, or symbolically, $84 + \square = 150$. Children could represent 84 with base-ten blocks and then "count on" as they add tens and ones to get to 150. Others will recognize that they can start with the 150, then remove eight tens and four ones to see how many are left.

Children with good number sense might try thinking this through mentally while operating at a symbolic level. Many children will think (using an easier example, $34 + \square = 87$), "34 plus 50 gives me 84, then 3 more gives me 87." Note that this is the left-to-right method again. Others may go through a thought process like:

$$
\begin{array}{r} 34 \\ + \text{--} \\ \hline 87 \end{array}
\qquad
\boxed{\begin{array}{l} 4 + ? = 7 \\ 4 + 3 = 7 \end{array}}
\qquad
\begin{array}{r} 34 \\ + \text{ --}3 \\ \hline 87 \end{array}
$$

$$
\boxed{\begin{array}{l} 30 + ? = 80 \\ 30 + 50 = 80 \end{array}}
\qquad
\begin{array}{r} 34 \\ + 53 \\ \hline 87 \end{array}
$$

FIGURE 9-20

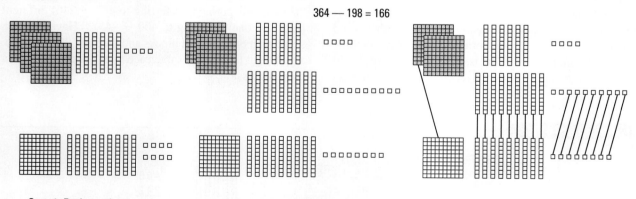

364 — 198 = 166

Step 1: Both numbers   Step 2: Regrouping   Step 3: Match

Later the subtractive form below could be used. The thought process is the same, it just moves from the bottom up instead of from the top down.

$$
\begin{array}{r}
87 \\
-\;-\;- \\
\hline
34
\end{array}
$$

When regrouping is involved (as in the original problem, 150 − 84), the thought process might go like this:

$$
\begin{array}{r}
1\,5\,0 \\
-\;-\;- \\
\hline
8\,4
\end{array}
$$

I can't add to 4 to get 0, so I will regroup

$$
\begin{array}{r}
1\,\overset{4}{\cancel{5}}\,^{1}0 \\
-\;-\;- \\
\hline
8\,4
\end{array}
$$

4 + ? = 10
4 + 6 = 10

$$
\begin{array}{r}
1\,\overset{4}{\cancel{5}}\,^{1}0 \\
-\;-\;-6 \\
\hline
8\,4
\end{array}
$$

I can't add to 80 to get 40 but the one hundred is 10 tens so I've got 14 tens

80 + ? = 140
80 + 60 = 140

$$
\begin{array}{r}
1\,\overset{4}{\cancel{5}}\,^{1}0 \\
-\;-6\,6 \\
\hline
8\,4
\end{array}
$$

Activity 9-8 parallels Activity 9-7 but involves subtraction. Students should work in a group or with a partner and discuss reasons for their choice of number.

Other subtraction algorithms

Equal additions. The equal additions algorithm was taught in North America until the mid-1900s (Brownell, 1947; Brownell & Moser, 1949). Its use then declined

FIGURE 9-21

	Decomposition			Equal additions	

Decomposition (left):
$$
\begin{array}{r}
\overset{2}{3}\;\overset{3}{\cancel{4}}\;\overset{1}{6} \\
-\;1\;\;7\;\;8 \\
\hline
1\;\;6\;\;8
\end{array}
$$

Equal additions (right):
$$
\begin{array}{r}
3\;\;\overset{1}{4}\;\;\overset{1}{6} \\
-\;\overset{2}{1}\;\overset{8}{\cancel{7}}\;8 \\
\hline
1\;\;6\;\;8
\end{array}
$$

and the decomposition method prevailed. In some parts of the world, the equal additions algorithm is taught and so teachers should be aware of it and understand how it works. When taught meaningfully, both the equal additions and the decomposition algorithms are effective. The two methods are compared in Figure 9-21.

Using the equal additions method, a child might reason: "I can't subtract 8 from 6 so I will add 10 ones. Since I added 10 to the top number I must add 10 to the bottom number. I will increase the 7 tens to 8 tens. 8 from 16 is 8. Now I can't subtract 8 tens from 4 tens so I'll add 10 tens to the top number and 10 tens in the form of one hundred to the bottom number. 8 tens from 14 tens is 6 tens and 2 hundreds from 3 hundreds leaves one hundred."

Note that this method is based on a compensation property. What is added to one number (the minuend) must be added to the other number (the subtrahend) to keep the difference the same. This algorithm, then, is based more on the properties and structure of the number system whereas the decomposition algorithm is based more on the structure of the numeration system. Children can easily be convinced of the validity of the compensation property through an exercise like the one in Activity 9-9.

Left to right. When using concrete materials, some children naturally want to operate left to right. Subtracting left to right may be just as fast and accurate as right to left. Certainly it is more useful when a rounded answer or an estimate is desired.

✳ ACTIVITY 9-8

CALCULATOR GAME (SUBTRACTION)

MATERIALS:
calculator for each student

PROCEDURE:
1. One person writes three numbers on paper for all others to see.
2. Without the others seeing, find the difference between two of the numbers on your calculator.
3. Write the difference on paper for the others to see.
4. The others decide, by estimation, which two numbers were subtracted and then check their guesses on their calculator.
5. Take turns doing the activity several more times.

✳ ACTIVITY 9-9

COMPENSATION INVESTIGATION

PROCEDURE:
1. Find the difference

$$
\begin{array}{ccccccccc}
8 & 9 & 10 & 8 & 18 & 28 & 18 & 19 & 20 \\
-3 & -4 & -5 & -3 & -13 & -23 & -13 & -14 & -15
\end{array}
$$

2. Write a sentence about what you notice.

FIGURE 9-22

$$
\begin{array}{r}
3\ 4\ 6 \\
-\ 1\ 7\ 8 \\
\end{array}
$$

$$
\begin{array}{r}
3\ 4\ 6 \\
6 \\
-\ 1\ 7\ 8 \\
\end{array}
$$

$$
\begin{array}{r}
3\ 4\ 6 \\
3\,{}^{1}6 \\
-\ 1\ 7\ 8 \\
\end{array}
$$

$$
\begin{array}{r}
3\ 4\ 6 \\
2\,{}^{1}3\,{}^{1}6 \\
-\ 1\ 7\ 8 \\
\end{array}
$$

$$
\begin{array}{r}
3\ 4\ 6 \\
2\,{}^{1}3\,{}^{1}6 \\
-\ 1\ 7\ 8 \\
\hline
1\ 6\ 8 \\
\end{array}
$$

a   b   c   d   e   f

Initially, children might construct an algorithm like the one shown here.

$$
\begin{array}{r}
3\,{}^{1}4\,{}^{1}6 \\
-\ 1\ 7\ 8 \\
\hline
2\ \,\llap{/}7\ 8 \\
{}_{1}\ \ {}_{6} \\
\end{array}
$$

The steps are similar to those in addition. A child might verbalize the process this way: "300 minus 100 is 200. I'll record a 2 in the hundreds column. I can't subtract 7 tens from 4 tens so I'll rename one of the two remaining hundreds as 10 tens giving me 14 tens. This leaves one hundred (crosses out the 2 and records a 1 beside it). 7 tens from 14 tens is 7 tens. I'll record 7 in the tens place. I can't subtract 8 from 6 so I'll take one of the 7 tens and make it 10 ones. I've now got 6 tens (crosses out the 7 and records a 6 beside it) and 16 ones. 8 from 16 is 8, so the answer is 168."

With experience children will learn to look to the place value position to the right before they record. If regrouping is necessary they will record one less in the current place value position and add 10 to the next lower place value position in the minuend. Their work will then appear as shown here.

$$
\begin{array}{r}
3\,{}^{1}4\,{}^{1}6 \\
-\ 1\ 7\ 8 \\
\hline
1\ 6\ 8 \\
\end{array}
$$

Low stress. The steps in the low-stress subtraction algorithm are illustrated in Figure 9-22. Each step (a, b, c, . . ., f) is explained below.

a. Initial exercise.

b. Minuend and subtrahend separated to create a working space.

c. Begin rewriting minuend doing all regrouping first.

d. 8 cannot be taken from 6 so regroup the 4 tens as 3 tens and 10 ones. Record in working space as shown.

e. 7 cannot be taken from 3 so regroup the 3 hundreds as 2 hundreds and 10 tens. Record in working space as shown.

f. Do all the subtractions.

Note that all the regroupings have been done first, then the subtractions. Sometimes alternating as we usually do with the conventional algorithm can cause errors. Note also that once all the regroupings have been done the subtractions can be done in any order: left-to-right, right-to-left, or randomly. All regroupings could be done first in the conventional algorithm, but that is rarely done.

If the 346 in Step f seems distracting to children, they can put a line through it after all regroupings and before starting the subtraction.

Multiplication

Several approaches to multiplication were developed in Chapter 7. All of these help children build a concept for multiplication. When it comes to developing a multiplication algorithm, the array representation is probably the most effective because it enables one to easily represent large numbers. Figure 9-23 illustrates 25 × 34 using the base-ten blocks. Imagine children trying to sketch or construct 25 sets of 34 objects or show 25 hops of 34 units along a number line!

As for addition and subtraction, no differentiation will be made between cases involving regrouping and no

FIGURE 9-23

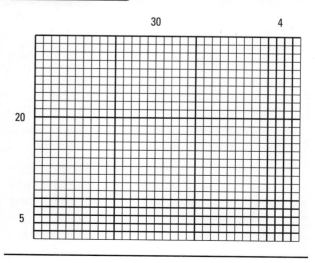

FIGURE 9-24

(a)   (b)   (c)

regrouping. There are very few cases in which regrouping is not required in multiplication. Furthermore, children have used models such as the base-ten blocks to trade between place value positions before. Therefore, trading in multiplication can be treated as a natural part of the process. Again, it is important to allow children to solve different kinds of problems on their own prior to formal instruction in the development of a "standard" algorithm (Burns, 1991; Huinker, 1989; Weiland, 1985).

One-digit multiplier   Children's first multiplication computations should arise from real-life problems involving one-digit multipliers. A problem such as the following could serve as a stimulus:

The principal bought 3 cases of sodas for the Grade 2 party. Each case had 24 cans. How many cans were purchased?

Children can set out a rectangular array using as few base-ten pieces as possible as shown in Figure 9-24(a) and observe (mentally or on paper) that the answer is 60 (3×20) plus 12 (3×4) or 72. They will recognize from previous experiences that 3×20 is 3 groups of 2 tens and the result is 6 tens. To this end, encourage children to verbalize what they have done in different ways and encourage the use of *place value language* illustrated below using the blocks as a model. The following sequence of activities suggests a possible approach.

1. Ask the children to construct a 2-by-6 rectangle using as few base-ten blocks as possible. See Figure 9-24(b). They will be able to do this by using only unit cubes.

Encourage children to use place value language like: "2 ones times 6 ones equals 12 ones."

2. Have the children construct a 2-by-60 rectangle using as few pieces as possible. See Figure 9-24(c). They should be able to say, "2 ones times 6 tens equals 12 tens." From these kinds of experiences children will be able to generalize:
    * 3×10 is 3 tens or 30.
    * 3×20 is 3×2 tens, which makes 6 tens or 60.

It is important to allow children ample time to solve numerous problems concretely while recording in *their own way* what they did. In the process encourage them to describe their work using the place value language.

Once children feel comfortable with place value language, products could then be recorded and regrouped in a place value chart as shown below.

H	T	O		H	T	O
		6				6
×	2			×		2
	˼2				˼2	0
	1	2		1	2	0

Notice that the lines used to indicate regrouping begin to look like the steps in the traditional paper-and-pencil algorithm. Recording using paper and pencil is, in fact, the next step in the development. Children should now be able to make connections among concrete representation, place value language, and symbolic recording as suggested in Figure 9-25.

FIGURE 9-25

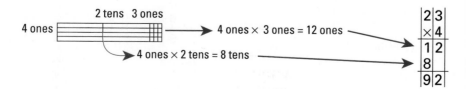

4 ones   2 tens 3 ones   4 ones × 3 ones = 12 ones
                                    4 ones × 2 tens = 8 tens

$$\begin{array}{r} 2\,3 \\ \times\,4 \\ \hline 1\,2 \\ 8 \\ \hline 9\,2 \end{array}$$

Activity 9-10 will help children with the connections suggested in Figure 9-25. A set of problem cards with problems similar to the one about the principal and the soft drinks at the beginning of this section will need to be prepared in advance.

For many children, it is helpful to retain the place value chart format—at least the use of vertical lines to separate the place value positions as shown to the right in Figure 9-25 rather than going directly to the traditional format. Children should have many experiences with the three-way connection shown in Figure 9-25 and with writing the paper-and-pencil algorithm listing both partial products before the algorithm is shortened.

When children are ready, the final step with one-digit multipliers is to record the final product in one line. The difference is not recording the 12 obtained when 3 ones are multiplied by 4 ones as before, but to record the 2 ones and keep a separate record of the 1 ten and add it to the number of tens obtained when the 2 tens are multiplied by the 4 ones. This record may be kept mentally, recorded above the 2 as in the conventional method, or even below the 2. By placing the two methods of recording side-by-side as illustrated in Figure 9-26, children will be able to connect the two and see that the 1 ten in each case (see the arrow) is the same. The connection and transition might be facilitated if children are allowed to use either format. Examples similar to those shown in Figure 9-27 could be used for a class discussion. A child

FIGURE 9-26

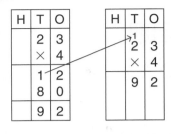

could be asked to tell how the procedures are different or similar. Children should also be asked to explain the meaning of the "small" 3 and "small" 2 and to identify their corresponding number in the left-hand chart.

Two-digit multiplier Do not rush to two-digit multipliers. Be sure children can solve problems with one-digit multipliers and can explain the procedure before introducing problems with two-digit multipliers. Two required extensions to children's place value language are described and illustrated below when the multiplicand is also a two-digit number.

1. "2 tens times 7 ones equals 14 tens"
   (This is the commutative form of the "ones × tens = tens" concept learned with one-digit multipliers.)

$$\begin{array}{r} 67 \\ \uparrow \\ \times\ 25 \end{array}$$

2. "2 tens times 6 tens equals 12 hundreds."

$$\begin{array}{r} 67 \\ \uparrow \\ \times\ 25 \end{array}$$

Children should have many opportunities to use the above place value language in the context of base-ten blocks before doing any recording. To help children with

---

✳ ACTIVITY 9-10

PROBLEM CARDS

MATERIALS:
a set of problem cards; base-ten blocks

PROCEDURE:
Work in groups of 3

1. Choose a problem card.

2. One person uses the blocks to show the problem.

3. Another describes the partial products shown by the blocks. Use language such as "4 ones times 2 tens equals 8 tens."

4. The third person records the problem and its solution in written form.

5. Change roles and do another problem.

FIGURE 9-27

H	T	O
	3	6
×	6	
	3	6
1	8	0
2	1	6

H	T	O
	³3	6
×	6	
2	1	6

2	7
×	3
2	1
6	0
8	1

²2	7
×	3
8	1

FIGURE 9-28

Th	H	T	O
		6	7
	×	2	5
		3	5
	3	0	0
	1	14	
	1	4	
	1	12	
1	2		

← From 1-digit multiplier

From place value language
"2 tens times 7 ones is 14 tens"
"14 tens" regrouped

From place value language
"2 tens times 6 tens is 12 hundreds"
"12 hundreds" regrouped

the "tens × tens = hundreds" concept, have them set out several arrays with the blocks showing multiplication with multiples of 10 as shown below. When children are encouraged to talk about their array, expressions such as "2 tens times 6 tens makes 12 hundreds" will develop.

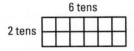

6 tens

2 tens

This type of array can now be extended to represent a problem like 25 × 67 (similar to Figure 9-23). Children should have many experiences representing this type of problem with base-ten blocks, recording their work in their own way. Children could then transfer their individual method of recording to a place value chart much like the one suggested for one-digit multipliers. The arrows

and boldface print in Figure 9-28 show the two new partial products from 25 × 67.

Again, children need to see the connections between the concrete, place value language, and the paper-and-pencil algorithm. This connection is shown in Figure 9-29. This figure is more readily interpreted if one considers the dimensions of the base-ten pieces rather than the area. For example, the rod consists of 10 units (area) and has dimensions 1 × 10. One dimension of an array composed of a rod and a flat would be 11 (10 from the flat plus 1 from the rod) or 1 ten and 1 unit. This same interpretation applies to Figure 9-24.

Most children will be able to make these connections if they progress meaningfully through the general sequence suggested. That is, children should first represent a problem and its solution with a concrete model. They should be encouraged to explain the concrete representation in words (written or oral) and then challenged to record their work in some way using symbols. Finally, an algorithmic format is developed.

Note that the written record can be recorded left to right or right to left, the only difference being the order of the partial products. Some children might record their work in horizontal form prior to the vertical format: (5 × 7) + (5 × 60) + (20 × 7) + (20 × 60).

After children have had adequate experiences representing two-digit multiplication problems using the base-ten blocks and writing a corresponding algorithm for the representation, they will begin to shorten the algorithm. Normally only two partial products are recorded. If children have already written one-line products for multiplication with single-digit multipliers as suggested earlier, the two-digit case should not be difficult. The teacher can encourage children along this line by extending an invitation such as "try to find a shorter way to record a multiplication with four partial products."

Using the 25 × 67 example above, children could begin the transition by focusing only on the 5 and treating the problem as 5 × 67 (previous section). They could

FIGURE 9-29

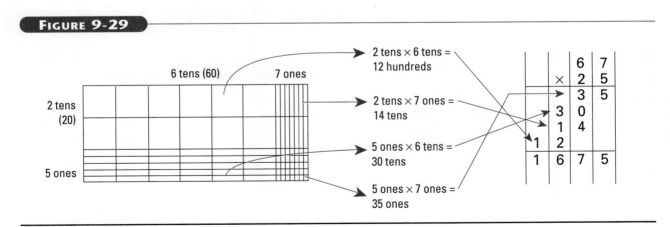

2 tens × 6 tens = 12 hundreds

2 tens × 7 ones = 14 tens

5 ones × 6 tens = 30 tens

5 ones × 7 ones = 35 ones

FIGURE 9-30

		Step 1		
Th	H	T	O	
		³6	7	
×		2	5	
	3	3	5	

		Step 2		
Th	H	T	O	
	¹			
		6	7	
×		2	5	
1	3	4		

	Combined			
Th	H	T	O	
	¹	³		
		6	7	
×		2	5	
	3	3	5	
1	3	4		
1	6	7	5	

then focus on the 2 tens as the multiplier. Since tens × ones = tens, the first digit in the second partial product will be placed in the tens position. There are 14 tens (2 tens × 7 ones) so the 4 tens will be recorded and the remaining 10 tens will be regrouped and recorded as 1 hundred in the hundreds column as in Figure 9-28. These shorter steps are illustrated in Figure 9-30.

The connection between the long form (four partial products) and the shortened form (two partial products) should be apparent to children. To ensure this, the teacher might present both forms side-by-side as shown in Figure 9-31 and ask children to explain the similarities and differences. Children may draw arrows as in Figure 9-31 to show the connection between the two forms.

Some children may wish to append the zero in the units place for the second partial product as shown here.

$$
\begin{array}{r}
28 \\
\times\, 46 \\
\hline
168 \\
1120 \\
\hline
1288
\end{array}
$$

Appended zero

The place value language suggested in this chapter leads more to leaving the zero off: "4 tens × 8 ones = 32 tens" focuses on the <u>tens</u> position for the result. If you think of 40 × 8 = 320, then the zero in the ones place is a natural

result. The difference is subtle and in the end it becomes largely a matter of preference. A student should use the form that she or he is most comfortable with. One advantage of appending the zero is that it appears "neater" and may help children place succeeding digits in the correct position when the lines are removed.

Three- and more digit multipliers Children who are confident with two-digit multipliers should be able to move to three-digit multipliers on their own if they need to. The main extension is in the use of the place value language developed for one- and two-digit multipliers. Although calculators will normally be used to solve multiplication problems with large numbers, children could be invited to "prove" they know how to multiply large numbers by writing a few examples in horizontal form using the distributive property and in vertical form.

STANDARDS LINK 9-9
Although the exploration of computation with larger numbers is appropriate, excessive amounts of time should not be devoted to proficiency. (NCTM, 1989, p. 47)

Zero in the multiplier A zero in the multiplier should not be troublesome for children if they understand the role of zero in multiplication. Using an example such as 30 × 27, a class discussion could lead children to suggest the shortened form as shown below.

$$
\begin{array}{r}
27 \\
\times\, 30 \\
\hline
00 \\
81 \\
\hline
810
\end{array}
\longrightarrow
\begin{array}{r}
27 \\
\times\, 30 \\
\hline
810
\end{array}
$$

27 × 30 should be thought of as (27 × 3) × 10, but one writes the zero first, rather than after multiplying by 3.

FIGURE 9-31

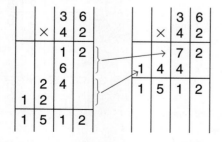

Zero in the multiplicand In a two-digit whole number multiplicand, the only place zero can occur is in the units position. This is generally not a source of difficulty as long as children understand the role of zero in multiplication. The zero is treated like any other digit. Alternatively, children might apply the commutative law and transform the question into the example in the previous paragraph.

In a three-digit multiplicand, a zero in the tens position sometimes proves troublesome for some children. A common tendency is to ignore the zero. That is, 7×205 is treated as 7×25 to obtain 175 as the product.

$$\begin{array}{r} 3 \\ 205 \\ \times\,7 \\ \hline 175 \end{array}$$

In anticipation of this misconception, teachers can engage children in different activities. Children should be encouraged to estimate an answer. Rounding the 205 to 200, they would estimate an answer a little more than 1400. Clearly, 175 is not close to 1400. Using a *place value chart* format should also help children keep the regrouping in the correct position, particularly if they use the place value language along with the chart. That is, 7 ones $\times$ 5 ones is 35 ones, write 5 ones and regroup the 30 ones as 3 *tens,* not hundreds, as demonstrated in the error above.

Th	H	T	O
¹	2	³0	5
	$\times$		7
1	4	3	5

A child could also compare her or his answer, 175, with the multiplicand, 205, and ask, "Does it make sense for the product to be less than 205?" Another comparison activity might involve asking children to explain how the questions below are different.

$$\begin{array}{ccc} 25 & 205 & 250 \\ \times\,7 & \times\,7 & \times\,7 \end{array}$$

Zeros in the multiplier and multiplicand for larger numbers (e.g., 206×348 and 509×408) could also be discussed.

Other algorithms We have advocated exposing children to different computational procedures because it helps them understand that any algorithm is simply a series of steps that will solve a computational problem and that no one algorithm has any kind of "special" power.

Experience with different algorithms also promotes reasoning and flexible thinking.

Low stress. The low-stress multiplication algorithm developed by Hutchings (1976) is a left-to-right algorithm that employs a "drop notation." For example, the basic facts would be recorded as shown here. Note from the last example that single-digit products also are written in drop notation using a leading zero.

$$\begin{array}{cccc} 9 & 6 & 8 & 4 \\ \times\,6 & \times\,7 & \times\,5 & \times\,2 \\ \hline 5 & 4 & 4 & 0 \\ 4 & 2 & 0 & 8 \end{array}$$

In the algorithm, all that is recorded are the basic facts. To compute the product, 6×427, one begins at the left and records the product of 6×4 as shown below.

$$\begin{array}{r} 427 \\ \times\,6 \\ \hline 2 \\ 4 \end{array}$$

Note that the 2 in 24 is recorded one position to the left of the 4 hundreds because ones $\times$ hundreds = hundreds. The 24 hundreds are then 2 thousands plus 4 hundreds. The remaining steps are shown below.

$$\begin{array}{ccc} 427 & 427 & 427 \\ \times\,6 & \times\,6 & \times\,6 \\ \hline 21 & 214 & 214 \\ 42 & 422 & 422 \\ & & \hline \\ & & 2562 \end{array}$$

Try a few examples of your own. For examples with larger numbers the reader is referred to Hutchings (1976).

The advantage of the low-stress algorithm over the conventional algorithm include:

- the elimination of almost all the mental work involved in regrouping.
- all the multiplication is done before any addition. In the conventional algorithm the regrouped number has to be added to the product, thus, there often is an alternating series of multiply-add, multiply-add steps.
- only basic facts are recorded.
- specific errors are more easily located since each step is recorded.

Some children may have a little difficulty with the alignment of digits in the proper place value positions. The use of squared paper until a student becomes comfortable with the algorithm usually overcomes this difficulty.

FIGURE 9-32

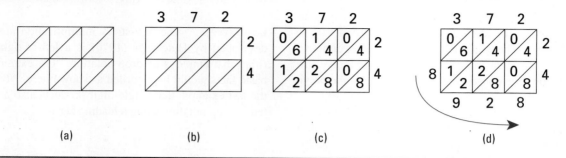

(a)   (b)   (c)   (d)

Lattice.   Some programs introduce the lattice method of multiplication as enrichment or to add some variety. The procedure works like this:

- Prepare an $n \times m$ grid of squares or rectangles with diagonals through each as shown in Figure 9-32(a). The n and m represent the number of digits in the two factors.
- Write the digits from the two factors above and to the right as shown in Figure 9-32(b).
- In each rectangle, enter the product of the corresponding digits from the two factors. See Figure 9-32(c). Enter the tens digit in the upper left portion of the rectangle and the ones digit in the lower right. If the product is a single digit, enter 0 in the upper left section.
- Beginning at the lower right, add all the digits in each diagonal. When the sum is a two-digit number, regroup to the next diagonal in the normal way.
- The product is the sequence of digits obtained in the previous step, reading from upper left to lower right as indicated by the arrow in Figure 9-32(d).

A teacher might challenge students to reflect on this algorithm and try to relate it to a conventional algorithm. This could be done through a diagram such as the one in Figure 9-33. An historical computing device, *Napier's rods* (sometimes called *Napier's bones*), is related to the lattice method of multiplication. The reader is invited to read elsewhere about the nature and operation of Napier's rods.

Enrichment extensions   Two partial products are normally used in the standard multiplication algorithm for a two-digit multiplier to minimize memory requirements. It is possible to write the products as a one-line product without any partial products. Some students may enjoy the challenge.

$$\begin{array}{r} 426 \\ \times\ 37 \\ \hline 15\ 762 \end{array}$$

The procedure involves keeping track of all the ways each place value position can be obtained. This requires a high level of proficiency with place value language. The first position to consider is the ones position. Using 37×426 as an example, the only way ones are obtained is from ones $\times$ ones. There are 42 ones. Record the 2 and remember (in memory, on your fingers, or on paper) the 4 tens. Next consider all the ways of getting tens. Ones $\times$ tens and tens $\times$ ones are the only ways to get tens. We have 7 ones $\times$ 2 tens = 14 tens and 3 tens $\times$ 6 ones = 18 tens plus the 4 tens from the previous calculation. That is 36 tens. Record the 6 in the tens position and remember the 3 hundreds. Next consider ways of obtaining hundreds. 7 ones $\times$ 4 hundreds = 28 hundreds, 3 tens $\times$ 2 tens = 6 hundreds plus 3 hundreds makes 37 hundreds. Record the 7 hundreds and remember the 3 thousands. The reader should continue this process to arrive at the one-line product: 15 762. You may wish to try several other examples, including some three-digit multipliers.

All students could be encouraged to use a calculator to explore some patterns such as those in Activity 9-11. Children should explain (written or orally) their observations.

Connections   Many concepts run like "threads" through the mathematics curriculum from early elementary through high school and beyond. For example, when

FIGURE 9-33

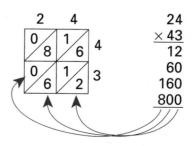

✳ ACTIVITY 9-11

PATTERNS

MATERIALS:
a calculator

PROCEDURE:
1. Use your calculator to help you discover the pattern in each set. When you see the pattern, complete the remainder of the exercises without your calculator.

32 × 101 = 3232	17 × 101 = _____
52 × 101 = _____	_____ × 101 =

Explain:

23 × 11 = 253	27 × 11 = _____
37 × 11 = _____	54 × 11 = _____
55 × 11 = _____	74 × 11 = _____

Explain:

214 × 111 = 23754	141 × 111 = _____
305 × 111 = _____	342 × 111 = _____

Explain:

Does the pattern hold for 467 × 111?

high school students expand $(a + b)(c + d)$ as $ac + ad + bc + bd$, they are actually doing the same thing they did in elementary school when they identified and listed the four partial products in an exercise such as 27 × 35. In fact, they may well use a diagram similar to the representation with base-ten blocks (Figure 9-34).

The expansion of $(a + b)^2 = a^2 + 2ab + b^2$ is just a special case of the above.

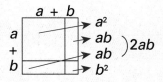

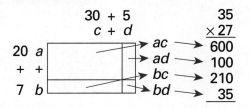

FIGURE 9-34

Division

While the process of division is a "natural" part of children's experiences, computational procedures have proven to be difficult for children to learn. There are several reasons for this; probably the most significant is that not only do children need to know the division basic facts but they also need to be able to multiply and subtract efficiently.

A large amount of time is spent in elementary and middle school trying to help children master the division algorithm. This is unjustifiable given that adults will reach for a calculator when a long division computation is needed.

Instruction on division computation should emphasize one-digit divisors so that children can develop an understanding of the steps involved. Some experience with two-digit divisors also is necessary, particularly to help children develop skill in estimating partial quotients. Extending this to a four-digit dividend can provide all the experience needed to become proficient with paper-and-pencil division computation. Beyond that all of us reach for a calculator, so why shouldn't students? This position has to be interpreted in context and as a generalization. There are times when division with larger numbers is required to solve a problem and a calculator may not be available. These "large computations," however, should not be the focus of instruction.

One-digit divisors Always begin with a real-life problem. For example:

Five children agreed to share equally all the apples they collected on Halloween. They collected 27 apples. How many apples did each person get?

The above problem results in a remainder. Sharing situations in which there is no remainder are rare and they can be treated as a special case of the general algorithm.

Although we did not discuss this level of problem in Chapter 7, children will very likely have encountered it and will resort to base-ten blocks or counters to illustrate the sharing process. Learning the paper-and-pencil algorithm is essentially learning a means of recording what is done concretely. Using place value language and the base-ten blocks is a natural and efficient way to do this.

The first step is to introduce children to a "different" way of writing 27 ÷ 5 as shown here.

$$5\overline{)27}$$

When solving division questions such as 27 divided by 5, the phrase "5 goes into 27" should not be used (it has no meaning). Rather, language that is appropriate for the context should be used such as "27 apples to be shared among 5 people" or "5 groups to share 27 apples." In a measurement context, expressions such as "27 apples to be separated into groups of 5" might be used.

Table 9-1 illustrates one way the sharing and place value language could be translated into a paper-and-pencil recording process.

Cheek and Olson (1986) use the setting of a group of robbers attempting to equally share some bills obtained in a robbery. Some real-life setting needs to be used to develop the computational procedure, but a more socially acceptable setting such as children distributing play money for a game should be used.

Using the same process with a three-digit dividend might be more illustrative. The reader should set out the base-ten blocks and manipulate them in step with the sequence in Table 9-2 in which 739 things shared among six children is illustrated.

The process for a measurement setting could be similar. 739 ÷ 6 means subtracting six things at a time from 739. However, with experience, children can begin by

TABLE 9-1

TRANSITION FROM CONCRETE TO SYMBOLIC RECORD VIA SHARING LANGUAGE

CONCRETE	LANGUAGE	RECORD
	Can I share the 2 tens equally among the 5 people? No.	5)27
	If I exchange them for 20 units, making 27 units, I can share the units.	5)27
	Each person gets 5 units. Since I am sharing units, I record the 5 in the units position.	5 5)27
	How many units have I shared? 25.	5 5)27 25
	How many left to be shared? 2. Can I share any more units? No.	5 5)27 25 — 2

subtracting six hundreds. The language in the first cell in Table 9-2 could be: "Can I subtract 6 hundreds? Yes. How many times? Once. Where do I record this? Since I've subtracted hundreds, the record goes in the hundreds position, above the 7." The language in the remaining cells would be modified in a similar way.

Children need to work through many problems involving one-digit divisors and two- and three-digit dividends. Teachers should not rush into introducing division with two-digit divisors until children can clearly verbalize and model what they are doing as they solve one-digit divisor problems with paper and pencil.

Cases with zero Two special cases involving zero have traditionally given children trouble. Many difficulties could be avoided if place value language was carefully developed.

Zero in the dividend. In a problem such as 709 ÷ 6, 6 of the 7 hundreds are shared, the 1 hundred that each group gets is recorded as before. Again the 1 hundred left over is exchanged for 10 tens. These tens have no other tens to be combined with so there are simply 10 tens to be distributed among the 6 groups. Thus, when place value language is used, there is no real difference with what was done before.

$$
\begin{array}{r}
1 \\
6\overline{)709} \\
6 \\
\hline
10 \\
\bullet \\
\bullet \\
\bullet
\end{array}
$$

TABLE 9-2

PLACE VALUE LANGUAGE TO PAPER-AND-PENCIL RECORD

LANGUAGE	RECORD
Can I share the 7 hundreds among 6 children? Yes! How many hundreds does each child get? 1. Where do I record this? Since each child gets 1 *hundred,* the record goes in the hundreds position, above the 7.	$6\overline{)739}$ $\dfrac{1}{6\overline{)739}}$
How many hundreds were shared? 6. Are there any hundreds left to be shared? Yes, 1. Can this 1 hundred be shared equally? No.	$\begin{array}{r} 1 \\ 6\overline{)739} \\ 6 \\ \hline 1 \end{array}$
If I exchange the 1 hundred for 10 tens, I can share more. How many tens to be shared? 10 + 3 or 13.	$\begin{array}{r} 1 \\ 6\overline{)739} \\ 6 \\ \hline 13 \end{array}$
How many tens will each child get? Where do I record this? Since it was tens that were being shared I will record it in the tens position above the three.	$\begin{array}{r} 12 \\ 6\overline{)739} \\ 6 \\ \hline 13 \end{array}$
How many tens were shared? 12. How many tens left to be shared? 1.	$\begin{array}{r} 12 \\ 6\overline{)739} \\ 6 \\ \hline 13 \\ 12 \\ \hline 1 \end{array}$
I can regroup the 1 ten as 10 ones, making 19 ones. How many ones will each child get? 3. How many ones were shared? 18. How many ones are left to be shared? 1. Can I share these equally? No.	$\begin{array}{r} 123 \\ 6\overline{)739} \\ 6 \\ \hline 13 \\ 12 \\ \hline 19 \\ 18 \\ \hline 1 \end{array}$

Zero in the quotient.   A zero in the quotient can also be troublesome in that children sometimes forget to record the zero. Again, however, if the value of what is being shared is emphasized, the problem should be minimized. Including place value separator lines as in Table 9-3 will also help students. Children should use the base-ten blocks to demonstrate each step in computing $625 \div 6$.

A case such as $6\overline{)609}$ embodies both "problem" situations. There are no leftover hundreds to keep. Again, if children use the place value language they will now say that there are no tens to share so a zero is recorded in the tens place to indicate this.

Not enough hundreds to share   In a problem such as $429 \div 5$, using the traditional approach, some children experience some difficulty with the place value of digits in the quotient. Careful use of the place value language and the line separators should minimize the difficulty. Children who are experiencing difficulty could be directed to place the leading zero over the 4 in 429 to indicate that there are zero hundreds as shown in the illustration. It will not take children long to realize that this is not necessary.

$$0$$
$$5\overline{)4\,|\,2\,|\,9}$$

Short division   With one-digit divisors, children sometimes are taught a form of "short division" in which subtraction is done mentally and the regrouping is recorded as shown here.

Step 1	*Completed short division*
1	$1\,2\,1\,4\,\text{R}\,1$
$6\overline{)7_{1}2\,8\,5}$	$6\overline{)7_{1}2\,8_{2}5}$

In this example, the 7 thousands can be shared by distributing one to each of the 6 groups. This leaves 1 thousand or 10 hundreds. The 10 hundreds are recorded next to the 2, making 12 hundreds to be shared. Note that the sharing of place value pieces does not change, only how a paper-and-pencil record is kept. For a measurement setting, the paper-and-pencil record would be identical but children would use language like "I can subtract 6 thousands . . . ." to work through the process.

Making sense of remainders   All of the examples in this section involved remainders. It is customary to report remainders in one of two ways as shown below. In the first case, the remainder is simply reported as a remainder. In the second example, the remainder is reported as a fraction of the divisor and is an integral part of the quotient.

$1\,0\,4\,\text{R}\,1$	$1\,0\,4\tfrac{1}{6}$
$6\overline{)6\,2\,5}$	$6\overline{)6\,2\,5}$

TABLE 9-3

DIVISION WITH 0 IN THE QUOTIENT

LANGUAGE	RECORD
I can share the 6 hundreds among 6 people; each person gets 1 hundred. There will be zero hundreds left.	1 $6\overline{)6\,|\,2\,|\,5}$ 6 0
I cannot share the 2 tens among 6 people. Each person will get zero tens so I will record the zero in the tens position above the 2.	$1\,|\,0$ $6\overline{)6\,|\,2\,|\,5}$ 6 $0\,|\,2$
The 2 tens left over can be shared if they are exchanged for 20 ones making 25 ones. Each person gets 4 ones.	$1\,|\,0\,|\,4$ $6\overline{)6\,|\,2\,|\,5}$ 6 $0\,|\,2\,|\,5$
24 of the 25 ones can be shared. There is 1 left over.	$1\,|\,0\,|\,4$ $6\overline{)6\,|\,2\,|\,5}$ 6 $0\,|\,2\,|\,5$ $2\,|\,4$ 1

Either of the above are acceptable responses if the computation is strictly a symbolic process. When the computation arises from a real-life context, the remainder must be interpreted in the context of the problem and handled in a way that is appropriate to that context. Consider the following 4 cases.

- **Case 1: Part of the answer.**

  I have a 29 inch length of the ribbon from which I want to make 5 award ribbons of equal length. How long will each ribbon be?

  Here the answer, 5 R4, does not make sense because there is no need to have wasted material. In this case the answer $5\frac{4}{5}$ inches makes more sense. The "remainder" is part of the answer.

- **Case 2: Include remainders.**

  Seven parents have volunteered to drive Mrs. Clemenson's class on their field trip to the zoo. There are 31 people going on the trip, including the parents. How many people will be in each car?

  Neither 4 R3 nor $4\frac{3}{7}$ make any sense in this case. What would actually happen is that 4 cars would take 4 people and 3 cars would have 5 people. No one will be left behind. Again, there really is no remainder. The "remainder" has to be included by evenly distributing it among as many groups as necessary.

- **Case 3: Round up.**

  A grocery store sells spaghetti sauce at 2 jars for $1.39. How much would a customer pay for one jar?

  Again, neither 69 R1 nor $69\frac{1}{2}$ make any sense. The quotient would be rounded up and the customer would pay 70¢ for one jar.

- **Case 4: Ignore remainder.**

  37 children try out for three teams. If 11 players are allowed on each team, how many teams can be formed?

  Clearly, neither 3 R4 nor $3\frac{4}{11}$ are appropriate answers. Four children cannot be included on a team. They can be scorekeepers, timers, or equipment managers, but have to be "ignored" as part of the teams.

Two-digit divisors the role of estimation becomes much more significant when children need to use a divisor with two (or more) digits. Consider a computation

such as 493 ÷ 62. Children can take several approaches to estimating the quotient.

1. *Rounding.* By rounding the divisor to the nearest 10, a logical estimate is 8 since 8×60 is 480. However, $8 \times 62 = 496$, which is larger than the dividend.

2. *Ignore the last digit in both the divisor and the dividend.* This results in the exercise, 49 ÷ 6. Again, 8 is a reasonable, but too high an estimate.

3. *Round the divisor up to the nearest 10.* The above example would be thought of as 493 ÷ 70. Since 7×70 is 490, a reasonable estimate is 7, which works well. However, if the problem would have been 503 ÷ 62, the estimate would still be 7 because $7 \times 70 = 490$ and $8 \times 70 = 560$, which exceeds the dividend. However, 7 is too small in this case.

4. *Round the divisor up and round the dividend down to the nearest compatible number.* This produces the most conservative estimate, often too low. Using the previous example, the quotient estimate would be based on 420 ÷ 70. In this case 6 is the best estimate but it is too small. We shall return to this problem shortly.

The language corresponding to the steps in the algorithm is essentially the same as for the one-digit divisor. A sample of the language associated with each step in computing 493 ÷ 62 is described in Table 9-4.

Employing the compatible number strategy along with rounding up the divisor will produce conservative estimates as long as the compatible number is less than the dividend. In fact, many times an estimate that is too small will occur with this combined strategy. This is a problem more for adults than for children who are familiar with this phenomenon in real life. For example, a child may share some sweets with other members of a group by giving each person two sweets. More can still be equally shared so another round of sharing takes place. The same process can be used with the division algorithm. The only question is how to record successive sharing of the same place value pieces. If a child had used 420 as the compatible number for the dividend, the first estimate of the quotient would be 6. Figure 9-35 shows how the paper-and-pencil record might be kept.

The final result of the algorithm must be recorded in either form (a) or form (b) in Figure 9-36.

The measurement approach In the real world, children experience measurement situations as well as sharing problems. The computational procedure for solving a measurement-type division problem may result in a

TABLE 9-4

CONNECTING PLACE VALUE LANGUAGE AND SYMBOLIC RECORD FOR TWO-DIGIT DIVISORS

LANGUAGE	RECORD
I cannot share 4 hundreds among 62 groups. I cannot share 49 tens among 62 groups, but I can share 493 ones among 62 groups.	62)4 9 3
I will estimate how many ones I can share by rounding the 62 groups to 70.	Think 70 →62)493
What number is compatible with 70 that I can use for the dividend? 490	Think 70 →62)493← Think 490 70)490
7 × 70 is 490 so I can distribute 7 ones to each group. Recording the 7 in the ones position since I am distributing ones.	7 62)493
How many ones were distributed to the 62 groups? 7 × 62 = 434.	7 62)493 434
How many ones are left? 59. Can I distribute any more ones? No. There is a remainder of 59.	7 62)493 434 59

similar algorithm to the sharing approach but the language the children use is different. Table 9-5 illustrates a measurement approach.

CHECKING CALCULATIONS

Children should be encouraged to develop a "check-my-work" mind-set although they are often reluctant to do so. Pointing out the increased accuracy that results from checking and showing a variety of checking strategies help overcome this reluctance. Estimation provides one

check on computational accuracy. The calculator provides a fast and easy way to check computations. Having children interchange the order of the addends (commutative property) is another way children could check addition.

A common strategy for checking subtraction is based on the inverse relationship between addition and subtraction. If you add the difference to the subtrahend you should get the minuend because the sum of the two subgroups is equal to the number in the total group.

Casting out nines, while not 100 percent reliable, is a "novel" approach to checking that children enjoy trying

FIGURE 9-35

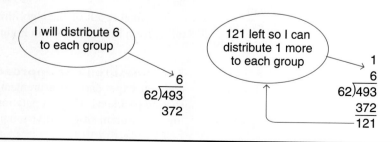

I will distribute 6 to each group

6
62)493
372

121 left so I can distribute 1 more to each group

1
6
62)493
372
121

FIGURE 9-36

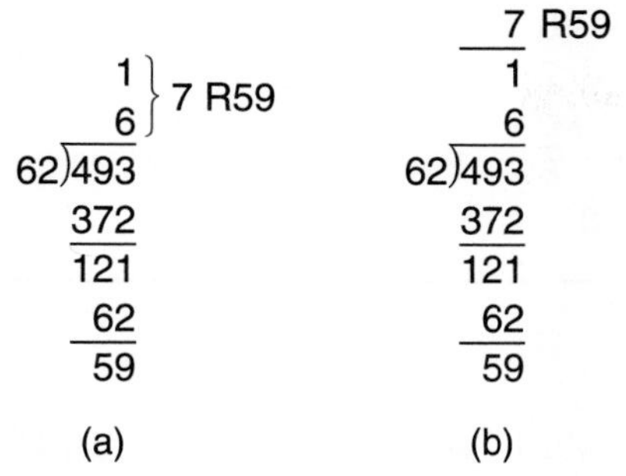

$$
\left.\begin{array}{r} 1 \\ 6 \end{array}\right\} 7\ R59
$$

$$
62\overline{)493} \\ 372 \\ \overline{121} \\ 62 \\ \overline{59}
$$

(a)

$$
\begin{array}{r} 7\ R59 \\ 1 \\ 6 \end{array}
$$

$$
62\overline{)493} \\ 372 \\ \overline{121} \\ 62 \\ \overline{59}
$$

(b)

and at the same time they may gain some additional insight into the whole number system. For addition the procedure involves calculating the sum of the digits in each addend. If this sum has more than one digit, repeat the process. Then calculate the sum of each of the single dig-

its obtained from each addend. If necessary, reduce this to a one-digit number as shown in (a) in Figure 9-37. Now take the sum of the digits in the sum. Reduce this to a one-digit number in the same way as shown in (b) in Figure 9-37. If the sum was correct, (a) and (b) will be the same.

This process can also be used for subtraction and multiplication. The difference is that the single digits obtained by casting out nines are subtracted or multiplied rather than added. Frequently you will end with situations like $3 - 7$. In this case one of the nines can be added back in as illustrated in Figure 9-38.

Multiplication is commonly used to check division because of the inverse relationship between these operations. Division, because it involves a more difficult algorithm, is not often used to check multiplication although it could be.

Checking division by use of multiplication requires consideration of the remainder. Since the remainder is the "left over" from an equal distribution, the number in each

TABLE 9-5

LANGUAGE TO SYMBOLIC RECORD (MEASUREMENT APPROACH)

LANGUAGE	RECORD
Can I subtract 62 thousands? No. But I can subtract 62 hundreds after I regroup the 6 thousands as 60 hundreds.	$62\overline{)6507}$
How many times can I subtract 62 hundreds? One time, I record this 1 in the hundreds column since I am subtracting hundreds.	$\begin{array}{r}1\\62\overline{)6507}\end{array}$
How many hundreds left? 3	$\begin{array}{r}1\\62\overline{)6507}\\62\\\overline{3}\end{array}$
I will regroup these as 3 tens. I now have 30 + 0 or 30 tens. Can I subtract 62 tens? No, so I record a zero in the tens place.	$\begin{array}{r}10\\62\overline{)6507}\\62\\\overline{30}\end{array}$
I will regroup these 30 tens as 300 ones. I have 300 + 7 or 307 ones.	$\begin{array}{r}10\\62\overline{)6507}\\62\\\overline{307}\end{array}$
Can I subtract 62 ones? Yes. How many times? $280 \div 70$ *(compatible numbers)* is 4, so I'll try 4. I am subtracting ones so I will record the 4 in the ones column.	$\begin{array}{r}104\\62\overline{)6507}\\62\\\overline{307}\end{array}$
How many ones have I subtracted? 4×62 is 248. How many ones left? 59. Can I subtract any more sets of 62? No, so there is a remainder of 59.	$\begin{array}{r}104\\62\overline{)6507}\\62\\\overline{307}\\248\\\overline{59}\end{array}$

FIGURE 9-37

$$357 \longrightarrow 3 + 5 + 7 = 15 \longrightarrow 1 + 5 = 6 \longrightarrow 6$$
$$236 \longrightarrow 2 + 3 + 6 = 11 \longrightarrow 1 + 1 = 2 \longrightarrow 2$$
$$\underline{495} \longrightarrow 4 + 9 + 5 = 18 \longrightarrow 1 + 8 = 9 \longrightarrow \underline{0}$$
$$ 8 \longrightarrow \text{(a)}$$
$$1088 \longrightarrow 1 + 0 + 8 + 8 = 17 \longrightarrow 1 + 7 = 8 \longrightarrow 8 \longrightarrow \text{(b)}$$

group is multiplied by the number of equal groups, and then the remainder added back in. A child who did the computation shown here would check by multiplying 22×17 to get 374 and then add 20 to make 394. Clearly something is incorrect. If the correct quotient, 107 R20, had been obtained, the check would have been $22 \times 107 = 2354$; $2354 + 20 = 2374$, the original dividend.

$$\begin{array}{r} 17 \ \text{R20} \\ 22\overline{)2374} \\ \underline{22} \\ 174 \\ \underline{154} \\ 20 \end{array}$$

Error Patterns

Ashlock (1998) notes that errors can be helpful in the process of learning if they are used to analyze patterns of errors. Error pattern analysis gives teachers information to use to modify instruction to meet students' needs.

According to Ashlock, teachers "need to examine each student's paper diagnostically: look for patterns, hypothesize possible causes, and verify your ideas. Approach a student's written work as if each paper is itself a problem or puzzle to be solved" (1998, p. 10). Students' errors often are a result of overgeneralizing or making generalizations based on limited amounts of data. For example, when regrouping in addition, it doesn't matter when the number "carried" is added. In the work shown below, the sum in the tens column is

$1 + 7 + 5$, which can be added in any order for a result of 13 tens.

$$\begin{array}{r} ^{1} \\ 78 \\ + 56 \\ \hline \end{array}$$

But consider the error in the multiplication problem below:

$$\begin{array}{r} ^{1} \\ 42 \\ \times 6 \\ \hline 302 \end{array}$$

This student makes an error in working with the 1 ten that we regrouped after multiplying 6×2: rather than multiplying 6 times 4 and adding 1, the student incorrectly adds the 1 to the 4, then multiplies 5 by 6, for an answer of 30 in the tens column. This error could be due to an overgeneralization of the addition algorithm described above.

How might a teacher help this student? Several approaches might be taken. Review the meaning of multiplication by using models. Remind students that 6 times 42 could mean 6 rows with 42 in each row. Construct this model with base-ten blocks (see Figure 9-39).

CONSOLIDATING SKILLS

Once children have developed computational procedures, they need many activities that will help to consolidate their understanding and to develop proficiency in terms of accuracy and speed. Doing straightforward computa-

FIGURE 9-38

Stop here, or add 9 back in to avoid negative

$$372 \longrightarrow 3 + 7 + 2 = 12 \longrightarrow 1 + 2 = 3 \longrightarrow 9 + 3 = 12$$
$$\underline{- 196} \longrightarrow 1 + 9 + 6 = 16 \longrightarrow 1 + 6 = 7 \longrightarrow 7$$
$$176 \longrightarrow 1 + 7 + 6 = 14 \longrightarrow 1 + 4 = 5 \longrightarrow 5$$

FIGURE 9-39

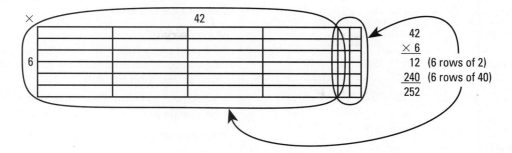

The Annenberg/CPB Math and Science Collection

VIDEO LINK 9-2
Whole Number Computation

Brief Summary: In "Choose a Method," teacher Mary Holden's fourth- and fifth-grade students are using different computational methods to solve problems.

1. Why do you think Ms. Holden relates money to the value of the blocks?
2. Describe the types of problems Ms. Holden asks the students to solve. Why do you think she chose those problems?
3. How do the students use base-ten blocks to solve computation problems such as 5 × $0.23?
4. How does the teacher relate estimation and the notion of "reasonableness" to the computation problems?
5. Describe the different methods students use to solve these computation problems.
6. What were the benefits of students working in groups during this lesson?

Video Source. Teaching Math: A Video Library, K–4; Tape 7 from The Annenberg/CPB Math and Science Collection.

tions is all right once in a while, but a teacher needs to have a large repertoire of ideas and activities for practice purposes. The following six categories are only examples of the different types of activities a teacher might use.

Puzzles

Puzzles provide an interesting and novel way for children to practice computation (Neufeld, 1991). Children will receive a great deal of practice with addition and subtraction as they attempt to complete the puzzle in Activity 9-12. How do they get practice with subtraction?

In the puzzle in Figure 9-40 children are to trace a path from the upper left cell to the lower right cell by joining

cells that contain a number divisible by 7. Cells may be joined vertically, horizontally, or diagonally.

Games

Many games are useful for consolidation purposes. Games where winning is based on mental strategy rather than on chance should be used. Activity 9-13 is one example.

Some variations on Activity 9-13 could include:

- Worksheets with 3 three-digit numbers, 3 two-digit numbers, etc.
- Go for the lowest sum.
- Use subtraction. (Use one less digit in the subtrahend than in the minuend to reduce the possibility of negative numbers.)

✳ ACTIVITY 9-12

HONEYCOMB SUM

MATERIALS:

PROCEDURE:
1. Make each column sum to 38. You can use only the numbers 1 through 19. Use each number only once.
2. Can you do it a different way?

FIGURE 9-40

START
↓

					7 AS A DIVISOR		
7	1005	634	904	1111	156	63	427
238	268	928	56	1215	297	5123	5
494	84	1015	96	140	307	77	7963
47	2047	82	5326	217	3131	9876	357
721	6055	214	63	3333	384	197	4242
128	9	4014	546	753	2114	595	1584
539	4021	535	246	2499	872	287	59
749	587	2121	8642	37	3977	861	4536

↑
FINISH

- Use multiplication or division.
- Will your strategy be different if balls are *not* replaced?

Activity 9-14 encourages children to apply some "number-sense-thinking" about possible combinations while providing some practice with the algorithms involving small numbers. Many of the combinations will not involve division because division will not produce a whole number. Nevertheless, children will need to consider division and make a mental decision as to whether it will divide evenly.

Two of the dice must be specially prepared as well as a variety of game boards. Numbers from 1 to 1296 can be used randomly to create the game boards. How can 1 be achieved? How can 1296 be achieved? A sample game board is shown in Figure 9-41.

Like all bingo-type cards, the card in Figure 9-41 will not contain responses for some shakes of the dice. If a combination cannot be found in a reasonable time, play goes to the next player. Does the card in Figure 9-41 have a response for a shake of 5, 9, 17?

Riddles

Riddles are another motivating way for children to practice computation. The solution to a riddle similar to the one suggested in Chapter 8 could be developed with larger numbers to provide addition and subtraction com-

✳ ACTIVITY 9-13

GREATEST SUM

MATERIALS:
- 10 ping pong balls with numerals 0, 1, 2, . . ., 9. (Cards could be used but they tend to stick together, reducing randomness.)
- Worksheet as below. (Several grids can be placed on one page to facilitate multiple games.)

PROCEDURE:

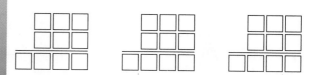

1. Select a leader to draw balls. (If a whole class activity, the teacher may act as leader.)
2. The leader draws a ball and announces the number on it. All players write this number in one of the addend boxes on the worksheet. Once a number has been placed, it cannot be moved or changed.
3. Replace the ball and shake the bag.
4. Repeat steps 2 and 3 until all addend boxes are filled.
5. Compute the sum.
6. The winners are all those with the greatest sum.

putation practice. Once you have found (or created) a riddle it is not difficult to construct exercises as in Activity 9-15 and Figure 9-42. Knowing the answer to a riddle, the teacher can simply create the kind of questions the class or small group of children need practice with and then associate each letter with the answer to a computation. The difficulty level can be changed to suit the level of the class. The exercises could also be altered to include decimals or common fractions.

Computer Software

Research suggests that the use of the computer does enhance computational performance (Cathcart, 1990, 1991). Computer software is one more ingredient in a teacher's repertoire of ideas to provide variety in practice activities.

Math Blaster provides computational practice with larger numbers as well as basic facts. Three products from MECC (Minnesota Educational Computing Corporation) products are inexpensive, readily available to

✳ ACTIVITY 9-14

ALL-OPS

MATERIALS:
- 3 dice: 1 regular (numbers 1–6)
          1 with numbers 7–12
          1 with numbers 13–18
- Game board for each player.

OBJECT:
To be the first to place 5 markers in a row, column, or diagonal.

PROCEDURE:
1. One player shakes all 3 dice.
2. All players then use the 3 numbers showing, and any combination of the four operations to try to produce a number on their card.
3. Each player must have one other player verify his or her work.
4. Take turns rolling the dice.

FIGURE 9-41

ALL-OPS

4	88	19	38	89
1024	55	76	106	8
60	3	I Can	111	635
149	91	384	9	63
904	210	788	500	1296

schools, and provide good computational practice. Questions in *Conquering Whole Numbers* involve regrouping. If a student makes two errors on the same question, intermediate regrouping steps are included on the screen and a student is eventually "forced" to respond correctly. Three games are included which provide additional practice as well as motivation and challenge. *Addition Logician* is similar except that it deals only with addition and the games are interspersed throughout a problem set. One component of MECC's *Subtraction Puzzles* simulates a balloon trip to Paris. Progress is made as computations such as those in Figure 9-43 are correctly entered.

One activity in *Estimation* (MECC) involves estimating products or quotients. The student can control the number of problems (5–30), but more importantly, the time allowed to make an estimate (5–30 s). The time can be set short enough to discourage paper-and-pencil computation, yet long enough to allow an analysis of the question and the application of an appropriate estimation strategy.

Control is permitted over the level of question. For multiplication, the choices are:

- one-digit × two-digit
- two-digit × 3-digit, product < 1000
- two-digit × two-digit, product > 1000
- mixture of all

FIGURE 9-42

How does a monster count to 20?

$4\overline{)136}$ → S $5\overline{)1600}$ → A

$8\overline{)280}$ → G $7\overline{)2975}$ → C

$9\overline{)5319}$ → N $6\overline{)144}$ → F

$6\overline{)1458}$ → T $7\overline{)105}$ → O

$9\overline{)801}$ → L $5\overline{)65}$ → E

$3\overline{)396}$ → I $8\overline{)3064}$ → R

$$\overline{15}\ \overline{591}\ \overline{132}\ \overline{243}\ \overline{34}$$

$$\overline{24}\ \overline{132}\ \overline{591}\ \overline{35}\ \overline{13}\ \overline{383}\ \overline{34}$$

✳ ACTIVITY 9-15

WHY DOES A HUMMINGBIRD HUM?

PROCEDURE:

1. Do each computation, then use the code to find the matching letter. The first one is done as an example.

CODE:

37 – W	122 – C	232 – H
54 – N	123 – O	241 – K
73 – M	154 – R	259 – E
78 – T	162 – D	287 – S
83 – I	163 – L	341 – A

$36 + 47 = \underline{83} \ \underline{I}$ $386 - 145 = \underline{\ \ } \ \underline{\ \ }$

$143 - 65 = \underline{\ \ } \ \underline{\ \ }$ $618 - 564 = \underline{\ \ } \ \underline{\ \ }$

$64 + 98 = \underline{\ \ } \ \underline{\ \ }$ $66 + 9 + 48 = \underline{\ \ } \ \underline{\ \ }$

$12 + 69 + 42 = \underline{\ \ } \ \underline{\ \ }$ $100 - 63 = \underline{\ \ } \ \underline{\ \ }$

$345 - 86 = \underline{\ \ } \ \underline{\ \ }$ $155 - 77 = \underline{\ \ } \ \underline{\ \ }$

$402 - 115 = \underline{\ \ } \ \underline{\ \ }$ $155 + 77 = \underline{\ \ } \ \underline{\ \ }$

$92 - 38 = \underline{\ \ } \ \underline{\ \ }$ $167 + 92 = \underline{\ \ } \ \underline{\ \ }$

$97 + 26 = \underline{\ \ } \ \underline{\ \ }$ $108 - 71 = \underline{\ \ } \ \underline{\ \ }$

$212 - 134 = \underline{\ \ } \ \underline{\ \ }$ $254 - 131 = \underline{\ \ } \ \underline{\ \ }$

$88 + 66 = \underline{\ \ } \ \underline{\ \ }$

$115 + 47 = \underline{\ \ } \ \underline{\ \ }$

$136 + 295 - 144 = \underline{\ \ } \ \underline{\ \ }$

Similarly for division, the choices are:

- 3-digit ÷ one digit
- 3-digit ÷ two-digit
- 4-digit ÷ two-digit
- mixture of all

Other Algorithms

The *Russian Peasant* algorithm can be presented in the form of a story. Provide the following background to the story. A certain Russian peasant (fictional, of course) who had attended school only occasionally, was in charge of a cabbage farm for the Russian Czar. He could add well, double a number, and divide by 2, but had no idea what to do with remainders so he ignored them. He had no formal knowledge of fractions. He had an intuitive idea that somehow multiplication (doubling) was the opposite of dividing by 2. Odd and even numbers were also recognized by this peasant.

FIGURE 9-43

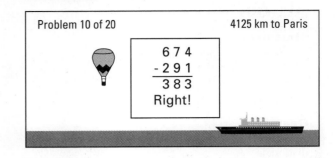

$$\begin{array}{r} 674 \\ -291 \\ \hline 383 \end{array}$$
Right!

Early one spring this Russian peasant was pacing off his field to determine how many cabbage plants he needed for transplanting. Just as he finished, the overseer came riding up on his big white horse and demanded, "How many cabbage plants do you need this spring?"

"We-l-l-l sir, I'm not sure. I know I've got room for 25 rows and I can put 36 in each row."

"How many is that!" demanded the overseer.

"I-l-l-I'm-m-m not sure, sir."

"I'm going down the road to see the next farmer. If you don't know how many plants you need by the time I get back, I'll have your head."

The poor peasant sat down to see if he could figure out how many cabbage plants he needed.

He wrote: **25**   **36**

"Well, I could double the 36. That would give me 72. No, I need a lot more than that. Since I doubled 36, maybe I better halve 25.   ~~12~~   ~~72~~

Let's see, that is 12." (Remember he didn't know what to do with remainders.)

"Perhaps I should do that again."   ~~6~~   ~~144~~
(He continued this process   **3**   **288**
until he got to 1 on the   **1**   **576**
left-hand side.)

"U-m-m-m, I'm sure I need more than 576 plants. Oh, yes, that astrologer friend of mine told me that numbers associated with even numbers are unlucky."

"I'll strike out the 12 and 6 rows.
I can't see that helps me.   **25**   **36**

I wonder what would happen if   **12**   **72**
I added this side (pointing to the   **6**   **144**
right-hand column)?" He adds   **3**   **288**
36 288, and 576 to get 900.   **1**   **576**

Just then the overseer comes   **900**
riding back on his big white
horse.

Ask the children to do an example on their own and to tell how they know their answer is correct. To determine the correctness of the answer, children will likely use a conventional algorithm, thus practicing multiplication with it. If you challenged them with the query, "I wonder if there are any numbers for which the Russian Peasant method doesn't work?", they will receive considerable self-motivating and self-checking practice.

Philipp (1996) describes the benefits of teachers talking with children and their families about the algorithms they use to solve problems. Many people, especially those who learned mathematics in another country, use different algorithms than those customarily taught in this country. According to Philipp, this "legitimizes the mathematics learning of either the child or a member of the child's family but also presents an opportunity to honor this learning in both the child's eyes and, depending on what is done with the information, in the eyes of all the students in the class." (p. 129)

Problem Solving

A teacher should strive to present interesting problem solving settings so students will practice doing computations in meaningful contexts. Managing a school store is an example of a good context.

CONCLUSION

Solving a problem involving computation can be done in a number of ways and children should be encouraged to develop their own computational procedures. This takes some time, but it is time well spent.

In developing computational procedures, try to capture as many serendipitous events as possible to provide a meaningful context. These are current, involve the children, and often have some bearing on their lives. For example:

All the Grade 3 children in Twin Rivers School are going to the zoo. How many tickets need to be purchased?

The children could find out how many classes have grade three students and how many in each, and then do the computation.

In general, students will proceed through several phases as they learn computational procedures. They should begin by finding the answer through the manipulation of base-ten blocks or other concrete material. Children should then be encouraged to record in their own way the process they used to find the answer. Over time this recording will become more symbolic and concise, but still it is done in the child's own way. Later, children can be guided into recording in the most concise form (standard algorithm). Even here there

can be variation because algorithms are not universally common.

Throughout the process of developing computational procedures, children should be encouraged to use estimation and mental computation. This helps children learn computational strategies and develops number sense. Estimation and mental computation can also provide a check on the accuracy of paper-and-pencil or calculator computation. As such they become a part of the looking-back phase of problem solving. Calculators should be available to help children solve problems, particularly with larger numbers.

Children also need practice to become proficient with computational procedures. The key is to employ a *variety* of interesting activities for practice.

For Your Journal

When you have finished studying this chapter, reflect on these questions in your math journal:

1. Estimate each sum and describe the thinking processes you see.

258	4921
819	2121
234	866
560	7295
602	

2. For each list of exercises below, describe the error pattern, complete the remaining problems using the error pattern, and describe a remediation plan for each type of error.

I.

347	468	516	739	604
− 189	− 342	− 209	− 485	− 368
242	126	313		

II.

28	394	476	366	37
36	+ 242	+ 708	+ 547	21
+ 21	5136	11714		+ 55
715				

3. Visit elementary classrooms and talk with children about the algorithms they or members of their families use to solve problems. Describe these algorithms and compare them with the traditional algorithm taught in this country.

For Your Portfolio

When you have finished studying this chapter, complete these activities to include in your professional portfolio:

1. Visit elementary classrooms and make copies (with the teacher's permission) of children's written work

using algorithms to solve problems. Identify the errors made and any patterns in those errors. Discuss what you might do if you were their teacher to enhance their understanding.

2. Write a lesson to help students connect meaning to symbols for an algorithm of your choice.

Resources for Teachers

Books about Algorithms

Ashlock, R. B. (1998). *Error patterns in computation (7th ed.).* Upper Saddle River, NJ: Simon & Schuster.

Morrow, L. J., & Kenney, M. J. (Eds.). (1998). *The teaching and learning of algorithms in school mathematics.* Reston, VA: National Council of Teachers of Mathematics.

Links to the Internet

Math League Help Topics

http://www.mathleague.com/help/help.htm

Contains hints for using algorithms for computation with whole numbers.

CHAPTER 10

Developing Fraction Concepts

What are fractions, and what should students know about them? As with many other mathematics topics, traditionally there has been a rush to introduce abstract symbols before students understand the underlying concepts. This section will explain what fractions are and what students need to learn about them. ○

Focus Questions

When you have finished studying this chapter, you should be able to answer these questions:

1. What should children understand about fractions?

2. What three models can be used in teaching the part-whole interpretation of fractions? What teaching considerations are involved? Give an example of each.

3. What strategies can teachers use to help children understand how to compare fractions?

4. Why is it important to help children understand the equivalence of fractions?

What Are Fractions?

The term *rational number* is rarely expressed in elementary classes. This is because fractional and decimal numbers are emphasized, whereas other interpretations of rational numbers such as ratio, rate, and percent usually are not formally studied at that level. In this chapter, the focus is on fractions. (Decimals, integers, and other interpretations of rational numbers are addressed in subsequent chapters.)

STANDARDS LINK 10-1

In grades K–4, the mathematics curriculum should include fractions and decimals so that students can

- develop concepts of fractions, mixed numbers, and decimals;
- develop number sense for fractions and decimals;
- use models to relate fractions to decimals and to find equivalent fractions;
- use models to explore operations on fractions and decimals;
- apply fractions and decimals to problem situations. (NCTM, 1989, p. 57)

STANDARDS LINK 10-2

In grades 5–8, the mathematics curriculum should include the study of number systems and number theory so that students can

- understand and appreciate the need for numbers beyond the whole numbers;
- develop and use order relations for whole numbers, fractions, decimals, integers, and rational numbers . . . . (NCTM, 1989, p. 91)

The fractions studied in elementary school are rational numbers that express the indicated quotient ($\frac{a}{b}$) of one whole number a by a counting number b (non-zero number). In algebra, the definition is broadened and fractions are more appropriately defined as the indicated quotient of an algebraic expression divided by another. From this definition, one can see that numbers such as $\frac{\pi}{5}$ and $-\frac{4}{5}$ also are fractions.

The term *fraction* is derived from a Latin word meaning "to break." From this literal meaning, it is assumed that an early concept of fractions was a broken whole or something "less than a whole." One can find ample support for using this primitive interpretation when introducing fractions to children.

In "parts of a whole" the metaphor used is fractions as things rather than as numbers. One-fifth of a pizza is a certain-sized piece of pizza and not necessarily a number that answers the question "how much?" The idea of fractional parts representing numbers emerges over time. Having students respond to the questions "how much?" or "what is the share?" in instances of sharing a whole can lead to thinking about fractions as numbers. Measurement explicitly uses the numeric value of fractions.

What Do Students Know About Fractions?

What do we know of the fraction understanding of students in the United States? The sixth National Assessment of Educational Progress (NAEP) noted that most fourth-, eighth-, and twelfth-grade students tested were able to correctly choose pictorial representations for simple fractions, but they had more difficulty representing equivalent fractions (Kouba, Zawojewski, & Struchens, 1997). Only about two-thirds of the eighth graders tested were able to correctly choose a picture showing an equivalent fraction or choose an equivalent fraction for a given picture.

NAEP results also showed that students had difficulty comparing fractions in items such as the following, for example:

Jose ate 1/2 of a pizza. Ella ate 1/2 of a pizza. Jose said that he ate more pizza than Ella, but Ella said they both ate the same amount. Use words and pictures to show that Jose could be right (Dossey, Mullis, & Jones, 1993).

Over half of the fourth-grade students did not answer this item correctly, and only about one-fourth of the students gave satisfactory responses to this question. Some students felt that Jose could not be right, since "one-half is always equal to one-half." Students who answered correctly were able to recognize that Jose's pizza might have been larger than Ella's, which would mean that Jose's statement was correct. Items such as this point to the importance of teachers' helping children understand fraction concepts.

Hiebert and Behr (1988) recommended that increased attention be devoted to developing the meaning of fraction symbols, developing concepts such as order and equivalence that are important in fostering a sense of the relative size of fractions, and helping children connect their intuitive understandings and strategies to more general, formal methods.

According to Bezuk and Bieck (1993), "instruction [is crucial] to strengthen students' understandings before progressing to operations on fractions, rather than assuming that students already understand these topics" (p. 119).

Mack (1990) noted that students often possess informal, real-world knowledge about fractions that they are able to use to understand fraction symbols and procedures. Teachers should help students connect their real-world experiences with fractions to classroom work with fractions to strengthen students' understanding.

What Should Students Understand About Fractions?

Students must understand several aspects about fraction concepts and relationships before beginning fraction computation. The prerequisite topics include understanding fraction concepts, comparing fractions and developing number sense about fractions, and recognizing equivalence. These topics will be discussed in detail in this chapter.

> **STANDARDS LINK 10-3**
> The K–4 instruction should help students understand fractions and decimals, explore their relationship, and build initial concepts about order and equivalence. Because evidence suggests that children construct these ideas slowly, it is crucial that teachers use physical materials, diagrams, and real-world situations in conjunction with ongoing efforts to relate their learning experiences to oral language and symbols. This K–4 emphasis on basic ideas will reduce the amount of time currently spent in the upper grades in correcting students' misconceptions and procedural difficulties. (NCTM, 1989, p. 57)

DEVELOPING FRACTION CONCEPTS AND NUMBER SENSE

Number Sense with Fractions

Number sense with fractions develops over a long period of time; therefore, elementary and middle school teachers need to focus on this topic. A first goal is for students to develop conceptual understanding of fractions as numbers. Then there are various abilities that students must acquire in order to work effectively with fractions. These abilities include:

1. The ability to represent numbers using words, models, diagrams and symbols and make connections among various representations;

2. The ability to give other names for numbers and justify the procedures used to generate the equivalent forms;

3. The ability to describe the relative magnitude of numbers by comparing them to common benchmarks, giving simple estimates, ordering a set of numbers, and finding a number between two numbers.

> **STANDARDS LINK 10-4**
> An awareness of the relative size of fractions fosters number sense and enhances basic understandings. (NCTM, 1989, p. 58)

Guidelines for developing these abilities together with conceptual understanding are included in this chapter.

Assessing fraction number sense When assessing fraction number sense, have students model fractions concretely, pictorially, and symbolically. At times, present a task in one mode and have students respond in another mode. Some tasks for assessing fraction number sense are presented here:

Task 1 Represent six-tenths with the fraction circles. Can you show six-tenths on a number line?

Task 2 Can you read this number? (Show $\frac{2}{5}$ on a card.) Can you draw a picture to show what it means? Explain what the 2 and the 5 mean.

Task 3 If the following diagram shows $\frac{3}{5}$ of a set, draw the whole set. Could another set be used? Explain.

Task 4 If this length is four-tenths, draw length one.

_____

If this part is three-tenths, draw the whole.

_____

Task 5 Can you give this fraction another name?
$\frac{3}{5}$
Another name? (Vance, 1990)

Writing is a powerful way to assess students' understandings (NCTM, 1989). Teachers are encouraged to ask students to write about the mathematics they are doing. For example, children's responses to a simple direction such as "write about what you did" or "write about what you learned" can reveal much about a child's fraction understandings. Two examples of children's responses to the invitation to write a story about one-half or one-third are presented in Figure 10-1.

FIGURE 10-1

One Half

One day I went to the "It Store" and I bought 14 scratch 'n' sniff stickers. The next day I went to my friend's house and we traded stickers. We traded and I gave her 7 stickers, or half of the stickers.

(The 14 stickers were drawn with 7 crossed out.)

P.S. Half means you have two equal parts and you take one away. Then you have half.

Jack, Grade 3

Half

My mommy got a pizza for me and my brother. My mommy cut it in eight pieces.

I had 2 pieces and my brother 2 pieces of pizza. All together, we ate half the pizza.

Beth, Grade 3

Developing the meaning of *half* Children come to school knowing the term *half* as they have used it in their sharing experiences. However, this does not mean that they know the fractional term *half* in its precise meaning, that is, half is one of two equal parts. Several activities to help develop the concept of half are described below. The first involves sets rather than a region model. It is included here because of its focus on half.

1. Sharing for two:
   - Set the context by relating a story such as: "Jane and Jill are sisters and they frequently have things to share. They each are to get half of the things."
   - Ask the students to tell how the sisters will share
     - 6   pieces of gum
     - 10   baseball cards
     - 12   dimes
     - 8   barrettes.
   - Encourage the children to verbalize. Listen for expressions like "They shared the gum and they each got the same amount. So they each got half the gum."

2. Cutting in half:
   - Obtain a knife and two oranges, two apples, two soft cookies or other objects suitable for cutting.
   - Explain that you are going to cut each orange in two parts.
   - Cut one orange into two parts, as equal as possible, then ask, "How have I cut this orange? What can you say about the pieces?"
   - Cut the other orange into two obviously unequal parts, then ask, "How have I cut this orange? What can you say about the pieces?"
   - Encourage the children to verbalize. Some expressions could include:

     This orange is cut in two parts that are the same size. The parts are equal.

     The orange is cut in half. Each piece is one-half the orange. The other orange is not cut in half because the pieces are not the same size. The pieces are not equal.

     In the verbalization above, note the dual expressions "same size" and "equal." For some time, both should be used to develop and consolidate the meaning of the term *equal*.

3. Partitioning a square in half:
   - You will need a large colored square cut from heavy paper, art foam, or other suitable material and several narrow strips of white poster board to demonstrate "cutting" lines. The strips should be at least as long as the diagonal of the square.
   - Set the context by asking the children to pretend that one day their mother baked a small square cake for them to share with a friend.
   - Ask the children to explore the possibilities of "cutting the cake" in two parts that are the same amount. The white strips are to be used to show cuts on the cake.
   - Ask the children to indicate or record the cuts they think produce parts that show the same amount. The recording can be done in two ways: Provide students with squares drawn on a piece of paper and have them draw the cutting line and/or provide a square for the students to trace on paper and then mark the partitioning line.

For the purpose of a class discussion, the teacher could draw a series of squares on a transparency. Children in turn can show one way to cut the cake in two parts that are the same amount. Each type of cut is discussed. Ask questions such as "Does this cut show two parts that are the same amount?" "How can you tell?" "How much cake will each of you get?"

The teacher can explain the meaning of half as follows and then have the children verbalize the various expressions.

Cutting in half means that we show two parts that are the same amount. The parts are the same size. When a figure has been cut in half, each part is half the shape, a half, *or* one-half.

✳ ACTIVITY 10-1

PARTITIONING FIGURES IN HALF

MATERIALS:
several of each of the following figures for each child; small sticks to show cutting lines

PROCEDURE:
1. Use sticks to divide each figure in half.
2. Can some of the figures be divided in two ways? In more than two ways?

The last expression should be encouraged for it helps name other fractions such as two-halves, three-halves, etc.

This activity can be extended by repeating it using a rectangle, an equilateral triangle, a regular pentagon, a hexagon, or an octagon as suggested in Activity 10-1. Have children record their partitionings on paper, and then share and discuss the conclusions they have reached.

Activity 10-2 can be used to assess a child's mental development level as well as to develop the concept of half. Some students in Grades 5 and 6 are unable to rea-

✳ ACTIVITY 10-3

MEANING OF NUMBER TERMS

MATERIALS:
paper and pencil

PROCEDURE:
Draw a picture to show what each of the following terms means to you.

two   second   half

five   fifth   fifths

---

son that "if the figures are the same size (congruent), and the parts within each are the same size, then all the parts are the same amount or have the same area." The activity should be used after students have had experiences in partitioning squares, rectangles, triangles, and pentagons.

Fraction Names

When the fraction names are first learned, that is, halves, thirds, fourths, etc., it can be anticipated that there might be confusion with the ordinal numbers. Thus, comparisons between, for example, second and half, third and thirds, fourth and fourths, etc., should be made. An activity similar to Activity 10-3 may be worthwhile.

In early fraction work, the fraction words should be used without the symbols. Students can record findings such as "one-sixth of the pie has been eaten" or "one-half

✳ ACTIVITY 10-2

DETERMINING IF PARTS ARE THE SAME SIZE

MATERIALS:
pairs of partitioned figures as shown

PROCEDURE:
1. A student is shown the partitioned figures in pairs as in the diagram.

2. Look at these two figures. Are parts a and b the same size? (or, Do parts a and b show the same amount?)

Is part (a) the same size as part (b)?	Is part (a) the same size as part (b)?	Is part (a) the same size as part (b)?	Is part (a) the same size as part (b)?
Yes No	Yes No	Yes No	Yes No

and one-fourth is the same as three-fourths." This manner of recording makes students focus on "what objects are being considered" and not merely on "how many." In time, recording work with fractions can be abbreviated to "1 half + 1 fourth = 3 fourths." Formal symbolization should be required only when students demonstrate an understanding of fractions through problem-solving activities.

Teachers should not assume that students who use fractional terms properly in some context have an understanding of fractions. Children who use fraction terms such as *half* and *quarter* frequently use them in a narrow sense and sometimes use them erroneously. "Split the cookie in half in three pieces" and "Break it in half in four pieces" are common verbalizations by young children. It is recommended that teachers provide opportunities for students to use familiar fractional terms in order to determine what meaning each child affixes to them. For example, a child may use the term *half* when referring to an action as in "half it" or "cut it in half" and not to name a part. Another child may use the term *half* to name parts when a whole is divided in two, three, or more parts. Frequently, the parts need not be the same size to be labeled half. This knowledge is important before moving on to further work with fractions.

Fraction symbols should be introduced only when students understand the meaning of the terms *one-half, one-third, one-fourth,* etc. Peck and Jencks (1981) present an interesting way of developing an understanding of fraction symbols with young children. They have children first read $\frac{1}{3}$ as "share among 3," then $\frac{2}{3}$ as "share among 3, cover 2." This process causes children to think of the denominator first, then the numerator, implying that the language "two-thirds" is "backward" to the thinking process. It is interesting to note that in Chinese, fractions are read by naming the denominator first. This might be an advantage in learning fractions.

Fraction symbolism   Fraction symbols should be introduced when students can use fractions in problem situations involving regions, parts of a set, and in measurement. Fraction symbols should be written with a horizontal bar, although a slanted bar is used on keyboards. The *Math Explorer* calculator also displays a slanted bar.

> **STANDARDS LINK 10-5**
> Fraction symbols, such as $\frac{1}{4}$ and $\frac{3}{2}$, should be introduced only after children have developed the concepts and oral language necessary for symbols to be meaningful and should be carefully connected to both the models and oral language. (NCTM, 1989, p. 58)

There is no reason students should learn the terms *numerator* and *denominator* when fraction symbols are introduced. Referring to the "top number" and "bottom number" in a fraction symbol would be an understandable designation for children.

Comparisons can be made in order to connect each number in the fraction symbol with the fraction language children have been using. For example, have students count fraction circles. As they count, write the fraction words on the board as in the second column below.

	one-sixth	1 sixth	$\frac{1}{6}$
	two-sixths	2 sixths	$\frac{2}{6}$
	three-sixths	3 sixths	$\frac{3}{6}$
	four-sixths	4 sixths	$\frac{4}{6}$
	five-sixths	5 sixths	$\frac{5}{6}$
	six-sixths	6 sixths	$\frac{6}{6}$

Ask: What is a short form we have been using when writing fractions: Then, write the third column on the board. Finally, write the last column, explaining that there is a still shorter form in which to write fractions.

The teacher should facilitate discussion by matching the "two" and both "2s" in the same row and asking what each represents. Repeat with the "sixths" and "6." Ask: "Why was the term *sixth* repeated when you counted? Why were the counting numbers used?"

For students who understand fraction parts, the following explanation of the fraction symbol should be adequate:

In fractions, the top number counts the parts and the bottom number tells what sized parts are being counted.

In order to consolidate the idea, have students count eighths and record the fractions in pictorial, written, and symbolic forms. Subsequently, students can be told that they can use any of the fraction forms whenever they are recording their work. In time, only the fraction symbols will be used.

Different units The meaning of fractions is developed by considering different units. Units are generally represented by continuous (regions) and discrete (a set of distinct objects) quantities. A unit also can be:

- continuous but divisible (e.g., a chocolate bar cut into squares to be shared among three siblings),
- a discrete set with divisible elements (e.g., 6 cookies to be shared among 4 children), or
- a discrete set with separate subsets (e.g., 5 boxes of candy, 12 candies per box to be shared among 4 people).

A unit may also, for particular problems, consist of part of a whole or more than one whole. These are not simple concepts for young students. See Figure 10-2.

Different Interpretations of Fractions

Fractions can be interpreted in several ways. Kieren (1980) identifies four meanings: part-while, quotient, ratio, and operator (multiplicative aspect), as shown in Figure 10-3. The part-whole interpretation is the one highlighted in elementary mathematics programs. This is not to conclude that young children are unable to understand other interpretations, however.

Part-whole interpretations The part-whole meaning of fractions comprises different units:

1. the whole can be a region (an object to be shared or an area to be divided),
2. a set of objects, or
3. a unit of linear measure.

Teaching considerations about each type are presented below.

Region model. There is substantial agreement that the region model of fractions should be learned before the model of "parts of a set" (Hollis, 1984; Payne, 1984; Skypek, 1984). Traditionally, regular geometric regions have been judged to be good fraction models because any unit fraction can be readily represented. It is suggested that students be allowed to experiment with partitioning different figures or regions rather than work solely with pre-partitioned figures. Without the personal experience of partitioning figures into equal parts, students are unable to use the model in problem-solving activities (Kieren, Nelson, & Smith, 1985; Pothier and Sawada, 1984).

Equality of parts. Children often are satisfied that parts "look the same size" when modeling fractions. For example, a regular pentagon or a heart shape partitioned by a horizontal "half cut" is often declared to be shared equally. See Figure 10-4. Therefore, in early fraction work, students should be required to construct parts that are congruent, that is, the same size and shape. At a later time, students will come to see (in area measurement) that non-congruent parts of regions can be equal.

For example, consider a set of tangrams, illustrated in Figure 10-5. Notice that there are three different tangram shapes that represent one-eighth of the whole tangram square. These three shapes are not congruent, but they each cover one-eighth of the area of the whole tangram square, so they each are one-eighth of the tangram. This example provides another opportunity to discuss with children that fractions do not have to be congruent to be the same part of the whole.

Children's judgments about the equality of parts in a few situations are presented in Figure 10-6.

Pothier and Sawada (1990) recommend that teachers provide students with opportunities to practice partitioning physical objects into equal-sized parts, rather than just drawing lines on the outlines of shapes. Do this by positioning coffee stirrers on top of uncut circles or rectangles, asking students to place the stirrers to show where the whole should be cut to make thirds, for example.

Parts drawn on cut-out figures can be tested for congruency by folding, or by dividing, cutting, and then superimposing the parts. Older students can measure the angles and sides of the parts produced. Activity 10-4 provides children with an opportunity to explore the iteration of equal parts. The following two teacher-directed activities aim to develop the concept of equality of parts in fractions.

1. Developing the Concept of Equality of Parts in Fractions
   - Materials: Figures drawn on paper to represent giant cookies: a heart, an equilateral triangle, a regular pentagon.
   - Provide students with at least two heart-shaped cookies and direct them to show how a cookie could be shared equally between 2 friends.
   - Focusing on a vertical cut, ask, "How can you prove each person gets the same amount?" (or, prove the pieces are equal?) Suggest that children fold one part over the other to see if the parts are equal.
   - Ask, "Can you cut the cookie a different way so each person gets the same amount?"
   - Focusing on a horizontal cut, ask, "Would each person get the same amount now?" Have students cut the shape on the fold line and superimpose the two parts.

FIGURE 10-2

(a) A continuous quantity

These regions are considered continuous quantities. The parts are measured rather than counted.

(b) Sets of discrete objects as the unit

 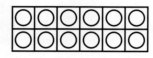

These are sets of discrete objects; that is, one can count the objects in each set.

(c) The unit is a continuous quantity that has been divided

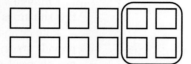

A Hershey bar cut-up. Gerry's share is these 4 pieces, or one-third of the bar.

(d) The unit is a discrete set with the elements divisible

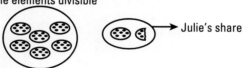 Julie's share

Four children share six cookies. What is each person's share? Julie's share is one and one-half cookies.

(e) The unit is a discrete set with divisible subsets

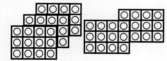 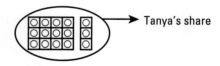 Tanya's share

A set of 5 boxes of candy with 12 candies per box, to be shared among 4 friends. How much does each person get?
Tanya's share is one and one-fourth boxes of candies.

(f) Part of a whole as a unit

What portion is one-half of the remaining pie? Three-fourths of the pie is the unit. One-half of three-fourths is three-eighths.

(g) The unit is more than a whole

The shaded parts show how much pizza Paul has eaten. Paul has eaten one and one-fourth mini pizzas.

FIGURE 10-3

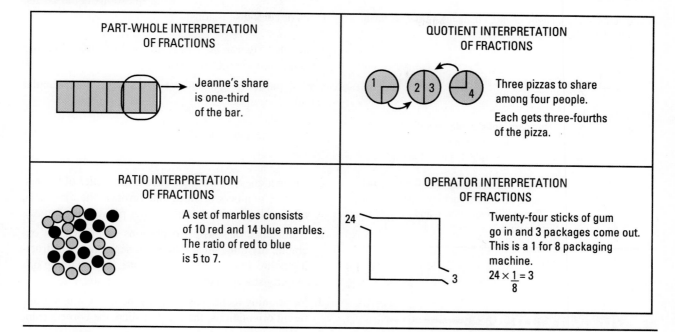

The panels in Figure 10-3:

PART-WHOLE INTERPRETATION OF FRACTIONS
Jeanne's share is one-third of the bar.

QUOTIENT INTERPRETATION OF FRACTIONS
Three pizzas to share among four people.
Each gets three-fourths of the pizza.

RATIO INTERPRETATION OF FRACTIONS
A set of marbles consists of 10 red and 14 blue marbles. The ratio of red to blue is 5 to 7.

OPERATOR INTERPRETATION OF FRACTIONS
Twenty-four sticks of gum go in and 3 packages come out. This is a 1 for 8 packaging machine.
$24 \times \frac{1}{8} = 3$

- Ask, "How are you sure the parts are equal? Why?"
- Say, "When we're sure the parts are equal, we can say that each part is one-half of the cookie."
- Repeat the procedures with a triangle, a pentagon, and other figures.
2. Equality of Parts: One-fourth
   - Materials: A square, a triangle, a parallelogram, a pentagon, a heart, and other figures.
   - Say: "Let's try two cuts on different figures to find out if they produce equal parts."
   - In each case ask, "Can the parts be called one-fourth of the figure? Why or why not?"

The following story could be used to assess children's understanding of equality in fractions:

A boy named Don told me that a heart-shaped cake cut into 4 parts like this [demonstrate a vertical and a horizontal halving line] makes parts equal because "this stick is in the middle of this one." What would you say to Don?

Children's responses can reveal whether they are focusing on the partitioning techniques or on the parts produced when assessing equality of parts.

A teacher who plans partitioning activities for students will learn which fractional parts are easy and which are difficult for children to attain on a circle, square, or other regular geometric figure. Students should be allowed to discover for themselves, for example, how to attain thirds and fifths on a circle or fifths on a pentagon. In time, students should be able to partition a region to model unit fractions with even and odd denominators.

The activity of partitioning figures should be repeated at different times during the year and at different grade

FIGURE 10-5

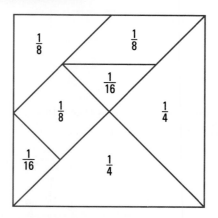

FIGURE 10-4

FIGURE 10-6

Statements to explain why children think the parts they have produced are the same size (equal).

Barry (7 years)

"All the same size. Not the same shape."

Ryan (7 years)

"*This part* looks smaller but it's just the same size because like I split it in half this way and I split it in half this way."

Joshua (7 years)

"I think I could do four!" He partitions the triangle. "It looks bigger but it isn't bigger . . . Cause it's thinner here and thicker here."

✷ ACTIVITY 10-4

GIVEN A PART, DRAW THE WHOLE

MATERIALS:
figures drawn on paper

PROCEDURE:

1. If this is one-fifth of a chocolate bar, what size is the whole bar?

2. This is three-fourths of a cake. Draw the whole cake.

3. This is three-eighths of a cheese block. Draw the whole block.

levels since further partitioning experiences will lead to more discoveries. The following questions could be the focus of class discussions.

- On what figures is it easy to attain thirds? fourths? fifths? sixths? eighths? tenths?
- What partitioning techniques work best on a particular figure?

Successful partitioning of regions requires capabilities such as:

1. An awareness of some geometric properties of figures, such as numbers of sides and vertices, the diagonals, midpoints of sides, and the center point of the figure.

2. Knowledge of possible operations on figures, for example, dividing sides into equal segments, constructing points in the interior of a figure, and attaining differently shaped parts within a given figure.

3. Partitioning techniques such as the half cut using different orientations, the parallel slice, the corners truncation, and the radial cut as shown in Figure 10-7.

These capabilities emerge slowly over time and provide students with one model for fractional numbers.

One excellent model for representing fractions is fraction circles. These are available commercially as sets of plastic circles partitioned into different numbers of equal-sized pieces. Sets of fraction circles also can be made economically from paper; draw circles on white paper and then duplicate each different denominator onto different colors of paper, which students can cut out (see Blackline Masters 6, 7, and 8). Laminating the paper before cutting will help retain the shape of the pieces and extend their usefulness.

Fraction circles are the model that perhaps is most familiar to children, but this is a difficult model for students

FIGURE 10-7

The half cut

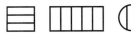

The parallel slice

The corners truncation

The radial cut

FIGURE 10-8

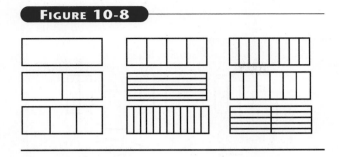

to construct on their own. Using pre-made sets thus provides students with a convenient, easy-to-understand model for fractions.

The commercial set of *Fraction Factory Pieces* is another example of the region model. The set is made of colored plastic rectangular pieces representing a whole and its fractional parts ($\frac{1}{2}$, $\frac{1}{3}$, $\frac{1}{4}$, $\frac{1}{5}$, $\frac{1}{6}$, $\frac{1}{8}$, $\frac{1}{10}$, and $\frac{1}{12}$) as shown in Figure 10-8. Exploratory activities can be planned for students using the materials as in Activity 10-5.

Part-of-a-Set Model

The difficulty of the *part-of-a-set* model for fractions resides in naming the result of partitioning rather than in the action itself. For example, children can easily share 20 candies among four friends but when asked *what* part of the candies each one gets, "five" or "one-fifth" is apt to be the reply. Students must learn that the question "how many" warrants a whole-number answer, whereas the questions "how much" and "what part" have fraction number answers.

When working with sets, students find it easier to identify, for example, one-tenth of a set of ten than to find one-fifth of ten objects. Students appear to think of "fifth" as "five." Thus, when finding one-fifth of ten, they partition the set in two groups of five rather than in

five groups of two. The idea to learn is that, for example, when talking about fifths, the whole is partitioned into five parts. The number of objects in each fifth depends upon the size of the set. See Figure 10-9. Activities 10-6 to 10-12 should be helpful in developing this important idea.

From Activity 10-6, students should observe that, because *thirds* is the fraction part, the set is *always* divided into *three parts*.

For Activity 10-7, students should draw pictures of what they have done and write statements such as:

Twelve buttons are one-half of 24 buttons.

One-fourth of 24 buttons is 6.

Children might respond to Activity 10-8 with a construction and statements such as:

Here are twelve discs.

I can make four groups of three.

Therefore, three is one-fourth of twelve.

✳ ACTIVITY 10-6

FINDING A FRACTIONAL PART OF A SET: PICTORIAL

MATERIALS:

1. 🐝🐝🐝🐝🐝🐝🐝🐝🐝🐝🐝🐝
2. 🐝🐝🐝🐝🐝🐝🐝🐝🐝🐝🐝🐝
3. 🐝🐝🐝
4. 🐝🐝🐝🐝🐝🐝
5. 🐝🐝🐝🐝🐝🐝🐝🐝🐝
   🐝🐝🐝🐝🐝🐝🐝🐝🐝
6. 🐝🐝🐝🐝🐝🐝🐝🐝🐝🐝🐝🐝
   🐝🐝🐝🐝🐝🐝🐝🐝🐝🐝🐝🐝
   🐝🐝🐝🐝🐝🐝🐝🐝🐝
   🐝🐝🐝🐝🐝🐝🐝🐝🐝

PROCEDURE:
1. Show two-thirds of each of the sets shown above.
2. Write a statement about each set.

✳ ACTIVITY 10-5

FRACTIONAL PARTS OF A WHOLE

MATERIALS:
Fraction Factory Pieces

PROCEDURE:
1. Find how many
   thirds are in a whole
   fifths are in a whole
   tenths are in a whole
   twelfths are in a whole

2. Do you notice a pattern?

3. Write a statement about what you have found.

FIGURE 10-9

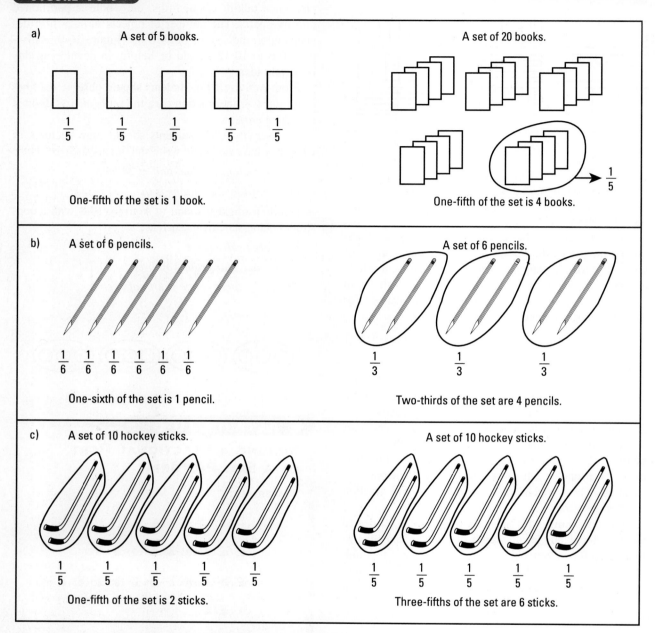

a)

A set of 5 books.

$\frac{1}{5}$ $\frac{1}{5}$ $\frac{1}{5}$ $\frac{1}{5}$ $\frac{1}{5}$

One-fifth of the set is 1 book.

A set of 20 books.

$\frac{1}{5}$

One-fifth of the set is 4 books.

b)

A set of 6 pencils.

$\frac{1}{6}$ $\frac{1}{6}$ $\frac{1}{6}$ $\frac{1}{6}$ $\frac{1}{6}$ $\frac{1}{6}$

One-sixth of the set is 1 pencil.

A set of 6 pencils.

$\frac{1}{3}$ $\frac{1}{3}$ $\frac{1}{3}$

Two-thirds of the set are 4 pencils.

c)

A set of 10 hockey sticks.

$\frac{1}{5}$ $\frac{1}{5}$ $\frac{1}{5}$ $\frac{1}{5}$ $\frac{1}{5}$

One-fifth of the set is 2 sticks.

A set of 10 hockey sticks.

$\frac{1}{5}$ $\frac{1}{5}$ $\frac{1}{5}$ $\frac{1}{5}$ $\frac{1}{5}$

Three-fifths of the set are 6 sticks.

Two students' solutions to the problem in Activity 10-10 are presented below:

$\frac{1}{3}$ $\frac{1}{3}$ $\frac{1}{3}$

The library bought 12 nonfiction books. I know this because if 4 books are $\frac{1}{3}$, then $\frac{3}{3}$ is 12 books.

Janice, Grade 6

12 nonfiction books were bought. If 4 computer books are one-third of all the nonfiction books, I need two more thirds.

A third = 4 so 3 × 4 = 12.

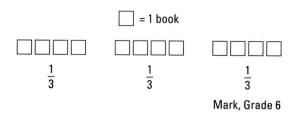

☐ = 1 book

$\frac{1}{3}$ $\frac{1}{3}$ $\frac{1}{3}$

Mark, Grade 6

✳ ACTIVITY 10-7

FINDING A FRACTIONAL PART OF A SET: CONCRETE

MATERIALS:
a set of 24 buttons for each student and 8 small plates or "mats"

PROCEDURE:
Place buttons on the plates to show:

1. one-half of 24 (use 2 plates).
2. one-fourth of 24 (use 4 plates).
3. one-sixth of 24 (use 6 plates).
4. one-eighth of 24 (use 8 plates).

✳ ACTIVITY 10-8

NAMING THE FRACTIONS

MATERIALS:
a set of 20 discs or other small objects

PROCEDURE:
Use the discs (or other objects) to answer the following:

1. What part of 12 is 3?
2. What part of 6 is 2?
3. What part of 20 is 4?
4. What part of 20 is 5?

✳ ACTIVITY 10-9

FINDING A PART OF A SET

PROCEDURE:
1. Solve the following problem. Draw a picture to show how you arrived at an answer.

Three-fifths of the ten books on the shelf are mysteries. How many are mystery books?

✳ ACTIVITY 10-10

FINDING THE WHOLE SET: FIXED TOTAL

PROCEDURE:
1. Solve the following problem. Draw a diagram to show how you arrived at an answer.

The school library has acquired some new books. The 4 books about computers are one-third of the nonfiction books. How many nonfiction books were bought?

A child might respond to the problem in Activity 10-11 in the following way:

Because I have to find $\frac{3}{8}$ and $\frac{1}{6}$ of a set, I'll choose 24 as the number of bows in the bag because 8 and 6 are factors of 24 so it's easy to find eighths and sixths of 24.

$\frac{3}{8}$ of 24 is 9 $\frac{1}{6}$ of 24 is 4

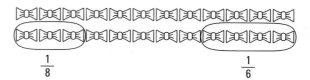

$$\frac{1}{8} \qquad\qquad \frac{1}{6}$$

9 and 4 = 13. Therefore, 11 bows were white.
$\frac{11}{24}$ of the bows were white.

If Ellen had bought a bag of 48 bows, she would have 22 white bows.

✳ ACTIVITY 10-11

FINDING THE WHOLE SET: VARIABLE TOTAL

PROCEDURE:
1. Solve the following problem. Show how you arrived at an answer.

Ellen purchased a bag of bows to put on Christmas presents. She found that three-eighths of the bows were red and one-sixth were green. How many (the remaining bows) were white? What fraction of the total number of bows were white?

✳ ACTIVITY 10-12

DRAW THE WHOLE SET

PROCEDURE:
Draw pictures to help you answer these questions.

1. Kevin has a collection of model airplanes. Three-tenths of his collection is three airplanes. How many airplanes does Kevin have in his collection?

2. Sharon enjoys taking pictures. She has taken 9 pictures, which is one-fourth of the pictures she can take with that roll of film. How many pictures can Sharon take with that roll of film?

3. Tanya has a paper route. Having delivered twelve papers means that she has one-third of the papers left to deliver. How many papers does Sharon deliver each day?

Measurement model. The measurement model can be exemplified using tape, ribbon, or other appropriate material. Students can be asked, for example, to find fractional parts of a given strip of paper.

Folding is one way to find fractional parts of strips of paper. Activity 10-13 could be used for this purpose.

One conclusion students should come to as a result of doing Activity 10-13 is that when comparing two unit fractions, the one with the smaller denominator is the larger fraction.

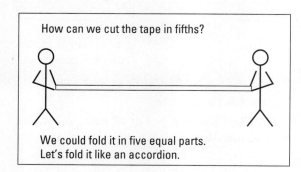

Fraction Bars and *Cuisenaire Rods* are two commercial sets of materials that can be used by students to help them discover fraction concepts using the measurement model. Fraction Bars are a set of plasticized paper strips, six inches long, partitioned to show twelfths (13 bars), tenths (11 bars), sixths (7 bars), fifths (6 bars), fourths (5 bars), thirds (4 bars), and halves (3 bars) (see Blackline Master 9). The thirteen bars for twelfths are pictured in Figure 10-10.

✳ ACTIVITY 10-13

FOLDING STRIPS TO FIND FRACTIONAL PARTS

MATERIALS:
a set of paper strips about 30 inches long for each student

PROCEDURE:
1. Fold the strips to find the following fractions:

$$\frac{1}{2}, \frac{1}{4}, \frac{1}{3}, \frac{1}{5}, \frac{1}{6}, \frac{1}{8}, \frac{1}{10}.$$

2. Use your set of fraction strips to compare the following pairs of fractions:
   (a) one-half and one-third
   (b) one-third and one-fourth
   (c) one-fourth and one-fifth
   (d) one-fifth and one-sixth

   What conclusion do you reach?

FIGURE 10-10

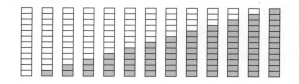

Cuisenaire Rods are a set of three-dimensional colored plastic or wooden rods of proportional lengths from 1 cm to 10 cm.

Books describing activities accompany both sets of materials. Activities 10-14 to 10-18 present sample activities.

✳ ACTIVITY 10-14

COMPARING FRACTIONS–A

MATERIALS:
Fraction Bars

PROCEDURE:
1. Use fraction bars to compare the following:
   (a) 1 part out of 3 and 1 part out of 4
   (b) 5 parts out of 6 and 3 parts out of 4
   (c) 1 part out of 2 and 5 parts out of twelve

✳ ACTIVITY 10-15

COMPARING FRACTIONS–B

MATERIALS:
Fraction Bars

PROCEDURE:
1. Find fraction bars that have a greater shaded amount than a blue bar with 3 parts shaded.

2. Find fractions which have less shading than a red bar with 1 part shaded.

✳ ACTIVITY 10-16

COMPARING FRACTIONS–C

MATERIALS:
Cuisenaire Rods

PROCEDURE:
1. Select the orange rod as the unit. Write fractional names for three other rods in terms of your unit.

2. Choose a different rod as the unit and do the same task.

✳ ACTIVITY 10-17

FRACTIONS ON A NUMBER LINE

MATERIALS:
number lines

PROCEDURE:
1. Draw three number lines the same length.

2. Divide one line in eighths, one line in tenths, and one in twelfths.

3. Use your number lines to order the following sets of fractions.

$$\frac{1}{3} \ \frac{5}{8} \ \frac{3}{5} \qquad \frac{9}{12} \ \frac{6}{10} \ \frac{5}{8}$$

$$\frac{4}{8} \ \frac{3}{10} \ \frac{5}{12} \qquad \frac{7}{8} \ \frac{11}{12} \ \frac{9}{10}$$

✳ ACTIVITY 10-18

GIVEN A PART, FIND THE WHOLE

PROCEDURE:
1. A part of a line is drawn. Draw the whole line.

   one-third of a line _____

   one-fifth of a line _____

   two-sixths of a line _____

   three-tenths of a line _____

A number line is frequently employed when using a measurement model. In this case, it is the distance from zero that is being named rather than points (Figure 10-11).

Area model. The area model is based on the idea that fractional parts may have the same area but might not necessarily be congruent. Consider the rectangles below. Each rectangle is divided into four parts. But are the parts fourths? Most students would agree that Rectangles A, B, and C are divided in fourths, but they may disagree about Rectangle D, since two of the parts are shaped differently than the other two parts.

How might students determine whether the four parts in Rectangle D are the same size? One way is to cut one of the triangular pieces as indicated below and rearrange it to form a small rectangle—which will be exactly the same size and shape as the two small rectangular pieces. This shows that all four pieces have the same area, so Rectangle D *is* divided into fourths.

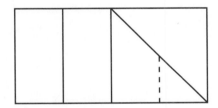

Other examples of shapes that have been cut into fractional parts using the area model are shown on the following page. How might you verify that each part has the same area as other parts within the whole?

Rectangle A:

Rectangle B:

Rectangle C:

Rectangle D:

FIGURE 10-11

Measurement Model

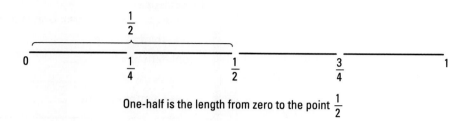

One-half is the length from zero to the point $\frac{1}{2}$

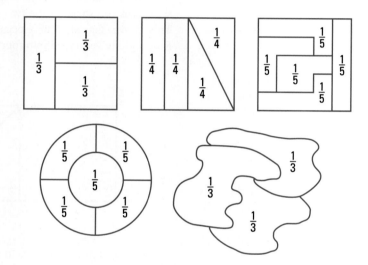

DEVELOPING COMPARISON AND ORDERING OF FRACTIONS

Another important fraction topic is comparison and ordering. This refers to a student's ability to judge the relative size of two or more fractions and to arrange two or more fractions in order based on their size.

Comparing and Ordering Fractions

Students need opportunities to *compare* and *order* fractions. Fractions should be compared by representing them concretely and pictorially before using an algorithm (Figure 10-12).

Experiences in comparing fractions at the concrete and pictorial levels will help students develop an intuitive sense of the numeric value of fractions. Formal symbolic work can then proceed (see Activities 10-19 to 10-21).

✳ ACTIVITY 10-19

COMPARING FRACTIONS

PROCEDURE:
1. Which is greater? $\frac{4}{5}$ or $\frac{2}{3}$
2. How do you know?
3. Use materials or draw a picture to show you are right.

✳ ACTIVITY 10-20

ORDERING FRACTIONS

PROCEDURE:
1. Order the fractions from smallest to largest.

$$\frac{1}{3} \qquad \frac{3}{8} \qquad \frac{5}{16} \qquad \frac{1}{2} \qquad \frac{5}{12}$$

2. Write how you know.

FIGURE 10-12

Which is the largest fraction:
2 fourths, 4 tenths, or 4 sixths?

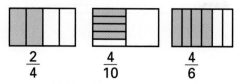

$$\frac{2}{4} \qquad \frac{4}{10} \qquad \frac{4}{6}$$

4 sixths is the largest.

Order the fractions from smallest to largest:
1 half, 2 thirds, 5 sixths, 3 fourths, 5 eighths.

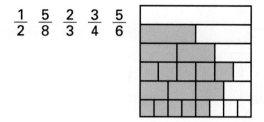

$$\frac{1}{2} \quad \frac{5}{8} \quad \frac{2}{3} \quad \frac{3}{4} \quad \frac{5}{6}$$

Students can be asked to compare a set of fractions with the same denominator, with the same numerator, and with different numerators and denominators to help them develop fraction number sense (see examples below). Then, they could model the fractions to verify their work as pictured in Figure 10-13.

Examples:

$$\frac{3}{12}, \frac{6}{12}, \frac{2}{12}, \frac{9}{12}, \frac{12}{12}, \frac{4}{12}.$$

$$\frac{2}{7}, \frac{2}{3}, \frac{2}{9}, \frac{2}{5}, \frac{2}{10}, \frac{2}{15}.$$

$$\frac{2}{3}, \frac{3}{4}, \frac{4}{5}, \frac{5}{6}, \frac{6}{7}, \frac{7}{8}.$$

$$\frac{5}{6}, \frac{3}{8}, \frac{2}{3}, \frac{1}{4}, \frac{2}{6}, \frac{3}{5}.$$

Activities 10-22 to 10-24 also help to develop a sense of fraction size.

✳ ACTIVITY 10-21

SYMBOLIC FRACTIONS

PROCEDURE:
1. Which is smaller?

$$\frac{2}{5} \text{ or } \frac{2}{10} \qquad \frac{3}{5} \text{ or } \frac{4}{7}$$

2. Draw a picture to show that you are right.

✳ ACTIVITY 10-22

VARIATIONS ON A THEME

PROCEDURE:
1. Write fractions that get closer and closer to 1, staying above 1.
2. Write a fraction that gets closer and closer to 1, by alternating above and below 1.

✳ ACTIVITY 10-23

GETTING CLOSE TO $\frac{3}{4}$

Given set A = $\{\frac{1}{2}, \frac{1}{3}, \frac{1}{4}, \frac{1}{5}, \frac{1}{6}, \frac{1}{7}, \ldots\}$, get close (and closer) to $\frac{3}{4}$ using three numbers from the set and the operation of addition.

✳ ACTIVITY 10-24

TARGET NUMBER IS $1\frac{1}{2}$

Given set B = $\{\frac{1}{2}, \frac{1}{3}, \frac{2}{3}, \frac{1}{4}, \frac{2}{4}, \frac{3}{4}, \frac{1}{5}, \frac{2}{5}, \frac{3}{5}, \frac{4}{5}\}$, try to construct $1\frac{1}{2}$.

For variation in Activity 10-23 more than one operation can be used or four or more numbers can be used from the given set.

Variations in Activity 10-24 could include:

- Change the target number.
- Use as few or as many numbers from set B as you can.
- Numbers can (or cannot) be used more than once.

When comparing fractions at the symbolic level, the power of the notion of equivalent fractions is recognized. Common denominators are found for the given fractions and then the numerators are compared.

A child's work for Activity 10-19 might look like this:

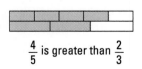

$\frac{4}{5}$ is greater than $\frac{2}{3}$

Using a calculator to compare fractions
The *Math Explorer* calculator can assist in comparing and ordering fractions. The process is as described in the previous section by first renaming the fractions to be compared so they will have a common denominator.

FIGURE 10-13

COMPARING FRACTIONS

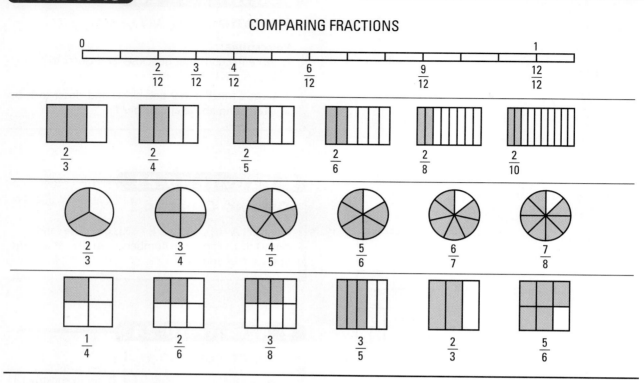

STANDARDS LINK 10-6

Children also should use reasoning to determine that $\frac{1}{5}$ is larger than $\frac{1}{8}$ or $\frac{1}{10}$ since fifths are larger than eighths or tenths. Students should recognize that, for example, $\frac{3}{4}$ is between $\frac{1}{2}$ and 1 and that $\frac{1}{3}$ is large compared to $\frac{1}{10}$, about the same size as $\frac{1}{4}$, and small compared to $\frac{5}{6}$. They can also explore fractions that are close to 0, close to $\frac{1}{2}$, or close to 1. . . . . Experiences with the relative size of numbers promote the development of number sense. (NCTM, 1989, p. 58)

Relative Size of Fractions

In learning the relative size of fractions, students should first compare fractions concretely and pictorially. Comparisons are made relative to certain benchmark numbers such as one, one-half, and zero. Activities 10-25 through 10-32 provide examples.

Improper Fractions and Mixed Numbers

An interpretation of fractions as numbers less than one probably led to a distinction between such fractions and those representing numbers greater than one. The terms

✳ ACTIVITY 10-25

RELATIVE SIZE OF FRACTIONS (PICTORIAL: REGION)

PROCEDURE:

1. About what size is the shaded part in each figure?

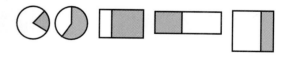

✳ ACTIVITY 10-26

WHAT MAKES ALMOST ONE? (CONCRETE: REGION)

PROCEDURE:

1. Use fraction pie pieces to help you find two different fractions that make almost one.

2. Can you find another pair of fractions that make almost one?

✳ ACTIVITY 10-27

WHAT MAKES JUST OVER ONE? (CONCRETE: MEASUREMENT)

PROCEDURE:

1. Use Fraction Bars to help you group two different fractions to make just over one. Can you find other pairs of fractions that make just over one?

✳ ACTIVITY 10-28

FRACTIONS THAT ADD UP TO ALMOST ONE (SYMBOLIC)

PROCEDURE:

1. Use the numbers 1, 2, 3, 4, 5, 6, 8, 10 to make two fractions that add up to almost one.

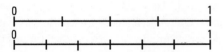

Example:

Three-fourths and one-sixth makes almost one.

2. Can you make other fraction pairs that add up to almost one?

✳ ACTIVITY 10-29

WHAT MAKES ALMOST ONE HALF? (CONCRETE: MEASUREMENT)

PROCEDURE:

1. Use Fraction Bars to group two fractions that make almost one half.

2. Can you find other pairs?

✳ ACTIVITY 10-30

WHAT MAKES ALMOST ONE HALF? (CONCRETE: REGION)

PROCEDURE:

1. Use Fraction Factory pieces to help you find pairs of fractions that make almost one-half.

✳ ACTIVITY 10-31

WHAT MAKES ALMOST ONE HALF? (SYMBOLIC)

PROCEDURE:

1. Using the numbers 1, 3, 4, 5, 8, 10 write pairs of fractions that make almost one half.

✳ ACTIVITY 10-32

FRACTIONS THAT ARE ABOUT ZERO, ONE-HALF, OR ONE

PROCEDURE:

1. Which of these fractions are close to zero, one-half, or one?

$\frac{12}{20}$	$\frac{1}{50}$	$\frac{2}{10}$	$\frac{8}{9}$	$\frac{3}{5}$
$\frac{6}{7}$	$\frac{1}{25}$	$\frac{15}{32}$	$\frac{4}{14}$	$\frac{6}{15}$
$\frac{99}{100}$	$\frac{15}{16}$	$\frac{4}{9}$	$\frac{2}{100}$	$\frac{11}{23}$

proper fraction and *improper* fraction have been assigned, respectively, to the two kinds of fractions (Figure 10-14).

It is not an easy task for young students to represent improper fractions concretely or diagrammatically. For example, the shaded portion in Figure 10-15 often is labeled $\frac{4}{6}$ rather than $\frac{4}{3}$.

Any fraction that is greater than one can be written as an improper fraction or as a *mixed number*. A mixed number is a way of expressing a number greater than 1 as a whole number and a fraction. Addition is implied in a mixed numeral even though the symbol + is not written.

FIGURE 10-14

PROPER FRACTIONS

$$\frac{1}{2}, \frac{2}{3}, \frac{4}{5} \cdots$$

For every $\frac{a}{b}$, a < b

IMPROPER FRACTIONS

$$\frac{3}{2}, \frac{4}{3}, \frac{5}{4}, \frac{5}{5} \cdots$$

For every $\frac{a}{b}$, a > b or a = b

FIGURE 10-15

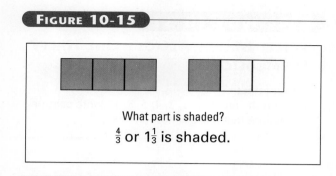

What part is shaded?

$\frac{4}{3}$ or $1\frac{1}{3}$ is shaded.

Example: $3\frac{2}{5}$ → $3 + \frac{2}{5}$

The process of changing a mixed number to an improper fraction can be demonstrated as follows:

Example: Change $\frac{18}{5}$ to a mixed number.
Recall: $1 = \frac{5}{5}$
Think: $18 = 5 + 5 + 5 + 3$
Therefore, $\frac{18}{5}$ can be written as $\frac{5}{5} + \frac{5}{5} + \frac{5}{5} + \frac{3}{5}$
which $= 1 + 1 + 1 + \frac{3}{5}$
       $= 3 + \frac{3}{5}$ or $3\frac{3}{5}$

In repeatedly working through this process, students may see that what is essentially being done is dividing 18 by 5 to obtain the quotient $3\frac{3}{5}$. From this analysis emerges the *quotient* interpretation of fractions, that is, $\frac{18}{5}$ is the same as 18 divided by 5.

The process of changing a mixed number to an improper fraction is similar to the process of checking a division exercise.

Example: $14 \div 3 = 4$ R2 or $4\frac{2}{3}$
Check: $(3 \times 4) + 2 = 14$

The mixed number (quotient) $4\frac{2}{3}$ has been changed to an improper fraction by multiplying the two factors (divisor and quotient) and adding the remainder to obtain the product 14 (dividend).

Using the *Math Explorer* calculator Converting improper fractions to mixed numbers can be performed on the *Math Explorer* calculator by using the [Ab/c] key.

Example: Change $\frac{8}{5}$ to a mixed number
Enter 8 [/] 5 [Ab/c] Display 1 u 3/5
(The u separates the whole number from a fraction.)

UNDERSTANDING EQUIVALENT FRACTIONS

Another important fraction topic is equivalent fractions, a concept that refers to the notion that different fractions can represent the same amount. For example, $\frac{1}{2}$ and $\frac{2}{4}$ are

different fractions that represent the same amount; however, to many children these are two completely different fractions. Many children believe that $\frac{2}{4}$ must be more, since the numbers are bigger. Indeed, understanding equivalent fractions is another important prerequisite to fraction computation and helps children evaluate the reasonableness of answers.

Equivalent Fractions

The notion that every number can be expressed in different ways is of critical importance when dealing with fractions. When assigning different names for a specified fraction, we say that we are writing *equivalent fractions.*

Children should understand unit fractions and composite fractions before they are introduced to equivalent fractions. For example, students should be able to readily compare fractions such as $\frac{1}{4}$ and $\frac{1}{6}$; $\frac{7}{10}$ and $\frac{5}{10}$; $\frac{2}{4}$ and $\frac{2}{8}$.

Bezuk and Bieck (1993) recommend that teachers discuss the meaning of the word *equivalent* ("equal value") and also discuss how equivalent fractions are both alike and different. They also recommend that teachers help students generalize from their experiences with manipulatives the symbolic algorithm for finding equivalent fractions.

STANDARDS LINK 10-7
Children need to use physical materials to explore equivalent fractions and compare fractions. For example, with folded paper strips, children can easily see that $\frac{1}{2}$ is the same amount as $\frac{3}{6}$ and that $\frac{2}{3}$ is smaller than $\frac{3}{4}$. (NCTM, 1989, p. 58)

STANDARDS LINK 10-8
Teachers should strive to make this process consistently positive; too often, students are taught that $\frac{2}{4} = \frac{1}{2}$, only to be informed later than $\frac{2}{4}$ is a "wrong answer" when the "correct" answer is $\frac{1}{2}$. Discussing the appropriateness of certain representations in a given situation, such as the fact that it is better to write "$\frac{68}{100}$ dollars" on a check than reduce to "$\frac{17}{25}$ dollars," helps students recognize that there is no single, uniform way to represent a fraction but that the "best" way depends largely on the situation. Students learn, for example, that $\frac{15}{100}$, $\frac{3}{20}$, 0.15, and 15% are all representations of the same number, appropriate for a fraction of a dollar on a bank check, the probability of winning a game, the tax on a purchase of $2.98, and a discount, respectively. (NCTM, 1989, p. 88)

Although the idea of equivalent fractions can be introduced early to children, mastery of the concept should not be expected until upper elementary grades or later (Driscoll, 1984).

Children can engage in activities with fraction circles, Fraction Factory pieces, or fraction bars to discover for themselves that fractions such as one-half and two-fourths name the same amount. They can fold paper strips or rectangles to discover equivalent fractions. Several activities to help children understand equivalent fractions are presented in this section (see Activities 10-33 to 10-35)

1. Equivalent Fractions
   - Provide each student with narrow strips of paper.
   - Ask the students to fold one strip of paper into 2 equal pieces. Have them identify the fractional parts and label the midpoint as $\frac{1}{2}$ and the endpoint as $\frac{2}{2}$.

     Note that the $\frac{1}{2}$ is the distance from the beginning point to the center and the $\frac{2}{2}$ is the distance from the beginning point to the end.
   - Have students fold a second strip of paper in fourths, open it up, and name the four parts on the foldlines and the end points as $\frac{1}{4}, \frac{2}{4}, \frac{3}{4}, \frac{4}{4}$.
   - Direct students to fold a third strip of paper in eighths and label each part produced in eighths. The strips should be labeled as in the diagram.

			$\frac{1}{2}$			$\frac{2}{2}$
	$\frac{1}{4}$		$\frac{2}{4}$	$\frac{3}{4}$		$\frac{4}{4}$
$\frac{1}{8}$	$\frac{2}{8}$	$\frac{3}{8}$	$\frac{4}{8}$	$\frac{5}{8}$	$\frac{6}{8}$	$\frac{7}{8}$	$\frac{8}{8}$

   - Ask students to find equal lengths on the strips that have been labeled differently. The idea that fractional lengths can be named differently or that fractions can have more than one name should be highlighted in the discussion. Equality statements could be written on the board.

   Example: $\frac{1}{2}$ and $\frac{2}{4}$ are the same length.
   $\frac{2}{2}, \frac{4}{4}$, and $\frac{8}{8}$ all indicate the same length.

2. Finding Equivalent Fractions
   - Have students use fraction bars to find equal lengths with different names.

   Examples:
   Orange and blue bars
     9 twelfths is the same length as 3 fourths
   Green and red bars
     1 half equals 3 sixths

✳ ACTIVITY 10-33

EQUIVALENT FRACTIONS

PROCEDURE:
1. What part of the bar is shaded?

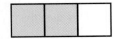

2. Divide each part of the bar in half. What part is shaded now? Write an equivalent fraction.

3. Divide each part of these bars in half. Write equivalent fractions for the shaded parts.

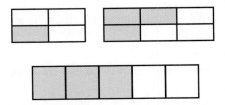

✳ ACTIVITY 10-34

WRITING EQUIVALENT FRACTIONS

MATERIALS:
a sheet of paper on which three rectangles have been drawn.

PROCEDURE:
1. Draw thirds on the first rectangle.
2. Draw sixths on the second rectangle.
3. Draw twelfths on the third rectangle.
4. Write equality statements about what you observe in your figures.

Example: 2 thirds = 4 sixths.

3. Finding Equivalent Fractions
   - Provide Fraction Factory pieces for each group of children.
   - Direct students to select the black rectangle.
   - Ask them to use other pieces to cover half of the black rectangle in at least two different ways.
   - Have them cover other fractional parts of the rectangle in at least two different ways.

✴ ACTIVITY 10-35

FINDING EQUIVALENT FRACTIONS

MATERIALS:
a set of twelve chips, four of one color and eight of another color.

PROCEDURE:
1. Use the set of chips to show the fractions:
   2 sixths   1 third   4 twelfths

2. Draw a picture to show how you grouped the chips to show each fraction.

3. What can you say about each fraction?

- Have students write equality statements about what they have done.
- Have students read aloud what they have written.
- The statements could be displayed on a bulletin board under the caption: Fractions Have More Than One Name.

4. Equivalent Fractions
   - Provide a set of buttons in two colors for each student.
   - Have students arrange 12 buttons, 6 of each color, in a two-row array.
     What part of the buttons are white?
     (one-half)

- Can you group the buttons another way so that you can give a different fraction name to the group of white buttons?
- Have students repeat the last step.

Possible solutions include the following:

- Provide students with 24 buttons, 12 of each color. Ask the students to find equivalent fractions for one-half; for two-thirds.

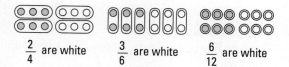

$\frac{2}{4}$ are white $\frac{3}{6}$ are white $\frac{6}{12}$ are white

- Given an appropriate number of buttons, the process can be repeated for any unit or composite fraction.

5. Renaming Fractions (adapted from Jensen and O'Neil, 1982)
   - For this activity, each group of students will need egg cartons separated into 2, 4, 6, 8, and 12 "cups" and small objects to represent eggs.
   - Have the children choose a 4-cup tray and place 2 eggs in it. Ask: "What part of the tray is filled?" (elicit $\frac{1}{2}$; $\frac{2}{4}$)
   - Continue in this manner, using in turn, a 6-, 8-, and a 12-cup tray. Each time, have students indicate in several ways what part of the tray is filled. (12-cup tray, 6 eggs: $\frac{1}{2}, \frac{2}{4}, \frac{3}{6}, \frac{6}{12}$).
   - Have students record their work on paper.
   - Ask, "What conclusions do you reach about the fractions you have written?"

Renaming and Simplifying Fractions

The idea that each fraction number can be represented in different numeric form is an important one for students to learn. (Example: $\frac{1}{2} = \frac{2}{4} = \frac{3}{6} = \frac{4}{8}$ . . .)

Some students may detect the pattern and articulate a rule for easily *renaming a fraction* (writing equivalent fractions) such as, multiplying each part of the fraction numeral by the same number. What may not be readily evident to students is that the multiplicative identity element, one, is being used in a different form, that is, as $\frac{2}{2}, \frac{3}{3}, \frac{4}{4}$, etc. Middle school students should comprehend the following reasoning.

Any number that multiplies one or is multiplied by one equals one.

Examples: $6 \times 1 = 6$ $\frac{1}{2} \times 1 = \frac{1}{2}$
         $1 \times 45 = 45$ $1 \times \frac{2}{5} = \frac{2}{5}$

Represent "1" as $\frac{2}{2}, \frac{3}{3}, \frac{4}{4}$, etc.

If $\frac{1}{2} \times 1 = \frac{1}{2}$ If $\frac{1}{2} \times 1 = \frac{1}{2}$
and $\frac{1}{2} \times \frac{2}{2} = \frac{2}{4}$ and $\frac{1}{2} \times \frac{3}{3} = \frac{3}{6}$
Then, $\frac{1}{2} = \frac{2}{4}$ Then, $\frac{1}{2} = \frac{3}{6}$

Facility in renaming fractions is of utmost importance when comparing fractions and as a preparation for computation.

Simplifying fractions is the process of renaming a fraction through division. The fraction is divided by the multiplicative identity element represented in fraction form. The choice of representation for the identity element depends on the fraction being simplified, that is, a divisor common to each term of the fraction numeral must be used.

Examples:
$\frac{4}{6} \div 1 = \frac{4}{6}$ $\frac{5}{15} \div 1 = \frac{5}{15}$

$\frac{4}{6} \div \frac{2}{2} = \frac{4 \div 2}{6 \div 2} = \frac{2}{3}$ $\frac{5}{15} \div \frac{5}{5} = \frac{5 \div 5}{15 \div 5} = \frac{1}{3}$

The algorithmic work of renaming fractions should be accompanied for some time by concrete (Figure 10-16) or pictorial (Figure 10-17) representations of the process.

Renaming and simplifying fractions with a calculator
After students understand the process of renaming and simplifying fractions, they can be allowed to use a calculator with that capability to assist them in problem solving. In renaming fractions with the *Math Explorer* calculator, the procedure is as follows:

Example:

Write an equivalent fraction for $\frac{3}{8}$.

Enter 3 $\boxed{/}$ 8 $\boxed{\times}$ 2 $\boxed{/}$ 2 $\boxed{=}$ Display: 6/16

The fact that the multiplicative identity is employed (1 written as 2/2 in this case) in renaming fractions will be emphasized when using a calculator. A student who merely multiplies a fraction by a whole number factor will note that the denominator has not changed.

Example:

Simplifying a fraction can be performed in two ways:

Enter: 2 $\boxed{/}$ 16 $\boxed{\times}$ 2 $\boxed{=}$ Display: 4/16

1) the calculator can choose the common factor or
2) the student can do so.

FIGURE 10-16

Using Cuisenaire Rods

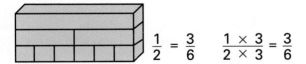

$$\frac{1}{2} = \frac{3}{6} \qquad \frac{1 \times 3}{2 \times 3} = \frac{3}{6}$$

Using Fraction Factory Pieces

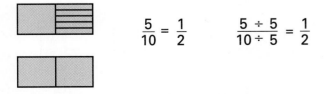

$$\frac{5}{10} = \frac{1}{2} \qquad \frac{5 \div 5}{10 \div 5} = \frac{1}{2}$$

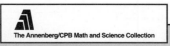
VIDEO LINK 10-1
Fraction Tracks

Brief Summary: In "Fraction Tracks," Hilory Paster's fifth graders are playing the Fractions Tracks game, a cooperative game for two players in which students draw fraction cards from a deck and move markers on their gameboard, trying to get all six markers from zero to one by moving them the distance specified on the card drawn. Figure 10-18 shows the gameboard. While playing the game, students often have to re-name the fraction they draw as an equivalent fraction or as the sum of two or more fractions.

1. What preliminary activities does the teacher do to prepare her students to be successful at the game?
2. How does the teacher use questioning to enhance students' understanding of the game and of equivalent fractions?
3. What modes of representation are used in this lesson?
4. How does Ms. Paster check for understanding while students are playing the game?
5. How does this lesson help the teacher assess her students' understanding of equivalent fractions?
6. Why does Ms. Paster ask students to rephrase other students' explanations?
7. How could this lesson be extended?
8. What might the teacher plan for the next lesson?

Video Source. Teaching Math: A Video Library, 5–8; Tape 1 from The Annenberg/CPB Math and Science Collection.

Example: Simplify $\frac{4}{24}$

Enter 4 $\boxed{/}$ 24 $\boxed{\text{Simp}}$

The calculator displays $\boxed{\text{Simp}}$ N/D → n/d in the left corner indicating that the fraction can be simplified. The two ways to proceed to simplify the fraction are:

1. Calculator chooses the common factor

   Enter = to get 2/12

   The calculator reduces the fraction to the next simpler term. If N/D → n/d still is displayed, that means that the fraction can be simplified further. Pressing the Simp and the = keys again simplifies the fraction to the next simpler term.

   In order to find out which factor the calculator used, enter the $\boxed{x \rightleftharpoons y}$ key and the factor will be displayed. Enter the $\boxed{x \rightleftharpoons y}$ key again to display the simpler fraction.

FIGURE 10-17

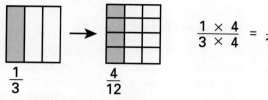

Renaming Fractions

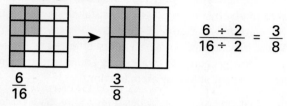

$$\frac{1 \times 4}{3 \times 4} = \frac{4}{12}$$

Simplifying Fractions

$$\frac{6 \div 2}{16 \div 2} = \frac{3}{8}$$

2. Student chooses the common factor:

Enter 2 (a common factor of 4 and 24)

Enter ☐= to obtain 2/12

To reduce the fraction further, press 2 (a common factor of 2 and 12) and ☐= to obtain the simplest fraction 1/16. If a number is entered that is not a common factor of the two fraction terms, the calculator will simply display the fraction again.

Example: 4/24 Enter ☐Simp 5 ☐= Display is 4/24

CONCLUSION

Fractions are an important part of the mathematics curriculum. Understanding fraction concepts, comparison, ordering, number sense, and equivalence lays the foundation for later work with fraction computation and prepares children for using mathematics in their everyday lives.

For Your Journal

When you have finished studying this chapter, reflect on these questions in your math journal:

FIGURE 10-18

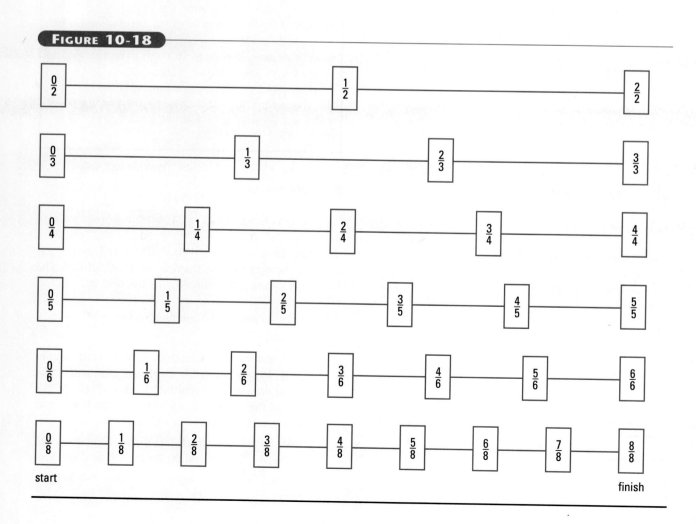

1. Think back on your own experiences learning about fractions. Describe how you were taught about the topics in this chapter and discuss your understandings of these topics. Will the way you were taught have any effect on how you will teach these topics to children?

2. Draw a diagram to illustrate the equivalence of $\frac{1}{2}$ and $\frac{3}{6}$ and explain why these fractions are equivalent.

3. Informally interview one or two intermediate-grade children to assess their understanding of fraction concepts, comparison, and/or equivalence. Describe their understandings.

For Your Portfolio

When you have finished studying this chapter, complete these activities to include in your professional portfolio:

1. Write a lesson to help children understand comparison of fractions, using the benchmarks of 0, $\frac{1}{2}$, and/or 1.

2. Write a lesson to help children understand the concept of equivalence using manipulative materials and making connections to symbols.

Resources for Teachers

Children's Book

Mathews, L. (1979). *Gator pie*. Littleton, MA: Sundance Publishing.

Books on Fractions

Brodie, J. (1995). *Constructing ideas about fractions, Grades 3–6*. Mountain View, CA: Creative Publications.

Corwin, R., Russell, S., & Tierney, C. (1990). *Seeing fractions: A unit for the upper elementary grades*. Sacramento, CA: California Department of Education.

Cramer, K., Behr, M., Post, T., & Lesh, R. (1997). *Rational Number Project: Fraction lessons for the middle grades level 1*. Dubuque, Iowa: Kendall/Hunt Publishing Company.

Cramer, K., Behr, M., Post, T., & Lesh, R. (1997). *Rational Number Project: Fraction lessons for the middle grades level 2*. Dubuque, Iowa: Kendall/Hunt Publishing Company.

Curcio, F. R., & Bezuk, N. S. (1994). *Understanding rational numbers and proportions: Curriculum and Evaluation Standards for School Mathematics Addenda Series Grade 5–8*. Reston, VA: National Council of Teachers of Mathematics.

Lappan, G., Fitzgerald, W., Winter, M., & Phillips, E. (1986). *Middle Grades Mathematics Project: Similarity and equivalent fractions*. Menlo Park, CA: Addison-Wesley Publishing Company.

Ward, S. (1995). *Constructing ideas about fractions, decimals, and percents*. Mountain View, CA: Creative Publications.

Links to the Internet

Ask Dr. Math (Fractions and Decimals)

http://forum.swarthmore.edu/dr.math/tocs/fractions. elem.html

Contains a list of interesting questions about fractions and decimals and Dr. Math's answers.

ProTeacher: Fractions and Decimals

http://www.proteacher.com/ 100014.shtml

Contains lesson plans on fractions and decimals.

Explorer: Fractions

http://explorer.scrtec.org/explorer/explorer-db/browse/static/Mathematics/browse/f34.html

Contains many lessions on and lists of other resources for fractions.

No Matter What Shape Your Fraction Are In

http://math.rice.edu/~lanius/Patterns/

Contains many lessons on and lists of other resources for fractions.

Fresh-Baked Fractions

http://www.funbrain.com/fract/index.html

Contains games on finding equivalent fractions.

CHAPTER 11

Developing Fraction Computation

- Prerequisites for operations on fractions
- Operation sense
- Meaning of each operation on fractions
- Modeling operations on fractions

Focus Questions

When you have finished studying this chapter, you should be able to answer these questions:

1. What are the prerequisites for operations on fractions?

2. What does it mean to help students develop operation sense?

3. What does each operation on fractions mean? Discuss a real-world situation that exemplifies each operation on fractions.

4. What models help children understand operations on fractions?

Fraction computation is arguably the mathematics topic with which most adults have had the *least* success and the *most* bad memories! The traditional curricular emphasis on mastering algorithms for adding, subtracting, multiplying, and dividing fractions without first developing understanding led to this frustration and lack of achievement.

One reason for the difficulty many students have with fraction computation is that students often are expected to compute with fraction symbols before they have developed a good understanding of fractions and related concepts. The temptation to have students progress quickly to working symbolically with fraction computation may arise from the thinking that since the students already know how to add, subtract, multiply, and divide whole numbers, it follows that they are ready to use these operations to compute with fractions.

But often this is not the case. Most students have great difficulty linking what they already know about operations on whole numbers with operations on fractions. Teachers must help students make these connections by carefully designing instruction to link these concepts. If these connections are not made, students will not be able to predict what a reasonable answer might be or make sense of the process, forcing them to memorize meaningless procedures. Too often, the result is frustration and lack of learning.

Some suggest that operations on fractions should be relegated to calculators, maintaining that calculators have eliminated the need for any instruction on fraction computation. It is true that the availability and power of calculators certainly reduces the level of paper-and-pencil mastery of fraction computation that students must achieve. But the availability of technology also increases the importance of students' developing **operation sense,** which refers to an understanding of the meaning of operations, as well as the need for the ability to determine the reasonableness of solutions. ○

STANDARDS LINK 11-1
In grades K–4, the mathematics curriculum should include fractions and decimals so that students can

- use models to explore operations on fractions and decimals;
- apply fractions and decimals to problem situations. (NCTM, 1989, p. 57)

STANDARDS LINK 11-2
In grades 5–8, the mathematics curriculum should develop the concepts underlying computation and estimation in various contexts so that students can

- compute with whole numbers, fractions, decimals, integers, and rational numbers;
- develop, analyze, and explain procedures for computation and techniques for estimation; . . .
- select and use an appropriate method for computing from among mental arithmetic, paper-and-pencil, calculator, and computer methods;
- use computation, estimation, and proportions to solve problems;
- use estimation to check the reasonableness of results. (NCTM, 1989, p. 94)

Teachers must carefully consider what students need to know concerning fraction computation. There are four goals of instruction regarding fraction computation:

1. Students need to recognize situations that involve operations on fractions.
2. Students need to find the answer to fraction computation problems by using models.
3. Students need to estimate the answer and understand the reasonableness of results to fraction computation problems.
4. Students need to find an exact answer to fraction computation problems.

Notice that finding an exact answer is only one goal of instruction. The other three goals are equally important, and will help students be successful in finding exact answers. This chapter will present ways to help students attain these four goals.

STANDARDS LINK 11-3
The mastery of a small number of basic facts with common fractions (e.g., $\frac{1}{4} + \frac{1}{4} = \frac{1}{2}$; $\frac{3}{4} + \frac{1}{2} = 1\frac{1}{4}$; and $\frac{1}{2} \times \frac{1}{2} = \frac{1}{4}$) . . . contributes to students' readiness to learn estimation and for concept development and problem solving. This proficiency in the addition, subtraction, and multiplication of fractions and mixed numbers should be limited to those with simple denominators that can be visualized concretely or pictorially and are apt to occur in real-world settings; such computation promotes conceptual understanding of the operations. This is not to suggest, however, that valuable instruction time should be devoted to exercises like $\frac{17}{24} + \frac{5}{18}$ or $5\frac{3}{4} \times 4\frac{1}{4}$, which are much harder to visualize and unlikely to occur in real-life situations. Division of fractions should be approached conceptually. An understanding of what happens when one divides by a fractional number (less than or greater than 1) is essential. (NCTM, 1989, p. 96)

Prerequisites for Fraction Computation

What must students understand *before* beginning work on fraction computation? There are two prerequisites for fraction computation:

1. Understanding of fraction concepts, comparison, and equivalence.
2. Understanding of the meaning of operations on whole numbers.

Attempts to teach students to perform fraction computation prior to their attainment of these prerequisites will result in frustration for both the student and his or her teacher. Students will be forced to mindlessly memorize procedures, rather than understanding what they are doing and why. Instead of rushing toward algorithms, teachers should spend time helping students master the prerequisites, which will enable them to perform fraction computation with a greater degree of understanding and success.

INTRODUCING COMPUTATION

Developmental Activities

As children work through introductory fraction activities, they progress from thinking of fractions as "parts of things" to operating with them as numbers, each with a precise place on the number line.

Throughout developmental activities, it is recommended that students be required to construct concrete representations of fraction quantities and, from the representations, to record their findings on paper. Using concrete models to assist in problem solving should be looked upon as the norm in elementary classrooms. Therefore, appropriate manipulative materials should be available to students for as long as they find them helpful.

Although regular figures such as triangles, rectangles, pentagons, hexagons, octagons, and decagons are good models to show fractional parts, the circular shape is more versatile because any unit fraction can easily be represented (Figure 11-1). Also, the circles can be used to model fraction computation.

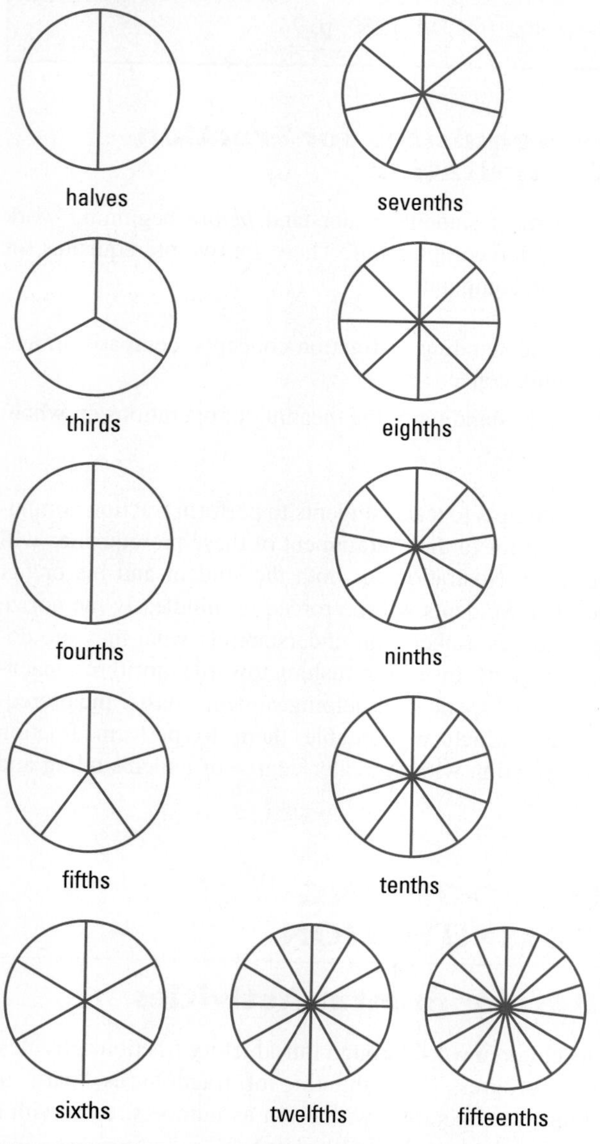

Introductory computation activities should have students work with fractions in different contexts because a narrow view of what fractions are (e.g., fractions are parts of a whole) is thought to be a reason for the generally unsatisfactory performance in fraction work (Hope & Owens, 1987). The part-whole, measurement, and part of a set interpretations should be embodied in different problem-solving situations. In time, the quotient, operator (multiplicative aspect), and ratio interpretations will also be explored (Kieren, 1976).

Allow adequate time for the algorithmic computation processes to emerge from students' active explorations with concrete and pictorial representations.

> ### STANDARDS LINK 11-4
> Physical materials should be used for exploratory work in adding and subtracting basic fractions, solving simple real-world problems, and partitioning sets of objects to find fractional parts of sets and relating this activity to division. For example, children learn that $\frac{1}{3}$ of 30 is equivalent to "30 divided by 3," which helps them relate operations with fractions to earlier operations with whole numbers. (NCTM, 1989, p. 59)

About Algorithms

The complexity of the algorithms for computing with whole numbers can be said to depend on the numbers used in the computation. For example, in subtraction, students find it difficult to subtract numbers with zeros such as $4002 - 307$. In multiplication, it is easier to find the product with a one-digit multiplier than with a two-digit multiplier; in division, single-digit divisors are easier than two-digit divisors when working through the long division algorithm, and zeros in the quotient add to the complexity. Because of these difficulties for students, the algorithms for computing with whole numbers generally are developed in stages over several grade levels.

The algorithms for computing with fractions are simple when compared with whole number computation algorithms. Because of their simplicity, students may readily learn algorithmic rules that enable them to compute with fractions. However, when procedures are not understood, some students become confused about which rule to use in a particular computation situation. They do not remember which fraction to invert or when common denominators are needed.

The goal is to have students learn to compute with fractions in a meaningful way. Therefore, students' first computations with fractions should be with concrete and pictorial models.

FIGURE 11-1

halves   sevenths

thirds   eighths

fourths   ninths

fifths   tenths

sixths   twelfths   fifteenths

Connecting Operations on Whole Numbers with Operations on Fractions

There are several different interpretations of operations on whole numbers, as was discussed in Chapter 7. Several of those interpretations work well for helping students understand operations on fractions, but a few are a bit confusing. Figure 11-2 shows examples of word problems using whole numbers and word problems using fractions for many of the different interpretations of the operations. These interpretations will be discussed in more detail throughout this chapter.

FIGURE 11-2

WORD PROBLEMS FOR FRACTIONS

Addition:

Tom ate $\frac{1}{2}$ of an apple pie yesterday and $\frac{1}{4}$ of an apple pie today. How much pie did Tom eat altogether?   (Join)

Number sentence: $\frac{1}{2} + \frac{1}{4} =$ _____

Subtraction:

Alberto has $\frac{3}{4}$ of a chocolate chip cookie and Juana has $\frac{1}{4}$ of a cookie. How much more does Alberto have?   (Comparison)

Number sentence: $\frac{3}{4} - \frac{1}{4} =$ _____

Alberto has $\frac{3}{4}$ of a chocolate chip cookie. He ate $\frac{1}{4}$ of a whole cookie. How much cookie does Alberto have left?   (Separate)

Number sentence: $\frac{3}{4} - \frac{1}{4} =$ _____

Multiplication:

There is $\frac{2}{3}$ of a chocolate pie in the refrigerator. Peter ate $\frac{1}{2}$ of it. What part of the whole pie did Peter eat?   (Area and Array)

Number sentence: $\frac{1}{2} \times \frac{2}{3} =$ _____

Shawntrice had 4 bags of cookies, with $\frac{1}{2}$ of a cookie in each bag. How many cookies did Shawntrice have?   (Repeated addition)

Number sentence: $4 \times \frac{1}{2} =$ _____

Division:

Steve has 4 cups of sugar. He needs $\frac{2}{3}$ of a cup of sugar to make one batch of his favorite cookies. How many batches of cookies can Steve make?   (Measurement/repeated subtraction)

Number sentence: $4 \div \frac{2}{3} =$ _____

Steve has 4 cups of sugar. That is enough to bake $\frac{2}{3}$ of batch of his favorite cookies. How much sugar will he need to make 1 batch of cookies?   (Partitive/fair sharing)*

Number sentence: $4 \div \frac{2}{3} =$ _____

---

*Notice that partitive division/fair sharing is NOT very easy to understand with fractions!

Properties

Learning to compute with fractions at the middle school level will include "testing" whether fractions possess the same properties as whole numbers. Through explorations, students will conclude that the commutative and associative properties hold for addition and multiplication; that multiplication is distributive over addition; and that the closure property holds true for addition, multiplication, and division. The new property from whole number computation is the closure property for division, that is, any fractional number can be divided by any fractional number except zero to obtain a quotient within the system.

ADDITION AND SUBTRACTION OF FRACTIONS

The concepts of addition and subtraction of fractions are the same as for addition and subtraction of whole numbers. Students will know that for problems wherein two fraction addends are given, the operation required to solve the problem is addition; likewise, when a fraction addend and a fraction or whole number sum is given, the operation of subtraction will provide the missing addend. As with whole numbers, addition fraction problems can be "join" problems; subtraction problems can be "separate" or "comparison" problems.

Developing Addition Procedures

Students in grades 3 and 4 enjoy finding addition sentences when working with concrete materials such as fraction bars, Fraction Factory pieces, and fraction circles (Figure 11-3). After a number of "simple" examples have been constructed, they voluntarily progress to find more complicated ones such as fractions with unlike denominators and some with more than two addends.

The addition sentences provided by the students could be classified as "easy" ones and "complicated" or "tricky" ones. Picking up on a student's example involving unlike denominators, a teacher could ask, "How did you figure that out? Could you write those fractions a different way?"

Example: $\frac{1}{4} + \frac{2}{3} = \frac{11}{12}$
Possible thinking:
I found that 1 fourth is the same as 3 twelfths and that 2 thirds is the same as 8 twelfths. So we can write:

1 fourth	$\rightarrow$	3 twelfths
+ 2 thirds	$\rightarrow$	8 twelfths
		11 twelfths *or*

$$\frac{3}{12} + \frac{8}{12} = \frac{11}{12}$$

FIGURE 11-3

Modeling Addition of Fractions

Part of a Whole
Fraction Bars

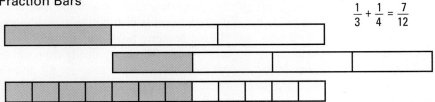

$$\frac{1}{3} + \frac{1}{4} = \frac{7}{12}$$

Fraction Factory Pieces

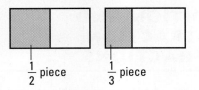

$\frac{1}{2}$ piece $\frac{1}{3}$ piece

$$\frac{1}{2} + \frac{1}{3} = \frac{5}{6}$$

Fraction Circles

$\frac{1}{2}$ $\frac{3}{8}$ $\frac{1}{2}$ ⎰ $\frac{3}{8}$ $\frac{1}{2} + \frac{3}{8} = \frac{7}{8}$

Fraction Rods

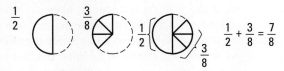

$\frac{1}{4}$ $\frac{1}{3}$

$\frac{1}{4}$ $\frac{1}{3}$ $\frac{1}{4} + \frac{1}{3} = \frac{7}{12}$

Part of a Set
How much is $\frac{1}{3} + \frac{3}{4}$?

Thirds and fourths can be modeled with a set of 12.

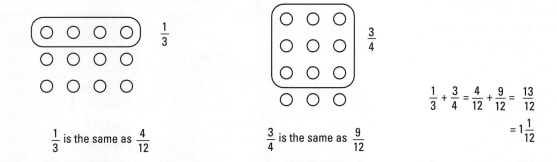

$\frac{1}{3}$ $\frac{3}{4}$

$\frac{1}{3}$ is the same as $\frac{4}{12}$ $\frac{3}{4}$ is the same as $\frac{9}{12}$

$$\frac{1}{3} + \frac{3}{4} = \frac{4}{12} + \frac{9}{12} = \frac{13}{12}$$
$$= 1\frac{1}{12}$$

Activities 11-1 to 11-6 have students construct addition sentences using Fraction Bars. The activities could be repeated to advantage using a different set of materials such as fraction pies, fraction squares, or a set of objects. Other addition problems could be embedded in familiar contexts such as parts of a dozen eggs (12 as lowest common denominator [LCD]), parts of a day (24 as LCD), or parts of an hour or minute (60 as LCD). More structured tasks are described in Activities 11-5 to 11-10.

Following several sessions of constructing addition equations (Activities 11-1 to 11-6), different addition statements could be collected and organized on a chart or bulletin board. The display could be the focus of a class discussion with the intention of having students verbalize how they know the sentences are true.

Addition algorithms Addition of fractions should not be problematic for students if fraction concepts are well understood, that is, if students can talk and write about fraction numbers, compare and estimate fractional quantities, and readily verify their work with concrete or pictorial representations.

Adding unlike fractions. Computing unlike fractions should evoke an automatic move to rewrite the fractions as same-sized denominators before proceeding with addition. The special characteristic of equivalent fractions enables one to add any set of fractions by first rewriting each fraction so that all fractions in the expression have same-sized denominators before proceeding with addition.

✸ ACTIVITY 11-1

FRACTION ADDITION SENTENCES

MATERIALS:
Fraction Bars

PROCEDURE:
1. Use the fraction bars to help you add different fractions.

   Record the addition sentences you make.

✸ ACTIVITY 11-2

FINDING A SUM OF 1

MATERIALS:
Fraction Bars

PROCEDURE:
1. Use the fraction bars to help you find two fractions that equal 1.
2. How many different pairs of fraction addends can you find to equal 1?

✸ ACTIVITY 11-3

FINDING A SUM OF 1 WITH MORE THAN 2 ADDENDS

MATERIALS:
Fraction Bars

PROCEDURE:
1. Use the fraction bars to help you write addition sentences that add up to 1 using more than two fraction addends.

   Example: 1 fourth + 1 third + 1 sixth + 3 twelfths is the same as 1 bar (or equals 1).

✸ ACTIVITY 11-4

FINDING A MISSING ADDEND

PROCEDURE:
1. Can you find out which fraction goes in the blank space to make a true statement?

   2 thirds + _____ = 11 twelfths

   1 fifth + _____ = 3 tenths

✸ ACTIVITY 11-5

ADDING FRACTIONS

MATERIALS:
Fraction Bars

PROCEDURE:
1. Use fraction bars to help you add $\frac{1}{2} + \frac{1}{5}$.
2. Do some other examples.

✸ ACTIVITY 11-6

FINDING PARTICULAR SUMS

PROCEDURE:
1. Write addition sentences with a sum of 15 sixteenths.
2. Write addition sentences using different-sized fractions with 11 twelfths as the sum.

✳ ACTIVITY 11-7

ADDING FRACTIONS

PROCEDURE:

1. Use fraction families (equivalent fractions) to add $\frac{3}{4} + \frac{1}{5}$.

2. Do some other addition problems.

Possible solution:

$$
\begin{array}{lll}
3 \text{ fourths} & \rightarrow & 15 \text{ twentieths} \\
\underline{1 \text{ fifth}} & \rightarrow & \underline{4 \text{ twentieths}} \\
& & 19 \text{ twentieths or } \frac{19}{20}
\end{array}
$$

✳ ACTIVITY 11-8

FINDING THE LOWEST COMMON DENOMINATOR

PROCEDURE:

1. Find the lowest common denominator to help you find the sum of $\frac{2}{5} + \frac{1}{6}$.

2. Do some other examples.

Possible solution:

$$
\begin{array}{lll}
2 \text{ fifths} & \rightarrow & 12 \text{ thirtieths} \\
\underline{1 \text{ sixth}} & \rightarrow & \underline{5 \text{ thirtieths}} \\
& & 17 \text{ thirtieths}
\end{array}
$$

✳ ACTIVITY 11-9

FRACTION ADDITION

MATERIALS:
Fraction Bars

PROCEDURE:
Do any of these fraction pairs add up to 1?
Use fraction bars to help you find the answer.

$$\frac{1}{6} + \frac{10}{12} = \qquad \frac{3}{4} + \frac{3}{12} = \qquad \frac{2}{3} + \frac{2}{6} =$$

✳ ACTIVITY 11-10

FRACTION ADDITION

Write fraction addition statements with sums less than 1.

Write fraction addition statements with sums greater than 1 but less than 2.

Students should be encouraged to formulate computation rules. Students' procedural descriptions might be like the following:

Examples:

$\frac{1}{5} + \frac{3}{5} =$ _____ *I'm adding fifths so I find how many fifths in all.*

$\frac{2}{3} + \frac{1}{2} =$ _____ *I have 2 thirds and 1 half, so I change the fractions so they are the same-sized parts, then I add the number of parts in each group.*

The inclination to merely add across numerators and denominators should be offset by having students verbalize and explain the meaning of composite fractions.

Examples:

$\frac{3}{10}$ *means 3 parts, each 1 tenth in size.*

$\frac{3}{10} = 1$ *tenth* $+ 1$ *tenth* $+ 1$ *tenth or*

3×1 *tenth*

$\frac{3}{10} = \frac{1}{10} + \frac{1}{10} + \frac{1}{10}$ *or* $3 \times \frac{1}{10}$

Addition:

$$
\begin{array}{lr}
& 3 \text{ tenths} \\
+ & 5 \text{ tenths} \\
\hline
& 8 \text{ tenths}
\end{array}
$$

Therefore, $\frac{3}{10} + \frac{5}{10} = \frac{8}{10}$ *(and not* $\frac{8}{20}$*)*

Finding common denominators. Addition of unlike fractions involves finding a common denominator of the fraction addends. There are several ways to find common denominators of two or more fractions.

1. Finding the common denominator of two fractions using fraction bars (see Figure 11-4).

$$\frac{1}{4} + \frac{2}{3} = ?$$

$$\frac{1}{4} + \frac{2}{3} = \frac{3}{12} + \frac{8}{12} = \frac{11}{12}$$

2. At the symbolic level, common denominators can be found by first listing successive multiples of the given denominators and then identifying a common multiple. Usually, one selects the lowest common multiple (LCM) so that the sum will be in simplest form.

Example: $\frac{1}{4} + \frac{2}{3}$

Denominators	Multiples
4	4, 8, 12, 16, 20, . . .
3	3, 6, 9, 12, 15, 18, . . .

The lowest common multiple of 4 and 3 is 12.

Therefore, $\frac{1}{4} + \frac{2}{3} = \frac{3}{12} + \frac{8}{12} = \frac{11}{12}$

FIGURE 11-4

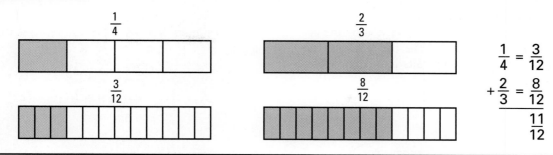

3. Common denominators can be found by listing equivalent fractions until a common denominator is found.

Example:
$\frac{1}{4} + \frac{2}{3}$

$$\frac{1}{4} \rightarrow \frac{1}{4}, \frac{2}{8}, \boxed{\frac{3}{12}}, \frac{4}{16}, \frac{5}{20}, \cdots$$

$$\frac{2}{3} \rightarrow \frac{2}{3}, \frac{4}{6}, \frac{6}{9}, \boxed{\frac{8}{12}}, \frac{10}{15}, \cdots$$

The fractions $\frac{3}{12}$ and $\frac{8}{12}$ have a common denominator, thus,
$\frac{1}{4} + \frac{2}{3} = \frac{3}{12} + \frac{8}{12} = \frac{11}{12}$

4. The lowest common denominator of two or more fractions can also be identified by finding the prime factors of the denominators and computing the product of the maximum set of unique prime factors.

Example:
$\frac{1}{4} + \frac{1}{6}$

Denominators	Prime factors
4	2×2
6	2×3

The maximum set of unique prime factors is $2 \times 2 \times 3$, that is, the prime factors of 4 are in the set and the prime factors of 6 are in the set.

Product: $2 \times 2 \times 3 = 12$

The LCD of 4 and 6 is 12.

$$2 \times \boxed{2} \times 3$$
prime factors of 4   prime factors of 6

Students should be allowed to use the method they prefer to find a common denominator of a set of fractions.

When working with fraction bars or other materials, students may record addition sentences as follows:

Examples:
$\frac{1}{2} + \frac{1}{4} = (\frac{1}{4} + \frac{1}{4}) + \frac{1}{4} = \frac{3}{4}$
  or $\frac{2}{4} + \frac{1}{4} = \frac{3}{4}$

$\frac{1}{6} + \frac{1}{2} = \frac{1}{6} + (\frac{1}{6} + \frac{1}{6} + \frac{1}{6}) = \frac{4}{6}$
  or $\frac{1}{6} + \frac{3}{6} = \frac{4}{6}$ or $\frac{2}{3}$

Developing an addition algorithm. Algorithms for adding unlike fractions require finding a common denominator for the fraction addends. If the lowest common denominator is desired, one of the methods described in the preceding section can be employed.

Example:
$\frac{3}{4} + \frac{5}{6}$

The multiples of 4 are 4, 8, 12, 16, . . .
The multiples of 6 are 6, 12, 18, . . .

Twelve is the LCM of 4 and 6 and, therefore, it is the lowest common denominator for renaming the fractions $\frac{3}{4}$ and $\frac{5}{6}$.

$\frac{3}{4} = \frac{?}{12}$ Since 4 was multiplied by 3 to obtain 12, the numerator 3 must also be multiplied by 3 to obtain the number of twelfths $\frac{3}{4}$ equals.

$\frac{5}{6} = \frac{?}{12}$ Similarly, 5 must be multiplied by 2 to obtain the number of twelfths $\frac{5}{6}$ equals.

$\frac{3}{4} + \frac{5}{6} = \frac{9}{12} + \frac{10}{12} = \frac{19}{12}$ or $1\frac{7}{12}$

In algorithmic form, this process demonstrates that each fraction is essentially being multiplied by one, the identity element for multiplication.

$$\frac{3}{3} = 1 \qquad \frac{2}{2} = 1$$

$$\frac{3}{4} + \frac{5}{6} = \frac{3 \times \boxed{3}}{4 \times \boxed{3}} + \frac{5 \times \boxed{2}}{6 \times \boxed{2}} = \frac{9}{12} + \frac{10}{12} = \frac{19}{12}$$

When adding fractions, it is not necessary to find the lowest common denominator. An algorithm for finding a common denominator consists of writing equivalent fractions by multiplying each term of a fraction by the denominator of the other fraction. The like fractions can then be added. The algorithm results in a common denominator but not necessarily the lowest.

Example:

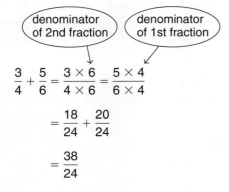

$$\frac{3}{4} + \frac{5}{6} = \frac{3 \times 6}{4 \times 6} = \frac{5 \times 4}{6 \times 4}$$

$$= \frac{18}{24} + \frac{20}{24}$$

$$= \frac{38}{24}$$

The procedure can be abbreviated to

$$\frac{3}{4} + \frac{5}{6} = \frac{(3 \times 6) + (5 \times 4)}{4 \times 6} = \frac{18 + 20}{24} = \frac{38}{24}$$

This leads to the generalization:

$$\frac{a}{b} + \frac{c}{d} = \frac{ad + bc}{bd}$$

Addition of mixed numbers. Addition of mixed numbers can be approached from the perspective of adding whole numbers since, in both instances, the numbers are indicated sums.

Example:

$$
\begin{aligned}
76 &= \ 7 \text{ tens} + 6 \text{ ones} \\
+ \ 61 &= \ 6 \text{ tens} + 1 \text{ one} \\
\hline
&= 13 \text{ tens} + 7 \text{ ones} \quad \text{or } 137
\end{aligned}
$$

Example:

$$
\begin{aligned}
3\tfrac{1}{5} &= 3 + \tfrac{1}{5} \\
+ \ 2\tfrac{2}{5} &= 2 + \tfrac{2}{5} \\
\hline
& \quad 5 + \tfrac{3}{5} \quad \text{or} \quad 5\tfrac{3}{5}
\end{aligned}
$$

Just as some whole number additions require regrouping, so do some fraction additions.

Example:

$$
\begin{aligned}
47 &\quad 40 + \ 7 \\
+ \ 25 &\rightarrow 20 + \ 5 \\
\hline
72 &\quad 60 + 12 = 60 + 10 + 2 = 72
\end{aligned}
$$

Example:

$$
\begin{aligned}
3\tfrac{1}{5} &= 3 + \tfrac{8}{40} \\
+ \ 1\tfrac{7}{8} &= 1 + \tfrac{35}{40} \\
\hline
& \quad 4 + \tfrac{43}{40} \\
&= 4 + \tfrac{43}{40} \\
&= 4 + \tfrac{40}{40} + \tfrac{3}{40} \\
&= 4 + 1 + \tfrac{3}{40} \\
&= 5\tfrac{3}{40}
\end{aligned}
$$

The Annenberg/CPB Math and Science Collection

VIDEO LINK 11-1
Fraction Tracks

Brief Summary: In "Fraction Tracks," Hilory Paster's fifth-graders are playing the Fraction Tracks game, in which they need to move chips from one side of the board to the other by using equivalent fractions. Figure 11-5 shows the gameboard. In the Fraction Tracks game, a cooperative game for two players, students draw fraction cards from a deck and move markers on their gameboard, trying to get all their markers from zero to one by moving the length specified on the card drawn. In the game, students often have to rename the fraction they draw as an equivalent fraction or as the sum of two or more fractions.

1. How does this game help students understand addition of fractions and common denominators?
2. How does this lesson help the teacher assess her students' understanding of common denominators?
3. How could this game be modified to provide students more practice with addition of fractions?

Video Source. Teaching Math: A Video Library, 5–8; Tape 1 from The Annenberg/CPB Math and Science Collection.

Developing Subtraction Procedures

The procedures for developing subtraction of fractions parallel those for addition. It would seem, therefore, that students who are competent with fraction addition would be equally successful with subtraction. However, there are reports that indicate students make more errors in subtracting fractions involving renaming than in whole number subtraction with renaming; also, subtraction seems to be the most difficult of the four basic operations with fractions.

Early subtraction activities First subtraction activities should have students writing subtraction statements from their work with manipulative materials. Students could be asked to write fraction subtraction stories

FIGURE 11-5

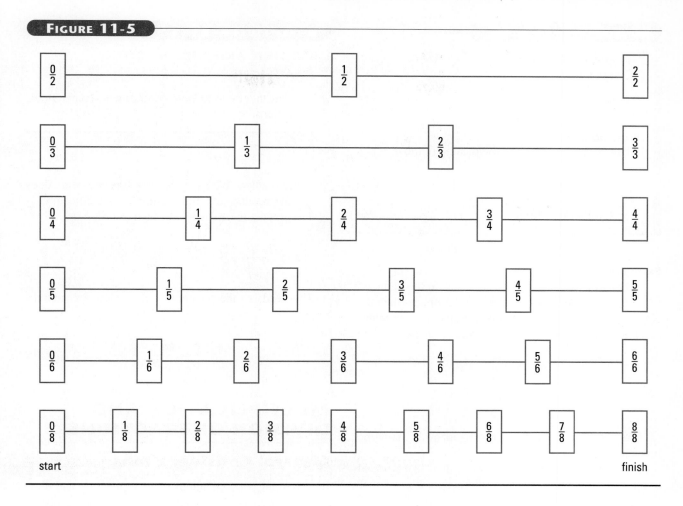

start   finish

(Activity 11-11) to demonstrate understanding of fractions and the subtraction operation.

After students have had experiences in writing subtraction sentences from their work with concrete materials, they can be asked to do specific subtraction problems. Activities 11-12 to 11-15 have students modeling subtraction sentences to find the missing addend. Each activity should be followed with a class dialogue.

Renaming fractions The process of writing equivalent fractions is sometimes called "renaming fractions." In fraction subtraction, another renaming process is introduced that parallels renaming in whole number subtraction. For example, when subtracting 28 from 175, the 7 tens and 5 ones are renamed as 6 tens and 15 ones before the subtraction is carried out. Similarly, renaming is required in some fraction subtractions.

✳ ACTIVITY 11-11

SUBTRACTION FRACTION STORIES

PROCEDURE:

1. Write a story about three friends eating part of a cake that has been cut in 8 equal pieces. Use fraction circle pieces to help you think of sharing the cake, then draw a picture of the cake before any pieces were eaten and after the friends had their share.

2. Write a fraction story about someone who decides to donate some books from a set of 36 books. Tell what part of the set of books was given away and what part was left.

✳ ACTIVITY 11-12

SUBTRACTING FRACTIONS (CONCRETE)

MATERIALS:
fraction circle pieces

PROCEDURE:

1. Use fraction circle pieces to find

$$\tfrac{5}{8} - \tfrac{1}{4} = ? \qquad \tfrac{3}{4} - \tfrac{1}{2} = ?$$

Solve other examples.

✴ ACTIVITY 11-13

FINDING THE MISSING ADDEND (CONCRETE)

MATERIALS:
fraction bars

PROCEDURE:
1. Use fraction bars to find the missing number.

$$\frac{3}{4} - \underline{\quad} = \frac{5}{8} \qquad \frac{4}{5} - \underline{\quad} = \frac{7}{15}$$

Solve other examples.

Example: $5\frac{3}{8} - 2\frac{7}{8}$.

Although the subtrahend ($2\frac{7}{8}$) is less than the minuend ($5\frac{3}{8}$), the fraction part of the subtrahend is greater than the corresponding part of the minuend. Renaming the minuend facilitates the operation. The process can be:

$$5\frac{3}{8} = 4 + \frac{8}{8} + \frac{3}{8} = 4\frac{11}{8}$$
$$- 2\frac{7}{8} = \quad\quad 2 + \frac{7}{8} = 2\frac{7}{8}$$
$$\overline{\quad\quad\quad\quad\quad 2\frac{4}{8} = 2\frac{1}{2}}$$

Take care that students do not erroneously show the procedures as $5\frac{3}{8} = 4\frac{13}{8}$

In whole number subtraction, it is a "ten" that is added to the ones column; in fraction subtraction, it is a "one" that is added to the fraction part of the addend. The "one" is expressed with the same denominator as the fraction addend.

Symbolic fraction algorithm   The procedures for the development of a meaningful subtraction algorithm parallel those for an addition algorithm. A subtraction algorithm that is commonly presented in textbooks is:

$$\frac{3}{4} - \frac{1}{6} = ?$$

$$\frac{3 \times 6}{4 \times 6} - \frac{1 \times 4}{6 \times 4} = \frac{18}{24} - \frac{4}{24} = \frac{14}{24} = \frac{7}{12}$$

In the example, the common denominator is found by multiplying each term of a fraction by the denominator of

✴ ACTIVITY 11-14

SUBTRACTING FRACTIONS

Write as many subtraction statements as you can with a difference of $\frac{1}{8}$; $\frac{1}{10}$; $\frac{1}{12}$.

✴ ACTIVITY 11-15

ADDING AND SUBTRACTING FRACTIONS

Draw rectangles to help you find sum and differences of fractions.

---

the other fraction. We have seen that this procedure does not always produce the lowest common denominator.

The procedure can be abbreviated as follows:

$$\frac{(3 \times 6) - (1 \times 4)}{4 \times 6} = \frac{18 - 4}{24} = \frac{14}{24} = \frac{7}{12}$$

This leads to the generalized algorithm for subtraction:

$$\frac{a}{b} - \frac{c}{d} = \frac{ad - bc}{bd}$$

MULTIPLICATION AND DIVISION OF FRACTIONS

General Considerations

In developing the operations of multiplication and division with fractions, ideas can be drawn from the operations with whole numbers. For example, multiplication can be interpreted as repeated addition while division can be presented as repeated subtraction.

Two common misunderstandings related to multiplication and division of fractions are that "multiplication makes bigger" and "division makes smaller." This means that many students expect the product to be greater than both factors in multiplication of fractions problems, as it is in multiplication of whole numbers. Similarly, students expect the quotient to be smaller than the divisor and the dividend in division of fractions problems, as it is in division of whole numbers. For example, many students expect that $6 \div \frac{1}{2}$ is 3, since they believe the answer to a division problem is smaller than the numbers in the problem. But this generalization is true only for whole number division. According to Bezuk and Bieck (1993), a goal of instruction should be "to enable students to determine the reasonableness of the results of operations on fractions" (p. 131). Instruction must lead students to recognize that these generalizations are incorrect and help them make sense of answers to fraction computation problems.

There is the potential risk of learning how to multiply and divide fractions by rote because the algorithmic rules are simple. For multiplication, the colloquial rule is "multiply top numbers and then bottom numbers" and for division it is "change the sign and invert the second fraction." Students who thus learn to compute with fractions often have to wait years before the mystery of fraction computation is revealed and understanding emerges.

> ### STANDARDS LINK 11-5
> The transition from whole numbers to fractions and decimals can be difficult for students. Although they may multiply the numerators and then the denominators, for example, they often do not understand why a similar procedure does not work in adding fractions. Concrete or representational models can help students clarify those anomalies. (NCTM, 1989, p. 92)

> ### STANDARDS LINK 11-6
> Operation sense should be expanded with such examples as, Is $\frac{2}{3} \times \frac{5}{4}$ more or less than $\frac{2}{3}$? More or less than $\frac{5}{4}$? (NCTM, 1989, p. 89)

Developing Fraction Multiplication

When students are learning to solve fraction multiplication problems, they should be asked to use concrete materials or draw diagrams and to write some kind of symbolic record of the solution process. This could be a word description, mathematical symbols, or a combination of both. Examples of diagrams and possible solution records are presented in the activities and problems that follow.

There are several different types of fraction multiplication problems:

- multiplying a fraction by a whole number
- multiplying a whole number by a fraction
- multiplying a fraction by a fraction
- multiplying mixed numbers.

Each type is discussed below.

Multiplying a fraction by a whole number
Probably the easiest multiplication situation for students to interpret is to multiply a fraction by a whole number. This type can be related to whole number multiplication.

Examples:

- 3×4 means 3 groups with 4 objects in each group or 3 groups of 4 objects which is 12 objects.

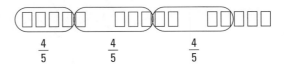

$$3 \times 4 = 12$$

- $3 \times \frac{4}{5}$ means 3 groups of 4 fifths or 12 fifths.

Bags of caramels, 5 candies in each bag

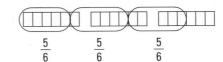

$$\frac{4}{5} \qquad \frac{4}{5} \qquad \frac{4}{5}$$

12 fifths in all, or 2 and $\frac{2}{5}$ bags.

Algorithm: $3 \times \dfrac{4}{5} = \dfrac{3 \times 4}{5} = \dfrac{12}{5}$ or $2\frac{2}{5}$

- $3 \times \frac{5}{6}$ means 3 times 5 sixths

Chocolate Bar

$$\frac{5}{6} \qquad \frac{5}{6} \qquad \frac{5}{6}$$

15 sixths in all, or 2 bars and $\frac{1}{2}$ of another bar.

Algorithm: $3 \times \dfrac{5}{6} = \dfrac{3 \times 5}{6} = \dfrac{15}{6} = 2\frac{3}{6} = 2\frac{1}{2}$

Activity 11-16 and Problem 1 presented below should assist students in understanding why the value of the product is between the whole number factor and the fraction

✳ ACTIVITY 11-16

MULTIPLICATION: TIMES AS MUCH

MATERIALS:
fraction circles to represent pizzas

PROCEDURE:
1. Take one third of a pizza.
2. Now take twice as much pizza. How much is 2 times $\frac{1}{3}$?
3. Make your share three times as large as two thirds. How much pizza is this? How much is 3 times $\frac{2}{3}$?
4. How much pizza is a share 4 times as large as two thirds?
5. Write multiplication sentences for your findings.

FIGURE 11-6

A SOLUTION TO ACTIVITY 11-16

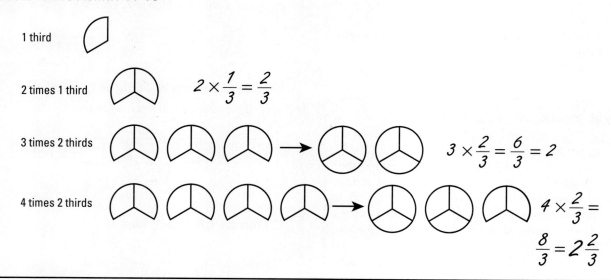

1 third

2 times 1 third $2 \times \dfrac{1}{3} = \dfrac{2}{3}$

3 times 2 thirds $3 \times \dfrac{2}{3} = \dfrac{6}{3} = 2$

4 times 2 thirds $4 \times \dfrac{2}{3} =$ $\dfrac{8}{3} = 2\dfrac{2}{3}$

factor. When the whole number is one, the product equals the fraction factor.

A possible solution to Activity 11-16 is shown in Figure 11-6.

Problem 1 is a simple problem that can be solved in several ways. Four possible solutions are presented.

Problem 1:

The remaining Ritz crackers in a box were all broken and Carl's mother gave him 7 half crackers. Carl receives the equivalent of how many crackers?

Possible solution strategies:

1. A student could use real crackers or paper circles cut in half, then assemble them to make whole crackers/circles. The product could then be easily determined.

2. A student could reason:

   Two halves make one. With 7 halves, Carl has 3 whole crackers with an extra half. So, Carl's mother gave him the same amount as 3 and $\frac{1}{2}$ crackers.

3. Repeated addition can be employed to solve the problem.

$$\frac{1}{2} + \frac{1}{2} + \frac{1}{2} + \frac{1}{2} + \frac{1}{2} + \frac{1}{2} + \frac{1}{2} = \frac{7}{2} \text{ or } 3\frac{1}{2}$$

$$1 \;+\; 1 \;+\; 1 \;+\; \frac{1}{2} = 3\frac{1}{2}$$

4. The problem can be solved multiplicatively.

$$7 \times \frac{1}{2} = \frac{7 \times 1}{2} = \frac{7}{2} \text{ or } 3\frac{1}{2}$$

Multiplying a whole number by a fraction

Problems 2, 3, and 4 are about taking a fractional part of a set. After solving a number of similar problems, students should come to realize that taking a fractional part of something implies multiplication. Thus, "$\frac{3}{4}$ of 8" means 8 multiplied by $\frac{3}{4}$ or $\frac{3}{4} \times 8$. The statements "$\frac{3}{4}$ times 8" and "$\frac{3}{4}$ of 8" both are appropriate for the expression $\frac{3}{4} \times 8$. In situations in which the multiplier is not a whole number, the multiplication symbol is more frequently read as "of" rather than "times."

Problem 2:

Kim has a collection of 15 books. One third of them are science fiction. How many books are science fiction?

In this situation, the multiplier is a fraction and the multiplicand a whole number. Because the commutative property holds true for fraction multiplication, it is expected that the product will be between the whole number factor and the fraction.

Repeated addition is not an appropriate solution strategy for Problem 2, but setting up an array is.

Possible solution strategy:

Tiles, representing books, can be set up in one row of 15 or in three rows of five.

 $\dfrac{1}{3}$

$\dfrac{1}{3}$

$\dfrac{1}{3}$

There are three thirds in the whole set.

One third of 15 is 5 books.

$$\frac{1}{3} \times 15 = 5$$

Kim has 5 science fiction books.

Algorithm: $\frac{1}{3} \times 15 = \frac{1 \times 15}{3} = \frac{15}{3} = 5$

Problem 3:

Two fifths of the 20 baseball cards Andy has are of New York Yankees. How many Yankees cards does Andy own?

A student's thinking and subsequent record of the solution process might be as follows:

The problem question is: What is two fifths of 20?

One fifth means one of five equal parts.

Two fifths means two of five equal parts.

First, I'll find out what is one fifth of 20.

Twenty divided by 5 is 4.

Therefore, one fifth of 20 is 4.

$\frac{1}{5}$ *of 20 is 4* $\frac{2}{5}$ *of 20 is 8*

Andy has 8 baseball cards of the Yankees.

Algorithm: $\frac{2}{5} \times 20 = \frac{2 \times 20}{5} = \frac{40}{5} = 8$

With the student's reasoning that the problem can be solved by dividing 20 by 5, the following step in the algorithm can be discussed: $\frac{1}{5} \times 20 = \frac{1 \times 20}{5} = \frac{20}{5} = 4$

Problem 4:

Monique had 8 candies and she ate $\frac{3}{4}$ of them during recess. How many candies does she have left?

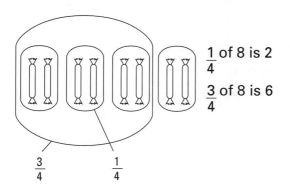

$\frac{1}{4}$ of 8 is 2

$\frac{3}{4}$ of 8 is 6

$\frac{3}{4}$ $\frac{1}{4}$

Solution process:

Monique ate 6 candies and has 2 candies left.

Algorithm: $\frac{3}{4} \times 8 = \frac{3 \times 8}{4} = \frac{24}{4} = 6$

The idea that whole numbers can be expressed in fraction form can be discussed and another step in the development of the algorithm can follow.

$$8 = \frac{8}{1}$$

Therefore, in the problem above, one can write

$$\frac{3}{4} \times 8 = \frac{3}{4} \times \frac{8}{1} = \frac{3}{4} \times \frac{8}{1} = \frac{24}{4} = 6$$

Multiplying a fraction by a fraction When two proper fractions are multiplied, the product is smaller than either factor. This may be incongruous to students' thinking about multiplication. Therefore, care should be taken to provide realistic problem situations so that students will realize why fraction multiplication works this way.

Constructing an array is an appropriate strategy to help solve a problem when both factors are fractions. Consider the situations in Problems 5 to 7.

Problem 5:

How much is $\frac{1}{2}$ of $\frac{1}{3}$ of a candy bar?

Possible solution process:

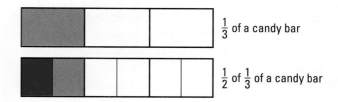

$\frac{1}{3}$ of a candy bar

$\frac{1}{2}$ of $\frac{1}{3}$ of a candy bar

Therefore, one half of one third is one sixth.

Algorithm: $\frac{1}{2} \times \frac{1}{3} = \frac{1 \times 1}{2 \times 3} = \frac{1}{6}$ or $\frac{1}{2} \times \frac{1}{3} = \frac{1}{6}$

Problem 6:

When Jane's friend arrived for a visit, Jane had just finished eating one fourth of 8 chocolate-coated raisins. Jane and her friend each ate one half of the remaining raisins. What part of the 8 raisins did Jane's friend eat?

Possible solution process:

The problem question is: $\frac{1}{2}$ of $\frac{3}{4}$ = ?

The raisins can be arranged in a rectangular array.

Jane had eaten $\frac{1}{4}$ or 2 raisins.

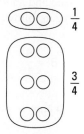

Six raisins are $\frac{3}{4}$ of the set of 8 raisins.

If one thinks of the 6 raisins, one can say: $\frac{1}{2}$ of 6 is 3.

But, if one thinks of $\frac{3}{4}$ of a whole set, the question to ask is

What is $\frac{1}{2}$ of $\frac{3}{4}$? or $\frac{1}{2} \times \frac{3}{4}$ = ?

Three raisins are 3 eighths of the whole set of raisins.

Algorithm: $\frac{1}{2} \times \frac{3}{4} = \frac{1 \times 3}{2 \times 4} = \frac{3}{8}$

Jane's friend ate three raisins which is three eighths of the whole set of raisins.

When multiplying two fractions, the process involves taking a *part of a part* but the product is a part of the original unit. This operational trait of the changing unit can be problematic for students; therefore, it is important to provide clear examples. Having students talk about their problem-solving process is an effective way to find out how they are thinking about fractions. Figure 11-7 shows how to model fraction multiplication with rectangles.

Problem 7:

How many eggs is $\frac{1}{4}$ of $\frac{2}{3}$ of a dozen eggs?

Possible solution process:

Two thirds of a dozen eggs is 8 eggs.

One fourth of 8 eggs is two eggs.

Therefore, one fourth of two thirds is two twelfths.

Algorithm: $\frac{1}{4} \times \frac{2}{3} = \frac{1 \times 2}{4 \times 3} = \frac{2}{12}$ or $\frac{1}{4} \times \frac{2}{3} = \frac{2}{12}$

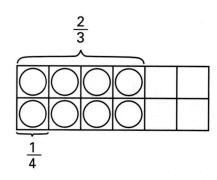

Problems 2, 3, and 4 all exemplify multiplying a whole number by a fraction. Problem 2 is solved concretely with the answer derived from the array. In Problems 3 and 4, principles used in the multiplication algorithm are highlighted:

- a whole number can be written in fraction form
  $20 = \frac{20}{1}$
- division is involved
  $\frac{20}{5}$ means 20 divided by 5
- numerators are multiplied
  $\frac{1}{5} \times 20 = \frac{20}{5}$

In Problems 5, 6, and 7, both factors are fractions. Concrete or pictorial solutions to similar problems can lead students to formulate the algorithmic rule: multiply numerators together and denominators together.

As students solve problems, some of their "algorithms" could be written on the board or on an overhead transparency to provide the focus for a class dialogue. Reflecting on their problem-solving processes and discussing them with classmates can lead to insights about related procedures and to a refinement of the procedures. Thus, students can develop an algorithm for multiplying fractions that will be meaningful to them.

Multiplying mixed numbers Whole number multiplication can be used to exemplify the process of multiplying mixed numbers. Use of the distributive property is evident in the following two examples.

Example 1:

$$23 \times 45 = (20 + 3) \times (40 + 5)$$
$$= (20 \times 40) + (20 \times 5) +$$
$$(3 \times 40) + (3 \times 5)$$
$$= 800 + 100 + 120 + 15$$
$$= 1035$$

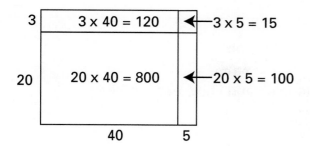

Partial products are 800, 100, 120, and 15. Adding them gives 1035.

Example 2:

$$3\frac{2}{5} \times 4\frac{1}{3} = \left(3 + \frac{2}{5}\right) \times \left(4 + \frac{1}{3}\right)$$

$$= (3 \times 4) + \left(3 \times \frac{1}{3}\right) + \left(\frac{2}{5} \times 4\right) + \left(\frac{2}{5} \times \frac{1}{3}\right)$$

$$= 12 + \frac{3}{3} + \frac{8}{5} + \frac{2}{15}$$

$$= 12 + 1 + 1\frac{3}{5} + \frac{2}{15}$$

$$= 14 + \frac{9}{15} + \frac{2}{15}$$

$$= 14\frac{11}{15}$$

The sum of the partial product is $12 + 1 + \frac{8}{5} + \frac{2}{15} = 13\frac{26}{15} = 14\frac{11}{15}$

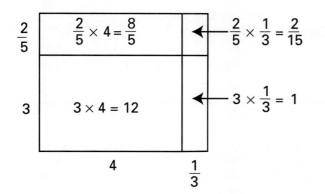

Another way to approach multiplication of mixed numbers is to change each mixed number to an improper fraction and then multiply the two fractions.

Example 3:

Understanding that $3 = \frac{15}{5}$ and $4 = \frac{12}{3}$, the student might write:

$$3\frac{2}{5} \times 4\frac{1}{3} = \left(\frac{15}{5} + \frac{2}{5}\right) \times \left(\frac{12}{3} + \frac{1}{3}\right)$$

$$= \frac{17}{5} \times \frac{13}{3}$$

$$= \frac{221}{15}$$

$$= 14\frac{11}{15}$$

Other considerations

Simplifying. When students begin to work symbolically with fraction multiplication, they are encouraged to simplify the factors before proceeding to multiply. Simplifying should be thought of as a process of renaming or exchange and not cancellation (Example 1). Thinking of simplifying as cancellation can lead to errors in computation. For example, if students are told to "cancel like factors" as in Example 2 below, students may go on to erroneously cancel common digits as in Example 3.

Example 1:

$\frac{2}{6} \times \frac{3}{8} =$

Thinking process:

Rename $\frac{2}{6}$ as $\frac{1}{3}$, then simplify

$\frac{2}{6} \times \frac{3}{8} = \frac{1}{3} \times \frac{3}{8} = \frac{3}{3 \times 8} = \frac{3}{3} \times \frac{1}{8} = \frac{1}{8}$

or

$\frac{2}{6} \times \frac{3}{8} = \frac{2 \times 3}{6 \times 8} = \frac{6}{6 \times 8} = \frac{1}{8}$

Example 2:

$\frac{2}{6} \times \frac{3}{8} =$

$\frac{2}{6} \times \frac{3}{8} = \frac{\cancel{2}}{\cancel{2} \times 3} \times \frac{\cancel{3}}{2 \times 4} = \frac{1}{8}$

Example 3 (Incorrect procedure):

$\frac{2\cancel{3}}{\cancel{3}5} = \frac{2}{5}$

There are a few cases when indeed the like digits can be cancelled and the resulting fraction will be a correct simplification. Examples: $\frac{16}{64} = \frac{1}{4}$ and $\frac{26}{65} = \frac{2}{5}$.

An investigation to find other fractions for which this procedure holds true should lead to the realization that the procedure works only for a very small number of cases. Therefore, the procedure should be thought to be generally incorrect.

Reciprocals. Like whole numbers, fractions have a reciprocal or multiplicative inverse (except a fraction with a numerator of 0). The definition of multiplication

Fraction Multiplication

$\frac{1}{5} \times \frac{1}{2}$ Draw two congruent rectangles and show each fraction.

Then draw a third rectangle congruent to the others and shade $\frac{1}{5}$ and $\frac{1}{2}$ of the rectangle as shown below.

$\frac{1}{10}$

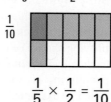

The part where the shading intersects shows $\frac{1}{5}$ of $\frac{1}{2}$.

$\frac{1}{5}$ of $\frac{1}{2}$ is $\frac{1}{10}$.

$$\frac{1}{5} \times \frac{1}{2} = \frac{1}{10}$$

$\frac{1}{2} \times \frac{3}{4}$ Draw two congruent rectangles. Show $\frac{1}{2}$ on one rectangle and $\frac{3}{4}$ on the other rectangle as shown.

Draw another rectangle, congruent to the others and show eighths as pictured.

Shade in $\frac{1}{2}$ of the rectangle, then $\frac{3}{4}$.

The part where the shading intersects shows $\frac{1}{2}$ of $\frac{3}{4}$.

$$\frac{1}{2} \times \frac{3}{4} = \frac{3}{8}$$

The twice-shaded part is $\frac{3}{8}$ of the figure.

---

can be used to demonstrate to students that the product of a fraction and its multiplicative inverse equals one.

Example:

Is there a factor that, when multiplied by $\frac{3}{4}$, will give the product one?

$\frac{3}{4} \times n = 1$

The reciprocal of $\frac{3}{4}$ is $\frac{4}{3}$.

$\frac{3}{4} \times \frac{4}{3} = \frac{3 \times 4}{4 \times 3} = \frac{1}{12} = 1$

In general terms, $\frac{a}{b} \times \frac{b}{a} = 1$.

This procedure is helpful in understanding the fraction division algorithm.

Developing Fraction Division

When working with whole numbers it was observed that division problems can be of two types: measurement and partitioning. Likewise, fraction division problems can be of the two types. A teacher would be wise to review with students both problem types before introducing fraction division problems to ensure that students understand the problems and that they will, therefore, be able to concentrate on the division process. Problems 8 and 9 below are examples of measurement division problems; Problem 10 is a partition problem.

Division problems involving fraction divisors and whole number dividends are easiest and should be presented first. Both even and uneven division should be modeled. Division problems with fraction and whole number divisors are exemplified below.

Whole number divided by a fraction: even division

Problem 8:
Randy has 6 sticks of gum. He wants to break each in half-sized pieces. How many pieces will he get?

Possible solution process:

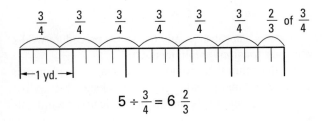

$6 \div \frac{1}{2} = 12$

Whole number divided by a fraction: uneven division

Problem 9:
Jane is responsible for wrapping small packages for the local fall fair. She is cutting a roll of ribbon in $\frac{3}{4}$ yd. lengths to make bows for the packages. How many pieces of ribbon $\frac{3}{4}$ yd. long will she get from 5 yards of ribbon?

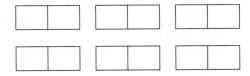

$$5 \div \frac{3}{4} = 6 \frac{2}{3}$$

Possible solution process:
Jane will get 6 pieces of ribbon $\frac{3}{4}$ yd. long. She will have $\frac{2}{3}$ of another piece.

Fraction divisor and whole number dividend

Problem 10:
For her birthday, Molly received a box of chocolates with 32 chocolates in it. After her family had some, Molly calculated that $\frac{3}{4}$ of the chocolates remained. One day, she shared the remaining chocolates equally among herself

and five friends. What part of the box of chocolates did each friend receive?

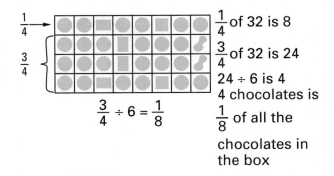

$\frac{1}{4}$ of 32 is 8

$\frac{3}{4}$ of 32 is 24

24 ÷ 6 is 4

4 chocolates is $\frac{1}{8}$ of all the chocolates in the box

$$\frac{3}{4} \div 6 = \frac{1}{8}$$

Possible solution process:
Each friend received $\frac{1}{8}$ of the chocolates or 4 chocolates ($\frac{1}{8} = \frac{4}{32}$).

Fraction divisor and dividend When students are able to concretely represent problems with a whole number divisor or dividend, they can be asked to solve problems that have fraction divisors and dividends. Quotients may be whole numbers or fractions. Problem 11 is an example with a whole number quotient.

Problem 11:
Max has $\frac{1}{2}$ quart of lemonade. He wants to pour $\frac{1}{6}$ quart in small glasses. How many servings of lemonade will Max have?

Possible solution process:

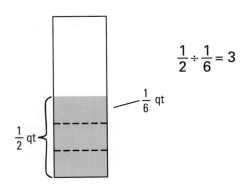

$$\frac{1}{2} \div \frac{1}{6} = 3$$

Max will have 3 servings of lemonade.

Mixed number dividend

Problem 12:
Mrs. Hanson bought $2\frac{1}{2}$ yards of magnetic tape to use in displaying a set of geometric figures on the classroom metallic board. She wants to cut each yard into equal pieces, that is, each piece is to be $\frac{1}{12}$ yard long. How many pieces $\frac{1}{12}$ yd. long can Mrs. Hanson get?

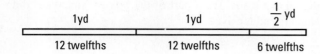

Possible solution strategy:

12 pieces $\frac{1}{12}$ yd long in 1 yard

24 pieces in two yards

6 pieces in $\frac{1}{2}$ yard

Therefore, Mrs. Hanson can get 30 pieces of tape.

Problems with composite fractions for both divisor and dividend are more challenging to represent pictorially and students' work deserves careful supervision. Examples are shown in Figure 11-8 using a rectangular model.

Developing a symbolic division algorithm
In the preceding sections, several problems were presented with concrete or diagrammatic solution processes. As students demonstrate the ability to solve division problems, encourage them to record their work in mathematical sentences. At appropriate times, class discussions can serve to draw students' attention to patterns or relationships in their solution procedures. A class could produce answers to sets of problems similar to the different types exemplified in Problems 8 to 12. Subsequently, the equations could be listed on the board to be examined by the class. Observations should be verbalized and discussed. The following activities illustrate this strategy.

1. Provide each pair of students with a fraction division question similar to $6 \div \frac{1}{2}$ to solve by drawing a diagram. The student pairs check each other's work.

   Examples: $6 \div \frac{1}{2} = \qquad 5 \div \frac{1}{2} = \qquad 3 \div \frac{1}{3} =$
   $\qquad\quad 6 \div \frac{1}{5} = \qquad 4 \div \frac{1}{3} = \qquad 5 \div \frac{1}{4} =$

   • When all pairs have completed the work, write the equations on the board.

   • Invite students to examine the equations and write about their observations.

   • Ask students to share their observations. [The whole number (dividend) and the denominator of the divisor are multiplied.]

   • Ask students to write a multiplication equation for each division equation.

2. Follow the procedures above but use a different set of questions.

   Examples: $5 \div \frac{3}{4} = \frac{20}{3} \qquad 3 \div \frac{2}{3} = \frac{9}{2}$
   $\qquad\quad 4 \div \frac{2}{3} = \frac{12}{2}$

   Question: How can you obtain $6\frac{2}{3}$ from $5 \div \frac{3}{4}$? See Figure 11-9. Observation: Multiply the dividend and the denominator of the divisor, then divide this number by the numerator of the divisor.

   The rule may be verbalized: Change the question to a multiplication and invert the divisor, and then multiply the two numbers.

   Algorithm: $5 \div \frac{3}{4} = 5 \times \frac{4}{3} = \frac{20}{3} = 6\frac{2}{3}$

Students can subsequently test if this procedure works whenever fractions are divided.

An algorithm that provides a meaningful explanation of the "invert and multiply rule" is to change the divisor to one using reciprocals and the multiplicative identity element.

Example: $\frac{2}{3} \div \frac{4}{5} =$

Expressed as a complex fraction, the procedure is:

$$\dfrac{\dfrac{2}{3}}{\dfrac{4}{5}} = \dfrac{\dfrac{2}{3} \times \dfrac{5}{4}}{\dfrac{4}{5} \times \dfrac{5}{4}} = \dfrac{\dfrac{2}{3} \times \dfrac{5}{4}}{1} = \dfrac{2}{3} \times \dfrac{5}{4}$$

→ This is equal to one, the multiplicative identity element.

FIGURE 11-8

$\frac{3}{4} \div \frac{1}{2}$ How many $\frac{1}{2}$ fit into $\frac{3}{4}$?

There are $1\frac{1}{2}$ halves that fit into $\frac{3}{4}$.

$\frac{1}{2} \div \frac{3}{5}$ How many $\frac{3}{5}$ fit into $\frac{1}{2}$?

There are $\frac{5}{6}$ of $\frac{3}{5}$ that fit into $\frac{1}{2}$.

$\frac{4}{5} \div \frac{2}{3}$ How many $\frac{2}{3}$ fit into $\frac{4}{5}$?

There are $1\frac{2}{10}$ of $\frac{2}{3}$ that fit into $\frac{4}{5}$.

FIGURE 11-9

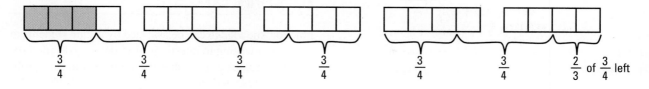

$$5 \div \frac{3}{4} = 6\frac{2}{3}$$

Throughout the development of computation algorithms, teachers should keep in mind that the aim in fraction computation is conceptual understanding of the operations and not memorization of algorithmic procedures. The fractions used in problems should be those that can be visualized concretely or pictorially and are likely to be met in everyday situations (NCTM, 1989).

COMPUTING FRACTIONS WITH A CALCULATOR

Calculators that display fractions, as, for example, the Texas Instruments *Math Explorer,* can be used to advantage by students to help develop computational competence. Systematic explorations can be made to discover patterns and relationships.

Examples:

- Find $\frac{1}{2}$ of these fractions: $\frac{2}{3}, \frac{3}{4}, \frac{4}{5}, \frac{5}{6}, \ldots$
- Find $\frac{1}{3}$ of these fractions: $\frac{2}{5}, \frac{2}{6}, \frac{2}{7}, \frac{2}{8}, \ldots$
- Divide these fractions by 2: $\frac{1}{2}, \frac{1}{3}, \frac{1}{4}, \frac{1}{5}, \ldots$
- Divide these fractions by 2: $\frac{2}{8}, \frac{3}{8}, \frac{4}{8}, \frac{5}{8}, \ldots$

Ask students to compare answers to finding $\frac{1}{2}$ of a number and dividing by 2.

Students can be invited to draw diagrams or model the sentences they solve with a calculator. When using the *Math Explorer* to add and subtract fractions, the calculator displays the answer with the lowest common denominator.

Example:

$$2 \boxed{/} 3 \boxed{+} 5 \boxed{/} 8 = \text{Display: } 31/24$$

To convert the improper fraction $\frac{31}{24}$ to a mixed number, follow the procedure:

$$31/24 \boxed{\text{Ab/c}} = \text{Display: 1 u 7/24 (1 unit and 7/24)}$$

In multiplying fractions, the calculator displays the product of the numerators and that of the denominators. In division, the calculator uses the invert and multiply rule. To simplify the answers in multiplication and division, the function key $\boxed{\text{Simp}}$ is used.

Example:

	Display		Display
$5 \boxed{/} 8 \boxed{\times} 2 \boxed{/} 3 = 10/24$		$\boxed{\text{Simp}}$	5/12
$4 \boxed{/} 7 \boxed{\div} 2 \boxed{/} 3 = 12/14$		$\boxed{\text{Simp}}$	6/7

MENTAL ARITHMETIC AND ESTIMATION

A judicious amount of mental arithmetic and estimation exercises should accompany fraction computation and problem-solving activities. Sets of exercises such as the following examples can easily be developed for brief practice sessions.

Example 1: Mental arithmetic

Problem		**Possible thinking processes**
$5\frac{3}{4} + 3\frac{1}{2}$	$\rightarrow$	$8, 9, 9\frac{1}{4}$
$7 - 2\frac{1}{3}$	$\rightarrow$	$5, 4\frac{2}{3}$
$\frac{1}{7} \times 280$	$\rightarrow$	$\frac{280}{7} = 40$
$8 \div \frac{1}{3}$	$\rightarrow$	$8 \times 3 = 24$

Example 2: Estimation

Problem		**Possible thinking processes**
$\frac{3}{5} + \frac{9}{10} + \frac{1}{23}$	$\rightarrow$	$\frac{1}{2} + 1 + 0 \rightarrow 1\frac{1}{2}$
$6\frac{1}{8} - 2\frac{4}{7}$	$\rightarrow$	$4, 3\frac{1}{2}$
$1\frac{1}{2} \times 5\frac{6}{7}$	$\rightarrow$	$1\frac{1}{2} \times 6 \quad \rightarrow 6 + 3 = 9$
$6\frac{1}{5} \div \frac{1}{2}$	$\rightarrow$	$6 \div \frac{1}{2} \quad \rightarrow 12$
$\frac{2}{3} \div \frac{7}{8}$	$\rightarrow$	divisor is close to 1, quotient is greater than $\frac{2}{3}$ but less than 1

FIGURE 11-10

Assessment Questions

1. Is this correct? $\frac{1}{2} + \frac{1}{8} = 1$ Tell how you know.

2. Is this correct? $\frac{5}{6} - \frac{2}{3} = 1$ Tell how you know.

3. Which quotient is the greatest? Explain how you know.

   8 divided by 1   8 divided by $\frac{1}{2}$ 8 divided by $\frac{1}{4}$

4. Which quotient is the least? Explain how you know.

   The number of threes in 24. The number of thirds in 24. The number of twos in 24.

FIGURE 11-11

Question: Is $\frac{10}{16}$ equal to $\frac{5}{8}$? Tell how you know.

Martha's response:

$\frac{10}{16}$ *is equal to* $\frac{5}{8}$. *One way I know this is by looking at the* $\frac{5}{8}$ *and the* $\frac{10}{16}$. *As you can see with* $\frac{5}{8}$ *all you are doing is doubling the 5 and the 8 to get* $\frac{10}{16}$ *and you can see they are equal.*

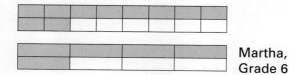

Martha, Grade 6

FIGURE 11-12

Problem:

Samantha and Jennifer have ordered a large pizza. Samantha is able to eat one third of the pizza and Jennifer eats two fifths of the pizza. How much of the pizza was not eaten?

Ajay's response:

$\frac{1}{3}$ $\frac{2}{5}$ $\frac{1}{3} = \frac{5}{15}$ $\frac{2}{5} = \frac{6}{15}$

In this problem, I figured it would be easier to relate the fifths and thirds to the lowest common denominator, fifteenths. I found that one third is equal to five fifteenths and two fifths is equivalent to six fifteenths. Six fifteenths plus five fifteenths is eleven fifteenths. Therefore four fifteenths is left.

Ajay, Grade 6

ASSESSING FRACTION KNOWLEDGE

Fraction knowledge can be assessed by asking students to respond in writing to questions or to develop detailed solution processes to problems. Some questions and problems are presented in Figures 11-10 to 11-12. Examples of responses received from students are presented in Figures 11-11 and 11-12.

Martha's response (Figure 11-11) of "all you are doing is doubling the 5 and the 8 ($\frac{5}{8}$)" without the accompanying diagram might lead one to think that she is merely reciting a rule. However, her drawing serves to verify (probably to herself as much as to the teacher) that indeed the answer to the question is yes. Ajay (Figure 11-12) shows that he understands the fraction addition algorithm; also, his mathematical language is commendable.

CONCLUSION

In this chapter mathematical ideas about fractions have been presented. Teaching considerations have been offered together with a number of activities to help students develop conceptual understanding and number sense about fraction computation. An important point is to make extensive use of concrete materials to model fractions and computational work with fractions and to connect operations on fractions with operations on whole numbers. Work with concrete and pictorial models should extend throughout the elementary grades and possibly well into the middle grades, particularly if computation activities are delayed until then.

For Your Journal

When you have finished studying this chapter, reflect on these questions in your math journal:

1. For each operation, write a word problem and draw a picture showing how to solve the problem using a model.

2. How can a teacher help students understand fraction computation?

3. What does it mean for a person to have "operation sense"?

For Your Portfolio

When you have finished studying this chapter, complete these activities to include in your professional portfolio:

1. Visit a fifth- or sixth-grade classroom. Informally interview several students about their understanding of fraction operations. Write a summary of their understandings and ideas about the instructional activities you might plan to enhance their understanding.

2. Write a lesson to introduce a fraction operation of your choice. Pay particular attention to the real-world situations and models used in the lesson.

Resources for Teachers

Books on Fraction Computation

Berman, B., & Friederwitzer, F. (1988). *Activities for fraction circles plus.* USA: Dale Seymour Publications.

Brodie, J. (1995). *Constructing ideas about fractions, grades 3–6.* Mountain View, CA: Creative Publications.

Charles, L., & Roper, A. (1990). *Activities for fraction circles plus.* Mountain View, CA: Creative Publications.

Corwin, R., Russell, S., & Tierney, C. (1990). *Seeing fractions: A unit for the upper elementary grades.* Sacramento, CA: California Department of Education.

Walker, K., Reak, C., & Stewart, K. (1995). *20 thinking questions for fraction circles, grades 3–6.* Mountain View, CA: Creative Publications.

Walker, K., Reak, C., & Stewart, K. (1995). *20 thinking questions for fraction circles, grades 6–8.* Mountain View, CA: Creative Publications.

Ward, S. (1995). *Constructing ideas about fractions, decimals, and percents.* Mountain View, CA: Creative Publications.

Links to the Internet

Ask Dr. Math (fractions and decimals)
http://forum.swarthmore.edu/dr.math/tocs/fractions.elem.html

Contains a list of interesting questions on fractions and decimals and Dr. Math's answers.

ProTeacher: Fractions and Decimals
http://www.proteacher.com/100014.shtml

Contains lesson plans on fractions and decimals.

Explorer: Fractions
http://explorer.scrtec.org/explorer/explorer-db/browse/static/Mathematics/browse/f34.html

Contains many lessons on and lists of other resources for fractions.

CHAPTER 12

Developing Decimal Concepts and Computation

Focus Questions

When you have finished studying this chapter, you should be able to answer these questions:

1. How can you use models to help children understand decimals and operations on decimals?

2. How are decimals related to whole numbers and fractions?

3. What does each operation on decimals mean? Give a real-world situation that exemplifies each operation on decimals.

"Because decimal fractions look similar to the familiar whole numbers, it seems reasonable to predict that children . . . might understand them without much difficulty. However, appearance is deceiving. The research on learning decimal fractions agrees on one point: There is a lack of conceptual understanding."

(Owens & Super, 1993, p. 137)

What do we know of U.S. students' understanding of decimal concepts and computation? The sixth National Assessment of Educational Progress (NAEP) assessment noted that most fourth-, eighth-, and twelfth-grade students tested had fairly weak understanding of these topics. Only about half of the eighth-graders tested were able to correctly identify the fraction closest to 0.52 (Kouba, Zawojewski, & Struchens, 1997).

Similarly, the results to the following item were disappointing: George buys two calculators that cost $3.29 each. If there is no tax, how much change will he receive from a $10 bill? Only 21% of the fourth graders were able to correctly answer this question.

STANDARDS LINK 12-1

In grades K–4, the mathematics curriculum should include fractions and decimals so that students can

- develop concepts of fractions, mixed numbers, and decimals;
- develop number sense for fractions and decimals;
- use models to relate fractions to decimals and to find equivalent fractions;
- use models to explore operations on fractions and decimals;
- apply fractions and decimals to problem situations. (NCTM, 1989, p. 57)

Research on children's learning of decimals consistently shows a lack of understanding of the concepts related to decimals, which leads to difficulty in determining the reasonableness of answers. Hiebert and Wearne (1986) found that students often lack "a link between their conceptual knowledge (of decimals) and a notion that written answers should be reasonable" (p. 220).

There are two different approaches to helping children learn decimals: building on place-value knowledge, and building on fraction knowledge. While it is tempting to assume (or hope) that children will easily connect what they know about place value to decimals, this can result in fairly low-level performance and a lack of understanding, particularly if concepts are taught procedurally. The place-value approach encourages students to build on their knowledge of place value, for example, by "lining up" the places when adding and subtracting decimals. But this approach has limitations, especially regarding multiplication and division of decimals, in which students do not need to "line up" the decimal points. Instruction that merely focuses on "moving the decimal point" is difficult for students to understand, resulting in a lack of ability to estimate solutions and determine their reasonableness.

The second approach to helping children learn decimals is to connect understanding of decimals with students' existing fraction understanding. This approach helps children develop conceptual knowledge of decimals as well as an understanding of the meaning of operations on decimals. For example, when multiplying 0.3×0.7, why will there be two decimal places in the answer? The traditional procedural response to this is "because you count the number of decimal places in both factors." But *why* is this true? Because 0.3 can be written as $\frac{3}{10}$ (see the insert below) and 0.7 can be written as $\frac{7}{10}$, and $\frac{3}{10} \times \frac{7}{10}$ means we're finding 3 tenths of 7 tenths, which is $\frac{21}{100}$, which can be written as 0.21 (which has two decimal places). This sort of connection must be made if children are to understand rather than merely memorize procedures, which too often are quickly forgotten.

$$0.3 \times 0.7 = \underline{}$$

$$0.3 = \tfrac{3}{10}$$

$$0.7 = \tfrac{7}{10}$$

$$\tfrac{3}{10} \times \tfrac{7}{10} = \tfrac{21}{100} = 0.21$$

So $0.3 \times 0.7 = 0.21$

This chapter presents an integrated approach to instruction on decimals, connecting place-value understanding and fraction understanding to help children develop a strong foundation in decimal concepts and operations. ○

INSTRUCTIONAL CONSIDERATIONS

Connections to Familiar Concepts

In introducing decimal numeration to students, it is important to make connections to familiar concepts. Decimals are closely related to *whole numbers* in that the characteristics of whole number numeration apply to decimals. Also, the computation algorithms are basically the same for whole numbers and decimals. However, to understand decimals quantitatively, one must develop *fractional number* concepts. Ordinarily, fraction concepts are developed before decimals and introduced; in this sequence, one draws upon fractional number knowledge. For example, the decimal number 0.2 can also be expressed as the fraction $\frac{2}{10}$.

Whole number connection   Learning to read and interpret whole numbers involves learning the characteristics of the Hindu-Arabic numeration system. These characteristics were presented in Chapter 6. It may be worthwhile to review the characteristics when children begin to work with decimals. Then, investigations to find out if the characteristics also describe decimal numbers can be part of the development of decimal number concepts.

Place value.   An understanding of the place value system for whole numbers is a prerequisite for reading and interpreting decimals. When learning whole number place value, children group numbers in ten and multiples of ten. They learn that for whole numbers, the value of a place is *ten times* the value of the place to its immediate right. Another way to state this relationship is to say that the value of a place in a numeral is *one tenth* the value of the place to its immediate left. This latter relationship is important in interpreting decimal numbers. The value of the place to the right of the tens is one tenth of ten or one; the value of the place to the right of the ones is one tenth of one or one tenth. Kieren (1984) cautions that acting out fractional regrouping may not be easy for children when he states that "we should not assume that the grouping-ungrouping action that allows one to go from ones to tens to hundreds will also allow one to go from ones to tenths to hundredths; dividing up is simply different from ungrouping" (p. 3). Allow students time to explore such regroupings concretely.

Whole numbers. Compare the value of each 1 in the numeral 115. What is the relationship of the leftmost 1 and the 1 on its right? Modeling the number 115 with bundled sticks and singles shows that the value of the leftmost 1 is ten times the value of the 1 on its right.

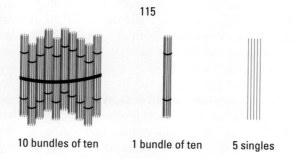

115

| 10 bundles of ten | 1 bundle of ten | 5 singles |

The middle digit, or the 1 to the immediate left of the 5, can be represented by one bundle of ten sticks. It has the value of ten. To show the value of the leftmost 1, group together ten groups of ten sticks. Its value is hundred, or ten times ten. Its value is *ten times* the value of the 1 on its right.

One can also ask, what is the relationship of the 1 on the immediate left of the five to the leftmost 1? Modeling the numbers shows that the 1 next to the 5 is *one tenth* the value of the 1 on its left.

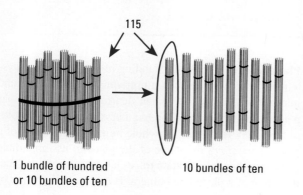

115

1 bundle of hundred
or 10 bundles of ten   10 bundles of ten

The leftmost 1 has the value of hundred. To show the value of the 1 on its right, take a large bundle (ten groups of ten) and separate it into ten bundles of ten. One small bundle (a group of ten sticks) shows the value of the 1 to the left of the 5. Its value is *one tenth* the value of the leftmost 1.

Students who understand and can verbalize the "ten times" and the "one-tenth" relationships between adjacent digits in whole numbers are ready to interpret decimal numeration.

Decimal numbers. Consider 21.1 as an example. The 1 before the decimal point has the value of one. It can be represented with a square.

The value of the 1 on the right of the decimal point can be represented by dividing a square (1) in ten parts.

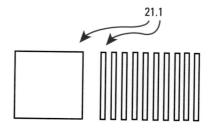

21.1

The value of the 1 on the right of the decimal point is *one tenth* the value of the 1 to the left of the decimal point. This maintains the place-value relationship established above.

As a second example, consider the number 2.11. Using a square to represent 1 unit (as above), the process of subdividing can be extended a step further to demonstrate the value of the rightmost 1 in the number 2.11.

The rightmost 1 has a value of *one-hundredth*. It is one-tenth the value of the 1 on its left. One-hundredth is one-tenth of one-tenth.

The familiar whole number place-value chart can be extended to include decimal places as in Figure 12-1. Notice that the chart is symmetric about the ones place and not the decimal point.

Middle school students may appreciate the patterns inherent in the symbolic representation of place values as in Figure 12-2.

FIGURE 12-1

THOUSANDS	HUNDREDS	TENS	ONES	TENTHS	HUNDREDTHS	THOUSANDTHS
2	3	6	4.	1	2	7

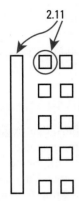

2.11

The following two exercises will assist students to develop meaning of decimal numbers by connecting them to whole numbers.

1. Begin by asking students to respond to the following questions:
   • How many hundreds in 66 600? (six hundred sixty-six)
   • How many tens in 6660? (six hundred sixty-six)
   • How many ones in 666? (six hundred sixty-six)
   Next, continue the pattern using decimals.
   • How many tenths in 66.6? (six hundred sixty-six)
   • How many hundredths in 6.66? (six hundred sixty-six)
   • How many thousandths in 0.666? (six hundred sixty-six)

2. Have students read and write numbers in the following manner:
   • 444 000   four hundred forty-four thousands
   • 44 400   four hundred forty-four hundreds
   • 4440   four hundred forty-four tens
   • 444   four hundred forty-four
   Then, continue the pattern using decimals.
   • 44.4   four hundred forty-four-tenths
   • 4.44   four hundred forty-four-hundredths
   • 0.444   four hundred forty-four-thousandths

Reading numbers as described in the second exercise helps to reinforce the fact that no matter where the decimal point is, each digit is ten times as much as the digit on its right and one-tenth of the digit on its left.

The different reading sequences should also be noticed:

• Whole numbers reading sequence: thousands, hundreds, tens, ones

• Decimal reading sequence: tenths, hundredths, thousandths

Additive quality. To develop the idea that decimals, like whole numbers, are additive, have students first show different ways to write specified whole numbers, then decimal numbers. For example:

Whole numbers

$$45 = 40 + 5$$

$$643 = 600 + 40 + 3$$
or 6 hundreds + 4 tens + 3
$$= 500 + 140 + 3$$
or 5 hundreds + 14 tens + 3
$$= 600 + 30 + 13$$
or 6 hundreds + 3 tens + 13

FIGURE 12-2

10^3	10^2	10^1	10^0	10^{-1}	10^{-2}	10^{-3}
1000	100	10	1	$\frac{1}{10}$	$\frac{1}{100}$	$\frac{1}{1000}$
7	8	2	3.	5	4	5

Decimal numbers

$$0.45 = 0.4 + 0.05$$
$$\text{or 4 tenths + 5 hundredths}$$
$$= 0.40 + 0.05$$
$$\text{or 40 hundredths + 5 hundredths}$$

$$6.43 = 6 + 0.4 + 0.03$$
$$\text{or 6 + 4 tenths + 3 hundredths}$$
$$= 5 + 1.4 + 0.03$$
$$\text{or 5 + 14 tenths + 3 hundredths}$$
$$= 6 + 0.3 + 0.13$$
$$\text{or 6 + 3 tenths + 13 hundredths}$$

Multiplicative quality. The multiplicative aspect of decimal numbers can be highlighted when students learn to write decimals in expanded notation. For example:

$$452.69 \rightarrow (4 \times 100) + (5 \times 10) + (2 \times 1) +$$
$$(6 \times 0.1) + (9 \times 0.01)$$
$$\rightarrow (4 \times 100) + (5 \times 10) + (2 \times 1) +$$
$$(6 \times \tfrac{1}{10}) + (9 \times \tfrac{1}{100})$$

Fraction number connection Pause a moment and order the following fractions from least to greatest:

$$\frac{5}{100} \qquad \frac{5}{1000} \qquad \frac{51}{100} \qquad \frac{501}{100\,000} \qquad \frac{5}{1000} \qquad \frac{150}{1000} \qquad \frac{1005}{100\,000}$$

How does this task compare to that of ordering decimals? Many students find ordering fractions when the denominators are powers of ten easier than ordering decimals. Why is this so? One reason may be that it is easier to visualize the size of a fraction such as $\frac{51}{100}$ (51 parts of 100 parts) than it is to concretize "point five one" (0.51).

The common practice of reading decimals by naming the digits rather than expressing them properly as decimal fractions thwarts the ability to view decimals as fractional numbers.

STANDARDS LINK 12-4

Decimal instruction should include informal experiences that relate fractions to decimals so that students begin to establish connections between the two systems. For example, if students recognize that $\frac{1}{2}$ is the same amount as 0.5, they can use this relationship to determine that 0.4 and 0.45 are a little less than $\frac{1}{2}$ and that 0.6 and 0.57 are a little more than $\frac{1}{2}$. Such activities help children develop number sense for decimals. (NCTM, 1989, p. 59)

Another factor that can contribute to the difficulty in ascertaining the value of a decimal number is the paucity of concrete and semi-concrete experiences that students have when working with decimal numbers. In the past,

some mathematics programs have not encouraged extensive modeling of either decimals or fractions. In practice, it is believed that modeling decimals has occurred even less than modeling fractions, particularly as parts of a whole.

Students who understand fractions prior to studying decimals should be able to make connections between the two systems of representing rational numbers.

Example: $8.45 \rightarrow 8$ and $0.4 + 0.05$
$$\text{or 8 and } 0.45$$
$$\rightarrow 8 \text{ and } \tfrac{4}{10} + \tfrac{5}{100}$$
$$\text{or 8 and } \tfrac{45}{100} \rightarrow 8\tfrac{45}{100}$$

Reading and Writing Decimals

In elementary classrooms, one frequently hears children reading decimals as, for example, "two decimal six" or "two point six" (for 2.6). Some teachers accept this (some textbooks recommend it!) and children go on to say things like "3 point 4 plus 5 point 2 equals 7 point 6." On the lips of adults, statements like these do not perturb us. However, if children use such expressions when learning the meaning of decimal numbers, it is possible they may not readily develop understanding of the quantitative value of decimal numbers. The practice is tantamount to reading whole numbers by naming the digits that form a number as, for example, reading 647 as "six four seven." The expression "six hundred forty-seven" conveys some understanding of the value of each digit in the numeral. The same is true when reading decimals. Children should be required to state the quantitative value of digits when they read a decimal numeral.

Examples: 4.5   Read as "four and five-tenths."
0.35   Read as "zero and thirty-five-hundredths" or "thirty-five-hundredths."

Decimal point In fraction form, it is easy to distinguish between the whole number and the fraction part (e.g., $4\frac{5}{10}$). With decimal numeration, the denominator is not visible; therefore, a sign is needed to denote when a fraction part of a number is indicated. The sign is the decimal point and is read "and" when reading decimal numbers. As stated in Chapter 6, it is not proper to use "and" when reading whole numbers.

Example: 100, 101, 102, . . .
Not correct:
"one hundred, one hundred *and* one, one hundred *and* two, . . ."
Correct:
"one hundred, one hundred one, one hundred two, . . ."

Decimal names Take care to pronounce the decimal terms distinctly (possibly slightly exaggerating the "th" and "ths" term endings) so that children will be able to discriminate between them and whole number terminology.

Example: ten and tenth; tens and tenths
hundred and hundredth; hundreds
and hundredths
thousand and thousandth, . . .

In early work with decimals, it is recommended that decimal numerals be written on the board or a chart for reference (a teacher can point to the parts) when communicating decimal numbers orally. This will aid students in matching the "th" and "ths" term endings with the numeric place values and to distinguish them from whole number place-value terms.

Decimal notation Decimal notation has changed over the years and even today is not uniform throughout the world. In the United States, a point is used and is placed immediately after (to the right of) the ones digit; people in some European countries use a comma in the same position. This is the reason the use of a comma to separate number periods has been discontinued (see Chapter 6 for the proper way to record numbers).

Example: English French
0.05 0,05
245.63 245,63

This symbolization transfers to monetary values.

Example: $4.95 4,95$
$56.08 56,08$
$0.05 0,05$

When reading a number, the decimal point is read as "and."

Example: 6.5 or 6,5
Read as: six *and* five tenths
$1.49 or 1,49$
Read as: one dollar *and* forty-nine cents

If children read decimals properly, writing decimals will be a simple exercise. Reading decimals properly also enhances children's ability to readily identify denominators, which enables them to think of decimals as fractional numbers.

Children may more easily visualize a fraction in concrete terms than a decimal. For example, it is easier to visualize $\frac{3}{4}$ of something than 0.75. Thinking about deci-

mals as fractions (rather than manipulating digits) helps to develop decimal number sense. Teaching ideas for developing decimal number sense through concrete and semi-concrete models are provided in the next section of this chapter.

The following activities provide practice in reading and writing decimal numbers.

1. Reading and writing decimals
   - Provide a calculator for each student and a calculator for use on an overhead projector.
   - Dictate the decimal number, *seven and fifty-five-hundredths.*
   - Ask students to enter the number in their calculators.
   - Then display the number on an overhead projector calculator (or on a transparency if a calculator is not available) for the students to self-check.
   - Repeat the procedure with other numbers:
     three and four-hundredths
     sixty and sixteen-thousandths
     two hundred three and five-hundredths

2. Reading decimal numbers
   - Display a decimal numeral on an overhead projector calculator or write it on the board.
     Example: 4.65
   - Ask a student to read the number.
   - Repeat with other numerals:
     40.08   0.095   0.002   306.36   500.05

3. Writing decimal numbers
   - Write several decimal numerals on the board.
     Examples: 0.405   60.05   300.003
   - Have students write the numbers in words.

DEVELOPING DECIMAL NUMBER SENSE

It is important to devote time to developing the meaning of decimal numbers through concrete and semi-concrete models. Several examples are described here together with suggestions for activities.

STANDARDS LINK 12-5
The approach to decimals should be similar to work with fractions, namely, placing a strong and continued emphasis on models and oral language and then connecting this work with symbols. This is necessary if students are to make sense of decimals and use them insightfully. Exploring ideas of tenths and hundredths with models can include preliminary work with equivalent decimals, counting sequences, the comparing and ordering of decimals, and addition and subtraction. (NCTM, 1989, p. 59)

Base-Ten Blocks

Children will have used base-ten blocks when learning to interpret whole numbers and their operations. These materials also can be used to represent decimal numbers provided students are able to cognize that different blocks can be selected to represent the unit.

A "tens" block as the unit A first activity could be to select a tens block (called a "rod" or a "long") to represent the unit. Questions such as the following can be asked:

- If this piece represents (or is worth) one, what is the value of this piece (small cube)?
- What is the value of two of these small cubes? three small cubes? . . . ten small cubes?

Change the questioning to:

- If this piece (a rod) is one, show me one tenth; three tenths; nine tenths.

A "hundreds" block as the unit Take a "hundreds" block (called a "square" or a "flat"). Say:

- Now let's say that this square block is one or one whole. Can you find a block that is one-tenth of this square block?
- Can you show two-tenths of this square block with the blocks? three-tenths? . . . ten-tenths?

Change the questioning to:

- I have five rods (tens) here. What part of the square are they?
- I have one small cube in my hand. Can you tell what part of the square this small cube is? Why do you call it that?

A "thousands" block (large cube) as the unit Children can be invited to write relation statements about the various blocks when a thousands block is designated as the unit. They can be challenged to write as many different relationships as they can. Two other activities with base-ten blocks follow:

1. A square as the unit
   - Designate a square as the unit.
   - Write the numeral 2.5 on the board (or display it on an overhead projector calculator or transparency).
   - Have students model the number with the blocks. Students can check each other's work.
   - Ask a child to tell what number has been modeled.
   - Repeat with other numerals such as:
     1.6   0.2   0.12   0.06   0.56

2. Choose a unit
   - Tell children to select a block as the unit and then to represent a number with the blocks. Have them record what they have done.

   Possible sample work:

   I chose the square as one. I made the number 2.25. This is how I made the number.

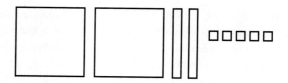

I chose the large cube as one. I made the number 0.036. This is how I made the number.

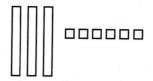

Decimal Squares

The commercial kit, *Decimal Squares* consists of colored paper squares (1 dm) prepartitioned in tenths (red), hundredths (green), and thousandths (yellow). The ten tenths squares are shaded to represent 0.1, 0.2, . . . , 1.0. The hundredths and thousandths squares are shaded to represent multiples of five and ten fractional parts. Students can use the squares to compare decimal fractions (Activities 12-1 to 12-3) and for simple addition and subtraction. Teachers can construct a similar model using decimal grids (see Blackline Master 10), which can be used to represent one whole, tenths, and hundredths.

Measurement Sticks

Measurement is one real-world application of decimal number knowledge. It is not necessary for students to know the different basic unit prefixes to read measurements as part of a unit of measure.

Students can be provided with non-calibrated meter, decimeter and centimeter sticks. (The decimeter and centimeter pieces can be cut from stiff cardboard.) Students should be able to articulate the relationships among the linear pieces.

✴ ACTIVITY 12-1

COMPARING DECIMAL FRACTIONS: TENTHS AND HUNDREDTHS

MATERIALS:
A set of Decimal Squares (red and green) for each student

PROCEDURE:
1. Select a red square. Now find a green square with the same amount shaded. Write a statement about the two amounts.
   Example: *Eight-tenths and eighty-hundredths are the same amount.*
2. Find other pairs of decimal squares that show the same amount shaded and write a statement about the pairs of decimal fractions.

✴ ACTIVITY 12-2

COMPARING DECIMAL FRACTIONS: TENTHS AND THOUSANDTHS

MATERIALS:
Decimal Squares (red and yellow)

PROCEDURE:
1. Select a red square. Then find a yellow square with the same amount shaded. Write a statement about the two decimal fractions.
2. Find other pairs of decimal squares with the same amount shaded and write statements about the pairs of decimal fractions.

The following activities require more teacher direction.

1. Modeling linear measurements
   - You will need a meter stick, 10 decimeter sticks, 10 centimeter sticks and a collection of ribbon pieces.
   - Relate a scenario such as the following:
     While cleaning a closet one day, you find a box of pieces of ribbon. You decide to measure them and label each length.

✴ ACTIVITY 12-3

COMPARING DECIMAL FRACTIONS: INEQUALITIES

MATERIALS:
Decimal Squares for each student

PROCEDURE:
1. Select two decimal square cards. After examining them, write a statement about the two decimal fractions represented.
   Examples:
   Three-hundredths is less than one-tenth.
   0.03 is less than 0.1
   Four-hundredths is greater than twenty-five-thousandths.
   0.04 is greater than 0.025
2. Compare other pairs of decimal fractions and write statements in words and in symbolic form.

- Provide students in small groups with several ribbon lengths and a set of measurement sticks. Direct them to measure each piece of ribbon with the materials, then write the length to the nearest hundredth of a meter on a piece of paper and affix it to the ribbon. Example: 1.24 m.

2. Decimal measurements
   - First model some lengths with meter, decimeter, and centimeter sticks.
   - Give pairs of students a written direction as follows: Draw a line with chalk on the classroom floor that is 1.2 meters long.
   - Have students tell the length in two ways. For example:
     The length is 1 and 2 tenths meters.
     The length is 1 and 20 hundredths meters.

A metric chart could be constructed and displayed on a bulletin board and subsequently used to read different lengths (or weights or capacities) using decimal numbers. The chart may depict metric names and matching place-value names or symbols (Figure 12-3).

FIGURE 12-3

KILOMETER	HECTOMETER	DEKAMETER	METER	DECIMETER	CENTIMETER	MILLIMETER
1000	100	10	1	0.1	0.01	0.001

Graph Paper

Graph paper marked in 10 cm squares is useful for showing different decimal fractions. The paper can be centimeter or millimeter graph paper (see Blackline Master 15). Students can be asked to shade parts of the squares to show different decimal fractions, to compare decimal fractions, or to show addition and subtraction of decimal fractions.

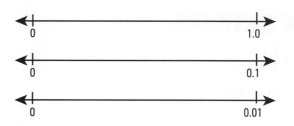

1. Modeling decimal fractions pictorially (hundredths)
   • Provide children with several pieces of centimeter graph paper marked in 10 cm squares.
   • Direct students to show decimal fractions on the pieces of graph paper by coloring or shading.

   Examples: 0.4, 0.45, 0.5, 0.05, 0.25

> **STANDARDS LINK 12-6**
> To provide students with a lasting sense of number and number relationships, learning should be grounded in experience related to aspects of everyday life or to the use of concrete materials designed to reflect underlying mathematical ideas. Students should encounter number lines, area models, and graphs as well as representations of numbers that appear on calculators and computers (e.g., forms of scientific notation). Students should learn to identify equivalent forms of a number and understand why a particular representation is useful in a given setting. (NCTM, 1989, p. 87)

2. Modeling decimal fractions pictorially (thousandths)
   • Provide children with millimeter graph paper marked in 10 cm squares.
   • Direct students to show decimal fractions on the graph paper by coloring or shading.

   Examples: 0.35, 0.08, 0.075, 0.009, 0.016

Working with millimeter graph paper will communicate to students how relatively small the third place value in a decimal fraction really is. Another way to get students to realize the relative sizes of decimal fraction place values is to have them partition a centimeter hundred square in thousandths and then in ten thousandths. Procedures for this exercise are described below.

1. Provide students with a 10 cm square piece of centimeter graph paper.
2. Direct them to shade in the amount of 0.57142 by first shading in 5 tenths, next 7 hundredths, then 1 thousandth, then 4 ten thousandths, and finally 2 hundred thousandths. Students will soon realize that it is difficult to designate the area for ten thousandths.
3. Discussion: What did you learn from this exercise?

Number line A number line is a good model to demonstrate the density property of decimals. Provide students with number lines drawn on paper and have them write several numbers between 0 and the given number. For example:

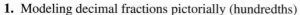

From this kind of exercise, students will realize that it is always possible to name decimal numbers between any two given numbers.

A number line also can be used to write decimal numbers in specified increments such as 0.1, 0.5, or 0.01. This type of activity helps students count from one place value to another larger one as from hundredths to tenths. This is not a trivial task for students because of the whole number influence. With whole numbers, when counting up, one goes from tens to hundreds; with decimals, one goes from hundredths to tenths.

Give children appropriate number lines drawn on paper. Ask them to

• begin with 0.8, count by tenths.
• begin with 7.5, count by 5 tenths.
• begin with 0.56, count by tenths.

Two examples of students' counting errors are:
12.08, 12.09, 13.00
20.97, 20.98, 20.99, 30.00

Activities 12-4 through 12-6 contain additional number line activities.

Money

Some teachers use coins to model decimal computation. Recording amounts in dollars and cents does involve decimal fractions but care must be taken that students see the

✳ ACTIVITY 12-4

LABELING POINTS ON A NUMBER LINE

Write numbers for A, B, and C on each line.

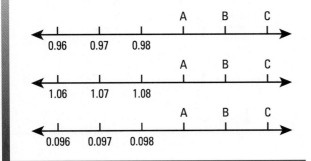

✳ ACTIVITY 12-5

MARKING PRECEDING AND SUBSEQUENT POINTS

Mark the indicated numbers on the number line. Then mark 2 preceding and 2 following numbers.

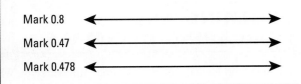

Mark 0.8

Mark 0.47

Mark 0.478

connection between the coins and the fractional part of a decimal number. For example, children do not readily relate $2.25 to 2 dollars and 25 hundredths of a dollar or a dime to one tenth of a dollar. If money is used as a model for decimals, children need to think of dimes and pennies as fractional parts of a dollar.

Examples: 5 pennies = 5 hundredths of a dollar
3 dimes = 3 tenths of a dollar

Provide students with pennies, dimes, and a dollar coin (play money is fine). Ask them to first display the following sets of coins and then to write the decimal number that they represent.

- 1 dollar, 4 dimes (1.40 or 1.4)
- 3 dimes, 5 pennies (0.35)
- 15 pennies (0.15)
- 2 dimes, 12 pennies (0.32)

✳ ACTIVITY 12-6

COUNTING

Write 15 numerals for each.

- counting by 0.02. Begin with 1.
- counting by 0.1. Begin with 0.95.
- counting by 0.05. Begin with 0.05.
- counting by 0.01. Begin with 0.197.

✳ ACTIVITY 12-7

RECORDING PRICES

Sara and her brother Bill have set up a lemonade stand at the beach. They want to make a sign to indicate the price of large, medium, and small glasses of lemonade. What are two ways Sara and Bill can show the prices?

Large glass: ninety-five cents

Medium glass: seventy-five cents

Small glass: fifty cents

It is not uncommon to find in commercial advertisements an incorrect use of decimal notation when recording costs. For example, the price of a commodity item is indicated as .25¢. The assumption is that .25¢ means the same as $0.25 when in fact it means 25-hundredths of a cent, that is, less than one cent! Activity 12-7 can help students practice recording money properly.

The expected answer to Activity 12-7 would be $0.95 or 95¢, $0.75 or 75¢, and $0.50 or 50¢.

Other Materials to Model Decimals

Most base-ten models can be used to represent decimal numbers. For example, students may like to work with pocket charts or a vertical abacus. If such materials are used, the ones place should be indicated in some manner on the materials (Figure 12-4).

EQUIVALENT DECIMALS

Usually, more attention is given to equivalent fractions than to equivalent decimals in mathematics programs. Equivalent fractions are necessary for fraction computation, whereas one can work through decimal computations without thinking of equivalent decimals. Nonetheless,

FIGURE 12-4

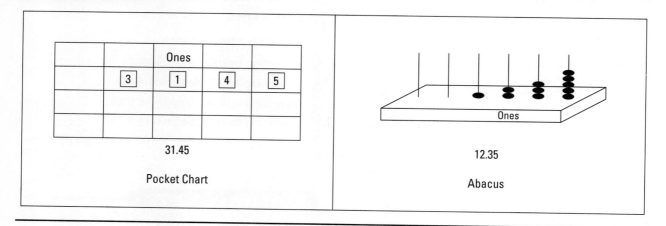

equivalent decimals help students understand decimal computation.

If the process of naming equivalent decimals is connected to that of writing equivalent fractions, there is nothing new to learn. The fact that each decimal fraction can be written differently will not be surprising to students.

Example:
$\frac{4}{10} = \frac{40}{100} = \frac{400}{1000}$

The fraction $\frac{4}{10}$ was multiplied by "one" in the form of $\frac{10}{10}$ and $\frac{100}{100}$ respectively. In a decimal numeral, the process is the same although the denominator is not visible.

Example: 0.4 = 0.40 = 0.400

These numerals are read as 4 tenths = 40 hundredths = 400 thousandths. This is similar to the equivalent fractions above.

A concrete "proof" of the equivalency could be demonstrated by using base-ten blocks and comparing, for example, 4 tenths (4 rods) and 40 hundredths (40 ones) on a square unit (a hundreds flat) [Figure 12-5].

Students who have had experiences in modeling decimal fractions and in recording amounts in different ways

(e.g., 5 tenths or 50 hundredths; 0.5 or 0.50) should develop a sense of the size of decimal numbers. In particular, they should be able to compare tenths and hundredths and to rename one decimal fraction to an equivalent form. They will have a mental referent for the process. The generalization that adding zeros to decimal fractions produces numbers of equivalent value is not difficult to conceptualize.

ORDERING AND COMPARING DECIMALS

Students who have developed decimal number sense will be able to order decimals. Students who do not understand decimals sometimes use erroneous thinking strategies when ordering decimals. One line of thinking is that "longer is greater" as, for example, 0.65 is less than 0.0345 because "65" is shorter than "345." Another false method of comparison is that "shorter is greater" as, for example, *0.3 is greater than 0.41 because tenths are greater than hundredths* (Vance, 1986b). It is wise for a teacher to ask students to tell how they arrive at solutions in order to learn their thinking processes.

Students can be taught to compare decimals by focusing, in turn, on each place-value position beginning from the left and moving to the right until a comparison can be made. This is similar to the process of comparing whole numbers.

FIGURE 12-5

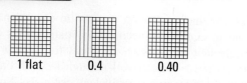

1 flat   0.4   0.40

Examples:
1. 1.52 and 1.48

    Comparison: ones place—same digit;

    tenths place—5 tenths and 4 tenths.

    Therefore, 1.52 > 1.48

✱ ACTIVITY 12-8

CONSTRUCTING AND ORDERING DECIMALS

MATERIALS:
Four small cards for each student with the numerals 0, 1, 2, and a decimal point written on the cards.

PROCEDURE:
1. Use the cards to show as many different decimal numbers as you can.

   Examples: 0.12   1.02

   Discuss with the class whether numerals such as 012. or .120 are allowed.

2. Record each number as you make it.

3. When you are sure you cannot make any more numbers, order all your numbers from least to greatest.

✱ ACTIVITY 12-9

ORDERING DECIMALS

MATERIALS:
Five small cards for each student with the numerals 0, 1, 2, 3, and a decimal point written on the cards.

PROCEDURE:
1. Use the cards to show at least five decimals that are less than one.

   Write each numeral as you make it.

   Order your decimals from least to greatest.

2. Use your cards to show at least five decimals that are more than one-tenth.

   Write each numeral as you make it.

   Order your decimals from greatest to least.

---

2. 0.0156 and 0.85

   Comparison: 0 tenths and 8 tenths or
                 1 hundredth and 85 hundredths
                 Therefore, 0.0156 < 0.85

3. 0.314 and 0.28

   Comparison: 31 hundredths and 28 hundredths
                 Therefore, 0.314 > 0.28

Another method used to order decimals is to write equivalent decimal fractions.

Example:
Order the following decimals from least to greatest.

1.06   0.36   0.06   0.0306   0.0063

Changing all the numbers to the same-sized decimal fraction, one obtains

1.0600   0.3600   0.0600   0.0306   0.0063

It is now easy to list the numbers in order of size. Activities 12-8 and 12-9 provide practice in constructing and ordering decimals.

COMPUTATION

Understanding computation with decimals requires an understanding of place value, decimal concepts, and computation of fractions. Investing time in developing that understanding before beginning decimal computa-

tion will pay off in enhanced understanding and increased achievement for students.

Students who have developed an understanding of decimal concepts and place value will have no difficulty adding and subtracting decimals. For multiplication and division, there is a need to practice the operations with ten and multiples of ten as a factor. The ability to mentally multiply and divide by ten, hundred, etc., greatly facilitates the operations of multiplication and division, particularly in ascertaining the reasonableness of an answer.

Students with a sense of the quantitative value of decimal numbers can be expected to compute with greater accuracy than when computation is done by applying meaningless rules.

Addition and Subtraction

Addition and subtraction of decimals should be related to addition and subtraction of whole numbers and of fractions. As discussed in Chapters 7 and 11, solving word problems set in familiar, real-world situations helps children understand operations and judge the reasonableness of answers. An easy-to-understand interpretation of addition is the "join" interpretation, in which two quantities are combined. The "separate" and "comparison" interpretations of subtraction, in which two quantities are separated or compared, also are easy to understand.

Addition and subtraction of decimals should be introduced by posing problems based on "join" and "separate" situations involving quantities measured in decimal units, such as lengths of ribbon, pounds of food, and money. Figure 12-6 contains sample word problems for addition and subtraction of decimals and compares them with similar problems involving fractions. Notice the similarities between the problem contexts.

FIGURE 12-6

	WORD PROBLEM WITH FRACTIONS	NUMBER SENTENCE	WORD PROBLEM WITH DECIMALS	NUMBER SENTENCE
Addition (JOIN)	Tom ate $\frac{1}{2}$ of an apple pie yesterday and $\frac{1}{4}$ of an apple pie today. How much pie did Tom eat altogether?	$\frac{1}{2} + \frac{1}{4}$ = _____	Tom ate 0.25 pound of turkey and 0.10 pound of cheese. How much food did Tom eat altogether?	0.25 + 0.10 = _____
Subtraction (SEPARATE)	Alberto has $\frac{3}{4}$ of a cookie. He ate $\frac{1}{4}$ of a whole cookie. How much cookie does Alberto have left?	$\frac{3}{4} - \frac{1}{4}$ = _____	Maria had 0.37 meter of ribbon. She used 0.25 meter to make a bow. How much ribbon does Maria have left?	0.37 − 0.25 = _____
Subtraction (COMPARISON)	Alberto has $\frac{3}{4}$ of a cookie and Juana has $\frac{1}{4}$ of a cookie. How much more does Alberto have?	$\frac{3}{4} - \frac{1}{4}$ = _____	Maria has 0.37 meter of red ribbon and 0.25 meter of blue ribbon. How much more red ribbon does she have than blue ribbon?	0.37 − 0.25 = _____

Addition questions can be represented on 10 cm graph paper squares. Students can shade in a set of addends and subsequently "read" the number shaded.

The children have measured the mass of some paperback story books in the classroom. The four books that Therese and Monica weighed had a mass of 0.25 kg, 0.3 kg, 0.17 kg, and 0.09 kg. What is the mass of the four books? Show the shadings on graph paper.

0.25
0.3
0.17
0.09

   OR

The mass of the books is 0.81 kg.

If students are required to add several sets of numbers by shading the amounts, they probably will find that it helps to shade in the tenths first, then to add the hundredths and shade them in as tenths plus hundredths, as in the second grid above. For example, for the numbers listed above, a student would first shade in 1, 2, and 3 tenths to make 6 tenths; next, he or she would shade in 2 tenths plus 1 hundredth for a total of 0.81 shaded. This procedure causes one to think of the value of each digit and should help students learn how to properly write ragged decimals in vertical columns.

When adding ragged decimals, students can be encouraged to write equivalent decimal fractions by adding zeros as required.

Example:
Given: 0.4 + 0.078 + 0.1056 + 0.23
Change to: 0.4000 + 0.0780 + 0.1056 + 0.2300

This method can be thought of as adding the numerators of same-sized decimal fractions.

In subtraction, when the subtrahend is expressed in tenths and the minuend is in hundredths or thousandths, it is a common practice to rename the decimal fractions to the same-sized fractions (all hundredths or thousandths, etc.) by adding zeros to facilitate using the standard algorithm.

Two alpine skiers finished a race with the following time scores: 13.50 seconds and 12.96 seconds. What is the time difference of their scores?
Solution process:
Subtract: 13.50 − 12.97
The subtraction algorithm is the same as with whole numbers.

Addition and subtraction questions with mixed decimals can be modeled with base-ten blocks. A concrete demonstration of regrouping is easily carried out with these materials (Figure 12-7).

Other concrete and semi-concrete material used to add and subtract whole numbers can be used to add and subtract decimals provided there is a way of showing place values smaller than the ones place.

Regrouping in addition and subtraction can also be carried out with dollar and dime coins. These are visually

FIGURE 12-7

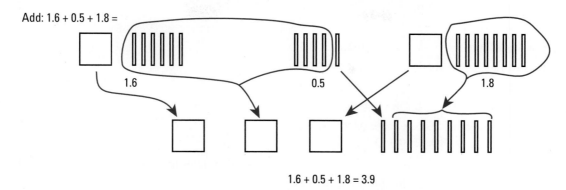

ADDING MIXED DECIMALS WITH BASE-TEN BLOCKS

Add: 1.6 + 0.5 + 1.8 =

1.6   0.5   1.8

1.6 + 0.5 + 1.8 = 3.9

non-proportional materials however, and, therefore, should not be the first materials used.

Multiplication

> **STANDARDS LINK 12-7**
> Similarly, students should learn to compute decimal products like 0.3 × 0.6, especially as a means of locating the decimal point. Although such problems train students to estimate more difficult computations, valuable instructional time should not be devoted to calculating products such as 0.31 × 0.588 with paper and pencil. (NCTM, 1989, p. 96)

As with addition and subtraction, multiplication and division of decimals should be related to those operations on whole numbers and on fractions. The interpretations of multiplication and division of decimals that are easiest to understand are repeated addition, area and array multiplication, and measurement division (repeated subtraction). Recall that repeated addition problems involve repeatedly adding quantities that are the same size, while area and array problems involve finding the area of a rectangular region. Measurement division, also known as repeated subtraction, involves measuring out groups of a certain size from a whole. Figure 12-8 contains sample word problems for multiplication and division of decimals and compares them with similar problems involving fractions. Notice the similarities between the problem contexts.

FIGURE 12-8

	WORD PROBLEM WITH FRACTIONS	**NUMBER SENTENCE**	**WORD PROBLEM WITH DECIMALS**	**NUMBER SENTENCE**
Multiplication (REPEATED ADDITION)	Shawntrice had 4 bags of cookies, with $\frac{1}{2}$ of a cookie in each bag. How many cookies did Shawntrice have?	$4 \times \frac{1}{2} =$ _____	Shawntrice had 4 bags of sliced cheese, with 0.75 pound of cheese in each bag. How much cheese did Shawntrice have?	4×0.75 = _____
Multiplication (AREA AND ARRAY)	There is $\frac{2}{3}$ of a chocolate pie in the refrigerator. Peter ate $\frac{1}{2}$ of it. What part of the whole pie did Peter eat?	$\frac{1}{2} \times \frac{2}{3} =$ _____	Peter has a garden that is 2.5 meters long and 1.5 meters wide. What is the area of Peter's garden?	2.5×1.5 = _____
Division (MEASUREMENT— REPEATED SUBTRACTION)	Steve has 4 cups of sugar. He needs $\frac{2}{3}$ of a cup of sugar to make one batch of his favorite cookies. How many batches of cookies can Steve make?	$4 \div \frac{2}{3} =$ _____	Steve has $4.00. He wants to buy several candy bars that cost $0.65 each. How many candy bars can Steve buy?	$4.00 \div 0.65$ = _____

Multiplication of decimals should be introduced with simple problems involving tenths and gradually progress to smaller decimal fractions.

A suggested sequence for multiplication of decimals is:

1. tenths by a whole number $\qquad$ 4×0.2; 3×0.4
2. hundredths by a whole number $\qquad$ 3×0.05
3. tenths by tenths $\qquad$ 0.4×0.6
4. hundredths by tenths $\qquad$ 0.3×0.04; 0.4×0.15
5. hundredths by hundredths $\quad$ 0.05×0.09; 0.04×0.56; 0.12×0.23

Multiplication questions such as the first two can be represented concretely with base-ten blocks using a square (hundreds block) as the unit.

Example: $4 \times 0.2 = 0.8$

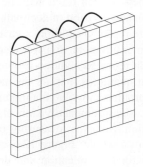

Read: 4 times two tenths = eight tenths

Example: $3 \times 0.4 = 1.2$
Read: 3 times four tenths = twelve tenths

Similarly, hundredths multiplied by a whole number can be represented with blocks.

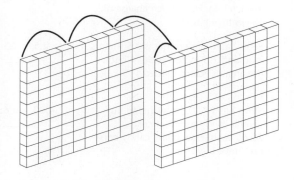

Example: $5 \times 0.05 = 0.25$

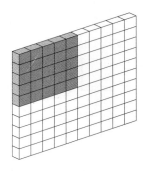

Read: 5 times five hundredths = 25 hundredths

Multiplication of a decimal number by a whole number can also be pictured on a number line as in Figure 12-9.

When multiplying tenths by tenths, it is helpful to interpret the question as, for example, four tenths of three tenths. A representation of this problem with base-ten blocks through a teacher-guided lesson could be as follows:

- Designate a square (hundreds block) as the unit.
- Ask the students to show 3 tenths in two ways using the blocks.

a.

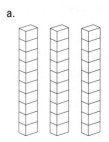

b.

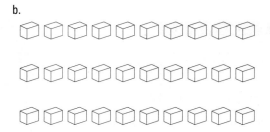

- Ask, "Which arrangement allows four tenths of three tenths to be removed?" (The thirty hundredths should be chosen.)
- Ask the children to identify four tenths of three tenths.
- Ask, "how can we state what number this is?" (twelve hundredths)

$$0.4 \times 0.3 = 0.12$$

FIGURE 12-9

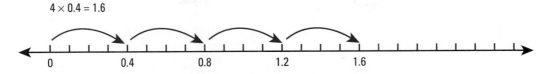

MULTIPLYING DECIMALS

$4 \times 0.4 = 1.6$

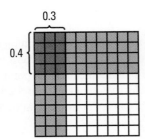

The process can be shown pictorially on a 10 cm square piece of graph paper (Figure 12-10).

There is a commercial set of Decimal Squares made of colored acetate for use on an overhead projector. Decimal multiplication can be represented by overlaying two squares as in shading grid paper. The region where the shaded parts overlap represents the product (Figure 12-11).

Multiplying decimals by powers and multiples of ten is an important skill to develop. Progressing from concrete representations to paper-and-pencil work to mental calculations, students should develop a rule for the placement of the decimal point in products when multiplying by a power of ten (Figure 12-12).

FIGURE 12-10

A PICTORIAL REPRESENTATION OF MULTIPLICATION

$0.4 \times 0.3 = 0.12$

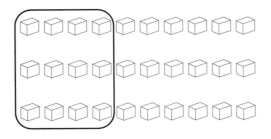

The product is the part of the unit that is shaded twice

A place-value chart can be used to justify the rule for multiplying by 10 (by 100, and by 1000).

Example:

Hundreds	Tens	One	Tenths	Hundredths
		3	2	5
	3	2	5	
3	2	5		

Since the value of each position is ten times that of the position to its right, multiplying by ten "moves" each digit one place to the left. This is equivalent to "moving" the decimal point one place to the right.

Example: $3.25 \times 10 = 32.5$
$32.5 \times 10 = 325.$

A number of concrete experiences followed by written statements will assist students in generalizing a rule for locating the decimal point in products. The concrete modeling can proceed in a systematic way so that students notice patterns that will help them develop rules (see Figure 12-13). The following are examples of lists that students can write as they multiply decimals concretely or pictorially.

4×1 tenth $= 4$ tenths	$4 \times 0.1 = 0.4$
4×2 tenths $= 8$ tenths	$4 \times 0.2 = 0.8$
4×3 tenths $= 12$ tenths	$4 \times 0.3 = 1.2$
4×4 tenths $= 16$ tenths	$4 \times 0.4 = 1.6$
4×5 tenths $= 20$ tenths	$4 \times 0.5 = 2.0$

4 tenths $\times$ 1 tenth $= 4$ hundredths
$\qquad 0.4 \times 0.1 = 0.04$
4 tenths $\times$ 2 tenths $= 8$ hundredths
$\qquad 0.4 \times 0.2 = 0.08$
4 tenths $\times$ 3 tenths $= 12$ hundredths
$\qquad 0.4 \times 0.3 = 0.12$
4 tenths $\times$ 4 tenths $= 16$ hundredths
$\qquad 0.4 \times 0.4 = 0.16$
4 tenths $\times$ 5 tenths $= 20$ hundredths
$\qquad 0.4 \times 0.5 = 0.20$

FIGURE 12-11

0.5 shaded   0.3 shaded $0.5 \times 0.3 = 0.15$

The product is the part of the unit that is shaded twice.

FIGURE 12-12

MULTIPLYING WITH POWERS OF TEN

$10 \times 0.3 = 3$ $100 \times 1.85 = 185$

$100 \times 0.6 = 60$ $400 \times 0.28 = 112$

Rule: Move the decimal point the same number of places to the right of its original position as there are zeros in the multiple-of-ten multiplier.

FIGURE 12-13

PROBLEM	DECIMAL PLACES		PRODUCT	DECIMAL PLACES IN PRODUCT
	First Factor	Second Factor		
3×0.2	0	1	0.6	1
3.1×4.71	1	2	14.601	3
0.3×5.2	1	1	1.56	2
0.25×0.11	2	2	0.0275	4

Patterns can be generated with a calculator when studying multiplication with decimals. The following are examples.

$$
\begin{array}{ll}
\text{Enter } 5 \times 0.1 = & \text{display: } 0.5 \\
0.5 \times 0.1 = & 0.05 \\
0.05 \times 0.1 = & 0.005 \\
0.005 \times 0.1 = & 0.0005
\end{array}
$$

If the calculator has a multiplicative constant, one needs only to press "=" after the first multiplication to generate the products listed above.

Example: 5×0.1

Students could use a calculator to complete a table as in Figure 12-13 and then look for a pattern to help them articulate a rule for placing the decimal point in products. One needs to be selective about the numbers chosen for such an exercise because for some numbers it appears that the rule does not work.

Problem: $0.24 \times 39.5 = ?$

According to the rule, there should be three decimal places in the product. However, a calculator response is 9.48. Students need to be aware of how their calculator displays numbers. In this case, the calculator drops final zeros after a decimal point.

Middle school students may appreciate the following explanation of why the number of places to the right of the decimal point in each factor is summed up and used to place the decimal point in the product.

Example:

$$2.36 \times 3.4 = 8.024 \qquad 2.36 = \tfrac{236}{100} \qquad 3.4 = \tfrac{34}{10}$$

$$\frac{236 \times 34}{10^2 \times 10^1} = \frac{8024}{10^3} = \tfrac{8024}{1000} = 8.024$$

Division

Students who know a division algorithm for whole numbers should be able to divide with decimals.

Early division problems should involve whole number divisors.

Example: $5\overline{)25.75}$ $\qquad$ $12\overline{)292.2}$

Using the principle that adding zeros does not change the value of the decimal, the second problem could easily be carried out to an even division. Division with decimal number divisors could be introduced with a problem and dialogue similar to that presented in Figure 12-14.

Problems involving decimal fraction divisors in the hundredths and mixed decimal numbers should be presented to students to discuss and solve. The following generalization should eventually be articulated: Multiplying both the divisor and the dividend by the same multiple of ten does not affect the answer. The connection to equivalent decimals should be made as well (also to equivalent fractions, if appropriate at the time).

Example: $0.62\overline{)744}$ is like $\dfrac{744}{0.62}$

Writing equivalent fractions, we have

$$\frac{774}{0.62} \qquad \frac{7440}{6.2} \qquad \frac{74400}{62}$$

Decimal form: $0.62\overline{)744}$ $\qquad$ $6.2\overline{)7440}$

$$62\overline{)74400}$$

Although it is usual to rewrite the decimal division so that the divisor is a whole number, some students may wish to change both divisor and dividend to whole numbers before dividing.

FIGURE 12-14

TEACHING SCENARIO

Problem: Sheilagh has bought 12 m of ribbon to make bows to decorate flower pots. It takes 0.8 m of ribbon to make one bow. Sheilagh wants to figure out how many bows can be made with the length of ribbon she has.

Sheilagh first writes the problem question as

$$0.8\overline{)12}$$

Then she thinks: There are 10 tenths in 1 m

therefore 12 m = 120 tenths.

Using this knowledge, she rewrites the question as 120 tenths divided by 8 tenths

$$8\overline{)120}$$

Sheilagh then divides and finds that 12 m of ribbon can make 15 bows.

Questions to ask:
- What do you think of Sheilagh's work?
- Why is it proper to change the division question as Sheilagh did?
- Could Sheilagh have written a different division question and still have arrived at the answer?

Example: $0.36\overline{)2.695}$

$$\frac{2.695 \times 1000}{0.36 \times 1000} \rightarrow \frac{2695}{360} \rightarrow 360\overline{)2695}$$

Decimal form: $0.36 \times 1000 = 360$
$2.695 \times 1000 = 2695$

Therefore, $0.36\overline{)2.695} \rightarrow 360\overline{)2695}$

If students come to use the expression "move the decimal point *n* places to the right in the two numbers" when dividing decimals, a teacher should question them to find out if they understand why that "works."

Some students make errors in division situations that require zeros in the dividend. A good way to have students represent such division questions is to use money. Educational 1000-, 100-, and 10-dollar bills, and 1-dollar coins, dimes, and pennies can be distributed to groups of students to have them solve division problems by sharing amounts of money among different-sized groups of people. The situation of winning a lottery can provide a context for dividing up large amounts. By working through a problem such as $7387.20 to be shared among 24 people using "play" money, students will see the necessity of a zero in the dividend.

Estimating with Decimals

In their daily lives, students probably will estimate with decimals more frequently than they will calculate exact answers. It is therefore important that they learn estimation skills.

What are some of the techniques that facilitate estimation with decimal numbers? First of all, students must be able to read and write multi-digit decimal numbers and understand place value of decimal fractions. They must also be able to order and compare decimals, and they must be able to round decimals (Vance, 1986a).

Students should have practice rounding decimal numbers. Two strategies to use are using the leading digit and using the rounded leading digit in a number.

Examples:

	Number	**Rounded**
Leading digit	365.75	300
	0.0463	0.04
Rounded leading digit	365.75	400
	0.0463	0.05

Estimates for sums and differences of decimal numbers can be obtained by using either the leading digit or the rounded leading digit strategy. Students should recognize which strategies will give estimates that are more than or less than the actual numbers. This knowledge will enable them to decide when to use which strategy. Have them consider situations such as the following and decide which strategy they would use.

- You want to be certain that you have sufficient cash to pay for groceries.
- You know the amount the family pays for electricity per month and you want an estimate of the yearly cost.
- You have measurements to the nearest meter of the distance run by an athlete in a certain time during practice sessions. You want an approximation of the average distance she runs in that time span.

In multiplication questions, the leading digit strategy can produce significantly lower estimates than the actual product.

Example:

	485×0.23		
leading digit	400×0.2	$\rightarrow$	80
rounding	500×0.2	$\rightarrow$	100
actual	485×0.23	$\rightarrow$	111.55

It appears that the rounded digit strategy gives an estimate that is closer to the actual product than the leading digit strategy. When rounding digits, one can round both factors up or round one factor up and the other factor down.

Example:

783×0.26	$\rightarrow$	800×0.3	$\rightarrow$	240
or	$\rightarrow$	800×0.2	$\rightarrow$	160
or	$\rightarrow$	700×0.3	$\rightarrow$	210
actual			$\rightarrow$	203.64

In this case, the closest estimate is 210.

In division, when estimating quotients, it is a common practice to round both numbers in the same direction (up or down).

Example:

$0.28\overline{)675.94}$	$\rightarrow$	$0.3\overline{)700}$	$\rightarrow$	2333.30
or		$0.2\overline{)600}$	$\rightarrow$	3000.0
actual			$\rightarrow$	2414.07

In this case, the best estimate is the first one. If one used compatible numbers (evenly divisible), the division question would become $0.3\overline{)690}$ to arrive at an estimate of 2300.

WRITING FRACTIONS AS DECIMALS

Decimal number sense is enhanced by studying decimals in relationship to fractions. Exploring the decimal forms of different fractions in a systematic way is an opportunity to discover patterns and relationships.

Examples:

1. $\frac{3}{10} = 0.3$ $\quad \frac{3}{100} = 0.03$ $\quad \frac{3}{1000} = 0.003$

   $\frac{45}{10} = 4.5$ $\quad \frac{45}{100} = 0.45$ $\quad \frac{45}{1000} = 0.045$

2. Change the denominator to a power of ten

   $\frac{2}{5} = \frac{4}{10} = 0.4$

   $\frac{3}{20} = \frac{15}{100} = 0.15$

   $\frac{1}{8} = \frac{125}{1000} = 0.125$

3. Divide

   $\frac{3}{8} = 8)\overline{3.000}$

Using the *Math Explorer* Calculator

The *Math Explorer* calculator has the function $\boxed{\text{F} \rightleftharpoons \text{D}}$ to change fractions to decimals or decimals to fractions in one step.

Example: To change $\frac{1}{3}$ to a decimal enter

$\frac{1}{3}$ $\boxed{\text{F} \rightleftharpoons \text{D}}$ Display: 0.3333333

Some fraction sequences that students could write as decimals are presented in Activity 12-10.

✳ ACTIVITY 12-10

WRITING FRACTIONS AS DECIMALS

MATERIALS:
calculator

PROCEDURE:
Use a calculator to change several of the following fraction sequences to decimals. Look for patterns. Write the decimals.

1. $\frac{1}{2}, \frac{1}{3}, \frac{1}{4}, \frac{1}{5}, \frac{1}{6}, \frac{1}{7}, \frac{1}{8}, \frac{1}{9}$.

2. $\frac{1}{3}, \frac{2}{3}, \frac{1}{4}, \frac{2}{4}, \frac{3}{4}, \frac{1}{5}, \frac{2}{5}, \frac{3}{5}, \frac{4}{5}$.

3. All the proper fractions with 7 as denominator.

4. $\frac{1}{13}, \frac{1}{17}, \frac{1}{19}, \frac{1}{23}, \frac{1}{29}, \frac{1}{37}$.

5. $\frac{1}{9}, \frac{2}{9}, \frac{3}{9}, \frac{4}{9}, \frac{5}{9}, \frac{6}{9}, \frac{7}{9}, \frac{8}{9}$.

6. $\frac{1}{11}, \frac{2}{11}, \frac{3}{11}, \frac{4}{11}, \frac{5}{11}, \ldots$

After completing the activity, have students examine the sets of decimals for patterns. Discuss these as a class.

When changing decimals to fractions, the *Math Explorer* calculator works only with terminating decimals.

Terminating and Repeating Decimals

When changing fractions to decimals by division, students will notice that some divide evenly and others do not. In the case of even division, the decimals produced are said to be *terminating decimals*. In uneven division, the decimals produced are called *repeating decimals*. It is possible to tell whether a fraction will result in a terminating or repeating decimal by finding the prime factors of its denominator. Fractions whose denominators have 2 and/or 5 as their prime factors will be terminating decimals; fractions with denominators that have other prime factors (not 2 or 5) will be repeating decimals.

In a repeating decimal, the group of digits that repeat is known as the *repetend*. The repetend is indicated by a bar over the repeating digits.

Example:

$\frac{2}{3}$ $\quad 0.666666\ldots$ $\quad 0.\overline{6}$

$\frac{1}{12}$ $\quad 0.0833333\ldots$ $\quad 0.08\overline{3}$

$\frac{1}{7}$ $\quad 0.142857142857\ldots$ $\quad 0.\overline{142857}$

WRITING DECIMALS AS FRACTIONS

Terminating decimals are easily written as fractions.

Examples: $0.5 = \frac{5}{10}$

$\qquad\qquad 0.125 = \frac{125}{1000} = \frac{1}{8}$

To write repeating decimals as fractions is a more involved process. The following two examples present a procedure for changing a repeating decimal to a fraction.

Example 1: Write the decimal $0.\overline{6}$ in fraction form.

Steps: 1. Let $n = 0.66666\ldots$

2. $10n = 6.66666\ldots$

3. Subtract n from $10n$ and solve for n

$$10n = 6.6666\ldots$$
$$\underline{-\ n = 0.6666\ldots}$$
$$9n = 6$$
$$n = \frac{6}{9} = \frac{2}{3}$$

Example 2: Write the decimal $0.2\overline{35}$ in fraction form.

Steps: 1. Let $n = 0.2353535\ldots$
   2. $1000n = 235.3535\ldots$
   3. $10n = 2.3535\ldots$
   4. Subtract $10n$ from $1000n$ and solve for n.

$$1000n = 235.353535\ldots$$
$$10n = 2.353535\ldots$$
$$990n = 233$$
$$n = \tfrac{233}{990}$$

Since every fraction can be expressed in decimal form whether terminating or repeating and vice versa, it follows that the set of fractions is equivalent to the set of decimals. Since decimals are read in base-ten place values, that is, in tenths, hundredths, etc., while fractions can have any whole number as denominators, students may think that there are fewer decimals than fractions.

SCIENTIFIC NOTATION

Middle school students will learn to express numbers in a special notation called *scientific notation*. Scientific notation reduces the number of digits to record in a numeral by expressing numbers as the product of two factors; the first factor is a number greater than or equal to 1 and less than 10 and the second factor is a power of ten.

- The United States produces approximately 42 000 000 tons of garbage every year. This amount expressed in scientific notation is 4.2×10^7
- The diameter of an electron is 0.00 000 000 000 056 354 cm or 5.6354×10^{-13}.

Although scientific notation generally is used when dealing with very large or very small numbers, any number can be expressed in that notation. Study the following examples to find out what happens to the decimal point when a number is greater than one and when a number is greater than zero but smaller than one.

6	$\rightarrow$	6×10^0
386.5	$\rightarrow$	3.865×10^2
0.2006	$\rightarrow$	2.006×10^{-1}
0.00007	$\rightarrow$	7×10^{-5}

In 386.5, the four digits are called significant digits because they appear when the number is expressed in scientific notation; in 0.0007, the 7 is significant because it alone appears in scientific notation. It is possible to compute numbers written in scientific notation using the laws of exponents.

CONCLUSION

The focus of this chapter has been developing understanding of decimals. The main goal of instruction is to develop understanding of decimals in order to operate intelligently and effectively with them. Students should come to view decimals as an extension of place-value numeration and as another way to symbolize fractions. Activities have been presented to help students develop a good sense of decimals so that, together with fractions, they enable students to use these rational numbers to solve problems.

For Your Journal

When you have finished studying this chapter, reflect on these questions in your math journal:

1. What concepts about decimals should children understand? Draw pictures showing how to use a model to illustrate each concept.
2. Write a word problem for each operation and draw a picture showing how to solve the problem using a model.
3. How can a teacher help students understand decimals and decimal computation?

For Your Portfolio

When you have finished studying this chapter, complete these activities to include in your professional portfolio:

1. Write a lesson to help children understand a decimal concept of your choice.
2. Write a lesson to introduce decimal computation (for an operation of your choice) by linking this topic to fraction computation.
3. Visit an intermediate-grade classroom and informally interview several children to assess their understanding of decimal concepts and computation. Write a short paper describing their understanding and discuss what you would do next if you were their classroom teacher.

Resources for Teachers

Books on Decimals

Bennett, A. (1982). *Decimal squares: Step by step teacher's guide*. USA: Scott Resources, Inc.

Creative Publications. (1994). *Beyond Activities Project Mathematics replacement curriculum: Getting to the point! Investigating decimals*. Mountain View, CA: Creative Publications.

Links to the Internet

Real Worth Math

http://www.realworldmath.com/index.htm

Contains an integrated simulation of travel for grades 3–8 in which students apply the concepts of measurement, multiplication, division, decimals, and time by planning vacations across given states.

Explorer: Decimals

http://explorer.scrtec.org/explorer/explorer-db/browse/static/Mathematics/browse/f40.html

Contains links to lessons and activities involving decimals.

Energy Conservation Enhancement Project

http://ecepl.usl.edu/ecep/math/h/h.htm

Contains activity guides presented by the Energy Conservation Enhancement Project that include using decimals to calculate the energy bill of a homeowner.

CHAPTER 13

Understanding Ratio, Proportion, and Percent

SPEED
55
LIMIT

Other than familiar signs such as the one shown, real-world examples involving the ratio concept include the following:

- Two candy bars for 97¢.
- The map scale is 1 : 1 000 000.
- Sales tax is 7%.

Ratio, proportion, and percent are important topics in the mathematics program in the middle grades. Meaningful instruction builds on and extends understanding of fractions and decimals, and emphasizes problem solving and applications in real-world situations. This chapter describes and illustrates the key concepts for these topics, points out potential sources of difficulty, and suggests teaching strategies and problem settings for use in the classroom.

RATIO AND RATE

A *ratio* is a comparison of two numbers or quantities. As illustrated in the examples presented at the beginning of this chapter, the ratio concept arises in many practical and scientific situations and in several different mathematical contexts. When the measuring units describing two quantities being compared are different, the ratio is called a *rate*. Many everyday examples involve speed (Lisa ran 100 m in 12 sec.) or price (12 ears of corn for $2.50). When the second term is 1, the rate is referred to as the *unit rate*. Thus typing 40 words per minute and earning $5.50 an hour are unit rates.

In the early grades children learn about comparison subtraction situations. In Grade 5 or 6, ratio is introduced as another way of comparing two quantities. For example, given 6 balls and 3 bats, we could say that there are three more balls than bats, but we also note that there are twice as many balls as bats or that there are two balls for every bat. The idea of ratio involves *multiplicative* rather than additive comparisons.

There has been a disappointingly low level of understanding about ratio and proportions among students in the United States (Cramer, Post, & Currier, 1993; Hoffer & Hoffer, 1992). The sixth National Assessment of Educational Progress (NAEP) assessment also noted a low level of success by fourth-, eighth-, and twelfth-grade students (Kouba, Zawojewski, & Struchens, 1997). Most students incorrectly solved ratio problems by performing a one-step operation.

For example, consider the following problem given to fourth-graders.

A package of birdseed costs $2.58 for 2 pounds. A package of sunflower seeds costs $3.72 for 3 pounds. What is the difference in the cost per pound?

Most fourth-grade students chose an answer of $1.14, which is the difference between the two costs listed in the problem, neither of which is the cost *per pound*. Only 8% of the fourth graders answered this problem with the correct answer of $0.05, which is the difference between the cost per pound of birdseed ($1.29) and the cost per pound of sunflower seeds ($1.24). These results indicate a need for increased emphasis on understanding and reasonableness in instruction about ratios and rates.

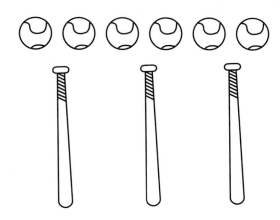

Language and Notation

To introduce the language and notation, the teacher might refer to a picture or a sketch of 3 pelicans and 2 frogs. The students are told that the *ratio* of pelicans to frogs in this picture is 3 to 2 and that this can be written $3:2$ or $\frac{3}{2}$. They can then be asked to state and write the ratio of frogs to pelicans $(2:3)$ and the ratio of pelicans to animals $(3:5)$. Note that this last ratio is a *part-to-whole comparison*, while the other two are *part-to-part comparisons*. The two numbers in a ratio are referred to as the *first term* and the *second term*.

PROPORTION

Aaron reasons: "If 3 oranges cost 60¢, then 6 oranges would cost $1.20 and one orange would cost 20¢" (see diagram at bottom of page).

A *proportion* is a statement that two ratios are equal. Finding unit rates and making scale drawings are examples of proportion problems.

Proportional Reasoning

The ability to understand ratios is one aspect of *proportional reasoning,* which is considered to be an indicator of a shift from concrete to formal operational levels of thought. Proportional reasoning involves both qualitative and quantitative thinking and concerns prediction and multiple comparisons (Lesh, Post, & Behr, 1989).

Ratio is a difficult concept because it involves a relationship between two quantities. At first children tend to focus on only one of the parts of a ratio. Quintero (1987) found that many nine-year-olds will predict that 6 tablespoons of white sugar mixed with 8 tablespoons of brown sugar would be lighter in color than 4 tablespoons of white sugar mixed with 3 tablespoons of brown sugar, because 6 is larger than 4.

Considerable research has been conducted to investigate children's thinking as they solve proportion problems. A version of one widely used task, "Mr. Short and Mr. Tall" (Karplus, Karplus, & Wollman, 1974), is described in Figure 13-1. On items such as this many children use an incorrect addition strategy, focusing on the difference between the numbers rather than on their ratio. Thus they will say 8 paper clips are needed since there are 2 more buttons. Even students who have been taught ratio and proportion will sometimes use this method, particularly if the ratio involved is not a simple one such as $1:2$.

Ratio and Rational Number

Number and ratio are different concepts, but the word "*ratio*nal" and the use of the fraction symbol for a ratio suggest that there are overlapping elements. Since a fraction represents a part-to-whole relationship, fractions are types of ratios. In the previous example, the ratio of pelicans to animals is 3 to 5 and three fifths of the animals are pelicans. The two ideas are essentially the same and both are represented by the symbol $\frac{3}{5}$. However, 2 frogs to 3 pelicans is a part-to-part comparison and, in this situation, the ratio 2 to 3 is quite different from the fraction $\frac{2}{3}$. We note further in this example that while the ratios 2 to 3 and 3 to 2 can both be used to express the relationship between the numbers of pelicans and frogs, the fractions $\frac{2}{3}$ and $\frac{3}{2}$ name different rational numbers.

Students should also appreciate that combining ratios is not the same as adding fractions. To illustrate, suppose there are 2 boys and 3 girls in one group and 3 boys and 4 girls in another group. If the two groups joined, the ratio of boys to girls would be 5 to 7. However, the sum of the numbers $\frac{2}{3}$ and $\frac{3}{4}$ is definitely not $\frac{5}{7}$! Similarly, while the ratio of boys to children could be expressed as $\frac{5}{12}$, it would be incorrect to write $\frac{2}{5} + \frac{3}{7} = \frac{5}{12}$. Arithmetic operations such as addition are performed on numbers.

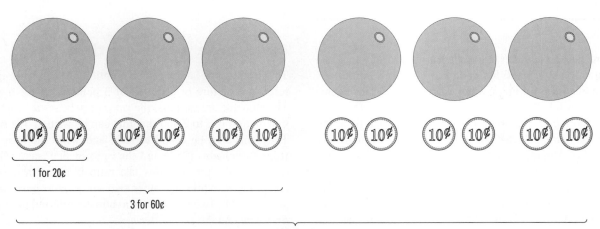

1 for 20¢

3 for 60¢

6 for $1.20

FIGURE 13-1

Mr. Short (shown) is 4 buttons high.

Mr. Tall (not shown) is 6 buttons high.

Use paper clips to measure Mr. Short (6).

How many paper clips high will Mr. Tall be?

On easy proportion questions some students will consistently use repeated addition rather than multiplication. Consider the following problem:

Snakes are fed according to their length. If the 5-inch-long snake is fed 2 cubes of food, how many cubes of food should the 10-inch and 15-inch snakes be fed?

A common solution is to add 2 cubes of food for the 10-inch snake and 2 more for the 15-inch snake, rather than multiplying 2 times 2 and 3 times 2 (Hart, 1989). Students who use addition rather than multiplication have difficulty solving proportions involving more complex relationships.

Equal Ratios

Introductory experiences for equal ratios include activities involving number patterns and repeated addition. For example, children in the early grades could be asked to make a table showing the relationship between the number of horses and the number of legs. The children might use toy animals to make sketches in solving the problem.

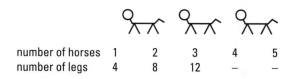

number of horses	1	2	3	4	5
number of legs	4	8	12	–	–

It is important that older students see the multiplicative relationship in the number pairs. They should be able to use multiplication directly to determine how many legs 9 horses have and use division to figure out how many horses there are if there are 28 legs. Frequent group oral questions such as, "If a video costs 4 dollars to rent, how much would it cost to rent 7 videos?" and "If 3 student movie tickets cost 15 dollars, how much would one ticket cost?" should be asked.

As students examine the horses and legs table above, they note that if 1 horse has 4 legs, then 2 horses have 8

legs, and so on. The teacher states that the ratios 1 to 4 and 2 to 8 are *equal* and writes:

$$1:4 = 2:8 \text{ or } \frac{1}{4} = \frac{2}{8}$$

Students should be encouraged to discover and verbalize the procedure for generating equal ratios: multiply both terms by the same (counting) number. They should also explore what happens when the same number is added to both terms and conclude that the resulting ratios are usually not equal. For example:

$$\frac{1}{4} \neq \frac{(1 + 2)}{(4 + 2)}$$

Students will likely see the connection with the rule for writing equivalent fractions. The use of the same notation for ratios and fractions could be discussed in this context. Finding a lower-terms ratio is accomplished by dividing both terms by the same number; the connection to the procedure for simplifying fractions is immediate. This idea is applied in finding a unit rate as in the following problem.

Brian types 100 words in 4 minutes. How many words is that per minute?

Since $\frac{100}{4} = \frac{25}{1}$, *the unit rate is 25 words per minute.*

In Activity 13-1 students write equal ratios suggested by a diagram.

✴ ACTIVITY 13-1

MARBLE RATIOS

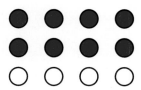

• What is the ratio of blue marbles to white marbles in the picture? Can you write the ratio in more than one way?

• Now write the ratio of blue marbles to marbles in as many ways as you can.

Beginning questions requiring students to find a missing term in a pair of equal ratios should involve only whole number multiplication as in the following problem.

If the ratio of children to adults is 17 to 2 and there are 6 adults, how many children are there?

If we let n *represent the number of children,*

$$\frac{17}{2} = \frac{n}{6}$$

Since 6 = 2 × 3, n *= 17 × 3 = 51. There are 51 children.*

Comparing Ratios

Which mixture will be lighter in color—3 parts white sugar to 5 parts brown sugar or 2 parts white sugar to 3 parts brown sugar? Questions such as this can be used to motivate the idea of renaming the two ratios so that they have the same second term. Thus to compare $\frac{3}{5}$ and $\frac{2}{3}$ we might look at $\frac{9}{15}$ and $\frac{10}{15}$. We conclude that the ratio of white to brown sugar is greater in the second mixture. The second mixture will be slightly lighter in color, although this would be difficult to discern.

This is, of course, the same procedure as that learned for comparing two fractions. A common second term or denominator is a common multiple of the two second terms or denominators. In some cases it is easiest to use the least common multiple. For example, to compare $\frac{3}{4}$ and $\frac{5}{8}$ we would likely consider $\frac{6}{8}$ and $\frac{5}{8}$, and for $\frac{3}{4}$ and $\frac{5}{6}$ we might write $\frac{9}{12}$ and $\frac{10}{12}$. However, students should appreciate that any common multiple of the two second terms will work, and that a particularly easy one to find is the product of the two numbers. Thus $\frac{3}{4}$ and $\frac{5}{6}$ could also be compared as $\frac{18}{24}$ and $\frac{20}{24}$, where 24 is the product of 4 and 6.

In a basketball game Amy made 3 of 5 free throws and Diane made 4 of 7 attempts. Which performance was better?

We write equal ratios with 5 × 7 as the second term.

$$\frac{3}{5} \qquad\qquad \frac{4}{7}$$

$$\frac{3 \times 7}{5 \times 7} \quad \frac{5 \times 4}{5 \times 7}$$

$$\frac{21}{35} \qquad \frac{20}{35}$$

Amy's shooting was slightly better than Diane's.

Number sense thinking, similar to that used in comparing fractions, can also be used to compare ratios. For example, the relations $\frac{4}{7} > \frac{4}{9}$, $\frac{5}{6} < \frac{6}{7}$, and $\frac{3}{5} > \frac{4}{9}$ are true whether the symbols apply to fractions or to ratios. While these relations can be verified by computing equal ratios, students should be challenged to use quantitative explanations. A student might think about the above relations as follows: 4 hits out of 7 times at bat is better than 4 hits out of 9; if I have made 5 of 6 free throws during a game and make my next one, I will be 6 for 7; 3 out of 5 is more than half while 4 out of 9 is less than half.

Cross Products

Given several pairs of equal ratios such as $\frac{3}{6} = \frac{5}{10}$, students can be challenged to find a relationship among the four terms. They should be able to discover that the *cross products* are equal: $3 \times 10 = 6 \times 5$.

Students should also be able to explain why this relationship holds. Comparing $\frac{3}{6}$ and $\frac{5}{10}$ by finding equal ratios with 60 as the second term, we multiply both terms of the first ratio by 10 and both terms of the second ratio by 6, giving 3×10 and 6×5, respectively, as the first terms. Thus, computing cross products provides a simple test for determining if two ratios (or fractions) are equal. We can tell, for example, that $\frac{2}{3} \neq \frac{3}{4}$ because $2 \times 4 \neq 3 \times 3$.

In addition, if three of the four terms in a proportion are given, the fourth can be calculated directly using the cross product relationship. This method is particularly useful where non-integer ratios are involved.

If 3 pounds of apples cost $4.00, how many pounds could you get for $6.00?

$\frac{3}{4} = \frac{n}{6}$

4 × n = 3 × 6 = 18; n = 18 ÷ 4 = 4.5. You would get 4.5 pounds.

Note that instead of considering the pounds to dollar ratios, we could have written the proportion $\frac{3}{n} = \frac{4}{6}$ which relates the pound to pound ratio and the dollar to dollar ratio. Two other proportions that model this situation and lead to the same computations are created by interchanging the first and second terms: $\frac{4}{3} = \frac{6}{n}$ and $\frac{n}{3} = \frac{6}{4}$.

A more direct way to solve the first proportion above is to reason that since 6 is 1.5 times 4, $n = 3 \times 1.5 = 4.5$. But in most real-life situations the numbers are large or "messy" and the cross product method, with a calculator to perform the multiplication and division, is the most efficient procedure. In the above example, the apples would more likely be priced at 3 pounds for $3.95 rather than $4.00.

The majority of proportion problems in the intermediate grades should have solutions that do not require the use of cross products. While the cross product algorithm is a powerful tool, students should appreciate that many problems can be solved in more than one way and be encouraged to look for alternative solutions. See Activity 13-2 and the soup problem that follows.

A recipe for soup for 8 people calls for 6 onions. How many onions should be used in preparing soup for 12 people?

$\frac{8}{6} = \frac{12}{n}$

Then 8n = 6 × 12 = 72 and n = 9.

Therefore, 9 onions are needed.

There are several things that might be discussed by a class after examining this solution. First, the proportion $\frac{8}{6} = \frac{12}{n}$ can be solved without using cross products. One way is to note that $\frac{8}{6} = \frac{4}{3}$ and consider $\frac{4}{3} = \frac{12}{n}$. Since $12 = 4 \times 3$, $n = 3 \times 3$. Second, we could have also considered the ratios, 8 people to 12 people and 6 onions to n onions, and written the proportion $\frac{8}{12} = \frac{6}{n}$. Two other

proportions describing the same situation are $\frac{6}{8} = \frac{n}{12}$ and $\frac{12}{8} = \frac{n}{6}$. In all three cases the numerical ratio can be simplified. Finally, we could reason that since there are 4 more people and 4 is half of 8, you would make a recipe and a half. Therefore, you would need 6 plus 3 onions.

STANDARDS LINK 13-4

Instruction should stress informal but effective methods for solving proportions, including ways to identify integer multiples in ratios and processes in which changing one of the ratios to an equivalent unit ratio is an intermediate step. Cross-multiplication methods should be deferred until students understand these methods in algebraic terms. (NCTM, 1989, p. 96)

Scale Drawings

Reading maps and plans, enlarging or reducing pictures, and finding corresponding dimensions of similar geometric figures all involve the idea of a *scale*. A scale drawing is a smaller or larger representation of an object. The scale is the ratio of a dimension in the drawing to the corresponding dimension of the actual object. Three sample problems and solutions follow.

Below is a scale drawing of a bee. Find the bee's actual length.

Scale $\frac{3}{1}$

The length of the bee in the scale drawing is about 48 mm. Therefore the bee's length is one third of 48 mm, which is about 16 mm. The related proportion is $\frac{3}{1} = \frac{48}{n}$.

The scale on a city street map reads

1 in. = 3 miles
1:3

Find the distance between two schools 7 in. apart on the map.

✳ **ACTIVITY 13-2**

TRAVEL ON

Solve the following problem in at least two different ways.

A car travels 212 km in 4 hours. At this rate of speed, how far would it travel in 7 hours?

7 in. represents 7×3 miles $= 21$ miles. So the schools are about 21 miles apart. The related proportion is $\frac{1}{3} = \frac{7}{n}$.

In the diagram the second triangle is an enlargement of the first. Find the scale ratio of the enlargement.

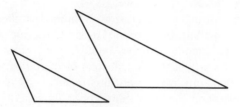

Using a ruler we find that the bases of the triangles measure 2 cm and 3 cm. Therefore the scale ratio for the enlargement is $3:2$ (or 150%). Measuring the longest side of the smaller triangle we find that its length is 3 cm. We can compute the length of the corresponding side of the enlarged triangle using a proportion and then compare the answer with the measured length.

$\frac{2}{3} = \frac{3}{n}$. *The length is found to be 4.5 cm.*

Comparison Shopping

Determining which size of package gives the most product for the money is another type of problem involving ratios that can be solved in several ways. The data in the following example were taken from the bread counter in a major supermarket.

A 16-ounce loaf of bread costs $1.99, while a 24-ounce loaf costs $2.49. Which loaf of bread is the better buy?

The unit price is the cost of 1 ounce of bread. The unit price of the smaller loaf is $1.99/16 = $0.12 per ounce, and the unit price of the larger loaf is $2.49/24 = $0.10 per ounce. Since the larger loaf has a lower unit price, it is the better buy.

This solution involves complex calculations that would usually be done using a calculator. A shopper in a store might use mental arithmetic to solve this problem as follows: The 16-ounce loaf is 1 pound and the 24-ounce loaf is $1\frac{1}{2}$ pounds. One and a half of the smaller loaves would cost $1.99 plus half of $1.99, which is about $2 + $1 = $3. The larger loaf costs only $2.49, which is less than $3, so the larger loaf is the better buy.

The class should discuss why the largest size package does not always have the lowest unit price, and also why

---

the lowest unit price might not always represent the "best buy" (Activity 13-3).

PERCENT

Percents are used in many everyday life situations. They are also frequently misused. For example, a store advertises prices reduced by 100% (rather than 50%), an interest rate of .13% is offered (rather than 13%), and a newspaper reports murders up by 200% (correct, but they went from 1 to 3).

What do we know of U.S. students' understanding of percents? The sixth National Assessment of Educational Progress (NAEP) noted a low level of performance by eighth- and twelfth-grade students, whose average total correct ranged between 33% and 40% on questions involving percent (Kouba et al., 1997). A particular concern was the high number of students giving unreasonable answers. For example, students were asked to find the total cost of a used car bought for $5375 plus 15% tax. Twenty-five percent of the eighth-graders and 20% of the twelfth-graders selected an answer of $806, which is the correct amount of tax, but not the correct *total cost* of the car. As with ratio and proportion, these disappointing results point to a need for increased emphasis on understanding and reasonableness in instruction about percents.

Meaning and Notation

A *percent* is a part-to-whole ratio which has 100 as its second term. For example, seven percent means seven parts per hundred which is written $7:100$ or $\frac{7}{100}$. We introduce the notation 7%, noting the connection between the percent symbol and the numeral 100.

> 7 per hundred
> 7 percent
> 7:100
> 7%

A 7 percent tax on a $100 item is $7. The $100 is referred to as the *base,* 7 percent is the *rate* and $7 is the

FIGURE 13-2

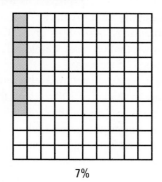
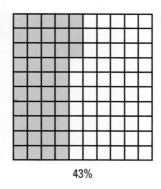
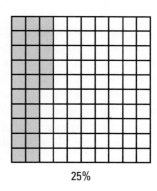

| 7% | 43% | 25% |

---

percentage. Since percents are part-to-whole ratios, they can also be thought of as fractions with denominators of 100. Expressed as common or decimal fractions, percents can be treated as numbers and used in arithmetic computations.

Number Sense

Introductory activities should help students form visual images and develop a quantitative feel for numbers expressed as percents. An effective pictorial model is a 10 by 10 grid which students shade to represent various percents (Figure 13-2). Corresponding activities at the concrete level involve placing small cubes on the flat of the base-ten materials.

Special emphasis should be placed on 1%, 50%, and 100%. Other important benchmarks are 10% and 25%. Students naturally come to associate these ratios with their corresponding common fractions. Percents less than 1 (such as $\frac{1}{2}$%) and percents greater than 100 (such as 150%) can also be represented using the grid model (Figure 13-3).

The following activities, which use an unmarked rectangle, can help students develop estimation skills with percents.

1. Shade about 50%, 10%, 75%, 2%, 97%, 35%.

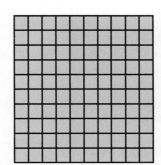

2. About what percent has been shaded in each rectangle?

FIGURE 13-3

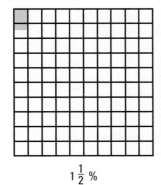
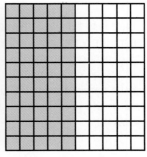

| $1\frac{1}{2}$ % | 150% |

Fraction and Decimal Equivalents

A key idea in mathematics is that numbers can be represented in many ways. A rational number can be expressed as a fraction, a decimal, or a percent. As students show percents on a 10-by-10 grid and reflect on the language they use to describe their representations, the fraction and decimal names for the numbers will become apparent. For example, since 9% means 9 out of 100, it is nine hundredths, which is written $\frac{9}{100}$ in fraction notation and 0.09 in decimal notation.

9%   nine hundredths $\frac{9}{100}$ 0.09

Further, $150\% = \dfrac{150}{100} = 1.5 = \dfrac{3}{2} = 1\frac{1}{2}$

Decimals as Percents Writing a decimal as a percent involves finding an equivalent decimal in hundredths. For example,

three tenths = thirty hundredths = thirty percent

0.3 = 0.30 = 30%

Generalizing from examples such as 17 hundredths = 17 percent (0.17 = 17%), students find that to change a decimal to a percent, you multiply by 100, which means "moving" the decimal point two places to the right. Thus 0.135 = 13.5% and 9.1 = 910%. To express a percent as a decimal the opposite rule is employed: divide by 100. Thus 6.9% = 0.069.

Fractions as Percents Students can be challenged to apply their understanding to find ways of writing a fraction as a percent. A basic method is to find an equivalent fraction having a denominator of 100. For example,

$$\frac{2}{5} = \frac{40}{100} = 40\%$$

Another procedure is to first write the fraction in decimal form and then multiply this number by 100. Students recall that one way of accomplishing the first step is to divide the numerator by the denominator: $2 \div 5 = 0.4 = 40\%$. Multiplying the numerator by 100 before dividing by the denominator would give the same answer: $200 \div 5 = 40$, which means 40%.

$$\begin{array}{r} 0.4 \\ 5)\overline{2.0} \\ 2.0 \\ \hline 0 \end{array} \qquad \begin{array}{r} 40 \\ 5)\overline{200} \\ 20 \\ \hline 00 \end{array}$$

In most cases the computation would be carried out with the aid of a calculator. To express $\frac{3}{8}$ as a percent, press $3 \div 8 =$ and mentally multiply the answer 0.375 by 100. Alternatively, pressing $300 \div 8 =$ gives 37.5. Students can later be shown that on most simple calculators, pressing $3 \div 8\%$ gives 37.5 directly.

Some fractions have repeating decimal representations. When students attempt to shade $\frac{1}{3}$ of 100 squares, they find they shade 33 whole squares and a third of one square. Thus $\frac{1}{3} = 33\frac{1}{3}\%$. Rounding to the nearest whole number, we say that $\frac{1}{3}$ is about 33%. Calculators should be used to help find approximate percent equivalents for fractions with repeating decimal representations. For example,

$$\frac{5}{12} = 0.41666 \ldots, \text{ which the student rounds to 42\%.}$$

Percents as Fractions Expressing a percent as a fraction with a denominator of 100 is accomplished by applying the definition of percent: $67\% = \frac{67}{100}$. In some cases the resulting fraction can be written in simpler form:

$$8\% = \frac{8}{100} = \frac{2}{25}$$

$$87.5\% = \frac{87.5}{100} = \frac{875}{1000} = \frac{7}{8}.$$

The *Math Explorer* calculator (Texas Instruments) is programmed to carry out these computations.

Keystrokes	Display
87.5%	0.875
F⟷D	875/1000
Simp =	175/200
Simp =	35/40
Simp =	7/8

There are several computer programs that deal with equivalent percents, decimals, and fractions. Activity 13-4 describes a card game, "Math Rummy" (Brown, 1973), which provides practice in recognizing fraction, decimal, and percent names of common numbers. To prepare a deck of 52 cards, make a list of 13 numbers, each of which has four equivalent forms. For example: $20\% = \frac{20}{100} = \frac{1}{5} = 0.2$.

Finding the Percent of a Number

Computing sales tax, discount, commission, and interest are examples of everyday situations involving finding a percent of a number. To help students understand that the

✳ ACTIVITY 13-4

MATH RUMMY

MATERIALS:
deck of 52 cards comprising 13 numbers in 4 equivalent forms.

PROCEDURE:
Two, three, or four players can play. The object of the game is to lay all your cards down.

1. Begin by dealing 7 cards to each player. The remainder of the pack is placed facedown on the table. The top card is then placed faceup next to the pack to begin the discard pile.

2. The first player may either draw the top card from the facedown pile or pick up the top card on the discard pile. The player must then discard a card, and the play goes to the next player.

3. When one player has accumulated three cards of equivalent value, these are laid faceup on the table. The player who has the fourth equivalent value for the set lays that card faceup on the table in front of himself or herself. The player next to the one who laid down the three equivalent cards continues the play.

4. When the pack is gone, the discard pile is turned over and becomes the pack.

5. The first player to lay down all his or her cards wins that hand. Each player receives 5 points for every card laid down and −5 points for every card still held.

6. The game is over when one player has 100 points.

operation involved is multiplication, a problem such as the following might be presented:

In our class of 28 students, 50% went skiing during winter break. How many of our class members went skiing?

Students know that 50% is a half and that one half *of* 28 is expressed by $\frac{1}{2} \times 28$. The general procedure then is to express the percent in either fraction or decimal form and multiply by the other given number.

Early examples should involve percents that have simple fraction or decimal equivalents (such as 50%, 25%, 10%, 200%), together with numbers chosen so that the computation can be carried out using mental arithmetic procedures for multiplying a whole number by a unit fraction or power of ten.

$$50\% \text{ of } 28 = \frac{1}{2} \times 28 = \frac{28}{2} = 14$$

$$25\% \text{ of } 80 = \frac{1}{4} \times 80 = \frac{80}{4} = 20$$

$$10\% \text{ of } 70 = \frac{1}{10} \times 70 = \frac{70}{10} = 7$$

$$100\% \text{ of } 63 = 63$$

$$200\% \text{ of } 45 = 2 \times 45 = 90$$

$$30\% \text{ of } 80 = 0.3 \times 80 = 24$$

$$10\% \text{ of } 235 = 0.1 \times 235 = 23.5$$

$$1\% \text{ of } 469 = 0.01 \times 469 = 4.69$$

Since most real-life computations will be carried out with a calculator, students need to learn to estimate answers and judge the reasonableness of results. This requires a good sense of number and the ability to do mental arithmetic with rounded or "special" numbers. Examples such as the following should be discussed and practiced.

49% of 85	about $\frac{1}{2}$ of 84
102% of 543	a little more than 543
31% of 68	about $\frac{1}{3}$ of 69 or 0.3 × 70
9.5% of 752	a little less than 75
36% of 851	about 0.4 × 800

To estimate a 6% sales tax on a purchase of $135.97, the shopper might think: 10% is about $14; 6% would be a bit more than half or about $8. With a calculator: 135.97 × 0.06 = gives 8.1582; the tax is $8.16. Later, students learn that they can use the percent key rather than the decimal form of the percent: 135.97 × 6% gives 8.1582 directly.

The following activity is described by Vance (1982). Grade 7 students, working in pairs, were given department store catalogs (and calculators) and told that they had $400 to purchase clothing. They were to assume a 20% discount on prices listed and 6% sales tax. The students began by identifying several items they wanted to buy. They would then find the total cost, compute the discount and the sale price, and finally compute the tax and find the total cost. After comparing this figure with $400, they would add or delete items and repeat the process. The problem soon became that of finding the maximum list price that would lead to a final cost of not more than

$400 after the discount and tax were considered. Several interesting alternative procedures and hypotheses were generated and evaluated by the various groups as they worked towards a solution.

1. Could you simply subtract 14% (20% − 6%) from the list price to get the final cost price? (No)

2. Do you get the same final answer if you first add the tax and then subtract the discount (on the list plus the tax), rather than doing it the other way? (Surprisingly, yes)

3. Can you compute the sale price in one step? (Yes, multiply by 0.8)

4. Given the sale price, can you compute the final cost in one step? (Yes, multiply by 1.06)

Given the last two results, some groups wrote the following equation:

final cost = list price × 0.8 × 1.06 = list price × 0.848.

They were then able to compute the maximum list price directly:

$$\$400 \div 0.848 = \$471.70.$$

Several students came close to this figure by using guess and check repeatedly.

Finding the Percent

The Owls soccer team won 13 of 20 games played last season. What percent of its games did the team win?

Finding what percent one number is of another amounts to expressing the corresponding fraction as a percent. Thus $\frac{13}{20} = \frac{65}{100} = 65\%$. As previously discussed this can be done on a calculator by dividing 13 by 20 and (mentally) multiplying by 100, by dividing 1300 by 20, or by pressing $13 \div 20\%$. Before students are shown this last calculator procedure, they need to have many experiences computing easy examples and estimating answers to more difficult questions. Consider the following sample questions and solutions.

$$\frac{3}{5} = \frac{60}{100} = 60\%$$

$\frac{4}{7}$ is close to half so it is just over 50%

$\frac{23}{70}$ is about $\frac{1}{3}$ so it is about 33%

$\frac{8}{9}$ is almost 1 so it is a little less than 100%

$\frac{3}{478}$ is small—under 1%

Other Procedures for Solving Percent Problems

In the previous two sections instructional strategies for finding the percentage and the rate were presented. For both types of problems the solutions follow directly from the meaning of percent. Three other approaches to solving percent problems are now considered: the proportion method, the equation method, and the unitary analysis method.

The proportion method The statement 30% of 70 = 21 can be written as a proportion:

$$\frac{30}{100} = \frac{21}{70}.$$

Therefore, given two of the three numbers 30, 21, and 70, we can compute the third using cross products. To find 30% of 70, we let n represent the percentage and solve the proportion $\frac{30}{100} = \frac{n}{70}$. To find what percent 21 is of 70 we let n represent the rate and solve the proportion $\frac{n}{100} = \frac{21}{70}$.

While this can be a meaningful and very powerful method, it should not be introduced until students have learned to find a percent of a number and what percent one number is of another as previously discussed. Writing a proportion is an excellent way of solving problems in which the base is to be found.

Of the Grade 6 students in a school, 21 usually walk to school. This represents 30% of the Grade 6 students.

How many Grade 6 students are there?

$\frac{30}{100} = \frac{21}{n}$

30n = 2100

n = 70. There are 70 Grade 6 students.

To help students see the structure of a proportion problem and estimate the answer, Dewar (1984) suggests having them complete a comparison scale. The steps for the previous example are shown in Figure 13-4. From the two scales it appears reasonable that since 30 is just less than a third of 100, n should be a bit more than 3 times 21.

The equation method The statement 30% of 70 = 21 is represented by the equation 30% × 70 = 21. Given two of these three numbers, the third can be

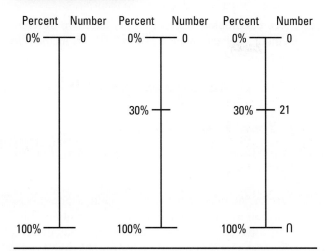

Adapted from Dewar, 1984.

computed by inspection or using inverse operations. To find what percent 21 is of 70, we solve for the variable n in the equation $n \times 70 = 21$. Since $n = 0.3$, the rate is 30%.

If the base is unknown, we solve for n in the equation $0.3 \times n = 21$. Neither this method nor rules such as "to find the base divide the number by the percent" should be formally taught to elementary school students. These learners should, however, be encouraged to use their understanding of percent and the "guess and check" strategy to find answers to questions such as the following:

50% of _____ = 32

6 is 10% of _____

78 is 120% of a number. What do you know about the number?

The unitary analysis method The unitary analysis or unit method was once popular in schools in the United States. It is presented here because it illustrates logical reasoning and mental computation strategies. Examples for each of the three types of percent problems follow.

Find 5% of 700.

1% of 700 is 7.
Therefore 5% of 700 is 5 × 7 = 35.

What percent is 2 of 5?

5 is 100% of the total.
Therefore 1 is 20% of the total. (100% ÷ 5)
And 2 is 2 × 20% = 40% of the total.

60 is 20% of what number?

20% of the number is 60.

Therefore 1% of the number is 3. (60 ÷ 20)
And 100% of the number is 300.

The numbers in these examples are easy to work with. In many problems, however, the intermediate steps involve cumbersome fractions or decimals. For this reason, the method is not generally taught formally today.

ASSESSMENT AND INSTRUCTION

Assessing Proportional Reasoning

An important aspect of proportional reasoning is the ability to discriminate between proportional and nonproportional situations. Cramer, Post, and Currier (1993) reported that most of the preservice teachers in a mathematics methods course wrote a proportion to solve the following problem:

Sue and Julie were running equally fast around a track. Julie started first. When she had run 9 laps, Sue had run 3 laps. When Julie completed 15 laps, how many laps had Sue run?

In addition to missing-value problems, such as the "Mr. Short and Mr. Tall" task, and numerical comparison problems, such as predicting the relative strength of orange juice given different mixtures of concentrate and water, qualitative prediction or comparison situations such as the following can be used to assess proportional reasoning.

If today Eric ran fewer laps in more time than he did yesterday, was his speed faster, slower, the same, or can't you say for sure?

If Lisa ran more laps than Craig and she ran for less time, who was the faster runner—Lisa, Craig, they ran the same speed, or can't you say for sure?

Everyday Life Problem Settings

Newspaper and magazine articles, as well as radio and television reports, are continuing sources of up-to-date information on topics of interest to young people, such as sports, entertainment, and environmental concerns. Such data can be used in concept and skill development activities related to ratio and percent. For example, students could write various part-to-part and part-to-whole ratios based on the number of medals won by a country at the recent Olympic Games: Winter—2 gold, 3 silver, and 2 bronze; Summer—6 gold, 5 silver, and 7 bronze, for example.

Students who collect sports cards or follow professional teams might be asked to explain what certain statistics mean and how they are computed:

- a hitter's batting average of .317
- a pitcher's earned run average of 2.85
- a team's powerplay percentage of 21%
- a quarterback's passing percentage of 62%
- a player's 3-point shooting percentage of 46%

Different students could be encouraged to keep various statistics on games in a sport in which they participate or are spectators. Problems or student projects based on data from printed sources could then be generated and solved by class members.

Another source of information is data collected in surveys conducted by students. For example, the number of people who prefer certain soft drinks, watch certain TV shows, or recycle paper can be reported and compared in ratio or percent form. Activities such as these have obvious connections to topics and concepts in the data analysis strand, which focuses on collecting, representing, and interpreting quantitative information (see Chapter 16).

CONCLUSION

In this chapter, procedures for developing the concepts of ratio, proportion, and percent have been described. Suggestions for effective instruction have emphasized higher-level reasoning, number sense, and real-world applications. Students should rely on conceptual understanding rather than mechanical rules when solving problems, and they should know that problems can be solved in many different ways. Mental computation and estimation skills need to be developed for these topics. Calculators should be used for complex computations.

For your Journal

When you have finished studying this chapter, reflect on these questions in your math journal:

1. Why do students have low levels of achievement on ratio, proportion, and percent problems? What might a classroom teacher do to help strengthen students' understandings of these topics?

2. Imagine you are an intermediate-grade or middle-school teacher. The parents of one of your students are concerned that you have not yet taught their child the

"cross-multiply-and-divide" method for solving proportions. What would you say to them?

3. Solve the problem below using at least two different methods. Reflect on each method. Which method do you prefer, and why?

6 is 40% of what number?

For Your Portfolio

When you have finished studying this chapter, complete these activities to include in your professional portfolio:

1. Visit an intermediate-grade or middle school classroom and informally interview several children. Have them solve and describe their solution methods for a few ratio, proportion, and percent problems. Write a short description of their solution strategies and their understandings of these kinds of problems. If you were their teacher, what would you plan for their next lessons about these topics?

2. Write a lesson plan to help children understand the meaning of ratio and/or proportion by linking it to their everyday lives.

3. Write a lesson plan to help children understand and use unit rates to solve proportion problems.

4. Write a lesson plan to help children understand percents by using a model.

Resources for Teachers

Books on Ratio and Proportion

Curcio, F. R., & Bezuk, N. S. (1994). *Understanding rational numbers and proportions: Curriculum and evaluation standards for School Mathematics Addenda Series, Grades 5–8*. Reston, VA: National Council of Teachers of Mathematics.

Links to the Internet

Fibonacci Numbers and the Golden Section
http://www.mcs.surrey.ac.uk/Personal/R.Knott/Fibonacci/fib.html

Contains information about Fionacci numbers and the Golden section (or ratio), including how they appear in nature and how to calculate them.

Math Forum:
http://forum.swarthmore.edu/dr.math/faq/faq.fractions.html

Contains answers to frequently asked questions about percents.

CHAPTER 14

Developing Geometric Thinking and Spatial Sense

The study of geometry at the elementary level is an opportunity to connect mathematics to the environment. Through explorations of shapes and figures, children learn how to describe their world in an orderly manner (NCTM, 1989). The mode of study should be informal with the gradual implementation of more systematic and rigorous study as the age and experience of the student increases.

The ideas presented in this chapter are about "getting to know" objects in the world so that eventually they can be measured and quantified. Working with concrete objects leads to intuitive discoveries of geometric properties and relationships.

The geometry component of the mathematics program at the elementary level includes, in part, the study of varied three-dimensional (3-D) shapes and two-dimensional (2-D) figures. As children mature, they are able to recognize different shapes and figures, name them and describe them, deduce properties, and eventually express relationships both within and between shapes and figures. The study of geometry also is about developing spatial sense, that is, the ability to mentally picture objects and to maintain accurate perception of the objects under different orientations (Owens, 1990).

What do we know of U.S. students' understanding of geometry and spatial sense? The sixth National Assessment of Educational Progress (NAEP) noted that fourth-grade students were able to identify properties of simple geometric figures but had more difficulty with more complex figures and with producing more extensive written explanations (Struchens & Blume, 1997). As with other topics, teachers must give students many opportunities to experience a variety of geometric concepts with hands-on materials and to encourage students to communicate about those concepts. ○

STANDARDS LINK 14-1

In grades K–4, the mathematics curriculum should include two- and three-dimensional geometry so that students can

- describe, model, draw, and classify shapes;
- investigate and predict the results of combining, subdividing, and changing shapes;
- develop spatial sense;
- relate geometric ideas to number and measurement ideas;
- recognize and appreciate geometry in their world. (NCTM, 1989, p. 48)

STANDARDS LINK 14-2

In grades 5–8, the mathematics curriculum should include the study of the geometry of one, two, and three dimensions in a variety of situations so that students can

- identify, describe, compare, and classify geometric figures;
- visualize and represent geometric figures with special attention to developing spatial sense;
- explore transformations of geometric figures;
- represent and solve problems using geometric models;
- understand and apply geometric properties and relationships;
- develop an appreciation of geometry as a means of describing the physical world. (NCTM, 1989, p. 112)

TABLE 14-1

VAN HIELE LEVELS OF GEOMETRIC THINKING

LEVEL	DESCRIPTION
0-Visualization	Students recognize shapes by their global, holistic appearance.
1-Analysis	Students observe the component parts of figures (e.g., a parallelogram has opposite sides that are parallel) but are unable to explain the relationships between properties within a shape or among shapes.
2-Informal deduction	Students deduce properties of figures and express interrelationships both within and between figures.
3-Formal deduction	Students create formal deductive proofs.
4-Rigor	Students rigorously compare different axiomatic systems.

DEVELOPMENT OF GEOMETRIC THINKING

The van Hiele Levels of Geometric Thought

The work of two Dutch educators, Dina van Hiele-Geldof and Pierre van Hiele (pronounced "van HEE-Ley"), is influencing the teaching of geometry. The van Hieles were concerned about the difficulties their students were having with geometry (Geddes & Fortunato, 1993), so they conducted research aimed at understanding students' levels of geometric thinking to determine the kinds of instruction that can best help students.

The van Hieles observed five levels of geometric thinking, listed in Table 14-1 (Crowley, 1987). Each level describes what students understand related to geometry. Most elementary school students are at van Hiele Levels 0 or 1; some middle school students are at Level 2. The

sixth NAEP noted that "most of the students at all three grade levels (fourth, eighth, and twelfth) appeared to be performing at the 'holistic' level (Level 0) of the van Hiele levels of geometric thought" (Struchens & Blume, 1997, p. 166).

Students at Level 0 think about shapes in terms of what they resemble. For example, a student at this level might describe a triangle as a "clown's hat." The student, however, might not recognize the same triangle after it is rotated 180 degrees, saying, "It's not a triangle because a triangle can't stand on its head." Students at Level 0 are able to sort shapes into groups that "seem to be alike" (Van de Walle, 1998, p. 346).

Students at Level 1 think about groups or classes of shapes, such as parallelograms. They are able to describe characteristics that make a shape a parallelogram, such as its having four sides, with opposite sides parallel. Students at this level are able to understand that all shapes in a group such as parallelograms have the same properties, and they can describe those properties.

Students at Level 2 not only think about properties of shapes, they are also able to notice relationships between properties. Students at this level understand informal deductive discussion about shapes and their properties (Van de Walle, 1998).

Students at Level 3 think about relationships between properties of shapes and also understand relationships between axioms, definitions, theorems, corollaries, and postulates. At this level, students are able to "work with abstract statements about geometric properties and make conclusions based more on logic than intuition" (Van de Walle, p. 346). This is the level at which two-column proofs, often done in high school geometry courses, are understood. Unfortunately, however, few high school students function at this level of geometric thinking.

Students at Level 4 think about "deductive axiomatic systems" of geometry (Van de Walle, 1998, p. 347). This is the level at which college mathematics majors think about geometry.

Comments on the Levels of Thought

There are several important points to be made about the van Hiele levels of geometric thought. These are adapted from the work of Crowley (1987), Van de Walle (1998), and Geddes and Fortunato (1993).

- The levels are not age-dependent, but, instead, are related more to the experiences students have had.

- The levels are sequential; that is, students must pass through the levels in order as their understanding increases.

- In order to move from one level to the next, students need to have many experiences in which they are actively involved in exploring and communicating about their observations of shapes, properties, and relationships.

- Language must match the student's level of understanding for learning to take place. If the language used in instruction is above the student's level of thinking, the student may only be able to learn procedures and memorize relationships without truly understanding geometry.

Thus, it is important for teachers to use the van Hiele levels in order to plan instruction on geometry and spatial sense that is appropriate and relevant to students' level of thinking.

OTHER INSTRUCTIONAL NOTES

Developing the Language

The formal language of geometry develops over time. Therefore, use of informal terms and expressions should be accepted in the elementary grades. For example, both teacher and students can use such terms as "corners," "square corners," "flips," and "slides." These terms eventually will be replaced, respectively, with the formal terms "vertices," "right angles," "reflections," and "translations." By frequently talking about what they are doing, children's descriptions will become more precise and correct.

VIDEO LINK 14-1
Geometry and Spatial Sense

Brief Summary: In "Thanksgiving Quilt," teacher Elaine McAlear's first-graders are making quilts from geometric shapes.

1. How was communication used in this lesson? How did it support the development of students' understanding?

2. What did the teacher do to support the students' working in pairs?

3. What is the teacher's role in this lesson? What do you think her objectives were for this lesson?

4. What were you able to learn about children's understanding from this lesson? What lessons might the teacher do next with this class?

Video Source. Teaching Math: A Video Library, K–4; Tape 8 from The Annenberg/CPB Math and Science Collection.

Method of Instruction

There is strong agreement among educators that geometry learning for elementary school students should be informal, involving explorations, discovery, guessing, and problem solving. The capabilities of formulating precise descriptive statements using formal terminology and symbols are developed from many geometric experiences. Indeed, a child may progress through more than one grade level before she or he can intelligently use both symbols and precise terminology to communicate an idea or relationship.

While the study of geometry is to be informal in elementary school, experiences should not be haphazard and totally unstructured, however. There should be a sequence of activities that is developed systematically so that some direction and progress become evident to the students and that students' thinking progresses through the van Hiele levels.

In order to make good decisions about the type of activity suitable for students, a teacher must try to discern their geometric thinking level. Engaging students in "open-ended" geometry explorations is one way to accomplish this. The following are examples of open-ended tasks:

- Draw as many different four-sided figures as you can. Write about how they are different and how they are the same.

- Choose a block. Use sticks and marshmallows to make a skeleton model of the shape.

- How many different ways can you connect six square tiles with at least one side attached?

Open-ended tasks such as these allow all students to engage in a common activity. Although their output from these tasks will differ, students will have had a common experience that could profitably be followed by a class discussion. Such sharing enables some students to see relationships, that, left to themselves, they might not have seen.

As students engage in discovery-oriented activities, a teacher can, as she or he mingles with the students, ask questions such as, "What do you notice?" "How would you describe this?" and "Can you make a different one?" Responses can provide insight into a child's thinking level.

Connecting with the World

Geometry is an opportunity to connect mathematics to the child's world. Choose activities that involve the recognition and classification of shapes and figures, and operations on objects that are familiar to the child. A collection of boxes and other containers that the children bring to school can be the focus of discussions about different shapes and figures. Likewise, a "geometry walk" on a city street or on a nature trail can serve to connect geometry work to the environment.

Geometric ideas such as patterns, symmetry, and similarity can be explored in the school environment or neighborhood in both living and non-living things. Upper elementary and middle school students can, for example, explore packaging possibilities for different commodities in response to environmental concerns.

> ### STANDARDS LINK 14-3
> In learning geometry, children need to investigate, experiment, and explore with everyday objects and other physical materials. Exercises that ask children to visualize, draw, and compare shapes in various positions will help develop their spatial sense. Although a facility with the language of geometry is important, it should not be the focus of the geometry program but rather should grow naturally from exploration and experience. (NCTM, 1989, p. 48)

LEARNING ABOUT TOPOLOGY

A child's world view is first topological, that is, the child sees objects as changeable depending on perspective or position (Piaget, Inhelder, & Szeminska, 1960). Gradually, the view changes to recognition of the rigidity of objects despite transformations in space.

Topology is the study of the properties of figures that remain unchanged even under distortions excluding tear-

ing or cutting. Aspects of topology should be included in elementary school geometry programs.

Things That Change and Things That Do Not Change

Robinson (1975) uses a balloon with markings on it and has children indicate which features change and which do not as the balloon is being inflated. For example, a round balloon with facial features drawn on it can serve to exemplify the following properties that do not change when the balloon is inflated:

- Something *inside* something (the eyes in the face)
- Something *not closed* (nose drawn this way)
- Something involving *order* (the nose above the mouth)
- Something *intersecting* (eyelashes with the eyes)
- Something *connected* and something *not connected* (any of the features on the face) (Robinson, 1975, p. 213)

Things that could change when the balloon is being inflated would be that one eye might be larger than the other or the mouth could become nonsymmetrical.

After real balloons have been examined, Robinson suggests that children be shown pictures of balloons with faces drawn on them properly and improperly and asked to tell which picture the balloon could look like (Figure 14-1). This activity can be repeated with other characters drawn on a balloon or piece of sheet rubber. Children can experiment with pieces of sheet rubber that have figures drawn on them to find out how they can transform the figures by stretching (Robinson, 1975).

Place and Order

The concepts of *place, order, betweeness, inside,* and *outside,* can also be studied using real objects or pictures. For example, a teacher could set up classroom furniture, equipment, or children in a way that children could respond to questions in the following manner: "Tom is sitting *on* the rug." "Annette is *behind* the chair." "The geoboards are *inside* the cupboard." "The box of centicubes is *under* the table." Suitable large pictures can replace real objects for similar activities. Children can be taken outside and asked to describe what they notice. Statements showing order like the following should be encouraged: "The fir tree is *after* the maple tree." "The white house is *between* the brick house and the store."

Mazes and Networks

Mazes of suitable complexity can be presented to young children to solve while upper elementary children can

FIGURE 14-1

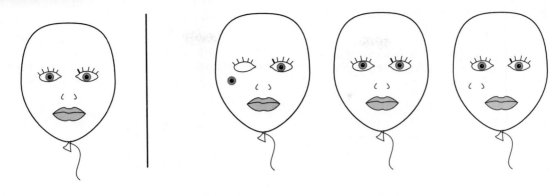

Could the balloon face look like this? If not, what's wrong?*

*Pictures and questions are adapted from G. E. Robinson (1975). "Geometry." In Joseph N. Payne (Ed.), *Mathematics Learning in Early Childhood*. Yearbook. National Council of Teachers of Mathematics. Reston, VA: NCTM. Used with permission.

work with networks. A study of networks will reveal which can be traversed and which cannot. A "traversable" network is one that can be traced in one continuous motion without going over a line twice. Try to discover which types of networks can be transversed by experimenting with figures that have:

- all even vertices (two or four lines meeting at a point);
- all odd vertices (three or five lines meeting at a point);
- only two odd vertices, others even; and
- more than two odd vertices.

Some networks are portrayed in Figure 14-2.

Distortion of Figures

Earlier, activities about distortion of figures were presented using the example of inflating a balloon. Besides

FIGURE 14-2

EXAMPLES OF NETWORKS

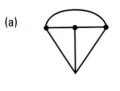 (a)

 (b)

 (c)

 (d)

stretching, distortions can be achieved by twisting, bending, and shrinking. Experimenting with Möbius strips is one type of activity that involves figure distortion by twisting. See Activity 14-1.

LEARNING ABOUT EUCLIDEAN GEOMETRY

Three-Dimensional Shapes

Concurrent with activities of a topological nature, children can begin the study of rigid shapes or ideas related to Euclidean geometry. Children in Kindergarten and Grade 1 should be involved in manipulating different 3-D shapes to find out similarities and differences. When children explore 3-D shapes, they should be asked to describe them: some shapes can roll; some have flat faces; some have pointed corners. The sophistication of the responses will depend on the child's geometric knowledge. Possible descriptions of faces are:

- some faces are round, some have pointed corners;
- some faces are squares, some are triangles;
- some faces have four sides, some have three sides.

Children learn to recognize 2-D figures and name them (van Hiele Level 0) well before they are able to articulate their properties (van Hiele Level 1). Middle school students should be able to classify 3-D shapes and 2-D figures by explaining some relationships between properties within a shape or figure and among shapes or figures (van Hiele Level 2).

✳ ACTIVITY 14-1

EXPLORATIONS WITH MÖBIUS STRIPS

MATERIALS:
Use strips of narrow adding machine tape approximately 1 m in length. Mark each end of the strip with a large dot on the same side.

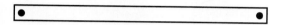

PROCEDURE:
1. Take one strip, twist it once, then glue the ends together (the dots should touch each other).
   * Cut the strip in half following the lengthwide direction. Describe the results.

   * Use another strip and locate a line that is about one-third of the way across the strip. Cut along this line until you reach the "end." Describe what happened.

   * What would happen if you wanted to make one side of a strip one color and the other side another color? Try this and describe what you found.
2. Make Möbius strips with two twists, and conduct cutting and coloring experiments.

STANDARDS LINK 14-4
Geometry helps us represent and describe in an orderly manner the world in which we live. Children are naturally interested in geometry and find it intriguing and motivating; their spatial capabilities frequently exceed their numerical skills, and tapping these strengths can foster an interest in mathematics and improve number understandings and skills. (NCTM, 1989, p. 48)

Polyhedra   Polyhedra are three-dimensional shapes with *faces* made up of polygons, that is, plane figures (two-dimensional) with three, four, five, or more straight sides. In a polyhedron, the lines where the sides of two polygons meet are the *edges* of the shape, and the point where edges meet are the *vertices* of the polyhedron.

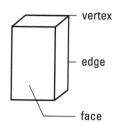

Regular polyhedra.   *Regular polygons* are plane figures with sides that are all the same length and angles of equal measure, as, for example, an equilateral triangle or a square. A *regular polyhedron* is one whose faces consist of the same kind of regular congruent polygons (e.g., all squares or all triangles) with the same number of edges meeting at each vertex of the figure (Billstein, Libeskind, & Lott, 1990). It is possible to construct five regular polyhedra. They are:

Shape	Type and Number of Faces
Tetrahedron	four equilateral triangles
Octahedron	eight equilateral triangles
Icosahedron	twenty equilateral triangles
Hexahedron	six squares
Dodecahedron	twelve regular pentagons

The study of polyhedra is thought to have begun with Pythagoras (582–500 B.C.). Historians relate that Pythagoras probably brought his knowledge of the cube, the tetrahedron, and the octahedron from Egypt, but the icosahedron and the dodecahedron seem to have been developed in his own society. The study of the five regular polyhedra was passed on to the school of Plato, a Greek philosopher (427–347 B.C.), and subsequently these polyhedra became known as the *Platonic Solids* (Figure 14-3).

Semi-regular polyhedra.   Another set of polyhedra, known as the *Archimedean solids,* are semi-regular shapes composed of more than one kind of regular polygons. There are thirteen semi-regular solids, all ascribed to Archimedes (287–212 B.C.), who wrote about the entire set. Semi-regular solids are shown in Figure 14-4.

Truncated and stellated polyhedra.   The study of polyhedra did not terminate with the discovery of the solids. In more modern times, the systematic study of

FIGURE 14-3

PLATONIC SOLIDS

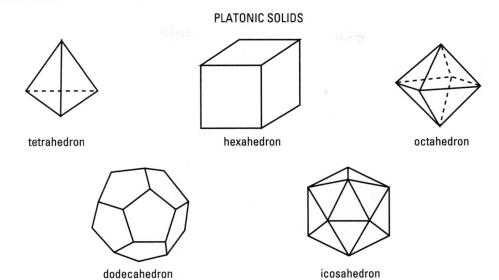

tetrahedron   hexahedron   octahedron

dodecahedron   icosahedron

FIGURE 14-4

SEMI-REGULAR SOLIDS

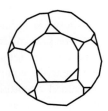

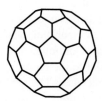

FIGURE 14-5

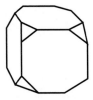

Stella Octangula   Truncated Cube   Stellated Octahedron

solids by the astronomer Johannes Kepler (1571–1630) led him to create other solids through a process called *stellating*. This process consists in building onto solids to form different solids. For example, attaching a tetrahedron to each face of an octahedron produces a solid known as the stella octangula or the eight-pointed star. See Figure 14-5. It also is possible to modify solids by cutting off sections in a systematic way. This process is known as *truncating* and also can lead to the formation of new solids. Figure 14-5 also shows examples of a stellated icosahedron and a truncated cube. Stellating and truncating solids are appropriate activities for upper elementary and middle school students.

FIGURE 14-6

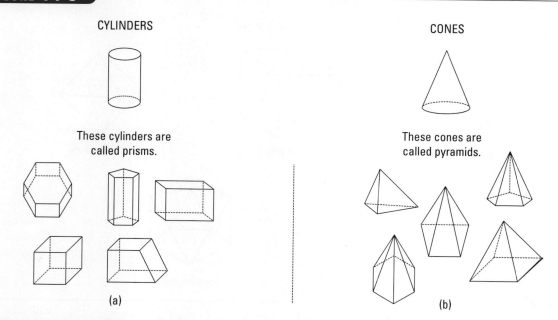

CYLINDERS

These cylinders are
called prisms.

(a)

CONES

These cones are
called pyramids.

(b)

Cylinders. *Cylinders,* such as those shown in Figure 14-6(a), are distinguished from other 3-D shapes by two properties: they have two bases that are congruent and in parallel planes, and all lines (called elements) joining corresponding points on the bases are parallel (Van de Walle, 1998). Cylinders can be right or oblique. A *right cylinder* has its elements perpendicular to the bases.

Prisms are shapes with polygons as bases. The type of base is the name given to the prism: a rectangular prism has rectangles as bases; a cube is a square prism with all faces square. All faces of prisms, except the bases, are rectangles (the one exception is a prism with a rectangular base).

From the description of cylinders, it is seen that prisms fit the description and, therefore, belong to the set of cylinders. However, in everyday usage, we think of cylinders as shapes with two parallel circular bases joined by a curved surface. Prisms usually are thought of as being distinct from the set of cylinders.

Cones. *Cones,* such as those shown in Figure 14-6(b) are 3-D shapes, each with at least one face called the base and a vertex that is outside the base. A line (element) can be drawn from any point on the base to the vertex (Van de Walle, 1998). Cones also are named according to the shape of their base: cones with circular bases are called *circular cones* (commonly known simply as "cones"), whereas cones with polygonal bases are called *pyramids.* Pyramids have all faces as triangles, except the base (the one exception being a triangular-based pyramid). Although pyramids belong, by definition, to the set of cones, usually they are thought about as distinct from cones.

FIGURE 14-7

POLYHEDRON	FACES	VERTICES	EDGES
Tetrahedron			
Cube			
Octahedron			
Triangular Prism			
Square Pyramid			
What relationship do you notice among the shapes?			

Discovering Euler's rule. There exists a special relationship among the number of faces (*F*), vertices (*V*), and edges (*E*) of polyhedra known as Euler's rule. The relationship is such that given the value of two of the three variables (*F, V, E*), one can calculate the value of the third variable. Examine some models and complete a table similar to the one in Figure 14-7; then look for a pattern in the data.

LEARNING ABOUT THREE-DIMENSIONAL SHAPES

> **STANDARDS LINK 14-5**
> Students discover relationships and develop spatial sense by constructing, drawing, measuring, visualizing, comparing, transforming, and classifying geometric figures. Discussing ideas, conjecturing, and testing hypotheses precede the development of more formal summary statements. In the process, definitions become meaningful, relationships among figures are understood, and students are prepared to use these ideas to develop informal arguments. (NCTM, 1989, p. 112)

✳ ACTIVITY 14-2

DESCRIBING SHAPES

MATERIALS:
an assortment of 3-D shapes

PROCEDURE:
1. Find shapes that can roll.
2. Find shapes that cannot roll.
3. How are the shapes different? How are they the same?

✳ ACTIVITY 14-3

CLASSIFYING SHAPES

MATERIALS:
a set of 3-D shapes

PROCEDURE:
1. Put the shapes in two different groups.
2. Tell why the shapes in each group belong together.

Comparing Polyhedra

Children can be given a collection of various 3-D shapes and asked to classify and describe them. Some classification activities are described below. Each activity has children verbalize what they notice about shapes. A teacher should attempt to provide frequent opportunities for students to express geometric ideas orally. Activity 14-2 is appropriate for primary children while Activity 14-5 can be challenging for upper elementary students. This kind of task can provide information about a student's geometric thinking level.

Constructing 3-D Shapes

A study of 3-D shapes should involve students in construction activities. Polyhedra can be constructed using various mediums such as Play-doh and stiff paper. Stu-

✳ ACTIVITY 14-4

COMPARING TWO SHAPES

MATERIALS:
a set of 3-D shapes

PROCEDURE:
1. Choose two shapes and
   • tell how they are alike.
   • tell how they are different.

✳ ACTIVITY 14-5

WRITING ABOUT SHAPES

MATERIALS:
a set of 3-D shapes

PROCEDURE:
1. Examine a shape and write several statements about its characteristics.

✳ ACTIVITY 14-6

CONSTRUCTING 3-D SHAPES WITH PLAY-DOH

MATERIALS:
a set of 3-D shapes

PROCEDURE:
1. Select a 3-D shape.
2. Construct a similar shape using Play-doh.

FIGURE 14-8

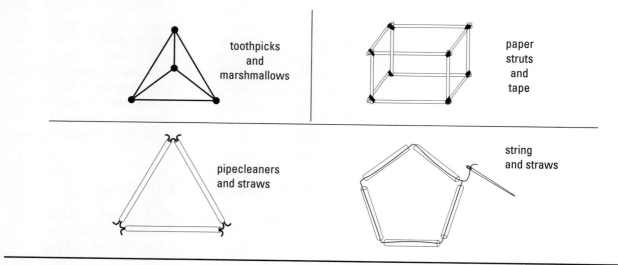

toothpicks
and
marshmallows

paper
struts
and
tape

pipecleaners
and straws

string
and straws

dents can construct *skeleton* or *edge models* of polygons and polyhedra using different materials. These can include:

- toothpicks and miniature marshmallows or small gum drops,
- struts made of rolled paper and taped together,
- straws and pipecleaners or some thin cord (crochet cotton, twine, or elastic thread).

See Figure 14-8.

As students construct polyhedra from nets they have drawn (Activity 14-7), they will learn that the beauty of the finished product is proportional to the care taken in measuring, drawing, and cutting the nets.

A set of polygons with tabs made from stiff paper (Figure 14-9) enables students to engage in investigative

✳ ACTIVITY 14-7

CONSTRUCTING POLYHEDRA FROM NETS

MATERIALS:
nets of shapes drawn on paper

PROCEDURE:
1. Cut out nets of shapes. See Figure 14-9.
2. By folding and taping, construct models of polyhedra.
3. As an alternative, draw 1 cm tabs around some edges of the nets, and then construct models of polyhedra by cutting and pasting.

✳ ACTIVITY 14-8

CONSTRUCTING POLYHEDRA

MATERIALS:
equilateral triangles with tabs, elastics

PROCEDURE:
1. Using a set of equilateral triangles and elastics, try to construct some polyhedra.
2. Can you construct a shape with 4 triangles? with 8 triangles? Can you name the shapes?
3. An icosahedron is made up of 20 equilateral triangles. Try to construct one.

✳ ACTIVITY 14-9

CONSTRUCTING POLYHEDRA: EXPERIMENTING WITH IRREGULAR POLYGONS

MATERIALS:
a set of isosceles triangles with tabs, elastics

PROCEDURE:
1. Try to construct a 3-D shape using a set of isosceles triangles and elastics.
2. Can you construct a shape with 4 triangles? with 8 triangles?
3. Can you construct another shape?
4. Comment on the regularity and nonregularity of the shape(s).

FIGURE 14-9

NETS

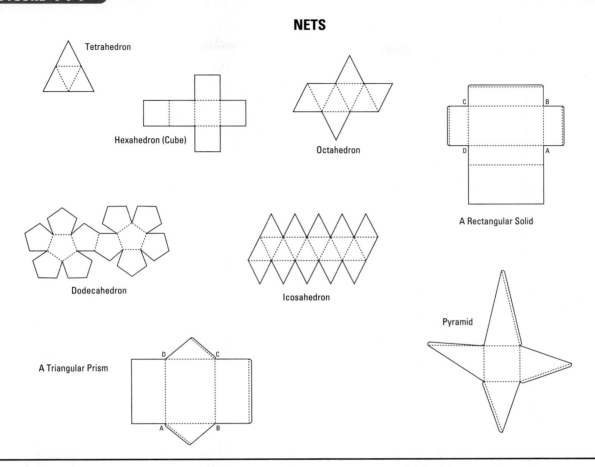

Tetrahedron

Hexahedron (Cube)

Octahedron

A Rectangular Solid

Dodecahedron

Icosahedron

Pyramid

A Triangular Prism

work regarding the composition of polyhedra. If available, the commercial set of *Polydrons* are excellent pieces for explorations in polyhedra. Students can experiment with regular and nonregular polygons and try to construct shapes.

Constructions should be followed by descriptions and comparisons, and discussions about successful and unsuccessful construction attempts. Activities 14-8 through 14-12 are sample investigations students can be asked to do using the materials described in Figure 14-10.

✹ ACTIVITY 14-10

CONSTRUCTING SEMI-REGULAR POLYHEDRA

MATERIALS:
squares and equilateral triangles with tabs, elastics

PROCEDURE:
1. Can you construct a 3-D shape using equilateral triangles and squares with the same side length? Describe your shape.*

2. Compare your shape with an icosahedron. What are the similarities? the differences?

*Students could be provided with a picture of the semi-regular shape that they are to construct.

✹ ACTIVITY 14-11

CONSTRUCTING PYRAMIDS AND PRISMS

MATERIALS:
various polygons with tabs, elastics

PROCEDURE:
1. Using different polygons and elastics, construct three different pyramids.

2. Construct three different prisms.

3. Tell how the pyramids are different; how they are similar.

4. Tell how the prisms are different; how they are similar.

FIGURE 14-10

1. Cut out regular triangles.
2. Draw an 8 mm tab on each side.
3. Punch a hole near each vertex and clip off the point. Fold each tab outward.
4. Use elastic bands to construct 3-D shapes.
5. Cut out squares, and other kinds of polygons. Follow steps 2 through 4.

✳ ACTIVITY 14-12

CONSTRUCTING POLYHEDRA— EXPLORATIONS

MATERIALS:
parallelograms

PROCEDURE:
1. Can you construct a 3-D shape with parallelograms?
2. Describe the shape.
3. Compare it with a rectangular prism.

FIGURE 14-11

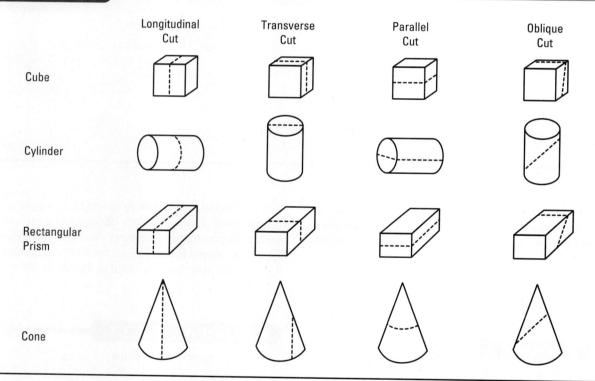

	Longitudinal Cut	Transverse Cut	Parallel Cut	Oblique Cut
Cube				
Cylinder				
Rectangular Prism				
Cone				

Polyhedra can also be constructed with modeling clay. The stroke of a knife through a clay model serves to exemplify a plane passing through at given angles. In this manner, truncated figures can be formed to display different sections of solids. Students can experiment with different cuts on a solid as shown in Figure 14-11. A dissection activity is presented in Activity 14-13.

LEARNING ABOUT TWO-DIMENSIONAL FIGURES

Polygons

Polygons can be described as two-dimensional figures with straight-line segments. Polygons are examples of *simple closed geometric curves* composed of straight line

✳ ACTIVITY 14-13

DISSECTION OF A CUBE

MATERIALS:
modeling clay, knife

PROCEDURE:

1. What various polygons do you get when a plane cuts through a cube? Experiment to find out.

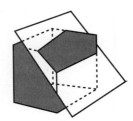

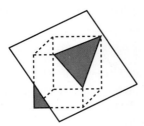

- Are all cross sections of a cube bounded by quadrilaterals?
- What kinds of polygonal regions could be cross sections of a cube?
- Find as many types of cross sections as you can.
- What is the last number of edges that a cross section can have?
- What is the greatest number of edges that a cross section can have?

2. Make predictions for the answers to the following questions. Then, using a clay model of a cube and a knife, verify your predictions. Record both your predictions and your final answers.

3. Make predictions about the cross sections of a rectangular solid, a cone, and a right cylinder. Verify your predictions in the same manner as for the cube.

---

segments. A geometric curve in a plane may be straight or curved. Therefore, parallelograms and circles are both simple closed curves. They are simple curves because no lines in the figure cross each other; only one region is formed. Examples of open and closed curves, and simple and complex curves are shown in Figure 14-12. The line segments of a polygon are *sides* and each point where two line segments meet is a *vertex*.

Polygons can be *convex* or *concave*. A convex polygon is one whose interior angles are all less than 180 degrees, that is, any two points in a figure can be connected by a line segment that will be completely within the figure. A nonconvex polygonal region is concave. See Figure 14-13.

Convex polygons are named according to the number of sides:

Number of Sides	Name of Polygon
3	triangle
4	quadrilateral
5	pentagon
6	hexagon
7	heptagon
8	octagon
9	nonagon
10	decagon

FIGURE 14-12

GEOMETRIC CURVES

(a)

Open Curves

(b)

Simple Closed Curves

(c)

Complex Closed Curves

Triangles Triangles are classified according to their sides and/or angle measure. Figure 14-14 shows a classification of triangles according to angles and sides.

Children's experiences with triangles should be with all types, of different sizes, and in different orientations. A geoboard is a good tool for explorations with plane figures. Constructions on a geoboard can be recorded on dot paper. Activities 14-14 through 14-16 have students explore different triangles.

FIGURE 14-13

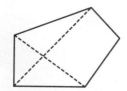

(a)   Convex Polygons.
All angles are less than 180°

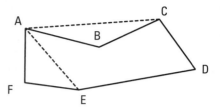

(b)   Concave Polygons
Segment AC is outside the figure.
Interior angle ABC is greater than 180°

The Annenberg/CPB Math and Science Collection

VIDEO LINK 14-2
Geometry and Spatial Sense

Brief Summary: In "Pattern Blocks," teacher Rose Christiansen's second-graders are exploring and making designs with pattern blocks.

1. Why did the teacher begin by having the students explore the pattern blocks? What did she do while the students were exploring?
2. What modes of representation were used in the pattern block game? How did these help develop students' understanding?
3. What role did communication play in this lesson? How did students communicate about shapes?
4. What did students learn by doing the "Cover the Hexagon" activity? What lessons might the teacher do next with this class?

Video Source. Teaching Math: A Video Library, K–4; Tape 8 from The Annenberg/CPB Math and Science Collection.

As a related activity to Activity 14-14, provide students with a set of plane figures as in Figure 14-15. Ask them to find the triangles. Follow this with a class discussion by asking, "In what ways are some alike? Different?"

Quadrilaterals   Like triangles, quadrilaterals are also classified according to their sides and/or angle measure.

A *parallelogram* is a polygon with each pair of opposite sides parallel. A *rectangle* fulfills that requirement and therefore, is also a parallelogram, but it is a special parallelogram that has right angles. A *rhombus* also has opposite sides parallel and is also a special parallelogram because it has equal sides. A *square* also is a parallelogram. A square has four right angles, therefore, it is a rectangle; and it has equal sides so it is a rhombus.

Children will recognize properties of shapes according to their geometric thinking level. For example, primary grade children may only articulate the number of sides and corners; upper elementary children may note that sides are equal or parallel and that angles are right or equal; middle school students will be able to provide

FIGURE 14-14

DIFFERENT TRIANGLES

(a)

equilateral
(all sides equal)

(b)
isosceles
(two sides equal)

(c)
scalene
(no sides equal)

(d)

right triangle
(1 angle = 90 degrees)

(e)

acute triangle
(angles < 90 degrees)

(f)

obtuse triangle
(1 angle > 90 degrees)

formal descriptions and classify figures in "families" such as the family of parallelograms. See Figure 14-16. Concise definitions of quadrilaterals are included in Figure 14-17.

In preparation for an oral activity, display a set of different polygons. Ask the children to choose a figure and examine it. Then ask, "What can you say about the figure?" Activities 14-17 through 14-20 suggest some explorations with polygons, including quadrilaterals.

FIGURE 14-15

FIND THE TRIANGLES

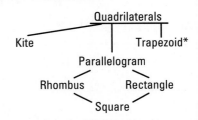

✷ ACTIVITY 14-14

DRAWING DIFFERENT TRIANGLES

MATERIALS:
paper, pencil, and ruler

PROCEDURE:
1. Draw three different triangles.
2. How are they different?
3. How are they alike?
4. Draw others that are different.

FIGURE 14-16

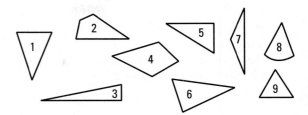

```
                    Quadrilaterals
         Kite            |           Trapezoid*
                   Parallelogram
            Rhombus              Rectangle
                      Square
```

* A trapezoid is sometimes defined as a quadrilateral with only one pair of parallel sides; in this case, a parallelogram is not a trapezoid.

✷ ACTIVITY 14-15

CONSTRUCTING TRIANGLES

MATERIALS:
geoboards, elastics, dot paper

PROCEDURE:
1. Make different triangles on a geoboard.
2. Draw a picture of the triangles you make on dot paper.

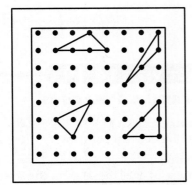

3. Is there one type of triangle that you cannot make on the geoboard? Why?

FIGURE 14-17

Parallelogram	A quadrilateral with opposite sides parallel.
Rectangle	A parallelogram with 90-degree angles.
Square	A rectangle with equal sides.
Rhombus	A parallelogram with all sides equal.
Trapezoid	A quadrilateral with at least one pair of parallel sides.
Isosceles Trapezoid	A trapezoid with 2 nonparallel sides equal.
Kite	A quadrilateral with 2 pairs of adjacent sides equal.

✳ ACTIVITY 14-16

DESCRIBING TRIANGLES

MATERIALS:
a geoboard

PROCEDURE:

1. Make different triangles like these on a geoboard, then draw them on dot paper.

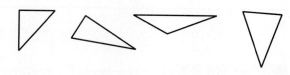

2. Describe each triangle.

The Annenberg/CPB Math and Science Collection

VIDEO LINK 14-3
Geometry and Spatial Sense

Brief Summary: In "Shapes from Squares," the second- and third-graders in teacher Marco Ramirez's class are making different shapes by folding a square. Their task is to make as many different shapes as they can, but they can fold the paper only on a pre-folded crease.

1. Describe how Mr. Ramirez communicates with students to help further their understanding. How does he help students who are "stuck"? How does he support the development of students' understanding?
2. How do partners help each other?
3. What was done to support the mathematics learning of students who still are learning English?
4. What is the teacher's role in this lesson? What do you think his objectives were for this lesson?
5. What were you able to learn about children's understanding from this lesson? What lessons might the teacher do next with this class?

Video Source. Teaching Math: A Video Library, K–4; Tape 8 from The Annenberg/CPB Math and Science Collection.

Diagonals. Exploring the number of diagonals in different figures is another aspect of the study of polygons. A *diagonal* is a line segment joining any two nonadjacent vertices of a figure with the line segment completely in the interior of the figure (Henderson & Collier, 1973).

✳ ACTIVITY 14-17

RECTANGLES

MATERIALS:
polygons as shown below

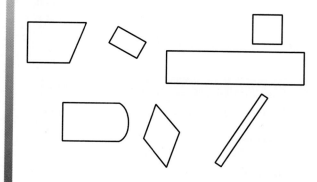

PROCEDURE:

1. Which of the figures are rectangles?
2. Tell why you think the non-rectangles are not rectangles.

✳ ACTIVITY 14-18

COMPARING POLYGONS

MATERIALS:
a set of polygons

PROCEDURE:

1. Select a polygon. Write about the figure, mentioning as many characteristics as you can.
2. Choose another polygon and write about how it is different from and how it is similar to the first one.

✳ ACTIVITY 14-19

DESCRIBING POLYGONS

MATERIALS:
a set of five different polygons

PROCEDURE:

1. Make a list of all the different characteristics you notice as you examine the figures.
2. Which polygons have one or more characteristics in common?

✳ ACTIVITY 14-20

NAMING FIGURES

MATERIALS:
the twelve figures shown below

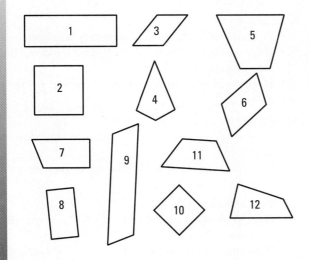

PROCEDURE:
1. Examine the twelve figures.
2. How many figures can you name? Can you give more than one name for some figures?

For example, in the diagram below, the line segment FD is a diagonal, whereas the line segment AC is not. Activity 14-21 is about diagonals.

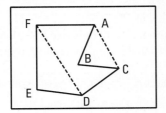

Circles A *circle* is a plane figure that has all its points the same distance from a fixed point called the *center* of the circle. The distance from the center to the edge of the circle is called a *radius,* and a segment connecting two points on the edge of the circle is a *chord.* A chord passing through the center of the circle is a *diameter;* the

✳ ACTIVITY 14-21

FINDING DIAGONALS

MATERIALS:
a set of convex polygons with 4, 5, 6, 7, 8, 9, and 10 sides drawn on paper

PROCEDURE:
1. Find the number of diagonals in a four-sided polygon; in a five-sided polygon; in a ten-sided polygon.
2. Look for a pattern that tells the number of diagonals in an *n*-sided polygon.

length of the circle (distance around) is the *circumference.*

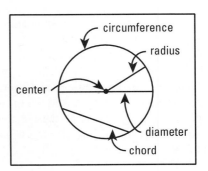

LEARNING ABOUT SYMMETRY, CONGRUENCE, AND SIMILARITY

Symmetry

The idea of *symmetry* can first be introduced to children with examples from nature, art, and pictures of familiar objects. Folding is a means of testing for line symmetry. For example, by folding, one will find out that a square has four lines of symmetry, a rectangle has two lines of symmetry, while a parallelogram has none.

Figures can be classified according to the number of lines of symmetry in each. A *line of symmetry* separates a figure into two congruent parts such that each point in one part is reflected in the other part. For polygons, lines of symmetry can be of three types: a line connecting two vertices; a line connecting a vertex to a midpoint of a side; or a line connecting the midpoints of two sides.

A mira is a good instrument to test for lines of symmetry in a figure. A mira is a piece of colored plexiglass that allows one to view the reflection of a figure through the glass rather than on it, as with a mirror.

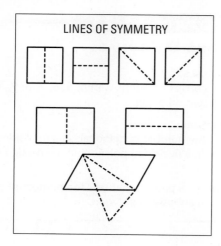

Students can be asked to create symmetrical designs with pattern blocks, construct some symmetrical figures on a geoboard, or draw some on graph paper. Activities 14-22 and 14-23 are about creating symmetrical figures using pattern blocks and graph paper.

The following eight numbered activities have students examine familiar objects (leaves, windows), pictures of familiar objects (magazine pictures), and geometric figures for symmetry. Students are asked to construct symmetrical pictures and figures. In all these activities, it is important to listen to students as they tell what they observe and what they are doing.

1. Symmetry
   • Provide students with a set of leaves to examine.
   • Have them discuss what they observe. Listen for observations about "sameness" within a shape

("I think this side is the same as this side because. . . .")

2. Symmetry
   • Provide students with a set of pictures from magazines, some symmetrical, others not.
   • Have students examine them, looking for some that are the same on two sides of a central line.
   • Have students tell what they notice.

3. Symmetry
   • Provide a set of pictures of homes or windows.
   • Have students examine them to find windows that are symmetrical.
   • Have them tell why they think some are not symmetrical.

4. Symmetry
   • Have students construct symmetrical figures on a geoboard.
   • Have them tell how they know the figures are symmetrical.

5. Line Symmetry
   • Have students draw different figures on paper that have line symmetry.
   • Have them cut out the figures and test for symmetry by folding.

6. Line Symmetry
   • Provide students with a set of different polygons drawn on paper.
   • Have them examine the figures for lines of symmetry and tell where each line of symmetry is.
   • Listen to find out how students describe each line of symmetry in a figure.

7. Symmetry
   • Tell students to draw figures on paper with only one line of symmetry.
   • Ask, "Can you draw figures with two lines of symmetry? Can you draw one with three lines of symmetry? With more than three lines of symmetry?"

8. Drawing Triangles and Quadrilaterals
   Tell students to
   • draw a triangle with only one line of symmetry.
   • draw a triangle with more than one line of symmetry.
   • draw a triangle with no lines of symmetry.
   Repeat the above steps with quadrilaterals.

✴ ACTIVITY 14-22

MAKING SYMMETRICAL DESIGNS WITH PATTERN BLOCKS

MATERIALS:
pattern blocks

PROCEDURE:
1. Select a triangle and surround it with triangles and squares. How many lines of symmetry does the figure have?

2. Select a square and surround it with triangles. How many lines of symmetry does the figure have?

3. Select one of the blocks and surround it with other blocks to make regular figures. Count the lines of symmetry each of the figures have.*

*Idea from Eperson, 1982a.

Upper elementary and middle school students can study 3-D shapes for planes of symmetry. A 3-D shape has *plane symmetry* if a plane passing through the figure bisects it such that every point of the figure on one side of the plane has a reflection image on the other side of the plane. Activity 14-24 explores planes of symmetry.

✷ ACTIVITY 14-23

SYMMETRICAL PATTERNS ON GRAPH PAPER

MATERIALS:
graph paper

PROCEDURE:
1. Draw 3-by-3 squares on graph paper. Shade three of the small squares so that the figure created has one line of symmetry. Two examples are shown here.

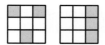

2. How many different patterns with one line of symmetry can you make by shading in three small squares?

3. Can you make patterns with two lines of symmetry?

4. Shade in four small squares and make figures with one line of symmetry; with two lines of symmetry.

5. Can you make figures with more than two lines of symmetry?

6. Compare your work with your classmates.*

*Idea from Eperson, 1982b.

Some 3-D shapes and 2-D figures have *rotational symmetry*. A shape is said to have rotational symmetry if, when rotated about a point for an amount less than 360°, the rotated shape matches the original shape. For example, a square has 90°, 180°, and 270° rotational symmetry (Figure 14-18). Students can be asked to examine shapes and figures for rotational symmetry. For example, in explorations with figures, they will find that some figures have rotational symmetry but no line symmetry (e.g., a parallelogram), some have line symmetry but not rotational symmetry (e.g., an isos-

celes triangle), and that regular polygons have both line and rotational symmetry, whereas, some figures have neither.

Congruence and Similarity

Congruent figures are those that have the same size and shape, that is, all corresponding angles and the length of corresponding sides are equal. Superimposing figures is one way to test for congruency. Another is by measuring sides and angles.

✷ ACTIVITY 14-24

PLANES OF SYMMETRY

MATERIALS:
a cube

PROCEDURE:
Consider a cube.

1. How many horizontal planes of symmetry does a cube have?

2. How many vertical planes of symmetry does a cube have?

3. How many planes of symmetry pass through each pair of opposite edges?

4. How many planes of symmetry can you find for a cube?

Consider other solids.

5. Has the tetrahedron the same number of planes of symmetry as the cube?

6. Does an octahedron, an icosahedron, or a dodecahedron have planes of symmetry?

7. Record your findings on a chart. Compare your findings with those of some classmates.

FIGURE 14-18

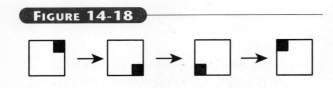

Similar figures have the same shape but not necessarily the same size. If two figures are congruent, they are also similar. Similar polygons have equal angles and proportional sides. Examples of similar figures can be obtained by enlarging or reducing a picture on a photocopying machine. Congruent and similar figures can be constructed on a geoboard and on graph paper.

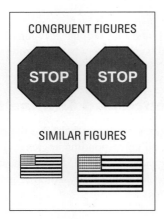

CONGRUENT FIGURES

STOP STOP

SIMILAR FIGURES

LEARNING ABOUT TRANSFORMATIONAL GEOMETRY

Rigid Transformations

The idea that objects can be moved from one position to another without changing shape and size is a fundamental part of the study of transformation geometry. Movements of an object where the object itself is not distorted or changed in any way are called *rigid transformations.* Rigid transformations can be contrasted with topological transformations (e.g., stretching) in which the shape and size of objects change.

Transformation geometry (also called motion geometry) can be introduced by discussing different movements observed in nature and in the environment such as a falling leaf, an airplane taking off, a boat moving on a river, or a door being opened.

Elementary students study three fundamental types of rigid transformations: translations, reflections, and rotations. Children usually name these motions "slides," "flips," and "turns," respectively. A *translation* is a movement along a straight line. It has direction and dis-

tance. The direction can be horizontal, vertical, or oblique. A *reflection* is the movement of a figure about a line outside the figure, on a side of the figure or intersecting with a vertex. A *rotation* is the movement of a figure around a point. The turning point may be inside the figure, on the figure, or outside the figure. See Figure 14-19.

Materials used in the following ten transformation geometry activities include a mira, paper cutouts, figure templates, tracing paper, attribute blocks, pattern blocks, and a geoboard.

1. Constructing Reflections
   * Provide students with a set of attribute blocks.
   * Have them construct a figure such as a house or animal.
   * Then have them construct a horizontal and vertical reflection of the figure.

2. Transformations on a Geoboard
   * Ask students to make a figure on a geoboard.
   * Show a slide of the figure; a flip; a turn.

3. Drawing Reflection Images
   * Provide students with a mira and some figures on a page.
   * Have them draw reflection images about given lines.

4. Modeling Transformations
   * Using several paper cutouts of nonsymmetrical figures such as a boat or a bird, have students explore different motions on their desks.
   * For example, have them demonstrate different slides (horizontal, vertical, oblique).
   * Have them record their work.

5. Constructing Reflections
   * Provide students with an irregular figure.
   * Have them draw the figure.
   * Then have them draw the figure showing a horizontal reflection; a vertical reflection; an oblique reflection.

6. Constructing Rotations
   * Provide students with a paper cutout of a nonsymmetrical figure such as an animal.
   * Have students explore with different rotations on their desks.

In time, students should be able to demonstrate a rotation about a point on a figure, a rotation about a point outside a figure, and a rotation about a point inside a figure.

7. Constructing Rotations
   * Provide students with a template of a small nonsymmetrical figure.
   * Have them trace the figure and then draw a half turn; a quarter turn clockwise; a quarter turn counterclockwise; combinations of rotations.

FIGURE 14-19

TRANSLATIONS (Slides)

horizontal slide

vertical slide

oblique slide

REFLECTIONS (Flips)

reflection about a line on
the figure

reflection about a line
not on the figure

reflection line intersects
with a vertex

ROTATIONS (Turns)

turning point
inside figure

turning point
on the figure

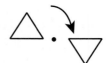
turning point
outside figure

8. Constructing Rotations
   - Direct students to make a figure with pattern blocks.
   - Have them make one that is a quarter turn of the first figure; a half turn; a three-quarter turn.

9. Constructing a Pattern Showing Transformations
   - Provide each student with a 4-by-4 square grid with each small square approximately 5 cm and a cut-out of a small figure.
   - Ask them to trace the figure in each square following a pattern of rigid motions (for example, horizontal reflections and vertical half turns).

10. Constructing a Pattern Showing Transformations
    - Provide each student with a figure to use as a template (or use tracing paper)
    - Invite students to create borders for a bulletin board by using translations, reflections, and rotations of a figure.

At the middle school level, students can conduct explorations with combinations of motions. Explorations to pursue include:

1. Draw any Figure A and then make two successive translations to produce Figures B and C. Compare Figures A and C. Is the result of a single translation different from the result of two successive translations? Why?

2. Draw any Figure A and then make two successive flips to produce Figures B and C. Compare Figures A and C. Are the results the same as for translations? Why not?

3. Compare the results of other successive motions.
   - a slide followed by a flip and a flip followed by a slide.
   - a turn followed by a flip and a flip followed by a turn.
   - other combinations and their reverse.

Write about your findings.

LEARNING ABOUT TESSELLATIONS

When considering *tessellations,* one generally thinks of a flat region being covered with repetitions of the same figure without any overlapping. A floor covered with square tiles is an example of a tessellation. Young children can be provided with a sufficient number of different types of regular figures and invited to explore which figures can cover a region (Activity 14-25). Triangles, convex quadrilaterals, and regular hexagons will tessellate by themselves, as well as varied kinds of irregular shapes (Figure 14-20). Students can be challenged to explore why some figures tessellate and not others. The exploration could begin with triangles by asking the question: "Will all types of triangles tessellate?" Next, the questions "Why do all rectangles tessellate?" and "Will all convex quadrilaterals tessellate?" can be explored. Further investigations can be done with other polygons and with combinations of figures; also, with modified polygons to create Escher-type designs. Explorations in Escher-type tessellations offer students opportunities to extend their understanding of symmetries, such as translation, reflection, rotation, and glide-reflection symmetry (Haak, 1976). Figure 14-21 shows the process of creating a simple Escher-type tessellation. Tessellation activities are described in Activities 14-25 through 14-28.

DEVELOPING SPATIAL SENSE

Spatial sense involves a visualization and an orientation factor (Owens, 1990). *Visualization* is the ability to mentally picture how objects appear under some rigid motion or other transformation. *Orientation* includes the ability to note positions of objects and to maintain accurate perception of the objects under different orientation. Research reveals that the two types of ability do not always reside within the same individual and that, generally, boys are better than girls on tests of spatial abilities (Owens, 1990).

Beginning at the primary level, geometry activities should aim to develop children's spatial abilities. Many of the activities described in this chapter can contribute to the development of visual perception. Activities involving tangrams and polyominoes and describing figures and dissecting figures help to develop spatial sense.

FIGURE 14-20

TESSELLATIONS

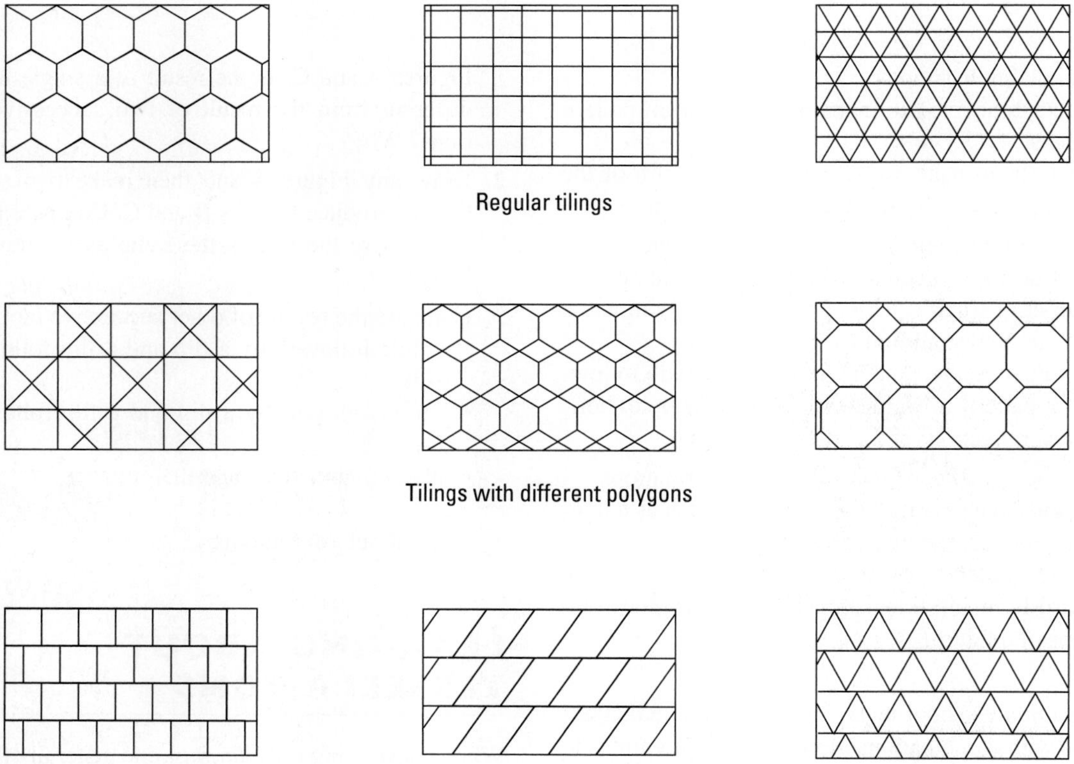

Regular tilings

Tilings with different polygons

Tilings that are not edge-to-edge

FIGURE 14-21

Constructing Escher-type Tessellations

Step 1. Select a polygon, for example, a square.

Step 2. Select a transformation, for example, a rotation. Label the vertices and sides of the square. Rotating the square four times around vertex C produces the diagram at the right. One can see that sides 2 and 3 fit together. If the four square pattern was translated horizontally and vertically, it would show that sides 1 and 4 fit together.

Step 3. Modify the square. The example shows that the piece removed from side 1 has been attached to side 4. Sides 2 and 3 could similarly be modified. The modified square has the same area as the original square and it will tessellate in the same manner as did the original square.

Step 4. Invite students to use their ingenuity to make cuts on a square to produce a tessellation. An example follows.

Source for diagrams: Haak (1976)

✷ ACTIVITY 14-25

TILING A FLOOR

MATERIALS:
a number of equilateral triangles, squares, and regular pentagons, hexagons, and octagons with sides of equal length

PROCEDURE:
1. Pretend that the shapes are ceramic tiles. What kind of shape could you use to tile a bathroom floor using only one kind of shape?
2. Could you tile a floor using two different shapes?
3. Draw pictures of different tiled floors.

✷ ACTIVITY 14-26

CONSTRUCTING TILING PATTERNS

MATERIALS:
a set of rectangular-shaped tiles in 2 colors

PROCEDURE:
1. Use the tiles to create an interesting pattern for a bathroom floor. Use tiles in three colors; four colors.

✷ ACTIVITY 14-27

CONSTRUCTING A QUILT BLOCK

MATERIALS:
sixteen 8 cm squares (8 white and 8 of a solid color) and a piece of paper 24 cm square

PROCEDURE:
1. Cut each square along one diagonal to form two congruent triangles.
2. Arrange the triangles in an interesting pattern to create a "block" pattern for a quilt.
3. When you have decided on a pattern, glue the triangles on a piece of paper.
4. Display your finished product on a bulletin board or on a large wall as a "quilt."

QUILT BLOCKS

✳ ACTIVITY 14-28

TESSELLATIONS

MATERIALS:
graph paper

PROCEDURE:
1. Draw an outline of a figure on the graph paper that will tessellate.

2. Color or shade in the figure.

3. By alternating white and color, create an interesting tiling pattern with the figure.

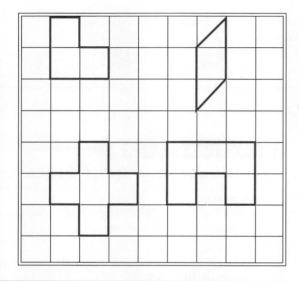

STANDARDS LINK 14-6

Spatial understandings are necessary for interpreting, understanding, and appreciating our inherently geometric world. Insights and intuitions about two- and three-dimensional shapes and their characteristics, the interrelationships of shapes, and the effects of changes to shapes are important aspects of spatial sense. Children who develop a strong sense of spatial relationships and who master the concepts and language of geometry are better prepared to learn number and measurement ideas, as well as other advanced mathematical topics. (NCTM, 1989, p. 48)

Tangram Puzzles

A *tangram* is a seven-piece puzzle consisting of five triangles, one square, and one parallelogram cut from a square and that can be arranged to create different shapes.

See Figure 14-22. Students can be asked to compare the tangram pieces:

- Compare the small triangle to the two larger triangles.
- Compare the small triangle to the parallelogram.
- Compare the square to the largest triangle.

STANDARDS LINK 14-7

Spatial sense is an intuitive feel for one's surroundings and the objects in them. To develop spatial sense, children must have many experiences that focus on geometric relationships; the direction, orientation, and perspectives of objects in space; the relative shapes and sizes of figures and objects; and how a change in shape relates to a change in size. These experiences depend on a child's ability to follow directions that use words like *above*, *below*, and *behind* and to progress to such activities as using a computer to reproduce a pattern-block design. (NCTM, 1989, p. 49)

Such comparisons can elicit fraction language as "the square is one half the size of a large triangle" or "a small triangle is one fourth the size of a large triangle."

A common activity is to use the pieces to construct or "cover" different figures as in Figure 14-22. Other activities can involve students constructing geometric figures with some or all the pieces as in the following examples:

- Use two tangram pieces to make a square. Can you make a square with two other pieces? With four pieces? With all seven pieces?
- Can you make a parallelogram with two pieces? With three pieces?
- How many different trapezoids can you make?
- Can you make a pentagon? A hexagon?

Students can be asked to keep a record of the different geometric figures they construct and how many tangram pieces they used.

Polyominoes

Polyominoes are arrangements of different numbers of squares: a triomino is constructed with three squares, a tetromino has four squares, a pentomino has five squares, etc. In Activity 14-29, students create figures using triominoes. The study can be extended to tetrominoes through, for example, the four-stamp problem.

FIGURE 14-22

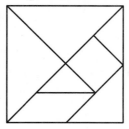

Tangram Puzzle Pieces

Use the tangram pieces to make the following figures.

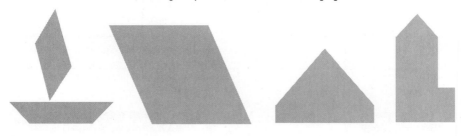

FOUR-STAMP PROBLEM

Stamps are sometimes printed in sheets of 100 stamps (10 rows of 10 stamps). How many different four-stamp arrangements could you buy?

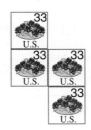

Pentominoes and hexominoes can be explored in the context of a packing box problem as described in Activity 14-30. Activities 14-31 and 14-32 also help to develop spatial sense. The twelve pentominoes that can be constructed (Activity 14-32) are depicted in Figure 14-23.

Describing Figures

An activity that has students verbalize what they visualize is to have them describe a figure through feeling. The students can be grouped in pairs and provided with an irregular figure cut from poster board. One student holds the figure under the desk cover (neither student has seen the figure) and through feeling it, describes the figure to a partner who attempts to draw the figure. The roles of de-

scribing and drawing can be interchanged. The exercise can be simple or complex depending on the figure.

The Annenberg/CPB Math and Science Collection

VIDEO LINK 14-4
Geometry and Spatial Sense

Brief Summary: In "Hexominoes," teacher Nan Sepeda asks her fifth-graders to make as many hexominoes (shapes made from six squares) as they can, and to decide how to categorize them.

1. How did students make hexominoes? What modes of representation did the students use?

2. What are the different ways that students sorted their hexominoes?

3. How did Ms. Sepeda react to the group that sorted their hexominoes by their resemblance to letters? How else might that situation have been handled?

4. What is the teacher's role in this lesson? What do you think her objectives were for this lesson?

What were you able to learn about children's understanding from this lesson? What lessons might the teacher do next with this class?

Video Source. Teaching Math: A Video Library, K–4; Tape 8 from The Annenberg/CPB Math and Science Collection.

✳ ACTIVITY 14-29

TRIOMINOES

MATERIALS:
a set of small ceramic or paper square tiles

PROCEDURE:

1. Try to visualize which of the figures below can be made from two triominoes. Test your responses.

2. Use your triominoes to make figures that can be covered with three triominoes. Draw the outline of the figures on graph paper.

3. Draw the outline of some 9 square-unit figures on graph paper that cannot be covered with 3 triominoes. Ask a classmate to "solve your puzzles."*

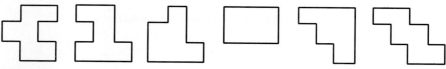

*Idea from Eperson, 1983.

✳ ACTIVITY 14-30

PACKING BOX PROBLEM

MATERIALS:
graph paper

PROCEDURE:

1. Imagine you are a box manufacturer and you want to ship boxes flattened out. How many possible ways can you do this?

   • Case I. The boxes you are presently making are without tops. If each side is a square, a box flattened out could resemble the pattern shown below.

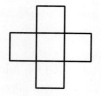

   Can you think of other patterns? Use graph paper and draw all possible patterns that can be made with five squares. (Two patterns are the same if they can be covered by the same paper cutout.) How many of your patterns fold into boxes? Draw a set of "box makes" for display.

   • Case II. Now think about patterns for boxes with tops. Draw as many patterns as you can for six-sided squares. How many of the patterns are nets of cubes? Draw a set of "nets of cubes" for display.

✳ ACTIVITY 14-31

QUADROMINOES

MATERIALS:
interlocking cubes

PROCEDURE:

1. Construct different arrangements using only three cubes.

2. How many did you find?

3. Now construct as many different arrangements as you can using four cubes (quadrominoes). Arrangements that are reflections or rotations of another are not considered different.

4. How many did you find?

✳ ACTIVITY 14-32

CONSTRUCTING PENTOMINOES

MATERIALS:
five square tiles, graph paper

PROCEDURE:

1. Use the tiles to construct different arrangements of five squares. Each tile has to connect with other tiles along a full side.

2. Draw the different arrangements on graph paper.

Another activity is to have a figure drawn on a card and to ask one student to describe the figure to a partner who draws the figure as she or he visualizes what is described (Sgroi, 1990). Another type of visualization is to provide students with a complex figure and ask them to find different figures within it. See Figures 14-24 and 14-25.

The activities described in Figures 14-26 and 14-27 are two kinds of activities that help develop visualization and orientation abilities.

Dissection Motion Operations

Spatial sense can be developed through dissection motion operations on figures. A *dissection motion operation* (DMO) is the operation of partitioning and then dissecting a figure for the purpose of rearranging the pieces

FIGURE 14-23

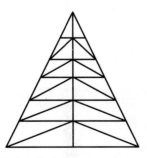

FIGURE 14-24

How many triangles do you
see in the figure?

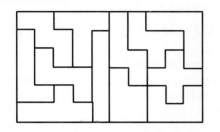

FIGURE 14-25

How many different-sized
squares can you make on a
5-by-5 geoboard?

FIGURE 14-26

VISUALIZING CUBES

1. Let us say that a 1-by-1-by-1 cube has "order 1." Suppose that you were to dip such a cube into a can of paint. How many sides of the cube would be covered with paint?

2. Now imagine a 2-by-2-by-2 cube or a cube of order 2. Again, suppose you dip the cube into a can of paint and after the paint has dried, you sawed along each of the lines of its faces to obtain eight smaller cubes. How many of the small cubes have six sides painted? How many of the small cubes have five sides painted? Four sides painted? Three sides? Two sides? One side? No side?

3. BIG DIP! Now consider a cube of order three. Once again, you follow the procedure of dipping and sawing. Can you answer the questions in part 2 for a cube of order three?

FIGURE 14-27

VISUALIZING PAPER UNFOLDED

Take large rectangular pieces of paper, fold each one, and cut holes as indicated in the diagrams.
------ indicates a fold.

Draw the picture of the paper as it would look when unfolded.

1.

2.

3.

4.

(Rahim & Sawada, 1986). DMO has not commonly been a part of geometry programs, although children use such motions spontaneously when partitioning figures to attain equal-sized parts (Pothier & Sawada, 1990).

Subsequent to Activity 14-34, students could be challenged to "prove" that the area of non-congruent parts of figures, as in the figures shown here, are equal by DMO.

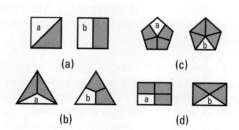

(a)   (c)

(b)   (d)

✳ ACTIVITY 14-33

DISSECTING FIGURES

MATERIALS:
several paper rectangles, the same size, for each student

PROCEDURE:
1. Select one rectangle.

2. Cut it in two pieces so that the pieces can be put together again to make a large triangle.

3. Cut other rectangles in two pieces to make
   • a parallelogram
   • a rhombus
   • a right-angled triangle
   • a trapezoid
   • other figures.

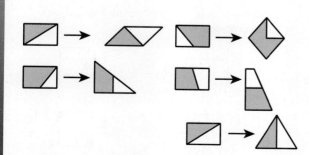

✳ ACTIVITY 14-34

DISSECTING SQUARES

MATERIALS:
scissors, paper

PROCEDURE:
1. Cut a square in four parts to make
   • a rhombus
   • a parallelogram
   • other figures.

LEARNING ABOUT COORDINATE GEOMETRY

Upper elementary schoolchildren are introduced to notions of coordinate geometry. A first introduction could be with real-life situations such as finding a seat in a theatre or sports arena, or a car in a parking lot. Rows and columns could be labeled with letters and numbers (e.g., Row F, Seat 8) and later changed to numbers only (e.g., Row 6, Column 8). The ordered pair notation (6,8) can be presented by drawing graphs. Students may connect locating points on a coordinate grid with the popular game *Battleship*. Activities for students can consist of drawing figures on a coordinate grid by plotting points from sets of given ordered pairs or by identifying points on a grid figure (Activities 14-35 and 14-36). Geoboards and pegboards are good materials for coordinate geometry activities.

✳ ACTIVITY 14-35

NAMING POINTS ON A GRID

MATERIALS:
a grid with points labeled as in the figure

PROCEDURE:
1. Name the points labeled A, B, C, D, and E.

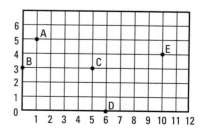

✳ ACTIVITY 14-36

LOCATING POINTS ON A GRID

MATERIALS:
graph paper

PROCEDURE:
1. Mark off a grid in at least 6-by-6 squares on the graph paper.
2. Label the axes.
3. Locate and label the following points on your grid. A (2,4); B (3,3); C (0,5); D (5,3); E (4,0)

LEARNING ABOUT CURVE STITCHING

String sculpture or curve stitching is the process of connecting sequences of points with straight lines in such a manner that curves are formed. The materials required are poster board or stiff paper, a needle, and colored embroidery thread. Steps for creating designs with angles and circles follow.

Angles
- Draw an acute angle on a square piece of poster board. On each arm of the angle, mark off 1 cm intervals. Label the points with a pencil as in the diagram.
- With a needle, punch holes along the arms at each interval.
- Thread a needle and tape the end of the thread on the underside of the card. Pull the needle up at Point A and then down at 1. Cross over to 2 underneath and pull up at 2, then go down at Point B. Then up at Point C, down at 3, up at 4, down at Point D, and so on.

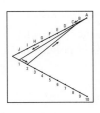 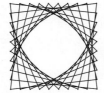 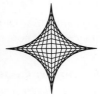

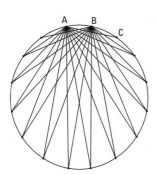

FIGURE 14-28

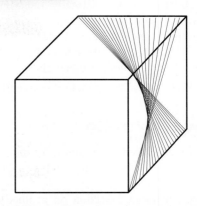

Circles
- Divide the circumference of a circle into twenty-four (or more) equal parts.
- Using needle and thread, begin at Point A, cross over and push down at Point B, then up at Point C, over to and down at Point A, up at Point D, over to and down at Point A, up at Point E, and so on.
- Upon completion, each point will be joined with every other point.

Varied designs can be constructed by changing the angle size and the distance between points. It is also possible to create three-dimensional curve stitching sculptures as shown in Figure 14-28.

The art of string sculpture can provide insights into relationships between lines and curves. It also exemplifies the aesthetics of geometry. String sculpture activities can be integrated with art classes.

CONCLUSION

In this chapter, introductory aspects of different geometries have been presented. Elementary students should be introduced to ideas of each type in an informal manner. As children's geometric thinking progresses, the topics should be discussed in a progressively more formal manner. The development of spatial abilities should be a focus of geometry activities at all grade levels. Teachers should pay particular attention toward helping students progress on the van Hiele levels of geometric thinking.

For Your Journal

When you have finished studying this chapter, reflect on these questions in your math journal:

1. Give an example of an activity at each of the five van Hiele levels of geometric thought.

2. Visit an elementary school classroom and a middle school classroom and informally interview several students to assess their understanding of geometry. Describe their understandings and misconceptions. Where would you place their thinking related to the van Hiele levels of geometric thought?

3. Explain how to develop spatial sense in children.

For Your Portfolio

When you have finished studying this chapter, complete these activities to include in your professional portfolio:

1. Examine a textbook's section on geometry and describe it in relation to the van Hiele levels.

2. Write a lesson plan to introduce a geometry concept of your choice to students at van Hiele Level 0. Then write a lesson to introduce a related topic to students at van Hiele Level 1.

3. Write a lesson plan to help children develop spatial sense.

Resources for Teachers

Children's Books

Burns, M. (1994). *The greedy triangle.* New York: Scholastic, Inc.

Ehlert, L. (1989). *Color zoo.* New York: J. B. Lippincott.

Ringgold, F. (1991). *Tar beach.* New York: Scholastic, Inc.

Tompert, A. (1990). *Grandfather Tang's story: A tale told with tangrams.* New York: Crown Publishers, Inc.

Books on Geometry

Del Grande, J. (1993). *Geometry and spatial sense: Curriculum evaluation standards for school mathematics addenda series grade K–6.* Reston, VA: National Council of Teachers of Mathematics.

Creative Publications. (1994). *Beyond activities project: mathematics replacement curriculum: Polyhedra-ville.* Mountain View, CA: Creative Publications.

Geddes, D. (1992). *Geometry in the middle grades: Curriculum evaluation standards for school mathematics addenda series grade 5–8.* Reston, VA: National Council of Teachers of Mathematics.

Picciotto, H. (1984). *Pentomino activities, lessons, and puzzles.* Sunnyvale, CA: Creative Publications.

Rectanus, C. (1994). *Math by all means: Geometry grade 2.* Sausalito, CA: Math Solutions Publications.

Rectanus, C. (1994). *Math by all means: Geometry grade 3.* Sausalito, CA: Math Solutions Publications.

Seymour, D., & Britton, J. (1989). *Introduction to tessellations.* Palo Alto, CA: Dale Seymour Publications.

Walker, K., Reak, C., & Stewart, K. (1995). *20 thinking questions for geoboards grades 3–6.* Mountain View, CA: Creative Publications.

Walker, K., Reak, C., & Stewart, K. (1995). *20 thinking questions for geoboards grades 6–8.* Mountain View, CA: Creative Publications.

Winter, M., Lappan, G., Phillips, E., & Fitzgerald, W. (1986). *Middle grades mathematics project: Spatial visualization.* Menlo Park, CA: Addison-Wesley Publishing Company.

Links to the Internet

Math Forum: Tessellation Tutorials

http://forum.swarthmore.edu/sum95/suzanne/tess.intro.html

Contains information about tessellations, including what they are and how to create them.

Geoboards in the Classroom

http://forum.swarthmore.edu/trscavo/geoboards/

Contains a unit on exploring the length and area of two-dimensional geometric figures using geoboards.

Tangrams

http://forum.swarthmore.edu/trscavo/tangrams.html

Contains a unit on finding the area of polygons without employing formulas by using tangrams.

Virtual Polyhedra

http://www.li.net/~george/virtual-polyhedra/vp.html

Contains information about polyhedra, including what they are and how to make paper models of polyhedra.

Explorer: Geometry

http://explorer.scrtec.org/explorer/explorer-db/browse/static/Mathematics/browse/f66.html

Contains many lessons on and lists of other resources for geometry.

CHAPTER 15

Developing Measurement Concepts and Skills

Key Concepts

- Standard units of measure
- Nonstandard units of measure
- Meaning of *length, area, volume, capacity, mass, time, temperature,* and *angle*

Focus Questions

When you have finished studying this chapter, you should be able to answer these questions:

1. What is the difference between standard and nonstandard units of measure?

2. What are some examples of situations in which measurement is needed? Choose at least one example for each attribute: length, area, volume, capacity, mass, time, temperature, and angle.

Measurement can be one of the most interesting and useful topics in the elementary curriculum. Children and adults use measurement ideas in their everyday lives, and questions involving measurement can be identified in virtually every subject taught during the school day. Learning the concepts and processes associated with measurement requires active participation in a wide variety of physical and mental situations; instruction naturally lends itself to a problem-solving approach. As children study measurement they apply concepts from number and geometry, and thus have opportunities to gain new insights and discover new connections within and between these mathematical topics (Lindquist, 1989).

What do we know of U.S. students' understanding of measurement? The sixth National Assessment of Educational Progress (NAEP) noted that most fourth- and eighth-grade students show an "incomplete conceptual understanding of area, sometimes confuse area and perimeter, and have difficulty applying area concepts to complex situations" (Kenney & Kouba, 1997, p. 142). Likewise, twelfth-grade students had limited understanding of the concepts of volume and surface area. As with other math topics, teachers must make sure that students understand concepts before proceeding to practice skills. In measurement, children must understand what it means to measure and what different types of measurement, such as length, perimeter, area, and volume, *mean* before focusing on formulas to calculate those measures.

This chapter consists of two major sections. The first discusses measurement concepts and processes along with a recommended instructional sequence. The second section presents teaching strategies and learning activities for each of the following elementary and middle school measurement topics: length, area, volume, capacity, mass, time, temperature, and angle.

STANDARDS LINK 15-1
In grades K–4, the mathematics curriculum should include measurement so that students can

- understand the attributes of length, capacity, weight, mass, area, volume, time, temperature, and angle;
- develop the process of measuring and concepts related to units of measurement;
- make and use estimates of measurement;
- make and use measurements in problem and everyday situations. (NCTM, 1989, p. 51)

STANDARDS LINK 15-2
In grades 5–8, the mathematics curriculum should include extensive concrete experiences using measurement so that students can

- extend their understanding of the process of measurement;
- estimate, make, and use measurements to describe and compare phenomena;
- select appropriate units and tools to measure to the degree of accuracy required in a particular situation;
- understand the structure and use of systems of measurement;
- extend their understanding of the concepts of perimeter, area, volume, angle measure, capacity, and weight and mass;
- develop the concepts of rates and other derived and indirect measurements;
- develop formulas and procedures for determining measures to solve problems. (NCTM, 1989, p. 116)

CONCEPTS AND INSTRUCTIONAL SEQUENCE

What Is Measurement?

While counting involves discrete objects, measuring involves continuous properties. A *measurable attribute* of an object or event, such as mass or time, is a characteristic that can be quantified by comparing it to a *unit*. The *process* of measuring is the same for each attribute: an appropriate unit is chosen and the object or event being measured is compared to the unit. The result of measuring is a number and a unit, such as 27 kg or 9.8 seconds.

To illustrate, if you had a large box to measure, you would first have to decide which attribute of the box you were interested in and then select a unit that possesses

that same attribute. If you wanted to know how long the box was, possible choices for the unit would include your hand span, a paper clip, or the centimeter. Depending on the unit chosen, the length of a given box might be 3 spans, 20 paper clips, or 62 cm. If you wanted to know how heavy the box was, you would use a balance scale to compare it with a unit of mass such as a book or the pound. To measure how much the box holds, you could find how many smaller boxes of a particular size would fit into it, or measure its length, width, and height in *centimeters* and compute the volume in *cubic centimeters* using the formula $V = lwh$.

STANDARDS LINK 15-3
Measurement is of central importance to the curriculum because of its power to help children see that mathematics is useful in everyday life and to help them develop many mathematical concepts and skills. Measuring is a natural context in which to introduce the need for learning about fractions and decimals, and it encourages children to be actively involved in solving and discussing problems. (NCTM, 1989, p. 51)

Instructional Sequence

While the meanings, units, instruments, and formulas associated with the various attributes are different, the process, concepts, and instructional sequence for each measurement topic are basically the same (Inskeep, 1976). First, the meaning of the attribute is developed through activities involving perception and direct comparison. Second, children begin to measure using arbitrary or nonstandard units. Third, they measure and estimate using standard units. Related experiences involve learning to use instruments and read scales and developing formulas to determine measurements. The following paragraphs present key concepts and principles for teaching measurement in each of these phases.

STANDARDS LINK 15-4
Children need to understand the attribute to be measured as well as what it means to measure. Before they are capable of such understanding, they must first experience a variety of activities that focus on comparing objects directly, covering them with various units, and counting the units. Premature use of instruments or formulas leaves children without the understanding necessary for solving measurement problems. (NCTM, 1989, p. 51)

Perception and direct comparison   This first stage is sometimes referred to as "premeasurement" since it does not require a unit and it does not involve assigning a number to the object being measured. Activities such as those that follow in this chapter allow children to experience the properties of the attribute and to use sight and touch to compare and order objects with respect to that property. The focus is on the development of conceptual understanding.

The use of appropriate *language* in direct comparison tasks is critical to allow the children to relate the concept to their experience and to distinguish among the various attributes. Deciding which of two objects is "bigger" depends on the meaning of the term "big." Children also appreciate the need for different words to describe different attributes. For determining length, the child can be asked which of two sticks is *longer*. The problem can be solved by placing the sticks side-by-side. For determining capacity, the child can be asked to determine which of two cups *holds more*. Pouring from one cup into the other allows the child to answer without knowing how much either cup holds. Similarly, questions such as the following can be used to introduce mass, area, and temperature: Which book is *heavier?* Which paper *covers more surface?* Which liquid is *hotter?*

Classical Piagetian *conservation* tasks can be used at this stage to provide insight into the child's thinking (Steffe & Hirstein, 1976). To test for conservation of length, the child is asked to find a stick as long as a given stick and to show this by placing them side-by-side. One stick is then moved forward and the child is asked if that stick is now longer than, shorter than, or as long as the other stick. Children who do not conserve length believe that the length of an object changes when it is moved.

The teacher should not attempt to "correct" non-conservers, and should not conclude that such children are not "ready" to learn basic measurement ideas and skills (Hiebert, 1984). Maturation and experience, particularly in settings in which children discuss their work with each other and the teacher, are factors that contribute to cognitive development, and over time children become conservers. Both non-conservers and conservers can benefit from comparison and other early measurement activities. Conservation tasks can also be presented as problems to be solved by the class or by small groups of children. It is through experiences such as these that children construct and modify their view of reality. Students can discuss conflicting answers and different reasons for them. Children who conserve generally give one

of three arguments to explain why the quantity still is the same after a transformation: (1) reversibility—"you can move it back the way it was"; (2) identity—"you didn't add any or take any away"; and (3) compensation—"this one sticks out more here but this one sticks out more here" (Cathcart, 1971).

Seriation tasks involve ordering three or more objects according to a particular attribute. For example, the child might be given six containers and asked to order them by capacity. While this requires a series of direct comparisons, other properties are also involved. The child uses *transitivity* when he or she reasons as follows: "I found that the bottle holds more than the jar and the jar holds more than the can, so I know that the bottle holds more than the can without actually pouring."

Nonstandard units   At this stage the question is "How big?" rather than "Which is bigger?" and invites the further question "Compared to what?" When children see a need for a referent, they are encouraged to choose a variety of units with which to measure the object. The first criterion for selecting an *appropriate* unit is that it has the same attribute as that to be measured. Thus a long thin object such as a pencil would be a good unit for measuring length but it would not be a very good unit for measuring area or angles. Another consideration is the size of the unit relative to the object to be measured. The unit should usually be smaller than the object but large enough so that the counting can be completed in a reasonable time and the resulting number has a reasonable magnitude; one would not want to measure the thickness of a page with an eraser or the length of a classroom with a paper clip.

An important concept is that physical measurement of continuous quantities is always *approximate* (Kastner, 1989). Children are exposed to this reality when they measure the length of a pen in paper clips and find that a whole number multiple of this unit does not exactly match the object's length. In the drawing shown, the length of the pen is closer to 5 paper clips than to 6; we can say that the pen is about 5 paper clips long, the pen is a bit more than 5 paper clips long, or to the nearest paper clip the length of the pen is 5. Similarly, children might find that the capacity of a large juice can is about 10 paper cups and that the mass of an eraser is a bit more than 5 pieces of chalk.

As children gain experience working with nonstandard units, they should be encouraged to *estimate* their answers before they measure. In particular, they should be challenged to predict the effect of using a larger or smaller unit: Will the number obtained be larger or smaller? Examining the results of measuring an object using several different units leads children to discover the inverse relationship between the size of the unit and the number of units required to match the object. Learners should be encouraged to verbalize this concept in their own words. A child might say, "If the unit is shorter, it will take more of them to be as long."

The idea of *subdividing* a unit so that the number of units more closely matches the object introduces the concept of *precision* in relation to the approximate nature of measurement. Dividing the unit into smaller parts results in a more precise answer. The length of the pen below is about 5 of the larger units and 10 of the smaller units.

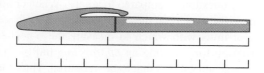

When two children accurately use the same unit to measure a particular object, both should get the same number. However, if they use different units, two different answers can be correct. It is helpful to discuss this idea when using body parts as arbitrary units. An example is measuring the width of the room in shoe lengths. Thus another characteristic of a good unit is that others can easily replicate and understand it. It is interesting to discuss historical measures such as the cubit (the distance from the elbow to the tip of the middle finger) in this connection.

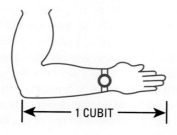

← 1 CUBIT →

Standard units Even though the children all get the same answers using arbitrary classroom units and know what these units mean, they can appreciate the problems associated with trying to communicate such measures outside their class or school. They might discuss telling their parents about a rock with a mass of 23 blocks or trying to buy a board 13 textbooks long. But students will come to see that it is difficult to communicate measurements done with nonstandard units to other people. So something else is needed.

That something is **standard units.** Standard units are units agreed upon and accepted by a group of people. In the United States, two systems of standard units are used: the customary system and the metric system. Table 15-1 lists common units of measure in each system to measure different attributes.

The customary system may seem to be easier to most adults, since it is widely used in the United States. But this system has difficult equivalences: for example, there are 5280 feet in a mile and there are 16 ounces in a pound. The equivalences in the metric system are much easier to learn, since the metric system is based on powers of ten. For example, there are 1000 millimeters in a meter and 1000 milliliters in a liter. In the metric system there are three prefixes for smaller units: *milli-* (which means one-thousandth), *centi-* (which means one-hundredth), and *deci-* (which means one-tenth). Likewise, there are three prefixes for larger units: *kilo-* (which means one thousand), *hecto-* (which means one hundred), and *deka-*

TABLE 15-1

COMMON UNITS OF MEASURE

ATTRIBUTE BEING MEASURED	CUSTOMARY SYSTEM	METRIC SYSTEM
Length	inch foot yard mile	millimeter centimeter meter kilometer
Area	square inch square foot square yard acre	square centimeter square meter hectare
Volume	cubic inch cubic foot cubic yard	cubic centimeter cubic meter
Capacity	fluid ounce cup quart gallon	milliliter liter
Weight	ounce pound ton	gram kilogram metric ton
Temperature	degrees Fahrenheit	degrees Celsius
Time	second minute hour day week month year	
Angles	degrees radians	degrees radians

(which means ten). So a student can use these prefixes to help him or her understand the following:

There are   1000 millimeters in 1 meter
              100 centimeters in 1 meter
              10 decimeters in 1 meter
And that   1 dekameter is equal to 10 meters
              1 hectometer is equal to 100 meters
              1 kilometer is equal to 1000 meters

These same equivalences are true for all different units of measure, including meters, grams, and liters, and make the metric system easy to use.

It is important that students learn to use both systems of measurement. Note, however, that the teacher should *not* spend important instructional time converting measurements from one system to the other. Instead, instruction should focus on developing understanding of and skill in measuring using both systems of units.

Knowledge of the units appropriate for a given task and the ability to decide when and how to *estimate* are components of "measurement sense" (Shaw & Cliatt, 1989). Thus a student would identify the kilometer or mile as opposed to the meter or centimeter or yard or foot as the most appropriate unit for describing distances between two cities, and would want to know only the approximate distance in order to estimate how long it would take to drive that far. Strategies used by good estimators include *referents* (using a known quantity such as your

TABLE 15-2

SCOPE AND SEQUENCE CHART FOR TEACHING MEASUREMENT

GRADE LEVEL	K	1	2	3	4	5	6
Length	direct comparison nonstandard units cm, in. ruler	m, ft	dm, yd	mm, km, mi perimeter rectangle			prefixes circle
Area		direct comparison nonstandard units	cm^2, $in.^2$	m^2, ft^2, yd^2 rectangle	km^2 parallelogram circle	mm^2	ha surface area
Volume			direct comparison nonstandard units	cm^3, $in.^3$	m^3, ft^3, yd^3	rectangular prism	$dm^3 = L$ $cm^3 = mL$ $m^3 = kL$
Capacity	direct comparison nonstandard units	L, C	mL	graduated beaker	pt, qt, gal	kL	
Mass	direct comparison balance	nonstandard units	kg	g	t	mg	g – mL kg – L t – kL
Time	sequencing events direct comparison nonstandard units calendar	minute hour second digital clock	dial clock	date notation	A.M., P.M. 24-h clock	time zones	
Temperature	weather	temperature direct comparison	°C, °F thermometer		Celsius referents		
Angles					right obtuse acute straight	degree protractor	interior angles in triangle

own height to estimate another person's height); *chunking* (estimating the area of a room by first breaking it into several workable parts); and *unitizing* (estimating the volume of a pitcher by mentally dividing it into smaller, equal parts such as glassfuls of 250 mL) (Lindquist, 1987). Students should have referents for common metric units (the person's mass in kilograms; a liter carton of milk; a millimeter is about the thickness of a dime; room temperature is about 70°F).

Relationships among metric units can often be discovered directly. For example, it takes ten centimeters to make a train one decimeter long. To successfully convert from one unit to another, the student needs to know the meaning of the prefixes, be able to multiply and divide by powers of ten, and understand that the larger unit will be associated with the smaller number. Generally, conversion questions should occur in the context of realistic problem-solving situations rather than as sets of contrived exercises.

Instruments In the elementary grades, students learn to use the following measuring instruments: ruler (length), pan balance (mass), graduated beaker (capacity), protractor (angles), thermometer (temperature), and clock (time). While these instruments are based on standard units, children should invent and construct their own instruments to simplify various tasks at earlier stages. For example, a balance is used to find which of two objects is heavier; a paper clip chain ruler is used to measure length in these arbitrary units; and a clear bottle is calibrated to show the water heights for whole numbers of paper cup units. Such devices help children see the connection between the attribute and the standard instrument. Careful teaching, demonstration, and appropriate student activities are required to insure that students use measuring instruments correctly and with understanding.

STANDARDS LINK 15-5
Estimation should be emphasized because it helps children understand the attributes and the process of measuring as well as gain an awareness of the sizes of units. Everyday situations in which only an estimate is required should be included. Since measurements are not exact, children should realize that it is often appropriate, for example, to report a measurement as between eight and nine centimeters or about three hours. (NCTM, 1989, p. 51)

Formulas According to Bright and Hoeffner (1993), "formulas should be a product of exploration and discovery" (p. 81). They recommend that students must have hands-on experiences with measuring, "with emphasis more on understanding the underlying concepts than on applying formulas" (p. 82).

In the intermediate grades, students learn and apply *formulas* for finding the perimeter, area, and volume of simple two- and three-dimensional figures. Students can often discover these relationships on their own. For example, students who have been finding the distance around a number of different polygons by measuring the individual sides notice that when a rectangle is involved, only two sides need to be measured; the perimeter can be found by doubling the sum of the length and the width or by adding twice the length and twice the width. Developing formulas in this way is meaningful and makes it possible for students to solve problems when rules are forgotten. Formulas for the area of a rectangle, parallelogram, and triangle and for the surface area and volume of a rectangular prism can similarly be discovered by students. The relationship between the circumference and the diameter of a circle (pi) can be explored by students at various grade levels. Primary children can use string to compare the distances around and across discs of varying sizes; intermediate students can measure these distances in millimeters and find their ratio using a calculator.

Problem solving and applications There are a number of interesting problems in which relationships between two attributes are investigated. For example, students can make as many different rectangles as they can having a fixed perimeter and find the area of each. Activities of this nature are appropriate at various grade levels since formulas and relationships do not depend on particular units. Practical real-life problems might include finding the cost of painting or carpeting a room. Cooking, carpentry, and outdoor education are other settings in which measurement skills can be learned and applied.

Summary of Teaching Sequence

The first part of this chapter described the measurement process and an instructional sequence for the important concepts and skills. The early emphasis is on developing understanding and vocabulary through activities involving visual perception, direct comparison, and measuring with arbitrary units. Later, students learn to estimate and measure with appropriate metric units, use measurement instruments, and discover formulas and relationships. Finally, teachers should use an active learning, problem-solving approach at all levels.

The remainder of the chapter describes sample teaching strategies and learning activities for the three stages of the instructional sequence for each of the attributes. Teachers can adapt questions and activities for use in whole class, small group, and individual learning settings.

TEACHING STRATEGIES AND LEARNING ACTIVITIES

Length

In studying linear measure we refer to the *length* of an object and to the *distance* between two objects. We also talk about the *height* of a building, the *width* of a hall, and the *thickness* of a piece of paper. Related vocabulary includes the terms *long* and *short, near* and *far, tall* and *short, narrow* and *wide,* and *thick* and *thin. Perimeter* is the total distance around a closed figure.

Research on children's knowledge of measuring has identified several difficulties (Wilson & Rowland, 1993). To assess children's understanding of the inverse relationship between the size of the unit and the number of units used, Grade 1 and 2 children were shown two identical strips. When one strip was covered with small units and the other with larger units, students said that the strip covered by the smaller units was longer because there were more units. In another study, Grade 3 students were told the number of sheets of paper used by two different people to measure the height of a door. Over half of the students claimed that the person who had used the most sheets had the longest sheets. On a task involving measuring with a ruler in an unfamiliar situation, most Grade 3 students and half of the Grade 7 students could not give the length of a line segment placed on a pictured ruler such that the end of the ruler was not aligned with the end of the segment.

Length: perception and direct comparison

Beginning activities focus on language and concept development (Jensen & O'Neil, 1981). The following are sample questions and directions a teacher might use with a group of children provided with a set of rods or cardboard strips cut to different lengths.

- Find a strip that is long (short). Find another strip that is longer (shorter) than this strip. Can you tell by looking? How do you place the strips to know? Find another strip as long as your strip. Show how you know these two strips have the same length.

- Now choose any strip and sort the other strips into three groups: longer, shorter, and the same length. Choose any five strips and put them in order from longest to shortest.

Many young children do not understand that the length of an object is the distance between the two endpoints. They focus on only one aspect of the situation and consider only the position of the endpoint. The test for conservation of length was described earlier in this chapter. After the child has stated whether the moved stick is longer, shorter, or the same length as the other stick, she or he is asked to "explain how you know."

The idea of the length of a curved path can be investigated with string. The child is asked to cut two pieces the same length. The teacher then bends one of them and asks if it is still the same length.

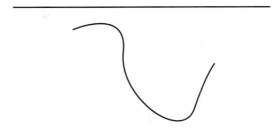

As a further activity, children can sort and order pieces of string of different lengths.

Activities and questions such as the following are useful for introducing related vocabulary and further exploring basic concepts.

- Name something in the room that is *near* to you (*far* from you). Find something that is nearer (farther). Is it farther from you to the door or from the door to you?

- Name someone who is *tall* (*short*). Who is taller, Marie or Peter? How do you know? Find a child who is taller, shorter, and *as tall as* Pam.

- We can see that Paul and Kim have the same *height*. (Have Paul stand on a chair.) Are Paul and Kim still the same height? Can you tell by looking? How do you know?

- Form a group of three or four children. Who is the tallest and who is the shortest? Show how you know. With their backs against the chalkboard, have the children in the group stand side-by-side in a line from tallest to shortest. Have another classmate mark the height of each member of the group on the chalkboard.

- Tell or write a story about the members of your family using the words *tall, taller, tallest, short, shorter, shortest.*

- If Jim is taller than Kate and Kate is taller than Don, is Jim shorter or taller than Don? Can you tell without seeing them together?

To introduce the idea that objects have more than one linear dimension and that the children need additional vocabulary to describe them, the teacher shows a pencil and a shorter, thicker crayon and asks the children which they think is *bigger.* The children might say that the pencil is longer but that the crayon is *thicker* or *fatter* or *wider.* The teacher then assembles a collection of pencils, felt pens, markers, and crayons and asks the children to sort them and to order them according to size. Next, the teacher can challenge the children to sort the objects in another way.

Length: nonstandard units As a transition to the idea of using a unit, the children can compare two lengths or distances where direct comparison is not possible. *Indirect comparison* involves comparing representations of the objects (Hiebert, 1984). Sample problems and possible solution strategies are as follows:

- Which is longer—the distance around your wrist or the length of an eraser? (String might be used.)
- Which is higher—the doorknob or the top of the filing cabinet? Since we cannot move the door or the filing cabinet, how can we find out? (The child might stand by the doorknob and use masking tape to mark a point on her body, then walk to the filing cabinet and compare its height with the tape mark.)
- Could we move the teacher's desk through the door without first tipping the desk on its side? (Provide an unmarked stick about a meter in length.)

To introduce the idea of measuring with a unit, each child can find how many paper clips it would take to make a train *as long* as his or her pencil. The teacher tells the class that they are *measuring the length* of their pencils in paper clips. He or she points out that a whole number of paper clips will not exactly match a pencil length, but that the number that most closely fits is to be reported. The teacher demonstrates the correct procedure for measuring with this unit, and also shows common errors and invites the children to tell what is wrong in each case.

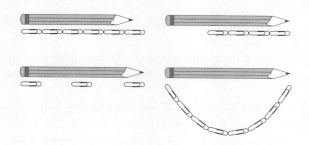

At first, teachers should provide the children with enough paper clips to measure the selected objects. Later, children may move a single paper clip along the object. This procedure is called "iteration of the unit." After children have had some practice, they are encouraged to estimate before they measure. Students can record their work in a chart such as the following.

Object	Estimate	Measure
pencil	9 paper clips	6 paper clips
eraser	_____	_____
book	_____	_____
_____	_____	_____

Another beneficial exercise is to invite children to use paper clips to make straight paths the same length as broken or curved paths. In one setting for this task, students are shown a "road" that has curves or bends and are instructed to use short rods to make a straight road that would be just as far to walk on.

The teacher then explains that the paper clip is a *unit* for measuring length and asks the children to suggest other objects that could be used as units. They then use several different units to measure the length of a page of their notebook and record their findings in a chart as follows.

Unit	Estimate	Measure
chalk	5	4
eraser	9	7
pencil	_____	_____
_____	_____	_____

During and following this activity, teachers should ask questions such as the following to focus attention on the role of the unit: Why did you get different answers for the length of the page? If you were told that the length of a page was 4, would you know how long the page was? What else would you need to know? Did you need more units for measuring the page when you used a long unit or a short unit? Why?

Other questions relate to the choice of an appropriate unit. Do you think an eraser would be a good unit for measuring the length of our classroom? Why or why not? Is a new pencil a good unit for measuring the length of a piece of chalk? Why or why not?

Body parts can also be used as nonstandard units of length. For example, children can use their *span* (the distance between the thumb and little finger on an outstretched hand) to measure the length of their desk. To increase their understanding the children should discuss the reason different children get different answers when they use this unit.

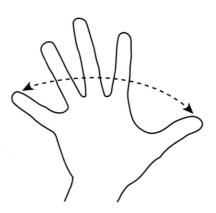

To introduce the idea of a *ruler,* have children make a paper clip chain. Then ask: "How do you think you can use your chain to measure the length of your pencil?" The children could also connect about ten interlocking cubes together and use this device to measure the lengths of various objects in cubes. They could discuss whether it is easier or harder to measure using individual cubes or the cube stick.

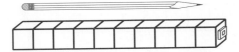

Students can use squared paper (Activity 15-1) and geoboards (Activity 15-2) to explore interesting and worthwhile problems involving the lengths of broken line segments and distances around polygons. Using string, students can find relationships among distances around a person's wrist, neck, and waist (Activity 15-3) and discover the relationship (pi) between the distance around and across circular objects (Activity 15-4).

Length: standard units   Children who have measured lengths using a variety of units can appreciate the need for a unit that can be understood and communicated beyond the classroom. The book *How Big is a Foot?* by Rolf Myller (1990) makes this point in a delightful way. The king in the story orders an apprentice to make him a bed 6 feet long and 3 feet wide. The apprentice uses his own foot to measure the bed, with predictable results.

The centimeter is usually the first standard unit taught to children. It is presented as a unit of length known throughout the world. Children become familiar with the size of the centimeter by using the small cubes from the base-ten blocks or interlocking centimeter cubes (called "centicubes") to measure objects. They should note that one of their fingernails is about a centimeter in length. They are told that the *symbol* for centimeter is cm and that five centimeters is written 5 cm. They then practice measuring and estimating length using this unit, recording their findings on a chart such as the following:

Object	Estimate	Measure
pencil	12 cm	14 cm
eraser	___ cm	___ cm
your span	___ cm	___ cm
_____	_____	_____

EXPLORING DISTANCES ON SQUARED PAPER

MATERIALS:
squared paper

PROCEDURE:
1. Copy Figures A and B on a piece of squared paper.

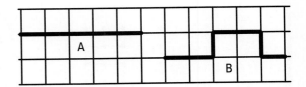

2. If the unit is the distance between two lines, the total length of Figure A is 5 units. Figure B has a length of 7 units.
   • By tracing over grid lines, draw some other figures and find their length.
   • How many different figures can you draw that have a total length of 10 units?

3. Figure C is closed. The distance around it is 16 units.
   • Draw some other closed figures by following grid lines and find the distance around each of them.
   • How many different closed figures can you draw that have a distance around of 12 units?

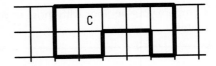

Before demonstrating the standard ruler, invite children to use the ten rod from the base-ten materials or a connected centicube stick to find lengths in centimeters (Thompson & Van de Walle, 1985). The first ruler they use should have centimeter markings without numbers along one edge, so they see that the unit on the ruler is represented by the space, not the mark. Children then learn to measure using the other edge that has numbers under the markings. The teacher needs to demonstrate the correct procedure for using this tool, emphasizing the importance of placing the zero mark at the beginning of the object. Students should also realize that a ruler with the

✴ ACTIVITY 15-2

PERIMETERS ON A GEOBOARD

MATERIALS:
geoboard or dot paper

PROCEDURE:
1. The distance around a closed figure is called its perimeter. How many different figures that have a perimeter of 10 units can you make on a 5 × 5 geoboard?

✴ ACTIVITY 15-3

WRIST, NECK, AND WAIST

MATERIALS:
string

PROCEDURE:
1. Use string to measure the distance around your wrist, neck, and waist.

2. Cut pieces of string matching these lengths and compare them.
   • How many wrist lengths are as long as a neck length?
   • How many wrists make a waist?

3. Compare your findings with those of your classmates.

✴ ACTIVITY 15-4

MEASURING A CIRCLE

MATERIALS:
different-sized circular shapes (bottle lids, cans, etc.), string

PROCEDURE:
1. For each shape, cut pieces of string as long as the distance across and the distance around the outside edge.

2. Use the shorter piece to measure the longer one. What do you notice for each shape?

front end broken off still can be used to find the length of an object (by subtraction or counting units between the endpoints).

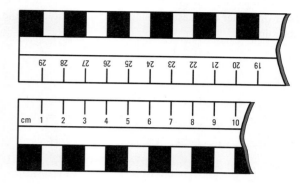

As a practice activity, children can work in pairs. One person draws a line segment on a piece of paper. The partner estimates its length in centimeters and then measures it using a ruler. The children then switch jobs. They might also try this with broken-line or curved paths. Similar activities can be done using inches.

The *meter* is introduced as a standard unit for measuring longer distances such as the length of the classroom. Activities such as the following help children gain an appreciation for the size of this unit and relate it to the centimeter.

• Use an unmarked meter stick to find a point on your body that is one meter from the floor. Put the meter stick on the floor. How many of your steps make a meter. Find objects in the classroom that are about one meter in length or have height of about one meter. How many meters long (wide) do you think the classroom is? Measure and compare the actual length with your estimate.

• Use a trundle wheel to measure the length of the hall, the distance around the gym, and so on. Estimate before you measure.

• How many centimeters does it take to make a meter. Estimate first, then look at the side of the meter stick marked in centimeters to find out. If an object is 2 m long, how many centimeters is that?

Similar activities can be done for feet, inches, and yards.

To measure in *decimeters* students can use the 10 cm Cuisenaire rod, the "long" from the base-ten materials, or a ten centicube stick. The meter stick pictured is marked to show the relationships among the meter, decimeter, and centimeter. The meaning of the prefixes *centi* and *deci* can be discussed in this connection.

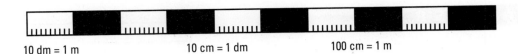

10 dm = 1 m   10 cm = 1 dm   100 cm = 1 m

In relation to the concept of precision, students can measure the length of the chalkboard to the nearest meter, decimeter, and centimeter. They can discuss which unit is most appropriate in this case and which of the three results is the most precise.

The *millimeter* is introduced as a unit to measure very small things such as insects. Two sample activities involving this unit are:

- Use a ruler marked in centimeters and millimeters to measure to the nearest millimeter the length of several objects or line segments drawn on paper.
- Make a stack of ten dimes. Measure the height of the stack. What is the approximate thickness of one dime?

Sample questions and activities relating to the *kilometer* are as follows:

- What place would be about one kilometer from your home (the school?) How long does it take you to walk (jog, run) a kilometer. Identify places that are about 2 km (10 km) apart.
- Use a road map or atlas to find the distances between your town or city and other cities you have visited or would like to visit. How far is it from Los Angeles to New York? from Chicago to Seattle? What is the distance around the earth? How far is it to the moon?

In Activities 15-5 through 15-8, students measure in metric units to collect data to develop formulas or discover relationships.

✳ ACTIVITY 15-5

PERIMETER OF A RECTANGLE

MATERIALS:
ruler, meter stick

PROCEDURE:
1. Find and record the *perimeter* of (distance around) your textbook, the door, a window, the top of the filing cabinet. Use appropriate units.
2. How many different sides did you need to measure to find the perimeter of these things? Write a sentence telling how to find the perimeter of a rectangle.

✳ ACTIVITY 15-6

CIRCUMFERENCE OF A CIRCLE

MATERIALS:
circular objects, tape measure, calculator

PROCEDURE:
1. Using a tape measure marked in millimeters, measure the *diameter* (distance across) and the *circumference* (distance around) of several circular objects. Enter these numbers in the chart and use a calculator to compute the ratios.

Circumference (C)	Diameter (d)	C ÷ d
273 mm	85 mm	3.21

2. Can you state a relationship between the diameter and the circumference of a circle?

✳ ACTIVITY 15-7

ARE YOU SQUARE?

MATERIALS:
meter stick or tape measure

PROCEDURE:
1. Measure your height and armspan (the distance between your outstretched fingertips) in centimeters. Are you square?
2. Compare with your classmates.

✳ ACTIVITY 15-8

BODY PARTS

MATERIALS:
tape measure

PROCEDURE:
1. Use a tape measure marked in centimeters to find the distance around your wrist, neck, and waist.

2. Do this for several people.

3. Can you state a relationship among these measurements for people?

Name	Wrist	Neck	Waist
————	————	————	————
————	————	————	————
————	————	————	————

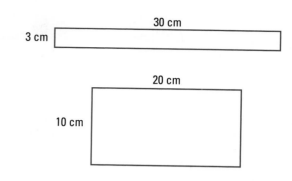

Area

Area is the amount of surface enclosed by a curve in the plane. We consider area when we hang wallpaper, carpet a floor, or wrap a present. While any plane region that tessellates can be used as a unit for measuring area, the standard unit is the measure of a square having an edge with a length of one unit. Students should learn about measuring area by covering figures with square tiles and by drawing figures on squared paper before being taught to use formulas. Units of area are derived from corresponding linear units.

Area: perception and direct comparison

To introduce the notion of area the teacher might show the class two rectangular pieces of cardboard, one measuring about 30 cm by 3 cm and the other 20 cm by 10 cm, and ask the question "Which is bigger?" Even though the first piece is longer, students will generally say that the other looks bigger in the sense that it *covers more surface.* They might also argue that the two areas could be compared directly if the long strip was cut into two pieces.

As a follow-up activity, students working in small groups can compare the areas of pairs of rectangles having the following dimensions: 10 cm by 6 cm and 8 cm by 8 cm; 6 cm by 8 cm and 12 cm by 4 cm.

To test for conservation of area, two squares of the same size are shown. The teacher cuts one square along a diagonal and rearranges the two pieces to form a triangle or parallelogram. Then the teacher asks the child whether the two shapes have the same area and to explain her or his answer.

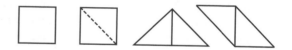

Area: nonstandard units

To introduce the idea of a unit of area, the teacher can ask the class how many pieces of construction paper would be required to cover the bulletin board. At their seats they could use small file cards to cover a page or the surface of their desks. Students could also find out how many of their hands it takes to cover their desks and then compare and discuss their results.

In another activity, students can be given small squares and asked if they can use these to find which two of three specially constructed figures cover the same amount of surface. The number of squares covering each figure is the area measure of the figure with respect to that unit.

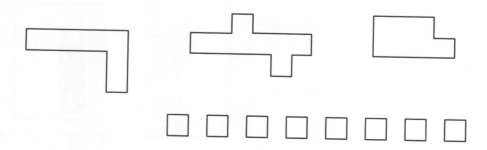

Given pattern blocks such as the six shapes shown, students can be asked to find how many copies of each shape are required to cover a card measuring about 10 cm by 13 cm.

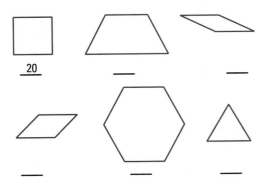

20

Asking students to use objects such as toothpicks and circular counters to cover a surface can lead to a discussion about the desirable characteristics of a unit of area. Key ideas are that the unit should possess the attribute of covering and that it should cover without overlapping; the figure tessellates the plane. Students should also use three different sizes of squares to measure a particular surface and note the relationship between the number of units needed and the size of the unit.

Several geoboard tasks involving area are shown in Activity 15-9. Activity 15-10 leads students to discover the formula for the area of a rectangle; other excellent activities with squared paper are described by Shaw (1983). In Activity 15-11 students use tiles to find the perimeters of rectangles having a fixed area. See BLMs 11 and 12 for a geoboard template and geoboard recording paper.

Area: standard units The basic units of area are the *square meter,* the square inch, and the square foot. To give students a feel for the square meter, outline a square 1 m by 1 m on the chalkboard or on the floor (with masking tape). Students need to know that the symbol m^2 is read "square meter" and not "meter squared." The class could determine the number of square meters of carpet needed to cover the classroom floor and the area of the gym floor in square meters. Similar activities can be done for square inches and square feet.

Students can become familiar with the *square centimeter* (cm^2) by using centimeter graph paper (Horak & Horak, 1982). One task is to find the approximate area of their hand by tracing around it on graph paper and counting squares. Students also can be asked to outline polygons enclosing specified numbers of square centimeters. For example, enclose a region with an area of 43 cm^2. Do this in several different ways. (See BLM 15 for centimeter grid paper.)

✳ ACTIVITY 15-9

GEOBOARD AREAS

MATERIALS:
a geoboard

PROCEDURE:
1. Copy the figure below on your geoboard. The unit is the square region formed as shown. The area of the figure is 7 units.

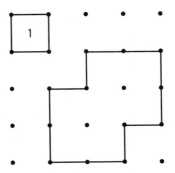

2. On your geoboard, enclose figures with areas of 3, 6, and 11 units.
3. On your geoboard, how many different figures can you make having an area of 5 units?
4. Find the perimeter of each figure in 3.

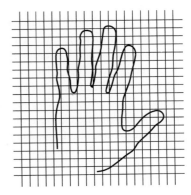

The faces of the small cube of the base-ten materials have sides 1 cm in length and thus each face has an area of 1 cm^2. The 10-by-10 flat is a *square decimeter.* By comparing these two blocks, students can find that 1 dm^2 = 100 cm^2. They should also be able to determine that 1 m^2 = 10 000 cm^2 by considering 100 rows of 100 square centimeters in a square meter.

✳ ACTIVITY 15-10

AREAS OF RECTANGLES

MATERIALS:
squared paper

PROCEDURE:

1. Draw several different rectangles on squared paper.

2. For each rectangle find the length and width in linear units and the area in square units.

Length	Width	Area
3	2	6
___	___	___
___	___	___

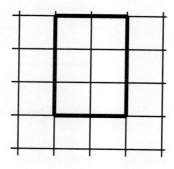

3. State a rule for finding the area of a rectangle given its length and width.

✳ ACTIVITY 15-11

PERIMETER AND AREA

MATERIALS:
36 square tiles

PROCEDURE:

1. Arrange 36 small square tiles to form a rectangular region with a base of 9 units and a height of 4 units as shown.

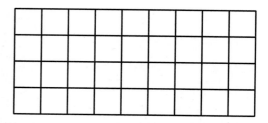

2. Find the perimeter and area of this figure.

3. Using all 36 squares each time, make as many other different rectangular regions as you can.

4. Record your findings.

Base	Height	Perimeter	Area
9	4	26	36
___	___	___	___

5. What did you notice about the perimeters and areas of the various figures?

6. Which shape gives the greatest perimeter?

From Activity 15-10, students found that the area of a rectangle is the product of its *length* and *width*. In Activity 15-11, the terms *base* and *height* were used for the two dimensions of a rectangle. These latter concepts are needed in developing formulas for the area of a parallelogram and a triangle. First, students can discover that a parallelogram can be transformed into a rectangle by cutting and sliding a triangular section as indicated in the diagram below.

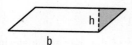 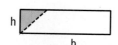

Thus the area of a parallelogram is the product of its base and height. It needs to be stressed that the height is the perpendicular distance from the base to the opposite side and not the length of an adjacent side. Furthermore, any of the sides can be considered as the base.

Students can use geoboards to investigate triangular areas. Students see that a right triangle can be enclosed in a rectangle and since the two resulting triangles are congruent, the area of the original triangle is half that of the rectangle. A triangle without a right angle can also be enclosed in a rectangle, as illustrated, and its area found by subtracting the areas of the right triangles formed from the area of the rectangle.

Area $= \dfrac{1 \times 2}{2} = 1$ Area $= 4 - 1 - 2 = 1$

In general, two copies of any triangle form a parallelogram as shown in the diagram. Students can reason that since the triangle and the parallelogram have the same base and height, the area of a triangle can be computed by finding half the product of its base and height.

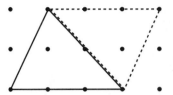

Activities 15-12 through 15-15 are problems and investigations relating to the areas of rectangles, parallelograms, and triangles. The surface area of a rectangular solid is introduced in Activity 15-16.

To help students see that the formula for the area of a circle, $A = \pi r^2$, is sensible, show a diagram in which a circle of radius r is inscribed in a square of side $2r$. The area of the square is $4r^2$. It appears that the area of the circle is about three-fourths of the area of the square, or about $3r^2$. Students can also draw circles on squared paper and find their approximate areas by counting squares. They will find that the ratio of the area to the square of the radius is a bit more than three.

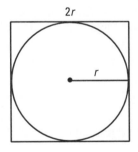

Volume

Volume measure associates a number with a closed space region. *Volume* is the amount of space occupied by a

✳ ACTIVITY 15-12

MAKING A FENCE

Julie has 100 m of fencing to make a pen for her horse. She wants the pen to be rectangular in shape. Find the dimensions of the pen that encloses the greatest area.

✳ ACTIVITY 15-13

PARALLELOGRAM AREAS

- How are the parallelograms the same?
- How are they different?
- Find the area of each.

three-dimensional object. *Interior volume* refers to the amount of space confined within the boundaries of a container such as a box. The unit is the measure of a cube having an edge with a length of one unit. Concept development activities include building solids with cubes and filling boxes with cubes (Hart, 1984). Units for volume are derived from linear units.

Volume: perception and direct comparison
To introduce the concept of cubic volume the teacher might hold up two solid rectangular prisms and ask which is "bigger." While linear dimensions and surface areas of these three-dimensional objects could be compared, the discussion should lead to the question of which one *occupies more space.* Two empty boxes, one of which fits within the other, are then shown and compared directly for *volume.* The teacher and students can generate a list of everyday examples of objects that have a large volume or a small volume, but in most cases direct comparison cannot be carried out and beginning instructional activities involve the use of nonstandard units.

To determine whether a child conserves volume, the teacher can use wooden cubes to build a solid shape, such as a $2 \times 3 \times 2$ prism. The teacher explains that she or he is making a house with blocks and that each block is a room. He or she instructs the child to copy the

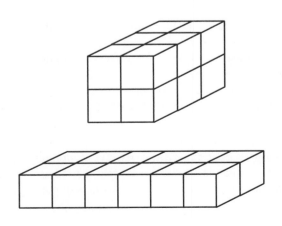

✳ ACTIVITY 15-14

GEOBOARD TRIANGLES

MATERIALS:
a geoboard

PROCEDURE:

1. Find the areas of these geoboard triangles by enclosing them in rectangles and subtracting the areas of the right triangles formed.

2. On a 25-nail geoboard it is possible to make 8 different triangles that have an area of 1. How many can you find?

 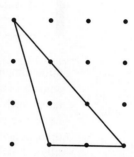 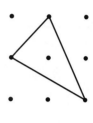

✳ ACTIVITY 15-15

AREAS OF TRIANGLES

MATERIALS:
a compass and a ruler

PROCEDURE:

1. Construct a triangle with sides measuring 9 cm, 10 cm, and 12 cm.

2. From each of the vertices construct the perpendicular to the opposite side.

3. Using the standard formula compute the area of the triangle three times, each time using a different side as base. Are the three answers the same?

4. Construct other triangles with sides of different lengths and repeat the activity.

✳ ACTIVITY 15-16

COVERING A BOX

MATERIALS:
a shoebox (or similar box), paper, scissors

PROCEDURE:

1. Cut pieces of paper to match each of the faces of the box. Use them to completely cover the box.

2. How many pieces of paper did you cut? How many different sizes were there?

3. Find the dimensions of each rectangular piece of paper in centimeters and compute the areas.

4. The *surface area* of a box is the sum of the areas of its faces. Find the surface area of the box in square centimeters.

5. State a rule for finding the surface area of a box given its length, width, and height.

teacher's house and to confirm that the two structures have the same number of rooms. The teacher then rearranges the 12 blocks to form a prism with different dimensions such as $6 \times 2 \times 1$ and asks the child if this house has more, fewer or the same number of rooms as the child's house. The child is asked to justify her or his explanation.

Volume: nonstandard units Common (2.5 cm cube) wooden or plastic blocks can be used as a unit of volume in many concept development activities. For one

task, the teacher constructs open boxes that can be filled by the cubes arranged in the following ways: $3 \times 3 \times 3$, $4 \times 3 \times 2$, and $5 \times 5 \times 1$. The students first predict which of the boxes will hold the most cubes and then carry out the measurement.

Students can also use the blocks to make solid shapes with a given volume (such as 7 or 13) and to make as many different rectangular solids as possible using a fixed number of blocks (12, for example). Activity 15-17

✳ ACTIVITY 15-17

VOLUME OF A RECTANGULAR SOLID

MATERIALS:
25 wooden or plastic cubes

PROCEDURE:

1. Use cubes to build the rectangular solid pictured here. Its length is 4, its width is 2, and its height is 2.

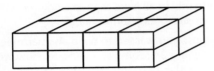

2. Find its volume by counting the number of blocks used to build the solid.

3. Build other rectangular solids with different dimensions.

4. Record their length, width, height, and volume.

Length	Width	Height	Volume
4	2	2	16
5	1	3	_____
_____	_____	_____	_____

5. Can you state a rule for finding the volume of a box given its length, width, and height?

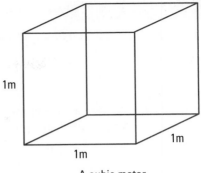

A cubic meter

The cubic centimeter (cm^3) is modeled by the small cube of the base-ten materials and by the centicube block. Students should use these blocks to build solids having volumes of given numbers of cubic centimeters. They should also use a ruler to measure the length, width, and height of a box to the nearest centimeter and compute the approximate volume in cubic centimeters.

The large cube of the base-ten materials provides a model for a *cubic decimeter* (dm^3). Comparing the small cube to the large cube, students find that $1 \ dm^3 = 1000 \ cm^3$.

Students can also determine that there are a million cubic centimeters in a meter. A centimeter cube can be placed inside the model of the cubic meter to help students visualize this large number.

is designed to lead students to discover the formula for the volume of a rectangular prism. In Activity 15-18 students investigate the surface areas of rectangular solids with a constant volume.

Teachers should discuss with students the problem associated with using spherical-shaped objects such as marbles or Ping-Pong balls as units of volume. Using different-sized cubes (such as sugar cubes and interlocking cubes) to measure the volume of a box provides a setting for reviewing the relationship between the unit size and the number of units needed.

Volume: standard units   A model for a *cubic meter* can be constructed using 12 meter-length sticks. After the teacher introduces the symbol m^3, the class might calculate the approximate volume of the classroom using its length, width, and height in meters. A similar activity can be done for yd^3 and ft^3.

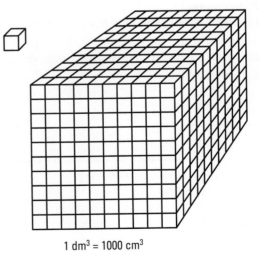

$1 \ dm^3 = 1000 \ cm^3$

Activity 15-19 describes an interesting small group problem-solving activity relating to the construction of an open box of maximum volume.

✱ ACTIVITY 15-18

SURFACE AREA OF A RECTANGULAR SOLID

MATERIALS:
24 wooden or plastic cubes

PROCEDURE:
1. Arrange 24 cubes to form a rectangular solid 4 blocks long, 2 blocks wide, and 3 blocks high.

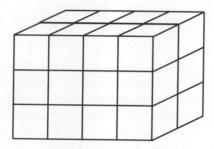

2. Find the prism's surface area—the total number of squares (the size of a face of a unit cube) needed to cover all faces of the prism.

3. Using all 24 cubes each time, make as many other different solid rectangular prisms as you can.

4. Record your findings.

Length	Width	Height	Surface Area
4	3	2	52
12	2	1	

5. These prisms all have the same volume. Which has the greatest/least surface area?

6. Suppose you wanted to build an apartment building containing 24 rooms of equal size. How would you arrange the 24 rooms? Consider factors such as cost, view, heating, availability of land, need for elevators, etc.

✱ ACTIVITY 15-19

MAKE THE BIGGEST BOX

MATERIALS:
centimeter grid paper 12 cm by 9 cm, scissors

PROCEDURE:
1. Cut a square of size 1 cm from each corner of the grid paper.

2. Fold the resulting edges to make an open box.

3. Find its volume.

4. What size square should you cut out of the corners of the original square to make the box with the greatest volume?

Length of Cut	Height	Length	Width	Volume
1 cm	1 cm	10 cm	7 cm	70 cm³
2 cm				

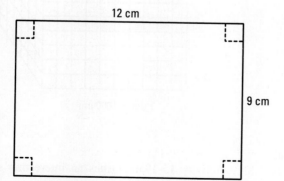

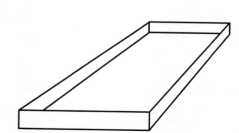

Capacity

While volume is the amount of space occupied by an object, the term *capacity* is often used to refer to the amount of space that can be filled. Capacity is usually used in connection with liquid measure. In the elementary curriculum, children learn about capacity in kindergarten and Grade 1, while cubic volume is first encountered in Grades 3 or 4.

Capacity: perception and direct comparison

To introduce the attribute of capacity, children can be shown two containers and asked which one *holds more*. If one container fits into the other, the children can see that the large container will hold more. If not, the question is answered by filling one container and pouring it into the other. Substances used to explore capacity in the classroom include dried peas, sand, and water. Children require a great deal of hands-on experience with a variety of cans, bottles, paper cups, and other containers of different sizes and shapes. The following instructions might be given:

• Find which container holds the most/least. Estimate first, then check by pouring.

• Can you find two different containers that hold about the same amount?

• Order the containers according to how much they hold.

To check for conservation, the teacher shows two identical glasses sitting side-by-side, pours water into one of the glasses, and asks a child to fill the other glass so that it contains the same amount. The child pours water into the glass until the water level is the same in the two glasses. The teacher then pours the water from the first glass into a tall narrow container and asks if it contains more water, less water or the same amount of water as the child's glass. The teacher then asks the child to explain or justify her or his answer.

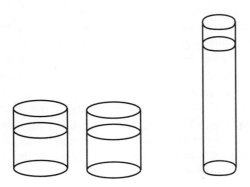

Capacity: nonstandard units
To describe *how much* a container holds, the child finds how many times a smaller container must be filled in order to hold the same

amount as the larger container. Again students should be encouraged to estimate before they measure and to record their results as they find the capacities of a variety of containers using a nonstandard unit. Children will find that the container will not be filled exactly by a whole number of units. They are instructed to measure to the nearest unit, but answers such as $4\frac{1}{2}$ cups are not uncommon.

Container	Estimate	Measure
mug	8 cups	10 cups
yogurt carton	————	————
————	————	————

Next, children can use units of different sizes to measure an object such as a cottage cheese container. They should predict what will happen when a smaller unit is used and explain why more of these units will be needed to fill the container.

Unit	Estimate	Measure
paper cup	4	5
ladle	————	————
————	————	————

A body unit for capacity is the "handful." Several different children can be asked to find how many handfuls of corn it takes to fill a margarine tub. Students can compare results and discuss the problems associated with using handfuls as a unit of measurement are discussed.

Children can make their own *calibrated beaker* by adhering a strip of masking tape to the length of a tall clear glass and marking with a felt pen the water level for 1, 2, 3, and 4 smaller containers. They can then use this device to find the approximate capacities of various containers with respect to the given unit.

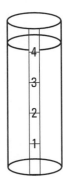

Capacity: standard units
A teacher can instruct children about measuring capacity in standard units by first telling them that a standard unit for measuring how much a container holds is a *liter* and that its symbol is L. Then show the children several different-shaped liter

containers and give them the opportunity to verify that the containers have the same capacity. An early activity with this unit is to sort a variety of containers using the categories "more than a liter," "about a liter," and "less than a liter." Familiar containers such as a 1 L water bottle should be displayed and referred to in connection with this unit. Similar activities can be done with quarts and gallons.

The *milliliter* (mL) is a very small unit and children usually first experience it by measuring with a set of uncalibrated beakers of sizes 500 mL, 250 mL, 100 mL, and 50 mL. Spoon sets including sizes 1 mL, 2 mL, 5 mL, 15 mL, and 25 mL can also be used to measure smaller amounts. Students can then learn to use graduated 1000 mL beakers marked in 100 mL or 50 mL intervals to measure capacity. They note that reading the scale is similar to using a ruler to measure length.

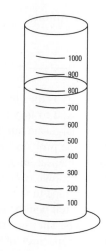

The problem in Activity 15-20 explores the relationship between volume and lateral surface area. Predict which one has the greater volume before performing the experiment. Computing the volumes of the two cylinders confirms that their ratio is 2 : 1.

Mass

Mass is a measure of the amount of matter in an object, while *weight* is the force of gravity acting on that mass. When astronauts orbit the earth in the space shuttle, their weight is less than it is on earth but their mass does not change. To compare two masses or to quantify mass, children first use a *two-pan balance*. Since this apparatus does not directly show what mass means, the concept is a difficult one for children to grasp. While the pound is a unit of weight in the customary system of measurement, the *kilogram* is a metric unit for mass. Compression scales and spring balances are calibrated to measure mass in standard units.

✳ ACTIVITY 15-20

COMPARING CYLINDERS

MATERIALS:
paper, scissors, popcorn

PROCEDURE:
1. Cut two pieces of paper 8 cm by 16 cm.
2. Roll each sheet to form a cylinder, one 8 cm high and the other 16 cm high.
3. Tape the edges together and stand them on a flat surface.
4. The two cylinders have the same lateral surface area. Do you think they have the same volume?
5. Fill each with popcorn to compare volumes.
6. Repeat with two papers 8 cm × 24 cm.

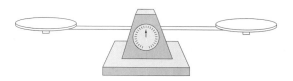

Mass: perception and direct comparison
To test for conservation of matter, the teacher can use clay to make two balls that the child judges to have the same amount of clay. The teacher then rolls one ball into a sausage shape and asks the child if it has more clay, less clay, or the same amount of clay as the other ball. The teacher then asks the child to elaborate on her or his answer.

To introduce the concept of mass, the teacher might hold a brick in one hand and a basketball in the other and ask "Which is bigger?" From their experience, children will likely know that although the ball has a larger volume, the brick is *heavier.* The teacher asks the class to name some things that are *heavy* and *light.* These ideas are further developed as the children hold objects and feel the pull of gravity. In most cases the masses of two objects cannot be compared by sight; they must be held to determine which is heavier. Activity 15-21 describes a task for partners.

The pan balance is helpful for making more accurate comparisons. Children should discuss why the side with the heavier object is lower. In Activity 15-22 children first estimate which of two objects is heavier, then check using a pan balance.

Mass: nonstandard units Objects that can be used as nonstandard units of mass include common wooden or plastic blocks, interlocking cubes, paper clips, and bolts or nuts. The children might be asked to estimate

✳ ACTIVITY 15-21

WHICH IS HEAVIER?

MATERIALS:
various objects

PROCEDURE:

1. Choose two objects.
2. Decide which is heavier by first looking, then by holding one object in each hand.
3. See if your partner makes the same decision.
4. Do this for other pairs of objects.
5. Record what you do and find.

Heavier	Lighter	Partner Agrees
book	ball	yes
scissors	stapler	no
_____	_____	_____

how many wooden blocks are *as heavy as* a glue stick, and to use the pan balance to measure. If five blocks are required, the teacher explains that the *mass* of the glue stick is about five blocks. The teacher should then repeat the procedure with several other objects.

Object	Estimate	Measure
glue stick	7 cubes	5 cubes
eraser	_____	_____
_____	_____	_____

✳ ACTIVITY 15-22

USING A PAN BALANCE TO COMPARE

MATERIALS:
pan balance, various objects

PROCEDURE:

1. Use the pan balance to compare pairs of objects. Estimate first. Then record which is heavier.

Objects	Estimate	Balance
book and ball	book heavier	book heavier
scissors and scotch tape	same	scissors heavier
_____	_____	_____

2. Arrange the objects in order from lightest to heaviest.
3. Are big things always heavier than small things? Why or why not?

To explore the relationship between the size of the unit and the number of units required to measure an object, the mass of a particular object, such as a glue stick, is then found using several different units.

Unit	Estimate	Measure
wooden cube	7	5
interlocking cube	12	15
bottle cap	_____	_____

Mass: standard units The *kilogram* (kg) is introduced as a standard unit for measuring mass. Sample activities include the following:

- Hold a kilogram mass. Use clay to make a ball with a mass of 1 kg. Check using a pan balance. Make another shape using this same clay. Is its mass still 1 kg? How do you know?
- Find things in the room that have a mass of about 1 kg, greater than 1 kg, and less than 1 kg. How many notebooks does it take to make a mass of 1 kg?
- At home use your bathroom scale to find your mass in kilograms. Ask your family members to do the same.

Similar activities can be done with pounds.

The *gram* (g) is one thousandth of a kilogram. The centicube is designed to have a mass of one gram. Children can use individual gram units to compare masses of objects, such as the small cube from the base-ten materials and a paper clip, and find the mass of various objects in grams.

Object	Estimate	Measure
nickel	10 g	5 g
eraser	_____	_____
pen	_____	_____
_____	_____	_____

Children can also use a set of standard masses (1 kg, 500 g, 200 g, 100 g, 50 g, 20 g, 10 g) to find the masses of various objects to the nearest 10 g.

Object	Estimate	Measure
glue bottle	200 g	250 g
stapler	_____	_____
_____	_____	_____

At home children should look for products that are packaged or sold by mass and report these to the class (e.g., a sack of sugar, a cake mix, a box of cereal, a candy bar, a bag of apples).

Students learn relationships between metric units of volume and mass when they find that the mass of a liter (cubic decimeter) of water is close to a kilogram. It follows that a milliliter (cubic centimeter) of water has a mass of one gram. Furthermore, since a cubic meter is a thousand cubic decimeters, the mass of water required to fill a tub of length, width, and height 1 m is 1000 kg, which is a *tonne* (t). Since an average football player has a mass of about 100 kg, it would take about ten of them to make a tonne.

Time

We use *time* to specify *when* an event occurred or will occur and also to describe *how long* an event lasted. Can you identify both aspects of time in the following sentence?

In 1988, Florence Griffith-Joyner set a new Olympic record of 10.62 sec. in the 100 m dash.

Judging the passage of time is not an easy task for children, and adults remark that "time flies when you're having fun." Learners should have many concept development experiences related to the *sequencing* of events and the *duration* of time periods before they are taught the complex process of *telling time* by reading a clock (Horak & Horak, 1983).

Time: perception and direct comparison

Questions such as the following help children develop concepts and vocabulary related to the sequencing of events:

- When you get dressed, which do you put on *first*—your shoes or your socks? When you get ready for bed do you brush your teeth *after* you put on your pajamas or *before* you put on your pajamas? What is the *last* thing you do before you go to bed?
- Name some things we do in class before lunch and some things we do after lunch.
- List in order five things you do after you wake up on Saturday mornings.

Early comparison tasks rely on memory. The teacher may describe two events and ask the child which takes longer or more time to complete. Examples are eating breakfast or walking to school, watching a cartoon or playing a soccer game. The class might also make a list of activities done during a school day (such as music, sharing time, and recess) and vote on which takes the least amount of time and which takes the most amount of time. A related task is to list several events in order according to how much time each takes.

To check for conservation of time, a teacher can place two toy animals side-by-side on a table. He or she then tells the child that the animals are going for a walk and to say when to start and when to stop. When the child says "go," the teacher hops the animals along the table so that they remain side-by-side. At "stop" the teacher asks the child if the animals started and stopped at the same time. The procedure is then repeated but with one animal taking longer hops so that when they stop, it will be further ahead. The teacher then asks the child if the animals started and stopped at the same time.

Although we cannot see time, it is sometimes possible to observe which of two events takes longer. To carry out direct comparisons of time, the two events must start simultaneously. Children are familiar with the idea that in a race the two runners must start at the same time. Comparing two different activities can help children focus on the concept of time duration rather than on "who won." For example, one child jumps up and down ten times while another stacks seven blocks. The class observes which event took more time to complete.

Time: nonstandard units

To establish the need for a unit for measuring time, the children should compare the times of two events that cannot be carried out concurrently; for example, the children may be asked how they might find out whether it takes Samantha longer to print her name neatly or tie the laces on her shoe. The problem then becomes one of determining how to measure *how long* an event takes.

Any repeated, regular action can serve as a nonstandard unit. One procedure is to have one child tap a pencil on a table according to a steady beat while another counts the taps. The number of taps required by other children to perform various tasks is then recorded. Later, children experiment with increasing and decreasing the rate of tapping, and discuss the relationship between this variable and the number of taps associated with a given event.

As an instrument for measuring time, children could make a *pendulum* by attaching a metal nut to a piece of string. Working in pairs, one partner counts the number of times the string swings back and forth while the other performs a task.

Task	Estimate	Measure
saying the alphabet	6 swings	5 swings
joining 10 interlocking cubes	_____	_____
_____	_____	_____

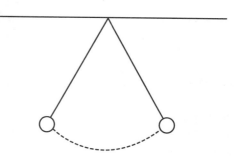

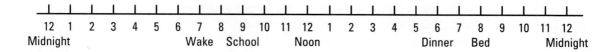

A *metronome* also is useful for measuring time. One person performs a task while others count the "ticks." The class can observe and discuss the effect of adjusting the device to tick at different speeds. The children might also use a *sand timer* to find how many times they can perform various actions, such as jumping up and down, before the sand runs out.

Time: standard units To introduce the *second* (s), the teacher should set the metronome so that its ticks are one second apart. If a metronome is not available, a pendulum of length 25 cm may be used. Children count in time with the metronome or the swing of the pendulum so that they are saying one number per second. They then measure the time required to do various tasks in seconds.

The following activities acquaint the children with the *minute:*

• Put your heads on your desks and close your eyes. I will tell you when a minute has passed. Now I will read to you for one minute. Next we will jump up and down for one minute. Did the length of these minutes seem the same to you? What are some things you can do that take about a minute? Less than a minute? More than a minute? Now close your eyes again and raise your hand when you think one minute has passed.

• Make a minute book. On each page describe something you can do in a minute or how many times you can do some activity in a minute. For example, how many sit-ups can you do in a minute? How many times can you bounce a ball?

If there is a dial clock in the classroom with a second hand, the minute can be related to the time it takes this hand to make a complete revolution. The class might also discuss the fact that this is equivalent to 60 seconds. Longer periods of time can then be referred to: recess is 15 minutes long; a music class lasts for 40 minutes.

The *hour* can be related to the child's experience as follows: lunch break is one hour; we go to school for three hours in the morning; movies are about two hours; you should get about ten hours of sleep each night. Children are familiar with the concept of a *day* and the ideas of *yesterday* and *tomorrow*. They might be asked to make a list showing how many of the 24 hours in a day they spend on the following activities: sleeping, eating, going to school, playing, doing chores, and watching television.

The *week, month,* and *year* are studied in connection with the *calendar.* In problems such as the following students use equivalencies among these units.

• How many years have you lived? How many months?

• Can you give your age in weeks? Days? Hours? Minutes? Seconds? You may want to use a calculator.

We now turn our attention from questions related to measuring *how long* an event took to questions about describing *when* an event occurred or is scheduled to occur. Children should be familiar with the dates of special events such as their birthday. The idea of *telling time* is motivated by the need to specify when events occur during the day. The related question is "What time is it?" To introduce this concept the teacher might draw an hour timeline on the board starting and ending at midnight. A dialogue such as the following might be used:

At 1 o'clock in the *morning,* most people are asleep. You probably wake up at about 7 o'clock. School starts at 9 o'clock and ends in the morning at 12 o'clock which is also called *noon.* An hour later it is 1 o'clock in the *afternoon.* School lets out at 3 o'clock. You might have dinner at 6 o'clock and go to bed at 8 o'clock. 12 o'clock at night is also called *midnight.*

We write 4 o'clock like this—4:00. Between 1 o'clock and 2 o'clock we indicate the number of minutes past the hour. If it is 23 minutes past 1 o'clock, we write the time like this—1:23. Four minutes past 1 o'clock is written 1:04 and one minute before 2 o'clock is 1:59. Times such as 1:23 are also read "one twenty-three."

Digital clocks show the time of day in this way. If a digital clock shows 5:40, what would it show 1 h later? 7 h later? 8 h later? 10 min later? 20 min later?

To introduce the *dial clock* the teacher might draw a horizontal 12-hour timeline and then discuss and draw how this looks when it is rearranged to form a circle with the number 12 at the top. He or she then shows a demonstration clock and asks questions such as the following: Which number is at the top (bottom)? Which number comes before 8? After 3? Before 12? After 12? The hour hand and the minute hand are identified and the positions of these hands for 5 o'clock, 8 o'clock, and 12 o'clock are shown. Children note how these clock times are the same and how they are different, and then use individual demonstration clocks to practice showing times on the hour.

To teach children to tell time between hours, teachers should use a clock with a minute scale as well as an hour scale (Thompson & Van de Walle, 1981). Prerequisite skills include counting by fives and reading a number line scale with numbers provided only for the multiples of five. Children first learn to place the minute hand for times such as 20 or 50 minutes past the hour, and later for 23 or 57 minutes past the hour. They should realize that at 5:40 the hour hand will be between 5 and 6, but precise placement is not important at this stage. Later they will relate the fraction of the circle traversed by the minute hand to the fractional part of the distance between two numbers moved by the hour hand. The ideas of "half past" and "quarter past" the hour and "before the hour" are taught after children can express all clock times "after the hour."

Other time topics usually found in the later elementary curriculum include A.M. and P.M. and the 24-hour clock.

Temperature

Temperature is a measure of how hot or cold an object is. A reading of a *thermometer,* the instrument used to measure temperature, does not reflect the quality of heat or temperature and this can cause difficulties for some students. The *Celsius scale* is commonly used for recording temperature in the metric system.

Temperature: perception and direct comparison Although temperature is not visible, large differences can be sensed by feel and we notice even relatively small changes in room temperatures. Questions using the terms "hot and cold" and "warm and cool" are used in concept development activities.

- Is it *hotter* in summer or in winter? Is it *cooler* on a sunny day or on a cloudy day? Is it *warmer* inside our classroom or outside today?
- How do you dress when you go outside on a *cold* day? Name something you drink when it is *cold/hot* outside. We use the word *temperature* when we talk about how hot or cold something is.

The teacher can collect and display pictures clearly indicating heat. The class could discuss how these pictures might be ordered using the idea of hot and cold. For a hands-on activity, the teacher prepares several containers with water of varying temperatures: hot and cold tap water, water at room temperature, and water from a refrigerator. The children feel the water in each container and order them from warmest to coldest.

The class can discuss what happens to water when it gets very hot and very cold, and how you can tell when some objects are very hot (for example, coals in a barbecue grill or an element of an electric stove).

Temperature: standard units No activities for measuring temperature using nonstandard units are suggested. Children will be familiar with hearing temperatures reported in *degrees Fahrenheit.* The teacher can state that the temperature in the room is about 70°F. The class should also discuss temperature readings on hot and cold days, the meaning of 32°F, and temperatures below zero.

Introduce the *thermometer* as an instrument for measuring temperature. To make a demonstration thermometer, join a piece of white ribbon and a piece of red ribbon and fit the ends through horizontal slits in a piece of cardboard. Mark a scale on the cardboard and slide the ribbon up and down to indicate the temperature rising and falling. The height of the red section indicates the temperature. The teacher should demonstrate how to read the scale, first at ten- or five-degree intervals and then to the nearest degree.

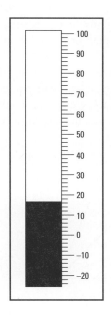

The teacher can explain that in a real thermometer the liquid in the tube expands as the temperature increases and the level rises. Children can then use a thermometer to find the temperature of water under several conditions to the nearest degree Fahrenheit.

	Estimate	**Measure**
water left sitting	20°C	18°C
hot tap water	_____	_____
cold tap water	_____	_____
ice water	_____	_____

Two useful benchmarks are the temperature at which water boils (212°F) and normal body temperature (about 98.6°F). As an ongoing activity students can record and graph the outside temperature (or the high and low temperatures) for a month. As a telecommunications project students could share these data with schools in different parts of the world.

Angle

As a geometric figure, an *angle* is the union of two rays that have the same endpoint. When we measure an angle we assign a number to the *spread* between the two arms, or rays. Angular measure can also be thought of in terms of the *amount of turning* about a point, which is used in defining the degree. In order for students to use a *protractor* correctly and understand what is being

measured, they first require experiences in comparing angles directly and in using arbitrary units of angular measure.

Angle: perception and direct comparison

Developing the concept of angle as a turn is particularly appropriate in the early elementary years (Wilson & Adams, 1992). Children can explore turning their bodies to make half, full, and quarter turns, and use their arms to represent clock hands. They can also examine and discuss angles made by a swinging door.

To introduce the notion of the size of an angle, the teacher might open a pair of scissors and direct attention to the *angle* formed by the two blades. He or she should ask the class whether they think this angle is "big" or "small" and how a bigger or smaller angle might be formed. The key idea is that the size of an angle has to do with the *spread* between the two blades, not their length. To make this point, compare angles formed by two pairs of scissors of different sizes, paying special attention to examples in which the angle formed by the larger scissors is smaller than the angle formed by the scissors with shorter blades.

Drawing representations of angles on a chalkboard or paper introduces the static view of angle. To develop basic concepts, the teacher might use an overhead projector to display two angles as indicated below and ask the class members which they think is bigger and how they might check their estimate.

Again, students find that they must focus on the relationship between the arms and not their length. Mention that, geometrically, the arms of an angle are rays and thus extend indefinitely. To compare the two angles, one first makes a tracing of one of them and directly compares the tracing with the other angle. When the vertices and one of the arms are matched, the other arm of the smaller angle lies in the interior of the larger angle.

Next, teachers can give students tracing paper and a sheet containing angles of various measures in a number of different positions, with instructions to order them according to size. Two of these angles should have the same measure.

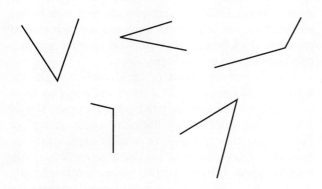

Angle: nonstandard units The teacher can draw an angle on the chalkboard and ask students how they might determine "how big" the angle is. One strategy that is often suggested is to use a ruler to measure the distance between the arms. It should be recognized that students can use this procedure to compare and quantify angular measure, provided that they take the measurement at a fixed distance from the vertex along the arm(s).

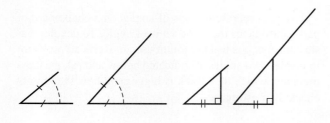

When students are reminded that an important characteristic of a unit is that it has the same attribute as that to be measured, they should realize that a small angle can be used as a unit. The question then is how many copies of this small angle fit inside the angle to be measured. A wedge cut from cardboard is useful as a unit to measure the angle on the chalkboard.

Students should predict and verify the result of using a smaller unit angle to measure the angle in question. As an activity students could prepare several copies of cardboard wedges representing angles of three different sizes. They then draw an angle on paper and measure it using the three different units. Teachers should remind students to estimate before measuring and to measure to the nearest unit.

Students can create an instrument for measuring angles by partitioning a paper half circle into equal sectors by folding. The teacher can then challenge them to use this "protractor" to find the measures of angles of various cardboard wedges.

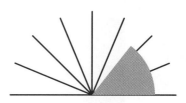

Angle: standard units Before students learn about the degree as a standard unit of angular measure, they can use the familiar *right angle* as a referent. This special angle can first be introduced in relation to body turns. Some students reason that since a quarter turn right is called a right angle, a quarter turn left is called a "left" angle. Later, students should be shown how to fold a piece of paper twice to produce a right angle. They then use this "right angle tester" to identify right angles on familiar objects at their desk and in the room, and to classify other angles as greater than or less than a right angle. To illustrate a *straight angle,* two right angles can be placed together. Tell students that an *acute* angle has a measure that is less than a right angle, and an *obtuse* angle has a measure greater than a right angle but less than a straight angle.

Students explore the measures of angles of triangles and quadrilaterals in Activities 15-23 and 15-24.

The *degree* can be defined as the amount of turning (or the size of unit angle) such that the measure of a quarter turn (or right angle) is 90°. It follows that the measure of a half turn (or straight angle) is 180° and the measure of a full turn is 360°.

Since the number 360 is not a power of ten, students may be interested in knowing the origin of the degree. This unit originated with the Babylonians who observed that the position of the sun changes by the same amount each day. They called the amount of turn the earth makes each day from the viewpoint of the sun one degree. Because 365 has few divisors, they decided to divide the circle into 360 parts instead (Newton, 1988).

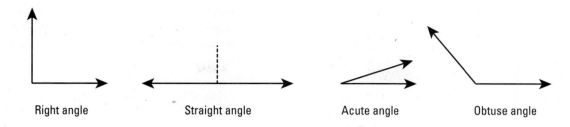

Right angle   Straight angle   Acute angle   Obtuse angle

✷ ACTIVITY 15-23

ANGLES OF TRIANGLES

MATERIALS:
straight edge

PROCEDURE:
1. Draw a triangle with a right angle.

2. Can you draw a triangle with two right angles? Why or why not?

3. Try to draw triangles with angles as follows:
   • one obtuse angle
   • two obtuse angles
   • three acute angles

4. If possible, draw a quadrilateral with:
   • exactly one right angle
   • exactly two right angles
   • exactly three right angles
   • four right angles.

At this point, teachers can ask the class to estimate the measures of various acute and obtuse angles drawn on the board by the teacher, and draw angles of approximately 45°, 60°, 135°, and 170°. The teacher then demonstrates how to use a *protractor* to measure angles in degrees, emphasizing the correct placement of the baseline and the vertex. Students practice using a protractor to measure angles and construct angles with given measures. Working in pairs, one student draws an angle and the other estimates and then measures it. Next, the students reverse roles. Later, students learn to measure and construct angles greater than 180°.

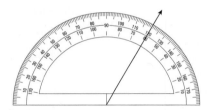

In Activity 15-25 students use protractors to investigate the sum of the interior angles of various polygons.

✷ ACTIVITY 15-24

TRIANGLE ANGLES

MATERIALS:
light cardboard, scissors

PROCEDURE:
1. Cut a triangle out of cardboard.

2. Cut off each of the corners and place the three angles together. What kind of angle is formed?

3. Repeat with a different-shaped triangle. Did you get the same result?

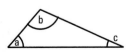   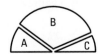

4. Cut a cardboard quadrilateral.

5. Cut off the four corners and place the four angles together. What did you find?

✷ ACTIVITY 15-25

SUM OF ANGLES IN A POLYGON

MATERIALS:
a straight edge, protractor

PROCEDURE:
1. Draw several different-shaped triangles.

2. Measure each of the interior angles and find the sum of the three angles of each triangle.

3. What do you notice?

4. Repeat for quadrilaterals, pentagons, and hexagons.

5. Can you find a pattern?

CONCLUSION

When we measure, we assign a number to a physical property of an object or to an event by comparing it with a unit. Beginning instruction in measurement stresses language development and involves activities that give meaning to the attribute: perception and physical materials are used to make direct and indirect comparisons. Measuring should be carried out first with nonstandard units, then with standard SI units. Students need to be able to identify appropriate units for given situations and estimate and use instruments or formulas to measure with those units. As they learn measurement concepts and skills, learners are actively involved in solving problems.

Measurement is a practical, useful skill. Students should appreciate the role it plays in their everyday lives and in modern society. Measurement ideas should be identified, applied, and reinforced in other school subjects including science, social studies, physical education, art, and music. Students should enjoy measuring and have confidence in their ability to use their knowledge and skills to solve problems in the real world.

For Your Journal

When you have finished studying this chapter, reflect on these questions in your math journal:

1. What are some examples of real-world situations in which nonstandard and standard units of measure are used? Discuss the reasons for each.

2. How does measuring with nonstandard units help students use standard units?

3. How were you taught to find perimeter, area, and volume when you were in elementary school? Compare and contrast your experiences with the recommendations of this chapter.

4. Visit a middle school classroom and informally interview several students to assess their understanding of area and perimeter. What were their understandings and misconceptions about these concepts?

For Your Portfolio

When you have finished studying this chapter, complete these activities to include in your professional portfolio:

1. Examine a textbook's section on measurement. Discuss it in relation to the content of this chapter. How is actual measurement provided for in the textbook activities?

2. Write a lesson plan to introduce nonstandard measurement of an attribute of your choice (either length, area, volume, capacity, mass, time, temperature, or angle).

3. Write a lesson plan to introduce standard measurement of an attribute of your choice (either length, area, volume, capacity, mass, time, temperature, or angle).

Resources for Teachers

Children's Books

McMillan, B. (1989). *Time to . . .* New York: Scholastic, Inc.

Olney, R., & Olney, P. (1984). *How long? to go, to grow, to know.* New York: William Morrow & Co.

Pluckrose, H. (1995). *Math counts: Length.* USA: Children's Press.

Books on Measurement

Geddes, D. (1994). *Measurement in the middle grades: curriculum evaluation standards for school mathematics addenda series grade 5–8.* Reston, VA: National Council of Teachers of Mathematics.

Rectanus, C. (1997). *Math by all means: Area and perimeter grades 5–6.* USA: Math Solutions Publications.

Shroyer, J., & Fitzgerald, W. (1986). *Middle grades mathematics project: Mouse and elephant: Measuring growth.* Menlo Park, CA: Addison-Wesley Publishing Company.

Links to the Internet

Explorer: Measurement

http://explorer.scrtec.org/explorer/explorer-db/browse/static/Mathematics/browse/f55.html

Contains many lessons on and lists of resources for measurement.

Shape Surveyor

http://www.funbrain.com/poly/index.html

Contains a game on finding area and perimeter.

CHAPTER 16

Collecting, Organizing, and Interpreting Data

Key Concepts

- Stages of graphing experiences
- Types of graphs
- Measures of central tendency
- Probability
- Using technology

Focus Questions

When you have finished studying this chapter, you should be able to answer these questions:

1. What are the stages of graphing experiences that children should encounter? Give an example of each stage.

2. What different types of graphs are used in organizing and interpreting data? Give an example of each type.

3. What are the three measures of central tendency? How can teachers help students to better understand each of these measures?

4. What are some ways to use technology to help in collecting, organizing, and interpreting data?

Data are all around us. Indeed, sometimes data overwhelm us. Children, too, are bombarded with all kinds of data that they would like to understand. How? What? When? Where? Who? Why? are real-life questions that often require the collection, organization, and interpretation of data in order to be answered.

What do we know of U.S. students' understanding of data analysis, statistics, and probability? The sixth National Assessment of Educational Progress (NAEP) assessment noted that most fourth-, eighth-, and twelfth-grade students tested were able to read and use data presented in tables. But students in all three grade levels tested had "difficulty communicating their reasoning about data representation" (Zawojewski & Heckman, 1997, p. 196). Teaching about data analysis must be more than just creating and reading graphs. Instruction must help students to understand, interpret, and apply reasoning in studying data.

In this chapter we will describe data collection techniques, examine methods for organizing and displaying data, and discuss ways of interpreting data to make predictions—all with the intent of designing mathematics instruction to help students use and interpret data in decision making. ○

COLLECTING AND ORGANIZING DATA

STANDARDS LINK 16-1
In grades K–4, the mathematics curriculum should include experiences with data analysis and probability so that students can

- collect, organize, and describe data;
- construct, read, and interpret displays of data;
- formulate and solve problems that involve collecting and analyzing data;
- explore concepts of chance. (NCTM, 1989, p. 54)

STANDARDS LINK 16-2
In grades 5–8, the mathematics curriculum should include exploration of statistics in real-world situations so that students can

- systematically collect, organize, and describe data;
- construct, read, and interpret tables, charts, and graphs;
- make inferences and convincing arguments that are based on data analysis;
- evaluate arguments that are based on data analysis;
- develop an appreciation for statistical methods as powerful means for decision making. (NCTM, 1989, p. 105)

There must be a reason for collecting data. Children need to have some question they want to answer—a question they agreed upon after a brainstorming session, perhaps, or a question that arises from a class discussion in some other subject area or from someone's recent experience. A provocative question by the teacher may also give rise to the need to collect data. For example, "Do more children have dogs than cats for pets?" or "I think vanilla is the most liked flavor of ice cream by students in this class." These questions arouse interest. Children want to find out—even to prove that the teacher's supposition is wrong.

Scenarios such as those just described suggest that we are involved with an investigation or research project rather than a short in-class activity. The first two steps in a research model appropriate for elementary school mathematics proposed by Bohan, Irby, and Vogel (1995) involve choosing a question to answer or problem to solve. The complete model consists of seven steps:

Step 1: Brainstorm for questions students would like answered.
Step 2: Choose one of the questions or problems.

Step 3: Predict what the outcome will be.
Step 4: Develop a plan to test the predicted outcome.
Step 5: Carry out the plan.
Step 6: Analyze the data. Is the hypothesis supported?
Step 7: Look back. Answer the question. Should the information be shared? With whom? How could it be shared?

STANDARDS LINK 16-3
A spirit of investigation and exploration should permeate statistics instruction. Children's questions about the physical world can often be answered by collecting and analyzing data. After generating questions, they decide what information is appropriate and how it can be collected, displayed, and interpreted to answer their questions. The analysis and evaluation that occur as children attempt to draw conclusions about the original problem often lead to new conjectures and productive investigations. This entire process broadens children's views of mathematics and its usefulness. (NCTM, 1989, p. 54)

It is very important that children collect their own data (Russell & Friel, 1989). This contributes ownership, interest, and reality to their experience. A class survey is one of the most obvious and easy ways of getting information with which all students can identify. The next section presents a number of ideas for surveys, including children's favorites—one of the most fruitful sources of data (Young, 1991). Children can make surveys on favorite pets, fruits, ice cream flavors, colors, and so on and graph the data. For some topics, they can extend the survey to include other classes or the whole school. For example, older children can take surveys of traffic outside the school, type of clothing worn by people who enter a nearby mall, or the amount of sugar or fiber in several brands of cereal.

Hofstetter and Sgroi (1996) used cereal boxes as the basis for a data management project. After collecting a variety of empty boxes of different brands of cereal, the children described the boxes (geometry) and then classified and ordered them using different criteria. Later, they analyzed and graphed the food content.

M&Ms or other candy can also be used by children as firsthand data (Browning, Channell, & Meyer, 1994; Brosnan, 1996). The students can predict the number of each color of candy to be found in one box, then count and graph for themselves.

In general, food seems to be a popular basis for data management activities. Hitch and Armstrong (1994) and Shannon (1995) also use it. In addition, children's literature can provide a rich source of ideas for data management projects (Litton, 1995). Bankard and Fennell (1991) and Brahier and Speer (1995) also provide some projects

FIGURE 16-1

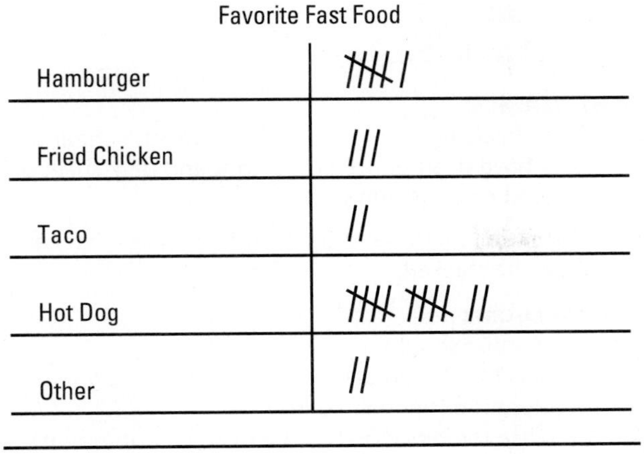

Favorite Fast Food

Hamburger	卌 l
Fried Chicken	lll
Taco	ll
Hot Dog	卌 卌 ll
Other	ll

GRAPHING DATA

Graphs summarize data in a concise and pictorial form. Graphing, while a legitimate mathematics education topic in its own right, is best thought of as an integrative component of the program. It is integrative within mathematics in that graphs can be used when developing other mathematical topics. Graphs, for instance, can be used as a means of generating computational exercises, for showing the number of prismatic as opposed to pyramidal shapes students can find in the classroom, the variability in the noon-hour temperature outside the classroom over a period of a week, and many other relationships. An understanding of ratios, proportions, percents, fractions, and other topics are often required in constructing or interpreting more advanced graphs.

Graphing is also integrative in the sense that it brings together mathematics and other curriculum subjects such as science, physical education, social studies, and so on. Thus, from a teaching point of view, graphing should not be thought of as a strand to be covered in a four-week unit, but as something to be done from September through June.

Students may be introduced to graphing as early as the first grade. Skills associated with graphing include constructing graphs, reading information from graphs, and interpreting the information by discussing or writing about it.

that would involve gathering data firsthand, then organizing and displaying them in graphical form.

The Internet and electronic mail can be interesting media for collecting data. Comparing data collected and shared by children from different countries can lead to some valuable learning in mathematics and beyond.

A useful technique for recording data is a tally. The teacher can demonstrate this technique to the whole class by taking a survey of students' favorite fast food, weekend activity, or some other topic. Demonstrate making a tally for each child's preference as in Figure 16-1.

Young children should also have opportunities to discover that the way data are organized varies with the kinds of questions one wants to ask. Figure 16-2 shows three ways in which data from a survey of class members' favorite fruit could be organized. Figure 16-2(a) would be the best display if you wanted to know Nathan's favorite fruit. On the other hand, if you were interested in the number of people who prefer oranges, or were determining the most popular fruit in the class, you would consult the display in either (b) or (c) of Figure 16-2.

> **STANDARDS LINK 16-4**
> Children should learn that data can be displayed in different ways and that depending on the question being asked, one type of display might be more appropriate than another. A variety of early experiences helps children build a foundation for creating conventional graphs. (NCTM, 1989, p. 55)

FIGURE 16-2

Fruit Survey

Name	Fruit
Wendy	Apples
Seyi	Oranges
Nathan	Bananas
Mavis	Oranges
John	Apples
	Grapes

(a)

Fruit Survey

Fruit	Choices
Oranges	✓ ✓ ✓ ✓ ✓ ✓ ✓
Apples	✓ ✓ ✓ ✓ ✓ ✓
Bananas	✓ ✓ ✓
Grapes	✓

(b)

Fruit Survey

Fruit	Frequency
Oranges	12
Apples	6
Bananas	3
Grapes	1

(c)

Early Experiences

Most graphic representations at the primary level will be some form of bar graph. Some introduction to coordinate graphing is often included before the end of the primary grades. At this level, children's graphing experiences generally progress through four overlapping stages: Concrete, Concrete-Pictorial, Pictorial-Abstract, and Abstract.

Concrete stage Children's early graphing experiences should involve constructing graphs with concrete materials. Each object such as a block should represent only one thing and children should compare only two events or things.

There are numerous dichotomous events that young children enjoy graphing. Some of these include:

- eye glasses—no eye glasses
- walked to school—rode to school
- left handed—right handed

When modeling graphs concretely, children like to be the objects. An initial query might be, "I wonder if more children walked to school than rode to school this morning." Children could form two straight lines, those who walked in one line and those who rode in the other. Depending on the ratio in the class, children may or may not be able to perceive a difference in the length of the line. If children formed two lines on the basis of whether they printed with their right hand or left hand, the lines would most likely be very different in length. In these examples, the line is analogous to a bar in a bar graph, so you may want to discuss the following aspects of graphing with the students:

- the beginning of the lines should be along the same line (axis).
- distance between students in line should be uniform.

While the children like to "act out" the graph, there are a number of disadvantages to this approach. The most significant is that the children have difficulty perceiving which line is longer because they are part of a line. They often need to "get out of line" to check, which can create problems with the line as it was initially constituted. Other disadvantages include the possible lack of uniformity in spacing and the possibility of the lines not starting at the same imaginary axis.

Experiences such as the one described in Activity 16-1 avoid these difficulties. This activity is probably best done in a group of about one-half the class; otherwise, the stacks of blocks used in the activity may be-

---

✳ ACTIVITY 16-1

CONCRETE GRAPH (LIGHT vs. Dark Hair)

MATERIALS:
- Two sheets of paper on which the words *light* and *dark* have been printed (or a light and dark sheet of colored construction paper).
- Selection of light- and dark-colored blocks that can easily be stacked.

PROCEDURE:
1. Each child should
   - select a block that he or she thinks most resembles his or her hair color.
   - place the block on the stack on the appropriate sheet as shown in the figure.
2. Talk about what the graph tells you.
3. Talk about things the graph does not tell you. (The teacher may need to ask a leading question such as, "Does this graph tell us how many children are absent today?")

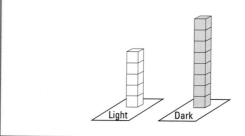

---

come too high and topple before all the blocks are placed. The two groups can compare their graphs afterward.

An activity that might serve as a transition to the next level would be to have children draw a picture of themselves on an index card. A query to the children might be, "Would you like to be younger or older than you are?" Each child would then tack his or her picture in the appropriate section of a bulletin board chart the teacher prepares beforehand. See Figure 16-3.

Since the pictures will be somewhat randomly placed in the boxes, it may not be easy to see if there is a difference. Children could count to decide, or they might be asked to organize the cards in each box into an array.

A by-product of this activity may be some further insight into the thoughts of your students. These thoughts could be elicited as an extension of the reading/interpretation questions. That is, you could follow a question like, "Do more children prefer to be younger or do more prefer to be older?" with, "Why would you like to be older (younger)?"

FIGURE 16-3

I Would Like to Be:

Younger | Older

Concrete-pictorial stage In this stage, children will use pictorial representation of objects in addition to concrete materials. They may compare more than two events but will still maintain the one-to-one correspondence between object or picture and what is being graphed.

The last example in the previous section was a transition to this level. To make it a true Level 2 activity, change the bulletin board chart to include three boxes as in Figure 16-4.

Children like to talk about their birthdays. They could make a block graph of birthday months. Normally a comparison of twelve things is too much for primary children, but birthdays may be an exception due to pertinence and interest. Furthermore, it will reinforce the students' learning of the months of the year. Figure 16-5 shows one

FIGURE 16-4

I Would Like to Be:

Younger | Older | Same Age

form that this graph might take. If you had photocopies of a child's photo, each child could tack his or her picture above the appropriate month to make a bulletin board graph.

Children's favorites is an excellent setting for a variety of Stage 2 graphing activities. Favorite flavor of ice cream is one possibility. An introductory motivational query might be, "I think most children in the class like chocolate ice cream the best." A bulletin board display like the one in Figure 16-6 could be prepared as well as several cutouts of each of the anticipated flavors. Ask the children to take one of the paper cones representing their favorite flavor and pin it above the appropriate model.

A primary grade teacher could capitalize on the variety of characteristics of buttons to develop Level 2 graphing experiences. For example, children in cooperative learning groups could each take a handful of buttons, put their selections together, and create a graph as in Figure 16-7. Some possible comparisons include:

- number of holes: 0, 2, 4
- flat versus raised
- material: plastic, metal, wood
- shapes: round, square, other
- texture: smooth, rough, fabric-covered, other

Encourage the children to "interpret" the graph by asking one or two leading questions such as "What does the graph tell you?" or "What can you learn from the graph?" Children might also discuss how this graph could help them if they were a button maker. Once children's writing skills have developed sufficiently, they could write a report about what they learned.

Pictorial-abstract stage At the third level, pictorial-abstract, primary children continue to make bar graphs with pictures, but they also make a transition to the abstract by using gummed stickers, colored cards, etc., to form the graph.

Any of the topics used in the previous two levels could be used at Level 3. Children could pin objects or pictures of objects on the bulletin board or on paper as before. Then they could construct the same graph by putting gummed stickers on a chart. In Figure 16-8(a), the children pinned pictures of their favorite fruit on a bulletin board chart. Figure 16-8(b) shows the same information with gummed stickers.

A transition to the next level could be developed by having children fill in squares, one square for each tally on their survey. This could easily be done with the favorite fruit activity. Provide children with a template as in Figure 16-9 (without the shading) and challenge them to figure out how they could represent the same information on this graph.

FIGURE 16-5

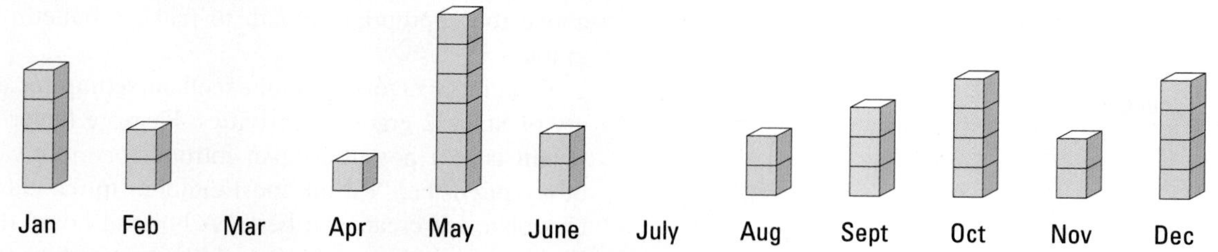

| Jan | Feb | Mar | Apr | May | June | July | Aug | Sept | Oct | Nov | Dec |

Pictographs. While most pictographs are a Level 4 (abstract) activity, they can be introduced at Level 3 in a setting in which the one-to-one correspondence is convenient. For example, children could be given the graph in Figure 16-10 and asked to read, interpret, and discuss it through questions such as:

- How many brothers and sisters does Heather have?
- Who has the most brothers and sisters?
- Does Kerri have more brothers and sisters than Heather?
- What else does the graph tell you?

To construct a simple one-to-one pictograph children could be given a template as shown in Figure 16-11. They would tally the number of library books in their desk, print their name in one of the rows, then draw one square for each book they found. Some may have no books, in which case they would only print their name. Students could follow this by writing a short paragraph about the graph.

Glyphs. *Glyphs,* another form of picture graph, are a great way to represent or communicate data. They have their origin in ancient hiero*glyph*ics or picture writing and have been used more recently in medical and scientific applications. Children and teachers in the primary grades are now using glyphs to represent information (Cartland, 1996; Harbaugh, 1995). Since glyphs are a form of picture graph they are easily incorporated into data management experiences.

Children find glyphs both easy and fun to construct. Harbaugh (1995) describes the process as follows:

> Simply (1) decide to create either a facial glyph or a shape glyph, (2) determine the various characteristics to be explained, (3) assign glyph features to the characteristics, (4) print the corresponding key, and (5) draw the glyph (p. 511).

The following example has been adapted from Cartland (1996). After seeing some hot air balloons float over the school, children might decide to use a hot

FIGURE 16-6

My Favorite Ice Cream

FIGURE 16-7

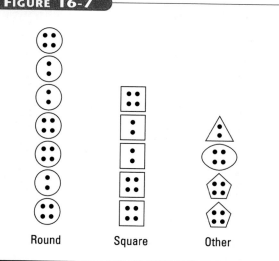

Round   Square   Other

FIGURE 16-8

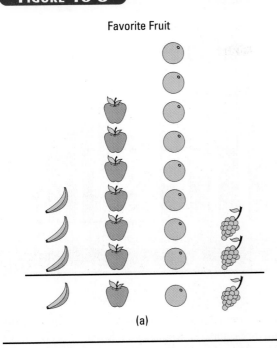

(a)

(b)

FIGURE 16-9

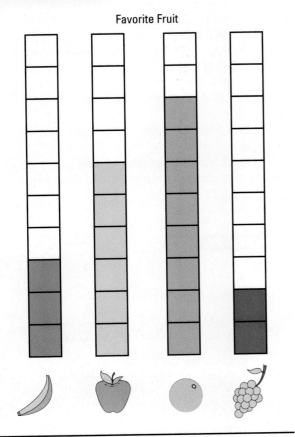

Favorite Fruit

FIGURE 16-10

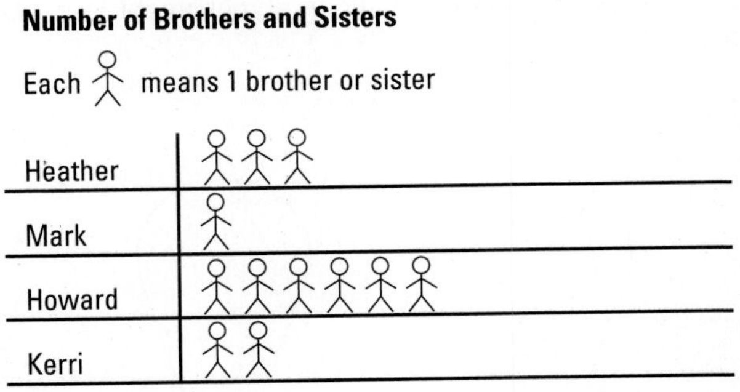

Number of Brothers and Sisters

Each ⚧ means 1 brother or sister

Heather	⚧ ⚧ ⚧
Mark	⚧
Howard	⚧ ⚧ ⚧ ⚧ ⚧ ⚧
Kerri	⚧ ⚧

FIGURE 16-11

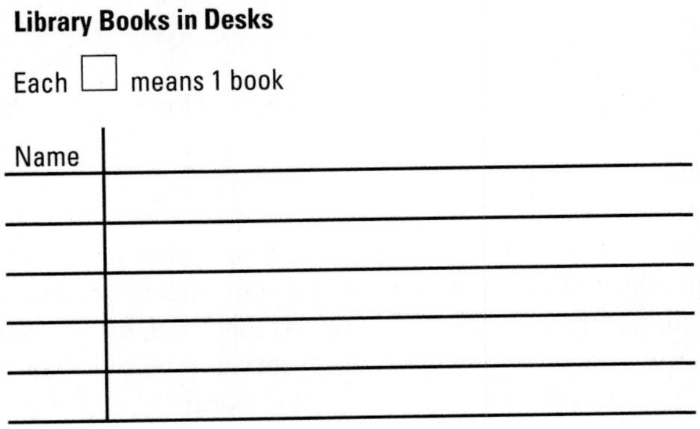

Library Books in Desks

Each ☐ means 1 book

| Name | |

air balloon shape for a glyph. Children might decide to use

1. a different basket shape to represent their position in the family.

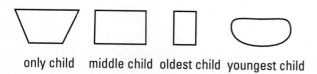

only child   middle child oldest child youngest child

2. the number of strings attaching the basket to the balloon to represent the number of people in their home.
3. the design on the basket to represent the main language spoken at home.

English: **+++**   Ukrainian: ✓✓✓

French: **▲▲▲**   Spanish: ✳✳✳

Vietnamese: Ŏ Ŏ Ŏ   Other: ◆◆◆

Two children's hot air balloon glyphs might look like this:

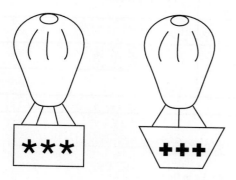

Harbaugh (1995) and Sacco, Copes, Sloyer, and Stark (1987) present other samples of glyphs that young children have constructed.

Abstract stage If adequate experiences have been provided in Levels 1 to 3, the move to abstract representation should be relatively easy. At this level, one-to-one correspondence of objects to events is replaced with a one-to-many correspondence. This normally requires a scale for one of the axes. Rectangular bars replace the colored squares and line graphs can be introduced.

Again, many of the topics graphed earlier could be used at this level. It is not the topic, but rather the way the

FIGURE 16-12

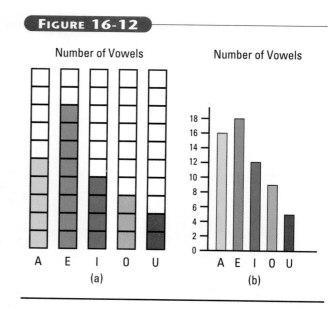

data are presented that determines the level. Consider the introductory query, "I wonder which vowel occurs most often in writing." At Level 3, children might select a sentence from their reader or library book, tally the occurrence of each vowel, and then color squares, one square for each occurrence as in Figure 16-12(a).

At Level 4 (abstract level), students could choose a paragraph and tally the occurrence of vowels as before. A paragraph may provide more vowels than they wish to handle on their graph using one square for each occurrence. A scale of 1 square representing 2 occurrences may be convenient. Later the squares can be replaced with rectangular bars. The graph shown in Figure 16-12(b) may result.

The one-for-many relationship leads naturally into pictographs in which the object may represent 2, 5, 10, or some other convenient number of things. Figure 16-13 shows a pictograph of the number of soda can tabs a few

FIGURE 16-13

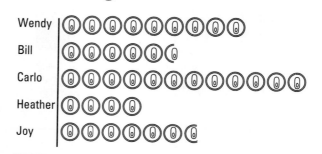

children brought to school as part of a class project investigating how much room 1000 soda can tabs would take up.

Another activity that would involve Level 4 graphing could be instigated with the query, "What kind of vehicle passes by our school most often?" This should be done on a day a parent volunteer or teacher-assistant is available to help. One or two small groups could go out with the parent or aide for a 20- or 30-minute period to collect the data by keeping a tally of the different kinds of vehicles that pass by.

Afterward, students could color a rectangular bar as in Figure 16-14, rather than preexisting squares. An excellent interpretation activity could involve writing a letter to the principal describing the vehicular activity and perhaps making some safety recommendations.

Line graphs are another way to represent information at Level 4. For example, children could record the outside temperature at a given time each day for a week. The data could be graphed using a bar graph as before. See Figure 16-15(a). Discuss how each data point can be joined with a line as shown in Figure 16-15(b). Line graphs are not so mysterious for young children if they understand this difference, namely that in a bar graph, data points determine the height of a rectangle (the bar) from the axis, whereas in a line graph the same data points are simply joined with a line. Figure 16-15(b) and Figure 16-15(c) show this distinction.

One important distinction, however, between line and bar graphs that children need to understand is that bars represent a category or event, whereas line graphs represent continuous data such as temperature. Both axes on a smooth line graph involve a continuous scale. In the case of a broken line graph, one scale may not be numeric but is at least ordered as in the case of the months of the year (see Figure 16-16).

FIGURE 16-15

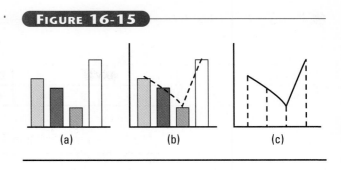

(a)   (b)   (c)

A good reading/interpretation activity is to give children a line graph with a title and the nature of the units for each axis and ask them to describe orally or in writing what is happening. This will also reinforce the continuous nature of the data. Activity 16-2 is an example of this type of exercise.

Once this basic understanding is developed, upper elementary and middle school children are ready for more advanced line graphs. But first, a transitional activity such as Activity 16-3 would help children think about the kind of continuous activity or relationship represented by both straight line and curved line graphs.

Upper elementary and junior high school students can use a multiple line graph to compare two or more things.

✳ ACTIVITY 16-2

GAS STOP

MATERIALS:
graph (below)

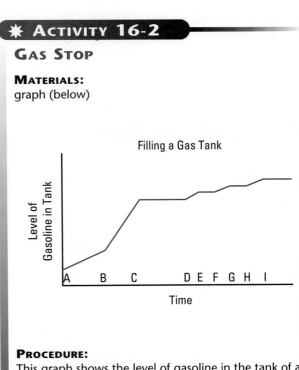

Filling a Gas Tank

PROCEDURE:
This graph shows the level of gasoline in the tank of a car as it is being filled. Write as interesting a story as you can about this.

Include what happened at points (Time) A, B, C, D, E, F, G, H, and I.

FIGURE 16-14

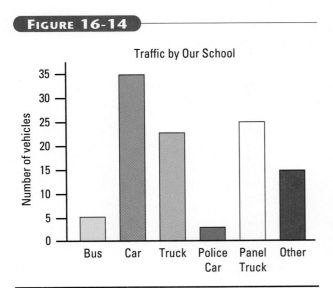

Traffic by Our School

FIGURE 16-16

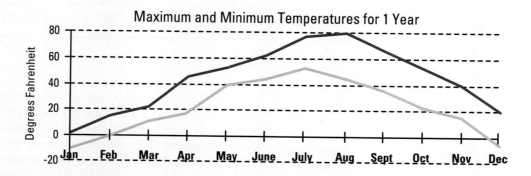

	Jan	Feb	Mar	Apr	May	June	July	Aug	Sept	Oct	Nov	Dec
Maximum	2	16	22	48	56	62	78	80	62	56	40	20
Minimum	−18	0	10	18	40	44	56	46	38	24	16	−6

For example, a group of children could obtain the maximum and minimum temperatures for each month of the year from the local weather office. They would plot two line graphs on the same chart, one showing the maximum, the other the minimum temperature each month and orally report their observations and conclusions to the class or prepare a written report. Upper elementary or junior high students who have had a little experience with a computer spreadsheet may volunteer to enter the data and have the computer produce the graph. Figure 16-16 shows a line graph and the spreadsheet from which it was generated.

Coordinate Graphing

Coordinate graphing is normally introduced at about the Grade 3 level. Smith (1986) found that "third graders are able to understand the concepts and master the skills required" (p. 11). He also recommends that, pedagogically, coordinate graphing should be presented "as an integrated unit rather than in a piecemeal fashion" (p. 11). Superimposing a grid on a "community" and using coordinates to locate buildings on a map might be an example of an integration of a social studies unit with mathematical skills.

✴ ACTIVITY 16-3

COLLECTING WATER

MATERIALS:
graphs (below)

PROCEDURE:
Write a story about each graph.

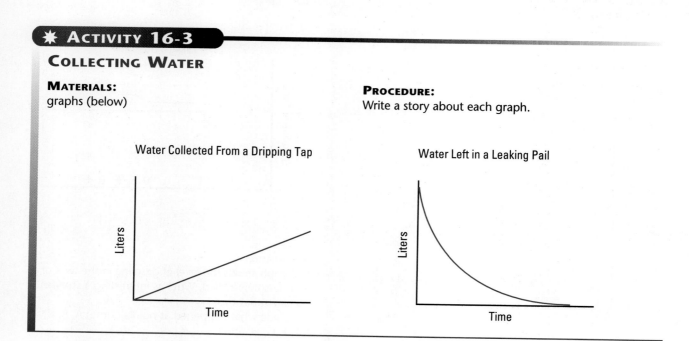

To introduce coordinate graphs, Smith (1986) suggests beginning with the geoboard. Children can decide on how to label each nail or peg on a 5-by-5 square geoboard. They might begin by simply labeling them from A through Y, as shown in Figure 16-17(a), 1 through 25. With some guidance they can be led to name just the rows and columns as in Figure 16-17(b). The need for the 0 coordinates can be elicited by presenting a grid similar to Figure 16-17(c) on the overhead projector. Place a small object such as a small plastic animal (it is all right that children will see only the outline) at a particular location and ask the students to tell you where the animal is hiding. After a few repetitions, place the animal on one of the points on one of the axes, say (0,3) and ask where the animal is hiding. Students could now suggest labels for the points on each of the axes.

Using the geoboard or dot paper, children can engage in activities such as copying shapes from coordinate descriptions and playing simple versions of tic-tac-toe and Battleship (Smith, 1986).

Initially the language needs to be the language of the child. A teacher might project a simple grid as in Figure 16-18 and ask the children to describe how to find the lost puppy if they are standing at the origin (0,0). They will likely use statements such as "go over 3 and up 2." Initial activities use terms such as "over," "across," "up," etc. Once children understand the concept it is relatively easy to introduce notation such as ($\rightarrow 3, \uparrow 2$), and then the standard notation (3,2). Once children reach this stage of understanding they can apply their understanding to some more practical or integrative activities as in Figure 16-19 (Smith, 1986).

Next, the grid can be expanded to include 10 or more coordinate points on each axis. Students could be given coordinates, asked to plot them, and join them in order to discover a design as in Figure 16-20. They could extend this by creating a design, recording and giving only the

FIGURE 16-18

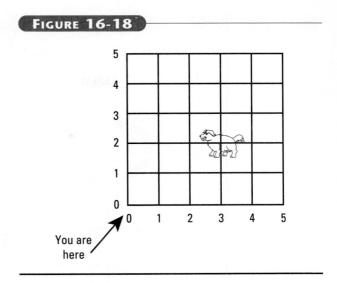

ordered coordinates to a friend, and asking the friend to draw the design.

Vissa (1987) suggests an activity in which the teacher gives the students half of a design on a coordinate grid. The students are to complete it and list the coordinates of each corner. Figure 16-21 is one example from her article. She also extends coordinate graphing to three-dimensions using an airplane in space and fish in a water tank (negative coordinates).

Circle or Pie Graphs

Circle or pie graphs appear frequently in newspapers, brochures, and many business documents. A circle graph clearly shows how a whole is broken into parts. Sources of revenue or a breakdown of expenditures are usually shown with a circle or pie graph. Temperatures are appropriate for a line graph but not normally for circle graphs.

FIGURE 16-17

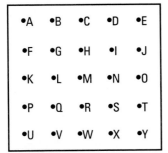

(a) Coordinates named A - Y

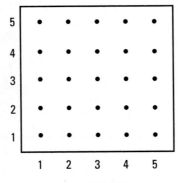

(b) Coordinates named by rows and columns

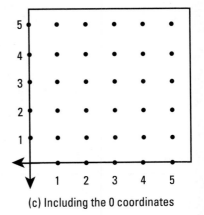

(c) Including the 0 coordinates

FIGURE 16-19

(a) What are the coordinates of the different sites?

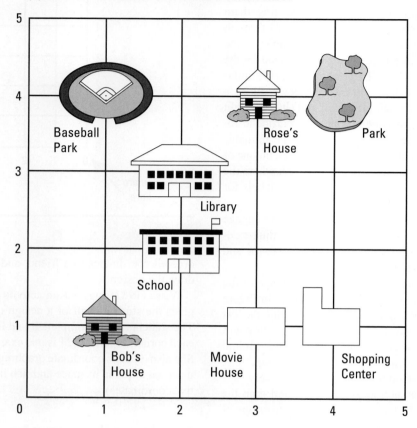

(b) What are the coordinates of the different sites?

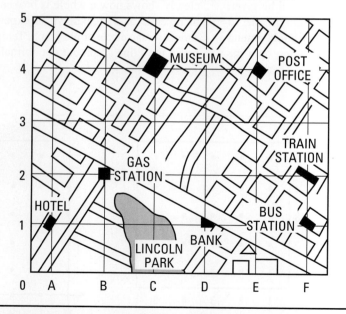

Source: From R. F. Smith (1986). Let's do it: Coordinate geometry for third graders. *Arithmetic Teacher, 33*(8), 6–11. Used with permission.

FIGURE 16–20

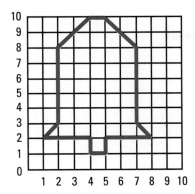

FIGURE 16–22

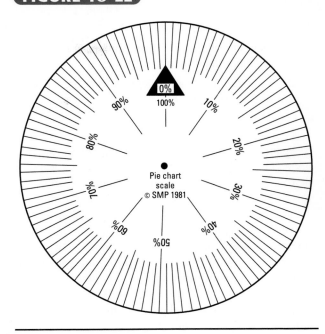

Likewise, a circle graph clearly portrays the amount of student time that is devoted to various activities during the day. A line graph of these data would not be as easy to understand. Although bar graphs could show this information, the relationship among the activities and of each activity to the whole is more clearly seen in a circle graph.

Reading and constructing circle graphs is generally delayed until Grade 6 or later because children need to have an understanding of fractions, percents, and angular measure before they can work with circle graphs in a meaningful way.

A device designed by the School Mathematics Project in England (cited by Ewbank, 1987) shown in Figure 16-22 may allow children to draw circle graphs in earlier grades before they have done much with angular measure.

Most school texts include a family budget as an example of a circle graph. In this case, the circle represents the total budget and each sector represents a budget category as a percent of the total budget. The family whose budget

is represented in Figure 16-23 spent 25 percent of its budget for food, 18 percent for clothing, and so on.

To construct a circle graph, children should be guided through 6 steps.

1. Collect the data and calculate the total.
2. Calculate the fractional part each data piece is of the total.

FIGURE 16–21

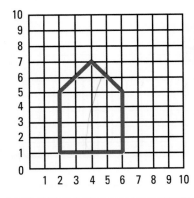

Name the shape. _____

List the coordinates
of each corner.

(___ , ___) (___ , ___)
(___ , ___) (___ , ___)
(___ , ___)

FIGURE 16–23

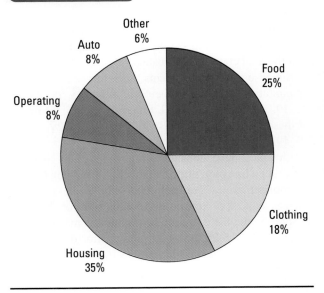

3. Express each fraction as a percent. This is not mandatory, although many circle graphs include the percent as part of the labeling process.

4. Calculate the number of degrees out of 360° that each fractional part represents.

5. Draw the graph, using the degrees from Step 4 to determine the size of each sector.

6. Label the graph and each sector.

Again, class surveys can provide data for constructing circle graphs. Children might survey the class (or a sample of the school population) to determine favorite sport, ice cream flavor, TV show, month or season of the year, etc. Rather than drawing bars as they did earlier, children would determine the fraction of students who responded in each category, calculate the corresponding angle, and construct the circle graph. Statistics from government documents and newspaper articles also provide suitable graphing data that is of interest to students. Again, children need to talk or write about what the graph tells them and, perhaps, what it does not tell.

Histograms, Line Plots, and Stem-and-Leaf Plots

Histograms, line plots, and *stem-and-leaf plots* are different forms of graphs often used to represent characteristics of a set of scores. They are often discussed and used in the context of statistical topics. We include them here because of their graphical nature. Another display, *box-and-whisker plots,* will be discussed later in this chapter. These forms of representation are often introduced in the later middle grades.

Histograms and line plots The histogram is a graphical representation of the frequency with which scores occur. To construct a histogram, separate the data into categories (usually equal intervals), tally the occurrence of each value in the appropriate category, and then plot the total count in each category.

Suppose a group of students found last year's monthly precipitation in inches in their city to be: 25, 19, 23, 35, 22, 19, 15, 24, 42, 29, 13, 9. Figure 16-24 is a histogram of these data using intervals: 0–9, 10–19, 20–29, 30–39, 40–49.

Line plots have replaced histograms in many cases. To construct a line plot, draw a number line and label it with appropriate values. For each data value, place a symbol, such as an X, above the corresponding point on the scale. If appropriate, the data may be rounded to make plotting easier. Figure 16-25 shows the precipitation data on a line plot. The grid format used in Figure 16-25 is not required but makes plotting easier, especially when some values

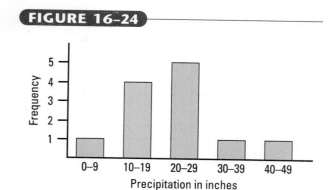

FIGURE 16-24

have higher frequencies than those occurring in the precipitation data.

Stem-and-leaf plots In the early 1990s the *stem-and-leaf* plot was introduced into the middle grades curriculum. To construct a stem-and-leaf plot, select a certain number of "front-end" digits at the beginning of each value to form the *stem*. The next digit to the right of the stem forms the *leaf*. For example, in the precipitation data above, the tens digits would be selected for the stems and the ones digits would form the leaves.

To form a stem-and-leaf display, first place the stems in either ascending or descending order as shown in Figure 16-26(a). Next, draw a vertical line to the right of the stems. Now place the leaves (units digits) to the right of the vertical line but on the same horizontal line as their corresponding stems. The precipitation data would look like Figure 16-26(b). The use of grid paper is not necessary but will ensure that the leaves are evenly spaced, making it easier to interpret the graph. Note the addition of a key to inform the reader of what the data values represent. For clarity and ease of reading, it is also wise to sort the leaves. The final stem-and-leaf display in this case is shown in Figure 16-26(c).

Note that these stem-and-leaf plots bear some resemblance to a histogram. However, in a stem-and-leaf display, all the data values are retained and can be identified,

FIGURE 16-25

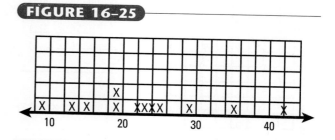

FIGURE 16–26

4|2 means 42 inches   4|2 means 42 inches

4	2				
3	5				
2	5	3	2	4	9
1	9	9	5	3	
0	9				

4	2				
3	5				
2	2	3	4	5	9
1	3	5	9	9	
0	9				

(a)   (b)   (c)

FIGURE 16–28

	GIRLS					BOYS			
			4 7	15	4				
		2 5 6 7	14	6 8				
1 2 5 6 6 8	13	1 4 4 6							
		2 4	12	0 4 4 7 9					
		3	11	7					

15 | 4 means 154 centimeters

the categories are not arbitrary, construction is easier, the data can be easily ordered, and other descriptive statistics can be calculated from the display.

Applications. Measurement activities provide an excellent setting for collecting data that could be displayed in a stem-and-leaf plot. An example from the *Curriculum Standards* (NCTM, 1989, p. 117) suggests that students use a meter tape to measure the length of a room to the nearest centimeter. Each student's measure could be recorded on the chalkboard and then pairs of students could construct a stem-and-leaf plot for the data.

Figure 16-27 illustrates a possible stem-and-leaf display resulting from this activity. Notice how the one extreme value is handled. Note also how the remainder of the data clusters between 85 and 86. These values still serve as stems, but the leaves between them are partitioned into pairs (0 and 1, 2 and 3, etc.) marked in this example, with a bullet (•).

Children could also measure their heights and/or masses and prepare a stem-and-leaf display of the class data (Bankard & Fennell, 1991). This may be an ideal

setting in which to develop a stem-and-leaf plot comparing two groups. Suppose the height measurements (cm) turned out to be:

Girls: 154, 136, 138, 113, 122, 145, 131, 136, 124, 132, 146, 135, 147, 157, 142

Boys: 117, 136, 148, 154, 146, 129, 124, 131, 124, 120, 134, 134, 127

Figure 16-28 is a stem-and-leaf display comparing these two sets of data.

Children enjoy collecting data over a reasonable period of time. (If the time frame is too long they lose interest.) For example, they might determine the wind velocity at a particular time each day for two weeks. Daily precipitation, maximum temperatures, value of a particular stock, and other things could provide data that could be displayed by a stem-and-leaf plot.

For each stem-and-leaf plot, students should make observations about and discuss, orally or in the form of a written paragraph, features such as:

- how wide a range there is in the data values.
- the smallest value—the largest value.
- how concentrated the values are.
- the symmetry of the distribution.
- gaps in the data.
- extreme values.
- what was learned from the plot.

Computer-Generated Graphs

There are a number of commercial graphing programs that elementary and middle school students can use easily.

Graphers (Sunburst) and *GraphPower* (Ventura Educational Systems) are two software packages that

FIGURE 16–27

95	4	
86		
•	8 9 9	
•	6 6 6 6 6 7 7 7	
•	4 4 5 5 5 5	
•	2 3	
85		
85	3 means 853 cm	

Source: Adapted from NCTM (1989):117. Used with permission.

younger students can use to produce a variety of types of graphs. *Data Insights* and *Statistics Workshop,* both available from Sunburst, are more suitable for middle school students. See Kader and Perry (1994) for some examples of graphs produced by the last two programs.

The Cruncher from Davidson and Associates is an example of a fairly simple spreadsheet/charting program suitable for the middle grades. It is appealing for classroom use because it is easy to learn, includes a variety of chart types, and allows a student to instantly see the effect that changing one cell in the spreadsheet has on a graph.

Most integrated productivity packages such as *MicrosoftWorks* (Microsoft) and *ClarisWorks* (Claris Corporation) also have graphing capabilities. Figure 16-29 shows two graphs of the same data produced by ClarisWorks.

The reader should consult supplier's catalogs for information on the newest versions of these and other software packages.

FIGURE 16–29

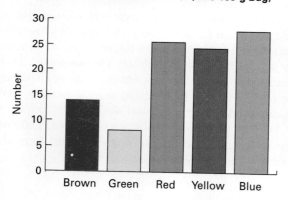

Color of Peanut Butter M&Ms (One 153 g Bag)

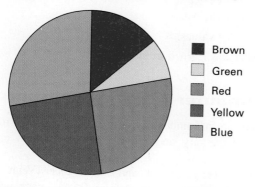

Color of Peanut Butter M&Ms (One 153 g Bag)

INTERPRETING DATA: STATISTICS

Statistics is a topic that is found with increasing frequency in elementary and middle school mathematics textbooks. Some years ago the *average* was about the only statistical topic introduced prior to junior high school. Now other topics such as median, mode, and even some rudimentary notions of dispersion can be found in elementary texts. Middle school students will study these topics in more depth, particularly the notion of dispersion or variation in data.

Descriptive statistics is a general term used to refer to the collection, organization, presentation, and interpretation of data. Even young children are exposed to statements that *describe* data. For example:

• "The average high temperature last week was only 13°F."

• "Most children in this room are 11 years old."

Shulte and Smart (1981, p. ix) identify five reasons statistics and probability should be included in the school mathematics program:

• they provide meaningful applications of mathematics at all levels;

• they provide methods for dealing with uncertainty;

• they give us some understanding of the statistical arguments, good and bad, with which we are continually bombarded;

• they help consumers distinguish sound use of statistical procedures from unsound or deceptive uses; and

• they are inherently interesting, exciting, and motivating topics for most students.

Frequency

The notion of how often something occurs was inherent in many of the graphing activities that involved collecting data and discussing the relative frequency of different events, as discussed earlier in this chapter. For example, oranges were more frequently mentioned as a favorite fruit than grapes; *e* occurred more frequently than any of the other vowels in a piece of writing; 5 buses, 35 cars, 22 trucks, 3 police cars, 25 panel trucks, and 15 other vehicles passed the school in one half hour.

Older students could make more elaborate frequency distributions. If each member of a team tossed counters at a target with possible scores ranging from 0 to 20, the team might prepare a distribution table like the one shown in Figure 16-30. A histogram could then be drawn for their data. Some students may prefer to tally each

FIGURE 16–30

Distribution of Team Scores		
Score	Tally	Frequency
0–4		
5–9		
10–14		
15–19		
20		

FIGURE 16–31

Size	Tally	Count
7	/	1
6	////	4
5	//	2
4	//	2
3	/	1

score and show the frequency through a stem-and-leaf display.

Central Tendency

Measures of *central tendency* attempt to describe what is "typical" or "average" in a set of data. At the elementary and middle school levels, three types or measures of central tendency are normally considered; mode, median, and arithmetical average (mean).

Mode The concept of the mode, but not the term, is introduced informally early in a child's school experience when a child examines a graph and reports:

- "September has the most birthdays."
- "Most members of the class like chocolate ice cream the best."
- "The vowel that occurs most often is *e*."

The mode is the most frequently occurring value in a set of data. Sometimes one or two values in a data set can distort the "typical" value described by the mean. In these cases the mode is sometimes the preferred measure of central tendency. For example, a shoe manufacturer is more interested in the most frequently sold shoe size than the mean size of shoes.

The mode is usually easily determined from a frequency distribution. For example, 10 children in a classroom reported the following shoe sizes: 6, 5, 4, 6, 7, 4, 6, 3, 5, 6. The mode is not easy to see in this list, but once a frequency table (Figure 16-31) is prepared the mode, 6, is apparent. Line plots as shown in Figure 16-25 and stem-and-leaf plots also provide good visual representation of the mode.

Median A second measure of central tendency, the *median,* is often not introduced until the middle grades. Computational procedures should be left until the middle grades, but the concept of the median should be intro-

duced to elementary school children because they "need many experiences with data sets and the median before they can understand how the mean represents the data" (Russell & Mokros, 1996, p. 362).

The median is the middle number in a set of numbers. Some children may have seen the highway sign, DO NOT CROSS MEDIAN. Here the term is used to refer to the section between two parts of the highway; that is, the middle position. Reference to the use of the term outside of mathematics may help children understand the concept.

The concept of the median can also be easily modeled. Suppose that in one learning group, five children record their ages on index cards: 11 10 13 12 10 . To find the median age, the children order the cards from youngest to oldest or vice versa: 10 10 11 12 13 . The children might discover the need for sorted data by first working with unsorted data. They will soon recognize that with unsorted data the middle card could have any number on it.

Students now simultaneously remove a card from each end and continue this process until there is only one card left. This card is the midpoint or middle value, since the cards were ordered.

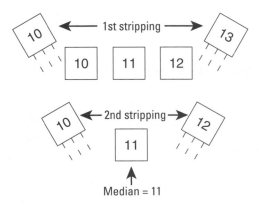

Median = 11

What happens if there is an even number of children in the group? Again the children order the cards and remove the first and last as before. This time, however, there will be two cards left in the middle and children should be challenged to talk about what the median should be.

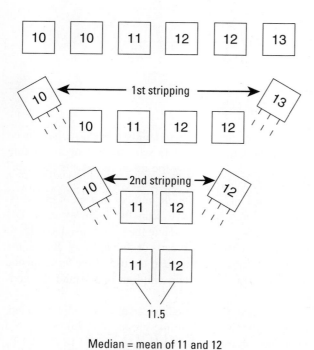

Median = mean of 11 and 12
or 11.5

From these manipulative experiences children should understand that the median is the midpoint of a set of values. If the number of values is odd, the median is the middle number; if the number of values is even, the median is the mean of the *two* middle values.

Mean   The mean is the most commonly used measure of central tendency. It is what most people speak of simply as the *average*. It is found by dividing the sum of a set of numbers by the number of numbers in the set. This is a

rule that is easily forgotten by children unless they have some understanding of the concept. A good introduction might be to have children engage in a discussion about "being average" (Paull, 1990). What does it mean? Is being average desirable? Is anyone average?

An understanding of the mean can be developed through concrete and visual manipulation (Rubenstein, 1989). Begin with two numbers. Using interlocking cubes, ask the children to build a tower with four blocks and another with eight blocks. They should now talk about what they would have to do to make both towers the same height, using only the blocks they have used to construct the towers. After several examples with two numbers, children should apply their strategy to three or four numbers, say, 3, 5, 7, and 9. Figure 16-32 illustrates the process of concretely determining the mean of these numbers. Later, children can attempt to apply the process and discuss a situation in which the cubes cannot be evenly shared. Allow the children to use their own language but the end result should be an understanding that the mean is simply one number that describes or characterizes all the numbers in the data set.

Once the children understand the concept, the teacher should provide an activity that more closely matches the computational algorithm. A problem such as the following would serve that purpose.

While trick-or-treating on Halloween, Trevor collected 4 chocolate bars, Heather collected 8, Betty got 3, and Harold found 5 in his sack. What is the average number of bars collected by the 4 children?

HINT: To find the average, put all 4 collections together and share them equally.

The process could be simulated with pictures or counters (Figure 16-33). First find the sum (put everybody's

FIGURE 16-32

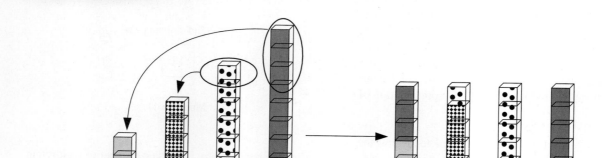

FIGURE 16-33

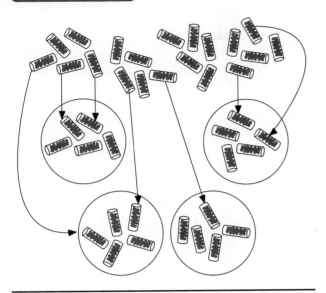

FIGURE 16-34

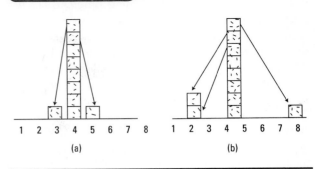

bars into one pile), then separate the total pile into 4 equal piles (the number of people to share). Finally, count to see how many bars each person received. This process parallels the computational algorithm. To help children discover the "add-'em-up and then divide" rule, Zawojewski (1988) suggests giving children

> a bundle of eight pencils of varying lengths and ask them to cut a straw to the length that they would estimate as the average length of all the pencils. After the estimates are in, lay the pencils end-to-end and cut a strip of adding machine tape the same length. This action illustrates the "add-em-up" step. Then fold the strip into eight equal parts to illustrate the division step. (p. 26)

Russell and Mokros (1996) use "construction" problems (given a statistic, children construct the data) to help children understand the concepts of central tendency. One type of problem involves an "unpacking" task to construct the data given the mean. They use an example in which the mean family size is 4. Assuming there were eight families, a line plot could be constructed by placing eight stick-on notes above the 4 on the line. At an early level, children could "unpack" the data by taking one stick-on note from the set and placing it above the 3. To balance this, the next one would go above the 5, and so on as in Figure 16-34(a).

After a series of symmetrical balancing as above, students might be asked what would happen if one family had 8 members. Clearly, one stick-on note could be moved above the 8 on the line, but it does not make sense to balance this with a note above zero. Russell and Mokros maintain that in their work "students have always come up

with the idea of moving two different stick-on notes down a total of 4 units so as to balance the upward move of 4" (p. 363). This is illustrated in Figure 16-34(b).

Integrating activities. Problems such as the following will stimulate small group discussion resulting in increased understanding of the mean, median, and mode. They will also stimulate discussion about the relationships among the measures.

> *Seven girls are at a slumber party. Their shoe sizes range from $5\frac{1}{2}$ to 9 (with half-sizes included). If the median shoe size for the girls is 7, what are some possible combinations of shoe sizes for the girls?*
>
> *The mean of five brothers' ages is 4, and the mode is 3. What are some possible ages for the five brothers? (Zawojewski, 1988, p. 26)*

See Loewen (1991) for some other integrating activities based on a card game.

Variation

Children are often interested in learning about the longest and shortest jump distances achieved at the school field day, the tallest and shortest heights in class, or the highest and lowest grades given on an examination. These children are inquiring about the *range* or the difference between the greatest and least number in a set of numbers. The range is a simple measure of the spread or dispersion of scores. The range of shoe sizes (Figure 16-31) is $7 - 3$ or 4. In addition to central tendency, spread or variation is another way to describe or characterize data.

The range, like the mean, is often not a good characterization of the data however because it is directly affected by extreme scores. For example, consider these two sets of data:

SET 1: 3, 3, 13, 13   Mean = 8; Range = 10

SET 2: 3, 8, 8, 13   Mean = 8; Range = 10

While the mean and range are the same for each set, the dispersion or scatter of scores is quite different. The first set has scores clustering around the extremes, while the second set has scores more uniformly distributed about the mean. Histograms, line plots, and stem-and-leaf plots discussed earlier in this chapter provide more useful representations of the variation in scores. Another representation, the box-and-whiskers plot, is discussed here.

Box-and-whisker plots In the NCTM *Curriculum Standards* for grades 5–8, box-and-whisker plots are mentioned as appropriate activities for these grades in both Standard 10 (Statistics) and Standard 13 (Measurement). A box-and-whiskers plot includes the median and charts the dispersion of data in a way that adds information about the spread of scores not directly available from a stem-and-leaf display. To construct a simple (sometimes referred to as a *skeletal*) box-and-whiskers plot, five values are required; median, *upper quartile, lower quartile, upper extreme,* and *lower extreme.* These terms will be explained in the following paragraphs as they are used. Note that the median is the middle quartile.

The median, quartiles, and extremes can be readily obtained by sorting the data into ascending order and adding a *depth* column beside the sorted data. The depth simply indicates how far a particular value is from the high or low end of the set of values. The lowest and highest value each have a depth of 1, the next highest and next lowest a 2, and so on. The life expectancy at birth for males in 15 selected countries (excluding Canada) is shown in Table 16-1 with the depth of each value listed to the left of the data.

When the number of data values is odd the median is the "deepest" value. The eighth value from both the top

and bottom is 71.45. If the equivalent statistic for Canada, 72.92, were incorporated into the list, both 71.50 and 71.45 would have a depth of 8. The median then would be the mean of 71.50 and 71.45 or 71.48.

The *upper* and *lower quartiles* are roughly the medians of the two halves of the data determined by the median. The quartiles can, therefore, be found by repeating the depth-finding process using the median as the starting point and going both directions. The following simplified examples should clarify the process.

Example 1

DATA	MEDIAN	DEPTH FOR UPPER QUARTILE	LOWER QUARTILE
63	1	1	
60	2	59.5 2	
59	3	← 2	
55	← 4	1	
48	3		47 2
46	2		← 2
45	1		1

Example 2

DATA	MEDIAN	DEPTH FOR UPPER QUARTILE	LOWER QUARTILE
63	1	1	
60	2	← 60 2	
59	← 3	1	
55	3		1
48	2		48 2
46	1		← 1

Example 3

DATA	MEDIAN	DEPTH FOR UPPER QUARTILE	LOWER QUARTILE
63	1	1	
60	2	60 2	
59	← 3	← 1	
55	2		55 1
48	1		← 2
			2

Using the life-expectancy data with 15 countries, the median has a depth of 8. The greatest depth for the upper quartile would be 4, corresponding to both 72.70 and 72.52. The upper quartile would then be the average of these, or 72.61 years. What is the value of the lower quartile? What are the upper and lower quartiles when the value for Canada, 72.92, is included?

The *extremes* (highest and lowest scores) are 74.54 and 65.09. The five values needed to construct a box-and-whiskers plot (Figure 16-35) are now available. Begin by drawing a number line horizontally or vertically that

---

TABLE 16-1

LIFE EXPECTANCY AT BIRTH FOR MALES

DEPTH	LIFE EXPECTANCY
1	74.54
2	73.62
3	72.75
4	72.70
5	72.52
6	72.09
7	71.50
8	71.45
7	71.34
6	71.00
5	70.41
4	70.41
3	69.69
2	67.04
1	65.09

Source: Statistics Canada (1989). *Canada Yearbook 1990.* Ottawa, ON: Publications Division, Statistics Canada, p. 3–18.

FIGURE 16–35

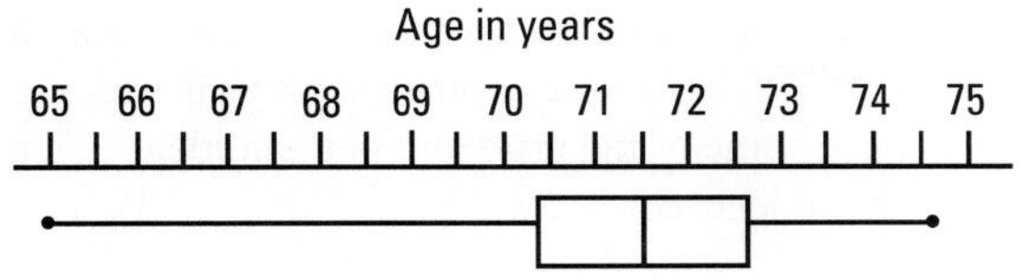

FIGURE 16–35

Age in years

encompasses both extremes and as many other reference points as desired. On the side of the line opposite the reference points construct a *box* (rectangle) with one pair of opposite sides perpendicular to the number line at the points corresponding to the quartiles as illustrated in Figure 16-35. Draw another line through the box parallel to the quartiles at the point on the number line corresponding to the median. Now draw a *whisker* (line) parallel to the number line from the midpoint of the side corresponding to the lower quartile to a point corresponding to the lowest value in the data set. Similarly draw a whisker from the upper quartile to the point corresponding to the greatest data value.

Two or more box-and-whisker plots could be superimposed on the same reference line. Box charts for the heights of boys and girls (data from Figure 16-28) could be placed side-by-side as shown in Figure 16-36.

Children and box-and-whisker plots. Box-and-whisker plots are relatively new in school curricula. For this reason, the preceding explanation was more extensive and formal than is necessary for children in the middle grades. To find the median, children already know that they need to work with sorted data. Rather than using

a depth column, they could simply count up from the bottom or down from the top to the middle value or middle pair of values. For the upper quartile, they could count down from the top to the score that represented one quarter of the scores. Similarly, they could count one quarter of the scores from the bottom to find the lower quartile. They could then draw the box-and-whisker plot.

Of greater importance than the precision of the construction is the interpretation or discussion that takes place as a result of the data. Children should write a paragraph or two stating their observations. If necessary, the teacher can draw attention to such features as the extremes, the range, and the range within which most of the scores fall (the box contains the middle 50%). Children should also discuss questions such as "What does a long box tell you?" and "What does a short box with long whiskers mean?"

We have provided some data for illustrative purposes. It is important, however, that children draw box-and-whisker plots for data they collect themselves. Activity 16-4, adapted from Brosnan (1996), provides one idea for doing this.

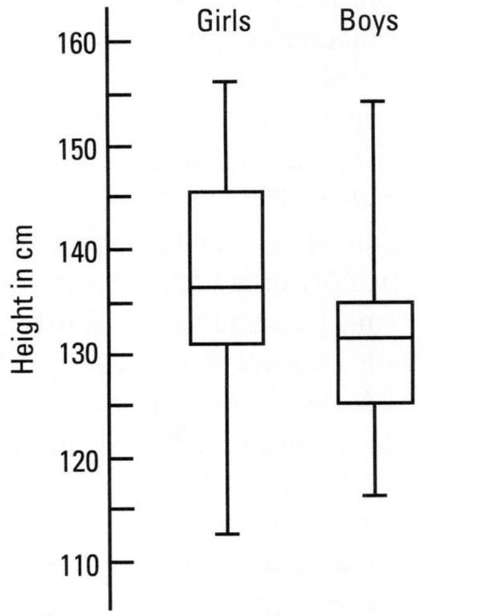

✳ ACTIVITY 16-4

COUNT THE RAISINS

MATERIALS:
14G box of raisins for each child, 1cm grid paper

PROCEDURE:
- Don't open the box. Each person write down an estimate of how many raisins he or she thinks is in the box.
  (The teacher records all the estimates from each group on the board.)
- Count the number of raisins in each box. (Again the teacher records the actual count for each box on the board.)
- Construct a back-to-back stem-and-leaf plot. One side will show the estimates, the other side the actual counts.
- Construct a box-and-whiskers plot for both the estimates and the counts. Use one number line to show both box plots.
- Answer these questions:
  1. Which actual count occurred most often? Which plot tells you this?
  2. What is the lowest count? The highest count? What is the range?
  3. What is the lowest estimate? The highest estimate? What is the range?
  4. How can you find the medians from your plots?
  5. What can you say about the estimates compared to the actual counts?

FIGURE 16–36

INTERPRETATION DATA: PROBABILITY

I think it will snow today.
If I drop this rock in the pool it will sink.
I want to roll a 4.

These probability-type statements could easily have been uttered by young children who are exposed to probability in their life outside school. In school we need to provide them with activities that will ensure misconceptions do not develop. Activities involving probability contribute to the development of problem-solving skills because children do experiments and collect and organize data in order to determine the probability of an event. Probability activities can also be used to reinforce other concepts and skills. Furthermore, activities in probability can be fun, adding motivation, excitement, and variety to the mathematics program. "Classroom activities involving probability should be active, involve physical materials, and furnish opportunities for questioning, problem solving, and discussion" (Fennell, 1990, p. 18). And according to Bright and Hoeffner (1993), "students need to be exposed to problems for which intuitions alone are insufficient for finding solutions" (p. 87).

STANDARDS LINK 16-5
In grades 5–8, the mathematics curriculum should include explorations of probability in real-world situations so that students can

- model situations by devising and carrying out experiments or simulations to determine probabilities;
- model situations by constructing a sample space to determine probabilities;
- appreciate the power of using a probability model by comparing experimental results with mathematical expectations;
- make predictions that are based on experimental or theoretical probabilities;
- develop an appreciation for the pervasive use of probability in the real world. (NCTM, 1989, p. 109)

Overview

Probability is the area of mathematics that analyzes the chance of something occurring. The probability that a given *event* will occur is the ratio of the number of *favorable* or *desirable outcomes* to the total number of *possible outcomes*. This is often written in the form:

$$P(\text{event}) = \frac{\text{Number of Desired or Favorable Outcomes}}{\text{Number of Total Possible Outcomes}}$$

For example, if you flip a coin, the probability of it landing with the head up is $\frac{1}{2}$, since there is one desired outcome (landing heads) and two possible outcomes (head, tail). This provides another setting in which children can use some of the ratio and percent ideas (Chapter 13) they have learned.

STANDARDS LINK 16-6
Probability, the measure of the likelihood of an event, can be determined theoretically or experimentally. Students in the middle grades must actively participate in experiments with probability so that they develop an understanding of the relationship between the numerical expression of a probability and the events that give rise to these numbers. (NCTM, 1989, p. 109)

In an experiment, events must be *random* and each event or outcome must have the same likelihood of occurring on each trial. To illustrate, each time you shake a die, each of the six outcomes is equally likely and the probability of the die landing with a 2 on top is the same for each trial. On the other hand, if you drew a card from a deck of ordinary playing cards, replaced it at the bottom of the deck and drew again, the probability of drawing the same card would not be the same the second time. The deck would need to be thoroughly shuffled after each draw to ensure randomness. This does not mean that all possible outcomes have the same probability. For example, if a styrofoam cup is tossed into the air and allowed to land on the table, the probability of its landing on its side is greater than on either its top or bottom, but the likelihood of its landing on its side does not change from toss to toss. Based on studies in the United States and England, it is evident that many children do not have a good understanding of randomness (Dessart, 1995).

Shaking a die is an example of a *sample space* with *equally likely* outcomes because each of the six faces has the same chance of turning up. Tossing a styrofoam cup involves a sample space with outcomes that are *not equally likely*. Experiments such as those involve events that are *independent*. The fact that a 2 turned up last time has no bearing on what will come up on the next shake of a die. The probability of getting a 2 is always $\frac{1}{6}$ regardless of how many times 2 came up previously. This is sometimes a difficult concept for adults to understand, let alone children. *Dependent* events are events in which the probability of a second outcome is different, given the nature of an earlier outcome. If a bag contains eight yellow and four red marbles, the initial probability of drawing a red marble at random is $\frac{4}{12}$ or $\frac{1}{3}$. If, after each draw, the marble is replaced and the bag is shaken, the

FIGURE 16-37

Draw number	1	2	3	4	5	6	7	8	9	10
Color										

probability of drawing a red marble on subsequent draws remains at $\frac{1}{3}$ since these events are independent. If, however, the marble is not replaced, the probability on subsequent draws changes. If a red marble was drawn on the first trial, the probability of a red on the second draw would now be $\frac{3}{11}$ since there are now 11 marbles in the bag, three of which are red. If a yellow marble was drawn on the first trial, the probability of a red on the second draw would now be $\frac{4}{11}$.

In some situations the number of favorable outcomes is equal to the number of possible outcomes. In this case the event is said to be *certain* and has a probability of 1. If there are no favorable outcomes, the event has a probability of 0 and is said to be *impossible*.

General Teaching Considerations

Early experiences Teachers can introduce some informal, non-numeric (no values) probability activities to young children to help them think about concepts such as certain, impossible, equally likely, more likely, and less likely. Terms such as these may or may not be used explicitly. *Prediction* and *experimentation* are major components of many of the activities in the early years.

Capitalize occasionally on the natural language of the children to help them think in probability terms. For example, a child may come bounding in one morning and say "It's going to rain today." Many times you will accept this statement, but on occasion you might respond "Are you *certain* it is going to rain today, or do you think it *might* rain today?"

The following four activities are samples of experiences children in the late primary grades might find interesting and which would help develop intuitive understanding as a foundation for later work.

1. What's in the bag?
   - Without the children's knowledge, place 3 blue blocks in a bag.
   - Tell the children that you have some blocks in the bag and that you are going to draw one out, note the color, and then replace it in the bag.
   - Ask the children to keep a record of the color drawn.

   - Draw and replace 2 or 3 times, then ask the children to make a prediction about the color of the block you will draw next time. Record their guesses.
   - Draw 2 or 3 more times. Ask again for a prediction for the color of the next block.
   - Ask, "Can anyone guess what is in the bag?" "What are the chances that I will draw a red block?"

2. One-of-Each
   - Place 1 red and 1 blue block in a bag, shake, and draw one block out.
   - Give the children a recording sheet like the one in Figure 16-37. Ask them to color the square under "1" the color of the first block drawn (see Figure 16-37).
   - Return the block to the bag, shake the bag and draw another block without looking and have the children color each square as you go along.
   - Do this a total of 10 times.
   - Ask, "How many red blocks were drawn?" "How many blue blocks were drawn?"

3. Guess the Color
   - Use the setting from the previous activity, but this time have the children record their guess of the outcome before a block is drawn. See Figure 16-38.
   - Have the children shade in the first square opposite "Guess" with either blue or red before the draw. After the draw they should color the square opposite "Color drawn" with the color of the block drawn.
   - After 10 draws, have the children complete the totals below the chart.

   Total guessed: _____ red and _____ blue.

   Total drawn: _____ red and _____ blue.

FIGURE 16-38

Draw number	1	2	3	4	5	6	7	8	9	10
Guess										
Color drawn										

4. Sort the Statements
- Give the children a set of cards with probability statements on them or have students make up their own statements. For example:

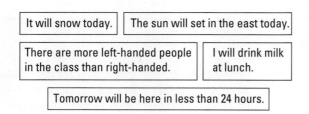

- Prepare containers so that the children can sort the statements into groups

- Have the children compare their groupings and discuss any differences.

Burbank (1987) outlines several useful activities. One that will help with the notion of the range of probability going from impossible (0) to certain (1) involves initially placing five cubes under five glasses. The students discuss the number of choices, number of cubes, and the chance of selecting a glass with a cube. Then they replace one cube with one ball and repeat the discussion, and then replace a second cube with a ball and again discuss the chances of selecting a cube. They continue until all five glasses have balls under them (no cubes) and again discuss the chances of picking a glass with a cube under it.

Upper elementary In the upper elementary grades children will begin to use some of the conventional probability terms and children can start to assign probability

---

✳ ACTIVITY 16-5

FLIP A WASHER

MATERIALS:
washers with masking tape on one side

PROCEDURE:
- Predict how many times the washer will land tape up in 10 tosses.
- Toss a washer 10 times and keep a record of how it lands.
- Compare your results with your prediction.
- Repeat the experiment several times and calculate a total for each outcome.
- Compare your results with those of another group and discuss similarities and differences.

---

values to some events. The emphasis still is on experimental probability as opposed to *theoretical* probability, although theoretical values can be assigned to some simple events such as flipping a coin or shaking a die. Some simple *simulations* can be done at this level. Children could also be exposed to examples of *fair* and *unfair* experiments or games. Here, and at higher grade levels, considerable integration of graphing and statistics with probability can take place.

Wilkinson and Nelson (1966) observed that children often demonstrate biases when dealing with familiar material such as coins or dice. Biases did not seem apparent when using thumb tacks, styrofoam cups, or other unfamiliar material. It might be wise, then, to start a more formal development of basic probability concepts in the upper elementary grades with relatively unfamiliar objects. Activity 16-5 is one example. Before starting this activity, a number of washers (or equivalent) will need to have a small piece of masking tape placed on one side.

Children who are ready to begin quantifying the probability of an outcome could complete a recording sheet as in Figure 16-39. Tossing a single die is essentially the same experiment except that the sample space now contains six possible outcomes rather than two. However, each outcome still is equally likely.

FIGURE 16-39

Outcome	After 10 Tosses		After 40 Tosses	
	Number	Fraction	Number	Fraction
Tape up		$\overline{10}$		$\overline{40}$
Tape down		$\overline{10}$		$\overline{40}$

FIGURE 16–40

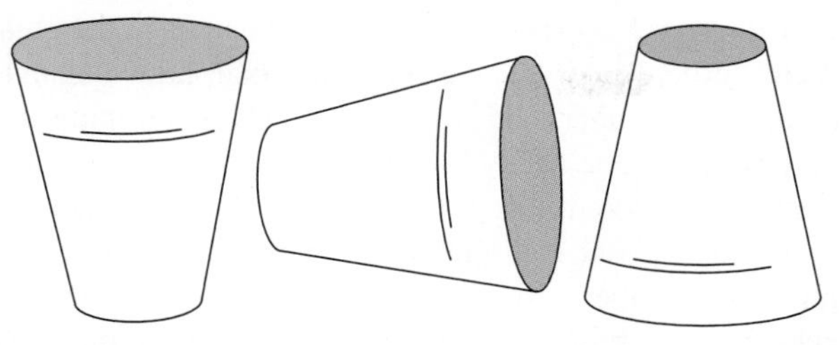

Experiments in which different outcomes have different chances of occurring add another element of interest for students. Figure 16-40 illustrates the three possible outcomes, each with a different probability, when a styrofoam cup is tossed. Students should toss the cup a large number of times in order to feel confident that they have a reasonable estimation of the actual probability.

Students should be challenged to think about factors that could affect the probability of a particular event. Would the probabilities be different if the cup landed on a piece of plush carpet? Would the size of the cup change the probabilities? These challenges could serve as the basis for a long-term project for one or two groups of students.

Tossing a thumb tack is another popular activity using unfamiliar probability materials with outcomes not equally likely. There are only two possible outcomes if students toss the tack on the floor or their desk. Here is a case in which tossing the tack on a plush carpet might not only change the probabilities associated with each outcome but it might also add a third possible outcome to the sample space, namely, the point going down into the carpet.

Activity 16-6 and the following teacher-directed activity also involve events that are not equally likely.

Drawing Numbered Balls
- Write the numeral 5 on one ping pong ball (or card), 6 on two balls, 7 on four balls, 8 on two balls, and 9 on one ball.
- Place all 10 balls in a bag. Tell the students that you have 10 balls in the bag, but give no other information.
- Have one student record the outcomes on the chalkboard or overhead as another student draws the balls from the bag.
- After 3 or 4 draws, solicit predictions as to what the 10 balls are.
- After approximately 20 draws, ask the recorder to organize the data on the chalkboard.
- Then tell the students that each ball had either a 5, 6, 7, 8, or 9 on it.
- Divide the children into groups to discuss and write a new prediction.
- Then have one student count the number of times each number was drawn and announce this to the class so students can compare the count with their prediction.

✳ ACTIVITY 16-6

HIT THE TARGET

MATERIALS:
- game board
- bingo chips or similar counters

PROCEDURE:
1. Take turns tossing a chip at the board 10 times from a distance of about 1 m, recording each time where the chip lands.

2. Guess how many times you would hit both A and B (overlap) if you tossed your counter 100 times.

3. Combine the results from 10 students and compare the total with your guess.

PART HIT	TALLY	FRACTION OF TOTAL HITS
Circle A but NOT B		$\frac{}{10}$
Circle B but NOT A		$\frac{}{10}$
Both A AND B (overlap)		$\frac{}{10}$
Outside Circles (on board)		$\frac{}{10}$
Off the board		$\frac{}{10}$

For Activity 16-6, children will need a game board similar to the one shown here. This activity should be done in groups of three or four.

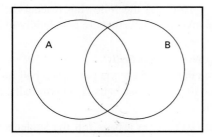

Teachers can incorporate probability discussions into some of the graphing and statistics activities suggested previously. For example, one activity suggested earlier in this chapter involved selecting a paragraph, recording the length of each word, and then graphing these data. Students could also use the data to calculate statistics such as the mean, median, and mode, to draw a stem-and-leaf display, and to make a box-and-whiskers plot. Some probability questions could then be explored. For example, suppose you were blindfolded and randomly placed the tip of your pencil anywhere on a page from a book. Suppose also that your pencil pointed to a word. Based on your data,

- What would be a "good" guess for the length of the word?
- What would be some "poor" guesses?
- What is the probability that the word has 1 letter? 3 letters? 8 letters?

Survey activities could also be expanded to include some probability questions. For example, students might take a survey of the class to determine how many students are left-handed. What is the probability that the next student to walk through the door is left-handed? Use the data from your room to guess how many students in the room next door are left-handed. Survey that class to find out. Use these data to predict how many students in the school are left-handed. Bankard and Fennell (1991) suggest a similar activity based on hair color.

Simulations are another popular probability activity. Simulating an experiment is known as the *Monte Carlo* method. Consider the following scenario.

A certain cookie manufacturer designs a set of six different hockey cards. One card is randomly inserted into each bag of cookies. On the average, how many bags of cookies would you have to buy to get at least one of each card?

(Assume that equal numbers of each card are printed and distributed.)

Teachers should challenge children to think of ways to simulate this problem. One suggestion is to place the digits 1 through 6 on six different cards. Then have the children shuffle the cards, place them in a bag, draw one out, record the number, and replace the card, continuing the process until one of each of the six numbers is drawn. Have the children note how many draws were made in order to get one of each card, repeat this complete process a number of times, and then calculate the mean to get a better estimate of the answer to the problem. Most problems can be simulated in a variety of ways. A regular die could also be used for this problem, since there are six different and equally likely outcomes.

Children in the upper elementary grades could also explore the concept of a *fair game*. For example, you might take a few minutes one day to suggest to your students that you will play a game with them. Shake a die; if it shows a number greater than 4 they win, otherwise you win. Each game consists of 10 shakes. Keep a tally on the chalkboard for each game and note the winner beside each set. It likely won't take long for someone to object to this game because "It's not fair!"

Middle grades In the middle and junior high school grades, more emphasis is placed on determining theoretical values, although the experimental aspect should not be neglected. More advanced work can be done with simulating events and with some of the other ideas developed earlier.

An activity commonly done at this level is to have students shake and roll a pair of dice and record the sum. Activity 16-7 is a good opportunity for students to compare experimental with theoretical probability.

A related but more complicated activity involves tossing two styrofoam cups. The three possible outcomes for one cup (top, bottom, side) are not equally likely and their theoretical probability cannot readily be determined. Furthermore, the probability will vary with the size of cup, type of landing surface, etc. Encourage students to toss the two cups many times in order to gain some assurance that their experimental probability is reasonable. If students worked in pairs and each pair tossed the cups 50 times and then pooled their results, they would have at least 500 tosses. Each group could complete a chart like the one shown here.

		Side	Top	Bottom
Cup 1	Side	$\frac{}{50}$	$\frac{}{50}$	$\frac{}{50}$
	Top	$\frac{}{50}$	$\frac{}{50}$	$\frac{}{50}$
	Bottom	$\frac{}{50}$	$\frac{}{50}$	$\frac{}{50}$

Cup 2

✳ ACTIVITY 16-7

DICE SUM

MATERIALS:
dice (different colors)

PROCEDURE:
1. Shake and roll a pair of dice 36 times. Tally and record each result in the first chart below. Write the probability for each outcome based on your experiment.

2. Now compare your results with the *theoretical probability.* Analyze how many possible ways there are for each sum to occur by completing the chart at right.

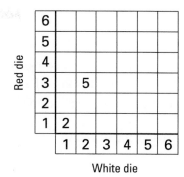

Red die / White die grid with: 1,2 entry; 3,5 entry

Outcome	2	3	4	5	6	7	8	9	10	11	12
Frequency											
Experimental Probability	36	36	36	36	36	36	36	36	36	36	36

Outcome	2	3	4	5	6	7	8	9	10	11	12
Frequency											
Theoretical Probability	36	36	36	36	36	36	36	36	36	36	36

3. Count the frequency of each sum and record it in the first line of the chart immediately above. Write the theoretical probability in the last line.

4. Compare the *experimental* with the *theoretical* results

by drawing a bar graph with the bars for each type of result adjacent and in a different color.

5. Write a paragraph describing similarities and differences.

Activity 16-8 is another type of experiment.

In some cases the probability of a second event is *dependent* on the result of an earlier event. These cases are more difficult for children to conceptualize. A tree diagram is helpful for analyzing this type of situation. An approach that should help children understand dependent events involves giving children a problem that they can simulate, and then having them develop and discuss a tree diagram of the problem.

For example, prepare two identical boxes, one with one hockey card and two baseball cards, the other with one of each. Label the bottom of the first box A, and the bottom of the second B; place a label on the bottom of each box so that the label is not visible when a box is selected. In groups of three, one student shuffles the boxes, one keeps a record, and the other randomly chooses a box, then randomly chooses a card from that box, and then checks the label so the recorder can keep

a proper record. Each group member should perform each role 10 times, then the group should discuss their results. One expected observation is that, if Box B is chosen, the chance of getting a hockey card is better than if Box A is chosen. After students have discussed this problem, develop a tree diagram for the problem (Figure 16-41).

Trial	Box A		Box B	
	H	B	H	B
1		✓		
2			✓	
3		✓		
4				✓

✳ ACTIVITY 16-8

FLIPPING A COIN

MATERIALS:
marker

PROCEDURE:

1. Flip a coin 5 times to move from START to one of the letter boxes at the bottom.

2. When you reach the bottom record the letter box you ended in.

3. Do the experiment 50 times.

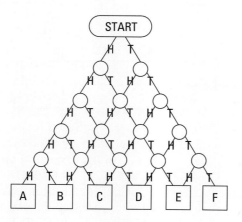

4. Graph the results of your 50 trials.

5. Which letter or letters did you finish on most often? Least often?

6. Write a paragraph about your experiment.

More advanced *simulation* activities are appropriate for the middle grades. Consider the following problem.

Ten hunters are in a blind together. All 10 are perfect shots. That is, they never miss. Ten Canada geese fly up at the same time. The 10 hunters rise together, randomly choose a goose, and simultaneously shoot. On the average, how many geese would survive?

In the earlier simulation, shaking a die or drawing a card from a set of six worked well. Although the cards would work here as well, teachers should challenge students to think of other ways to simulate this problem. Students may suggest that 10 students each should write the number of the goose he or she chooses (0 to 9 or 1 to 10) on a piece of paper. Then they could record all numbers chosen and determine which numbers were not chosen by any of the group.

This may also be an opportune time for children to explore a table of random numbers. Give students a table of random numbers and challenge them to use it to solve the hunters and geese problem. The partial table in Figure 16-42 suggests that you begin at any random position and list off the next 10 digits either horizontally or vertically. Digits from 0 to 9 not included in the list would represent the geese that survived. Repeat the experiment several times to answer the question, "On the *average*, how many geese would survive?"

The concept of a fair game was introduced earlier in this chapter. In the middle or junior high grades this concept can be expanded with some more involved examples. Bright, et al. (1981) describe eight pairs of games to introduce the notion of "fairness." Each game

FIGURE 16–41

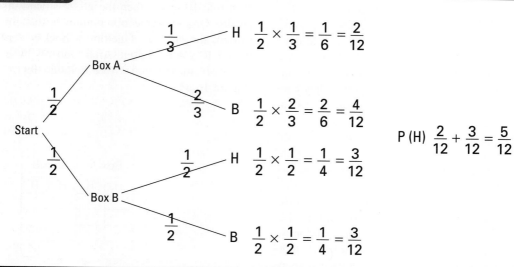

✳ ACTIVITY 16-9

FAIR GAMES

Game 1. Fractions Less Than or Equal to 1.

MATERIALS:

2 standard dice and a recording sheet.
   One player will be 'A,' the other 'B.'

PROCEDURE:

1. Roll the dice and make a fraction less than or equal to 1 with the numbers showing. If the fraction is in lowest terms, player A scores a point; otherwise, B scores a point.

2. Do this 20 times for one game. The player with the most points after 20 rounds is the winner.

3. Play several games, then answer these questions:
   • Did the same player win each time?
   • Do both players have the same chance of winning?
   • Is this a fair game?

Game 2. Proper and Improper Fractions

MATERIALS:

2 standard dice (one red and one green) and a recording sheet. (The number on the red die will be the numerator and the number on the green die will be the denominator.)
   One player will be 'A,' the other 'B.'

PROCEDURE:

1. Roll the dice. If the fraction formed is greater than 1, player A scores a point. If the fraction is less than 1, player B wins. If the fraction is equal to 1, both players score one point.

2. Repeat this 16 times for one game. The player with the most points after 16 rolls wins that game.

3. Play several games, then answer these questions:
   • Did the same player win each time?
   • Do both players have the same chance of winning?
   • Is this a fair game?

FIGURE 16–42

Partial Table of Random Numbers

10480	15011	01536	02011	81647
22368	46573	25595	85393	30995
24130	48360	22527	97265	76393
42167	93093	06243	61680	07856
37570	39975	81837	16656	06121

Beginning from the point of the pencil, 10 random numbers reading horizontally are: 5, 7, 3, 2, 5, 5, 9, 5, 8, 5. Digits not included are: 0, 1, 4, 6. For this trial, 4 geese survived.

requires two players. Activity 16-9 is an adaptation of one of the pairs of games. Note the reinforcement of fraction concepts.

TECHNOLOGY AND DATA

Analyzing data can lead to a significant amount of computational work. This may, at times, be used to reinforce paper-and-pencil computation. Since the emphasis, however, should not be on computation, but on obtaining, understanding, and using the calculated results, teachers should permit students to do most of the computation on a calculator or computer.

The graphing software mentioned earlier in this chapter can be used to graph collected data. The visual display facilitates and clarifies interpretation of the data. In most cases, computers construct graphs from data entered into a spreadsheet. A spreadsheet is also a useful medium for conceptualizing measures of central tendency and other statistics. Most spreadsheets have built-in functions for mean, median, mode, maximum, and minimum, as well as procedures for sorting data. Given a set of data, children could be encouraged to change one or more values, predict what effect the change will have on one or more of the measures of central tendency, and then observe the change or changes. This kind of exploration could help children understand the key ideas before they learn computational procedures (Wilson & Krapfl, 1995).

CONCLUSION

In today's technological age, the collection, organization, and interpretation of data is important to almost everyone of almost every age. Children need to have experiences with data analysis to help them deal with the large amount of information that is available to them.

Initially, children should collect data themselves through surveys or other means to answer questions they have identified. Later, they can gather information from secondary sources such as encyclopedias, newspapers, and the Internet.

Similarly, the first approach to probability needs to be experimental. Children should do experiments to determine the probability of particular events occurring. This active approach will make these topics interesting and enjoyable, but more importantly, it will enable children to develop conceptual understanding that will serve them well in their everyday lives and careers.

For Your Journal

When you have finished studying this chapter, reflect on these questions in your math journal:

1. What are some uses for each of the different types of graphs discussed? Describe situations in which some types of graphs are more appropriate or useful than others, and why.

2. What are the three measures of central tendency? How can teachers help students to understand each measure?

3. Visit a middle school classroom and informally interview several students to assess their understanding of data analysis, statistics, and/or probability. What are their understandings and misconceptions?

4. Examine a textbook's section on data analysis, statistics, and/or probability. discuss the textbook in terms of the concepts included in this chapter.

5. Imagine that you are a classroom teacher and a parent of one of your students is concerned that you are devoting too much instructional time to data analysis, statistics, and probability. How would you respond?

For Your Portfolio

When you have finished studying this chapter, complete these activities to include in your professional portfolio:

1. Write a series of lesson plans focusing on the stages of graphing experiences children should encounter.

2. Write a series of lesson plans to introduce the three measures of central tendency.

3. Use software to assist with the organization and interpretation of data.

Resources for Teachers

Books on Data and Statistics

Corwin, R., & Friel, S. (1990). *Used numbers: Statistics: Prediction and sampling.* Palo Alto, CA: Dale Seymour Publications.

Lindquist, M. M. (1992). *Making sense of data: Curriculum Evaluation Standards for School Mathematics Addenda Series, Grade K–6.* Reston, VA: National Council of Teachers of Mathematics.

Russell, S., & Corwin, R. (1989). *Used numbers: The shape of the data.* Palo Alto, CA: Dale Seymour Publications.

Russel, S., & Corwin, R. (1990). *Used numbers: Sorting: Groups and graphs.* Palo Alto, CA: Dale Seymour Publications.

Friel, S., Mokros, J., & Russell, S. (1992). *Used numbers: Statistics: Middles, means, and in-betweens.* Palo Alto, CA: Dale Seymour Publications.

Zawojewski, J. S. (1991). *Dealing with data and chance: Curriculum Evaluation Standards for School Mathematics Addenda Series, Grade 5–8.* Reston, VA: National Council of Teachers of Mathematics.

Books on Probability

Burns, M. (1995). *Math by all means: Probability, grades 3–4.* Sausalito, CA: Math Solutions Publications.

Phillips, E., Lappan, G., Winter, M., & Fitzgerla,d W. (1986). *Middle Grades Mathematics Project: Probability.* Menlo Park, CA: Addison-Wesley Publishing Company.

Shulte, A., & Choate, S. (1977). *What are my Chances, Book A.* Sunnyvale, CA: Creative Publications.

Links to the Internet

Government Information Sharing Project

http://govinfo.kerr.orst.edu/usaco-stateis.html

Contains information about the current U.S. census data, including profiles of geographical areas. Great source of data.

Exploring Data

http://forum.swarthmore.edu/workshops/usi/dataproject/

Contains lesson plans for collecting, analyzing, and displaying data, links to statistics software on the Web, and suggested discussion questions.

Explorer: Statistics and Probability

http://explorer.scrtec.org/explorer/explorer-db/browse/static/Mathematics/browse/ff75.html

Contains many lessons on and lists of other resources for statistics and probability.

CHAPTER 17

Developing Integers
and Algebraic Thinking

Key Concepts

- Models for understanding integers and operations on integers

- Meaning of variables

- Functions

Focus Questions

When you have finished studying this chapter, you should be able to answer these questions:

1. What models are useful for helping students understand operations on integers? Give an example of a model for each operation.

2. What should students know about variables?

3. What is a function?

The mathematics of the middle grades provides a transition between the concretely based elementary program and the more formal secondary curriculum. The topics discussed in this chapter—integers, variables, and functions—are important components in the study of algebra, a subject many students find difficult and confusing.

What do we know of U.S. students' understanding of algebra and functions? The sixth National Assessment of Educational Progress (NAEP) noted that more than half of the eighth-grade students tested successfully answered items dealing with algebra concepts treated informally. But most eighth- and twelfth-graders "had difficulty solving equations and inequalities other than fairly simple ones" (Blume & Heckman, 1997, p. 226). As with other NAEP findings, it is clear that we must do a better job helping students understand concepts and connect that understanding with necessary procedures and skills.

Algebra is often defined as generalized arithmetic. In the following sections the goal is to show how the whole number system can be extended, and concepts such as number sentence, pattern, and graphing developed, to enable students to learn and use the powerful language of algebra. Learned in a meaningful way, algebra can be a useful tool for solving many real world problems. ○

INTEGERS

Negative numbers have been known since ancient times (Crowley & Dunn, 1985). The Chinese had red and black computing rods to distinguish between positive and negative numbers respectively. (When accountants today speak about being in the "red" or "black," the terms have the opposite meanings.) The Hindus used negative numbers to represent debt and denoted a negative quantity by enclosing the number in a circle. From a mathematical perspective the motivation for constructing the system of integers is to provide numbers to rename expressions such as $2 - 3$ or to make sentences such as $\Box + 3 = 2$ true. Mathematicians of the sixteenth and seventeenth centuries were reluctant to accept negative numbers as "true" roots of equations and referred to them as "absurd" or "fictitious." By the eighteenth century, however, negative numbers were universally accepted.

A study of the integers, usually beginning in Grade 6 or Grade 7, provides students with a second opportunity to extend the whole number system. Previously they learned to use fractions and decimals to name numbers between the whole numbers and to give answers to division questions such as $3 \div 5$. Even though models for negative numbers are less concrete than those for fractions and decimals, students generally find that learning about the system of integers is easier than working with the positive rational numbers. The notation is much simpler, and usually only one- or two-digit numbers are used in examples and problems. Furthermore, the rules for operating on integers are easier to learn and apply than the corresponding algorithms with fractions. The challenge for the teacher is to assist students to understand *why* as well as *how* these rules work. The following sections suggest an approach that relates computational procedures to number properties and patterns, and to the meaning of the operations in the context of real-world applications.

Introducing the Integers

In everyday life there are many situations that require numbers that deal with direction as well as magnitude. Students know, for example, that a temperature of 5 degrees below zero is referred to as "minus five" and written $-5°F$. Young children encounter negative numbers when they use calculators to find answers for expressions such as $2 - 5$ or continue to "count down" past zero and see $-1, -2, -3$, and so on appear in the display.

The concept of a negative number is used when a person spends more money than he or she earns, and when a football team loses more yards than it gains. A hockey player's "plus-minus" statistic is the difference between the number of goals scored by and against that player's team when he or she is on the ice. Other real-world examples include profit and loss, above and below sea level, winning and losing points, golf scores above and below par, and positive and negative electrical charges.

Teachers can introduce negative numbers as *opposites* of counting numbers. The *opposite* of 3 is written -3 and is read *negative* 3 rather than *minus* 3 to make the distinction between the sign of the number and the operation of subtraction. The counting numbers, their opposites, and zero form the set of integers: $\ldots -3, -2, -1, 0, 1, 2, 3, \ldots$. Teachers can now also refer to the counting numbers as the positive integers; the number 3 is sometimes called *positive* 3 and written $+3$. The integer zero is neither positive nor negative. In the past the integers were sometimes referred to as "signed" or "directed" numbers.

To construct the integer *number line,* first mark a point 0, then measure equal segments to the right to determine points 1, 2, 3, . . . and to the left to determine points -1, $-2, -3, \ldots$.

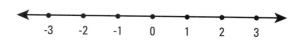

Opposites, such as 3 and -3 are equal distances from zero on the number line. Integers on the number line may also be thought of as directed distances (rather than points). As such they are represented by arrows that indicate both length and direction. Thus -3 can be represented as an arrow 3 segments in length and pointing left. Note that the arrow can be moved along the line to positions other than the 0 to -3 segment.

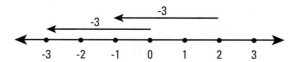

Ordering the Integers

The number line is a particularly useful model for establishing order relations for the integers. For the whole numbers the greater of two numbers is situated to the right of the other number on the number line; this idea is extended to the integers. As well as being asked to use words and symbols to indicate order relations between particular pairs of integers ($-3 < 2$, $-4 > -5$), teachers should encourage students to look for general results and express these in words or in writing. They might note, for example, that any negative number is less than zero and is also less than any positive number. The fact that $-7 < -4$, because -7 is further to the left on the number line, could also be discussed using familiar models: $-7°C$ is colder than $-4°C$; $7 in debt is worse than $4 in debt; 700 m below sea level is lower than 400 m below sea level.

Addition

Two approaches suggested for developing integer addition are the electric charges model (Grady, 1978) and the number line. Before providing any direct instruction, however, students should have opportunities to draw on their previous knowledge to construct solutions to addition problems. The teacher might begin with real-world situations involving earning and spending money: for example, "you earned $5 and you spent $7." Teachers should ask students to solve the problems and write corresponding number sentences (Chang, 1985). An alternative approach would be to give integer addition questions, such as $5 + -7 = \square$, in symbolic form and ask students to write real-life problems and find solutions for them.

Electric charges model   To model positive and negative charges concretely, teachers can use chips of two different colors, for example, white (positive) and black (negative), or they can represent the charges pictorially using the symbols $+$ and $-$. The key idea in the model is that a positive and a negative charge "cancel" each other. Symbolically, $1 + -1 = 0$. By combining re-

FIGURE 17-1

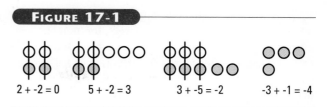

quired numbers of white and black chips, students easily find answers for different types of addition questions (Figure 17-1). Note that the diagram for $5 + -2$ can also be viewed as the solution to a comparison subtraction problem for whole numbers—how many more white chips than black chips? One student wrote in her journal after a lesson on addition of integers:

The interesting thing was how you would add a negative and a posetive you ended up with a lower number than you started with so it would be like subtracting (Vance, 1995, p. 14).

Number line model   To add on the number line, begin at the point represented by the first addend and move the distance and direction (positive—right and negative—left) indicated by the second addend. Thus for $2 + -5$, one begins at 2 and moves 5 spaces to the left. Students will find that while the number line solution for $-5 + 2$ looks different from that for $2 + -5$, the final result is the same (Figure 17-2).

Students who have had many experiences solving integer addition problems using these models begin to formulate mental procedures for getting answers. Teachers should ask individuals at this stage to verbalize how they determine the value and sign of the sum when the two integers have the same sign and when one is positive and one is negative.

Subtraction

The rule "to subtract an integer, add its opposite" is easy to remember and apply. However, rather than simply giving this rule, the teacher should provide opportunities for students to engage in problem-solving and sense-making experiences involving subtraction of integers. To begin,

FIGURE 17-2

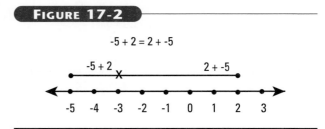

students working in small groups might be asked to make up problems and decide on answers for number sentences, such as $3 - 5 = \Box$ and $3 - -2 = \Box$, and explain their reasoning. Procedures for developing subtraction using patterns, the number line, and electric charges are discussed in the following paragraphs.

Number pattern approach Teachers can ask to continue patterns such as the following and discuss possible rules suggested by the results.

$$3 - 1 = 2 \qquad 3 - 2 = 1$$
$$3 - 2 = 1 \qquad 3 - 1 = 2$$
$$3 - 3 = 0 \qquad 3 - 0 = 3$$
$$3 - 4 = \Box \qquad 3 - -1 = \Box$$
$$3 - \Box = \Box \qquad 3 - \Box = \Box$$

Number line model Subtraction on the number line is in terms of missing addend addition. Recall that $5 - 2 = \Box$ can also be thought of as $2 + \Box = 5$. The solution, 3, is found on the number line by beginning at 2 and moving (3 spaces to the right) to 5. Similarly, $3 - 5 = \Box$ is equivalent to $5 + \Box = 3$. To solve we begin at 5 and move to 3. Since we have to move 2 spaces to the *left,* the solution is -2. This and other number line subtraction questions are shown in Figure 17-3.

Electric charges model The electric charges model of integers lends itself nicely to the "take away" interpretation of subtraction. To solve $5 - 2$, we start with 5 white chips and remove 2; the answer obviously is 3. To solve $-5 - -2$, we start with 5 black chips and remove 2 black chips; the 3 remaining black chips represent the answer -3. As with whole numbers, addition can be used to check the result: $-5 - -2 = -3$ because $-2 + -3 = -5$.

Using chips to solve problems such as $3 - 5$ requires another step that corresponds to renaming the minuend in order to be able to carry out the computation. Teachers can point out that this must sometimes be done when subtracting whole numbers $(43 - 16)$ or fractions $(\frac{4}{5} - \frac{3}{10})$.

Since adding zero $(1 + -1)$ to a number does not change its value, an integer can be named as the sum of two integers in many ways. For example, $3 = 4 + -1 = 5 + -2$, and so on. In the electric charges model the value of a set of chips remains the same if equal numbers of white and black chips are added to (or taken from) the pile. It follows that an integer, such as 3, can be represented by many different combinations of white and black chips.

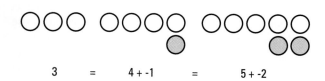

Now back to $3 - 5$. We cannot perform the subtraction starting with only 3 white chips, since we need to remove 5 white chips. Therefore we add equal numbers of white and black chips until we have enough white chips to remove 5. In this case we might add 2 chips of each color. Removing the 5 white chips leaves 2 black chips; the answer is -2. To solve $2 - -3$, we start with 2 white chips, then add 3 black chips (which are to be removed) and 3 white chips. After removing the black chips we are left with 5 white chips; the answer is 5 (Figure 17-4).

The rule Note that after the 3 negative chips are removed, the diagram for $2 - -3$ is the same as for $2 + 3$. Further, in solving $3 - 5$, if 5 positive chips and 5 negative chips had been added to the pile (instead of 2 of each type), the diagram would eventually look like $3 + -5$. The rule "to subtract an integer add its opposite" follows from an examination of several examples. Another approach is to have students find the answers to two related

---

FIGURE 17-3

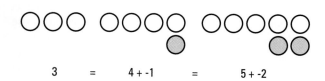

$$3 - 5 = \Box \leftrightarrow 5 + \Box = 3$$

$$3 - -2 = \Box \leftrightarrow -2 + \Box = 3$$

$$-1 - 3 = \Box \leftrightarrow 3 + \Box = -1$$

FIGURE 17-4

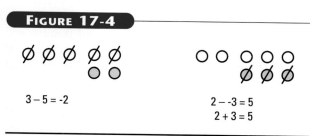

$$3 - 5 = -2$$

$$2 - -3 = 5$$
$$2 + 3 = 5$$

sets of questions using any of the methods previously developed.

$$5 - 2 = \square \qquad 5 + -2 = \square$$
$$3 - -4 = \square \qquad 3 + 4 = \square$$
$$-2 - 5 = \square \qquad -2 + -5 = \square$$
$$-6 - -2 = \square \qquad -6 + 2 = \square$$

The class then examines the two groups of questions and considers how they are the *same* (first number and answer) and how they are *different* (the first set consists of subtraction sentences, the other set addition sentences; the second numbers in corresponding sentences are opposites). Teachers might then ask students to verbalize a "short-cut" procedure for subtracting an integer. The result "to subtract an integer add its opposite" could then be compared to the rule "to divide by a fraction multiply by its opposite (reciprocal)."

Perhaps the most interesting aspect of this result is that the process of subtracting a negative number changes it to a positive number. The "postman stories" (Cohen, 1965) make an attempt to justify this conclusion by considering what happens when a postman takes back a bill that had been incorrectly delivered. If the bill is for $5, having it taken back leaves the person $5 richer; therefore $- -5 = 5$. Many students, however, feel that the result of this transaction is 0, since the person does not actually have the $5. A recently noted practical application of this relationship is the use of "negative deductions" on payroll slips to account for certain funds given to the employee. The teaching strategies that have been recommended for subtraction are intended to help students make connections between addition and subtraction, and between subtraction with whole numbers and subtraction with integers.

Multiplication

The rules for multiplying integers are very straightforward; the product of two positive or two negative integers is positive and the product of a positive and a negative integer is negative. When the first factor is positive, students can apply the interpretation of multiplication as repeated addition to find the product. For example, $3 \times -2 = -2 + -2 + -2$. Teachers can use both the electric charges model and the number line in this case.

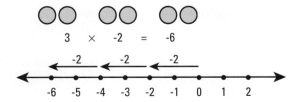

Products such as -3×2 or -3×-2 do not lend themselves well to physical models. The most meaningful approach involves extending whole number properties and patterns. A student could argue that since $3 \times -2 = -6$, -2×3 should also be -6, if we are to preserve the property that multiplication is commutative. A pattern leading to this same conclusion and a pattern suggesting that $-3 \times -2 = 6$ follow.

$$2 \times 3 = 6 \qquad -3 \times 2 = -6$$
$$1 \times 3 = 3 \qquad -3 \times 1 = -3$$
$$0 \times 3 = 0 \qquad -3 \times 0 = 0$$
$$-1 \times 3 = \square \qquad -3 \times -1 = \square$$
$$-2 \times 3 = \square \qquad -3 \times -2 = \square$$

Division

Sign rules for division are determined by considering the inverse relationship between division and multiplication. Students recall that the sentence $6 \div 2 = \square$ can be expressed as $2 \times \square = 6$. The three cases in which at least one of the integers is negative are as follows:

$$-6 \div 2 = -3 \text{ since } 2 \times -3 = -6$$
$$6 \div -2 = -3 \text{ since } -2 \times -3 = 6$$
$$-6 \div -2 = 3 \text{ since } -2 \times 3 = -6.$$

Thus the rules for determining the sign of the quotient of two integers are the same as those for multiplication.

Assessment

Assessment should be consistent with the goals of instruction. A test should include questions that require the students to relate integers to everyday life and to justify rules for the operations. Some test questions (Q) and sample responses (R) by sixth-grade and seventh-grade students follow:

Q: Write and solve a story problem for $-5 + 13$.

R: Pavel Bure was on the ice for 5 goals scored against his team during one game. The next game he was on for 13 goals his team scored. What was his $+/-$ rating? $-5 + 13 = 8$. He was $+8$.

Q: Write a question to make a problem using the following information. "At noon the temperature was $8°F$. At midnight the temperature was $-5°F$." Solve the problem.

R: How much did the temperature fall? (A diagram of a thermometer was drawn.) $8 - -5 = 13$. The temperature fell $13°$.

Q: Write a problem for 3 × −4. Solve using a number line.

R: Stephen had 3 library cards. If he owed $4.00 on each how much does he owe? (A number line showing 3 jumps of 4 starting at zero and moving to the left to −12 was drawn.) 3 × −4 = −12. He owed $12.00.

Q: Write and solve a story problem for −8 ÷ 2. Show how you would check that your answer is correct.

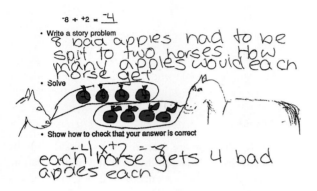

How would you assess the skill and understanding of the student who gave the above response to the division question?

Practice Settings

As discussed in the previous sections, students should be able to use models and mathematical reasoning to justify the rules for adding, subtracting, multiplying, and dividing integers. Students also need to be able to execute these procedures automatically when solving problems and learning algebraic concepts. Activity 17-1 is an example of a problem-solving activity that provides practice with integer operations.

✳ ACTIVITY 17-1

INTEGER TARGET

Use the first three listed integers together with two operations to make a number sentence having the fourth integer as the answer (target). The three numbers can appear in any order in the sentence.

EXAMPLE:	7	−2	−5	−6
SOLUTION:	(7 − −5) ÷ −2 = −6			
1. −9	4	3	−23	
2. −8	2	−7	3	
3. 6	−9	6	0	
4. −7	1	12	−2	

The remaining sections of this chapter describe a variety of activities requiring students to evaluate expressions, apply order of operations, illustrate properties of operations, solve equations and inequalities, and explore functions using tables, graphs, calculators, and computers. While the examples given involve whole numbers, most of the activities can be adapted to provide computational practice for integers.

VARIABLES

According to Peck and Jencks (1988), "algebra can and should arise as a by-product of making arithmetic sensible" (p. 85). There are two topics that are crucial to helping middle school students connect arithmetic with algebra: (1) the use of variables, which are letters that represent numbers, and (2) an "awareness of the mathematical method that is being symbolized by the use of both numbers and letters" (Kieran & Chalouh, 1993, p. 179). The second topic refers to thinking about the solution process or method rather than just finding the answer.

It is very important to help students understand *variables*. In primary grades, students encounter the notion of a variable when they solve missing addend problems and when they use words to generalize patterns. Mathematicians today think of a variable as a symbol for an element of a specified replacement set (Usiskin, 1988).

Instruction should focus on the exploration of key algebraic ideas in which students "(a) think about the numerical relations of a situation, (b) discuss them explicitly in simple everyday language, and (c) eventually learn to represent them with letters or other nonmisleading notation" (Kieran & Chalouh, 1993, pp. 181–182).

STANDARDS LINK 17-3

In grades 5–8, the mathematics curriculum should include explorations of algebraic concepts and processes so that students can

- understand the concepts of variable, expression, and equation;
- represent situations and number patterns with tables, graphs, verbal rules, and equations and explore the interrelationships of these representations;
- analyze tables and graphs to identify properties and relationships;
- develop confidence in solving linear equations using concrete, informal, and formal methods;
- investigate inequalities and nonlinear equations informally;
- apply algebraic methods to solve a variety of real-world and mathematical problems. (NCTM, 1989, p. 102)

STANDARDS LINK 17-4
Understanding the concept of variable is crucial to the study of algebra; a major problem in students' efforts to understand and do algebra results from their narrow interpretation of the term. (NCTM, 1989, p. 102)

STANDARDS LINK 17-5
Students need to be able to use variables in many ways. Two particularly important ways in grades 5–8 are using a variable as a placeholder for a specific unknown, as in $n + 5 = 12$, and as a representative of a range of values, as in $3t + 6$. (NCTM, 1989, p. 103)

Meanings

Letters are used to represent numbers in different mathematical contexts and consequently variables take on several different meanings. Variables can be used:

1. In equations as unknown numbers.
   Example: $3 + x = 7$
2. To state properties or generalizations.
   Example: $a + 0 = a$.
3. To describe functions or sequences.

Example: in:	n	7	4	12
out:	$3n - 1$	20	11	35

   Example: $2, 5, 8, . . ., 3n - 1$
4. In formulas to express relationships.
   Example: $C = \pi d$
5. In computer programs to indicate storage locations.
   Example: $B = B + 1$

In the first case the variable x is a placeholder for a specific unknown. The task is to solve for x; that is, find a single number that will replace x and make the sentence true. In the other cases the variable is a representative for a range of values. In the second case the statement is true for all numbers. In the third case the expression $3n - 1$ defines a function; given any number n as input, the output number corresponding to the rule "multiply n by 3 and subtract 1" can be determined. The expression can also be used to generate a sequence; successive terms are found by replacing the variable by 1, 2, 3, and so on. In the fourth case the formula expresses the relationship between the diameter and the circumference of a circle; the circumference varies as the diameter and, given one of the quantities, the other can be determined. In the fifth case the statement is an instruction to the computer to replace a storage location with a number that is one greater.

Misconceptions

There are several types of misunderstandings associated with the use of letters to represent numbers (Booth, 1988). Since 5 m means five meters and A, l, and w stand for area, length, and width in the formula $A = l \times w$, some students believe that the letters represent objects rather than numbers. In one study a subject said that $8y$ would have to mean eight yachts or yams or some other word starting with y. Writing $5 \times n$ as $5n$ also leads some students to write 56 when $n = 6$.

Wagner (1981) found that many students believe that changing the letter in an equation changes the problem. Subjects were shown the equations, $7 \times W + 22 = 109$ and $7 \times N + 22 = 109$, and asked whether W or N would have a larger value. Some students said that you can't tell without solving the equation. Others believed that the ordering of the letters corresponds to the ordering of the numbers, and stated that W would be larger because it comes after N in the alphabet. Many students have difficulty accepting algebraic expressions, particularly those containing addition or subtraction symbols, as answers to problems. A typical error is to rewrite $3 + 4b$ as $7b$.

Expressions and Number Sentences

Children first encounter expressions and number sentences when they study addition. For example, if 2 birds are joined by 3 other birds, the *expression* $2 + 3$ tells how many birds there now are. When we write the *number sentence* $2 + 3 = 5$, we are saying that 5 is another name for the number of birds. The *equals* sign means that $2 + 3$ and 5 are different names for the same number. Children should be shown that this relation can also be written in the form $5 = 2 + 3$, and they should have experiences writing number sentences such as $2 + 3 = 3 + 2$ and $2 + 3 = 4 + 1$. Asking students to examine families of basic facts having the same sum or product, or to write expressions to name a particular number in many different ways (Activity 17-2), allows these concepts to be discussed and reinforced.

An important point here is that an arithmetic expression such as $2 + 3$ can be an answer as well as an

✱ ACTIVITY 17-2

NAMING NINE

Name the number nine in as many ways as you can using two or more numbers and one or more operations.

EXAMPLES:		
	$3 + 6$	$5 + 2 + 2$
	$13 - 4$	$54 \div 6$
	$10 + 7 - 8$	$2 \times 4 + 1$

instruction to add. Students with this understanding will later be better able to accept algebraic expressions such as $3 + a$ and $x + y$ as correct and meaningful final representations. The ideas that the addition symbol can show the result of an operation as well as the action of addition, and that the equals sign can indicate an equivalence relation as well as represent a signal to give the answer are essential to algebraic understanding (Booth, 1988).

Evaluating Expressions

Throughout the elementary years students have many opportunities to interpret, write, and evaluate arithmetic expressions. As each of the four operations is introduced, learners have experiences connecting physical actions and real-world situations with mathematical expressions. Learning the basic facts and computational algorithms involves finding single numbers to rename expressions. It is important to note that textbook and teacher-made exercises requiring children to "add," "find the product," or "complete" may or may not include the equals sign. Regardless of the format, the intent is that the student find the "answer."

$$\begin{array}{c} 4 \\ +\,9 \end{array} \qquad 5 \times 8 = \underline{} \qquad 63 \div 7$$

Later exercises involve more than two numbers and/or more than one operation. These cases provide opportunities for students to discover important *properties* of the operation(s) and learn mathematical *conventions* that are essential for successful algebraic manipulation. The use of grouping symbols (parentheses and brackets) and order of operation rules are encountered at this time.

When only addition or multiplication is involved, students find that the numbers can be added or multiplied in any order. For example, $5 + 4 = 4 + 5$, and in computing $3 + 9 + 5$, any two of the numbers can be added first and the third number added to that sum. The use of *parentheses* can be introduced in this context:

$$(3 + 9) + 5 = 12 + 5;\ 3 + (9 + 5) = 3 + 14;$$
$$9 + (5 + 3) = 9 + 8.$$

Note that the use of parentheses is a convention within the symbolic language, while the order properties are inherent features of the number system. These order properties can be applied to make some computations easier. For example:

$$4 \times 37 \times 25 = (4 \times 25) \times 37 = 100 \times 37 = 3700.$$

The order properties can be explored with addition or multiplication "rabbits" (Activity 17-3). The four numbers are added or multiplied two at a time in three different ways to compute their sum or product. Students in the

middle grades should be encouraged to use fractions and integers as well as whole numbers in their examples.

When children study subtraction and division they find that the order in which the numbers are written *does* affect the value of the expression. In the initial phases of instruction for these operations, it is important that the difference between $5 - 2$ and $2 - 5$ (and $6 \div 2$ and $2 \div 6$) be discussed. Teachers should *not* say that "you always subtract the smaller number from the bigger number" (divide the bigger number by the smaller number") or that "$2 - 5$ (or $2 \div 6$) is impossible." It is true that $2 - 5$ and $2 \div 6$ cannot be renamed by whole numbers; students learn later that these expressions are named by the integer -3 and the fraction $\frac{2}{6}$, respectively. When more than two numbers are involved, students find that the answer depends on how the numbers are grouped. For example, $9 - 5 - 2$ can be either $(9 - 5) - 2 = 2$ or $9 - (5 - 2) = 6$.

Order of Operations

For the previous example students are told that if there are no parentheses, the *convention* is to work from left to right. An expression containing both addition and subtraction, without parentheses, is also evaluated from left to right (as if the numbers and operations were being read orally). For example: $12 - 5 + 2 + 4 - 3 + 6 = 16$. As a warm-up activity and to provide practice in mental arithmetic, the teacher might say "Follow me" and call out such expressions orally: twelve minus five plus two plus four minus three plus six. Each class member would write down his or her answer before the correct result is given.

When an expression contains addition and multiplication, students will find that the answer depends on the order in which the operations are performed. For example, the expression $3 + 4 \times 2$ has the value 14 if the addition is done first and 11 if the multiplication is done first. Students are told that the agreed-upon convention in situations such as this is that multiplication is done before addition. To indicate that the addition is to be done first, parentheses must be used: $(3 + 4) \times 2$. Division also is done before addition or subtraction: $24 - 6 \div 3 = 24 - 2 = 22$.

Standard order of operation rules are:

1. Operations in parentheses are done first.
2. Starting at the left, all multiplication and division is done.
3. Starting at the left, all addition and subtraction is done. For example: $3 \times 5 - (12 + 8) \div 4 = 10$.

In more complex expressions *brackets,* another type of grouping symbol, are also used. To evaluate an expression with parentheses and brackets, operations in

✳ ACTIVITY 17-3

ARITHMETIC RABBITS

PROCEDURE:
1. Draw a rabbit—4 squares, 2 ears, and 1 tail.

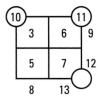

2. Write any four numbers in the four squares.

3. Add across and down and write the sums. Add diagonally and write the sums in the ears.

4. Add the two "across" sums. Write this number in the tail. Add the two "down" sums. Add the two "diagonal" sums. What do you notice?

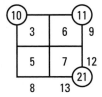

- Do this using your own four numbers. Is the final sum always the same? Why?
- Try this with multiplication instead of addition.
- Now try it using subtraction.

---

parentheses are done first and then the operation in the brackets is performed. For example:

$$[(4 + 6) \div 2 - 1] \times 3 = 12.$$

Simple calculators perform operations in the order entered: pressing $2 + 3 \times 4 =$ produces 20. This is referred to as *chain* computation. Also available for elementary school students are low-cost calculators that are designed to follow order of operation rules. For example, on the Texas Instruments *Math Explorer*, pressing $2 + 3 \times 4 =$ gives 14. Computers are programmed for order of operation conventions.

Several computer programs that provide practice with order of operations are available. In the strategy game "How the West Was One + Two × Three" (Sunburst), players create equations using three randomly generated numbers with two different operations of their choice to produce answers, in order to move a stagecoach or locomotive along a trail. For example, possible answers using the numbers 6, 2, and 5 include: $6 \div 2 + 5 = 8$; $(6 - 5) \times 2 = 2$; and $6 - 5 \times 2 = 4$.

A whole-class game that requires participants to write expressions using grouping symbols and order of opera-

tion rules is described by Erickson (1977). Five students suggest different numbers between 0 and 25. A sixth number is then given. The objective is to perform operations on the first five numbers to obtain the sixth. Any combination of the four operations is acceptable. The numbers can be considered in any order but each must be used exactly once. The first player to produce a correct equation wins.

For example: The five numbers are 6, 8, 23, 2, and 12 and the target number is 21. One solution is:

$$23 + 2 - 6 \times 8 \div 12 = 21.$$

A variation is to use the five numbers to make expressions for as many different numbers from 1 to 25 as possible (within a given time limit such as five minutes, an hour, or a week). This version is well suited for a cooperative group task. Possible expressions for 1, 9, and 25 are as follows:

$$12 + 8 + 6 - 23 - 2 = 1$$

$$(23 - 12 - 8) \times 6 \div 2 = 9$$

$$8 \div 2 - 12 \div 6 + 23 = 25$$

The commercial game "Krypto" (Creative Publications) for two to eight players is based on the same idea. The game includes a deck of 52 cards numbered as follows: three each 1–10, two each 11–17, and one each 18–25. Five cards are dealt to each player and a common objective card for all players is turned up. The first player to use his or her five numbers, together with any combination of the operations, to match the objective card number wins the hand.

Other games can be played using dice or number cubes. A player shakes three to five dice and uses the numbers together with any combination of the operations to make an equation. Activity 17-4 is of a similar nature.

A number of problem-solving activities requiring the use of grouping symbols to alter the order of operations are suggested by Sanfiorenzo (1991).

1. Use grouping symbols to make a sentence true.

   Example: $11 - 5 \times 2 + 3 = 30$

   Solution: $(11 - 5) \times (2 + 3) = 30$

2. Use grouping symbols to produce multiple values for an expression.

   Example: $4 + 8 \div 4 - 2$

   Solution: $(4 + 8) \div (4 - 2) = 6$

   $\quad\quad\quad (4 + 8) \div 4 - 2 = 1$

3. Find operations and use grouping symbols to make a sentence true.

   Example: $5 \bigcirc 4 \bigcirc 2 = 2$

   Solution: $(5 - 4) \times 2 = 2$

Properties of Operations

In the early grades students apply the *commutative* and *associative* properties of addition and multiplication but do not need to know these formal terms. In the middle and junior high years the terms can be introduced and the properties described using variables.

$$a + b = b + a \quad\quad\quad\quad a \times b = b \times a$$

$$(a + b) + c = a + (b + c) \quad (a \times b) \times c = a \times (b \times c)$$

Students who understand these symbolic statements will be able to express in their own words what each sentence says and give numerical examples. These students will realize that for a given example the same number must be used to replace a given letter wherever it appears, but also know that the same number can replace more than one letter. The key idea is that the statements are true for all numbers under consideration. While the properties are first examined for whole numbers, they are later found to also hold for the integers, the rational numbers, and the real numbers. Variables in this conception act as pattern generalizers. The goal is for the students to come to appreciate the power and simplicity of this symbolic representation of the ideas.

Students should also be able to give examples to show that these properties do not *generally* hold for subtraction and division but that they might for some numbers. Teachers can challenge students, for example, to find values of a, b, and c such that $(a - b) - c = a - (b - c)$.

The *distributive property of multiplication over addition* has important applications in both arithmetic and algebra. Figure 17-5 indicates that $3 \times 6 = 3 \times (2 + 4) = 3 \times 2 + 3 \times 4$. In general:

$$a \times (b + c) = a \times b + a \times c$$

$$(a + b) \times c = a \times c + b \times c$$

The distributive property is applied in the standard multiplication algorithm and in some mental multiplication strategies. For example, the standard vertical form computation for 29×6 involves thinking of 29 as $20 + 9$ and finding the sum of 6×9 and 6×20. This product can be found mentally by thinking of 29 as $30 - 1$, finding 6×30 and 6×1, and subtracting 6 from 180. This particular strategy illustrates the distributive property of multiplication over *subtraction*. Students can find that division also distributes over addition and subtraction, but only from the right. For example:

$$(6 + 9) \div 3 = 6 \div 3 + 9 \div 3$$

$$12 \div (2 + 4) \neq 12 \div 2 + 12 \div 4$$

Formulas

Students' first encounters with algebraic expressions usually involve *formulas* that contain more than one variable.

✳ ACTIVITY 17-4

FOUR 4's

Using four 4's each time, make expressions for each value from 0 through 10.

EXAMPLE: $(4 + 4) \div 4 + 4 = 6$

FIGURE 17-5

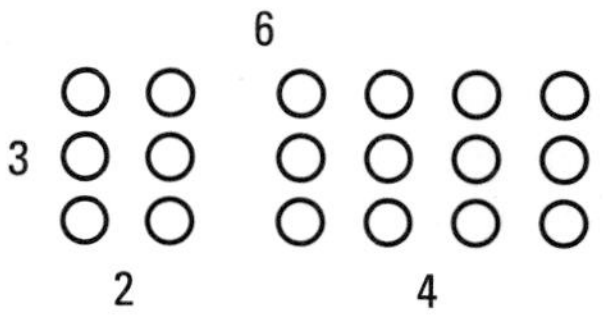

For example, students discover that the perimeter of a rectangle can be found by adding twice the length and twice the width, or by adding the length and width and doubling. After expressing this relationship in words, they write it using symbols: $P = 2l + 2w$ or $P = 2(l + w)$. The perimeters of different rectangles are then determined by substituting the values of their dimensions in the formula. Other well-known formulas include $V = lwh$ (volume of a rectangular prism), $A = \pi r^2$ (area of a circle), and $i = prt$ (simple interest).

Mathematical formulas abound in science, business, and everyday life. One example is a formula developed by IBM to produce "fail-safe" credit card numbers. The last digit of the number functions as a check on the possibility that an error is made in transcribing the number into the computer. The last digit is determined using the following formula:

1. Add the digits in the odd-numbered positions and double this sum.

2. Count the number of odd-numbered digits greater than 4.

3. Add the even-numbered digits, except the last digit.

4. The last digit is the difference between the sum of (1), (2), and (3) and the next highest multiple of ten.

Example: Consider card number 312-5600-196-431-2

1. $(3 + 2 + 6 + 0 + 9 + 4 + 1) \times 2 = 50$
2. The number of these digits greater than $4 = 2$
3. $1 + 5 + 0 + 1 + 6 + 3 = 16$
4. $50 + 2 + 16 = 68$. The last digit is 2.

The computer receiving the credit card number is programmed to check the numbers entered against this formula. About 98 percent of the most common transcription errors are caught using this procedure.

Algebraic Expressions

Moving from arithmetic expressions to algebraic expressions is accompanied by the introduction of new notation for multiplication and division. The symbol x is no longer used to indicate multiplication; "3 times a" is written $3a$, "3 times the sum of a and b" is written $3(a + b)$, and "3 times 4" is written $3(4)$ or $3 \cdot 4$. As noted earlier, this notation can be a source of confusion for students. For division the symbol $\frac{a}{b}$ is most commonly used to denote "a divided by b." Students first make this connection when they study fractions and decimals. For example, they see that both $6 \div 3$ and $\frac{6}{3}$ are 2, and they find that the fraction $\frac{3}{5}$ can be expressed as a decimal by performing $3 \div 5$. Thus $\frac{a}{b}$ can be either a number or an instruction to divide. The expression $(a + b) \div 3$ is written without parentheses $\frac{a+b}{3}$.

Students learn to write and interpret expressions involving variables. The phrase "4 more than a number" can be written $p + 4$; the letter p is a placeholder for a number. To evaluate the expression, a specific number is substituted for the variable p and the resulting number expression is evaluated. For $p = 2$ the value of the expression is 6; for $p = 5$ the value is 9; and so on. In evaluating expressions such as $3n + 6$ and $7 - (\frac{n}{2} - 3)$, order of operation rules must be applied. (For $n = 10$ the values are 36 and 5, respectively.)

Other skills learned in beginning algebra involve simplifying and expanding expressions. Students learn that a *term* is either a number, a variable, or a product or quotient including one or more variables. Terms are separated by addition or subtraction operation symbols. Thus in the expression, $7x - 3xy + y - 8 + 2x$, there are five terms. In this example $7x$, $3xy$, y, and 8 are *unlike terms,* while $7x$ and $2x$ are *like terms* because they contain the same variable x. Like terms can be combined to simplify an expression. Thus $7x + 2x$ can be written as $9x$, but the terms in $7x + y$ and $7x + 8$ cannot be combined. The distributive law is often used to write an expression in a different way. Writing $3(x + y)$ as $3x + 3y$ is sometimes referred to as *expanding*, while writing $3x + 3y$ as $3(x + y)$ may be called *taking out a common factor.*

> **STANDARDS LINK 17-6**
> Formal equation-solving methods can be developed from, and supported by, informal methods. These informal methods, which may include actions on concrete materials that are paralleled by symbolic actions, can lead to more formal procedures. If students develop formal procedures from informal methods grounded in real-world contexts, they can validate their own formal thinking and develop a basis for extending these algebraic ideas. (NCTM, 1989, p. 103)

Solving Equations

Many people feel that algebra is first taught in Grade 8 and involves solving equations to find "x, the unknown." However, the "missing number" idea of a variable is introduced to children in the early grades when they write numbers in boxes to complete "open" sentences such as $4 + \square = 7$ and $\square \times 9 = 45$.

Nibbelink (1990) outlined an instructional sequence for teaching equations that provides a gradual transition from arithmetic to algebra. In the early stages (up to the middle of Grade 2) he recommends working with basic facts in vertical rather than horizontal format, since young children can more easily discriminate up from down than right from left. Reversed readings rarely occur in vertical form, but many children read $\square - 5 = 3$ as $3 = 5 - \square$ and write 2 or even Σ (the mirror image of 2) in the box.

Step 1: *Hidden and missing numbers.* Story lines and special characters are used at this stage. For example, a cat wearing a large mitten covers a number with its paw and a gerbil eats a hole in the paper where a number was written (Figure 17-6).

Step 2: *Replaced numbers.* The character at this stage (which can begin about the middle of Grade 3) is a thief who steals numbers and leaves, as a mark, the letter of his or her first name at the scene of the crime. The idea is that the letter marks the spot and the task is to replace that letter with the number that will make the sentence true (Figure 17-7). In this context it is reasonable that a given letter can replace different numbers in different problems, and that in a given problem any one letter will always represent the same number.

Step 3: *Number aliases (unknowns).* The idea in this stage (beginning in the middle of Grade 4) is that numbers use aliases that are letters of the alphabet. Note that different numbers can use the same alias in different problems and that a given number can choose different pseudonyms from problem to problem. The task in $P + 8 = 13$ is to find which number is using the name P in this instance. The letter then is a name for a number. Solving equations is likened to detective work aimed at finding the true (number) identity of the letter.

Step 4: *Variables over specified domains.* The formal concept of a variable is studied in algebra courses.

In the early grades students find missing or unknown numbers in open number sentences by using their knowledge of basic facts or by applying the guess-and-check strategy. For example, if $m - 6 = 8$, then $m = 14$ because $14 - 6 = 8$. In the middle and junior high years, students begin to learn procedures to solve equations that rely on inverse relationships.

FIGURE 17-6

Hidden Number

Missing Number

$$\begin{array}{r} 2 \\ + \\ \hline 7 \end{array}$$

$$\begin{array}{r} \\ - 3 \\ \hline 5 \end{array}$$

FIGURE 17-7

$$\begin{array}{r} 23 \\ + B \\ \hline 29 \end{array}$$

Replaced numbers

$4 \times H = 28$

$T - 3 = 18$

Examining families of facts consisting of two addition and two subtraction facts using the same numbers can help students understand that addition and subtraction are *inverse* operations (Chapter 7). That is, subtraction undoes addition and vice versa. Similarly, multiplication and division are inverse operations.

$$\begin{array}{ll} 3 + 4 = 7 & 7 - 4 = 3 \\ 4 + 3 = 7 & 7 - 3 = 4 \end{array}$$

$$\begin{array}{ll} 3 \times 4 = 12 & 12 \div 4 = 3 \\ 4 \times 3 = 12 & 12 \div 3 = 4 \end{array}$$

When students study integers they learn that 3 and -3 are opposites, that is, $3 + -3 = 0$. From their knowledge of fractions they recall that 3 and $\frac{1}{3}$ are reciprocals, that is, $3 \times \frac{1}{3} = 1$. Thus to solve $n + 3 = 8$, one can either subtract 3 from or add -3 to both sides of the equation. In a similar vein, $3n = 15$ can be solved either by dividing both sides of the equation by 3 or by multiplying both sides of the equation by $\frac{1}{3}$.

Kieran (1988) found two different perspectives on solving equations among beginning (Grade 7) algebra students. One group substituted different numbers for the letter until they found one that made the sentence true. Another group used inverses of the operations and transposed terms to the other side to solve for the variable. She recommended that elementary school experiences with placeholders should emphasize the substitution method, because this method lends greater meaning to the idea that the letter is really a number in its own right within the equation.

Inequalities

An *equation* is a statement that two expressions are equal. An *inequality* is a statement that one expression is greater than (or less than) the other. In the early grades children learn to use the symbols $>$ and $<$ to write sentences expressing relationships between unequal numbers (for example, $2 < 5$ and $3 + 4 > 6$).

Solving an inequality containing a variable involves finding all possible values from the replacement set that will make the sentence true. For example, if the replacement set is the whole numbers, the solution set for $x + 1 < 4$ consists of the numbers 0, 1, and 2. If the replacement set for this inequality is the integers, the solution set consists of all integers less than 3—an infinite set. The solution in the set of rational numbers is expressed as: $x < 3$, x a rational number.

Equations such as $2 + n = 1$ and $2n = 3$ have no whole number solutions but do have answers in other number systems. The sentences $2 + x = x$ and $2 + x < x$ do not have solutions in any number system. Inequalities such as $x + 1 > x$ are true for all possible replacements of the variable. Such statements are known as *identities*.

Variables and Computer Programs

Computer science provides another setting in which students can learn about different uses of variables. In BASIC, variables are names of memory locations in the computer for storing values. The statement $B = 2$ in a program is an instruction to place the number 2 in the location named B. The statement $B = B + 5$ replaces the previous value in location B with a new value that is greater by 5. Obviously, the $=$ sign in this statement does not indicate equality in the usual sense.

In FOR . . . NEXT statements, a variable is used to represent a range of numbers. The following program when executed prints the numbers from 1 to 10.

```
10 FOR N = 1 TO 10

20 PRINT N

30 NEXT N
```

INPUT statements allow the user to evaluate expressions or formulas for different values of the variables. The following program computes and prints the volume of a rectangular prism when the user types in, as requested, the length, width, and height.

```
10  PRINT "ENTER LENGTH, WIDTH, AND
    HEIGHT"

20  INPUT L, W, H

30  V = L * W * H

40  PRINT "THE VOLUME IS" V
```

FUNCTIONS

The concept of function is one of the fundamental ideas in mathematics. In the school curriculum, function is viewed both as a concept—the study of regularity, and as a process—analyzing relationships (Howden, 1989). The idea was first introduced in the seventeenth century by Galileo who, in his work on motion, sought quantitative relationships to explain how things happen.

STANDARDS LINK 17-7

In grades 5–8, the mathematics curriculum should include explorations of patterns and functions so that students can

- describe, extend, analyze, and create a wide variety of patterns;
- describe and represent relationships with tables, graphs, and rules;
- analyze functional relationships to explain how a change in one quantity results in a change in another;
- use patterns and functions to represent and solve problems. (NCTM, 1989, p. 98)

STANDARDS LINK 17-8

During the middle years, the study of patterns and functions should focus on the analysis, representation, and generalization of functional relationships. These topics should first be explored as informal investigations. (NCTM, 1989, p. 98)

STANDARDS LINK 17-9

When students make graphs, data tables, expressions, equations, or verbal descriptions to represent a single relationship, they discover that different representations yield different interpretations of a situation. In informal ways, students develop an understanding that functions are composed of variables that have a dynamic relationship: Changes in one variable result in change in another. (NCTM, 1989, p. 98)

What Is a Function?

When the value of one thing depends on or varies with the value of another, we say that the first thing is a function of the second thing. For example, the height of a burning candle is a function of time: the longer the time it burns, the shorter the candle.

In general, a function is a rule of correspondence connecting the elements of one set (the domain of the function) with the elements of another set (the range of the function) such that each member of the domain corresponds to a unique member of the range. For example, the perimeter of a square is completely determined by the length of its side. For each value of a side, there is one and only one corresponding value for the perimeter. The domain and the range of this function are the nonnegative real numbers. The rule of correspondence in this case can

FIGURE 17-8

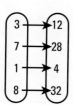

side s	perimeter 4 s
5	20
2	8
6	24
4	16

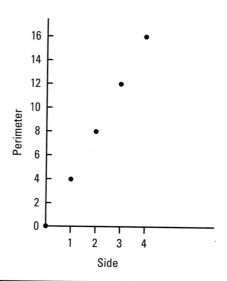

be expressed algebraically as an equation (formula), $P = 4s$. It can also be represented as an arrow diagram, a table, and a graph (Figure 17-8). Using formal functional language and notation, we say that the perimeter of a square is a function of the length of its side and write $f(s) = 4s$.

Not all functions can be represented as algebraic equations. Another way of defining a rule of correspondence is to give all possible pairings of elements in a table or arrow diagram, as in Figure 17-9(a). The relation defined by the arrow diagram in Figure 17-9(b) is not a function because the element 3 in the domain corresponds to two different elements, 5 and 8, in the range. The relation represented in Figure 17-9(c) is a function even though two different elements in the domain are paired with the same element in the range. The key attribute of a function is that each first element corresponds to only one second element.

Patterns and Relationships

In the primary grades, work relating to the function concept focuses on number patterns and mathematical relationships. For example, children could explore the prob-

lem of finding how many eyes there are in a small group or in the class (Howden, 1989). They might do this first by counting, drawing pictures, and/or using chips or blocks to model the process, and then make a table to record their findings (Figure 17-10). In the discussion the teacher should encourage the children to use words to describe the patterns and generalize the result. They might relate the "eyes" pattern to skip counting, counting by twos, or adding two each time. The idea of a functional relationship is encountered in predicting (without continuing the pattern) how many eyes ten children would have. In explaining his or her answer, a child might say that the number of eyes is equal to the number of people added to itself or doubled (multiplied by two). Writing the pattern rule as □ + □ or □ × 2 introduces the use of a variable as a placeholder for any (whole) number.

Similar problems involve finding the relationship between tricycles and wheels or hands and fingers. Students might also be asked to find real-world examples of relationships that match given rules, such as □ × 10.

How many toothpicks are needed to make 10 triangles? If the triangles are separate from one another, three toothpicks are needed for each triangle and the pattern rule is 3 × □. Suppose, however, that triangles can share

FIGURE 17-9

(a) a function

(b) not a function

(c) a function

FIGURE 17-10

children	1	2	3	4	10
eyes	2	4	6	8	—

a common side. Looking at the table we predict that 21 toothpicks are needed to make 10 triangles. The rule can be expressed as $2 \times \square + 1$.

triangles	1	2	3	4...	10
toothpicks	3	5	7	9...	—

Function Machines and Tables

A popular way of introducing functions in the elementary grades is through "function machines." The idea is that a number is fed into the machine, operated on by a rule, and the resulting number comes out of the machine. The rule "multiply by 3 and add 1" might first be described in words. Later this function would be represented using an algebraic expression: $3 \times \square + 1$ or $3n + 1$. The task is to find for given "input" numbers the associated "output" numbers and record these numbers in a table, as in Figure 17-11(a).

A related activity is "guess my rule" in which the objective is to determine the rule used to produce a given set of values. The teacher should include special functions such as the constant shown in Figure 17-11(b). The rule might be verbalized as "the answer is always 3."

Sequences

A number *sequence* is an ordered set of numbers such that there is a *first term,* a *second term,* a *third term,* and so on. The arrangement is from left to right and the terms are separated by commas. If the "in" values in a function table are 1, 2, 3 and so on, then the corresponding "out" values constitute a sequence. Thus a sequence is a function in which the "in" values are indicated by the position of the term (first—1, second—2, third—3, and so on). Some sequences can be described algebraically by finding a pattern that relates the number of the term to the term itself. The pattern rule is called the general or *n*th term of the sequence. For example, the *n*th term of the se-

quence of positive even numbers 2, 4, 6, . . . is $2n$. This means that every even number is the product of 2 and a counting number, and that a given term of the sequence is found by replacing n in the general term by the term number. Thus the 10th term is $2(10) = 20$.

Other elementary sequences and their *n*th terms are

Odd numbers:	1, 3, 5, . . ., $2n - 1$
Multiples of 5:	5, 10, 15, . . ., $5n$
Skip counting:	4, 10, 16, . . ., $6n - 2$
Square numbers:	1, 4, 9, . . ., n^2
Triangular numbers:	1, 3, 6, . . ., $\dfrac{n(n + 1)}{2}$

Given the first few terms of a sequence, students must find a pattern rule, write the next few terms and, where possible, give the *n*th term.

Calculator Functions

Most inexpensive calculators have built-in constant features that permit the user to evaluate expressions such as $n + 3$, $n - 3$, $3n$, and $n \div 3$ for different values of the variable by entering a number and pressing =. For example, $3n$ is established by keying $3 \times$. Successively pressing $5 =$, $8 =$, $12 =$ will produce 15, 24, 36 in the display. To establish $n - 3$, press $- 3 =$. This calculator feature might be explored in conjunction with function machines to illustrate the idea of a machine operating on input numbers according to a given rule to produce output numbers. Programmable calculators can, of course, handle more complex expressions.

Graphing

In geometry, students learn to plot ordered pairs of numbers on a coordinate system. A function can be represented graphically by thinking of the "in" and "out" elements in a table of values as the horizontal and the vertical coordinates, respectively, and plotting the points. The transition to naming the axes x and y is accomplished by expressing the rule as an equation in x and y and using these variables as column headings in a table of values. Consider $y = 4x - 3$.

x	y
1	1
2	5
3	7

First experiences in graphing functions often involve familiar formulas such as $P = 4s$, which relates the length of a side of a square and its perimeter (Figure 17-12). Students will see that the points lie on a line. At a

FIGURE 17-11

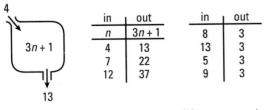

(a) function machine and table   (b) guess my rule

FIGURE 17-12

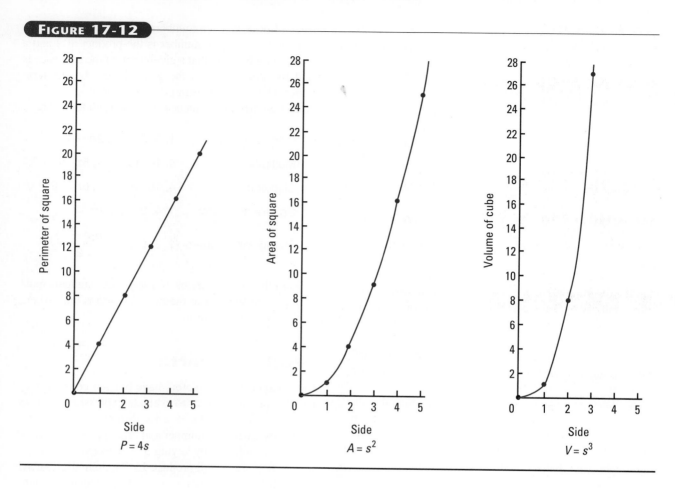

later time the points may be connected and extended. The teacher should encourage students to find how the relation "increasing the side by 1 increases the perimeter by 4" is manifest in the graph. Graphs representing the formulas for the area of a square ($A = s^2$) and the volume of a cube ($V = s^3$) can also be constructed (Figure 17-12). Students will find that these are not straight line graphs.

In considering the nature of these three graphs, teachers can suggest to students that they examine and compare the patterns of differences between successive terms.

side	0	1	2	3	4	5
perimeter of square	0	4	8	12	16	20
area of square	0	1	4	9	16	25
volume of cube	0	1	8	27	64	125

For the perimeter the first differences are 4. For the area the first difference pattern is 1, 3, 5, 7, 9, . . .; the second differences are the constant 2. For the volume the first, second, and third difference patterns are:

```
   1      7      19      37      61
      6      12      18      24
         6      6      6
```

Instruction and Assessment Activities

In addition to drawing graphs for formulas, students can take measurements or collect data for two related variables and plot the information on a graph. Problems of this nature include finding the relationship between height and armspan and between the distances around the wrist and neck (Figure 17-13). If appropriate graphing software is available, some students may wish to construct these graphs on a computer.

Problems involving relationships between measurement concepts such as perimeter and area or volume and surface area provide further opportunities for students to generate data, organize them in a table, and construct a graph (Phillips, 1991). For example, if you had 100 m of fencing to enclose a rectangular garden plot, what dimensions would you choose? To investigate this problem, selected integer values for the base and height might be systematically listed and the areas of corresponding rectangles computed. A graph showing the relationship between the base and the area of these rectangles could then be drawn (Figure 17-14).

The table and graph reveal that the rectangle with the greatest area is actually a square with sides of 25m. Long, narrow rectangles have small areas. In answering the

FIGURE 17-13

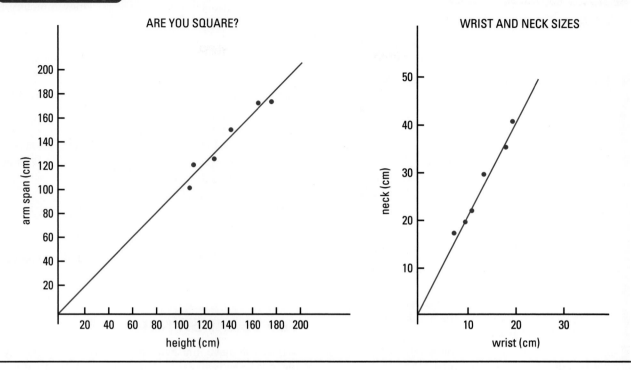

FIGURE 17-14

Perimeter = 100

Base	Height	Area
5	45	225
10	40	400
15	35	525
20	30	600
25	25	625
30	20	600
35	15	525
40	10	400
45	5	225

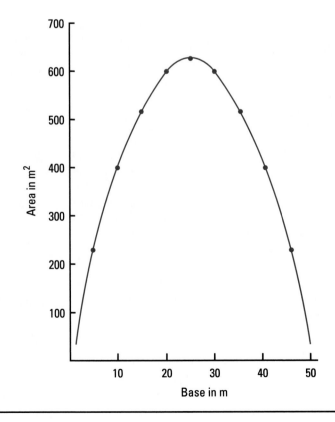

☀ ACTIVITY 17-5

WHAT COMES NEXT?

1. Write a description of how to build the fourth model in the series below.

2. Draw a diagram of the fourth model.

3. Describe any patterns you see in the models.

4. Make a chart of the number of cubes needed to build the first five models.

5. Draw a graph of the relationship between the number of the model and the number of cubes needed to construct it.

6. Use your graph to predict the number of cubes needed to build the 6th model.

original question of this example, other factors that might be considered in choosing the shape of the plot should also be identified.

The problem in Activity 17-5 requires students to describe a pattern in words, extend it visually, represent the relationship using a table and graph, and make a prediction based on the relationship.

CONCLUSION

The development of algebraic thinking in the mathematics curriculum begins in the early grades and occurs as a gradual building from informal to formal concepts (Schultz, 1991). Key ideas that run through the grades include pattern, variable, expression, equation, function, and graphing. The transition from arithmetic to algebra provides many opportunities for students to engage in problem solving and to make connections. Experiences such as those described in this chapter will help students continue to see mathematics as a sense-making activity as they study algebra in the middle school and high school years.

For Your Journal

When you have finished studying this chapter, reflect on these questions in your math journal:

1. Give an example of a model to help students understand each operation on integers. Draw a picture to show how to solve each problem using the model you chose.

2. Discuss how to help students develop understanding of variables.

3. Discuss several real-world situations that are functions.

4. Visit a middle school classroom and informally interview several students to assess their understanding of variables and integers. Ask the students questions such as the following:
   • What does the expression $3b$ mean?
   • What is n if: $n - 4 = 9$? $2n = n$? $2n = 1$?
   • What is greater: $2n$ or $n + 2$?   Explain.

Describe students' understandings and misconceptions.

For Your Portfolio

When you have finished studying this chapter, complete these activities to include in your professional portfolio:

1. Examine a textbook's section on operations on integers. Describe the models used in the textbook to represent operations on integers.

2. Using a model and an operation of your choice, write a lesson plan to introduce an operation with integers to middle-school students.

3. Write a lesson plan using a real-world situation to introduce the concept of variables to middle school students.

Resources for Teachers

Books on algebraic thinking

Charles, L. H. (1990). *Algebra thinking: First experiences.* Sunnyvale, CA: Creative Publications.

Picciotto, H. (1990). *The algebra lab: Middle school.* Sunnyvale, CA: Creative Publications.

Links to the Internet

Explorer: Algebraic ideas

http://explorer.scrtec.org/explorer/explorer-db/browse/static/Mathematics/browse/f83.html

Contains many lessons on and lists of other resources for algebraic ideas.

Blackline Masters

1. Base-Ten Blocks
2. Ten Frames
3. Hundreds Chart (0–99)
4. Hundreds Chart (1–100)
5. Ten-by-Ten Multiplication Array
6. Fraction Circles *(Whole, Halves, Thirds, Fourths)*
7. Fraction Circles *(Fifths, Sixths, Eighths, Ninths)*
8. Fraction Circles *(Tenths, Twelfths, Fifteenths, and Sixteenths)*
9. Fraction Bars *(Whole, Halves, Thirds, Fourths, Fifths, Sixths, Eighths, Ninths, Tenths, and Twelfths)*
10. Decimal Grids
11. Geoboard Template
12. Geoboard Recording Paper
13. Centimeter Dot Paper
14. Tangram
15. Centimeter Grid Paper
16. Inch Grid Paper

BLM-1 Base-Ten Blocks

BLM-2 Ten Frames

BLM-3   Hundreds Chart (0–99)

0	1	2	3	4	5	6	7	8	9
10	11	12	13	14	15	16	17	18	19
20	21	22	23	24	25	26	27	28	29
30	31	32	33	34	35	36	37	38	39
40	41	42	43	44	45	46	47	48	49
50	51	52	53	54	55	56	57	58	59
60	61	62	63	64	65	66	67	68	69
70	71	72	73	74	75	76	77	78	79
80	81	82	83	84	85	86	87	88	89
90	91	92	93	94	95	96	97	98	99

BLM-4   Hundreds Chart (1–100)

1	2	3	4	5	6	7	8	9	10
11	12	13	14	15	16	17	18	19	20
21	22	23	24	25	26	27	28	29	30
31	32	33	34	35	36	37	38	39	40
41	42	43	44	45	46	47	48	49	50
51	52	53	54	55	56	57	58	59	60
61	62	63	64	65	66	67	68	69	70
71	72	73	74	75	76	77	78	79	80
81	82	83	84	85	86	87	88	89	90
91	92	93	94	95	96	97	98	99	100

BLM-5   Ten-by-Ten Multiplication Array

BLM-6 Fraction Circles

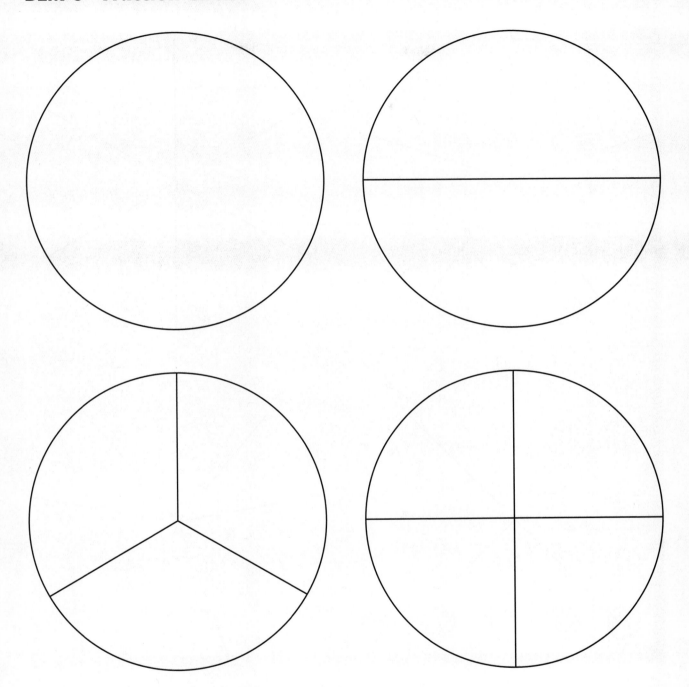

BLM-7 Fraction Circles

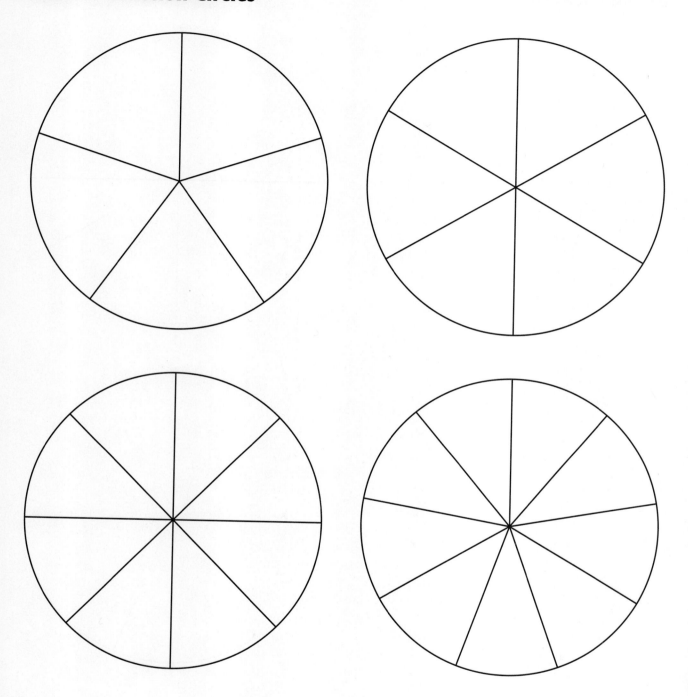

BLM-8   Fraction Circles

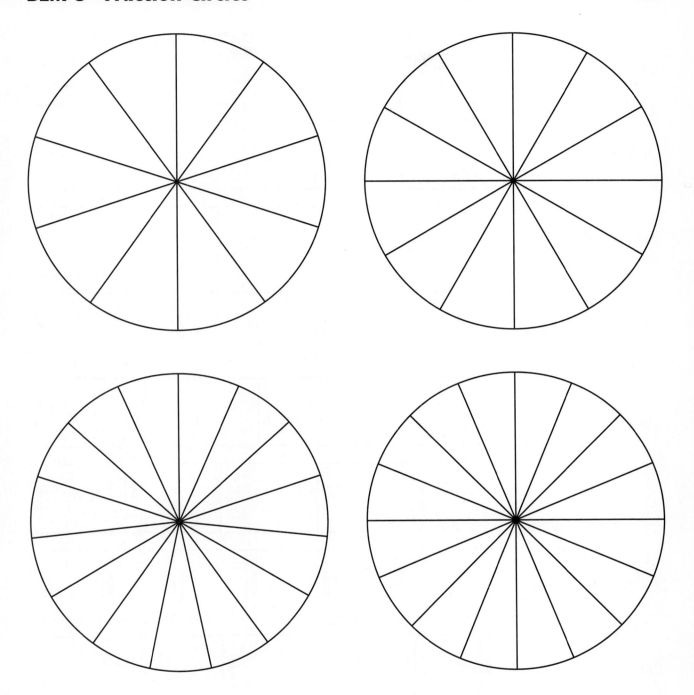

BLM-9 Fraction Bars

whole	

halves	$\frac{1}{2}$	$\frac{2}{2}$

thirds	$\frac{1}{3}$	$\frac{2}{3}$	$\frac{3}{3}$

fourths	$\frac{1}{4}$	$\frac{2}{4}$	$\frac{3}{4}$	$\frac{4}{4}$

fifths	$\frac{1}{5}$	$\frac{2}{5}$	$\frac{3}{5}$	$\frac{4}{5}$	$\frac{5}{5}$

sixths	$\frac{1}{6}$	$\frac{2}{6}$	$\frac{3}{6}$	$\frac{4}{6}$	$\frac{5}{6}$	$\frac{6}{6}$

eighths	$\frac{1}{8}$	$\frac{2}{8}$	$\frac{3}{8}$	$\frac{4}{8}$	$\frac{5}{8}$	$\frac{6}{8}$	$\frac{7}{8}$	$\frac{8}{8}$

ninths	$\frac{1}{9}$	$\frac{2}{9}$	$\frac{3}{9}$	$\frac{4}{9}$	$\frac{5}{9}$	$\frac{6}{9}$	$\frac{7}{9}$	$\frac{8}{9}$	$\frac{9}{9}$

tenths	$\frac{1}{10}$	$\frac{2}{10}$	$\frac{3}{10}$	$\frac{4}{10}$	$\frac{5}{10}$	$\frac{6}{10}$	$\frac{7}{10}$	$\frac{8}{10}$	$\frac{9}{10}$	$\frac{10}{10}$

twelfths	$\frac{1}{12}$	$\frac{2}{12}$	$\frac{3}{12}$	$\frac{4}{12}$	$\frac{5}{12}$	$\frac{6}{12}$	$\frac{7}{12}$	$\frac{8}{12}$	$\frac{9}{12}$	$\frac{10}{12}$	$\frac{11}{12}$	$\frac{12}{12}$

BLM-10   Decimal Grids

BLM-11 Geoboard Template

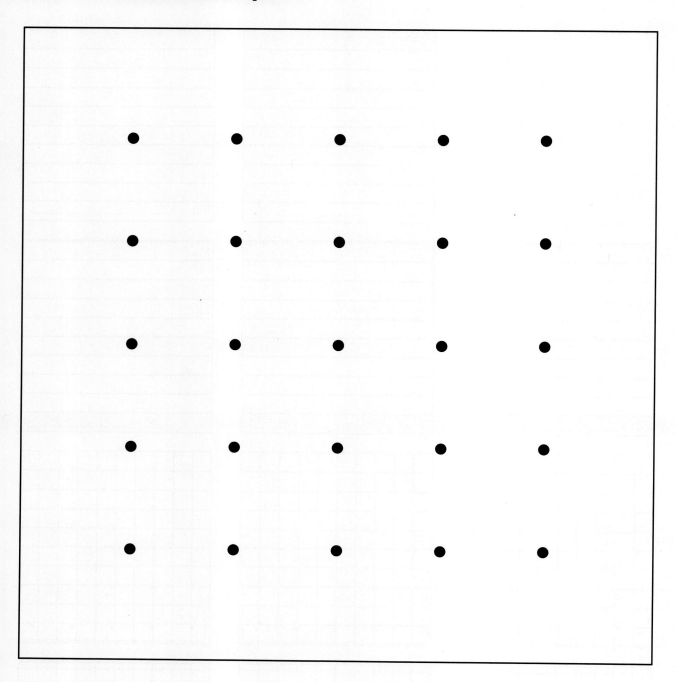

BLM-12   Geoboard Recording Paper

BLM-13 Centimeter Dot Paper

BLM-14 Tangram

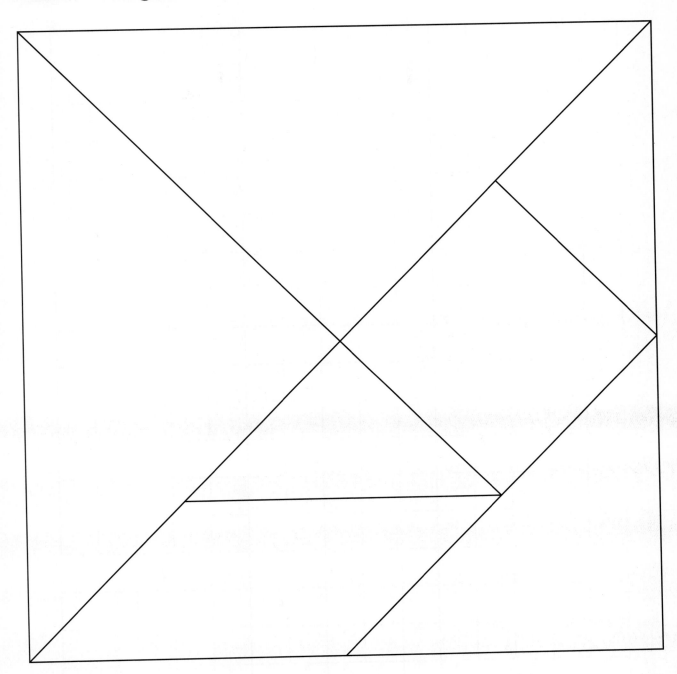

BLM-15 Centimeter Grid Paper

BLM-16 Inch Grid Paper

Chapter 1

Behr, M. J., Lesh, R., Post, T. R., & Silver, E. A. (1983). Rational number concepts. In R. Lesh & M. Landau (Eds.), *Acquisition of mathematics concepts and processes* (pp. 91–126). New York: Academic Press.

Brownell, W. A. (1947). An experiment on "borrowing" in third grade arithmetic. *Journal of Educational Research 41*(3), 161–171.

Brownell, W. A., & Moser, H. E. (1949). Meaningful vs. mechanical learning: A study in grade 3 subtraction. *Duke University Studies in Education 8,* 1–27.

Browning, C. A., & Channell, D. E. (1992). A "handy" database activity for the middle school classroom. *Arithmetic Teacher 40*(4), 235–238.

Corelli, R. (1989). A day in the year 2060. *Maclean's, 11,* 38–39.

Dossey, J. A., & Mullis, I. V. S. (1997). NAEP mathematics—1990–1992: The national, trial state, and trend assessments. In P. A. Kenney & E. A. Silver (Eds.) (1997). *Results from the Sixth Mathematics Assessment of the National Assessment of Educational Progress* (pp. 17–32). Reston, VA: National Council of Teachers of Mathematics.

Edmark Corporation (1993). *Millie's math house* [Computer Software]. Redmond, WA: Edmark Corp.

Friel, S. (1983). Lemonade's the name, simulation's the game. *Classroom Computer News 3,* 34–39.

Glennon, V. J. (1963). Some perspectives in education. In *Enrichment mathematics for the grades* (27th Yearbook). Washington, DC: National Council of Teachers of Mathematics.

Hembree, R., & Dessart, D. J. (1986). Effects of hand-held calculators in precollege mathematics education: A meta-analysis. *Journal for Research in Mathematics Education 17*(2), 83–99.

Hiebert, J. (1990). The role of routine procedures in the development of mathematical competence. In T. J. Cooney & C. R. Hirsch (Eds.), *Teaching and learning mathematics in the 1990s* (1990 Yearbook, pp. 31–40). Reston, VA: National Council of Teachers of Mathematics.

Hyde, J. S., Fennema, E., & Lamon, S. J. (1990). Gender differences in mathematics performance: A meta-analysis. *Psychological Bulletin, 109,* 139–155.

Jensen, R. J. (Ed.). (1993). *Research ideas for the classroom: Early childhood mathematics.* New York: Macmillan.

Kenney, P. A., & Silver, E. A. (Eds.). (1997). *Results from the Sixth Mathematics Assessment of the National Assessment of Educational Progress.* Reston, VA: National Council of Teachers of Mathematics.

Lapointe, A. E., Mead, N. A., & Phillips, G. W. (1989). *A world of differences: An international assessment of mathematics and science* (Report No. 19-CAEP-01). Princeton, NJ: Educational Testing Service.

Mathematical Sciences Education Board and National Research Council (1989). *Everybody counts: A report to the nation on the future of mathematics education.* Washington, DC: National Academy Press.

Mathematical Sciences Education Board and National Research Council. (1990). *Reshaping school mathematics: A philosophy and framework for curriculum.* Washington, DC: National Academy Press.

McKay, S. (1989). Fantastic hardware. *Maclean's, 11,* September, 40, 42.

McKenzie, W. S. (1990). Meaning: The common element in both reading and mathematics. *Ontario Mathematics Gazette 28*(3), 8–13.

Meyer, M. R. (1989). Gender differences in mathematics. In M. M. Lindquist (Ed.), *Results from the Fourth Mathematics Assessment.* Reston, VA: National Council of Teachers of Mathematics.

Meyer, M. R., & Fennema, E. (1992). Girls, boys, and mathematics. In T. R. Post (Ed.), *Teaching mathematics in grades K–8: Research-based methods* (pp. 443–464). Boston, MA: Allyn and Bacon.

Morgan, M. T., & Robinson, N. (1976). The "Back to the Basics" movement in education. *Canadian Journal of Education 1*(2), 1–11.

Mullis, I. V. S. (1997). *Benchmarking to international achievement: Attaining excellence: TIMSS as a starting point to examine student achievement.* Washington, DC: U.S. Department of Education, Office of Educational Research and Improvement.

National Council of Teachers of Mathematics (1977). "Position Statement on Basic Skills." *Arithmetic Teacher 25* (1 October): 18.

National Council of Supervisors of Mathematics. (1977). Position statement on basic skills. *Arithmetic Teacher 25*(1), 18–22.

National Council of Teachers of Mathematics. (1980). *An agenda for action.* Reston VA: National Council of Teachers of Mathematics.

National Council of Teachers of Mathematics. (1989). *Curriculum and evaluation standards for school mathematics.* Reston, VA: National Council of Teachers of Mathematics.

National Council of Teachers of Mathematics. (1991). *Professional standards for teaching mathematics.* Reston, VA: National Council of Teachers of Mathematics.

National Council of Teachers of Mathematics. (1991, February). *Position statement on calculators and the education of youth.* Reston, VA: National Council of Teachers of Mathematics.

National Council of Teachers of Mathematics. (1994). *Position statement on the use of technology in the learning and teaching of mathematics.* Reston, VA: National Council of Teachers of Mathematics.

National Council of Teachers of Mathematics. (1995). *Assessment standards for school mathematics.* Reston, VA: National Council of Teachers of Mathematics.

National Council of Supervisors of Mathematics. (1988). Essential mathematics for the 21st century. Unpublished paper.

Owens, D. T. (Ed.). (1993). *Research ideas for the classroom: Middle grades mathematics.* New York: Macmillan Publishing.

Reys, B. J., & Reys, R. E. (1987). Calculators in the classroom: How can we make it happen? *Arithmetic Teacher 34*(6), 12–14.

Suydam, M. N. (1984). Research report: Manipulative materials. *Arithmetic Teacher 31*(5), 27.

Travers, K. J., & McKnight, C. C. (1984). *International Association for the Evaluation of Educational Achievement—Second Study of Mathematics—The International Mathematics Curriculum.* Urbana-Champaign, IL: International Coordinating Center.

U.S. Department of Education, National Center for Education Statistics (1996). *Pursuing excellence: A Study of U.S. eighth-grade mathematics and science teaching, learning, curriculum, and achievement in international context.* Washington, DC: U.S. Government Printing Office.

U.S. Department of Education, National Center for Education Statistics (1997). *Pursuing excellence: A Study of U.S. fourth-grade mathematics and science achievement in international context.* Washington, DC: U.S. Government Printing Office.

Chapter 2

Artzt, A. L., & Newman, C. M. (1990). Implementing the Standards: Cooperative learning. *Mathematics Teacher 83*(6), 448–452.

Artzt, A. L., & Newman, C. M. (1990). *How to use cooperative learning in the mathematics class.* Reston, VA: National Council of Teachers of Mathematics.

Ashlock, R. B., Johnson, M. L., Wilson, J. W., & Jones, W. L. (1983). *Guiding each child's learning of mathematics: A diagnostic approach to instruction.* Columbus, OH: Merrill.

Azzolino, A. (1990). Writing as a tool for teaching mathematics: The silent revolution. In T. J. Cooney & C. R. Hirsch (Eds.), *Teaching and learning mathematics in the 1990s* (1990 NCTM Yearbook, pp. 92–100). Reston, VA: National Council of Teachers of Mathematics.

Bartels, B. H. (1995). Promoting mathematics connections with concept mapping. *Mathematics Teaching in the Middle School 1*(7), 542–549.

Behr, M. J., Lesh, R., Post, T. R., & Silver, E. A. (1983). Rational number concepts. In R. Lesh & M. Landau (Eds.), *Acquisition of mathematics concepts and processes* (pp. 91–126). New York: Academic Press.

Burton, G. M. (1985). Writing as a way of knowing in a mathematics education class. *Arithmetic Teacher 33*(4), 40–45.

Butler, K. (1988). Learning styles. *Learning 17*(4), 30–34.

Clements, D. H., & McMillen, S. (1996). Rethinking "concrete" manipulatives. *Teaching Children Mathematics 2*(5), 270–275.

Confrey, J. (1990). What constructivism implies for teaching. In R. B. Davis, C. A. Maher, & N. Noddings (Eds.). *Constructivist views on the teaching and learning of mathematics.* (*Journal for Research in Mathematics Education,* Monograph No. 4, pp. 107–122). Reston, VA: National Council of Teachers of Mathematics.

Davidson, D. M., & Pearce, D. L. (1988). Using writing activities to reinforce mathematics instruction. *Arithmetic Teacher 35*(8), 42–45.

Davidson, N. (1990a). Small-group cooperative learning in mathematics. In T. J. Cooney & C. R. Hirsch (Eds.). *Teaching and learning mathematics in the 1990s* (1990 NCTM Yearbook, pp. 52–61). Reston, VA: National Council of Teachers of Mathematics.

Davidson, N. (1990b). *Cooperative learning in mathematics: A handbook for teachers.* Reading, MA: Addison-Wesley Publishing.

Evans, C. S. (1984). Writing to learn in math. *Language Arts 61* (8 December), 828–835.

Fennell, F., & Ammon, R. (1985). Writing techniques for problem solvers. *Arithmetic Teacher 33*(1), 24–25.

Gagne, R. M. (1985). *The conditions of learning and theory of instruction.* New York: Holt, Rinehart & Winston.

Ginsburg, H. P., & Baron, J. (1993). Cognition: Young children's construction of mathematics. In R. J. Jensen (Ed.), *Research ideas for the classroom: Early childhood mathematics* (pp. 3–21). New York: Macmillan.

Goldin, G. A. (1990). Epistemology, constructivism, and discovery learning in mathematics. In R. B. Davis, C. A. Maher, & N. Noddings (Eds.), *Constructivist views on the teaching and learning of mathematics.* (*Journal for Research in Mathematics Education,* Monograph No. 4, pp. 31–47). Reston, VA: National Council of Teachers of Mathematics.

Good, T. L., Reys, B. J., Grouws, D. A., & Mulryan, C. M. (1989/90). Using work-groups in mathematics instruction. *Educational Leadership 47*(4), 56–62.

Hanselman, C. A. (1996). Using brainstorming webs in the mathematics classroom. *Mathematics Teaching in the Middle School 1*(9), 766–777.

Hart, L. C., Schultz, K., Najee-ullah, D., & Nash, L. (1992). The role of reflection in teaching. *Arithmetic Teacher 40*(1), 40–42.

Hiebert, J. (1990). The role of routine procedures in the development of mathematical competence. In T. J. Cooney & C. R. Hirsch (Eds.), *Teaching and learning mathematics in the 1990s* (1990 Yearbook, pp. 31–40). Reston, VA: National Council of Teachers of Mathematics.

Holmes, E. E. (1990). Motivation: An essential component of mathematics instruction. In T. J. Cooney & C. R. Hirsch (Eds.), *Teaching and learning mathematics in the 1990s* (1990 Yearbook, pp. 101–107). Reston, VA: National Council of Teachers of Mathematics.

Kamii, C. (1990). Constructivism and beginning arithmetic (K–2). In T. J. Cooney & C. R. Hirsch (Eds.). *Teaching and learning mathematics in the 1990s.* (1990 Yearbook, pp. 22–30). Reston, VA: National Council of Teachers of Mathematics.

Kennedy, L. M., and S. Tipps (1991). *Guiding children's learning of mathematics* (6th ed.). Belmont, CA: Wadsworth.

Lerman, S. (1989). Constructivism, mathematics and mathematics education. *Educational Studies in Mathematics 20*(2), 211–233.

McIntosh, M. E. (1991). No time for writing in your class? *Mathematics Teacher 84*(6), 423–433.

Morine-Dershimer, G. G. (1990). Instructional planning. In J. M. Cooper (Ed.), *Classroom teaching skills* (4th ed.) (pp. 17–49). Lexington, MA: D. C. Heath and Company.

National Council of Teachers of Mathematics. (1989). *Curriculum and evaluation standards for school mathematics.* Reston, VA: Author.

National Council of Teachers of Mathematics. (1991). *Professional standards for teaching mathematics.* Reston, VA: Author.

Oberholtzer-Sutton, G. (1992). Cooperative learning works in mathematics. *Mathematics Teacher 85*(1), 63–66.

Orlich, D. C., Harder, R. J., Callahan, R. C., Kauchak, D. P., Pendergrass, R. A., Keogh, A. J., and Gibson, H. (1990). *Teaching strategies: A guide to better instruction* (3rd ed.). Lexington, MA: D. C. Heath and Company.

Pa, N. A. N. (1986). Meaning in arithmetic from four different perspectives. *For the Learning of Mathematics 6*(1), 11–16.

Reuille-Irons, R., & Irons, C. J. (1989). Language experiences: A base for problem solving. In P. R. Trafton & A. P. Shulte (Eds.), *New directions for elementary school mathematics* (1989 NCTM Yearbook, pp. 85–98). Reston, VA: National Council of Teachers of Mathematics.

Riedesel, C. A. (1990). *Teaching elementary school mathematics* (5th ed.). Englewood Cliffs, NJ: Prentice Hall.

Ross, R., Kurtz, R. (1993). Making manipulatives work: A strategy for success. *Arithmetic Teacher 40* (5 January), 254–257.

Sawada, D. (1985). Mathematical symbols: Insight through invention. *Arithmetic Teacher 32*(6), 20–22.

Skemp, R. (1989). *Structured activities for primary mathematics* Vol. 1. London, UK: Routledge.

Stigler, J. W. (1988). Research into practice: The use of verbal explanation in Japanese and American classrooms. *Arithmetic Teacher 36*(2), 27–29.

Thompson, A. (1990). Letters to a math teacher. In N. Atwell (Ed.), *Coming to know: Writing to learn in the intermediate grades* (pp. 87–93). Concord, ON: Irwin Publishing.

Van de Walle, J. A. (1994). *Elementary school mathematics: Teaching developmentally* (2nd ed.). White Plains, NY: Longman.

Wentworth, N. M., & Monroe, E. E. (1995). What is the Whole? *Mathematics Teaching in the Middle School 1*(5), 356–360.

Chapter 3

Charles, R., & Lester, F. K. (1982). *Teaching problem solving: What, why, & how.* Palo Alto, CA: Dale Seymour Publications.

Charles, R. I., & Lester, F. K., Jr. (1984). An evaluation of a process-oriented program in mathematical problem solving in grades 5 and 7. *Journal for Research in Mathematics Education 18*(2), 83–97.

Fennell, F., & Ammon, R. (1985). Writing techniques for problem solvers. *Arithmetic Teacher 33*(1):24–25.

Ford, M. I. (1990). The writing process: A strategy for problem solvers. *Arithmetic Teacher 38*(3), 35–38.

Hembree, R., & March, H. (1993). Problem solving in early childhood: Building foundations. In R. J. Jensen (Ed.), *Research ideas for the classroom: Early childhood mathematics.* Reston, VA: National Council of Teachers of Mathematics.

Kroll, D. L., & Miller, T. (1993). Insights from research on mathematical problem solving in the middle grades. In D. T. Owens (Ed.), *Research ideas for the classroom: Middle grades mathematics* (pp. 58–77). New York: Macmillan.

Moser, J. M. (1992). Arithmetic operations on whole numbers: Addition and subtraction. In T. R. Post (Ed.), *Teaching mathematics in grades K–8: Research-based methods* (pp. 123–155). Boston: Allyn and Bacon.

Moses, B., Bjork, E., & Goldenberg, E. P. (1990). Beyond problem solving: Problem posing. In T. J. Cooney (Ed.). *Teaching and learning mathematics in the 1990s* (1990 Yearbook). Reston, VA: National Council of Teachers of Mathematics.

National Council of Teachers of Mathematics. (1989). *Curriculum and evaluation standards for school mathematics.* Reston, VA: Author.

National Council of Teachers of Mathematics (1991). *Professional standards for teaching mathematics.* Reston, VA: Author.

National Research Council (1989). *Everybody counts.* Washington, DC: National Academy Press.

Polya, G. (1949). On solving mathematical problems in high school. Reprinted in S. Krulik & R. E. Reys (Eds.), *Problem solving in school mathematics* (1980 Yearbook). Reston, VA: National Council of Teachers of Mathematics, 1–2.

Polya, G. (1957). *How to solve it* (2nd ed.). New York: Doubleday.

Pothier, Y. (1992). Writing to communicate mathematics. In D. Sawada (Ed.), *Communication in the mathematics classroom.* Edmonton, AB: Mathematics Council of the Alberta Teachers' Association.

Pothier, Y., & Sawada, D. (1990). Students value time and a patient teacher. *Mathematics in school 19*(3), 38–39.

Suydam, M. (1984). Research reports: Problem solving. *Arithmetic Teacher 31*(9), 36.

Van de Walle, J. A. (1998). *Elementary and middle school mathematics: Teaching developmentally* (3rd ed.). White Plains, NY: Longman.

Chapter 4

California Mathematics Council. (1996). *Constructive assessment in mathematics.* San Diego, CA: Author.

Collison, J. (1992). Using performance assessment to determine mathematical dispositions. *Arithmetic Teacher 39*, 40–47.

Crowley, M. L. (1993). Student mathematics portfolio: More than a display case. *Mathematics Teacher 86*, 544–547.

Lambdin, D. V., & Walker, V. L. (1994). Planning for classroom portfolio assessment. *Arithmetic Teacher 41*, 318–324.

National Council of Teachers of Mathematics. (1989). *Curriculum and evaluation standards for school mathematics.* Reston, VA: National Council of Teachers of Mathematics.

National Council of Teachers of Mathematics. (1995). *Assessment standards for school mathematics.* Reston, VA: National Council of Teachers of Mathematics.

Pandey, T. (1991). *A sampler of mathematics assessment.* Sacramento, CA: California Department of Education.

Stenmark, J. K. (Ed.). (1991). *Mathematics assessment: Myths, models, good questions, and practical suggestions.* Reston, VA: National Council of Teachers of Mathematics.

Chapter 5

Baker, A., & Baker, J. (1990). *Mathematics in process.* Portsmouth, NH: Heinemann Educational Books.

Baratta-Lorton, M. (1987). *Mathematics their way.* Palo Alto, CA: Addison-Wesley.

Barchas, S. E. (1975). *I was walking down the road.* New York: Scholastic Book Services.

Gelman, R., & Gallistel, C. R. (1978). *The child's understanding of number.* Cambridge, MA: Harvard University Press.

Hoffman, M. (1990). *Nancy no-size.* London, UK: Little Mannoth.

Hughes, M. (1986). *Children and number: Difficulties in learning mathematics.* Oxford, UK: Basil Blackwell.

Kamii, C., & Joseph, L. (1988). Teaching place value and double-column addition. *Arithmetic Teacher 35*(6), 48–52.

Labinowicz, E. (1980). *The Piaget primer: Thinking, learning, teaching.* Palo Alto, CA: Addison-Wesley.

Labinowicz, E. (1985). *Learning from children: New beginnings for teaching numerical thinking.* Palo Alto, CA: Addison-Wesley.

Marchand, L. C., Bye, M. P., Harrison, B., & Schroeder, T. L. (1985). *Assessing cognitive levels in the classroom.* Edmonton, AB: Alberta Education. (ERIC Document Reproduction Service No. ED 266 033.)

National Council of Teachers of Mathematics. (1989). *Curriculum and evaluation standards for school mathematics.* Reston, VA: Author.

Piaget, J. (1965). *The child's conception of number.* New York: W. W. Norton.

Oppenheim, J., & Reid, B. (1986). *Have you seen birds?* Richmond Hill, ON: Scholastic-TAB Publishers.

Parker, J. (1988). *I love spiders.* New York: Scholastic, Inc.

Serfoza, M. (1988). *Who said red?* New York: Scholastic Inc.

Skemp, R. (1989). *Structured activities for primary mathematics (vol. 1).* London, UK: Routledge.

Stinson, K. (1982). *Red is best.* Toronto, ON: Annick Press.

Van de Walle, J. A. (1994). *Elementary school mathematics: Teaching developmentally (2nd ed.).* White Plains, NY: Longman.

Wirtz, R. (1974). *Mathematics for everyone.* Washington, DC: Curriculum Development Associates.

Chapter 6

Bidwell, J. K. (1967). Mayan arithmetic. *Mathematics Teacher 60*(7), 762–768.

Cowle, I. M. (1970). Ancient systems of numeration—stimulating, illuminating. *Arithmetic Teacher 17*(5), 413–416.

Hampton-Burnett, P. (1981). A million! How much is that? *Arithmetic Teacher 29*(1), 49–50.

Kamii, C., & Joseph, L. (1988). Teaching place value and double-column addition. *Arithmetic Teacher 35*(6), 48–52.

National Council of Teachers of Mathematics. (1989). *Curriculum and evaluation standards for school mathematics.* Reston, VA: Author.

Payne, J. N. (1988). Research into practice: Place value for tens and ones. *Arithmetic Teacher 35*(6), 64–66.

Reys, R. E., Suydam, M. N., & Lindquist, M. M. (1984). *Helping children learn mathematics.* Englewood Cliffs, NJ: Prentice-Hall Inc.

Ross, S. (1986). *The development of children's place-value concepts in grades two through five.* Paper presented at the American Education Research Association, San Francisco.

Ross, S. (1989). Parts, wholes, and place value: A developmental view. *Arithmetic Teacher 36*(6), 47–51.

Skemp, R. (1989). *Structured activities for primary mathematics (Vol. 1).* London, UK: Routledge.

Smith, R. F. (1973). Diagnosis of pupil performance in place value tasks. *Arithmetic Teacher 20*(5), 403–408.

Chapter 7

Anghileri, J., & Johnson, D. C. (1992). Arithmetic operations on whole numbers: Multiplication and division. In T. R. Post (Ed.), *Teaching mathematics in grades K–8: Research-based methods* (pp. 157–200). Boston: Allyn and Bacon.

Burns, M. (1991). Introducing division through problem-solving experiences. *Arithmetic Teacher, 38*(8), 14–18.

Carey, D. A. (1991). Number sentences: Linking addition and subtraction word problems and symbols. *Journal for Research in Mathematics Education, 22*(4), 266–280.

Carpenter, T. P., & Moser, J. M. (1982). The development of addition and subtraction problem-solving skills. In T. P. Carpenter, J. M. Moser, & T. A. Romberg (Eds.), *Addition and subtraction: A cognitive perspective* (pp. 9–24). Hillsdale, NJ: Lawrence Erlbaum.

Fennema, E., Carpenter, T. P., Levi, L., Franke, M. L., & Empson, S. (1997). *Cognitively Guided Instruction: Professional development in primary mathematics.* Madison, WI: Wisconsin Center for Education Research.

Greer, B. (1992). Multiplication and division as models of situations. In D. A. Grouws (Ed.), *Handbook of research on mathematics teaching and learning* (pp. 276–299). New York: Macmillan.

Kouba, V. L., & Franklin, K. (1993). Multiplication and division: Sense making and meaning. In R. J. Jensen (Ed.), *Research ideas for the classroom: Early childhood mathematics* (pp. 103–126). New York: Macmillan.

National Council of Teachers of Mathematics. (1989). *Curriculum and evaluation standards for school mathematics.* Reston, VA: Author.

Page, A. (1994). Helping children understand subtraction. *Teaching Children Mathematics, 1*(3), 140–143.

Sowder, L. (1988). Children's solutions of story problems. *Journal of Mathematical Behavior, 7*(3), 227–238.

Stigler, J. W., Fuson, K. C., Ham, M., & Kim, M. S. (1986). An analysis of addition and subtraction word problems in American and Soviet elementary mathematics textbooks. *Cognition and Instruction, 3,* 153–171.

Trafton, P. R., & Zawojewski, J. S. (1990). Meaning of operations. *Arithmetic Teacher, 38*(3), 18–22.

Chapter 8

Baroody, A. J. (1984). Children's difficulties in subtraction: Some causes and questions. *Journal for Research in Mathematics Education, 15,* 203–213.

Feinberg, M. M. (1990, April 8). Using patterns to practice basic facts. *Arithmetic Teacher, 37,* 38–41.

Moser, J. M. (1992). Arithmetic operations on whole numbers: Addition and subtraction. In T. R. Post (Ed.), *Teaching mathematics in grades K–8: Research-based methods* (pp. 123–155). Boston: Allyn and Bacon.

National Council of Teachers of Mathematics. (1989). *Curriculum and evaluation standards for school mathematics.* Reston, VA: Author.

Rathmell, E. C. (1978). Using thinking strategies to teach the basic facts. In M. N. Suydam & R. E. Reys (Eds.), *Developing computational skills,* NCTM's 1978 yearbook (pp. 13–38). Reston, VA: National Council of Teachers of Mathematics.

Thornton, C. A. (1978). Emphasizing thinking strategies in basic fact instruction. *Journal for Research in Mathematics Education, 9,* 214–227.

Weill, B. F. (1978). Mrs. Weill's hill: A successful subtraction method for use with the learning-disabled child. *Arithmetic Teacher 26*(2), 34–35.

Watson, J. M. (1991). Models to show the impossibility of division by zero. *School Science and Mathematics 9*(8), 373–376.

Chapter 9

Ashlock, R. B. (1998). *Error patterns in computation* (7th ed.). Upper Saddle River, NJ: Merrill.

Atweh, B. (1982). Developing mental arithmetic. In L. Silvey & J. R. Smart (Eds.). *Mathematics for the middle grades*

(5–9), 1982 Yearbook (pp. 50–58). Reston, VA: National Council of Teachers of Mathematics.

Bidwell, J. K. (1991). Readers' dialogue: Susan's personal algorithm. *Arithmetic Teacher 39*(3), 1.

Bohan, H. J., & Shawaker, P. Bohan. (1994). Using manipulatives effectively: A drive down rounding road. *Arithmetic Teacher 41*(5), 246–248.

Brownell, W. A. (1947). An experiment on "borrowing" in third grade arithmetic. *Journal of Educational Research 41*(3), 161–171.

Brownell, W. A., & Moser, H. E. (1949). Meaningful vs. mechanical learning: A study in grade 3 subtraction. *Duke University Studies in Education 8,* 1–207.

Burns, M. (1991). Introducing division through problem-solving experiences. *Arithmetic Teacher 38*(8), 14–18.

Cathcart, W. G. (1990). Implementation of an Apple Center for Innovation and Year 1 Results. In L. Pereira-Mendoza & M. Quigley (Eds.). *Canadian Mathematics Education Study Group: Proceedings 1989 Annual Meeting* (pp. 87–98). St. Johns, NF: Memorial University of Newfoundland.

Cathcart, W. G. (1991). Achievement in a computer-rich environment. In S. Gayle (Ed.) *Proceedings: NECC 91* (pp. 188–194). Eugene, OR: International Society for Technology in Education.

Cheek, H. N., & Olson, M. (1986). A den of thieves investigates division. *Arithmetic Teacher 33*(9), 34–35.

Cochran, B. S., Barson, C. R., & Davis, R. D. (1970). Child-created mathematics. *Arithmetic Teacher, 17*(3), 211–215.

Hamic, E. J. (1986). Students' creative computations: My way or your way. *Arithmetic Teacher 34*(1), 39–41.

Harel, G., & Behr, M. (1991). Ed's strategy for solving division problems. *Arithmetic Teacher 39*(3), 38–40.

Huinker, D. M. (1989). Multiplication and division word problems: Improving students' understanding. *Arithmetic Teacher 37*(2), 8–12.

Hutchings, B. (1976). Low-stress algorithms. In R. E. Reys & L. D. Nelson (Eds.), *Measurement in school mathematics,* 1976 Yearbook (pp. 218–239). Reston, VA: National Council of Teachers of Mathematics.

Kouba, V. L., Zawojewski, J. S., & Struchens, M. E. (1997). What do students know about numbers and operations? In P. A. Kenney & E. A. Silver (Eds.) *Results from the Sixth Mathematics Assessment of the National Assessment of Educational Progress* (pp. 87–140). Reston, VA: National Council of Teachers of Mathematics.

Lee, K. S. (1991). Left-to-right computations and estimation. *School Science and Mathematics, 91*(5), 199–201.

Madell, R. (1985). Children's natural processes. *Arithmetic Teacher 32*(7), 20–22.

National Council of Teachers of Mathematics. (1989). *Curriculum and evaluation standards for school mathematics.* Reston, VA: National Council of Teachers of Mathematics.

Neufeld, K. A. (1991). Computational pizazz: Teach your students to create puzzles for their peers—Magic cross-out. *Ontario Mathematics Gazette 30*(2), 23–24.

Philipp, R. A. (1996). Multicultural mathematics and alternative algorithms: Using knowledge from many cultures. *Teaching Children Mathematics, 3*(3), 128–135.

Reys, B. J. (1985). Mental computation. *Arithmetic Teacher 32*(3), 43–46.

Reys, B. J. (1986). Teaching computational estimation: Concepts and strategies. In H. L. Schoen & M. J. Zweng (Eds.), *Estimation and mental computation,* 1986 Yearbook (pp. 31–44). Reston, VA: National Council of Teachers of Mathematics.

Reys, B. J., & Reys, R. E. (1986). One point of view: Mental computation and computational estimation—Their time has come. *Arithmetic Teacher 33*(7), 4–5.

Reys, B. J., & Reys, R. E. (1990). Estimation: Directions from the Standards. *Arithmetic Teacher 37*(7), 22–25.

Reys, R. E., Bestgen, B. J., Rybolt, J. F., Wyatt, J. W. (1982). Processes used by good estimators. *Journal for Research in Mathematics Education 13*(3), 183–201.

Reys, R. E., Reys, B. J., Nohda, N., Ishida, J., Yoshikawa, S., & Shimizu, K. (1991). Computational estimation performance and strategies used by fifth- and eighth-grade Japanese students. *Journal for Research in Mathematics Education 22*(1), 39–58.

Sawada, D. (1985). Mathematical symbols: Insight through invention. *Arithmetic Teacher 32*(6), 20–22.

Sowder, J. T. (1990, March 7). Mental computation and number sense. *Arithmetic Teacher 37,* 18–20.

Stanic, G. M. A., & McKillip, W. D. (1989). Developmental algorithms have a place in elementary school mathematics instruction. *Arithmetic Teacher 36*(5), 14–16.

Usiskin, Z. (1998). Paper-and-pencil algorithms in a calculator-and-computer age. In L. J. Morrow (Ed.), *The teaching and learning of algorithms in school mathematics* (NCTM's 1998 yearbook) (pp. 7–20). Reston, VA: National Council of Teachers of Mathematics.

Weiland, L. (1985). Matching instruction to children's thinking about division. *Arithmetic Teacher 33*(4), 34–35.

Young, J. L. (1984). Uncovering the algorithms. *Arithmetic Teacher 32*(3), 20.

Chapter 10

Bezuk, N. S., & Bieck, M. (1993). Current research on rational numbers and common fractions: Summary and implications for teachers. In D. T. Owens (Ed.), *Research ideas for the classroom: Middle grades mathematics* (pp. 118–136). New York: Macmillan.

Dossey, J. A., Mullis, I. V. S., & Jones, C. O. (1993). *Can students do mathematical problem solving? Results from constructed-response questions in NAEP's 1992 mathematics assessment.* Washington, DC: National Center for Education Statistics.

Driscoll, M. (1984). What research says. *Arithmetic Teacher, 31*(6), 34–35, 46.

Hiebert, J., & Behr, M. J. (1988). Capturing the major themes. In J. Hiebert & M. J. Behr (Eds.), *Number concepts and operations in the middle grades* (pp. 1–18). Hillsdale, NJ: Erlbaum.

Hollis, L. Y. (1984). Teaching rational numbers—Primary grades. *Arithmetic Teacher, 31*(6), 36–39.

Jensen, R., & O'Neil, D. R. (1982). That's eggzactly right. *Arithmetic Teacher, 29*(7), 8–13.

Kieren, T. E. (1980). The rational number construct—its elements and mechanisms. In T. E. Kieren (Ed.), *Recent research on number learning.* Columbus, OH: ERIC/SMEAC.

Kieren, T. E., Nelson, D., & Smith, G. (1985, April). Graphical algorithms in partitioning tasks. *Journal of Mathematical Behavior, 4:* 25–36.

Kouba, V. L., Zawojewski, J. S., & Struchens, M. E. (1997). What do students know about numbers and operations? In P. A. Kenney & E. A. Silver (Eds.), *Results from the Sixth Mathematics Assessment of the National Assessment of Educational Progress* (pp. 87–140). Reston, VA: National Council of Teachers of Mathematics.

Mack, N. K. (1990). Learning fractions with understanding. *Journal for Research in Mathematics Education, 21*(1), 16–32.

National Council of Teachers of Mathematics. (1980). *Curriculum and evaluation standards for school mathematics.* Reston, VA: National Council of Teachers of Mathematics.

Payne, J. N. (1984). Curricular issues: Teaching rational numbers. *Arithmetic Teacher, 31*(6), 14–17.

Peck, D. M., & Jencks, S. M. (1981). Share and cover. *Arithmetic Teacher, 28* (7 March): 38–41.

Pothier, Y. M., & Sawada, D. (1990). Partitioning: An approach to fractions. *Arithmetic Teacher, 38*(4), 12–16.

Skypek, D. H. B. (1984). Special characteristics of rational numbers. *Arithmetic Teacher, 31*(6), 10–12.

Vance, J. (1990). Rational number sense: Development and assessment. *Delta-K, 13* (2 August): 23–27.

Chapter 11

Bezuk, N. S., & Bieck, M. (1993). Current research on rational numbers and common fractions: Summary and implications for teachers. In D. T. Owens (Ed.), *Research ideas for the classroom: Middle grades mathematics.* New York: Macmillan, 118–136.

Hope, J. A., & Owens, D. T. (1987). An analysis of the difficulty of learning fractions. *Focus on Learning Problems in Mathematics 9* (Fall), 25–40.

Kieren, T. (1976). On the mathematical, cognitive, and instructional foundations of rational numbers. In R. E. Lesh (Ed.), *Number and measurement: Paper from a research workshop.* Columbus, OH: ERIC/SMEAC.

National Council of Teachers of Mathematics. (1989). *Curriculum and evaluation standards for school mathematics.* Reston, VA: National Council of Teachers of Mathematics.

Chapter 12

Hiebert, J., & Wearne, D. (1986). Procedures over concepts: The acquisition of decimal number knowledge. In J. Hiebert (Ed.), *Conceptual and procedural knowledge: The case of mathematics* (pp. 199–223). Hillsdale, NJ: Erlbaum.

Kieren, T. (1984). Helping children understand rational numbers. *Arithmetic Teacher, 31*(6), 3.

Kouba, V. L., Zawojewski, J. S., & Struchens, M. E. (1997). What do students know about numbers and operations? In P. A. Kenney & E. A. Silver (Eds.), *Results from the Sixth Mathematics Assessment of the National Assessment of Educational Progress* (pp. 87–140). Reston, VA: National Council of Teachers of Mathematics.

National Council of Teachers of Mathematics (1989). *Curriculum and evaluation standards for school mathematics.* Reston, VA: National Council of Teachers of Mathematics.

Owens, D. T., & Super, D. B. (1993). Teaching and learning decimal fractions. In D. T. Owens (Ed.), *Research ideas for the classroom: Middle grades mathematics* (pp. 137–158). New York: Macmillan.

Vance, J. (1986a). Ordering decimals and fractions: A diagnostic study. *Focus on Learning Problems in Mathematics, 8*(2), 51–59.

Vance, J. (1986b). Estimating decimal products: An instructional sequence. In H. L. Schoen (Ed.), *Estimation and mental computation* (1986 Yearbook). Reston VA: The National Council of Teachers of Mathematics.

Chapter 13

Brown, C. R. (1973). Math rummy. *Arithmetic Teacher 20*(1), 44–45.

Cramer, K., Post, T., & Currier, S. (1993). Learning and teaching ratio and proportion: Research implications. In D. T. Owens (Ed.), *Research ideas for the classroom: Middle grades mathematics* (pp. 159–178). New York: Macmillan.

Dewar, A. M. (1984). Another look at the teaching of percent. *Arithmetic Teacher 31*(7), 48–49.

Hart, K. (1989). Ratio and proportion. In J. Hiebert & M. Behr (Eds.). *Number concepts and operations in the middle grades.* Reston, VA: National Council of Teachers of Mathematics, 198–219.

Hoffer, A. R., & Hoffer, S. A. K. (1992). Ratios and proportional thinking. In T. R. Post (Ed.), *Teaching mathematics in grades K–8: Research-based methods* (pp. 303–330). Boston: Allyn and Bacon.

Karplus, E. F., Karplus, R., & Wollman, W. (1974). Ratio: The influence of cognitive style. *School Science and Mathematics 74*(6), 476–482.

Kouba, V. L., Zawojeski, J. S., & Struchens, M. E. (1997). What do students know about numbers and operations? In P. A. Kenney & E. A. Silver (Eds.), *Results from the Sixth Mathematics Assessment of the National Assessment of Educational Progress* (pp. 87–140). Reston, VA: National Council of Teachers of Mathematics.

Lesh, R., Post, T., & Behr, M. (1989). Proportional reasoning. In J. Hiebert & M. Behr (Eds.), *Number concepts and operations in the middle grades* (pp. 93–118). Reston, VA: National Council of Teachers of Mathematics.

National Council of Teachers of Mathematics. (1989). *Curriculum and evaluation standards for school mathematics.* Reston, VA: National Council of Teachers of Mathematics.

Quintero, A. H. (1987). Helping children understand ratios. *Arithmetic Teacher 34*(9), 17–21.

Vance, J. H. (1982). Individualizing instruction through multilevel problem-solving activities. *The Canadian Mathematics Teacher,* pp. 3–9.

Chapter 14

Billstein, R., Libeskind, S., & Lott, J. W. (1990). *A problem-solving approach to mathematics for elementary school teachers* (4th ed.). New York: The Benjamin Cummings Publishing Company, Inc.

Crowley, M. (1987). The van Hiele model of the development of geometric thought. In M. M. Lindquist & A. P. Shulte (Eds.), *Learning and teaching geometry, K–12.* Reston, VA: National Council of Teachers of Mathematics.

Eperson, C. B. (1982a). Puzzles, pastimes, problems. *Mathematics in School 11*(1), 15.

Eperson, C. B. (1982b). Puzzles, pastimes, problems. *Mathematics in School 11*(2), 10.

Eperson, C. B. (1983). Puzzles, pastimes, problems. *Mathematics in School 12*(2), 20–21.

Geddes, D., & Fortunato, I. (1993). Geometry: Research and classroom activities. In D. T. Owens (Ed.), *Research ideas for the classroom: Middle grades mathematics* (pp. 199–222). New York: Macmillan.

Haak, S. (1976). Transformational geometry and the artwork of M. C. Escher. *Mathematics Teacher 69*(8), 647–652.

Henderson, G. L., & Collier, C. P. (1973). Geometric activities for later childhood education. *Arithmetic Teacher 20*(10), 444–453.

National Council of Teachers of Mathematics. (1989). *Curriculum and evaluation standards for school mathematics.* Reston, VA: National Council of Teachers of Mathematics.

Owens, D. T. (1990). Research into practice: Spatial abilities. *Arithmetic Teacher 37*(6), 48–51.

Piaget, J., Inhelder, B., & Szeminska, A. (1960). *The child's conception of geometry.* New York: Basic Books Inc.

Pothier, Y., & Sawada, D. (1990). Students value time and a patient teacher. *Mathematics in School 19*(3), 38–39.

Rahim, M. H., & Sawada, D. (1986). Revitalizing school geometry through dissection-motion operations. *School Science and Mathematics 86*(3), 235–246.

Robinson, G. E. (1975). Geometry. In J. N. Payne (Ed.), *Mathematics learning in early childhood.* Reston, VA: National Council of Teachers of Mathematics.

Sgroi, R. J. (1990). Communicating about spatial relationships. *Arithmetic Teacher 37*(6), 21–24.

Struchens, M. E., & Blume, G. W. (1997). What do students know about geometry? In P. A. Kenney & E. A. Silver (Eds.), *Results from the sixth mathematics assessment of the National Assessment of Educational Progress* (pp. 165–193). Reston, VA: National Council of Teachers of Mathematics.

Van de Walle, J. A. (1998). *Elementary and middle school mathematics: Teaching developmentally* (3rd ed.). New York: Longman.

Chapter 15

Bright, G. W., & Hoeffner, K. (1993). Measurement, probability, statistics, and graphing. In D. T. Owens (Ed.), *Research ideas for the classroom: Middle grades mathematics* (pp. 78–98). New York: Macmillan.

Cathcart, W. G. (1971). The relationship between primary students' rationalization of conservation and their mathematical achievement. *Child Development, 42,* 755–765.

Hart, K. (1984). Which comes first: Length, area or volume? *Arithmetic Teacher, 31*(9), 16–18, 26–27.

Hiebert, J. (1984). Why do some children have trouble learning measurement concepts? *Arithmetic Teacher, 31*(7), 19–24.

Horak, V. M., & Horak, W. J. (1982). Making measurement meaningful. *Arithmetic Teacher, 30*(3), 18–23.

Horak, V. M., & Horak, W. J. (1983). Teaching time with slit clocks. *Arithmetic Teacher, 30*(5), 8–12.

Inskeep, J. E. 91976). Teaching measurement to children. In D. Nelson (Ed.), *Measurement in school mathematics* (pp. 60–86). Reston, VA: National Council of Teachers of Mathematics.

Jensen, R., & O'Neil, D. R. (1981). Meaningful linear measurement. *Arithmetic Teacher, 29*(1), 6–12.

Kastner, B. (1989). Number sense: The role of measurement applications. *Arithmetic Teacher, 36*(6), 40–46.

Kenney, P. A., & Kouba, V. L. (1997). What do students know about measurement? In P. A. Kenney & E. A. Silver (Eds.), *Results from the Sixth Mathematics Assessment of the National Assessment of Educational Progress* (pp. 141–163). Reston, VA: National Council of Teachers of Mathematics.

Lindquist, M. M. (1987). Estimation and mental computation: Measurement. *Arithmetic Teacher, 34*(5), 16–17.

Lindquist, M. M. (1989). The measurement standards. *Arithmetic Teacher, 37*(2), 22–26.

Myller, R. (1990). *How big is a foot?* New York: Dell Publishing.

National Council of Teachers of Mathematics. (1989). *Curriculum and evaluation standards for school mathematics.* Reston, VA: National Council of Teachers of Mathematics.

Newton, J. E. (1988). From pattern-block play to Logo programming. *Arithmetic Teacher, 35*(9), 6–9.

Shaw, J. M. (1983). Exploring perimeter and area using centimeter squared paper. *Arithmetic Teacher, 31*(4), 4–11.

Shaw, J. M., & Cliatt, J. P. (1989). Developing measurement sense. In P. R. Trafton (Ed.), *New directions for elementary school mathematics* (pp. 149–155). Reston, Virginia: National Council of Teachers of Mathematics.

Steffe, L. P., & Hirstein, J. J. (1976). Children's thinking in measurement situations. In D. Nelson (Ed.), *Measurement in school mathematics* (pp. 35–39). Reston, VA: National Council of Teachers of Mathematics.

Thompson, C. S., & Van de Walle, J. (1981, April 8). A single-handed approach to telling time. *Arithmetic Teacher, 28,* 4–9.

Thompson, C. S., & Van de Walle, J. (1985). Learning about rulers and measuring. *Arithmetic Teacher, 32*(8), 8–12.

Wilson, P. S., & Adams, V. M. (1992). A dynamic way to teach angle and angle measure. *Arithmetic Teacher, 39*(5), 6–13.

Wilson, P. S., & Rowland, R. E. (1993). Teaching measurement. In R. J. Jensen (Ed.), *Research ideas for the classroom: Early childhood mathematics* (pp. 171–194). New York: Macmillan.

Chapter 16

Bankard, D., & Fennell, F. (1991). Ideas. *Arithmetic Teacher, 39*(1), 26–33.

Bohan, H., Irby, B., & Vogel, D. (1995). Problem solving: Dealing with data in the elementary school. *Teaching Children Mathematics, 1*(5), 256–260.

Brahier, D. J., & Speer, W. R. (1995). Investigations: Nuts about mathematics. *Teaching Children Mathematics, 2*(4), 228–232.

Bright, G. W. Harvey, J. G., & Wheeler, M. M. (1981). Fair games, unfair games. In A. P. Shulte & J. R. Smart (Eds.), *Teaching statistics and probability* (pp. 49–59). Reston, VA: National Council of Teachers of Mathematics.

Bright, G. W., & Hoeffner, K. (1993). Measurement, probability, statistics, & graphing. In D. T. Owens (Ed.), *Research ideas for the classroom: Middle grades mathematics* (pp. 78–98). New York: Macmillan.

Brosnan, P. A. (1996). Implementing data analysis in a sixth-grade classroom. *Mathematics Teaching in the Middle School. 1*(8), 622–628.

Browning, C. A., Channell, D. E., & Meyer, R. A. (1994). Preparing teachers to present techniques of exploratory data analysis. *Mathematics Teaching in the Middle School, 1*(2), 166–172.

Burbank, I. K. (1987). Probability without formulas and equations. *Delta-K, 26*(2), 32–39.

Cartland, P. (1996). What's in a glyph? *Teaching Children Mathematics, 2*(6), 324–328.

Dessart, D. J. (1995). Randomness: A connection to reality. In P. A. House & A. F. Coxford (Eds.), *Connecting mathematics across the curriculum* (1995 Yearbook, pp. 177–181). Reston, VA: National Council of Teachers of Mathematics.

Ewbank, W. A. (1987, December 4). Readers' dialogue: Accurate pie graphs. *Arithmetic Teacher, 35,* 4.

Fennell, F. (1990). Implementing the Standards: Probability. *Arithmetic Teacher, 38*(4), 18–22.

Harbaugh, K. (1995). Glyphs? Don't let them scare you! *Teaching Children Mathematics, 1*(8), 506–511.

Hitch, C., & Armstrong, G. (1994). Daily activities for data analysis. *Arithmetic Teacher, 41*(5), 242–245.

Hofstetter, E. B., & Sgroi, L. A. (1996). Data with snap, crackle, and pop. *Mathematics Teaching in the Middle School, 1*(9), 760–764.

Kader, G., & Perry, M. (1994). Learning statistics with technology. *Mathematics Teaching in the Middle School, 1*(2), 130–136.

Litton, N. (1995). Graphing from A to Z. *Teaching Children Mathematics, 2*(4), 220–223.

Loewen, A. C. (1991, March 1). M and M and Ms: An alternative context for teaching mean, median and mode. *delta-K, 29,* 36–40.

National Council of Teachers of Mathematics. (1989). *Curriculum and evaluation standards for school mathematics.* Reston, VA: National Council of Teachers of Mathematics.

Paull, S. (1990). Not just an average unit. *Arithmetic Teacher, 38*(4), 54–58.

Rubenstein, R. N. (1989). Building statistical concepts through visualization and verbalization. *Ontario Mathematics Gazette, 28*(2), 10–15.

Russell, S. J., & Friel, S. N. (1989). Collecting and analyzing real data in the elementary school classroom. In P. R. Trafton & A. P. Shulte (Eds.), *New directions for elementary school mathematics* (1989 Yearbook, pp. 134–148). Reston, VA: National Council of Teachers of Mathematics.

Russell, S. J., & Mokros, J. (1996). What do children understand about average? *Teaching Children Mathematics, 2*(6), 360–364.

Sacco, W., Copes, W., Sloyer, C., & Stark, R. (1987). *Glyphs: Getting the picture.* Dedham, MA: Janson Publications.

Shannon, B. K. J. (1995). Our diets may be killing us. *Mathematics Teaching in the Middle School, 1*(5), 376–382.

Shulte, A. P., & Smart, J. R. (Eds.). (1981). *Teaching statistics and probability.* Reston, VA: National Council of Teachers of Mathematics.

Smith, R. F. (1986). Let's do it: Coordinate geometry for third graders. *Arithmetic Teacher, 33*(8), 6–11.

Vissa, J. M. (1987). Coordinate graphing: Shaping a sticky situation. *Arithmetic Teacher, 35*(3), 6–10.

Wilkinson, J. D., & Nelson, O. (1966). Probability and statistics—Trial teaching in sixth grade. *Arithmetic Teacher, 13*(2), 100–106.

Wilson, M. R., & Krapfl, C. M. (1995). Exploring mean, median, and mode with a spreadsheet. *Mathematics Teaching in the Middle School, 1*(6), 490–495.

Young, S. L. (1991). Ideas. *Arithmetic Teacher, 38*(8), 26–33.

Zawojewski, J. S. (1988). Teaching statistics: Mean, median, and mode. *Arithmetic Teacher, 35*(7), 25–26.

Zawojewski, J. S., & Heckman, D. S. (1997). What do students know about data analysis, statistics, and probability? In P. A. Kenney & E. A. Silver (Eds.), (1997). *Results from the Sixth Mathematics Assessment of the National Assessment of Educational Progress* (pp. 195–223). Reston, VA: National Council of Teachers of Mathematics.

Chapter 17

Blume, G. W., & Heckman, D. S. (1997). What do students know about algebra and functions? In P. A. Kenney & E. A. Silver (Eds.), *Results from the Sixth Mathematics Assessment of the National Assessment of Educational Progress* (pp. 225–277). Reston, VA: National Council of Teachers of Mathematics.

Booth, L. R. (1988). Children's difficulties in beginning algebra. In A. F. Coxford (Ed.), *The ideas of algebra, K–12* (pp. 20–32). Reston, VA: National Council of Teachers of Mathematics.

Chang, L. (1985). Multiple methods of teaching the addition and subtraction of integers. *Arithmetic Teacher 33*(4), 14–19.

Cohen, L. S. (1965). A rationale in working with signed numbers. *Arithmetic Teacher 12*(7), 563–567.

Crowley, M. L., & Dunn, K. A. (1985). On multiplying negative numbers. *Mathematics Teacher 78*(4), 252–256.

Erickson, R. (1977). The old integer game. *Mathematics Teacher 70*(2):140–141.

Grady, M. B. (1978). A manipulative aid for adding and subtracting integers. *Arithmetic Teacher 26*(3), 40.

Howden, H. (1989). Patterns, relationships, and functions. *Arithmetic Teacher 37*(3), 18–24.

Kieran, C. (1988). Two different approaches among algebra learners. In A. F. Coxford (Ed.), *The ideas of algebra, K–12* (pp. 91–96). Reston, VA: National Council of Teachers of Mathematics.

Kieran, C., & Chalouh, L. (1993). Prealgebra: The transition from arithmetic to algebra. In D. T. Owens (Ed.), *Research ideas for the classroom: Middle grades mathematics* (pp. 179–198). New York: Macmillan.

National Council of Teachers of Mathematics. (1989). *Curriculum and evaluation standards for school mathematics.* Reston, VA: National Council of Teachers of Mathematics.

Nibbelink, W. H. (1990). Teaching equations. *Arithmetic Teacher 38*(3), 48–51.

Peck, D. M., & Jencks, S. M. (1988). Reality, arithmetic, and algebra. *Journal of Mathematical Behavior, 7*(1), 85–91.

Phillips, E. (1991). *Patterns and functions: Curriculum and Evaluation Standards for School Mathematics Addenda Series, Grades 5–8.* Reston, VA: National Council of Teachers of Mathematics.

Sanfiorenzo, N. R. (1991). Evaluating expressions: A problem-solving approach. *Arithmetic Teacher 38*(7), 34–38.

Schultz, J. E. (1991). Teaching informal algebra. *Arithmetic Teacher 37*(3), 34–37.

Usiskin, Z. (1988). Conceptions of school algebra and uses of variables. In A. F. Coxford (Ed.), *The ideas of algebra, K–12* (pp. 8–19). Reston, VA: National Council of Teachers of Mathematics.

Vance, J. H. (1995). Developing and assessing understanding of integer operations. *Delta-K 32*(3):10–14.

Wagner, S. (1981). Conservation of equation and function under transformation of variable. *Journal for Research in Mathematics Education 12*(2), 107–118.

A Special Offer from Merrill...
...Cuisenaire®'s Manipulative Starter Kit™

The most powerful mix of hands-on and overhead materials designed to get teaching mathematics off to a great start!

College students and professors!

Cuisenaire and Merrill/Prentice Hall are pleased to make an extraordinary offer to professors and students who use *Learning Mathematics in Elementary and Middle Schools* by Cathcart, Pothier, Vance and Bezuk — Cuisenaire's special Manipulative Starter Kit at a savings of more than **50% off the retail value.** Take advantage of this offer and make the most of your class!

The Cuisenaire® Manipulative Starter Kit. .

Twelve of the most widely used math manipulatives and a comprehensive 92-page resource book at a savings of more than 50%.

Teaching mathematics today means using a variety of manipulative materials to help children understand math concepts. The Cuisenaire *Manipulative Starter Kit* offers a selection of the most widely used manipulatives and overhead projector materials in classrooms today, and at a huge savings!

The *Manipulative Starter Kit* is your opportunity to learn how twelve different materials are used to introduce math concepts from kindergarten to eighth grade. A 92-page resource book, *Start with Manipulatives*, by Rosamond Welchman-Tischler comes complete with a handsome three-ring binder to encourage the addition of classroom notes and information from other resources. This clearly written concise guide begins with an overview of each manipulative, and then focuses on its pedagogical usefulness, indicating which math concepts are most appropriately taught with each model.

Equipped with this excellent resource and using the manipulatives from the kit, you will have everything needed to teach mathematics with methods and materials that support the standards set by the National Council of Teachers of Mathematics.

The *Manipulative Starter Kit* also includes a roomy attaché with shoulder strap and hand-grip. You will appreciate the ease of carrying the *Manipulative Starter Kit* in this versatile, reinforced nylon bag, which will serve you well throughout your student and teaching careers.

Each Manipulative Starter Kit includes:

Color Cubes
24 polished, hardwood cubes in four colors

Two-Color Counters
50 thick, smooth, two-sided plastic red/yellow counters

Fraction Circles
24-piece, plastic set of halves, thirds, fourths, sixths, and eighths in a clear storage tray

Cuisenaire® Rods
A set of 74 rods in ten colors in lengths from one to ten centimeters

Overhead Spinners
4 transparent spinners with printed circles and templates to draw halves, fourths, fifths, eights, and tenths

Overhead Counters
50 colorful, transparent circular pieces for use on overhead or as a hands-on manipulative

Overhead Pattern Blocks
A double set (96 pieces) of transparent plastic hexagons, squares, trapezoids, parrallelograms, rhombi, and triangles

Dice
One pair each of red, green, and white plastic dice

Mirrors
2 flexible plastic mirrors

Overhead Base Ten Blocks
A double set of 20 1 x 1 cm units, 20 1 x 1 cm tens, and 4 10 x 10 cm hundreds

Tangrams
A 7-piece set of high-quality plastic geometric shapes

Geoboard
Blue plastic geoboard with a 25-peg square lattice on one side and a circular lattice on the other

Why the shift to manipulatives?

Teaching and learning elementary mathematics has changed. Manipulative materials are now an integral part of daily classroom instruction. New teachers need first-hand experience with a range of such materials and with lessons that use them. Equally important, children benefit from a hands-on approach to learning mathematics, as studies continue to show. Comments in the *Curriculum and Evaluation Standards*, published by the National Council of Teachers of Mathematics, are most compelling:

"Teachers...need to make extensive and thoughtful use of physical materials..."

"Classrooms need to be equipped with a wide variety of physical materials and supplies."

"Classrooms should have ample quantities of such materials as counters; interlocking cubes; connecting links; base-ten, attribute, and pattern blocks; tiles; geometric models; rulers; spinners; colored rods; geoboards; balances; fraction pieces..."

The Cuisenaire *Manipulative Starter Kit* introduces classroom-tested methods of teaching with math manipulatives. And it contains everything you need to start teaching with these materials.

What makes the Manipulative Starter Kit so popular?

"The Manipulative Starter Kit gives pre-service teachers the tools to accurately model math concepts. The kit also allows them to study at home and allows for individual investigation."

Dr. Steven Wilkinson
Assistant Professor of Mathematics
Northeastern State University

Visit the Cuisenaire Learning Place!
http://www.cuisenaire.com

"This kit has become a critical component of our mathematics methods and materials courses for early childhood and elementary pre-service teachers. In many instances students truly understand mathematical concepts for the first time."

Dr. Claire Graham
Framingham State College

Cuisenaire Co. of America, Inc.
P.O. Box 5026
White Plains, NY 10602-5026
914-237-3142 • FAX 800-551-RODS

Cuisenaire® Manipulative Starter Kit Order Form

☐ I am a teacher education student.

☐ I am a college/university professor.

Name _____

College _____

Address _____

City _____ State_____ Zip _____

Phone _____ FAX _____ e-mail _____

Please send me _____ Manipulative Starter Kits (Item No. 011945) at $36.00 each, plus 10% shipping and handling, for a total of $ _____. *Please mention code MK99SK when ordering*

Charge this order to (check one) ☐ VISA   ☐ MasterCard

☐☐☐☐   ☐☐☐☐   ☐☐☐☐   ☐☐☐☐

Exp. Date_____ Phone (_____)_____

Signature _____

☐ My check for $ _____ is enclosed.

Make check payable to **Cuisenaire Co. of America, Inc.**
Please mail this order form to:

Order Processing Dept.
Cuisenaire Company of America
P.O. Box 5026
White Plains, NY 10602-5026

My permanent address, if different from above is:

_____

_____

Prices subject to change without notice.

ue $79.00)

Pre-Service Training Starts with Cuisenaire®

Start with Kits from Cuisenaire provide teachers-in-training with engaging hands-on experiences to make the challenging transition from college student to classroom teacher. Thousands of students at colleges and universities have used the *Manipulative Starter Kit*. And now, two new kits, *Start with Science TOOL KIT™* and *Start with Computer Technology Kit™*, use the same powerful teaching method to guarantee success!

Integrate Easily into any Curriculum

Start with Kits can be used along with any textbook or college course, or for self-study, so students can learn at their own pace to gain insight and confidence. Plus, each kit provides an outstanding selection of tools to implement a hands-on approach to learning.

Start with Science TOOLKIT™

Start with Science TOOLKIT enhances an understanding of science and science teaching skills, and stimulates an appreciation of science. The resource book, *Start with Science TOOLKIT*, is a guide to inquiry-based science, written by Jean Shaw and Debby Chessin for the K-8 pre-service teacher. The *Start with Science TOOLKIT* includes eight modules using a variety of tools to learn and teach more about physical science, life science, earth science, and environmental science.

Start with Computer Technology Kit™

The *Start with Computer Technology Kit* introduces pre-service teachers to the power of computer technology! It is designed for novices as well as more experienced computer-users to provide experiences with math software and Cuisenaire materials in the K-8 classroom.

ISBN 0-201-30495-3

Cuisenaire Company of America, Inc.
P.O. Box 5026
White Plains, NY 10602-5026